Introduction to Computer Science Using Python:
A Computational Problem-Solving Focus

Introduction to Computer Science Using Python: A Computational Problem-Solving Focus

Charles Dierbach

WILEY

VP & Executive Publisher:	Don Fowley
Executive Editor:	Beth Lang Golub
Assistant Editor:	Samantha Mandel
Marketing Manager:	Christopher Ruel
Marketing Assistant:	Ashley Tomeck
Photo Editor:	Hilary Newman
Cover Designer:	Thomas Nery
Associate Production Manager:	Joyce Poh
Production Editor:	Jolene Ling
Cover Illustration:	Norm Christiansen

This book was set in 10/12 Times LT Std by Aptara.

Founded in 1807, John Wiley & Sons, Inc. has been a valued source of knowledge and understanding for more than 200 years, helping people around the world meet their needs and fulfill their aspirations. Our company is built on a foundation of principles that include responsibility to the communities we serve and where we live and work. In 2008, we launched a Corporate Citizenship Initiative, a global effort to address the environmental, social, economic, and ethical challenges we face in our business. Among the issues we are addressing are carbon impact, paper specifications and procurement, ethical conduct within our business and among our vendors, and community and charitable support. For more information, please visit our website: www.wiley.com/go/citizenship.

Library of Congress Cataloging-in-Publication Data

Dierbach, Charles, 1953–
    Introduction to Computer Science Using Python: A Computational Problem-Solving Focus/Charles Dierbach.
        p. cm.
    Includes index.
    ISBN 978-0-470-55515-6 (pbk.)
1. Python (Computer program language)   I. Title.
    QA76.73.P98D547 2012
    005.13'3—dc23
                                                     2012027172

10 9 8 7 6 5 4 3 2

DEDICATION

To my wife Chen Jin, and our sons Jayden and Bryson.

Brief Contents

Contents

| 3 | Control Structures | 79 |

| 4 | Lists | 125 |

7   Modular Design   247

10 Object-Oriented Programming   383

11   Recursion   460

12   Computing and Its Developments   491

Preface

Book Concept

This text introduces students to programming and computational problem solving using the Python 3 programming language. It is intended primarily for a first-semester computer science (CS1) course, but is also appropriate for use in any course providing an introduction to computer programming and/or computational problem solving. The book provides a step-by-step, "hands on" pedagogical approach which, together with Python's clear and simple syntax, makes this book easy to teach and learn from.

The primary goal in the development of this text was to create a pedagogically sound and accessible textbook that emphasizes fundamental programming and computational problem-solving concepts over the minutiae of a particular programming language. Python's ease in the creation and use of both indexed and associative data structures (in the form of lists/tuples and dictionaries), as well as sets, allows for programming concepts to be demonstrated without the need for detailed discussion of programming language specifics.

Taking advantage of Python's support of both the imperative (i.e., procedural) and object-oriented paradigms, a "back to basics," "objects-late" approach is taken to computer programming. It follows the belief that solid grounding in imperative programming should precede the larger number of (and more abstract) concepts of the object-oriented paradigm. Therefore, objects are not covered until Chapter 5, and object-oriented programming is not introduced until Chapter 10. For those who do not wish to introduce object-oriented programming, Chapter 10 can easily be skipped.

How This Book Is Different

This text has a number of unique pedagogical features including:

♦ A *short motivation section* at the beginning of each chapter which provides a larger perspective on the chapter material to be covered.

♦ *Hands-on exercises* throughout each chapter which take advantage of the interactive capabilities of Python.

♦ A fully-developed computational problem solving example at the end of each chapter that places an emphasis on *program testing and program debugging*.

♦ A richly illustrated, final chapter on "*Computing and Its Developments*" that provides a storyline of notable individuals, accomplishments, and developments in computing, from Charles Babbage through modern times.

♦ A *Python 3 Programmers' Reference* in the back of the text which allows the book to serve as both a pedagogical resource *and* as a convenient Python reference.

Pedagogical Features

The book takes a step-by-step pedagogical approach. Each new concept is immediately followed by a pedagogical element that elucidates the material covered and/or challenges students' understanding. The specific pedagogical features of the book are listed below.

Summary Boxes

At the end of each subsection, a clearly outlined summary box is provided containing the most salient information of the material just presented. These concise summaries also serve as useful reference points as students review the chapter material.

Let's Try It Sections

Also at the end of each subsection, a short Let's Try It section is given in which students are asked to type in Python code (into the Python shell) and observe the results. These "hands on" exercises help to immediately reinforce material as students progress through the chapter.

Let's Apply It Sections

At the end of each major section, a complete program example is provided with detailed line-by-line discussion. These examples serve to demonstrate the programming concepts just learned in the context of an actual program.

Self-Test Questions

Also at the end of each major section, a set of multiple-choice/short-answer questions is given. The answers are included so that students may perform a comprehension self check in answering these.

A variety of exercises and program assignments are also included at the end of every chapter. These are designed to gradually ease students from review of general concepts, to code-writing exercises, to modification of significant-sized programs, to developing their own programs, as outlined below.

Chapter Exercises

At the end of each chapter, a set of simple, short-answer questions are provided.

Python Programming Exercises

Also at the end of each chapter, a set of simple, short Python programming exercises are given.

Program Modification Problems

Additionally, at the end of each chapter is a set of programming problems in which students are asked to make various modifications to program examples in the chapter. Thus, these exercises do not require students to develop a program from scratch. They also serve as a means to encourage students to think through the chapter program examples.

Program Development Problems

Finally, at the end of each chapter is a set of computational problems which students are to develop programs for from scratch. These problems are generally similar to the program examples given in the chapters.

Emphasis on Computational Problem Solving

The capstone programs at the end of each chapter show students how to go through the process of computational problem solving. This includes problem analysis, design, implementation, and testing, as outlined in Chapter 1. As a program is developed and tested, errors are intentionally placed in the code, leading to discussion and demonstration of program testing and debugging. Programming errors, therefore, are presented as a normal part of software development. This helps students develop their own program debugging skills, and reinforces the idea that program debugging is an inevitable part of program development—an area of coverage that is crucial for beginning programmers, and yet often lacking in introductory computer science books.

Given the rigor with which these problems are presented, the sections are somewhat lengthy. Since the capstones do not introduce any new concepts, they may be skipped if the instructor does not have time to cover them.

Guided Book Tour

Chapter 1 addresses the question "What is computer science?" Computational problem solving is introduced, including discussions on the limits of computation, computer algorithms, computer hardware, computer software, and a brief introduction to programming in Python. The end of the chapter lays out a step-by-step computational problem solving process for students consisting of problem analysis, program design, program implementation, and program testing.

Chapter 2 covers data and expressions, including arithmetic operators, discussion of limits of precision, output formatting, character encoding schemes, control characters, keyboard input, operator precedence and associativity, data types, and coercion vs. type conversion.

Chapter 3 introduces control structures, including relational, membership and Boolean operators, short-circuit (lazy) evaluation, selection control (if statements) and indentation in Python, iterative control (while statements), and input error checking. (For statements are not covered until Chapter 4 on Lists.) Break and continue statements are not introduced in this book. It is felt that these statements, which violate the principles of structured programming, are best not introduced to the beginning programmer.

Chapter 4 presents lists and for statements. The chapter opens with a general discussion of lists and list operations. This is followed by lists and tuples in Python, including nested lists, for loops, the built-in range function, and list comprehensions. Since all values in Python are (object) references, and lists are the first mutable type to which students are introduced, a discussion of shallow vs. deep copying is provided without explicit mention of references. The details of object representation in Python is covered in Chapter 6.

Chapter 5 introduces the notion of a program routine, including discussions of parameter passing (actual argument vs. formal parameters), value vs. non-value returning functions, mutable vs. immutable arguments, keyword and default arguments in Python, and local vs. global scope.

Chapter 6 introduces students to the concept of objects in programming. Here students see how objects are represented as references, and therefore are able to fully understand the behavior of assignment and copying of lists (initially introduced in Chapter 4), as well as other types. Turtle graphics is introduced (by use of the turtle module of the Python Standard Library) and is used to provide an intuitive, visual means of understanding the concept of object instances. This also allows students to write fun, graphical programs, while at the same time reinforcing the notion and behavior of objects.

Chapter 7 covers modules and modular design. It starts off by explaining the general notion of a module and module specification, including docstrings in Python. It is followed by a discussion of top-down design. It then introduces modules in Python, including namespaces, the importing of modules, module private variables, module loading and execution, and local, global, and built-in namespaces. The notion of a stack is introduced here via the development of a programmer-defined stack module.

Chapter 8 introduces text files and string processing. It starts with how to open/close, and read/write files in Python. Then the string-applicable sequence operations from Chapter 4 are revisited, and additional string methods are covered. Exception handling is introduced in the context of file handling, and some of the more commonly occurring Python Standard Exceptions are introduced.

Chapter 9 presents dictionaries (Python's associative data structure) and sets.

Chapter 10 introduces object-oriented programming. It begins with a discussion of classes, and the notion of encapsulation. Then, how classes are defined is presented, including discussion of special methods in Python. Inheritance and subtypes are discussed next, followed by a discussion of the use of polymorphism. Finally, the chapter ends with a brief introduction to class diagrams in UML.

Chapter 11 covers recursion and recursive problem solving, including discussion of recursion vs. iteration, and when recursion is appropriately used.

Chapter 12 concludes the book by providing an overview of the people, achievements and developments in computing. This chapter serves to "humanize" the field and educate students on the history of the discipline.

Online Textbook Supplements

All supplements are available via the book's companion website at www.wiley.com/college/dierbach. Below is the list of supplements that accompany this text:

♦ Instructor's manual, with answers to all exercises and program assignments

♦ PowerPoint slides, summarizing the key points of each chapter

♦ Program code for all programs in the book

♦ Test bank of exam questions for each chapter

A separate student companion site is available at the above web site which grants students access to the program code and additional files needed to execute and/or modify programs in the book. All other program code is available to instructors only.

Acknowledgments

I would first like to thank the people at Wiley & Sons. To Dan Sayre, for getting this project going; to my editor Beth Golub, for all her patience and guidance during the evolution of the book; and to Samantha Mandel, Assistant Editor, for her invaluable help. I would also like to thank Harry Nolan, Design Director, who took the time to ensure that the book design turned out as I envisioned; to Jolene Ling, Production Editor, who so graciously worked on the production of the book and the ensuing changes, and for seeing that everything came together.

There are many others to thank who have in some way contributed to this project. First, thanks to Harry Hochheiser, for all the motivating and informative discussions that eventually led me to Python, and ultimately the development of this book. Many thanks to my colleague Josh Dehlinger, who lent his extremely critical eye to the project (and took up the slack on many of my department duties!). Thanks to my department chair, Chao Lu, for his support, friendship, and for creating such a collegial and productive environment to work (and for funneling some of my duties to Josh!). And thanks to Shiva Azadegan, who first planted the idea of writing a book in my head, and for being such a supportive friend, as well as a wonderful colleague.

I would also like to acknowledge a couple of my outstanding graduate TAs in the Python course for all their help and enthusiasm on the project. I thank Crystal McKinney, for so freely offering her time to review chapters and offer her suggestions. I owe a great debt of thanks to Leela Sedaghat, who contributed to the project in so many ways—her insightful review of chapters, the enormous amount of time spent on verifying and obtaining image permissions, and her design of and contribution to the Python Programmers' Reference manual, which without her help, would never have been completed on time. Previous graduate students Ahbi Grover and Lanlan Wang also read earlier drafts of the book.

Finally, I thank the reviewers. Without them, the book could never be what it is now. First, special thanks to Claude Anderson of Rose-Hulman Institute of Technology. His meticulous review for technical errors, and his suggestions on pedagogy, have significantly contributed to the book. In addition, I thank each of the following individuals who served as reviewers on this project: James Atlas, University of Delaware; Richard Borie, University of Alabama; Tim Bower, Kansas State University Salina; Darin Brezeale, University of Texas at Arlington; Diana Cukierman, Simon Fraser University; Chris Heiden, St. Clair County Community College; Ric Heishman, George Mason University; Jennifer Kay, Rowan University; Debby Keen, University of Kentucky; Clayton Lewis, University of Colorado; Alan McLeod, Queen's University at Kingston; Ethan Miller, University of California, Santa Cruz; Joe Oldham, Centre College; Susan Mary Rosselet, Bemidji State University; Terry A. Scott, University of Northern Colorado; and Leon Tietz, Minnesota State University Mankato.

About the Author

Charles Dierbach is an Associate Professor of computer science at Towson University, and has regularly taught introductory undergraduate computer science courses for the past thirty-five years. He received his Ph.D. in Computer Science from the University of Delaware. While a lecturer there, he received the Outstanding Teaching Award from the undergraduate chapter of the ACM. At Towson, he served as Director of the Undergraduate Computer Science program for over ten years. In addition to teaching introductory computer science courses, Dr. Dierbach also teaches undergraduate and graduate courses in object-oriented design and programming.

## CHAPTER 1

Introduction

This chapter addresses the question "What is computer science?" We begin by introducing the essence of computational problem solving via some classic examples. Next, computer algorithms, the heart of computational problem solving, are discussed. This is followed by a look at computer hardware (and the related issues of binary representation and operating systems) and computer software (and the related issues of syntax, semantics, and program translation). The chapter finishes by presenting the process of computational problem solving, with an introduction to the Python programming language.

OBJECTIVES

After reading this chapter and completing the exercises, you will be able to:

♦ Explain the essence of computational problem solving

♦ Explain what a computer algorithm is

♦ Explain the fundamental components of digital hardware

♦ Explain the role of binary representation in digital computing

♦ Explain what an operating systems is

♦ Explain the fundamental concepts of computer software

♦ Explain the fundamental features of IDLE in Python

♦ Modify and execute a simple Python program

CHAPTER CONTENTS

MOTIVATION

Computing technology has changed, and is continuing to change the world. Essentially every aspect of life has been impacted by computing. Just-in-time inventory allows companies to significantly reduce costs. Universal digital medical records promise to save the lives of many of the estimated 100,000 people who die each year from medical errors. Vast information resources, such as Wikipedia, now provide easy, quick access to a breadth of knowledge as never before. Information sharing via Facebook and Twitter has not only brought family and friends together in new ways, but has also helped spur political change around the world. New interdisciplinary fields combining computing and science will lead to breakthroughs previously unimaginable. Computing-related fields in almost all areas of study are emerging (see Figure 1-1).

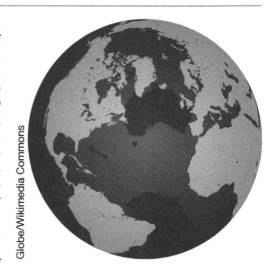

Globe/Wikimedia Commons

In the study of computer science, there are fundamental principles of computation to be learned that will never change. In addition to these principles, of course, there is always changing technology. That is what makes the field of computer science so exciting. There is constant change and advancement, but also a foundation of principles to draw from. What can be done with computation is limited only by our imagination. With that said, we begin our journey into the world of computing. I have found it an unending fascination—I hope that you do too. Bon voyage!

Various Computational-Related Fields		
Computational Biology	Computational Medicine	Computational Journalism
Computational Chemistry	Computational Pharmacology	Digital Humanities
Computational Physics	Computational Economics	Computational Creativity
Computational Mathematics	Computational Textiles	Computational Music
Computational Materials Science	Computational Architecture	Computational Photography
Computer-Aided Design	Computational Social Science	Computational Advertising
Computer-Aided Manufacturing	Computational Psychology	Computational Intelligence

FIGURE 1-1   Computing-Related Specialized Fields

FUNDAMENTALS

1.1   What Is Computer Science?

Many people, if asked to define the field of computer science, would likely say that it is about programming computers. Although programming is certainly a primary activity of computer science, programming languages and computers are only *tools*. What computer science is fundamentally about is **computational problem solving**—that is, solving problems by the use of computation (Figure 1-2).

This description of computer science provides a succinct definition of the field. However, it does not convey its tremendous *breadth and diversity*. There are various areas of study in computer science including software engineering (the design and implementation of large software systems), database management, computer networks, computer graphics, computer simulation, data mining, information security, programming language design, systems programming, computer architecture, human–computer interaction, robotics, and artificial intelligence, among others.

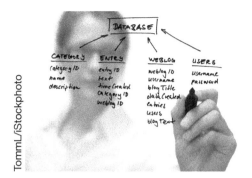

TommL/iStockphoto

FIGURE 1-2 Computational Problem Solving

The definition of computer science as computational problem solving begs the question: *What is computation?* One characterization of computation is given by the notion of an *algorithm*. The definition of an algorithm is given in section 1.2. For now, consider an algorithm to be a series of steps that can be systematically followed for producing the answer to a certain type of problem. We look at fundamental issues of computational problem solving next.

Computer science is fundamentally about computational problem solving.

1.1.1 The Essence of Computational Problem Solving

In order to solve a problem computationally, two things are needed: a *representation* that captures all the relevant aspects of the problem, and an *algorithm* that solves the problem by use of the representation. Let's consider a problem known as the **Man, Cabbage, Goat, Wolf problem** (Figure 1-3).

A man lives on the east side of a river. He wishes to bring a cabbage, a goat, and a wolf to a village on the west side of the river to sell. However, his boat is only big enough to hold himself, and either the cabbage, goat, or wolf. In addition, the man cannot leave the goat alone with the cabbage because the goat will eat the cabbage, and he cannot leave the wolf alone with the goat because the wolf will eat the goat. How does the man solve his problem?

There is a simple algorithmic approach for solving this problem by simply trying all possible combinations of items that may be rowed back and forth across the river. Trying all possible solutions to a given problem is referred to as a *brute force approach*. What would be an appropriate

FIGURE 1-3 Man, Cabbage, Goat, Wolf Problem

representation for this problem? Since only the relevant aspects of the problem need to be represented, all the irrelevant details can be omitted. A representation that leaves out details of what is being represented is a form of **abstraction**.

The use of abstraction is prevalent in computer science. In this case, is the color of the boat relevant? The width of the river? The name of the man? No, the only relevant information is *where* each item is at each step. The collective location of each item, in this case, refers to the *state* of the problem. Thus, the *start state* of the problem can be represented as follows.

```
man cabbage goat   wolf
[E,    E,     E,    E]
```

In this representation, the symbol E denotes that each corresponding object is on the east side of the river. If the man were to row the goat across with him, for example, then the representation of the new problem state would be

```
man cabbage goat   wolf
[W,    E,     W,    E]
```

in which the symbol W indicates that the corresponding object is on the west side of the river—in this case, the man and goat. (The locations of the cabbage and wolf are left unchanged.) A solution to this problem is a sequence of steps that converts the initial state,

```
[E,    E,    E,    E]
```

in which all objects are on the east side of the river, to the *goal state*,

```
[W,    W,    W,    W]
```

in which all objects are on the west side of the river. Each step corresponds to the man rowing a particular object across the river (or the man rowing alone). As you will see, the Python programming language provides an easy means of representing sequences of values. The remaining task is to develop or find an existing algorithm for computationally solving the problem using this representation. The solution to this problem is left as a chapter exercise.

As another example computational problem, suppose that you needed to write a program that displays a calendar month for any given month and year, as shown in Figure 1-4. The representation of this problem is rather straightforward. Only a few values need to be maintained—the month and year, the number of days in each month, the names of the days of the week, and the day of the week that the first day of the month falls on. Most of these values are either provided by the user (such as the month and year) or easily determined (such as the number of days in a given month).

The less obvious part of this problem is how to determine the day of the week that a given date falls on. You would need an algorithm that can compute this. Thus, no matter how well you may know a given programming language or how good a programmer you may be, without such an algorithm you could not solve this problem.

MAY 2012						
Sun	Mon	Tues	Wed	Thur	Fri	Sat
		1	2	3	4	5
6	7	8	9	10	11	12
13	14	15	16	17	18	19
20	21	22	23	24	25	26
27	28	29	30	31		

FIGURE 1-4 Calendar Month

In order to solve a problem computationally, two things are needed: a *representation* that captures all the relevant aspects of the problem, and an *algorithm* that solves the problem by use of the representation.

1.1.2 Limits of Computational Problem Solving

Once an algorithm for solving a given problem is developed or found, an important question is, "Can a solution to the problem be found in a reasonable amount of time?" If not, then the particular algorithm is of limited practical use.

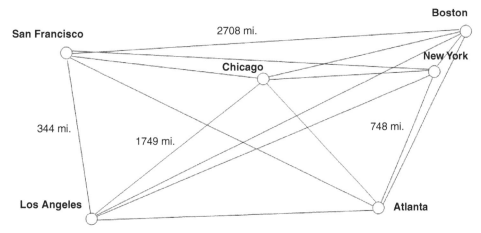

FIGURE 1-5 Traveling Salesman Problem

The **Traveling Salesman problem** (Figure 1-5) is a classic computational problem in computer science. The problem is to find the shortest route of travel for a salesman needing to visit a given set of cities. In a brute force approach, the lengths of all possible routes would be calculated and compared to find the shortest one. For ten cities, the number of possible routes is 10! (10 factorial), or over three and a half million (3,628,800). For twenty cities, the number of possible routes is 20!, or over two and a half quintillion (2,432,902,008,176,640,000). If we assume that a computer could compute the lengths of one million routes per second, it would take over 77,000 years to find the shortest route for twenty cities by this approach. For 50 cities, the number of possible routes is over 10^{64}. In this case, it would take more time to solve than the age of the universe!

A similar problem exists for the game of chess (Figure 1-6). A brute force approach for a chess-playing program would be to "look ahead" to *all* the eventual outcomes of every move that can be made in deciding each next move. There

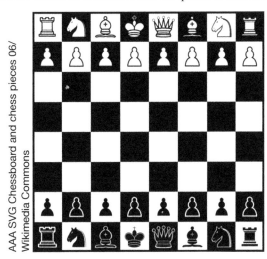

AAA SVG Chessboard and chess pieces 06/ Wikimedia Commons

FIGURE 1-6 Game of Chess

are approximately 10^{120} possible chess games that can be played. This is related to the average number of look-ahead steps needed for deciding each move. How big is this number? There are approximately 10^{80} atoms in the observable universe, and an estimated 3×10^{90} grains of sand to fill the universe solid. Thus, *there are more possible chess games that can be played than grains of sand to fill the universe solid!* For problems such as this and the Traveling Salesman problem in which a brute-force approach is impractical to use, more efficient problem-solving methods must be discovered that find either an exact or an approximate solution to the problem.

> Any algorithm that correctly solves a given problem must solve the problem in a reasonable amount of time, otherwise it is of limited practical use.

Self-Test Questions

1. A good definition of computer science is "the science of programming computers." (TRUE/FALSE)

2. Which of the following areas of study are included within the field of computer science?
   (a) Software engineering
   (b) Database management
   (c) Information security
   (d) All of the above

3. In order to computationally solve a problem, two things are needed: a representation of the problem, and an _____ that solves it.

4. Leaving out detail in a given representation is a form of _____.

5. A "brute-force" approach for solving a given problem is to:
   (a) Try all possible algorithms for solving the problem.
   (b) Try all possible solutions for solving the problem.
   (c) Try various representations of the problem.
   (d) All of the above

6. For which of the following problems is a brute-force approach practical to use?
   (a) Man, Cabbage, Goat, Wolf problem
   (b) Traveling Salesman problem
   (c) Chess-playing program
   (d) All of the above

ANSWERS: 1. False. 2. (d). 3. algorithm, 4. abstraction, 5. (b), 6. (a)

1.2   Computer Algorithms

This section provides a more complete description of an algorithm than given above, as well as an example algorithm for determining the day of the week for a given date.

1.2.1   What Is an Algorithm?

An **algorithm** is a finite number of clearly described, unambiguous "doable" steps that can be systematically followed to produce a desired result for given input in a finite amount of time (that is, it eventually terminates). Algorithms solve *general* problems (determining whether any given number is a prime number), and not specific ones (determining whether 30753 is a prime number). Algorithms, therefore, are general computational methods used for solving particular problem instances.

The word "algorithm" is derived from the ninth-century Arab mathematician, Al-Khwarizmi (Figure 1-7), who worked on "written processes to achieve some goal." (The term "algebra" also derives from the term "al-jabr," which he introduced.)

Computer algorithms are central to computer science. They provide step-by-step methods of computation that a machine can carry out. Having high-speed machines (computers) that can consistently follow and execute a given set of instructions provides a reliable and effective means of realizing computation. However, *the computation that a given computer performs is only as good as the underlying algorithm used.* Understanding what can be effectively programmed and executed by computers, therefore, relies on the understanding of computer algorithms.

Persian_khwarizmi/Wikimedia Commons

FIGURE 1-7   Al-Khwarizmi (Ninth Century A.D.)

An **algorithm** is a finite number of clearly described, unambiguous "doable" steps that can be systematically followed to produce a desired result for given input in a finite amount of time.

1.2.2   Algorithms and Computers: A Perfect Match

Much of what has been learned about algorithms and computation since the beginnings of modern computing in the 1930s–1940s could have been studied centuries ago, since the study of algorithms does not depend on the existence of computers. The algorithm for performing long division is such an example. However, most algorithms are not as simple or practical to apply manually. Most require the use of computers either because they would require too much time for a person to apply, or involve so much detail as to make human error likely. Because *computers can execute instructions very quickly and reliably without error*, algorithms and computers are a perfect match! Figure 1-8 gives an example algorithm for determining the day of the week for any date between January 1, 1800 and December 31, 2099.

Because computers can execute instructions very quickly and reliably without error, algorithms and computers are a perfect match.

To determine the day of the week for a given **month, day,** and **year**:

1. Let **century_digits** be equal to the first two digits of the year.

2. Let **year_digits** be equal to the last two digits of the year.

3. Let **value** be equal to **year_digits** + floor(**year_digits** / 4)

4. If **century_digits** equals 18, then add 2 to **value**, else
   if **century_digits** equals 20, then add 6 to **value**.

5. If the **month** is equal to January and **year** is not a leap year,
   then add 1 to **value**, else,

   if the **month** is equal to February and the **year** is a leap year, then
   add 3 to **value**; if not a leap year, then add 4 to **value,** else,

   if the **month** is equal to March or November, then add 4 to **value**, else,

   if the **month** is equal to May, then add 2 to **value**, else,

   if the **month** is equal to June, then add 5 to **value**, else,

   if the **month** is equal to August, then add 3 to **value**, else,

   if the **month** is equal to October, then add 1 to **value**, else,

   if the **month** is equal to September or December, then add 6 to **value**,

6. Set **value** equal to (**value + day**) mod 7.

7. If **value** is equal to 1, then the day of the week is Sunday; else

   if **value** is equal to 2, day of the week is Monday; else

   if **value** is equal to 3, day of the week is Tuesday; else

   if **value** is equal to 4, day of the week is Wednesday; else

   if **value** is equal to 5, day of the week is Thursday; else

   if **value** is equal to 6, day of the week is Friday; else

   if **value** is equal to 0, day of the week is Saturday

FIGURE 1-8 Day of the Week Algorithm

Note that there is no value to add for the months of April and July.

Self-Test Questions

1. Which of the following are true of an algorithm?
   (a) Has a finite number of steps
   (b) Produces a result in a finite amount of time
   (c) Solves a general problem
   (d) All of the above

2. Algorithms were first developed in the 1930–1940s when the first computing machines appeared. (TRUE/FALSE)

3. Algorithms and computers are a "perfect match" because: (Select all that apply.)
   (a) Computers can execute a large number of instructions very quickly.
   (b) Computers can execute instructions reliably without error.
   (c) Computers can determine which algorithms are the best to use for a given problem.

4. Given that the year 2016 is a leap year, what day of the week does April 15th of that year fall on? Use the algorithm in Figure 1-8 for this.

5. Which of the following is an example of an algorithm? (Select all that apply.)
   (a) A means of sorting any list of numbers
   (b) Directions for getting from your home to a friend's house
   (c) A means of finding the shortest route from your house to a friend's house.

ANSWERS: 1. (d). 2. False. 3. (a,b) 4. Friday. 5. (a,c)

1.3   Computer Hardware

Computer hardware comprises the physical part of a computer system. It includes the all-important components of the *central processing unit* (CPU) and *main memory*. It also includes *peripheral components* such as a keyboard, monitor, mouse, and printer. In this section, computer hardware and the intrinsic use of binary representation in computers is discussed.

1.3.1   Digital Computing: It's All about Switches

It is essential that computer hardware be reliable and error free. If the hardware gives incorrect results, then any program run on that hardware is unreliable. A rare occurrence of a hardware error was discovered in 1994. The widely used Intel processor was found to give incorrect results only when certain numbers were divided, estimated as likely to occur once every 9 billion divisions. Still, the discovery of the error was very big news, and Intel promised to replace the processor for any one that requested it.

The key to developing reliable systems is to keep the design as simple as possible. In digital computing, all information is represented as a series of digits. We are used to representing numbers using base 10 with digits 0–9. Consider if information were represented within a computer system this way, as shown in Figure 1-9.

FIGURE 1-9   Decimal Digitalization

In current electronic computing, each digit is represented by a different voltage level. The more voltage levels (digits) that the hardware must utilize and distinguish, the more complex the hardware design becomes. This results in greater chance of hardware design errors. It is a fact of information theory, however, that any information can be represented using only *two* symbols. Because of this, *all information within a computer system is represented by the use of only two digits, 0 and 1*, called **binary representation**, shown in Figure 1-10.

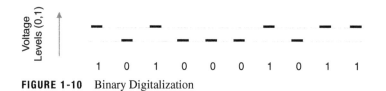

FIGURE 1-10   Binary Digitalization

In this representation, each digit can be one of only two possible values, similar to a light switch that can be either on or off. Computer hardware, therefore, is based on the use of simple electronic "on/off" switches called **transistors** that switch at very high speed. **Integrated circuits** ("chips"), the building blocks of computer hardware, are comprised of millions or even billions of transistors. The development of the transistor and integrated circuits is discussed in Chapter 12. We discuss binary representation next.

All information within a computer system is represented using only two digits, 0 and 1, called **binary representation.**

1.3.2   The Binary Number System

For representing numbers, any base (radix) can be used. For example, in base 10, there are ten possible digits (0, 1, . . ., 9), in which each column value is a power of ten, as shown in Figure 1-11.

10,000,000	1,000,000	100,000	10,000	1,000	100	10	1
10^7	10^6	10^5	10^4	10^3	10^2	10^1	10^0
						9	**9** = **99**

FIGURE 1-11   Base 10 Representation

Other radix systems work in a similar manner. **Base 2** has digits 0 and 1, with place values that are powers of two, as depicted in Figure 1-12.

128	64	32	16	8	4	2	1
2^7	2^6	2^5	2^4	2^3	2^2	2^1	2^0
0	**1**	**1**	**0**	**0**	**0**	**1**	**1**
0 +	64 +	32 +	0 +	0 +	0 +	2 +	1 = **99**

FIGURE 1-12   Base 2 Representation

As shown in this figure, converting from base 2 to base 10 is simply a matter of adding up the column values that have a 1.

The term **bit** stands for **bi**nary dig**it**. Therefore, every bit has the value 0 or 1. A **byte** is a group of bits operated on as a single unit in a computer system, usually consisting of eight bits. Although values represented in base 2 are significantly longer than those represented in base 10, binary representation is used in digital computing because of the resulting simplicity of hardware design.

The algorithm for the conversion from base 10 to base 2 is to successively divide a number by two until the remainder becomes 0. The remainder of each division provides the next higher-order (binary) digit, as shown in Figure 1-13.

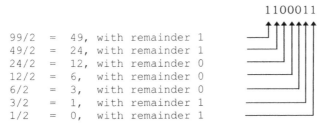

```
99/2  =  49, with remainder 1
49/2  =  24, with remainder 1
24/2  =  12, with remainder 0
12/2  =   6, with remainder 0
 6/2  =   3, with remainder 0
 3/2  =   1, with remainder 1
 1/2  =   0, with remainder 1
```

FIGURE 1-13   Converting from Base 10 to Base 2

Thus, we get the binary representation of 99 to be 1100011. This is the same as in Figure 1-12 above, except that we had an extra leading insignificant digit of 0, since we used an eight-bit representation there.

The term **bit** stands for binary digit. A **byte** is a group of bits operated on as a single unit in a computer system, usually consisting of eight bits.

1.3.3   Fundamental Hardware Components

The **central processing unit** (**CPU**) is the "brain" of a computer system, containing digital logic circuitry able to interpret and execute instructions. **Main memory** is where currently executing programs reside, which the CPU can directly and very quickly access. Main memory is volatile; that is, the contents are lost when the power is turned off. In contrast, **secondary memory** is nonvolatile, and therefore provides long-term storage of programs and data. This kind of storage, for example, can be magnetic (hard drive), optical (CD or DVD), or nonvolatile flash memory (such as in a USB drive). **Input/output devices** include anything that allows for input (such as the mouse and keyboard) or output (such as a monitor or printer). Finally, **buses** transfer data between components within a computer system, such as between the CPU and main memory. The relationship of these devices is depicted in Figure 1-14 below.

The **central processing unit** (**CPU**) is the "brain" of a computer, containing digital logic circuitry able to interpret and execute instructions.

1.3.4   Operating Systems—Bridging Software and Hardware

An **operating system** is software that has the job of managing and interacting with the hardware resources of a computer. Because an operating system is intrinsic to the operation a computer, it is referred to as **system software**.

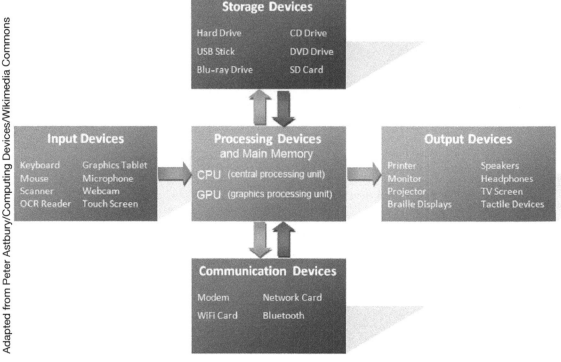

Adapted from Peter Astbury/Computing Devices/Wikimedia Commons

FIGURE 1-14 Fundamental Hardware Components

An operating system acts as the "middle man" between the hardware and executing application programs (see Figure 1-15). For example, it controls the allocation of memory for the various programs that may be executing on a computer. Operating systems also provide a particular user interface. Thus, it is the operating system installed on a given computer that determines the "look and feel" of the user interface and how the user interacts with the system, and not the particular model computer.

An **operating system** is software that has the job of managing the hardware resources of a given computer and providing a particular user interface.

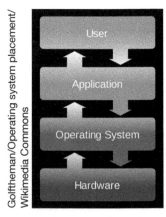

Golftheman/Operating system placement/Wikimedia Commons

FIGURE 1-15 Operating System

1.3.5 Limits of Integrated Circuits Technology: Moore's Law

In 1965, Gordon E. Moore (Figure 1-16), one of the pioneers in the development of integrated circuits and cofounder of Intel Corporation, predicted that as a result of continuing engineering developments, the number of transistors that would be able to be put on a silicon chip would double roughly every two years, allowing the complexity and therefore the capabilities of integrated circuits to grow exponentially. This prediction became known as **Moore's Law**. Amazingly, to this day that prediction has held true. While this doubling of performance cannot go on indefinitely, it has not yet reached its limit.

Courtesy of Intel Corporation

FIGURE 1-16   Gordon E. Moore

Moore's Law states that the number of transistors that can be placed on a single silicon chip doubles roughly every two years.

Self-Test Questions

1. All information in a computer system is in binary representation. (TRUE/FALSE)

2. Computer hardware is based on the use of electronic switches called _____.

3. How many of these electronic switches can be placed on a single integrated circuit, or "chip"?
   (a) Thousands
   (b) Millions
   (c) Billions

4. The term "bit" stands for _____.

5. A bit is generally a group of eight bytes. (TRUE/FALSE)

6. What is the value of the binary representation 0110.
   (a) 12
   (b) 3
   (c) 6

7. The _____ interprets and executes instructions in a computer system.

8. An operating system manages the hardware resources of a computer system, as well as provides a particular user interface. (TRUE/FALSE)

9. Moore's Law predicts that the number of transistors that can fit on a chip doubles about every ten years. (TRUE/FALSE)

ANSWERS: 1. True. 2. transistors. 3. (c). 4. binary digit. 5. False. 6. (c). 7. CPU. 8. True. 9. False

1.4 Computer Software

The first computer programs ever written were for a mechanical computer designed by Charles Babbage in the mid-1800s. (Babbage's Analytical Engine is discussed in Chapter 12). The person who wrote these programs was a woman, Ada Lovelace (Figure 1-17), who was a talented mathematician. Thus, she is referred to as "the first computer programmer." This section discusses fundamental issues of computer software.

1.4.1 What Is Computer Software?

Computer software is a set of program instructions, including related data and documentation, that can be executed by computer. This can be in the form of instructions on paper, or in digital form. While system software is intrinsic to a computer system, **application software** fulfills users' needs, such as a photo-editing program. We discuss the important concepts of syntax, semantics, and program translation next.

Royal Institution of Great Britain/Photo Researchers, Inc.

FIGURE 1-17   Ada Lovelace "The First Computer Programmer"

Computer software is a set of program instructions, including related data and documentation, that can be executed by computer.

1.4.2 Syntax, Semantics, and Program Translation

What Are Syntax and Semantics?

Programming languages (called "artificial languages") are languages just as "natural languages" such as English and Mandarin (Chinese). *Syntax* and *semantics* are important concepts that apply to all languages.

The **syntax** of a language is a set of characters and the acceptable arrangements (sequences) of those characters. English, for example, includes the letters of the alphabet, punctuation, and properly spelled words and properly punctuated sentences. The following is a syntactically correct sentence in English,

> "Hello there, how are you?" The following, however, is not syntactically correct,
> "Hello there, hao are you?"

In this sentence, the sequence of letters "hao" is not a word in the English language. Now consider the following sentence,

> "Colorless green ideas sleep furiously."

This sentence is syntactically correct, but is *semantically* incorrect, and thus has no meaning.

The **semantics** of a language is the meaning associated with each syntactically correct sequence of characters. In Mandarin, "Hao" is syntactically correct meaning "good." ("Hao" is from a system called pinyin, which uses the Roman alphabet rather than Chinese characters for writing Mandarin.) Thus, every language has its own syntax and semantics, as demonstrated in Figure 1-18.

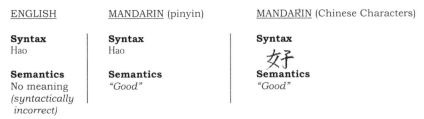

FIGURE 1-18 Syntax and Semantics of Languages

The **syntax** of a language is a set of characters and the acceptable sequences of those characters. The **semantics** of a language is the meaning associated with each syntactically correct sequence of characters.

Program Translation

A central processing unit (CPU) is designed to interpret and execute a specific set of instructions represented in binary form (i.e., 1s and 0s) called **machine code**. Only programs in machine code can be executed by a CPU, depicted in Figure 1-19.

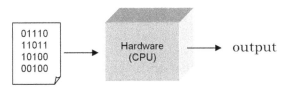

FIGURE 1-19 Execution of Machine Code

Writing programs at this "low level" is tedious and error-prone. Therefore, most programs are written in a "high-level" programming language such as Python. Since the instructions of such programs are not in machine code that a CPU can execute, a translator program must be used. There are two fundamental types of translators. One, called a **compiler**, translates programs directly into machine code to be executed by the CPU, denoted in Figure 1-20.

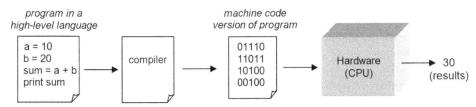

FIGURE 1-20 Program Execution by Use of a Compiler

The other type of translator is called an **interpreter**, which executes program instructions in place of ("running on top of") the CPU, denoted in Figure 1-21.

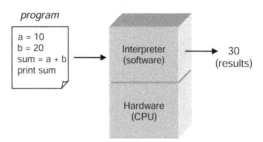

FIGURE 1-21   Program Execution by Use of a
Interpreter

Thus, an interpreter can immediately execute instructions as they are entered. This is referred to as **interactive mode**. This is a very useful feature for program development. Python, as we shall see, is executed by an interpreter. On the other hand, compiled programs generally execute faster than interpreted programs. Any program can be executed by either a compiler or an interpreter, as long there exists the corresponding translator program for the programming language that it is written in.

> A **compiler** is a translator program that translates programs directly into machine code to be executed by the CPU. An **interpreter** executes program instructions in place of ("running on top of") the CPU.

Program Debugging: Syntax Errors vs. Semantic Errors

Program debugging is the process of finding and correcting errors (**"bugs"**) in a computer program. Programming errors are inevitable during program development. **Syntax errors** are caused by invalid syntax (for example, entering `prnt` instead of `print`). Since a translator cannot understand instructions containing syntax errors, translators terminate when encountering such errors indicating where in the program the problem occurred.

In contrast, **semantic errors** (generally called **logic errors**) are errors in program logic. Such errors cannot be automatically detected, since translators cannot understand the intent of a given computation. For example, if a program computed the average of three numbers as follows,

$$(num1 + num2 + num3) / 2.0$$

a translator would have no means of determining that the divisor should be 3 and not 2. *Computers do not understand what a program is meant to do, they only follow the instructions given*. It is up to the programmer to detect such errors. Program debugging is not a trivial task, and constitutes much of the time of program development.

> **Syntax errors** are caused by invalid syntax. **Semantic (logic) errors** are caused by errors in program logic.

1.4.3 Procedural vs. Object-Oriented Programming

Programming languages fall into a number of *programming paradigms*. The two major programming paradigms in use today are *procedural (imperative) programming* and *object-oriented programming*. Each provides a different way of thinking about computation. While most programming languages only support one paradigm, Python supports both procedural and object-oriented programming. We will start with the procedural aspects of Python. We then introduce objects in Chapter 6, and delay complete discussion of object-oriented programming until Chapter 10.

> **Procedural programming** and **object-oriented programming** are two major programming paradigms in use today.

Self-Test Questions

1. Two general types of software are system software and _____ software.

2. The syntax of a given language is,
    (a) the set of symbols in the language.
    (b) the acceptable arrangement of symbols.
    (c) both of the above

3. The semantics of a given language is the meaning associated with any arrangement of symbols in the language. (TRUE/FALSE)

4. CPUs can only execute instructions that are in binary form called _____.

5. The two fundamental types of translation programs for the execution of computer programs are _____ and _____.

6. The process of finding and correcting errors in a computer program is called
    _____.

7. Which kinds of errors can a translator program detect?
    (a) Syntax errors
    (b) Semantic errors
    (c) Neither of the above

8. Two major programming paradigms in use today are _____ programming and _____ programming.

ANSWERS: 1. application. 2. (c). 3. False. 4. machine code. 5. compilers, interpreters. 6. program debugging. 7. (a). 8. procedural, object-oriented

---

COMPUTATIONAL PROBLEM SOLVING

1.5   The Process of Computational Problem Solving

Computational problem solving does not simply involve the act of computer programming. It is a *process*, with programming being only one of the steps. Before a program is written, a design for the program must be developed. And before a design can be developed, the problem to be solved must be well understood. Once written, the program must be thoroughly tested. These steps are outlined in Figure 1-22.

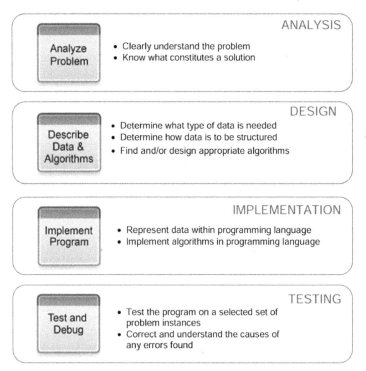

FIGURE 1-22   Process of Computational Problem Solving

1.5.1   Problem Analysis

Understanding the Problem

Once a problem is clearly understood, the fundamental computational issues for solving it can be determined. For each of the problems discussed earlier, the representation is straightforward. For the calendar month problem, there are two algorithmic tasks—determining the first day of a given month, and displaying the calendar month in the proper format. The first day of the month can be obtained by *direct calculation* by use of the algorithm provided in Figure 1-8.

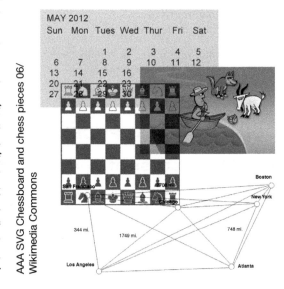

For the Man, Cabbage, Goat, Wolf (MCGW) problem, a brute-force algorithmic approach of trying all possible solutions works very well, since there are a small number of actions that can be taken at each step, and only a relatively small number of steps for reaching a solution. For both the Traveling Salesman problem and the game of chess, the brute-force approach is infeasible. Thus, the computational issue for these problems is to find other, more efficient algorithmic approaches for their

AAA SVG Chessboard and chess pieces 06/ Wikimedia Commons

solution. (In fact, methods have been developed for solving Traveling Salesman problems involving tens of thousands of cities. And current chess-playing programs can beat top-ranked chess masters.)

Knowing What Constitutes a Solution

Besides clearly understanding a computational problem, one must know what constitutes a solution. For some problems, there is only one solution. For others, there may be a number (or infinite number) of solutions. Thus, a program may be stated as finding,

♦ *A* solution

♦ An *approximate* solution

♦ A *best* solution

♦ *All* solutions

For the MCGW problem, there are an infinite number of solutions since the man could pointlessly row back and forth across the river an arbitrary number of times. A *best solution* here is one with the shortest number of steps. (There may be more than one "best" solution for any given problem.) In the Traveling Salesman problem there is only one solution (unless there exists more than one shortest route). Finally, for the game of chess, the goal (solution) is to win the game. Thus, since the number of chess games that can be played is on the order of 10^{120} (with each game ending in a win, a loss, or a stalemate), there are a comparable number of possible solutions to this problem.

1.5.2   Program Design

Describing the Data Needed

For the Man, Cabbage, Goat, Wolf problem, a list can be used to represent the correct location (east and west) of the man, cabbage, goat, and wolf as discussed earlier, reproduced below,

man cabbage goat   wolf
[W,   E,   W,   E]

For the Calendar Month problem, the data include the month and year (entered by the user), the number of days in each month, and the names of the days of the week. A useful structuring of the data is given below,

[*month, year*]
[31, 28, 31, 30, 31, 30, 31, 31, 30, 31, 30, 31]
['Sunday', 'Monday', 'Tuesday', 'Wednesday', 'Thursday', 'Friday', 'Saturday']

The month and year are grouped in a single list since they are naturally associated. Similarly, the names of the days of the week and the number of days in each month are grouped. (The advantages of list representations will be made clear in Chapter 4.) Finally, the first day of the month, as determined by the algorithm in Figure 1-8, can be represented by a single integer,

0 – Sunday, 1 – Monday, . . ., 6 – Saturday

For the Traveling Salesman problem, the distance between each pair of cities must be represented. One possible way of structuring the data is as a table, depicted in Figure 1-23.

For example, the distance from Atlanta to Los Angeles is 2175 miles. There is duplication of information in this representation, however. For each distance from *x* to *y*, the distance from *y* to *x* is

	Atlanta	Boston	Chicago	Los Angeles	New York City	San Francisco
Atlanta	-	1110	718	2175	888	2473
Boston	1110	-	992	2991	215	3106
Chicago	718	992	-	2015	791	2131
Los Angeles	2175	2991	2015	-	2790	381
New York City	888	215	791	2790	-	2901
San Francisco	2473	3106	2131	381	2901	-

FIGURE 1-23   Table Representation of Data

also represented. If the size of the table is small, as here, this is not much of an issue. However, for a significantly larger table, significantly more memory would be wasted during program execution. Since only half of the table is really needed (for example, the shaded area in the figure), the data could be represented as a list of lists instead,

[['Atlanta', ['Boston', 1110], ['Chicago', 718], ['Los Angeles', 2175], ['New York', 888],
  ['San Francisco', 2473]],
['Boston', ['Chicago', 992], ['Los Angeles', 2991], ['New York', 215], ['San Francisco', 3106]],
['Chicago', ['Los Angeles', 2015], ['New York', 791], ['San Francisco', 2131]],
['Los Angeles', ['New York', 2790], ['San Francisco', 381]],
['New York', ['San Francisco', 2901]]]

Finally, for a chess-playing program, the location and identification of each chess piece needs to be represented (Figure 1-24). An obvious way to do this is shown on the left below, in which each piece is represented by a single letter ('K' for the king, 'Q' for the queen, 'N' for the knight, etc.),

 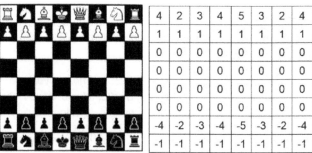

FIGURE 1-24   Representations of Pieces on a Chess Board

There is a problem with this choice of symbols, however—there is no way to distinguish the white pieces from the black ones. The letters could be modified, for example, PB for a black pawn and PW for a white pawn. While that may be an intuitive representation, it is not the best representation for a program. A better way would be to represent pieces using positive and negative integers as shown on the right of the figure: 1 for a white pawn and -1 for a black pawn; 2 for a white bishop and -2 for a black bishop, and so forth. Various ways of representing chess boards have been developed, each with certain advantages and disadvantages. The appropriate representation of data is a fundamental aspect of computer science.

Describing the Needed Algorithms

When solving a computational problem, either suitable existing algorithms may be found or new algorithms must be developed. For the MCGW problem, there are standard search algorithms that can be used. For the calendar month problem, a day of the week algorithm already exists. For the Traveling Salesman problem, there are various (nontrivial) algorithms that can be utilized, as mentioned, for solving problems with tens of thousands of cities. Finally, for the game of chess, since it is infeasible to look ahead at the final outcomes of every possible move, there are algorithms that make a best guess at which moves to make. Algorithms that work well in general but are not guaranteed to give the correct result for each specific problem are called *heuristic algorithms*.

1.5.3 Program Implementation

Design decisions provide *general* details of the data representation and the algorithmic approaches for solving a problem. The details, however, do not specify which programming language to use, or how to implement the program. That is a decision for the implementation phase. Since we are programming in Python, the implementation needs to be expressed in a syntactically correct and appropriate way, using the instructions and features available in Python.

1.5.4 Program Testing

As humans, we have abilities that far exceed the capabilities of any machine, such as using commonsense reasoning, or reading the expressions of another person. However, one thing that we are not very good at is dealing with detail, which computer programming demands. Therefore, while we are enticed by the existence of increasingly capable computing devices that unfailingly and speedily execute whatever instructions 'we give them, writing computer programs is difficult and challenging. As a result, *programming errors are pervasive, persistent and inevitable*. However, the sense of accomplishment of developing software that can be of benefit to hundreds, thousands, or even millions of people can be extremely gratifying. If it were easy to do, the satisfaction would not be as great.

Given this fact, software testing is a crucial part of software development. Testing is done incrementally as a program is being developed, when the program is complete, and when the program needs to be updated. In subsequent chapters, program testing and debugging will be discussed and expanded upon. For now, we provide the following general truisms of software development in Figure 1-25.

1. Programming errors are pervasive, persistent, and inevitable.

2. Software testing is an essential part of software development.

3. Any changes made in correcting a programming error should be fully understood as to why the changes correct the detected error.

FIGURE 1-25 Truisms of Software Development

Truism 1 reflects the fact that programming errors are inevitable and that we must accept it. As a result of truism 1, truism 2 states the essential role of software testing. Given the inevitability of programming errors, it is important to test a piece of software in a thorough and systematic manner. Finally, truism 3 states the importance of understanding *why* a given change (or set of changes) in a program fixes a specific error. If you make a change to a program that fixes a given problem but you don't know why it did, then you have lost control of the program logic. As a result, you may have corrected one problem, but inadvertently caused other, potentially more serious ones.

Accountants are committed to reconciling balances to the penny. They do not disregard a discrepancy of one cent, for example, even though the difference between the calculated and expected balances is so small. They understand that a small, seemingly insignificant difference can be the result of two (or more) very big discrepancies. For example, there may be an erroneous credit of $1,500.01 and an erroneous debit of $1,500. (The author has experienced such a situation in which the people involved worked all night to find the source of the error.) Determining the source of errors in a program is very much the same. We next look at the Python programming language.

1.6 The Python Programming Language

Now that computational problem solving and computer programming have been discussed, we turn to the Python programming language and associated tools to begin putting this knowledge into practice.

1.6.1 About Python

Guido van Rossum (Figure 1-26) is the creator of the Python programming language, first released in the early 1990s. Its name comes from a 1970s British comedy sketch television show called *Monty Python's Flying Circus*. (Check them out on YouTube!) The development environment IDLE provided with Python (discussed below) comes from the name of a member of the comic group.

Python has a simple syntax. Python programs are clear and easy to read. At the same time, Python provides powerful programming features, and is widely used. Companies and organizations that use Python include YouTube, Google, Yahoo, and NASA. Python is well supported and freely available at www.python.org. (See the Python 3 Programmers' Reference at the end of the text for how to download and install Python.)

1.6.2 The IDLE Python Development Environment

IDLE is an **integrated development environment** (**IDE**). An IDE is a bundled set of software tools for program development. This typically includes

Jason E. Kaplan

FIGURE 1-26 Guido van Rossum

an **editor** for creating and modifying programs, a **translator** for executing programs, and a **program debugger**. A debugger provides a means of taking control of the execution of a program to aid in finding program errors.

Python is most commonly translated by use of an interpreter. Thus, Python provides the very useful ability to execute in interactive mode. The window that provides this interaction is referered to as the **Python shell**. Interacting with the shell is much like using a calculator, except that, instead of being limited to the operations built into a calculator (addition, subtraction, etc.), it allows the entry and creation of any Python code. Example use of the Python shell is demonstrated in Figure 1-27.

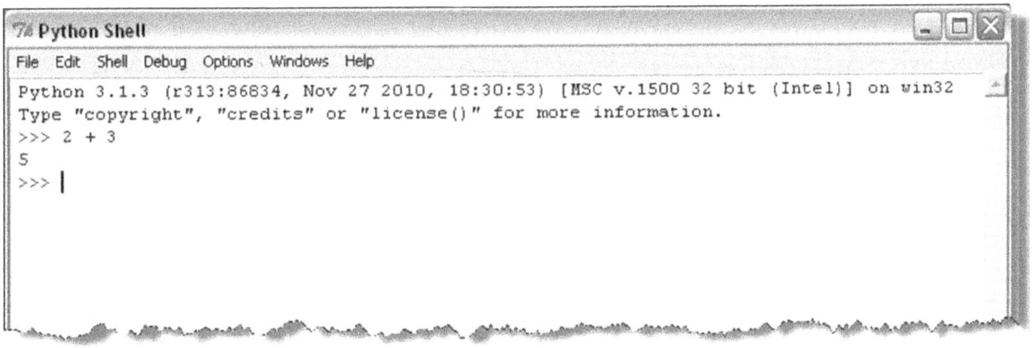

FIGURE 1-27   Python Shell

Here, the expression 2 + 3 is entered at the **shell prompt** (>>>), which immediately responds with the result 5.

Although working in the Python shell is convenient, the entered code is not saved. Thus, for program development, a means of entering, editing, and saving Python programs is provided by the program editor in IDLE. Details are given below.

An **Integrated Development Environment (IDE)** is a bundled set of software tools for program development.

1.6.3   The Python Standard Library

The **Python Standard Library** is a collection of *built-in modules*, each providing specific functionality beyond what is included in the "core" part of Python. (We discuss the creation of Python modules in Chapter 7.) For example, the math module provides additional mathematical functions. The random module provides the ability to generate random numbers, useful in programming, as we shall see. (Other Python modules are described in the Python 3 Programmers' Reference.) In order to utilize the capabilities of a given module in a specific program, an **import** statement is used as shown in Figure 1-28.

The example in the figure shows the use of the import math statement to gain access to a particular function in the math module, the factorial function. The syntax for using the factorial

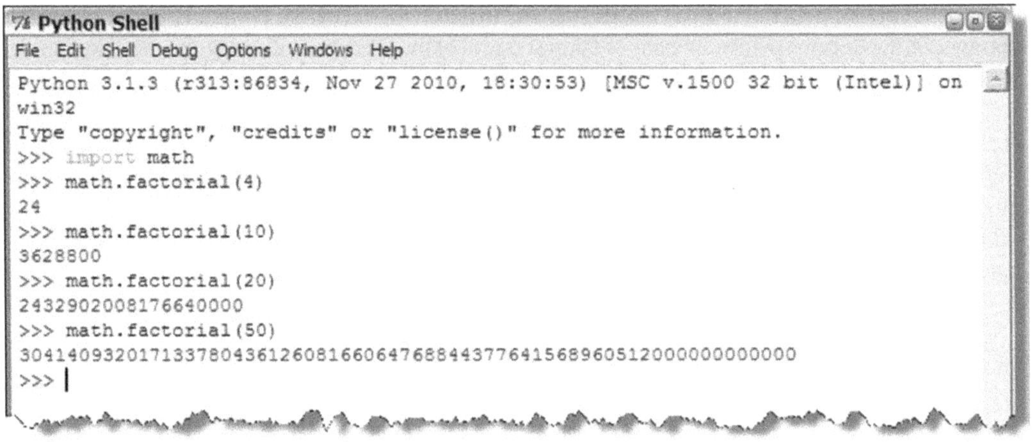

FIGURE 1-28 Using an import statement

function is `math.factorial(n)`, for some positive integer n. We will make use of library modules in Chapter 2. In section 1.7, we see how to enter and execute a complete Python program.

> The **Python Standard Library** is a collection of *modules*, each providing specific functionality beyond what is included in the core part of Python.

1.6.4 A Bit of Python

We introduce a bit of Python, just enough to begin writing some simple programs. Since all computer programs input data, process the data, and output results, we look at the notion of a variable, how to perform some simple arithmetic calculations, and how to do simple input and output.

Variables

One of the most fundamental concepts in programming is that of a *variable*. (Variables are discussed in detail in Chapter 2.) A simple description of a variable is "a name that is assigned to a value," as shown below,

$$n = 5 \qquad \text{variable n is assigned the value 5}$$

Thus, whenever variable n appears in a calculation, it is the current value that n is assigned to that is used, as in the following,

$$n + 20 \qquad (5 + 20)$$

If variable n is assigned a new value, then the same expression will produce a different result,

$$n = 10$$
$$n + 20 \qquad (10 + 20)$$

We next look at some basic arithmetic operators of Python.

A **variable** is "a name that is assigned to a value."

Some Basic Arithmetic Operators

The common arithmetic operators in Python are + (addition), − (subtraction), * (multiplication), / (division), and ** (exponentiation). Addition, subtraction, and division use the same symbols as standard mathematical notation,

$$10 + 20 \qquad\qquad 25 - 15 \qquad\qquad 20 / 10$$

(There is also the symbol // for truncated division, discussed in Chapter 2.) For multiplication and exponentiation, the asterisk (*) is used.

$$5 * 10 \quad \text{(5 times 10)} \qquad\qquad 2 ** 4 \quad \text{(2 to the 4th power)}$$

Multiplication is never denoted by the use of parentheses as in mathematics, as depicted below,

$$10 * (20 + 5) \quad \text{CORRECT} \qquad\qquad 10(20 + 5) \quad \text{INCORRECT}$$

Note that parentheses may be used to denote subexpressions. Finally, we see how to input information from the user, and display program results.

The common arithmetic operators in Python are + (addition), − (subtraction), * (multiplication), / (division), and ** (exponentiation).

Basic Input and Output

The programs that we will write request and get information from the user. In Python, the `input` function is used for this purpose,

```
name = input('What is your name?: ')
```

Characters within quotes are called *strings*. This particular use of a string, for requesting input from the user, is called a *prompt*. The `input` function displays the string on the screen to prompt the user for input,

```
What is your name?: Charles
```

The underline is used here to indicate the user's input.

The print function is used to display information on the screen in Python. This may be used to display a message,

```
>>> print('Welcome to My First Program!')
Welcome to My First Program!
```

or used to output the value of a variable,

```
>>> n = 10
>>> print(n)
10
```

or to display a combination of both strings and variables,

```
>>> name = input('What is your name?: ')
What is your name?: Charles
>>> print('Hello', name)
Hello Charles
```

Note that a comma is used to separate the individual items being printed, causing a space to appear between each when displayed. Thus, the output of the print function in this case is Hello Charles, and not HelloCharles. There is more to say about variables, operators, and input/output in Python. This will be covered in the chapters ahead.

In Python, input is used to request and get information from the user, and print is used to display information on the screen.

1.6.5 Learning How to Use IDLE

In order to become familiar with writing your own Python programs using IDLE, we will create a simple program that asks the user for their name and responds with a greeting. This program utilizes the following concepts:

♦ creating and executing Python programs
♦ input and print

First, to create a Python program file, select New Window from the File menu in the Python shell as shown in Figure 1-29:

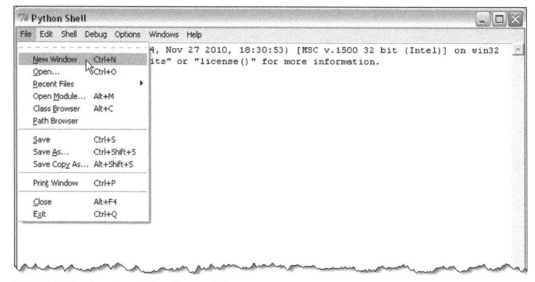

FIGURE 1-29 Creating a Python Program File

A new, untitled program window will appear:

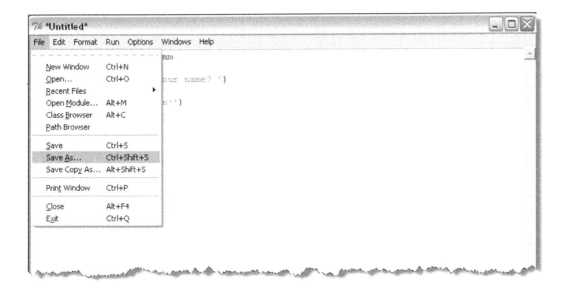

Type the following in the program window exactly as shown.

```
# My First Python Program

name = input('What is your name? ')
print('Hello', name)
print('Welcome to Python!')
```

When finished, save the program file by selecting Save As under the File menu, and save in the appropriate folder with the name MyFirstProgram.py.

To run the program, select Run Module from the Run menu (or simply hit function key F5).

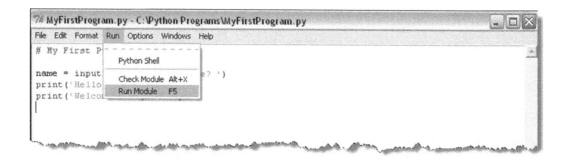

If you have entered the program code correctly, the program should execute as shown in Figure 1-30.

```
Python Shell
File  Edit  Shell  Debug  Options  Windows  Help
Python 3.1.3 (r313:86834, Nov 27 2010, 18:30:53) [MSC v.1500 32 bit (Intel)] on win32
Type "copyright", "credits" or "license()" for more information.
>>> ================================= RESTART =================================
>>>
What is your name? Charles
Hello Charles
Welcome to Python!
>>> |
```

FIGURE 1-30 Sample Output of MyFirstProgram.py

If, however, you have mistyped part of the program resulting in a syntax error (such as mistyping print), you will get an error message similar to that in Figure 1-31.

```
Python Shell
File  Edit  Shell  Debug  Options  Windows  Help
Python 3.1.3 (r313:86834, Nov 27 2010, 18:30:53) [MSC v.1500 32 bit (Intel)] on win32
Type "copyright", "credits" or "license()" for more information.
>>> ================================= RESTART =================================
>>>
What is your name? Charles
Hello Charles
Traceback (most recent call last):
  File "C:\Python Programs\MyFirstProgram.py", line 5, in <module>
    prnt('Welcome to Python!')
NameError: name 'prnt' is not defined
>>> |
```

FIGURE 1-31 Output Resulting from a Syntax Error

In that case, go back to the program window and make the needed corrections, then re-save and re-execute the program. You may need to go through this process a number of times until all the syntax errors have been corrected.

1.7   A First Program—Calculating the Drake Equation

Dr. Frank Drake conducted the first search for radio signals from extraterrestrial civilizations in 1960. This established SETI (Search for Extraterrestrial Intelligence), a new area of scientific inquiry. In order to estimate the number of civilizations that may exist in our galaxy that we may be able to communicate with, he developed what is now called the *Drake equation.*

The Drake equation accounts for a number of different factors. The values used for some of these are the result of scientific study, while others are only the result of an "intelligent guess." The factors consist of R, the average rate of star creation per year in our galaxy; p, the percentage of those stars that have planets; n, the average number of planets that can potentially support life for each star with planets; f, the percentage of those planets that actually go on to develop life; i, the percentage of those planets that go on to develop intelligent life; c, the percentage of those that have the technology communicate with us; and L, the expected lifetime of civilizations (the period that they can communicate). The Drake equation is simply the multiplication of all these factors, giving N, the estimated number of detectable civilizations there are at any given time,

$$N = R \cdot p \cdot n \cdot f \cdot i \cdot c \cdot L$$

Figure 1-32 shows those parameters in the Drake equation that have some consensus as to their correct value.

Drake Equation Factor Values		Estimated Values
Rate of star creation	R	7[†]
Percentage of stars with planets	p	40%
Average number of planets that can potentially support life for each star with planets	n	(no consensus)
Percentage of those that go on to develop life	f	13%
Percentage of those that go on to intelligent develop life	i	(no consensus)
Percentage of those willing and able to communicate	c	(no consensus)
Expected lifetime of civilizations	L	(no consensus)
[†] Estimate of NASA and the European Space Agency		

FIGURE 1-32   Proposed Values for the Drake Equation

1.7.1 The Problem

The value of 7 for R, the rate of star creation, is the least disputed value in the Drake equation today. Given the uncertainty of the remaining factors, you are to develop a program that allows a user to enter their own estimated values for the remaining six factors (p, n, f, i, c, and L) and displays the calculated result.

1.7.2 Problem Analysis

This problem is very straightforward. We only need to understand the equation provided.

1.7.3 Program Design

The program design for this problem is also straightforward. The data to be represented consist of numerical values, with the Drake equation as the algorithm. The overall steps of the program are depicted in Figure 1-33.

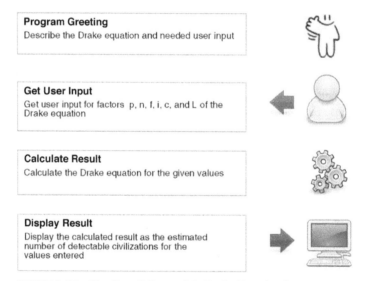

Program Greeting
Describe the Drake equation and needed user input

Get User Input
Get user input for factors p, n, f, i, c, and L of the Drake equation

Calculate Result
Calculate the Drake equation for the given values

Display Result
Display the calculated result as the estimated number of detectable civilizations for the values entered

FIGURE 1-33 The Overall Steps of the Drake Equation Program

1.7.4 Program Implementation

The implementation of this program is fairly simple. The only programming elements needed are input, assignment, and print, along with the use of arithmetic operators. An implementation is given in Figure 1-34. Example execution of the program is given in Figure 1-35.

First, note the program lines beginning with the hash sign, #. In Python, this symbol is used to denote a *comment statement*. A **comment statement** contains information for persons reading the program. Comment statements are ignored during program execution—they have no effect on the program results. In this program, the initial series of comment statements (**lines 1–23**) explain the Drake equation and provide a brief summary of the purpose of the program.

```
 1 # SETI Program
 2 #
 3 # The Drake equation, developed by Frank Drake in the 1960s, attempts to
 4 # estimate how many extraterrestrial civilizations, N, may exist in our
 5 # galaxy at any given time that we might come in contact with,
 6 #
 7 #     N = R * p * n * f * i * c * L
 8 #
 9 # where,
10 #
11 #     R ... estimated rate of star creation in our galaxy
12 #     p ... estimated percent of stars that have planets
13 #     n ... estimated average number of planets that can potentially support
14 #           life for each star with planets
15 #     f ... estimated percent of those planets that actually go on to develop life
16 #     i ... estimated percent of those planets go on to develop intelligent life
17 #     c ... estimated percent of those that are willing and able to communicate
18 #     L ... estimated expected lifetime of such civilizations
19 #
20 # Given that the value for R, 7 per year, is the least disputed of the values,
21 # the user will be prompted to enter estimated values for the remaining six
22 # factors. The estimated number of civilizations that may be detected in our
23 # galaxy will then be displayed.
24
25 # display program welcome
26 print('Welcome to the SETI program')
27 print('This program will allow you to enter specific values related to')
28 print('the likelihood of finding intelligent life in our galaxy. All')
29 print('percentages should be entered as integer values, e.g., 40 and not .40')
30 print()
31
32 # get user input
33 p = int(input('What percentage of stars do you think have planets?: '))
34 n = int(input('How many planets per star do you think can support life?: '))
35 f = int(input('What percentage do you think actually develop life?: '))
36 i = int(input('What percentage of those do you think have intelligent life?: '))
37 c = int(input('What percentage of those do you think can communicate with us?: '))
38 L = int(input('Number of years you think civilizations last?: '))
39
40 # calculate result
41 num_detectable_civilizations = 7 * (p/100) * n * (f/100) * (i/100) * (c/100) * L
42
43 # display result
44 print()
45 print('Based on the values entered ...')
46 print('there are an estimated', round(num_detectable_civilizations),
47       'potentially detectable civilizations in our galaxy')
```

FIGURE 1-34 Drake Equation Program

Comment statements are also used in the program to denote the beginning of each program section (**lines 25, 32, 40,** and **43**). These *section headers* provide a broad outline of the program following the program design depicted in Figure 1-33.

The program welcome section (**lines 25–30**) contains a series of print instructions displaying output to the screen. Each begins with the word `print` followed by a matching pair of parentheses. Within the parentheses are the items to be displayed. In this case, each contains a particular string of characters. The final "empty" print, `print()` on **line 30** (and **line 44**), does not display anything. It simply causes the screen cursor to move down to the next line, therefore creating a skipped line in the screen output. (Later we will see another way of creating the same result.)

```
Program Execution ...

Welcome to the SETI program
This program will allow you to enter specific values related to
the likelihood of finding intelligent life in our galaxy. All
percentages should be entered as integer values, e.g., 40 and not .40

What percentage of stars do you think have planets?: 40
How many planets per star do you think can support life?: 2
What percentage do you think actually develop life?: 5
What percentage of those do you think have intelligent life?: 3
What percentage of those do you think can communicate with us?: 5
Number of years you think civilizations last?: 10000

Based on the values entered...
there are an estimated 4.2 potentially detectable civilizations in
our galaxy
>>>
```

FIGURE 1-35 Execution of the Drake Equation Program

The following section (**lines 32–38**) contains the instructions for requesting the input from the user. Previously, we saw the input function used for inputting a name entered by the user. In that case, the instruction was of the form,

```
name = input('What is your name?:')
```

In this program, there is added syntax,

```
p = int(input('What percentage of stars do you think have planets?:'))
```

The input function always returns what the user enters as a string of characters. This is appropriate when a person's name is being entered. However, in this program, numbers are being entered, not names. Thus, in, the following,

```
What percentage of stars do you think have planets?: 40
```

40 is to be read as single number and not as the characters '4' and '0'. The addition of the int (...) syntax around the input instruction accomplishes this. This will be discussed more fully when numeric and string (character) data are discussed in Chapter 2.

On **line 41** the Drake equation is calculated and stored in variable num_detectable_ civilizations. Note that since some of the input values were meant to be percentages (p, f, i, and c), those values in the equation are each divided by 100. Finally, **lines 44–47** display the results.

1.7.5 Program Testing

To test the program, we can calculate the Drake equation for various other values using a calculator, providing a set of *test cases*. A **test case** is a set of input values and expected output of a given program. A **test plan** consists of a number of test cases to verify that a program meets all requirements. A good strategy is to include "average," as well as "extreme" or "special" cases in a test plan. Such a test plan is given in Figure 1-36.

Based on these results, we can be fairly confident that the program will give the correct results for all input values.

Input Values							Expected Results	Actual Results	Evaluation
	p	n	f	i	c	L			
Extreme Cases (no chance of contacting intelligent life)									
Zero Planets per Star	0	2	100%	1%	1%	10,000	0	0	passed
Zero percent of Planets Support Life	50%	0	100%	1%	1%	10,000	0	0	passed
Average Cases									
Average Case 1	30%	3	75%	1%	5%	5,000	12	12	passed
Average Case 2	50%	6	80%	5%	10%	10,000	840	840	passed
Extreme Cases (great chance of contacting intelligent life)									
Extreme Case 1	100%	10	100%	100%	100%	10,000	700,000	700,000	passed
Extreme Case 2	100%	12	100%	100%	100%	100,000	8,400,000	8,400,000	passed

FIGURE 1-36   Test Plan Results for Drake's Equation Program

CHAPTER SUMMARY

General Topics

Computational Problem Solving/Representation/
    Abstraction
Algorithms/Brute Force Approach
Computer Hardware/Transistors/Integrated Circuits/
    Moore's Law
Binary Representation/Bit/Byte/
    Binary-Decimal Conversion
Central Processing Unit (CPU)/Main and
    Secondary Memory
Input/Output Devices/Buses
Computer Software/System Software/
    Application Software
Operating Systems
Syntax and Semantics/Program Translation/
    Compiler vs. Interpreter

Program Debugging/Syntax Errors vs. Logic
    (Semantic) Errors
Procedural Programming vs. Object-Oriented
    Programming
The Process of Computational Problem Solving/
    Program Testing
Integrated Development Environments (IDE)/
    Program Editors/Debuggers
Comment Statements as Program Documentation
Test Cases/Test Plans

Python-Specific Programming Topics

The Python Programming Language/
    Guido van Rossum (creator of Python)
Comment Statements in Python

Introduction to Variables, Arithmetic Operators, `input` and `print` in Python

Introduction to Strings with the `input` Function in Python

Introduction to the Python Standard Library and the `import` Statement

The Python Shell/The IDLE Integrated Development Environment

The Standard Python Library

CHAPTER EXERCISES

Section 1.1

1. Search online for two computing-related fields named "computational X" other than the ones listed in Figure 1-1.

2. Search online for two areas of computer science other than those given in the chapter.

3. For the Man, Cabbage, Goat, Wolf problem:
   (a) List all the invalid states for this problem, that is, in which the goat is left alone with the cabbage, or the wolf is left alone with the goat.
   (b) Give the shortest sequence of steps that solves the MCGW problem.
   (c) Give the sequence of state representations that correspond to your solution starting with (E,E,E,E) and ending with (W,W,W,W).
   (d) There is an alternate means of representing states. Rather than a sequence representation, a set representation can be used. In this representation, if an item is on the east side of the river, its symbol is in the set, and if on the west side, the symbol is not in the set as shown below,

   {M,C,G,W}—all items on east side of river (start state)
   {C,W}—cabbage and wolf on east side of river, man and goat on west side
   { }—all items on the west side of the river (goal state)

   Give the sequence of states for your solution to the problem using this new state representation.
   (e) How many shortest solutions are there for this problem?

4. For a simple game that starts with five stones, in which each player can pick up either one or two stones, the person picking up the last stone being the loser,
   (a) Give a state representation appropriate for this problem.
   (b) Give the start state and goal state for this problem.
   (c) Give a sequence of states in which the first player wins the game.

Section 1.2

5. Using the algorithm in Figure 1-8, *show all steps* for determining the day of the week for January 24, 2018. (Note that 2018 is not a leap year.)

6. Using the algorithm in Figure 1-8, determine the day of the week that you were born on.

7. Suppose that an algorithm was needed for determining the day of the week for dates that only occur within the years 2000–2099. Simplify the day of the week algorithm in Figure 1-8 as much as possible by making the appropriate changes.

8. As precisely as possible, give a series of steps (an algorithm) for doing long addition.

Section 1.3

9. What is the number of bits in 8 bytes, assuming the usual number of bits in a byte?

10. Convert the following values in binary representation to base 10. *Show all steps.*
    (a) 1010   (b) 1011   (c) 10000   (d) 1111

11. Convert the following values into binary (base 2) representation. *Show all steps.*

    (a) 5   **(b)** 7   **(c)** 16   **(d)** 15   **(e)** 32

    (f) 33   **(g)** 64   **(h)** 63   **(i)** 128   **(j)** 127

12. What is in common within each of the following groups of binary numbers?

    (a) values that end with a "0" digit (e.g., 1100)

    (b) values that end with a "1" digit (e.g., 1101)

    (c) values with a leftmost digit of "1," followed by all "0s" (e.g., 1000)

    (d) values consisting only of all "1" digits (e.g., 1111)

13. Assuming that Moore's Law continues to hold true, where n is the number of transistors that can currently be placed on an integrated circuit (chip), and k*n is the number that can be placed on a chip in eight years, what is the value of k?

Section 1.4

14. Give two specific examples of an application program besides those mentioned in the chapter.

15. For each of the following statements in English, indicate whether the statement contains a syntax error, a logic (semantic) error, or is a valid statement.

    (a) Witch way did he go?

    (b) I think he went over their.

    (c) I didn't see him go nowhere.

16. For each of the following arithmetic expressions for adding up the integers 1 to 5, indicate whether the expression contains a syntax error, a semantic error, or is a valid expression.

    (a) `1 + 2 ++ 3 + 4 + 5`

    (b) `1 + 2 + 4 + 5`

    (c) `1 + 2 + 3 + 4 + 5`

    (d) `5 + 4 + 3 + 2 + 1`

17. Give one benefit of the use of a compiler, and one benefit of the use of an interpreter.

Section 1.5

18. Use the Python Interactive Shell to calculate the number of routes that can be taken for the Traveling Salesman problem for:

    (a) 6 cities   **(b)** 12 cities   **(c)** 18 cities   **(d)** 36 cities

19. Enter the following statement into the interactive shell:

```
print('What is your favorite color?')
```

Record the output. Now enter the following statement exactly as given,

```
printt('What is your favorite color?')
```

Record the output. Is this a syntax error or a logic error?

20. For the Traveling Salesman problem,

    (a) Update the list representation of the distances between cities in the table in Figure 1-23 to add the city of Seattle. The distances between Seattle and each of the other cities is given below.

        Atlanta to Seattle, 2641 miles, Boston to Seattle, 3032 miles, Chicago to Seattle, 2043 miles, LA to Seattle, 1208 miles, NYC to Seattle, 2832 miles, San Francisco to Seattle, 808 miles

    (b) Determine a reasonably short route of travel for visiting each city once and only once, starting in Atlanta and ending in San Francisco.

Section 1.6

21. Which of the following capabilities does an integrated development environment (IDE) provide?
    (a) Creating and modifying programs
    (b) Executing programs
    (c) Debugging programs
    (d) All of the above

22. The Python shell is a window in which Python instructions are immediately executed. (TRUE/FALSE)

23. Suppose that the math module of the Python Standard Library were imported. What would be the proper syntax for calling a function in the math module named `sqrt` to calculate the square root of four?

24. What is the value of variable n after the following instructions are executed?

```
j = 5
k = 10
n = j * k
```

25. Which of the following is a proper arithmetic expression in Python?
    (a) `10(15 + 6)`
    (b) `(10 * 2)(4 + 8)`
    (c) `5 * (6 - 2)`

26. Exactly what is output by the following if the user enters `24` in response to the input prompt.

```
age = input('How old are you?: ')
print('You are', age, 'years old')
```

PYTHON PROGRAMMING EXERCISES

P1. Write a simple Python program that displays the following powers of 2, one per line: 2^1, 2^2, 2^3, 2^4, 2^5, 2^6, 2^7, 2^8.

P2. Write a Python program that allows the user to enter any integer value, and displays the value of 2 raised to that power. Your program should function as shown below.

```
What power of two? 10
Two to the power of 10 is 1024
```

P3. Write a Python program that allows the user to enter any integer base and integer exponent, and displays the value of the base raised to that exponent. Your program should function as shown below.

```
What base? 10
What power of 10? 4
10 to the power of 4 is 10000
```

P4. Write a Python program that allows the user to enter a four-digit binary number and displays its value in base 10. *Each binary digit should be entered one per line, starting with the leftmost digit*, as shown below.

```
Enter leftmost digit: 1
Enter the next digit: 0
Enter the next digit: 0
Enter the next digit: 1
The value is 9
```

P5. Write a simple Python program that prompts the user for a certain number of cities for the Traveling Salesman problem, and displays the total number of possible routes that can be taken. Your program should function as shown below.

```
How many cities? 10
For 10 cities, there are 3628800 possible routes
```

PROGRAM MODIFICATION PROBLEMS

M1. Modify the sample "hello" Python program in section 1.6.5 to first request the user's first name, and then request their last name. The program should then display,

```
Hello firstname lastname
Welcome to Python!
```

for the *firstname* and *lastname* entered.

M2. Modify the Drake's Equation Program in section 1.7 so that it calculates results for a best case scenario, that is, so that factors p (percentage of stars that have planets), f (percentage of those planets that develop life), i (percentage of those planets that develop intelligent life), and c (percentage of those planets that can communicate with us) are all hard-coded as 100%. The value of R should remain as 7. Design the program so that the only values that the user is prompted for are how many planets per star can support life, n, and the estimated number of years civilizations last, L. Develop a set of test cases for your program with the included test results.

PROGRAM DEVELOPMENT PROBLEMS

D1. Develop and test a program that allows the user to enter an integer value indicating the number of cities to solve for the Traveling Salesman problem. The program should then output the number of years it would take to solve using a brute force-approach. Make use of the factorial function of the math module as shown in Figure 1-28. Estimate the total amount of time it takes by using the assumptions given in section 1.1.2.

D2. Based on the information provided about the game of chess in section 1.1.2, develop and test a program that determines how many years it would take for all possible chess games to be played if everyone in the world (regardless of age) played one (unique) chess game a day. Assume the current world population to be 7 billion.

## CHAPTER 2

Data and Expressions

With this chapter, we begin a detailed discussion of the concepts and techniques of computer programming. We start by looking at issues related to the representation, manipulation, and input/output of data—fundamental to all computing.

OBJECTIVES

After reading this chapter and completing the exercises, you will be able to:

◆ Explain and use numeric and string literal values

◆ Explain the limitations in the representation of floating-point values

◆ Explain what a character-encoding scheme is

◆ Explain what a control character is

◆ Explain and use variables, identifiers, and keywords

◆ Describe and perform variable assignment

◆ Describe and use operators and expressions

◆ Describe and use operator precedence and operator associativity

◆ Define a data type, and explain type coercion vs. type conversion

◆ Explain the difference between static and dynamic typing

◆ Effectively use arithmetic expressions in Python

◆ Write a simple straight-line Python program

◆ Explain the importance and use of test cases in program testing

CHAPTER CONTENTS

Motivation

Fundamental Concepts

2.4   Expressions and Data Types

Computational Problem Solving

2.5   Age in Seconds Program

MOTIVATION

The generation, collection, and analysis of data is a driving force in today's world. The sheer amount of data being created is staggering. Chain stores generate *terabytes* (see Figure 2-1) of customer information, looking for shopping patterns of individuals. Facebook users have created 40 billion photos requiring more than a *petabyte* of storage. A certain radio telescope is expected to generate an *exabyte* of information every four hours. All told, the current amount of data created each year is estimated to be almost two *zettabytes*, more than doubling every two years. In this chapter, we look at how data is represented and operated on in Python.

edge69/iStockphoto

Term†	Size (bytes)		Equivalent Storage
Kilobyte (KB)	10^3	1,000	Typewritten page†† (2 KB)
Kibibyte	2^{10}	1,024	
Megabyte (MB)	10^6	1,000,000	A small novel†† (1 MB)
Mebibyte	2^{20}	1,048,576	
Gigabyte (GB)	10^9	1,000,000,000	A pickup truck load of books†† (1 GB)
Gibibyte	2^{30}	1,073,741,824	
Terabyte (TB)	10^{12}	1,000,000,000,000	An academic research library†† (2 TB)
Tibibyte	2^{40}	1,099,511,627,776	
Petabyte (PB)	10^{15}	1,000,000,000,000,000	All U.S. academic libraries†† (2 PB)
Pebibyte	2^{50}	1,125,899,906,842,624	
Exabyte (EB)	10^{18}	1,000,000,000,000,000,000	All words ever spoken†† (5 EB)
Exbibyte	2^{60}	1,152,921,504,606,846,976	
Zettabyte (ZB)	10^{21}	1,000,000,000,000,000,000,000	Amount of data produced each year†††
Zebibyte	2^{70}	1,180,591,620,717,411,303,424	

† *Because of inconsistencies in the definition of Megabyte, Gigabyte, etc., the International Organization for Standards (ISO) has recommended the use of the terms Kilobyte, Megabyte, Gigabyte, etc. for 10^3, 10^6, 10^9 etc., and Kibibyte, Mebibyte and Gibibyte for 2^{10}, 2^{20}, 2^{30}, etc.* †† *School of Information Management and Systems, University of California Berkeley http://www2.sims.berkeley.edu/research/projects/how-much-info-2003/*
††† *The fifth annual IDC Digital Universe study, 2011 http://bit.ly/1bCBCJ*

FIGURE 2-1   Measurements of Data Size (bytes)

FUNDAMENTAL CONCEPTS

2.1 Literals

2.1.1 What Is a Literal?

To take something literally is to take it at "face value." The same is true of *literals* in programming. A **literal** is a sequence of one of more characters that stands for itself, such as the literal 12. We look at numeric literals in Python next.

> A **literal** is a sequence of one or more characters that stands for itself.

2.1.2 Numeric Literals

A **numeric literal** is a literal containing only the digits 0–9, an optional sign character (+ or −), and a possible decimal point. (The letter e is also used in exponential notation, shown in the next subsection). If a numeric literal contains a decimal point, then it denotes a **floating-point value**, or "**float**" (e.g., 10.24); otherwise, it denotes an **integer value** (e.g., 10). *Commas are never used in numeric literals.* Figure 2-2 gives additional examples of numeric literals in Python.

Numeric Literals						
integer values	floating-point values				incorrect	
5	5.	5.0	5.125	0.0005 5000.125	5,000.125	
2500	2500.	2500.0	2500.125		2,500	2,500.125
+2500	+2500.	+2500.0	+2500.125		+2,500	+2,500.125
−2500	−2500.	−2500.0	−2500.125		−2,500	−2,500.125

FIGURE 2-2   Numeric Literals in Python

Since numeric literals without a provided sign character denote positive values, an explicit positive sign character is rarely used. Next we look at how numeric values are represented in a computer system.

LET'S TRY IT

From the Python Shell, enter the following and observe the results.

```
>>> 1024           >>> −1024          >>> .1024
???                ???                ???

>>> 1,024          >>> 0.1024         >>> 1,024.46
???                ???                ???
```

> A **numeric literal** is a literal containing only the digits 0–9, a sign character (+ or −) and a possible decimal point. Commas are never used in numeric literals.

Limits of Range in Floating-Point Representation

There is no limit to the size of an integer that can be represented in Python. Floating-point values, however, have both a limited *range* and a limited *precision*. Python uses a double-precision standard format (IEEE 754) providing a range of 10^{-308} to 10^{308} with 16 to 17 digits of precision. To denote such a range of values, floating-points can be represented in scientific notation,

```
9.0045602e+5              (9.0045602 × 10⁵, 8 digits of precision)
1.006249505236801e8       (1.006249505236801 × 10⁸, 16 digits of precision)
4.239e−16                 (4.239 × 10⁻¹⁶, 4 digits of precision)
```

It is important to understand the limitations of floating-point representation. For example, the multiplication of two values may result in **arithmetic overflow**, a condition that occurs when a calculated result is too large in magnitude (size) to be represented,

```
>>> 1.5e200 * 2.0e210
>>> inf
```

This results in the special value inf ("infinity") rather than the arithmetically correct result 3.0e410, indicating that arithmetic overflow has occurred. Similarly, the division of two numbers may result in **arithmetic underflow**, a condition that occurs when a calculated result is too small in magnitude to be represented,

```
>>> 1.0e−300 / 1.0e100
0.0
```

This results in 0.0 rather than the arithmetically correct result 1.0e−400, indicating that arithmetic underflow has occurred. We next look at possible effects resulting from the limited precision in floating-point representation.

LET'S TRY IT

From the Python Shell, enter the following and observe the results.

```
>>> 1.2e200 * 2.4e100           >>> 1.2e200 / 2.4e100
???                             ???

>>> 1.2e200 * 2.4e200           >>> 1.2e−200 / 2.4e200
???                             ???
```

Arithmetic overflow occurs when a calculated result is too large in magnitude to be represented. **Arithmetic underflow** occurs when a calculated result is too small in magnitude to be represented.

Limits of Precision in Floating-Point Representation

Arithmetic overflow and arithmetic underflow are relatively easily detected. The loss of precision that can result in a calculated result, however, is a much more subtle issue. For example, 1/3 is equal to the infinitely repeating decimal .33333333 . . ., which also has repeating digits in base two, .010101010. . . . Since any floating-point representation necessarily contains only a finite number of digits, what is stored for many floating-point values is only an *approximation* of the true value, as can be demonstrated in Python,

```
>>> 1/3
.333333333333333
```

Here, the repeating decimal ends after the 16th digit. Consider, therefore, the following,

```
>>> 3 * (1/3)
1.0
```

Given the value of 1/3 above, we would expect the result to be .999999999999999, so what is happening here? The answer is that Python displays a *rounded* result to keep the number of digits displayed manageable. However, the representation of 1/3 as .333333333333333 remains the same, as demonstrated by the following,

```
>>> 1/3 + 1/3 + 1/3 + 1/3 + 1/3 + 1/3
1.999999999999998
```

In this case we get a result that reflects the representation of 1/3 as an approximation, since the last digit is 8, and not 9. However, if we use multiplication instead, we again get the rounded value displayed,

```
>>> 6 * (1/3)
2.0
```

The bottom line, therefore, is that no matter how Python chooses to display calculated results, the value stored is limited in both the range of numbers that can be represented and the degree of precision. For most everyday applications, this slight loss in accuracy is of no practical concern. However, in scientific computing and other applications in which precise calculations are required, this is something that the programmer must be keenly aware of.

LET'S TRY IT

From the Python Shell, enter the following and observe the results.

```
>>> 1/10                        >>> 6 * (1/10)
???                             ???

>>> 1/10 + 1/10 + 1/10          >>> 6 * 1/10
???                             ???

>>> 10 * (1/10)
???
```

Since any floating-point representation contains only a finite number of digits, what is stored for many floating-point values is only an *approximation* of the true value.

Built-in `format` Function

Because floating-point values may contain an arbitrary number of decimal places, the built-in `format` function can be used to produce a numeric string version of the value containing a specific number of decimal places,

```
>>> 12/5                          >>> 5/7
2.4                               0.7142857142857143
>>> format(12/5, '.2f')           >>> format(5/7, '.2f')
'2.40'                            '0.71'
```

In these examples, *format specifier* `'.2f'` rounds the result to two decimal places of accuracy in the string produced. For very large (or very small) values `'e'` can be used as a format specifier,

```
>>> format(2 ** 100, '.6e')
'1.267651e+30'
```

In this case, the value is formatted in scientific notation, with six decimal places of precision. Formatted numeric string values are useful when displaying results in which only a certain number of decimal places need to be displayed,

without use of format specifier
```
>>> tax = 0.08
>>> print('Your cost: $', (1 + tax) * 12.99)
Your cost: $ 14.029200000000001
```

with use of format specifier
```
>>> print('Your cost: $', format((1 + tax) * 12.99, '.2f'))
Your cost: $ 14.03
```

Finally, a comma in the format specifier adds comma separators to the result,

```
>>> format(13402.25, ',.2f')
13,402.24
```

We will next see the use of format specifiers for formatting string values as well.

LET'S TRY IT

From the Python Shell, enter the following and observe the results.

```
>>> format(11/12, '.2f')          >>> format(11/12, '.2e')
???                               ???

>>> format(11/12, '.3f')          >>> format(11/12, '.3e')
???                               ???
```

The built-in `format` function can be used to produce a numeric string of a given floating-point value *rounded* to a specific number of decimal places.

2.1.3 String Literals

Numerical values are not the only literal values in programming. **String literals**, or "**strings**," represent a sequence of characters,

```
'Hello' 'Smith, John' "Baltimore, Maryland 21210"
```

In Python, string literals may be *delimited* (surrounded) by a matching pair of either single (') or double (") quotes. Strings must be contained all on one line (except when delimited by triple quotes, discussed in Chapter 7). We have already seen the use of strings in Chapter 1 for displaying screen output,

```
>>> print('Welcome to Python!')
Welcome to Python!
```

Additional examples of string literals are given in Figure 2-3.

```
'A'                         - a string consisting of a single character
'jsmith16@mycollege.edu'    - a string containing non-letter characters
"Jennifer Smith's Friend"   - a string containing a single quote character
' '                         - a string containing a single blank character
''                          - the empty string
```

FIGURE 2-3   String Literal Values

As shown in the figure, a string may contain zero or more characters, including letters, digits, special characters, and blanks. A string consisting of only a pair of matching quotes (with nothing in between) is called the **empty string**, which is different from a string containing only blank characters. Both blank strings and the empty string have their uses, as we will see. Strings may also contain quote characters as long as different quotes are used to delimit the string,

```
"Jennifer Smith's Friend"
```

If this string were delimited with single quotes, the apostrophe (single quote) would be considered the matching closing quote of the opening quote, leaving the last final quote unmatched,

'Jennifer Smith's Friend' ... *matching quote?*

Thus, Python allows the use of more than one type of quote for such situations. (The convention used in the text will be to use single quotes for delimiting strings, and only use double quotes when needed.)

LET'S TRY IT

From the Python Shell, enter the following and observe the results.

```
>>> print('Hello')        >>> print('Hello")        >>> print('Let's Go')
???                       ???                       ???

>>> print("Hello")        >>> print("Let's Go!')    >>> print("Let's go!")
???                       ???                       ???
```

A **string literal**, or **string**, is a sequence of characters denoted by a pair of matching single or double (and sometimes triple) quotes in Python.

The Representation of Character Values

There needs to be a way to encode (represent) characters within a computer. Although various encoding schemes have been developed, the **Unicode** encoding scheme is intended to be a universal encoding scheme. Unicode is actually a collection of different encoding schemes utilizing between 8 and 32 bits for each character. The default encoding in Python uses **UTF-8**, an 8-bit encoding compatible with ASCII, an older, still widely used encoding scheme.

Currently, there are over 100,000 Unicode-defined characters for many of the languages around the world. Unicode is capable of defining more than 4 billion characters. Thus, all the world's languages, both past and present, can potentially be encoded within Unicode. A partial listing of the ASCII-compatible UTF-8 encoding scheme is given in Figure 2-4.

Space	00100000	32		A	01000001	65
!	00100001	33		B	01000010	66
"	00100010	34		C	01000011	67
#	00100011	35		.		
.				.		
.				Z	01011010	90
0	00110000	48		a	01100001	97
1	00110001	49		b	01100010	98
2	00110010	50		c	01100011	99
.				.		
.				.		
9	00111001	57		z	01111010	122

FIGURE 2-4 Partial UTF-8 (ASCII) Code Table

UTF-8 encodes characters that have an ordering with sequential numerical values. For example, 'A' is encoded as 01000001 (65), 'B' is encoded as 01000010 (66), and so on. This is true for character digits as well, '0' is encoded as 00110000 (48) and '1' is encoded as 00110001 (49). This underscores the difference between a numeric representation (that can be used in arithmetic calculations) vs. a number represented as a string of digit characters (that cannot), as demonstrated in Figure 2-5.

Numeric Value	String Value
01111100	001100010011001000110100
124	'1' '2' '4'

FIGURE 2-5 Numeric vs. String Representation of Digits

Python has means for converting between a character and its encoding. The ord function gives the UTF-8 (ASCII) encoding of a given character. For example, ord('A') is 65. The chr function gives the character for a given encoding value, thus chr(65) is 'A'. (Functions are discussed in Chapter 5.) While in general there is no need to know the specific encoding of a given character, there are times when such knowledge can be useful.

LET'S TRY IT

From the Python Shell, enter the following and observe the results.

```
>>> ord('1')          >>> chr(65)          >>> chr(97)
???                   ???                  ???

>>> ord('2')          >>> chr(90)          >>> chr(122)
???                   ???                  ???
```

Unicode is capable of representing over 4 billion different characters, enough to represent the characters of all languages, past and present. Python's (default) character encoding uses **UTF-8**, an eight-bit encoding that is part of the Unicode standard.

2.1.4 Control Characters

Control characters are special characters that are not displayed on the screen. Rather, they *control* the display of output (among other things). Control characters do not have a corresponding keyboard character. Therefore, they are represented by a combination of characters called an *escape sequence*.

An **escape sequence** begins with an **escape character** that causes the sequence of characters following it to "escape" their normal meaning. The backslash (\) serves as the escape character in Python. For example, the escape sequence '\n', represents the *newline control character*, used to begin a new screen line. An example of its use is given below,

```
print('Hello\nJennifer Smith')
```

which is displayed as follows,

```
Hello
Jennifer Smith
```

Further discussion of control characters is given in the Python 3 Programmers' Reference.

LET'S TRY IT

From the Python Shell, enter the following and observe the results.

```
>>> print('Hello World')          >>> print('Hello\nWorld')
???                               ???

>>> print('Hello World\n')        >>> print('Hello\n\nWorld')
???                               ???

>>> print('Hello World\n\n')      >>> print(1, '\n', 2, '\n', 3)
???                               ???

>>> print('\nHello World')        >>> print('\n', 1, '\n', 2, '\n', 3)
???                               ???
```

Control characters are nonprinting characters used to *control* the display of output (among other things). An **escape sequence** is a string of one or more characters used to denote control characters.

2.1.5 String Formatting

We saw above the use of built-in function `format` for controlling how numerical values are displayed. We now look at how the `format` function can be used to control how strings are displayed. As given above, the `format` function has the form,

```
format(value, format_specifier)
```

where *value* is the value to be displayed, and *format_specifier* can contain a combination of formatting options. For example, to produce the string `'Hello'` left-justified in a field width of 20 characters would be done as follows,

```
format('Hello', '<20') → 'Hello            '
```

To right-justify the string, the following would be used,

```
format('Hello', '>20') → '            Hello'
```

Formatted strings are left-justified by default. To center the string the `'^'` character is used: `format('Hello', '^20')`. Another use of the `format` function is to create strings of blank characters, which is sometimes useful,

```
format(' ', '30') → '                              '
```

Finally blanks, by default, are the *fill character* for formatted strings. However, a specific fill character can be specified as shown below,

```
>>> print('Hello World', format('.', '.<30'), 'Have a Nice Day!')
Hello World .............................. Have a Nice Day!
```

LET'S TRY IT

From the Python Shell, enter the following and observe the results.

```
>>> print(format('Hello World', '^40'))
???
>>> print(format('-','-<20'), 'Hello World', format('-','->20'))
???
```

Built-in function **format** can be used to control how strings are displayed.

2.1.6 Implicit and Explicit Line Joining

Sometimes a program line may be too long to fit in the Python-recommended maximum length of 79 characters. There are two ways in Python to do deal with such situations—implicit and explicit line joining. We discuss this next.

Implicit Line Joining

There are certain delimiting characters that allow a *logical* program line to span more than one physical line. This includes matching parentheses, square brackets, curly braces, and triple quotes. For example, the following two program lines are treated as one logical line,

```
print('Name:', student_name, 'Address:', student_address,
    'Number of Credits:', total_credits, 'GPA:', current_gpa)
```

Matching quotes (except for triple quotes, covered later) must be on the same physical line. For example, the following will generate an error,

```
print('This program will calculate a restaurant tab for a couple
        with a gift certificate, and a restaurant tax of 3%')
```

We will use this aspect of Python throughout the book.

> Matching parentheses, square brackets, and curly braces can be used to span a *logical* program line on more than one physical line.

Explicit Line Joining

In addition to implicit line joining, program lines may be explicitly joined by use of the backslash (\) character. Program lines that end with a backslash that are not part of a literal string (that is, within quotes) continue on the following line,

```
numsecs_1900_dob = ((year_birth - 1900) * avg_numsecs_year) + \
                   ((month_birth - 1) * avg_numsecs_month) + \
                   (day_birth * numsecs_day)
```

> Program lines may be explicitly joined by use of the backslash (\).

2.1.7 Let's Apply It—"Hello World Unicode Encoding"

It is a long tradition in computer science to demonstrate a program that simply displays "Hello World!" as an example of the simplest program possible in a particular programming language. In Python, the complete Hello World program is comprised of one program line,

```
print('Hello World!')
```

We take a twist on this tradition and give a Python program that displays the Unicode encoding for each of the characters in the string "Hello World!" instead. This program utilizes the following programming features:

➤ string literals ➤ print ➤ ord function

The program and program execution are given in Figure 2-6.

Program Execution ...

```
The Unicode encoding for 'Hello World!' is:
72 101 108 108 111 32 87 111 114 108 100 33
```

```
1  # This program displays the Unicode encoding for 'Hello World!'
2
3  # Program greeting
4  print("The Unicode encoding for 'Hello World!' is:")
5
6  # output results
7  print(ord('H'), ord('e'), ord('l'), ord('l'), ord('o'), ord(' '),
8        ord('W'), ord('o'), ord('r'), ord('l'), ord('d'), ord('!'))
```

FIGURE 2-6   Hello World Unicode Encoding Program

The statements on **lines 1**, **3**, and **6** are comment statements, introduced in Chapter 1. They are ignored during program execution, used to provide information to those reading the program. The print function on **line 4** displays the message 'Hello World!'. Double quotes are used to delimit the corresponding string, since the single quotes within it are to be taken literally. The use of print on **line 7** prints out the Unicode encoding, one-by-one, for each of the characters in the "Hello World!" string. Note from the program execution that there is a Unicode encoding for the blank character (32), as well as the exclamation mark (33).

Self-Test Questions

1. Indicate which of the following are valid numeric literals in Python.
   (a) 1024   (b) 1,024   (c) 1024.0   (d) 0.25   (e) .45   (f) 0.25+10

2. Indicate which of the following exceed the range and/or precision of floating-point values that can be represented in Python.
   (a) 1.89345348392e+301   (c) 2.0424e−320
   (b) 1.62123432632322e+300   (d) 1.323232435342327896452e−140

3. Which of the following would result in either overflow or underflow for the floating-point representation scheme mentioned in the chapter.
   (a) 6.25e+240 * 1.24e+10   (c) 6.25e+240 / 1.24e+10
   (b) 2.24e+240 * 1.45e+300   (d) 2.24e−240 / 1.45e+300

4. Exactly what is output by print(format(24.893952, '.3f'))
   (a) 24.894   (b) 24.893   (c) 2.48e1

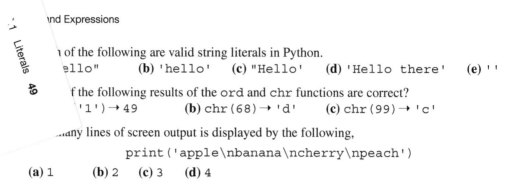

of the following are valid string literals in Python.

ello" **(b)** 'hello' **(c)** "Hello" **(d)** 'Hello there' **(e)** ''

f the following results of the ord and chr functions are correct?

'1') → 49 **(b)** chr(68) → 'd' **(c)** chr(99) → 'c'

..any lines of screen output is displayed by the following,

print('apple\nbanana\ncherry\npeach')

(a) 1 **(b)** 2 **(c)** 3 **(d)** 4

ANSWERS: 1. (a,c,d,e). 2. (c). 3. (b, overflow). (d, underflow). 4. (a) 5. (a,b,d,e). 6. (a,c). 7. (d)

2.2 Variables and Identifiers

So far, we have only looked at literal values in programs. However, the true usefulness of a computer program is the ability to operate on *different* values each time the program is executed. This is provided by the notion of a *variable*. We look at variables and identifiers next.

2.2.1 What Is a Variable?

A **variable** is a name (identifier) that is associated with a value, as for variable num depicted in Figure 2-7.

$$num \longrightarrow \boxed{10}$$

FIGURE 2-7 Program Variable

A variable can be assigned different values during a program's execution—hence, the name "variable." Wherever a variable appears in a program (except on the left-hand side of an assignment statement), *it is the value associated with the variable that is used*, and not the variable's name,

$$num + 1 \rightarrow 10 + 1 \rightarrow 11$$

Variables are assigned values by use of the **assignment operator**, =,

$$num = 10 \qquad num = num + 1$$

Assignment statements often look wrong to novice programmers. Mathematically, num = num + 1 does not make sense. In computing, however, it is used to increment the value of a given variable by one. It is more appropriate, therefore, to think of the = symbol as an arrow symbol, as shown in Figure 2-8.

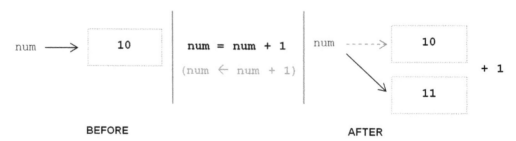

BEFORE   AFTER

FIGURE 2-8 Variable Update

When thought of this way, it makes clear that *the right side of an assignment is evaluated first, then the result is assigned to the variable on the left.* An arrow symbol is not used simply because there is no such character on a standard computer keyboard. Variables may also be assigned to the value of another variable (or expression, discussed below) as depicted in Figure 2-9.

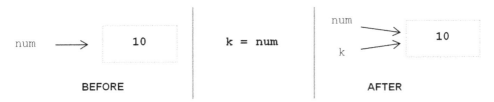

FIGURE 2-9   Variable Assignment (to another variable)

Variables num and k are both associated with the same literal value 10 in memory. One way to see this is by use of built-in function id,

>>> id(num)   >>> id(k)
505494040   505494040

The id function produces a unique number identifying a specific value (object) in memory. Since variables are meant to be distinct, it would appear that this sharing of values would cause problems. Specifically, if the value of num changed, would variable k change along with it? This cannot happen in this case because the variables refer to integer values, and integer values are *immutable*. An **immutable value** is a value that cannot be changed. Thus, both will continue to refer to the same value until one (or both) of them is reassigned, as depicted in Figure 2-10.

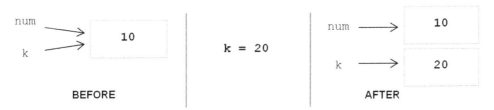

FIGURE 2-10   Variable Reassignment

If no other variable references the memory location of the original value, the memory location is *deallocated* (that is, it is made available for reuse).

Finally, in Python the same variable can be associated with values of different type during program execution, as indicated below.

```
var = 12        integer
var = 12.45     float
var = 'Hello'   string
```

LET'S TRY IT

From the Python Shell, enter the following and observe the results.

```
>>> num = 10                      >>> k = 30
>>> num                           >>> k
???                               ???
>>> id(num)                       >>> num
???                               ???
                                  >>> id(k)
>>> num = 20                      ???
>>> num                           >>> id(num)
???                               ???
>>> id(num)
???                               >>> k = k + 1
                                  >>> k
>>> k = num                       ???
>>> k                             >>> id(num)
???                               ???
>>> id(k)                         >>> id(k)
???                               ???
>>> id(num)
???
```

A **variable** is a name that is associated with a value. The **assignment operator**, =, is used to assign values to variables. An **immutable value** is a value that cannot be changed.

2.2.2 Variable Assignment and Keyboard Input

The value that is assigned to a given variable does not have to be specified in the program, as demonstrated in previous examples. The value can come from the user by use of the input function introduced in Chapter 1,

```
>>> name = input('What is your first name?')
What is your first name? John
```

In this case, the variable name is assigned the string 'John'. If the user hit return without entering any value, name would be assigned to the empty string (' ').

All input is returned by the input function as a string type. *For the input of numeric values, the response must be converted to the appropriate type.* Python provides built-in **type conversion functions int()** and **float()** for this purpose, as shown below for a gpa calculation program,

```
line = input('How many credits do you have?')
num_credits = int(line)
line = input('What is your grade point average?')
gpa = float(line)
```

Here, the entered number of credits, say '24', is converted to the equivalent integer value, 24, before being assigned to variable num_credits. For input of the gpa, the entered value,

say ' 3 . 2 ', is converted to the equivalent floating-point value, 3 . 2. Note that the program lines
above could be combined as follows,

```
num_credits = int(input('How many credits do you have? '))
gpa = float(input('What is your grade point average? '))
```

LET'S TRY IT

From the Python Shell, enter the following and observe the results.

```
>>> num = input('Enter number: ')        >>> num = input('Enter name: ')
Enter number: 5                          Enter name: John
???                                      ???

>>> num = int(input('Enter number: '))   >>> num = int(input('Enter name: '))
Enter number: 5                          Enter name: John
???                                      ???
```

All input is returned by the input function as a string type. Built-in functions int () and
float () can be used to convert a string to a numeric type.

2.2.3 What Is an Identifier?

An **identifier** is a sequence of one or more characters used to provide a name for a given program
element. Variable names line, num_credits, and gpa are each identifiers. Python is *case
sensitive*, thus, Line is different from line. Identifiers may contain letters and digits, but cannot
begin with a digit. The underscore character, _, is also allowed to aid in the readability of long identifier names. It should not be used as the *first* character, however, as identifiers beginning with an
underscore have special meaning in Python.

Spaces are not allowed as part of an identifier. This is a common error since some operating
systems allow spaces within file names. In programming languages, however, spaces are used to
delimit (separate) distinct syntactic entities. Thus, any identifier containing a space character
would be considered two separate identifiers. Examples of valid and invalid identifiers in Python
are given in Figure 2-11.

Valid Identifiers	Invalid Identifiers	Reason Invalid
totalSales	'totalSales'	quotes not allowed
totalsales	total sales	spaces not allowed
salesFor2010	2010Sales	cannot begin with a digit
sales_for_2010	_2010Sales	should not begin with an underscore

FIGURE 2-11 Identifier Naming

LET'S TRY IT

From the Python Shell, enter the following and observe the results.

```
>>> spring2014SemCredits = 15        >>> spring2014-sem-credits = 15
???                                  ???

>>> spring2014_sem_credits = 15      >>> 2014SpringSemesterCredits = 15
???                                  ???
```

An **identifier** is a sequence of one or more characters used to name a given program element. In Python, an identifier may contain letters and digits, but cannot begin with a digit. The special underscore character can also be used.

2.2.4 Keywords and Other Predefined Identifiers in Python

A **keyword** is an identifier that has predefined meaning in a programming language. Therefore, keywords cannot be used as "regular" identifiers. Doing so will result in a syntax error, as demonstrated in the attempted assignment to keyword and below,

```
>>> and = 10
SyntaxError: invalid syntax
```

The keywords in Python are listed in Figure 2-12. To display the keywords, type `help()` in the Python shell, and then type `keywords` (type `'q'` to quit).

and	as	assert	break	class	continue	def
del	elif	else	except	finally	for	from
global	if	import	in	is	lambda	nonlocal
not	or	pass	raise	return	try	while
with	yield	false	none	true		

FIGURE 2-12 Keywords in Python

There are other predefined identifiers that *can* be used as regular identifiers, but should not be. This includes `float`, `int`, `print`, `exit`, and `quit`, for example. A simple way to check whether a given identifier is a keyword in Python is given below,

```
>>> 'exit' in dir(__builtins__)     >>> 'exit_program' in dir(__builtins__)
True                                False
```

LET'S TRY IT

From the Python Shell, enter the following and observe the results.

```
>>> yield = 1000                     >>> print('Hello')
???                                  ???

>>> Yield = 1000                     >>> print = 10
???                                  >>> print('Hello')
                                     ???
```

A **keyword** is an identifier that has predefined meaning in a programming language and therefore cannot be used as a "regular" identifier. Doing so will result in a syntax error.

2.2.5   Let's Apply It—"Restaurant Tab Calculation"

The program below calculates a restaurant tab for a couple based on the use of a gift certificate and the items ordered. This program utilizes the following programming features:

➤ variables
➤ keyboard input
➤ built-in format function
➤ type conversion functions

An example execution of the program is given in Figure 2-13.

```
Program Execution ...

This program will calculate a restaurant tab for a couple with a gift
certificate, with a restaurant tax of 8.0 %
Enter the amount of the gift certificate: 200
Enter ordered items for person 1
Appetizer: 5.50
Entree: 21.50
Drinks: 4.25
Dessert: 6.00

Enter ordered items for person 2
Appetizer: 6.25
Entree: 18.50
Drinks: 6.50
Dessert: 5.50

Ordered items: $ 74.00
Restaurant tax: $ 5.92
Tab: $ -120.08
(negative amount indicates unused amount of gift certificate)
```

FIGURE 2-13   Execution of the Restaurant Tab Calculation Program

The program is given in Figure 2-14. **Lines 1–2** contain comment lines describing what the program does. The remaining comment lines provide an outline of the basic program sections. **Line 5** provides the required initialization of variables in the program, with variable `tax` assigned to 8% (`.08`). Variable `tax` is used throughout the program (in **lines 9, 35,** and **39**). Thus, if the restaurant tax needs to be altered, only this line of the program needs to be changed. (Recall that * is used to denote multiplication in Python, introduced in Chapter 1.)

Lines 8–9 display to the user what the program does. The control character \n as the last character of the print function causes a screen line to be skipped before the next line is displayed. The cost of the menu items ordered is obtained from the user in **lines 15–27**.

Lines 30 and 31 total the cost of the orders for each person, assigned to variables `amt_person1` and `amt_person2`. **Lines 34** and **35** compute the tab, including tax (stored in variable `tab`). Finally, **lines 38–41** display the cost of the ordered items, followed by the added restaurant tax and the amount due after deducting the amount of the gift certificate. The customers owe any remaining amount.

```
1  # Restaurant Tab Calculation Program
2  # This program will calculate a restaurant tab with a gift certificate
3
4  # initialization
5  tax = 0.08
6
7  # program greeting
8  print('This program will calculate a restaurant tab for a couple with')
9  print('a gift certificate, with a restaurant tax of', tax * 100, '%\n')
10
11 # get amount of gift certificate
12 amt_certificate = float(input('Enter amount of the gift certificate: '))
13
14 # cost of ordered items
15 print('Enter ordered items for person 1')
16
17 appetizer_per1 = float(input('Appetizier: '))
18 entree_per1 = float(input('Entree: '))
19 drinks_per1 = float(input('Drinks: '))
20 dessert_per1 = float(input('Dessert: '))
21
22 print('\nEnter ordered items for person 2')
23
24 appetizer_per2 = float(input('Appetizier: '))
25 entree_per2 = float(input('Entree: '))
26 drinks_per2 = float(input('Drinks: '))
27 dessert_per2 = float(input('Dessert: '))
28
29 # total items
30 amt_person1 = appetizer_per1 + entree_per1 + drinks_per1 + dessert_per1
31 amt_person2 = appetizer_per2 + entree_per2 + drinks_per2 + dessert_per2
32
33 # compute tab with tax
34 items_cost = amt_person1 + amt_person2
35 tab = items_cost + items_cost * tax
36
37 # display amount owe
38 print('\nOrdered items: $', format(items_cost, '.2f'))
39 print('Restaurant tax: $', format(items_cost * tax, '.2f'))
40 print('Tab: $', format(tab - amt_certificate, '.2f'))
41 print('(negative amount indicates unused amount of gift certificate)')
```

FIGURE 2-14   Restaurant Tab Calculation Program

A negative amount indicates the amount left on the gift certificate. Built-in function `format` is used to limit the output to two decimal places.

Self-Test Questions

1. Which of the following are valid assignment statements, in which only variable k has already been assigned a value?
    (a) n = k + 1   **(b)** n = n + 1   **(c)** n + k = 10   **(d)** n + 1 = 1

2. What is the value of variable num after the following assignment statements are executed?

    ```
    num = 0
    num = num + 1
    num = num + 5
    ```

3. Do variables num and k reference the same memory location after the following instructions are executed? (YES/NO)

```
num = 10
k = num
num = num + 1
```

4. Which of the following are valid identifiers in Python?
    (a) errors   **(b)** error_count   **(c)** error-count

5. Which of the following are keywords in Python?
    (a) and   **(b)** As   **(c)** while   **(d)** until   **(e)** NOT

6. Which one of the following is correct for reading and storing an integer value from the user?
    (a) n = int_input('Enter: ')   **(b)** n = int(input('Enter: '))

ANSWERS: 1. (a), 2. 6, 3. No, 4. (a,b), 5. (a,c), 6. (b)

2.3 Operators

Now that we have used numeric and string types in Python, we look at operations that may be performed on them.

2.3.1 What Is an Operator?

An **operator** is a symbol that represents an operation that may be performed on one or more *operands*. For example, the + symbol represents the operation of addition. An **operand** is a value that a given operator is applied to, such as operands 2 and 3 in the expression 2 + 3. A **unary operator** operates on only one operand, such as the negation operator in -12. A **binary operator** operates on two operands, as with the addition operator. Most operators in programming languages are binary operators. We look at the arithmetic operators in Python next.

An **operator** is a symbol that represents an operation that may be performed on one or more **operands**. Operators that take one operand are called **unary operators**. Operators that take two operands are called **binary operators**.

2.3.2 Arithmetic Operators

Python provides the arithmetic operators given in Figure 2-15.
    The +, −, * (multiplication) and / (division) arithmetic operators perform the usual operations. Note that the − symbol is used both as a unary operator (for negation) and a binary operator (for subtraction).

```
20 − 5        →        15      (− as binary operator)
−10 * 2       →       −20      (− as unary operator)
```

Arithmetic Operators		Example	Result
-x	negation	-10	-10
x + y	addition	10 + 25	35
x - y	subtraction	10 - 25	-15
x * y	multiplication	10 * 5	50
x / y	division	25 / 10	2.5
x // y	truncating div	25 // 10	2
		25 // 10.0	2.0
x % y	modulus	25 % 10	5
x ** y	exponentiation	10 ** 2	100

FIGURE 2-15   Arithmetic Operators in Python

Python also includes an exponentiation (**) operator. Integer and floating-point values can be used in both the base and the exponent,

```
2**4  → 16
2.5 ** 4.5  → 61.76323555016366
```

Python provides two forms of division. **"true" division** is denoted by a single slash, /. Thus, 25 / 10 evaluates to 2.5. **Truncating division** is denoted by a double slash, //, providing a truncated result based on the type of operands applied to. When both operands are integer values, the result is a truncated integer referred to as **integer division**. When as least one of the operands is a float type, the result is a truncated floating point. Thus, 25 // 10 evaluates to 2, while 25.0 // 10 becomes 2.0. This is summarized in Figure 2-16.

Operands		result type	example	result
/ Division operator	int, int	float	7 / 5	1.4
	int, float	float	7 / 5.0	1.4
	float, float	float	7.0 / 5.0	1.4
// Truncating division operator	int, int	truncated int ("integer division")	7 // 5	1
	int, float	truncated float	7 // 5.0	1.0
	float, float	truncated float	7.0 // 5.0	1.0

FIGURE 2-16   Division Operators in Python

An example of the use of integer division would be to determine the number of dozen doughnuts for a given number of doughnuts. If variable numDoughnuts had a current value of 29, the number of dozen doughnuts would be calculated by,

```
numDoughnuts // 12  → 29 // 12  → 2
```

Lastly, the **modulus operator** (%) gives the remainder of the division of its operands, resulting in a cycle of values. This is shown in Figure 2-17.

Modulo 7		Modulo 10		Modulo 100	
0 % 7	**0**	0 % 10	**0**	0 % 100	**0**
1 % 7	**1**	1 % 10	**1**	1 % 100	**1**
2 % 7	**2**	2 % 10	**2**	2 % 100	**2**
3 % 7	**3**	3 % 10	**3**	3 % 100	**3**
4 % 7	**4**	4 % 10	**4**	.	.
5 % 7	**5**	5 % 10	**5**	.	.
6 % 7	**6**	6 % 10	**6**	96 % 100	**96**
7 % 7	0	7 % 10	**7**	97 % 100	**97**
8 % 7	1	8 % 10	**8**	98 % 100	**98**
9 % 7	2	9 % 10	**9**	99 % 100	**99**
10 % 7	3	10 % 10	0	100 % 100	0
11 % 7	4	11 % 10	1	101 % 100	1
12 % 7	5	12 % 10	2	102 % 100	2

FIGURE 2-17 The Modulus Operator

The modulus and truncating (integer) division operators are complements of each other. For example, 29 // 12 gives the number of dozen doughnuts, while 29 % 12 gives the number of leftover doughnuts (5).

LET'S TRY IT

From the Python Shell, enter the following and observe the results.

```
>>> 10 + 35          >>> 4 ** 2           >>> 45 // 10.0
???                  ???                  ???

>>> -10 + 35         >>> 45 / 10          >>> 2025 % 10
???                  ???                  ???

>>> 4 * 2            >>> 45 // 10         >>> 2025 // 10
???                  ???                  ???
```

The **division operator**, /, produces "true division" regardless of its operand types. The **truncating division operator**, //, produces either an integer or float truncated result based on the type of operands applied to. The **modulus operator** (%) gives the remainder of the division of its operands.

2.3.3 Let's Apply It—"Your Place in the Universe"

The following program (Figure 2-18) calculates the approximate number of atoms that the average person contains, and the percentage of the universe that they comprise. This program utilizes the following programming features:

➤ floating-point scientific notation   ➤ built-in format function

```
Program Execution ...

This program will determine your place in the universe.
Enter your weight in pounds: 150
You contain approximately 3.30e+28 atoms
Therefore, you comprise 3.30e-51 % of the universe
```

```
 1  # Your Place in the Universe Program
 2
 3  # This program will determine the approximate number of atoms that a
 4  # person consists of and the percent of the universe that they comprise.
 5
 6  # initialization
 7  num_atoms_universe = 10e80
 8  weight_avg_person = 70  # 70 kg (154 lbs)
 9  num_atoms_avg_person = 7e27
10
11  # program greeting
12  print('This program will determine your place in the universe.')
13
14  # prompt for user's weight
15  weight_lbs = int(input('Enter your weight in pounds: '))
16
17  # convert weight to kilograms
18  weight_kg = 2.2 * weight_lbs
19
20  # determine number atoms in person
21  num_atoms = (weight_kg / 70) * num_atoms_avg_person
22  percent_of_universe = (num_atoms / num_atoms_universe) * 100
23
24  # display results
25  print('You contain approximately', format(num_atoms, '.2e'), 'atoms')
26  print('Therefore, you comprise', format(percent_of_universe, '.2e'),
27      '% of the universe')
```

FIGURE 2-18   Your Place in the Universe Program

Lines 1–4 describe the program. Needed variables num_atoms_universe, weight_avg_person, and num_atoms_avg_person are initialized in lines 7–9. The program greeting is on line 12. Line 15 inputs the person's weight. Line 18 converts the weight to kilograms for use in the calculations on lines 21–22 which compute the desired results. Finally, lines 25–27 display the results.

Self-Test Questions

1. Give the results for each of the following.
   (a) −2 * 3   (b) 15 % 4   (c) 3 ** 2

2. Give the exact results of each of the following division operations.
   (a) 5 / 4   (b) 5 // 4   (c) 5.0 // 4

3. Which of the expressions in question 2 is an example of integer division?

4. Do any two of the expressions in question 2 evaluate to the exact same result? (YES/NO)

5. How many operands are there in the following arithmetic expression?
   2 * 24 + 60 − 10
   (a) 4   (b) 3   (c) 7

6. How many binary operators are there in the following arithmetic expression?
   −10 + 25 / (16 + 12)
   (a) 2   (b) 3   (c) 4

ANSWERS: 1. (a) −6, (b) 3 (c) 9, 2. (a) 1.25 (b) 1 (c) 1.0, 3. (b), 4. no, 5. (a), 6. (b)

2.4 Expressions and Data Types

Now that we have looked at arithmetic operators, we will see how operators and operands can be combined to form expressions. In particular, we will look at how arithmetic expressions are evaluated in Python. We also introduce the notion of a *data type*.

2.4.1 What Is an Expression?

An **expression** is a combination of symbols that evaluates to a value. Expressions, most commonly, consist of a combination of operators and operands,

$$4 + (3 * k)$$

An expression can also consist of a single literal or variable. Thus, 4, 3, and k are each expressions. This expression has two *subexpressions*, 4 and (3 * k). Subexpression (3 * k) itself has two subexpressions, 3 and k.

Expressions that evaluate to a numeric type are called **arithmetic expressions**. A **subexpression** is any expression that is part of a larger expression. Subexpressions may be denoted by the use of parentheses, as shown above. Thus, for the expression 4 + (3 * 2), the two operands of the addition operator are 4 and (3 * 2), and thus the result it equal to 10. If the expression were instead written as (4 + 3) * 2, then it would evaluate to 14.

Since a subexpression is an expression, any subexpression may contain subexpressions of its own,

$$4 + (3 * (2 - 1)) \rightarrow 4 + (3 * 1) \rightarrow 4 + 3 \rightarrow 7$$

If no parentheses are used, then an expression is evaluated according to the rules of operator precedence in Python, discussed in the next section.

LET'S TRY IT

From the Python Shell, enter the following and observe the results.

```
>>> (2 + 3) * 4
???
```
```
>>> 2 + ((3 * 4) - 8)
???
```

```
>>> 2 + (3 * 4)
???
```
```
>>> 2 + 3 * (4 - 1)
???
```

An **expression** is a combination of symbols (or single symbol) that evaluates to a value. A **subexpression** is any expression that is part of a larger expression.

2.4.2 Operator Precedence

The way we commonly represent expressions, in which operators appear between their operands, is referred to as **infix notation**. For example, the expression 4 + 3 is in infix notation since the + operator appears between its two operands, 4 and 3. There are other ways of representing expressions called *prefix* and *postfix* notation, in which operators are placed *before* and *after* their operands, respectively.

The expression 4 + (3 * 5) is also in infix notation. It contains two operators, + and *. The parentheses denote that (3 * 5) is a subexpression. Therefore, 4 and (3 * 5) are the operands of the addition operator, and thus the overall expression evaluates to 19. What if the parentheses were omitted, as given below?

$$4 + 3 * 5$$

How would this be evaluated? These are two possibilities,

$$4 + \underline{3 * 5} \quad \rightarrow \quad 4 + 15 \quad \rightarrow \quad 19$$

$$\underline{4 + 3} * 5 \quad \rightarrow \quad 7 * 5 \quad \rightarrow \quad 35$$

Some might say that the first version is the correct one by the conventions of mathematics. However, each programming language has its own rules for the order that operators are applied, called **operator precedence**, defined in an **operator precedence table**. This may or may not be the same as in mathematics, although it typically is. In Figure 2-19, we give the operator precedence table for the Python operators discussed so far. (We will discuss the issue of associativity indicated in Figure 2-19 in the next section.)

Operator	Associativity
** (exponentiation)	right-to-left
- (negation)	left-to-right
* (mult), / (div), // (truncating div), % (modulo)	left-to-right
+ (addition), - (subtraction)	left-to-right

FIGURE 2-19 Operator Precedence of Arithmetic Operators in Python

In the table, higher-priority operators are placed above lower-priority ones. Thus, we see that multiplication is performed before addition when no parentheses are included,

$$4 + 3 * 5 \quad \rightarrow \quad 4 + 15 \quad \rightarrow \quad 19$$

In our example, therefore, if the addition is to be performed first, parentheses would be needed,

$$(4 + 3) * 5 \quad \rightarrow \quad 7 * 5 \quad \rightarrow \quad 35$$

As another example, consider the expression below. Following Python's rules of operator precedence, the exponentiation operator is applied first, then the truncating division operator, and finally the addition operator,

$$4 + 2 ** 5 // 10 \quad \rightarrow \quad 4 + 32 // 10 \quad \rightarrow \quad 4 + 3 \quad \rightarrow \quad 7$$

Operator precedence guarantees a consistent interpretation of expressions. However, it is good programming practice to use parentheses even when not needed if it adds clarity and enhances readability, without overdoing it. Thus, the previous expression would be better written as,

$$4 + (2 ** 5) // 10$$

LET'S TRY IT

From the Python Shell, enter the following and observe the results.

```
>>> 2 + 3 * 4                          >>> 2 * 3 // 4
???                                    ???

>>> 2 * 3 + 4                          >>> 5 + 42 % 10
???                                    ???

>>> 2 * 3 / 4                          >>> 2 * 2 ** 3
???                                    ???
```

Operator precedence is the relative order that operators are applied in the evaluation of expressions, defined by a given **operator precedence table**.

2.4.3   Operator Associativity

A question that you may have already had is, "What if two operators have the same level of precedence, which one is applied first?" For operators following the associative law, the order of evaluation doesn't matter,

$$(2 + 3) + 4 \rightarrow 9 \qquad 2 + (3 + 4) \rightarrow 9$$

In this case, we get the same results regardless of the order that the operators are applied. Division and subtraction, however, do not follow the associative law,

```
(a) (8 - 4) - 2 → 4 - 2 → 2      8 - (4 - 2) → 8 - 2 → 6
(b) (8 / 4) / 2 → 2 / 2 → 1      8 / (4 / 2) → 8 / 2 → 4
(c) 2 ** (3 ** 2) → 512          (2 ** 3) ** 2 → 64
```

Here, the order of evaluation does matter. To resolve the ambiguity, each operator has a specified **operator associativity** that defines the order that it and other operators with the same level of precedence are applied (as given in Figure 2-19). All operators in the figure, except for exponentiation, have left-to-right associativity—exponentiation has right-to-left associativity.

LET'S TRY IT

From the Python Shell, enter the following and observe the results.

```
>>> 6 - 3 + 2            >>> 2 * 3 / 4           >>> (2 ** 2) ** 3
???                      ???                     ???

>>> (6 - 3) + 2          >>> 12 % (10 / 2)       >>> 2 ** (2 ** 3)
???                      ???                     ???

>>> 6 - (3 + 2)          >>> 2 ** 2 ** 3
???                      ???
```

Operator associativity is the order that operators are applied when having the same level of precedence, specific to each operator.

2.4.4 What Is a Data Type?

A **data type** is a set of values, and a set of operators that may be applied to those values. For example, the integer data type consists of the set of integers, and operators for addition, subtraction, multiplication, and division, among others. Integers, floats, and strings are part of a set of predefined data types in Python called the **built-in types**.

Data types prevent the programmer from using values inappropriately. For example, it does not make sense to try to divide a string by two, `'Hello' / 2`. The programmer knows this by common sense. Python knows it because `'Hello'` belongs to the string data type, which does not include the division operation. The need for data types results from the fact that the same internal representation of data can be interpreted in various ways, as shown in Figure 2-20.

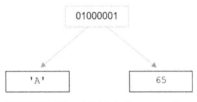

FIGURE 2-20 Multiple Interpretations of a Sequence of Bits

The sequence of bits in the figure can be interpreted as a character (`'A'`) or an integer (`65`). If a programming language did not keep track of the intended type of each value, then the programmer would have to. This would likely lead to undetected programming errors, and would provide even more work for the programmer. We discuss this further in the following section.

Finally, there are two approaches to data typing in programming languages. In **static typing**, a variable is declared as a certain type before it is used, and can only be assigned values of that type. Python, however, uses *dynamic typing*. In **dynamic typing**, the data type of a variable depends only on the type of value that the variable is currently holding. Thus, the same variable may be assigned values of different type during the execution of a program.

A **data type** is a set of values, and a set of operators that may be applied to those values.

2.4.5 Mixed-Type Expressions

A **mixed-type expression** is an expression containing operands of different type. The CPU can only perform operations on values with the same internal representation scheme, and thus only on operands of the same type. Operands of mixed-type expressions therefore must be converted to a common type. Values can be converted in one of two ways—by implicit (automatic) conversion, called *coercion*, or by explicit *type conversion*. We look at each of these next.

A **mixed-type expression** is an expression with operands of different type.

Coercion vs. Type Conversion

Coercion is the *implicit* (automatic) conversion of operands to a common type. Coercion is automatically performed on mixed-type expressions only if the operands can be safely converted, that is, if no loss of information will result. The conversion of integer 2 to floating-point 2.0 below is a safe conversion—the conversion of 4.5 to integer 4 is not, since the decimal digit would be lost,

2 + 4.5 → 2.0 + 4.5 → 6.5 safe (automatic conversion of int to float)

Type conversion is the *explicit* conversion of operands to a specific type. Type conversion can be applied even if loss of information results. Python provides built-in **type conversion functions** int() and float(), with the int() function truncating results as given in Figure 2-21.

$$\text{float}(2) + 4.5 \rightarrow 2.0 + 4.5 \rightarrow 6.5$$
$$2 + \text{int}(4.5) \rightarrow 2 + 4 \rightarrow 6$$

Conversion Function		Converted Result	Conversion Function		Converted Result
`int()`	int(10.8)	10	`float()`	float(10)	10.0
	int('10')	10		float('10')	10.0
	int('10.8')	ERROR		float('10.8')	10.8

FIGURE 2-21   Conversion Functions int() and float() in Python

Note that numeric strings can also be converted to a numeric type. In fact, we have already been doing this when using int or float with the input function,

```
num_credits = int(input('How many credits do you have? '))
```

Coercion is the *implicit* (automatic) conversion of operands to a common type. **Type conversion** is the *explicit* conversion of operands to a specific type.

2.4.6   Let's Apply It—"Temperature Conversion Program"

The following Python program (Figure 2-22) requests from the user a temperature in degrees Fahrenheit, and displays the equivalent temperature in degrees Celsius. This program utilizes the following programming features:

➤ arithmetic expressions   ➤ operator associativity   ➤ format function

Program Execution ...

This program will convert degrees Fahrenheit to degrees Celsius
Enter degrees Fahrenheit: 100
100.0 degrees Fahrenheit equals 37.8 degrees Celsius

```
1   # Temperature Conversion Program (Fahrenheit to Celsius)
2
3   # This program will convert a temperature entered in Fahrenheit
4   # to the equivalent degrees in Celsius
5
6   # program greeting
7   print('This program will convert degrees Fahrenheit to degrees Celsius')
8
9   #get temperature in Fahrenheit
10  fahren = float(input('Enter degrees Fahrenheit: '))
11
12  # calc degrees Celsius
13  celsius = (fahren - 32) * 5 / 9
14
15  # output degrees Celsius
16  print(fahrenheit, 'degrees Fahrenheit equals',
17        format(celsius, '.1f'), 'degrees Celsius')
```

FIGURE 2-22   Temperature Conversion Program

Lines 1–4 contain the program description. **Line 7** provides the program greeting. **Line 10** reads the Fahrenheit temperature entered, assigned to variable `fahren`. Either an integer or a floating-point value may be entered, since the input is converted to float type. **Line 13** performs the calculation for converting Fahrenheit to Celsius. Recall that the division and multiplication operators have the same level of precedence. Since these operators associate left-to-right, the multiplication operator is applied first. Because of the use of the "true" division operator /, the result of the expression will have floating-point accuracy. Finally, **lines 16–17** output the converted temperature in degrees Celsius.

Self-Test Questions

1. What value does the following expression evaluate to?
   ```
   2 + 9 * ((3 * 12) - 8) / 10
   ```
   (a) `27`   **(b)** `27.2`   **(c)** `30.8`

2. Evaluate the following arithmetic expressions using the rules of operator precedence in Python.
   (a) `3 + 2 * 10`   **(b)** `2 + 5 * 4 + 3`   **(c)** `20 // 2 * 5`   **(d)** `2 * 3 ** 2`

3. Evaluate the following arithmetic expressions based on Python's rules of operator associativity.
   (a) `24 // 4 // 2`   **(b)** `2 ** 2 ** 3`

4. Which of the following is a mixed-type expression?
   (a) `2 + 3.0`   **(b)** `2 + 3 * 4`

5. Which of the following would involve coercion when evaluated in Python?
   (a) `4.0 + 3`   (b) `3.2 * 4.0`

6. Which of the following expressions use explicit type conversion?
   (a) `4.0 + float(3)`   (b) `3.2 * 4.0`   (c) `3.2 + int(4.0)`

ANSWERS: 1. (b), 2. (a) 23 (b) 25 (c) 50 (d) 18, 3. (a) 3 (b) 256, 4. (a), 5. (a), 6. (a, c)

COMPUTATIONAL PROBLEM SOLVING

2.5   Age in Seconds Program

We look at the problem of calculating an individual's age in seconds. It is not feasible to determine a given person's age to the exact second. This would require knowing, to the second, when they were born. It would also involve knowing the time zone they were born in, issues of daylight savings time, consideration of leap years, and so forth. Therefore, the problem is to determine an *approximation* of age in seconds. The program will be tested against calculations of age from online resources.

2.5.1   The Problem

The problem is to determine the approximate age of an individual in seconds within 99% accuracy of results from online resources. The program must work for dates of birth from January 1, 1900 to the present.

2.5.2   Problem Analysis

The fundamental computational issue for this problem is the development of an algorithm incorporating approximations for information that is impractical to utilize (time of birth to the second, daylight savings time, etc.), while producing a result that meets the required degree of accuracy.

2.5.3   Program Design

Meeting the Program Requirements

There is no requirement for the form in which the date of birth is to be entered. We will therefore design the program to input the date of birth as integer values. Also, the program will not perform input error checking, since we have not yet covered the programming concepts for this.

Data Description

The program needs to represent two dates, the user's date of birth, and the current date. Since each part of the date must be able to be operated on arithmetically, dates will be represented by three integers. For example, May 15, 1992 would be represented as follows:

```
year = 1992     month = 5     day = 15
```

Hard-coded values will also be utilized for the number of seconds in a minute, number of minutes in an hour, number of hours in a day, and the number of days in a year.

Algorithmic Approach

The Python Standard Library module `datetime` will be used to obtain the current date. (See the Python 3 Programmers' Reference.) We consider how the calculations can be approximated without greatly affecting the accuracy of the results.

We start with the issue of leap years. Since there is a leap year once every four years (with some exceptions), we calculate the average number of seconds in a year over a four-year period that includes a leap year. Since non-leap years have 365 days, and leap years have 366, we need to compute,

```
numsecs_day = (hours per day) * (mins per hour) * (secs per minute)
numsecs_year = (days per year) * numsecs_day
avg_numsecs_year = (4 * numsecs_year) + numsecs_day) // 4      (one extra day
avg_numsecs_month = avgnumsecs_year // 12                       for leap year)
```

To calculate someone's age in seconds, we use January 1, 1900 as a basis. Thus, we compute two values—the number of seconds from January 1 1900 to the given date of birth, and the number of seconds from January 1 1900 to the current date. Subtracting the former from the latter gives the approximate age,

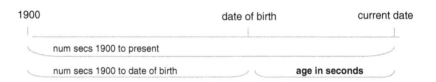

Note that if we directly determined the number of seconds between the date of birth and current date, the months and days of each would need to be compared to see how many full months and years there were between the two. Using 1900 as a basis avoids these comparisons. Thus, the rest of our algorithm is given below.

```
numsecs_1900_to_dob = (year_birth − 1900) * avg_numsecs_year +
                      (month_birth − 1) * avg_numsecs_month +
                      (day_birth * numsecs_day)

numsecs_1900_to_today = (current_year − 1900) * avg_numsecs_year +
                        (current_month − 1) * avg_numsecs_month +
                        (current_day * numsecs_day)

age_in_secs = num_secs_1900_to_today − numsecs_1900_to_dob
```

Overall Program Steps

The overall steps in this program design are in Figure 2-23.

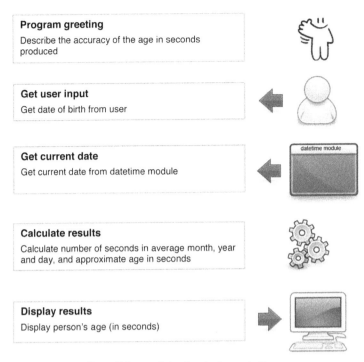

FIGURE 2-23 Overall Steps of the Age in Seconds Program

2.5.4 Program Implementation and Testing

Stage 1—Getting the Date of Birth and Current Date

First, we decide on the variables needed for the program. For date of birth, we use variables month_birth, day_birth, and year_birth. Similarly, for the current date we use variables current_month, current_day, and current_year. The first stage of the program assigns each of these values, shown in Figure 2-24.

```
1  # Age in Seconds Program (Stage 1)
2  # This program will calculate a person's approximate age in seconds
3
4  import datetime
5
6  # Get month, day, year of birth
7  month_birth = int(input('Enter month born (1-12): '))
8  day_birth = int(input ('Enter day born (1-31): '))
9  year_birth = int(input('Enter year born (4-digit): '))
10
11 # Get current month, day, year
12 current_month = datetime.date.today().month
13 current_day = datetime.date.today().day
14 current_year = datetime.date.today().year
15
16 # Test output
17 print('\nThe date of birth read is: ', month_birth, day_birth,
18         year_birth)
19
20 print('The current date read is: ', current_month, current_day,
21         current_year)
```

FIGURE 2-24 First Stage of Age in Seconds Program

Stage 1 Testing

We add test statements that display the values of the assigned variables. This is to ensure that the dates we are starting with are correct; otherwise, the results will certainly not be correct. The test run below indicates that the input is being correctly read.

```
Enter month born (1-12): 4
Enter day born (1-31): 12
Enter year born (4-digit): 1981

The date of birth read is: 4 12 1981
The current date read is: 1 5 2010
>>>
```

Stage 2—Approximating the Number of Seconds in a Year/Month/Day

Next we determine the approximate number of seconds in a given year and month, and the exact number of seconds in a day stored in variables avg_numsecs_year, avg_numsecs_month, and numsecs_day, respectively, shown in Figure 2-25.

```
1  # Age in Seconds Program (Stage 2)
2  # This program will calculate a person's approximate age in seconds
3
4  import datetime
5
6  ### Get month, day, year of birth
7  ##month_birth = int(input('Enter month born (1-12): '))
8  ##day_birth = int(input ('Enter day born (1-31): '))
9  ##year_birth = int(input('Enter year born (4-digit): '))
10
11 ### Get current month, day, year
12 ##current_month = datetime.date.today().month
13 ##current_day = datetime.date.today().day
14 ##current_year = datetime.date.today().year
15
16 # Determine number of seconds in a day, average month, and average year
17 numsecs_day = 24 * 60 * 60
18 numsecs_year = 365 * numsecs_day
19
20 avg_numsecs_year = ((4 * numsecs_year) + numsecs_day) // 4
21 avg_numsecs_month = avg_numsecs_year // 12
22
23 # Test output
24 print('numsecs_day ', numsecs_day)
25 print('avg_numsecs_month = ', avg_numsecs_month)
26 print('avg_numsecs_year = ', avg_numsecs_year)
```

FIGURE 2-25   Second Stage of Age in Seconds Program

The lines of code prompting for input are commented out (**lines 6–9** and **11–14**). Since it is easy to comment out (and uncomment) blocks of code in IDLE, we do so; the input values are irrelevant to this part of the program testing.

Stage 2 Testing

Following is the output of this test run. Checking online sources, we find that the number of seconds in a regular year is 31,536,000 and in a leap year is 31,622,400. Thus, our approximation of 31,557,600 as the average number of seconds over four years (including a leap year) is reasonable. The `avg_num_seconds_month` is directly calculated from variable `avg_numsecs_year`, and `numsecs_day` is found to be correct.

```
numsecs_day 86400
avg_numsecs_month = 2629800
avg_numsecs_year = 31557600
>>>
```

Final Stage—Calculating the Number of Seconds from 1900

Finally, we complete the program by calculating the approximate number of seconds from 1900 to both the current date and the provided date of birth. The difference of these two values gives the approximate age in seconds. The complete program is shown in Figure 2-26.

```
 1  # Age in Seconds Program
 2  # This program will calculate a person's approximate age in seconds
 3
 4  import datetime
 5
 6  # Program greeting
 7  print('This program computes the approximate age in seconds of an')
 8  print('individual based on a provided date of birth. Only dates of')
 9  print('birth from 1900 and after can be computed\n')
10
11  # Get month, day, year of birth
12  month_birth = int(input('Enter month born (1-12): '))
13  day_birth = int(input ('Enter day born (1-31): '))
14  year_birth = int(input('Enter year born (4-digit): '))
15
16  # Get month, day, year of birth
17  current_month = datetime.date.today().month
18  current_day = datetime.date.today().day
19  current_year = datetime.date.today().year
20
21  # Determine number of seconds in a day, average month, and average year
22  numsecs_day = 24 * 60 * 60
23  numsecs_year = 365 * numsecs_day
24
25  avg_numsecs_year = ((4 * numsecs_year) + numsecs_day) // 4
26  avg_numsecs_month = avg_numsecs_year // 12
27
28  # Calculate approximate age in seconds
29  numsecs_1900_dob = (year_birth - 1900 * avg_numsecs_year) + \
30                     (month_birth - 1 * avg_numsecs_month) + \
31                     (day_birth * numsecs_day)
32
33  numsecs_1900_today = (current_year - 1900 * avg_numsecs_year) + \
34                       (current_month - 1 * avg_numsecs_month) + \
35                       (current_day * numsecs_day)
36
37  age_in_secs = numsecs_1900_today - numsecs_1900_dob
38
39  # output results
40  print('\nYou are approximately', age_in_secs, 'seconds old')
```

FIGURE 2-26   Final Stage of Age in Seconds Program

We develop a set of test cases for this program. We follow the testing strategy of including "average" as well as "extreme" or "special case" test cases in the test plan. The test results are given in Figure 2-27.

Date of Birth	Expected Results	Actual Results	Inaccuracy	Evaluation
January 1, 1900	3,520,023,010 ± 86,400	1,468,917	99.96 %	failed
April 12, 1981	955,156,351 ± 86,400	518,433	99.94 %	failed
January 4, 2000	364,090,570 ± 86,400	1,209,617	99.64 %	failed
December 31, 2009	48,821,332 ± 86,400	-1,123,203	102.12 %	failed
(day before current date)	86,400 ± 86,400	86,400	0 %	passed

FIGURE 2-27   Results of First Execution of Test Plan

The "correct" age in seconds for each was obtained from an online source. January 1, 1900 was included in the test plan since it is the earliest date ("extreme case") that the program is required to work for. April 12, 1981 was included as an average case in the 1900s, and January 4, 2000 as an average case in the 2000s. December 31, 2009 was included since it is the last day of the last month of the year. Finally, a test case for a birthday on the day before the current date was included as a special case. (See sample program execution in Figure 2-28). Since these values are continuously changing by the second, we consider any result within one day's worth of seconds (± 84,000) to be an exact result.

```
This program computes the approximate age in seconds of an
individual based on a provided date of birth. Only ages for
dates of birth from 1900 and after can be computed

Enter month born (1-12): 4
Enter day born (1-31): 12
Enter year born: (4-digit)1981

You are approximately 518433 seconds old
>>>
```

FIGURE 2-28   Example Output of Final Stage Testing

The program results are obviously incorrect, since the result is approximately equal to the average number of seconds in a month (determined above). The only correct result is for the day before the current date. The inaccuracy of each result was calculated as follows for April 12, 1981,

((abs(expected_results – actual_results) – 86,400) / expected_results) * 100
= ((917,110,352 – 518,433) – 86400) / 917,110,352) * 100 = 99.93 %

Either our algorithmic approach is flawed, or it is not correctly implemented. Since we didn't find any errors in the development of the first and second stages of the program, the problem must be in the calculation of the approximate age in **lines 29–37**. These lines define three variables: numsecs_1900_dob, numsecs_1900_today, and age_in_secs. We can inspect the values of these variables after execution of the program to see if anything irregular pops out at us.

```
This program computes the approximate age in seconds of an
individual based on a provided date of birth. Only ages for
dates of birth from 1900 and after can be computed

Enter month born (1-12): 4
Enter day born (1-31): 12
Enter year born: (4-digit)1981

You are approximately 604833 seconds old
>>>

>>> numsecs_1900_dob
-59961031015
>>> numsecs_1900_today
-59960426182
>>>
```

Clearly, this is where the problem is, since we are getting negative values for the times between 1900 and date of birth, and from 1900 to today. We "work backwards" and consider how the expressions could give negative results. This would be explained if, for some reason, the second operand of the subtraction were greater than the first. That would happen if the expression were evaluated, for example, as

```
numsecs_1900_dob = (year_birth - (1900 * avg_numsecs_year)) + \
                   (month_birth - (1 * avg_numsecs_month)) + \
                   (day_birth * numsecs_day)
```

rather than the following intended means of evaluation,

```
numsecs_1900_dob = ((year_birth - 1900) * avg_numsecs_year) + \
                   ((month_birth - 1) * avg_numsecs_month) + \
                   (day_birth * numsecs_day)
```

Now we realize! Because we did not use parentheses to explicitly indicate the proper order of operators, by the rules of operator precedence Python evaluated the expression as the first way above, not the second as it should be. This would also explain why the program gave the correct result for a date of birth one day before the current date. Once we make the corrections and re-run the test plan, we get the following results shown in Figure 2-29.

Date of Birth	Expected Results	Actual Results	Inaccuracy
January 1, 1900	3,520,023,010 ± 86,400	3,520,227,600	< .004 %
April 12, 1981	955,156,351 ± 86,400	955,222,200	0 %
January 4, 2000	364,090,570 ± 86,400	364,208,400	< .009 %
December 31, 2009	48,821,332 ± 86,400	48,929,400	< .05 %
(day before current date)	86,400 ± 86,400	86,400	0 %

FIGURE 2-29 Results of Second Execution of Test Plan

These results demonstrate that our approximation of the number of seconds in a year was sufficient to get very good results, well within the 99% degree of accuracy required for this program. We would expect more recent dates of birth to give less accurate results given that there is less time that is approximated. Still, for test case December 31, 2009 the inaccuracy is less than .05 percent. Therefore, we were able to develop a program that gave very accurate results without involving all the program logic that would be needed to consider all the details required to give an exact result.

CHAPTER SUMMARY

General Topics

Numeric and String Literals
Limitations of Floating-Point Representation
Arithmetic Overflow and Underflow
Character Representation Schemes
    (Unicode/ASCII)
Control Characters
String Formatting Implicit and Explicit Line
    Joining/Variables and Variable Use/
    Keyboard Input/Identifier Naming/ Keywords
Arithmetic Operators/Expressions/Infix Notation
Operator Precedence and Associativity
Data Types/Static vs. Dynamic Typing

Mixed-Type Expressions/Coercion and
    Type Conversion

Python-Specific Programming Topics

Numeric Literal and String Literal Values in Python
Built-in `format` Function in Python
Variable Assignment and Storage in Python
Immutable Values in Python
Identifier Naming and Keywords in Python
Arithmetic Operators in Python
Operator Precedence and Associativity in Python
Built-in `int()` and `float()` Type Conversion
    Functions in Python

CHAPTER EXERCISES

Section 2.1

1. Based on the information in Figure 2-1, how many novels can be stored in one terabyte of storage?

2. Give the following values in the exponential notation of Python, such that there is only one significant digit to the left of the decimal point.
   (a) `4580.5034`   **(b)** `0.00000046004`   **(c)** `5000402.000000000006`

3. Which of the floating-point values in question 2 would exceed the representation of the precision of floating points typically supported in Python, as mentioned in the chapter?

4. Regarding the built-in `format` function in Python,
   (a) Use the `format` function to display the floating-point value in a variable named `result` with three decimal digits of precision.
   (b) Give a modified version of the format function in (a) so that commas are included in the displayed results.

5. Give the string of binary digits that represents, in ASCII code,
   (a) The string `'Hi!'`
   (b) The literal string `'I am 24'`

6. Give a call to `print` that is provided one string that displays the following address on three separate lines.

   John Doe
   123 Main Street
   Anytown, Maryland 21009

7. Use the `print` function in Python to output `It's raining today.`

Section 2.2

8. Regarding variable assignment,

   (a) What is the value of variables `num1` and `num2` after the following instructions are executed?

```
num = 0
k = 5
num1 = num + k * 2
num2 = num + k * 2
```

   (b) Are the values `id(num1)` and `id(num2)` equal after the last statement is executed?

9. Regarding the `input` function in Python,

   (a) Give an instruction that prompts the user for their last name and stores it in a variable named `last_name`.

   (b) Give an instruction that prompts the user for their age and stores it as an integer value named `age`.

   (c) Give an instruction that prompts the user for their temperature and stores it as a float named `current_temperature`.

10. Regarding keywords and other predefined identifiers in Python, give the result for each of the following,

   (a) `'int' in dir(__builtins__)`

   (b) `'import' in dir(__builtins__)`

Section 2.3

11. Which of the following operator symbols can be used as both a unary operator and a binary operator?

   $+, -, *, /$

12. What is the exact result of each of the following when evaluated?

   (a) `12 / 6.0`

   (b) `21 // 10`

   (c) `25 // 10.0`

13. If variable n contains an initial value of 1, what is the largest value that will be assigned to n after the following assignment statement is executed an arbitrary number of times?

```
n = (n + 1) % 100
```

14. Which of the following arithmetic expressions could potentially result in arithmetic overflow, where n and k are each assigned integer values?

   (a) `n * k`   **(b)** `n ** k`   **(c)** `n / k`   **(d)** `n + k`

Section 2.4

15. Evaluate the following expressions in Python.

   (a) `10 - (5 * 4)`

   (b) `40 % 6`

   (c) `- (10 / 3) + 2`

16. Give all the possible evaluated results for the following arithmetic expression (assuming no rules of operator precedence).

```
2 * 4 + 25 - 5
```

17. Parenthesize all of the subexpressions in the following expressions following operator precedence in Python.

   (a) `var1 * 8 - var2 + 32 / var3`

   (b) `var1 - 6 ** 4 * var2 ** 3`

18. Evaluate each of the expressions in question 17 above for `var1 = 10, var2 = 30,` and `var3 = 2.`

19. For each of the following expressions, indicate where operator associativity of Python is used to resolve ambiguity in the evaluation of each expression.

(a) `var1 * var2 * var3 - var4`

(b) `var1 * var2 / var3`

(c) `var1 ** var2 ** var3`

20. Using the built-in type conversion function `float()`, alter the following arithmetic expressions so that each is evaluated using floating-point accuracy. Assume that `var1`, `var2`, and `var3` are assigned integer values. Use the minimum number of calls to function `float()` needed to produce the results.

(a) `var1 + var2 * var3`

(b) `var1 // var2 + var3`

(c) `var1 // var2 / var3`

PYTHON PROGRAMMING EXERCISES

P1. Write a Python program that prompts the user for two integer values and displays the result of the first number divided by the second, with exactly two decimal places displayed.

P2. Write a Python program that prompts the user for two floating-point values and displays the result of the first number divided by the second, with exactly six decimal places displayed.

P3. Write a Python program that prompts the user for two floating-point values and displays the result of the first number divided by the second, with exactly six decimal places displayed in scientific notation.

P4. Write a Python program that prompts the user to enter an upper or lower case letter and displays the corresponding Unicode encoding.

P5. Write a Python program that allows the user to enter two integer values, and displays the results when each of the following arithmetic operators are applied. For example, if the user enters the values 7 and 5, the output would be,

```
7 + 5 = 12
7 - 5 = 2
7 * 5 = 35
7 / 5 = 1.40
7 // 5 = 1
7 % 5 = 2
7 ** 5 = 16,807
```

All floating-point results should be displayed with two decimal places of accuracy. In addition, all values should be displayed with commas where appropriate.

PROGRAM MODIFICATION PROBLEMS

M1. Modify the Restaurant Tab Calculation program of section 2.2.5 so that, instead of the restaurant tax being hard coded in the program, the tax rate is entered by the user.

M2. Modify the Restaurant Tab Calculation program of section 2.2.5 so that, in addition to displaying the total of the items ordered, it also displays the total amount spent on drinks and dessert, as well as the percentage of the total cost of the meal (before tax) that these items comprise. Display the monetary amount rounded to two decimal places.

M3. Modify the Your Place in the Universe program in section 2.3.3 for international users, so that the user enters their weight in kilograms, and not in pounds.

M4. Modify the Temperature Conversion program in section 2.4.6 to convert from Celsius to Fahrenheit instead. The formula for the conversion is $f = (c * 9/5) + 32$.

M5. Modify the Age in Seconds program so that it displays the estimated age in number of days, hours, and minutes.

M6. Modify the Age in Seconds program so that it determines the difference in age in seconds of two friends.

PROGRAM DEVELOPMENT PROBLEMS

D1. Losing Your Head over Chess

The game of chess is generally believed to have been invented in India in the sixth century for a ruling king by one of his subjects. The king was supposedly very delighted with the game and asked the subject what he wanted in return. The subject, being clever, asked for one grain of wheat on the first square, two grains of wheat on the second square, four grains of wheat on the third square, and so forth, doubling the amount on each next square. The king thought that this was a modest reward for such an invention. However, the total amount of wheat would have been more than 1,000 times the current world production.

Develop and test a Python program that calculates how much wheat this would be in pounds, using the fact that a grain of wheat weighs approximately 1/7,000 of a pound.

D2. All That Talking

Develop and test a Python program that determines how much time it would take to download all instances of every word ever spoken. Assume the size of this information as given in Figure 2-1. The download speed is to be entered by the user in million of bits per second (mbps). To find your actual connection speed, go to the following website (from Intel Corporation) or similar site,

www.intel.com/content/www/us/en/gamers/broadband-speed-test.html

Because connection speeds can vary, run this connection speed test three times. Take the average of three results, and use that as the connection speed to enter into your program. Finally, determine what is an appropriate unit of time to express your program results in: minutes? hours? days? other?

D3. Pictures on the Go

Develop and test a Python program that determines how many images can be stored on a given size USB (flash) drive. The size of the USB drive is to be entered by the user in gigabytes (GB). The number of images that can be stored must be calculated for GIF, JPEG, PNG, and TIFF image file formats. The program output should be formatted as given below.

```
Enter USB size (GB): 4

xxxxx images in GIF format can be stored
xxxxx images in JPEG format can be stored
xxxxx images in PNG format can be stored
xxxxx images in TIFF format can be stored
```

The ultimate file size of a given image depends not only on the image format used, but also on the image itself. In addition, formats such as JPEG allow the user to select the degree of compression for the image quality desired. For this program, we assume the image compression ratios given below. Also assume that all the images have a resolution of 800×600 pixels.

Thus, for example, a 800×600 resolution image with 16-bit (2 bytes) color depth would have a total number of bytes of $800 \times 600 \times 2 = 960{,}000$. For a compression rate of 25:1, the total number of bytes needed to store the image would be $960000/25 = 38400$.

Finally, assume that a GB (gigabyte) equals 1,000,000,000 bytes, as given in Figure 2.1.

Format	Full Name	Color Depth		Compression	
GIF	Graphics Interchange Format	256 colors	8 bits	lossless	5:1
JPEG	Joint Photographic Experts Group	16 million colors	24 bits	lossy	25:1
PNG	Portable Network Graphics	16 million colors	24 bits	lossless	8:1
TIFF	Tagged Image File Format	280 trillion colors	48 bits	lossless	n/a

Note that a "lossless" compression is one in which no information is lost. A "lossy" compression does lose some of the original information.

D4. Life Signs

Develop and test a program that prompts the user for their age and determines approximately how many breaths and how many heartbeats the person has had in their life. The average respiration (breath) rate of people changes during different stages of development. Use the breath rates given below for use in your program:

	Breaths per Minute
Infant	30–60
1–4 years	20–30
5–14 years	15–25
adults	12–20

For heart rate, use an average of 67.5 beats per second.

Control Structures

CHAPTER 3

In Chapter 2 we looked at the "nuts and bolts" of programming. In this chapter, we discuss the three fundamental means of controlling the order of execution of instructions within a program, referred to as sequential, selection, and iterative control.

OBJECTIVES

After reading this chapter and completing the exercises, you will be able to:

♦ Explain what a control structure is

♦ Explain the difference between sequential, selection, and iterative control

♦ Describe and use Boolean operators

♦ Explain the notion of logically equivalent Boolean expressions

♦ Explain what is meant by an infinite loop

♦ Explain the difference between a definite and indefinite loop

♦ Explain the use of indentation in Python

♦ Effectively use if statements in Python for selection control

♦ Effectively implement multi-way selection in Python

♦ Effectively use while statements in Python for iterative control

CHAPTER CONTENTS

Motivation

Fundamental Concepts

3.1 What Is a Control Structure?

3.2 Boolean Expressions (Conditionals)

3.3 Selection Control

3.4 Iterative Control

Computational Problem Solving

3.5 Calendar Month Program

MOTIVATION

The first electronic computers over sixty years ago were referred to as "Electronic Brains." This gave the misleading impression that computers could "think." Although very complex in their design, computers are machines that simply do, step-by-step (instruction-by-instruction), what they are told. Thus, there is no more intelligence in a computer than what it is instructed to do.

What computers can do, however, is to execute a series of instructions very quickly and very reliably. It is the speed in which instructions can be executed that gives computers their power (see Figure 3-1), since the execution of many simple instructions can result in very complex behavior. And thus this is the enticement of computing. A computer can accomplish any task for which there is an algorithm for doing so. The instructions could be for something as simple as sorting lists, or as ambitious as performing intelligent tasks that as of now only humans are capable of performing.

In this chapter, we look at how to control the order that instructions are executed in Python.

Term	Number of Floating Point Operations / Second		Device
Megaflops	10^6	1 million FLOPS	Supercomputers (1970s)
Gigaflops	10^9	1 billion FLOPS	CPU (single core)
Teraflops	10^{12}	1 trillion FLOPS	CPU (multi-core)
Petaflops	10^{15}	1 quadrillion FLOPS	Supercomputers (current)
Exaflops	10^{18}	1 quintillion FLOPS	Supercomputers in 2020 (projected)

FIGURE 3-1 Processing Speed—Floating-Point Operations per Second (FLOPS)

FUNDAMENTAL CONCEPTS

3.1 What Is a Control Structure?

Control flow is the order that instructions are executed in a program. A **control statement** is a statement that determines the control flow of a set of instructions. There are three fundamental forms of control that programming languages provide—*sequential control*, *selection control*, and *iterative control*.

Sequential control is an implicit form of control in which instructions are executed in the order that they are written. A program consisting of only sequential control is referred to as a "straight-line program." The program examples in Chapter 2 are all straight-line programs. **Selection control** is provided by a control statement that *selectively executes* instructions, while **iterative**

control is provided by an iterative control statement that *repeatedly executes* instructions. Each is based on a given condition. Collectively a set of instructions and the control statements controlling their execution is called a **control structure**.

Few programs are straight-line programs. Most use all three forms of control, depicted in Figure 3-2. We look at selection control and iterative control next.

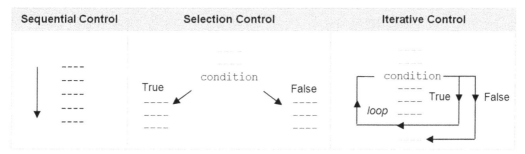

FIGURE 3-2 if Statement

A **control statement** is a statement that determines the control flow of a set of instructions. A **control structure** is a set of instructions and the control statements controlling their execution. Three fundamental forms of control in programming are **sequential**, **selection**, and **iterative control**.

3.2 Boolean Expressions (Conditions)

The **Boolean data type** contains two Boolean values, denoted as **True** and **False** in Python. A **Boolean expression** is an expression that evaluates to a Boolean value. Boolean expressions are used to denote the conditions for selection and iterative control statements. We look at the use of Boolean expressions next.

The **Boolean data type** contains two Boolean values, denoted as **True** and **False** in Python. A **Boolean expression** is an expression that evaluates to a Boolean value.

3.2.1 Relational Operators

The relational operators in Python perform the usual comparison operations, shown in Figure 3-3. Relational expressions are a type of Boolean expression, since they evaluate to a Boolean result. These operators not only apply to numeric values, but to any set of values that has an ordering, such as strings.

Note the use of the **comparison operator**, $==$, for determining if two values are equal. This, rather than the (single) equal sign, $=$, is used since the equal sign is used as the assignment operator. This is often a source of confusion for new programmers,

```
num = 10        variable num is assigned the value 10
num == 10       variable num is compared to the value 10
```

Relational Operators	Example	Result
== equal	10 == 10	True
!= not equal	10 != 10	False
< less than	10 < 20	True
> greater than	'Alan' > 'Brenda'	False
<= less than or equal to	10 <= 10	True
>= greater than or equal to	'A' >= 'D'	False

FIGURE 3-3 The Relational Operators

Also, != is used for inequality simply because there is no keyboard character for the ≠ symbol.

String values are ordered based on their character encoding, which normally follows a **lexographical (dictionary) ordering**. For example, 'Alan' is less than 'Brenda' since the Unicode (ASCII) value for 'A' is 65, and 'B' is 66. However, 'alan' is greater than (comes *after*) 'Brenda' since the Unicode encoding of lowercase letters (97, 98, . . .) comes *after* the encoding of uppercase letters (65, 66, . . .). Recall from Chapter 2 that the encoding of any character can be obtained by use of the ord function.

LET'S TRY IT

From the Python Shell, enter the following and observe the results.

```
>>> 10 == 20          >>> '2' < '9'          >>> 'Hello' == "Hello"
???                   ???                    ???

>>> 10 != 20          >>> '12' < '9'         >>> 'Hello' < 'Zebra'
???                   ???                    ???

>>> 10 <= 20          >>> '12' > '9'         >>> 'hello' < 'ZEBRA'
???                   ???                    ???
```

The relational operators ==, !=, <, >, <=, >= can be applied to any set of values that has an ordering.

3.2.2 Membership Operators

Python provides a convenient pair of **membership operators**. These operators can be used to easily determine if a particular value occurs within a specified list of values. The membership operators are given in Figure 3-4.

The in operator is used to determine if a specific value is in a given list, returning True if found, and False otherwise. The not in operator returns the opposite result. The list of values surrounded by matching parentheses in the figure are called *tuples* in Python. Tuples (and lists) are covered in Chapter 4.

Membership Operators	Examples	Result
in	10 in (10, 20, 30)	True
	red in ('red','green','blue')	True
not in	10 not in (10, 20, 30)	False

FIGURE 3-4 The Membership Operators

The membership operators *can also be used to check if a given string occurs within another string,*

```
>>> 'Dr.' in 'Dr. Madison'
True
```

As with the relational operators, the membership operators can be used to construct Boolean expressions.

LET'S TRY IT

From the Python Shell, enter the following and observe the results.

```
>>> 10 in (40, 20, 10)
???
```
```
>>> grade = 'A'
>>> grade in ('A','B','C','D','F')
???
```

```
>>> 10 not in (40, 20, 10)
???
```
```
>>> city = 'Houston'
>>> city in ('NY', 'Baltimore', 'LA')
???
```

```
>>> .25 in (.45, .25, .65)
???
```

Python provides membership operators in and not in for determining if a specific value is in (or not in) a given list of values.

3.2.3 Boolean Operators

George Boole, in the mid-1800s, developed what we now call *Boolean algebra*. His goal was to develop an algebra based on true/false rather than numerical values. Boolean algebra contains a set of **Boolean (logical) operators**, denoted by and, or, and not in Python. These logical operators can be used to construct arbitrarily complex Boolean expressions. The Boolean operators are shown in Figure 3-5.

Logical and is true only when *both* its operands are true—otherwise, it is false. Logical or is true when *either or both* of its operands are true, and thus false only when both operands are false. Logical not simply reverses truth values—not False equals True, and not True equals False.

x	y	x and y	x or y	not x
False	False	False	False	True
True	False	False	True	False
False	True	False	True	
True	True	True	True	

FIGURE 3-5 Boolean Logic Truth Table

One must be cautious when using Boolean operators. For example, in mathematics, to denote that a value is within a certain range is written as

$$1 <= num <= 10$$

In most programming languages, however, this expression does not make sense. To see why, let's assume that num has the value 15. The expression would then be evaluated as follows,

$$1 <= num <= 10 \quad \rightarrow \quad 1 <= 15 <= 10 \quad \rightarrow \quad True <= 10 \quad \rightarrow \quad ?!?$$

It does not make sense to check if True is less than or equal to 10. (Some programming languages would generate a mixed-type expression error for this.) The correct way of denoting the condition is by use of the Boolean and operator,

$$1 <= num \; and \; num <= 10$$

In some languages (such as Python), Boolean values True and False have integer values 1 and 0, respectively. In such cases, the expression 1 <= num <= 10 would evaluate to True <= 10 would evaluate to 1 <= 10, which equals True. This would not be the correct result for this expression, however. Let's see what we get when we do evaluate this expression in the Python shell,

```
>>> num = 15
>>> 1 <= num <= 10
False
```

We actually get the correct result, False. So what is going on here? The answer is that Python is playing a trick here. For Boolean expressions of the particular form,

$$value1 <= var <= value2$$

Python automatically rewrites this before performing the evaluation,

$$value1 <= var \; and \; var <= value2$$

Thus, it is important to note that expressions of this form are handled in a special way in Python, and would not be proper to use in most other programming languages.

One must also be careful in the use of and/or Boolean operators. For example, not (num == 0 and num == 1) is True for any value of num, as is (num != 0) or (num != 1), and therefore are not useful expressions. The Boolean expression num < 0 and num > 10 is also useless since it is always False.

Finally, Boolean literals True and False are never quoted. Doing so would cause them to be taken as string values ('True'). And as we saw, Boolean expressions do not necessarily contain Boolean operators. For example, 10 <= 20 is a Boolean expression. By definition, Boolean literals True and False are Boolean expressions as well.

LET'S TRY IT

From the Python Shell, enter the following and observe the results.

```
>>> True and False          >>> (10 < 0) and (10 > 2)
???                         ???
>>> True or False           >>> (10 < 0) or (10 > 2)
???                         ???
>>> not(True) and False     >>> not(10 < 0) or (10 > 2)
???                         ???
>>> not(True and False)     >>> not(10 < 0 or 10 > 2)
???                         ???
```

Boolean operators in Python are denoted by and, or, and not.

3.2.4 Operator Precedence and Boolean Expressions

The operator precedence (and operator associativity) of arithmetic operators was given in Chapter 2. Operator precedence also applies to Boolean operators. Since Boolean expressions can contain arithmetic as well as relational and Boolean operators, the precedence of all operators needs to be collectively applied. An updated operator precedence table is given in Figure 3-6.

Operator	Associativity
** (exponentiation)	right-to-left
- (negation)	left-to-right
* (mult), / (div), // (truncating div), % (modulo)	left-to-right
+ (addition), - (subtraction)	left-to-right
<, >, <=, >=, !=, == (relational operators)	left-to-right
not	left-to-right
and	left-to-right
or	left-to-right

FIGURE 3-6 Operator Precedence of Arithmetic, Relational, and Boolean Operators

As before, in the table, higher-priority operators are placed above lower-priority ones. Thus, we see that *all arithmetic operators are performed before any relational or Boolean operator,*

$$10 \ + \ 20 \ < \ 20 \ + \ 30 \quad \rightarrow \quad 30 \ < \ 50 \ \rightarrow \ \text{True}$$

In addition, *all of the relational operators are performed before any Boolean operator,*

$$10 \ < \ 20 \ \text{and} \ 30 \ < \ 20 \quad \rightarrow \quad \text{True and False} \ \rightarrow \ \text{False}$$

$$10 \ < \ 20 \ \text{or} \ 30 \ < \ 20 \quad \rightarrow \quad \text{True or False} \ \rightarrow \ \text{True}$$

And as with arithmetic operators, Boolean operators have various levels of precedence. Unary Boolean operator `not` has higher precedence than `and`, and Boolean operator `and` has higher precedence than `or`.

$$10 \ < \ 20 \ \text{and} \ 30 \ < \ 20 \ \text{or} \ 30 \ < \ 40 \ \rightarrow \ \text{True and False or True}$$

$$\rightarrow \ \text{False or True} \ \rightarrow \ \text{True}$$

$$\text{not} \ 10 \ < \ 20 \ \text{or} \ 30 \ < \ 20 \ \rightarrow \ \text{not True or False}$$

$$\rightarrow \ \text{False or False} \ \rightarrow \ \text{False}$$

As with arithmetic expressions, it is good programming practice to use parentheses, even if not needed, to add clarity and enhance readability. Thus, the above expressions would be better written by denoting at least some of the subexpressions,

```
(10 < 20 and 30 < 20) or (30 < 40)
(not 10 < 20) or (30 < 20)
```

if not all subexpressions,

```
((10 < 20) and (30 < 20)) or (30 < 40)
(not (10 < 20)) or (30 < 20)
```

Finally, note from Figure 3.6 above that all relational and Boolean operators associate from left to right.

LET'S TRY IT

From the Python Shell, enter the following and observe the results.

```
>>> not True and False              >>> 10 < 0 and not 10 > 2
???                                 ???
>>> not True and False or True      >>> not (10 < 0 or 10 < 20)
???                                 ???
```

3.2.5 Short-Circuit (Lazy) Evaluation

There are differences in how Boolean expressions are evaluated in different programming languages. For logical `and`, if the first operand evaluates to false, then regardless of the value of the second operand, the expression is false. Similarly, for logical `or`, if the first operand evaluates to true, regardless of the value of the second operand, the expression is true. Because of this, some programming languages do not evaluate the second operand when the result is known by the first operand alone, called **short-circuit (lazy) evaluation**. Subtle errors can result if the programmer is not aware of this. For example, the expression

`if n != 0 and 1/n < tolerance:`

would evaluate without error for all values of n when short-circuit evaluation is used. If programming in a language not using short-circuit evaluation, however, a "divide by zero" error would result when n is equal to 0. In such cases, the proper construction would be,

`if n != 0:`
`    if 1/n < tolerance:`

In the Python programming language, short-circuit evaluation is used.

> In **short-circuit (lazy) evaluation**, the second operand of Boolean operators and and or is not evaluated if the value of the Boolean expression can be determined from the first operand alone.

3.2.6 Logically Equivalent Boolean Expressions

In numerical algebra, there are arithmetically equivalent expressions of different form. For example, $x(y + z)$ and $xy + xz$ are equivalent for any numerical values x, y, and z. Similarly, there are *logically* equivalent **Boolean expressions** of different form. We give some examples in Figure 3-7.

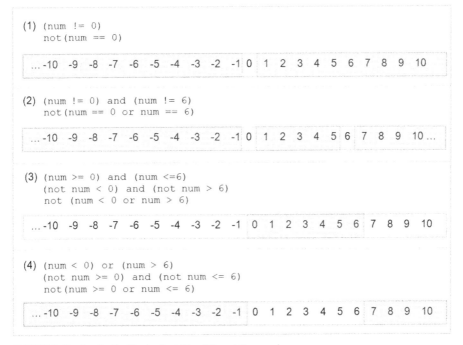

FIGURE 3-7 Logically Equivalent Conditional Expressions

The range of values satisfying each set of expressions is shaded in the figure. Both expressions in (1) are true for any value except 0. The expressions in (2) are true for any value except 0 and 6. The expressions in (3) are only true for values in the range 0 through 6, inclusive. The expressions in (4) are true for all values *except* 0 through 6, inclusive. Figure 3-8 lists common forms of logically equivalent expressions.

Logically Equivalent Boolean Expressions		
x < y	is equivalent to	not(x >= y)
x <= y	is equivalent to	not(x > y)
x == y	is equivalent to	not(x != y)
x != y	is equivalent to	not(x == y)
not(x and y)	is equivalent to	(not x) or (not y)
not(x or y)	is equivalent to	(not x) and (not y)

FIGURE 3-8   Forms of Logically Equivalent Boolean Expressions

The last two equivalences above are referred to as De Morgan's Laws.

LET'S TRY IT

From the Python Shell, enter the following and observe the results.

```
>>> 10 < 20                    >>> not(10 < 20 and 10 < 30)
???                            ???
>>> not(10 >= 20)              >>> (not 10 < 20) or (not 10 < 30)
???                            ???
>>> 10 != 20                   >>> not(10 < 20 or 10 < 30)
???                            ???
>>> not (10 == 20)             >>> (not 10 < 20) and (not 10 < 30)
???                            ???
```

There are logically equivalent **Boolean expressions** of different form.

Self-Test Questions

1. Three forms of control in programming are sequential, selection, and _____ control.

2. Which of the following expressions evaluate to `True`?
   (a) 10 >= 8 **(b)** 8 <= 10 **(c)** 10 == 8 **(d)** 10 != 8 **(e)** '8' < '10'

3. Which of the following Boolean expressions evaluate to `True`?
   (a) 'Dave' < 'Ed' **(b)** 'dave' < 'Ed' **(c)** 'Dave' < 'Dale'

4. What is the value of variable num after the following is executed?

```
>>> num = 10
>>> num = num + 5
>>> num == 20
>>> num = num + 1
```

5. What does the following expression evaluate to for name equal to 'Ann'?

```
name in ('Jacob', 'MaryAnn', 'Thomas')
```

6. Evaluate the following Boolean expressions using the operator precedence rules of Python.
(a) 10 >= 8 and 5 != 3 **(b)** 10 >= 8 and 5 == 3 or 14 < 5

7. Which one of the following Boolean expressions is not logically equivalent to the other two?
(a) not(num < 0 or num > 10)
(b) num > 0 and num < 10
(c) num >= 0 and num <= 10

ANSWERS: 1. Iterative. 2. (a,b,d). 3. (a). 4. 16. 5. False. 6. (a) True. (b) False. 7. (b)

3.3 Selection Control

A **selection control statement** is a control statement providing selective execution of instructions. A *selection control structure* is a given set of instructions and the selection control statement(s) controlling their execution. We look at the *if statement* providing selection control in Python next.

> A **selection control statement** is a control statement providing selective execution of instructions.

3.3.1 If Statement

An **if statement** is a selection control statement based on the value of a given Boolean expression. The if statement in Python is depicted in Figure 3-9.

if statement	Example use	

`if condition:`
    `statements`
`else:`
    `statements`
	`if grade >= 70:`
	    `print('passing grade')`
	`else:`
	    `print('failing grade')`
		`if grade == 100:`
		    `print('perfect score!')`

FIGURE 3-9 if Statement

Note that if statements may omit the "else" part. A version of the temperature conversion program from Chapter 2 using an if statement is given in Figure 3-10.

This program extends the original program by converting Celsius to Fahrenheit, as well as Fahrenheit to Celsius. The if statement (**line 13**) selects the appropriate set of instructions to execute based on user input ('F' for Fahrenheit to Celsius, and 'C' for Celsius to Fahrenheit). A statement that contains other statements, such as the if statement, is called a **compound statement**. We look at Python's use of indentation in compound statements next.

```
1    # Temperature Conversion Program (Celsius-Fahrenheit / Fahrenheit-Celsius)
2
3    # Display program welcome
4    print('This program will convert temperatures (Fahrenheit/Celsius)')
5    print('Enter (F) to convert Fahrenheit to Celsius')
6    print('Enter (C) to convert Celsius to Fahrenheit')
7
8    # Get temperature to convert
9    which = input('Enter selection: ')
10   temp = int(input('Enter temperature to convert: '))
11
12   # Determine temperature conversion needed and display results
13   if which == 'F':
14       converted_temp = (temp - 32) * 5/9
15       print(temp, 'degrees Fahrenheit equals', converted_temp, 'degrees Celsius')
16   else:
17       converted_temp = (9/5 * temp) + 32
18       print(temp, 'degrees Celsius equals', converted_temp, 'degrees Fahrenheit')
```

FIGURE 3-10   Temperature Conversion (Two-Way Conversion)

An **if statement** is a selection control statement based on the value of a given Boolean expression. Statements that contain other statements are referred to as a **compound statement**.

3.3.2   Indentation in Python

One fairly unique aspect of Python is that the amount of indentation of each program line is significant. In most programming languages, indentation has no affect on program logic—it is simply used to align program lines to aid readability. In Python, however, indentation is used to associate and group statements, as shown in Figure 3-11.

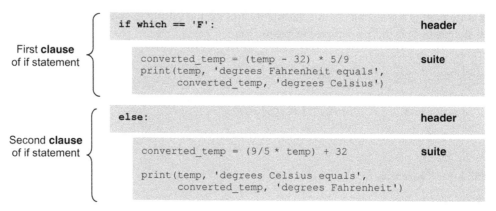

FIGURE 3-11   Compound Statement in Python

A **header** in Python is a specific keyword followed by a colon. In the figure, the if-else statement contains two headers, "if which == 'F':" containing keyword if, and "else:" consisting only of the keyword else. Headers that are part of the same compound statement must be indented the same amount—otherwise, a syntax error will result.

The set of statements following a header in Python is called a **suite** (commonly called a **block**). The statements of a given suite must all be indented the same amount. A header and its associated suite are together referred to as a **clause**. A compound statement in Python may consist of one or more clauses. While four spaces is commonly used for each level of indentation, any number of spaces may be used, as shown in Figure 3-12.

Valid indentation		Invalid indentation	

(a) `if condition:`
  `statement`
  `statement`
`else:`
  `statement`
  `statement`
	(b) `if condition:`
	    `statement`
	    `statement`
	`else:`
	      `statement`
	      `statement`
		(c) `if condition:`
		    `statement`
		    `statement`
		  `else:`
		    `statement`
		    `statement`
			(d) `if condition:`
			    `statement`
			    `statement`
			`else:`
			    `statement`
			   `statement`

FIGURE 3-12 Compound Statements and Indentation in Python

Both (a) and (b) in the figure are properly indented. In (a), both suites have the same amount of indentation. In (b), each suite has a different amount of indentation. This is syntactically correct (although not good practice) since the amount of indentation within each suite is consistent. Both (c) and (d) are examples of invalid indentation, and thus syntactically incorrect. In (c), the `if` and `else` headers of the if statement are not indented the same amount. In (d), the headers are indented the same amount. However, the statements within the second suite are not properly aligned. Finally, note that the suite following a header can itself be a compound statement (another if statement, for example). Thus, compound statements may be nested one within another. We look at nested compounded statements next.

LET'S TRY IT

From IDLE, create and run a Python program containing the code on the left and observe the results. Modify and run the code to match the version on the right and again observe the results. Make sure to indent the code exactly as shown.

```
grade = 90

if grade >= 70:
    print('passing grade')
else:
    print('failing grade')
```

```
grade = 90

if grade >= 70:
      print('passing grade')
   else:
      print('failing grade')
```

A **header** in Python starts with a keyword and ends with a colon. The group of statements following a header is called a **suite**. A header and its associated suite are together referred to as a **clause**.

3.3.3 Multi-Way Selection

In this section, we look at the two means of constructing multi-way selection in Python—one involving multiple nested if statements, and the other involving a single if statement and the use of `elif` headers.

Nested if Statements

There are often times when selection among more than two sets of statements (suites) is needed. For such situations, if statements can be nested, resulting in **multi-way selection**. An example of this is given in Figure 3-13.

Nested if statements	Example use
| ```
if condition:
    statements
else:
    if condition:
        statements
    else:
        if condition:
            statements

        etc.
``` | ```
if grade >= 90:
    print('Grade of A')
else:
    if grade >= 80:
        print('Grade of B')
    else:
        if grade >= 70:
            print('Grade of C')
        else:
            if grade >= 60:
                print('Grade of D')
            else:
                print('Grade of F')
``` |

FIGURE 3-13 Multi-way Selection Using if Statements

The nested if statements on the right result in a 5-way selection. In the first if statement, if variable grade is greater than or equal to 90, then 'Grade of A' is displayed. Therefore, its else suite is not executed, containing the remaining if statements. If grade is less than 90, the else suite is executed. If grade is greater than or equal to 80, 'Grade of B' is displayed and the rest of the if statements in *its* else suite are skipped, and so on. The final else clause is executed only if all the previous conditions fail, displaying 'Grade of F'. This is referred to as a *catch-all* case. As an example use of nested if statements and a check for invalid input in a program, we give a revised version of the temperature conversion program from Figure 3-10 in Figure 3-14.

```
1   # Temperature Conversion Program (Celsius-Fahrenheit / Fahrenheit-Celsius)
2
3   # Display program welcome
4   print('This program will convert temperatures (Fahrenheit/Celsius)')
5   print('Enter (F) to convert Fahrenheit to Celsius')
6   print('Enter (C) to convert Celsius to Fahrenheit')
7
8   # Get temperature to convert
9   which = input('Enter selection: ')
10  temp = int(input('Enter temperature to convert: '))
11
12  # Determine temperature conversion needed and display results
13  if which == 'F':
14      converted_temp = format((temp - 32) * 5.0/9.0, '.1f')
15      print(temp, 'degrees Fahrenheit equals', converted_temp, 'degrees Celsius')
16  else:
17      if which == 'C':
18          converted_temp = format((9.0/5.0 * temp) + 32, '.1f')
19          print(temp,'degrees Celsius equals',converted_temp,'degrees Fahrenheit')
20      else:
21          print('INVALID INPUT')
```

FIGURE 3-14 Temperature Conversion Program (Input Error Dectection)

In this version, there is a catch-all clause (**line 20**) for handling invalid input. We next look at a more concise means of denoting multi-way selection in Python.

LET'S TRY IT

From IDLE, create and run a simple program containing the code below and observe the results. Make sure to indent the code exactly as shown.

```python
credits = 45

if credits >= 90:
    print('Senior')
else:
    if credits >= 60:
        print('Junior')
    else:
        if credits >= 30:
            print('Sophomore')
        else:
            if credits >= 1:
                print('Freshman')
            else:
                print('* No Earned Credits *')
```

If statements can be nested in Python, resulting in **multi-way selection**.

The `elif` Header in Python

If statements may contain only one `else` header. Thus, `if-else` statements must be nested to achieve multi-way selection. Python, however, has another header called `elif` ("else-if") that provides multi-way selection in a *single* if statement, shown in Figure 3-15.

All the headers of an `if-elif` statement are indented the same amount, thus avoiding the deeply nested levels of indentation with the use of `if-else` statements. A final `else` clause may be used for "catch-all" situations. We next look at iterative control in Python.

```python
if grade >= 90:
    print('Grade of A')
elif grade >= 80:
    print('Grade of B')
elif grade >= 70:
    print('Grade of C')
elif grade >= 60:
    print('Grade of D')
else:
    print('Grade of F')
```

FIGURE 3-15 The `elif` Header in Python

LET'S TRY IT

From IDLE, create and run a Python program containing the code below and observe the results. Make sure to indent the code exactly as shown.

```
credits = 45

if credits >= 90:
    print('Senior')
elif credits >= 60:
    print('Junior')
elif grade >= 30:
    print('Sophomore')
elif grade >= 1:
    print('Freshman')
else:
    print('* No Earned Credits *')
```

If statements may contain any number of **elif headers**, providing for multi-way selection.

3.3.4 Let's Apply It—Number of Days in Month Program

The following Python program (Figure 3-16) prompts the user for a given month (and year for February), and displays how many days are in the month. This program utilizes the following programming features:

➤ if statement   ➤ elif header

Lines 1–4 provide the program header and program greeting. On **line 7**, variable `valid_input` is initialized to `True` for the input error-checking performed. **Line 10** prompts the user for the month, read as an integer value (1–12), and stores in variable `month`. On **line 15** the month of February is checked for. February is the only month that may have a different number of days—28 for a regular year, and 29 for leap years. Thus, when February (2) is entered, the user is also prompted for the year (**line 16**). If the `year` is a leap year, then variable `num_days` is set to 29—otherwise, it is set to 28.

Generally, if a year is (evenly) divisible by 4, then it is a leap year. However, there are a couple of exceptions. If the year is divisible by 4 but is also divisible by 100, then it is *not* a leap year—unless, it is also divisible by 400, then it is. For example, 1996 and 2000 were leap years, but 1900 was not. This condition is given below.

$$(year \% 4 == 0) \text{ and } (not (year \% 100 == 0) \text{ or } (year \% 400 == 0))$$

Thus, the conditions for which this Boolean expression is true are,

$$(year \% 4 == 0) \text{ and } not (year \% 100 == 0)$$

and

$$(year \% 4 == 0) \text{ and } (year \% 400 == 0)$$

Program Execution ...
This program will determine the number of days in a given month

Enter the month (1-12): 14
* Invalid Value Entered - 14 '*'
>>>

This program will determine the number of days in a given month

Enter the month (1-12): 2
Please enter the year (e.g., 2010): 2000
There are 29 days in the month

```python
# Number of Days in Month Program

# program greeting
print('This program will display the number of days in a given month\n')

# init
valid_input = True

# get user input
month = int(input('Enter the month (1-12): '))

# determine num of days in month

# february
if month == 2:
    year = int(input('Please enter the year (e.g., 2010): '))

    if (year % 4 == 0) and (not (year % 100 == 0) or (year % 400 == 0)):
        num_days = 29
    else:
        num_days = 28

# january, march, may, july, august, october, december
elif month in (1, 3, 5, 7, 8, 10, 12):
    num_days = 31

# april, june, september, november
elif month in (4,6,9,11):
    num_days = 30

# invalid input
else:
    print('* Invalid Value Entered - ', month, '*')
    valid_input = False

# output result
if valid_input:
    print('There are', num_days, 'days in the month')
```

FIGURE 3-16 Number of Days in Month Program

Line 24 checks if month is equal to 1, 3, 5, 7, 8, 10, or 12. If true, then num_days is assigned to 31. If not true, **line 28** checks if month is equal to 4, 6, 9, or 11 (all the remaining months except February). If true, then num_days is assigned to 30. If not true, then an invalid month (number) was entered, and valid_input is set to False. Finally, the number of days in the month is displayed only if the input is valid (**line 38**).

Self-Test Questions

1. All if statements must contain either an else or elif header. (TRUE/FALSE)

2. A compound statement is,
   (a) A statement that spans more than one line
   (b) A statement that contains other statements
   (c) A statement that contains at least one arithmetic expression

3. Which of the following statements are true regarding headers in Python?
   (a) Headers begin with a keyword and end with a colon.
   (b) Headers always occur in pairs.
   (c) All headers of the same compound statement must be indented the same amount.

4. Which of the following statements is true?
   (a) Statements within a suite can be indented a different amount.
   (b) Statements within a suite can be indented a different amount as long as all headers in the statement that it occurs in are indented the same amount.
   (c) All headers must be indented the same amount as all other headers in the same statement, and all statements in a given suite must be indented the same amount.

5. The elif header allows for,
   (a) Multi-way selection that cannot be accomplished otherwise
   (b) Multi-way selection as a single if statement
   (c) The use of a "catch-all" case in multi-way selection

ANSWERS: 1. False, 2. (b), 3. (a) (c), 4. (c), 5. (b)

3.4 Iterative Control

An **iterative control statement** is a control statement providing the repeated execution of a set of instructions. An *iterative control structure* is a set of instructions and the iterative control statement(s) controlling their execution. Because of their repeated execution, iterative control structures are commonly referred to as "loops." We look at one specific iterative control statement next, the while statement.

> An **iterative control statement** is a control statement that allows for the repeated execution of a set of statements.

3.4.1   While Statement

A **while statement** is an iterative control statement that repeatedly executes a set of statements based on a provided Boolean expression (condition). All iterative control needed in a program can be achieved by use of the while statement. Figure 3-17 contains an example of a while loop in Python that sums the first n integers, for a given (positive) value n entered by the user.

while statement	Example use

`while condition:`
`    suite`
	`sum = 0`
	`current = 1`
	
	`n = int(input('Enter value: '))`
	
	`while current <= n:`
	`    sum = sum + current`
	`    current = current + 1`

FIGURE 3-17   The while Statement in Python

As long as the condition of a while statement is true, the statements within the loop are (re)executed. Once the condition becomes false, the iteration terminates and control continues with the first statement after the while loop. Note that it is possible that the first time a loop is reached, the condition may be false, and therefore the loop would never be executed.

Suppose, for the example in the figure, that the user enters the value 3. Since variable `current` is initialized to 1 (referred to as a *counter variable*), the first time the while statement is reached, `current <= 3` is true. Thus, the statements within the loop are executed and `sum` is updated to `sum + current`. Since `sum` is initialized to 0, `sum` becomes 1. Similarly, `current` is updated and assigned to 2. After the first time through the loop, control returns to the "top" of the loop. The condition is again found to be true and thus the loop is executed a second time. In this iteration, both `sum` and `current` become 3. In the next iteration, the condition is still true, and therefore, the loop is executed a third time. This time, `sum` becomes 6 and `current` becomes 4. Thus, when control returns to the top of the loop, the condition is `False` and the loop terminates. The final value of `sum` therefore is `6 (1 + 2 + 3)`. This process is summarized in Figure 3-18.

Iteration	sum	current	current <= 3	sum = sum + current	current = current + 1
1	0	1	True	sum = 0 + 1 (1)	current = 1 + 1 (2)
2	1	2	True	sum = 1 + 2 (3)	current = 2 + 1 (3)
3	3	3	True	sum = 3 + 3 (6)	current = 3 + 1 (4)
4	6	4	False	loop termination	

FIGURE 3-18   Iterative Steps for Adding First Three Integers

A **while statement** is an iterative control statement that repeatedly executes a set of statements based on a provided Boolean expression.

3.4.2 Input Error Checking

The while statement is well suited for input error checking in a program. This is demonstrated in the revised version of the temperature conversion program from Figure 3-14, reproduced in Figure 3-19.

```
1  # Temperature Conversion Program (Celsius-Fahrenheit / Fahrenheit-Celsius)
2
3  # Display program welcome
4  print('This program will convert temperatures (Fahrenheit/Celsius)')
5  print('Enter (F) to convert Fahrenheit to Celsius')
6  print('Enter (C) to convert Celsius to Fahrenheit')
7
8  # Get temperature to convert
9  which = input('Enter selection: ')
10
11 while which != 'F' and which != 'C':
12     which = input("Please enter 'F' or 'C': ")
13
14 temp = int(input('Enter temperature to convert: '))
15
16 # Determine temperature conversion needed and display results
17 if which == 'F':
18     converted_temp = format((temp - 32) * 5/9, '.1f')
19     print(temp, 'degrees Fahrenheit equals', converted_temp, 'degrees Celsius')
20 else:
21     converted_temp = format((9/5 * temp) + 32, '.1f')
22     print(temp, 'degrees Celsius equals', converted_temp, 'degrees Fahrenheit')
```

FIGURE 3-19   Temperature Conversion Program (Invalid Input Checking)

The difference in this program from the previous version is that rather than terminating on invalid input, the program continues to prompt the user until a valid temperature conversion, 'F' or 'C', is entered. Thus, the associated input statement is contained within a while loop that keeps iterating as long as variable which contains an invalid value. Once the user enters a proper value, the loop terminates allowing the program to continue.

LET'S TRY IT

In IDLE, create and run a simple program containing the code below and observe the results. Make sure to indent the code exactly as shown.

```
n = 10                              n = 10
sum = 0                             sum = 0
current = 1                         current = 1

while current <= n:                 while current <= n:
    sum = sum + current                 sum = sum + current
    current = current + 1               current = current + 1

print(sum)                              print(sum)
???                                 ???
```

The while statement is well suited for input error checking.

3.4.3   Infinite loops

An **infinite loop** is an iterative control structure that never terminates (or eventually terminates with a system error). Infinite loops are generally the result of programming errors. For example, if the condition of a while loop can never be false, an infinite loop will result when executed. Consider if the program segment in Figure 3-17, reproduced in Figure 3-20, omitted the statement incrementing variable `current`. Since `current` is initialized to `1`, it would remain `1` in all iterations, causing the expression `current <= n` to be always be true. Thus, the loop would never terminate.

```
# add up first n integers
sum = 0
current = 1

n = int(input('Enter value: '))

while current <= n:
    sum = sum + current
```

FIGURE 3-20   Infinite Loop

Such infinite loops can cause a program to "hang," that is, to be unresponsive to the user. In such cases, the program must be terminated by use of some special keyboard input (such as ctrl-C) to interrupt the execution.

LET'S TRY IT

From IDLE, create and run a simple program containing the code below and observe the results. Make sure to indent the code exactly as shown. To terminate an executing loop, hit ctrl-C.

```
while True:
    print ('Looping')

???


n = 10
sum = 0
current = 1

while current <= n:
    sum = sum + current

print (sum)

???
```

```
n = 10
sum = 0
current = 1

while current <= n:
    sum = sum + current
    n = n - 1

print (sum)

???
```

An **infinite loop** is an iterative control structure that never terminates (or eventually terminates with a system error).

3.4.4 Definite vs. Indefinite Loops

A **definite loop** is a program loop in which the number of times the loop will iterate can be determined before the loop is executed. For example, the while loop introduced in Figure 3-17 is a definite loop,

```
sum = 0
current = 1
n = input('Enter value: ')
while current <= n:
    sum = sum + current
    current = current + 1
```

Although it is not known what the value of n will be until the input statement is executed, its value *is* known by the time the while loop is reached. Thus, it will execute "n times."

An **indefinite loop** is a program loop in which the number of times that the loop will iterate cannot be determined before the loop is executed. Consider the while loop in the temperature conversion program of Figure 3-19.

```
which = input("Enter selection: ")
while which != 'F' and which != 'C':
    which = input("Please enter 'F' or 'C': ")
```

In this case, the number of times that the loop will be executed depends on how many times the user mistypes the input. Thus, a while statement can be used to construct both definite and indefinite loops. In the next chapter we look at the for statement, specifically suited for the construction of definite loops.

> A **definite loop** is a program loop in which the number of times the loop will iterate can be determined before the loop is executed. A **indefinite loop** is a program loop in which the number of times the loop will iterate is not known before the loop is executed.

3.4.5 Boolean Flags and Indefinite Loops

Often the condition of a given while loop is denoted by a single Boolean variable, called a **Boolean flag**. This is shown in Figure 3-21.

Boolean variable `valid_entries` is a Boolean flag, controlling the while loop at **line 12**. If the mileage of the last oil change is greater than the current mileage, an error message is displayed (**lines 17–18**), and the while loop is re-executed. If the current mileage is greater than (or equal to) the mileage of the last oil change, `miles_traveled` is set to this difference and `valid_entries` is set to True, causing the loop to terminate. Thus, **lines 23–28** display either that they are due for an oil change, an oil change will soon be needed, or there is no immediate need for an oil change.

> A single Boolean variable used as the condition of a given control statement is called a **Boolean flag**.

```
 1  # Oil Change Notification Program
 2
 3  # display program welcome
 4  print('This program will determine if your car is in need of an oil change')
 5
 6  # init
 7  miles_between_oil_change = 7500   # num miles between oil changes
 8  miles_warning = 500        # how soon to warn of needed oil change
 9  valid_entries = False
10
11  # get mileage of last oil change and current mileage and display
12  while not valid_entries:
13      mileage_last_oilchange = int(input('Enter mileage of last oil change: '))
14      current_mileage = int(input('Enter current mileage: '))
15
16      if current_mileage < mileage_last_oilchange:
17          print('Invalid entry - current mileage entered is less than')
18          print('mileage entered of last oil change')
19      else:
20          miles_traveled = current_mileage - mileage_last_oilchange
21          valid_entries = True
22
23  if miles_traveled >= miles_oil_change:
24      print('You are due for an oil change')
25  elif miles_traveled >= miles_oil_change - miles_warning:
26      print('You will soon be due for an oil change')
27  else:
28      print('You are not in immediate need of an oil change')
```

FIGURE 3-21   Indefinite Loop Using a Boolean Flag

3.4.6   Let's Apply It—Coin Change Exercise Program

The Python program in Figure 3-22 implements an exercise for children learning to count change. It displays a random value between 1 and 99 cents, and asks the user to enter a set of coins that sums exactly to the amount shown. The program utilizes the following programming features:

➤ while loop   ➤ if statement   ➤ Boolean flag
➤ random number generator

On **line 3**, the `random` module is imported for use of function `randint`. This function is called (on **line 18**) to randomly generate a coin value for the user to match, stored in variable `amount`. **Lines 6–10** provide the program greeting. On **line 13** variable `terminate` is initialized to `False`, used to control when the main loop (and thus the program) terminates. On **line 14**, `empty_str` is initialized to the empty string literal `' '`, used to determine when the user has entered an empty line to end the coin entries. These two variables need only be initialized once, and therefore are assigned before the main while loop.

The game begins on **line 17**. Since Boolean flag `terminate` is initialized to `False`, the while loop is executed. Besides variable `amount`, `game_over` is initialized to `False`, and `total` is initialized to 0. Variable `game_over` serves as another Boolean flag to determine if the current game is to continue or not. The coin entry ends if either the user enters a blank line (indicating that they are done entering coins) in which case the result is displayed and `game_over` is set to `True` (**line 37–43**), or if the total amount accumulated exceeds the total amount to be matched (on **line 45–48**).

At the top of the while loop, a third Boolean flag is used, `valid_entry`. The value of this flag determines whether the user should be prompted again because of an invalid input—a value

```
Program Execution ...

The purpose of this exercise is to enter a number of coin values
that add up to a displayed target value.

Enter coins values as 1-penny, 5-nickel, 10-dime and 25-quarter.
Hit return after the last entered coin value.
-----------------
Enter coins that add up to 63 cents, one per line.

Enter first coin: 25
Enter next coin: 25
Enter next coin: 10
Enter next coin:
Sorry - you only entered 60 cents.

Try again (y/n)?: y
Enter coins that add up to 21 cents, one per line.

Enter first coin: 11
Invalid entry
Enter next coin: 10
Enter next coin: 10
Enter next coin: 5
Sorry - total amount exceeds 21 cents.

Try again (y/n)?: y
Enter coins that add up to 83 cents, one per line.

Enter first coin: 25
Enter next coin: 25
Enter next coin: 25
Enter next coin: 5
Enter next coin: 1
Enter next coin: 1
Enter next coin: 1
Enter next coin:
Correct!

Try again (y/n)?: n
Thanks for playing ... goodbye
```

FIGURE 3-22   Coin Change Exercise Program (*Continued*)

other than `'1'`, `'5'`, `'10'`, or `'25'`, or the empty string. Note the use of the membership operator `in` (**line 32**). Thus, once the user inputs an appropriate value, `valid_entry` is set to True (**line 33**)—otherwise, the message `'Invalid entry'` is displayed and `valid_entry` remains `False`, causing the loop to execute again. The list of valid entered values on line 32 includes variable `empty_str` since this is the value input when the user hits return to terminate their entry of coin values. When the empty string is found (**line 37**), the total coin value entered in variable `total` is compared with variable `amount` (the amount to be matched). If equal, the message `'Correct!'` is displayed (**line 39**)—otherwise, a message is displayed indicating how much they entered. This amount is always less than the required amount, since whenever variable `total` exceeds `amount`, the current game ends (**lines 46–48**).

```
 1  # Coin Change Exercise Program
 2
 3  import random
 4
 5  # program greeting
 6  print('The purpose of this exercise is to enter a number of coin values')
 7  print('that add up to to a displayed target value.\n')
 8  print('Enter coins values as 1-penny, 5-nickel, 10-dime and 25-quarter')
 9  print("Hit return after the last entered coin value.")
10  print('----------------')
11
12  # init
13  terminate = False
14  empty_str = ''
15
16  # start game
17  while not terminate:
18      amount = random.randint(1,99)
19      print('Enter coins that add up to', amount, 'cents, one per line.\n')
20      game_over = False
21      total = 0
22
23      while not game_over:
24          valid_entry = False
25
26          while not valid_entry:
27              if total == 0:
28                  entry = input('Enter first coin: ')
29              else:
30                  entry = input('Enter next coin: ')
31
32              if entry in (empty_str,'1','5','10','25'):
33                  valid_entry = True
34              else:
35                  print('Invalid entry')
36
37          if entry == empty_str:
38              if total == amount:
39                  print('Correct!')
40              else:
41                  print('Sorry - you only entered', total, 'cents.')
42
43              game_over = True
44          else:
45              total = total + int(entry)
46              if total > amount:
47                  print('Sorry - total amount exceeds', amount, 'cents.')
48                  game_over = True
49
50          if game_over:
51              entry = input('\nTry again (y/n)?: ')
52
53              if entry == 'n':
54                  terminate = True
55
56  print('Thanks for playing ... goodbye')
```

FIGURE 3-22   Coin Change Exercise Program

When **line 50** is reached, Boolean flag `game_over` may be either `True` or `False`. It is `True` when the user has indicated that they have entered all their coin values (by hitting return), or if the total of the coin values entered exceeds the value in variable `amount`—it is `False` otherwise. Therefore, flag variable `game_over` is used to determine whether the user should be prompted to play another game (**line 51**). If they choose to quit the program when prompted, then Boolean variable `terminate` is set to `True`. This causes the encompassing while loop at **line 17** to terminate, leaving only the final "goodbye" message on **line 56** to be executed before the program terminates.

Self-Test Questions

1. A while loop continues to iterate until its condition becomes false. TRUE/FALSE

2. A while loop executes zero or more times. TRUE/FALSE

3. All iteration can be achieved by a while loop. TRUE/FALSE

4. An infinite loop is an iterative control structures that,
   (**a**) Loops forever and must be forced to terminate
   (**b**) Loops until the program terminates with a system error
   (**c**) Both of the above

5. The terms *definite loop* and *indefinite loop* are used to indicate whether,
   (**a**) A given loop executes at least once
   (**b**) The number of times that a loop is executed can be determined before the loop is executed.
   (**c**) Both of the above

6. A Boolean flag is,
   (**a**) A variable
   (**b**) Has the value `True` or `False`
   (**c**) Is used as a condition for control statements
   (**d**) All of the above

ANSWERS: 1. True. 2. True. 3. True. 4. (c), 5. (b), 6. (d)

COMPUTATIONAL PROBLEM SOLVING

3.5   Calendar Month Program

3.5.1   The Problem

The problem is to display a calendar month for any given month between January 1800 and December 2099. The format of the month should be as shown in Figure 3-23.

MAY 2012						
Sun	Mon	Tues	Wed	Thur	Fri	Sat
		1	2	3	4	5
6	7	8	9	10	11	12
13	14	15	16	17	18	19
20	21	22	23	24	25	26
27	28	29	30	31		

FIGURE 3-23   Calendar Month Display

3.5.2   Problem Analysis

Two specific algorithms are needed for this problem. First, we need an algorithm for computing the first day of a given month for years 1800 through 2099. This algorithm is given in Chapter 1. The second needed algorithm is for appropriately displaying the calendar month, given the day of the week that the first day falls on, and the number of days in the month. We shall develop this algorithm. The data representation issues for this problem are straight forward.

3.5.3 Program Design

Meeting the Program Requirements

We will develop and implement an algorithm that displays the month as given. There is no require-ment of how the month and year are to be entered. We shall therefore request the user to enter the month and year as integer values, with appropriate input error checking.

Data Description

What needs to be represented in the program is the month and year entered, whether the year is a leap year or not, the number of days in the month, and which day the first of the month falls on. Given that information, the calendar month can be displayed. The year and month will be entered and stored as integer values, represented by variables `year` and `month`,

$$year\ =\ 2012 \qquad month\ =\ 5$$

The remaining values will be computed by the program based on the given year and month, as given below,

$$leap\_year \qquad num\_days\_in\_month \qquad day\_of\_week$$

Variable `leap_year` holds a Boolean (`True`/`False`) value. Variables `num_days_in_month` and `day_of_week` each hold integer values.

Algorithmic Approach

First, we need an algorithm for determining the day of the week that a given date falls on. The algo-rithm for this from Chapter 1 is reproduced in Figure 3-24.

We also need to determine how many days are in a given month, which relies on an algorithm for determining leap years for the month of February. The code for this has already been developed in the "Number of Days in Month" program in section 3.3.4. We shall also reuse the portion of code from that program for determining leap years, reproduced below.

```
if (year % 4 == 0) and (not (year % 100 == 0) or year % 400):
    leap_year = True
else:
    leap_Year = False
```

Let's review how this algorithm works, and try to determine the day of the week on which May 24, 2025 falls. First, variable `century_digits` (holding the first two digits of the year) is set to `20` and `year_digits` (holding the last two digits of the year) is set to `25` (**steps 1 and 2**). Variable `value`, in **step 3**, is then set to

$$value\ =\ year\_digits\ +\ floor(year\_digits\ /\ 4)$$
$$=\ 25\ +\ floor(25/4)\ \rightarrow\ 25\ +\ floor(6.25)\ \rightarrow\ 25\ +\ 6\ \rightarrow\ 31$$

To determine the day of the week for a given **month, day,** and **year:**

1. Let **century_digits** be equal to the first two digits of the year.

2. Let **year_digits** be equal to the last two digits of the year.

3. Let **value** be equal to **year_digits** + floor(**year_digits** / 4)

4. If **century_digits** equals 18, then add 2 to **value**, else
   if **century_digits** equals 20, then add 6 to **value**.

5. If the **month** is equal to January and the **year** is not a leap year,
   then add 1 to **value**, else,

   if the **month** is equal to February and the **year** is a leap year, then
   add 3 to **value**; if not a leap year, then add 4 to **value**, else,

   if the **month** is equal to March or November, then add 4 to **value**, else,

   if the **month** is equal to April or July, then add 0 to **value**, else,

   if the **month** is equal to May, then add 2 to **value**, else,

   if the **month** is equal to June, then add 5 to **value**, else,

   if the **month** is equal to August, then add 3 to **value**, else,

   if the **month** is equal to October, then add 1 to **value**, else,

   if the **month** is equal to September or December, then add 6 to **value**,

6. Set **value** equal to (**value** + **day**) mod 7.

7. If **value** is equal to 1, then the day of the week is Sunday; else

   if **value** is equal to 2, day of the week is Monday; else

   if **value** is equal to 3, day of the week is Tuesday; else

   if **value** is equal to 4, day of the week is Wednesday; else

   if **value** is equal to 5, day of the week is Thursday; else

   if **value** is equal to 6, day of the week is Friday; else

   if **value** is equal to 0, day of the week is Saturday

FIGURE 3-24 Day of the Week Algorithm (from Chapter 1)

In **step 4**, since `century_digits` is equal to `20`, `value` is incremented by `6`,

$$\texttt{value = value + 6} \rightarrow \texttt{31 + 6} \rightarrow \texttt{37}$$

In **step 5**, since the month is equal to May, `value` is incremented by 2,

$$\texttt{value = value + 2} \rightarrow \texttt{37 + 2} \rightarrow \texttt{39}$$

In **step 6**, `value` is updated based on the day of the month. Since we want to determine the day of the week for the 24th (of May), `value` is updated as follows,

$$
\begin{aligned}
\texttt{value} &= \texttt{(value + } \textit{day of the month}\texttt{) mod 7} \\
&= \texttt{(39 + 24) mod 7} \\
&= \texttt{63 mod 7} \\
&= \texttt{0}
\end{aligned}
$$

Therefore, by **step 7** of the algorithm, the day of the week for May 24, 2025 is a Saturday. A table for the interpretation of the day of the week for the final computed value is given in Figure 3-25.

1	2	3	4	5	6	0
Sunday	Monday	Tuesday	Wednesday	Thursday	Friday	Saturday

FIGURE 3-25 Interpretation of the Day of the Week Algorithm Results

Overall Program Steps

The overall steps in this program design are given in Figure 3-26.

3.5.4 Program Implementation and Testing

Stage 1—Determining the Number of Days in the Month/Leap Years

We develop and test the program in three stages. First, we implement and test the code that determines, for a given month and year, the number of days in the month and whether the year is a leap year or not, given in Figure 3-27.

FIGURE 3-26 Overall Steps of Calendar Month Program

```
 1   # Calendar Month Program (stage 1)
 2
 3   # init
 4   terminate = False
 5
 6   # program greeting
 7   print('This program will display a calendar month between 1800 and 2099')
 8
 9   while not terminate:
10       # get month and year
11       month = int(input('Enter month 1-12 (-1 to quit): '))
12
13       if month == -1:
14           terminate = True
15       else:
16           while month < 1 or month > 12:
17               month = int(input('INVALID INPUT - Enter month 1-12: '))
18
19           year = int(input('Enter year (yyyy): '))
20
21           while year < 1800 or year > 2099:
22               year = int(input('INVALID - Enter year (1800-2099): '))
23
24           # determine if leap year
25           if (year % 4 == 0) and (not (year % 100 == 0) or (year % 400 == 0)):
26               leap_year = True
27           else:
28               leap_year = False
29
30           # determine num of days in month
31           if month in (1, 3, 5, 7, 8, 10, 12):
32               num_days_in_month = 31
33           elif month in (4, 6, 9, 11):
34               num_days_in_month = 30
35           elif leap_year:   # February
36               num_days_in_month = 29
37           else:
38               num_days_in_month = 28
39
40           print ('\n', month, ',', year, 'has', num_days_in_month, 'days')
41
42           if leap_year:
43               print (year, 'is a leap year\n')
44           else:
45               print (year, 'is NOT a leap year\n')
```

FIGURE 3-27   First Stage of Calendar Month Program

The month and year entered by the user are stored in variables month and year. While loops are used at **lines 16** and **21** to perform input error checking. **Lines 25–28** are adapted from the previous Number of Days in Month program for determining leap years. **Lines 31–38** are similar to the previous program for determining the number of days in a month, stored in variable num_days_in_month. **Lines 42–45** contain added code for the purpose of testing. These instructions will not be part of the final program. The program continues to prompt for another month until −1 is entered. Thus, Boolean flag terminate is initialized to False (**line 4**) and set to True (**line 14**) when the program is to terminate.

Stage 1 Testing

We give output from the testing of this version of the program in Figure 3-28.

```
Enter month (1-12): 14
INVALID INPUT
Enter month (1-12): 1
Enter year (yyyy): 1800

1 , 1800 has 31 days
1800 is NOT a leap year
```

FIGURE 3-28 Example Output of First Stage Testing

The set of test cases for this stage of the program is given in Figure 3-29. The test cases are selected such that each month is tested within the 1800s, 1900s, and 2000s. The month of February has a number of test cases to ensure that the program is working for non-leap years (1985), "typical" leap years (1984), and exception years (1900 and 2000). The test plan also includes the "extreme" cases of January 1800 and December 2099 (the beginning and end of the range of valid months). All test cases are shown to have passed, and thus we can move on to stage 2 of the program development.

Calendar Month	Expected Results num days	leap year	Actual Results num days	leap year	Evaluation
January 1800	31	no	31	no	Passed
February 1900	28	no	28	no	Passed
February 1984	29	yes	29	yes	Passed
February 1985	28	no	28	no	Passed
February 2000	29	yes	29	yes	Passed
March 1810	31	no	31	no	Passed
April 1912	30	yes	30	yes	Passed
May 2015	31	no	31	no	Passed
June 1825	30	no	30	no	Passed
July 1928	31	yes	31	yes	Passed
August 2031	31	no	31	no	Passed
September 1845	30	no	30	no	Passed
October 1947	31	no	31	no	Passed
November 2053	30	no	30	no	Passed
December 2099	31	no	31	no	Passed

FIGURE 3-29 Results of Execution of Test Plan for Stage 1

Stage 2—Determining the Day of the Week

We give the next stage of the program in Figure 3-30. This version includes the code for determining the day of the week for the first day of a given month and year (**lines 40–71**), with the final print statement (**line 74**) displaying the test results. Note that for testing purposes, there is no need to convert the day number into the actual name (e.g., "Monday")—this "raw output" is good enough. Also, for this program, we will need to determine only the day of the week for the first day of any

```
 1 # Calendar Month Program (stage 2)
 2
 3 # init
 4 terminate = False
 5
 6 # program greeting
 7 print('This program will display a calendar month between 1800 and 2099'
 8
 9 while not terminate:
10     # get month and year
11     month = int(input('Enter month (1-12): '))
12
13     if month == -1:
14         terminate = True
15     else:
16         while month < 1 or month > 12:
17             month = int(input('INVALID INPUT - Enter month 1-12: '))
18
19         year = int(input('Enter year (yyyy): '))
20
21         while year < 1800 or year > 2099:
22             year = int(input('INVALID - Enter year (1800-2099): '))
23
24         # determine if leap year
25         if (year % 4 == 0) and (not(year % 100 == 0) or (year % 400 == 0)):
26             leap_year = True
27         else:
28             leap_year = False
29
30         # determine num of days in month
31         if month in (1,3,5,7,8,10,12):
32             num_days_in_month = 31
33         elif month in (4,6,9,11):
34             num_days_in_month = 30
35         elif leap_year:   # February
36             num_days_in_month = 29
37         else:
38             num_days_in_month = 28
39
40         # determine day of the week
41         century_digits = year // 100
42         year_digits = year % 100
43
44         value = year_digits + (year_digits // 4)
45
46         if century_digits == 18:
47             value = value + 2
48         elif century_digits == 20:
49             value = value + 6
50
```

FIGURE 3-30 Second Stage of Calendar Month Program (*Continued*)

given month, since all remaining days follow sequentially. Therefore, the day value in the day of the week algorithm part of the code is hard-coded to 1 (on **line 71**). Let's look at the code that implements the day of the week algorithm.

The algorithm operates separately on the first two digits and last two digits of the year. On **line 41**, integer division is used to extract the first two digits of the year (for example, 1860 // 100

```
51              if month == 1 and not leap_year:
52                  value = value + 1
53              elif month == 2:
54                  if leap_year:
55                      value = value + 3
56                  else:
57                      value = value + 4
58              elif month == 3 or month == 11:
59                  value = value + 4
60              elif month == 5:
61                  value = value + 2
62              elif month == 6:
63                  value = value + 5
64              elif month == 8:
65                  value = value + 3
66              elif month == 9 or month == 12:
67                  value = value + 6
68              elif month == 10:
69                  value = value + 1
70
71              day_of_week = (value + 1) % 7   # 1-Sunday, 2-Monday, ...,
72
73              # display results
74              print('Day of the week is', day_of_week)
```

FIGURE 3-30 Second Stage of Calendar Month Program

equals 18). On **line 42**, the modulus operator, %, is used to extract the last two digits (for example, 1860 % 100 equals 60). The rest of the program (through **line 71**) follows the day of the week algorithm given above.

Stage 2 Testing

We give a sample test run of this version of the program in Figure 3-31.

```
1
Enter month (1-12): 4
Enter year (yyyy): 1860
Day of the week is 1
Enter month (1-12): -1
>>>
```

FIGURE 3-31 Example Output of Second Stage Testing

Figure 3-32 shows the results of the execution of the test plan for this version of the program. It includes the same months as in the test plan for the first stage.

Since all test cases passed, we can move on to the final stage of program development.

Final Stage—Displaying the Calendar Month

In the final stage of the program (Figure 3-33), we add the code for displaying the calendar month.

The corresponding name for the month number is determined on **lines 74–97** and displayed (**line 100**). The while loop at **line 113** moves the cursor to the proper starting column by "printing"

Calendar Month	Expected Results first day of month	Actual Results first day of month	Evaluation
January 1800	4 (Wednesday)	4	Passed
February 1900	5 (Thursday)	5	Passed
February 1984	4 (Wednesday)	4	Passed
February 1985	6 (Friday)	6	Passed
February 2000	3 (Tuesday)	3	Passed
March 1810	5 (Thursday)	5	Passed
April 1912	2 (Monday)	2	Passed
May 2015	6 (Friday)	6	Passed
June 1825	4 (Wednesday)	4	Passed
July 1928	1 (Sunday)	1	Passed
August 2031	6 (Friday)	6	Passed
September 1845	2 (Monday)	2	Passed
October 1947	4 (Wednesday)	4	Passed
November 2053	0 (Saturday)	0	Passed
December 2099	3 (Tuesday)	3	Passed

FIGURE 3-32 Results of Execution of Test Plan for Stage 2

```
1 # Calendar Month Program
2
3 # init
4 terminate = False
5
6 # program greeting
7 print('This program will display a calendar month between 1800 and 2099')
8
9 while not terminate:
10     # get month and year
11     month = int(input('Enter month 1-12 (-1 to quit): '))
12
13     if month == -1:
14         terminate = True
15     else:
16         while month < 1 or month > 12:
17             month = int(input('INVALID - Enter month (1-12): '))
18
19         year = int(input('Enter year (yyyy): '))
20
21         while year < 1800 or year > 2099:
22             year = int(input('INVALID - Enter year (1800-2099): '))
23
```

FIGURE 3-33 Final Stage of Calendar Month Program (*Continued*)

```
24     # determine if leap year
25     if (year % 4 == 0) and (not(year % 100 == 0) or (year % 400 == 0)):
26         leap_year = True
27     else:
28         leap_year = False
29
30     # determine num of days in month
31     if month in (1,3,5,7,8,10,12):
32         num_days_in_month = 31
33     elif month in (4,6,9,11):
34         num_days_in_month = 30
35     elif leap_year:   # February
36         num_days_in_month = 29
37     else:
38         num_days_in_month = 28
39
40     # determine day of the week
41     century_digits = year // 100
42     year_digits = year % 100
43
44     value = year_digits + (year_digits // 4)
45
46     if century_digits == 18:
47         value = value + 2
48     elif century_digits == 20:
49         value = value + 6
50
51     if month == 1 and not leap_year:
52         value = value + 1
53     elif month == 2:
54         if leap_year:
55             value = value + 3
56         else:
57             value = value + 4
58     elif month == 3 or month == 11:
59         value = value + 4
60     elif month == 5:
61         value = value + 2
62     elif month == 6:
63         value = value + 5
64     elif month == 8:
65         value = value + 3
66     elif month == 9 or month == 12:
67         value = value + 6
68     elif month == 10:
69         value = value + 1
70
71     day_of_week = (value + 1) % 7  # 1-Sun, 2-Mon, ..., 0-Sat
72
```

FIGURE 3-33 Final Stage of Calendar Month Program (*Continued*)

the column_width number of blank characters (4) for each column to be skipped. The while loop at **line 119** displays the dates. Single-digit dates are output (**line 121**) with three leading spaces, and two-digit dates with two (**line 123**) so that the columns line up. Each uses the **newline suppression form of print**, print(..., end='') to prevent the cursor from moving to the next screen line until it is time to do so.

Variable current_day is incremented from 1 to the number of days in the month. Variable current_col is also incremented by 1 to keep track of what column the current date is being

```
73      # determine month name
74      if month == 1:
75          month_name = 'January'
76      elif month == 2:
77          month_name = 'February'
78      elif month == 3:
79          month_name = 'March'
80      elif month == 4:
81          month_name = 'April'
82      elif month == 5:
83          month_name = 'May'
84      elif month == 6:
85          month_name = 'June'
86      elif month == 7:
87          month_name = 'July'
88      elif month == 8:
89          month_name = 'August'
90      elif month == 9:
91          month_name = 'September'
92      elif month == 10:
93          month_name = 'October'
94      elif month == 11:
95          month_name = 'November'
96      else:
97          month_name = 'December'
98
99      # display month and year heading
100     print('\n', ' ' + month_name, year)
101
102     # display rows of dates
103     if day_of_week == 0:
104         starting_col = 7
105     else:
106         starting_col = day_of_week
107
108     current_col = 1
109     column_width = 4
110     blank_char = ' '
111     blank_column = format(blank_char, str(column_width))
112
113     while current_col <= starting_col:
114         print(blank_column, end='')
115         current_col = current_col + 1
116
117     current_day = 1
118
119     while current_day <= num_days_in_month:
120         if current_day < 10:
121             print (format(blank_char, '3') + str(current_day), end='')
122         else:
123             print (format(blank_char, '2') + str(current_day), end='')
124
125         if current_col <= 7:
126             current_col = current_col + 1
127         else:
128             current_col = 1
129             print()
130
131         current_day = current_day + 1
132
133     print('\n')
```

FIGURE 3-33 Final Stage of Calendar Month Program

displayed in. When `current_col` equals 7, it is reset to 1 (**line 128**) and `print()` moves the cursor to the start of the next line (**line 129**). Otherwise, `current_col` is simply incremented by 1 (**line 126**).

An example test run of this final version of the program is given in Figure 3-34.

```
This program will display a calendar month between 1800 and 2099

Enter month 1-12 (-1 to quit): 1
Enter year (yyyy): 1800

  January    1800
                 1   2   3   4
    5   6   7   8   9  10  11  12
   13  14  15  16  17  18  19  20
   21  22  23  24  25  26  27  28
   29  30  31

Enter month (1-12): -1
>>>
```

FIGURE 3-34   Example Output of Final Stage Testing

Something is obviously wrong. The calendar month is displayed with eight columns instead of seven. The testing of all other months produces the same results. Since the first two stages of the program were successfully tested, the problem must be in the code added in the final stage. The code at **line 74** simply assigns the month name. Therefore, we reflect on the logic of the code starting on **line 103**.

Lines 128–129 is where the column is reset back to column 1 and a new screen line is started, based on the current value of variable `current_col`,

```
if current_col <= 7:
    current_col = current_col + 1
else:
    current_col = 1
    print()
```

Variable `current_col` is initialized to 1 at **line 108**, and is advanced to the proper starting column on **lines 113–115**. Variable `starting_col` is set to the value (0-6) for the day of the week for the particular month being displayed. Since the day of the week results have been successfully tested, we can assume that `current_col` will have a value between 0 and 6. With that assumption, we can step though **lines 125–129** and see if this is where the problem is. Stepping through a program on paper by tracking the values of variables is referred to as **deskchecking**. We check what happens as the value of `current_col` approaches 7, as shown in Figure 3-35.

Now it is clear what the problem is—the classic *"off by one"* error! The condition of the while loop should be `current_col < 7`, *not* `current_col <= 7`. `Current_col` should be reset to 1 once the seventh column has been displayed (when `current_col` is 7). Using the

Current value of current_col	Value of condition current_col <= 7	Updated value of current_col
5	True	6
6	True	7
7	True	8
8	False	1
1	True	2
etc.		

FIGURE 3-35 Deskchecking the Value of Variable current_col

<= operator causes current_col to be reset to 1 only after an *eighth* column is displayed. Thus, we make this correction in the program,

```
if current_col < 7:
    current_col = current_col + 1
else:
    current_col = 1
print()
```

After re-executing the program with this correction we get the current output, depicted in Figure 3-36.

```
This program will display a calendar month between 1800 and 2099

Enter month 1-12 (-1 to quit): 1
Enter year (yyyy): 1800

  January    1800
                  1   2   3
    4   5   6   7   8   9  10
   11  12  13  14  15  16  17
   18  19  20  21  22  23  24
   25  26  27  28  29  30  31


Enter month (1-12): -1
>>>
```

FIGURE 3-36 Display Output of Final Stage of Calendar Month Program

Although the column error has been corrected, we find that the first of the month appears under the wrong column—the month should start on a Wednesday (fourth column), not a Thursday column (fifth column). The problem must be in how the first row of the month is displayed. Other months are tested, each found to be off by one day. We therefore look at **lines 113–115** that are responsible for moving over the cursor to the correct starting column,

```
while current_col <= starting_col:
    print(blank_column, end='')
    current_col = current_col + 1
```

We consider whether there is another "off by one" error. Reconsidering the condition of the while loop, we realize that, in fact, this is the error. If the correct starting column is 4 (Wednesday), then the cursor should move past three columns and place a 1 in the fourth column. The current condition, however, would move the cursor past *four* columns, thus placing a 1 in the fifth column (Thursday). The corrected code is given below.

```
while current_col < starting_col:
    print(' ', end='')
    current_col = current_col + 1
```

The month is now correctly displayed. We complete the testing by executing the program on a set of test cases (Figure 3-37). Although the test plan is not as complete as it could be, it includes test cases for months from each century, including both leap years and non-leap years.

Calendar Month	Expected Results first day of month	num days	Evaluation
April 1912	Sunday	30	Passed
February 1985	Monday	28	Passed
May 2015	Tuesday	31	Passed
January 1800	Wednesday	31	Passed
February 1900	Thursday	28	Passed
February 1984	Friday	29	Passed
January 2011	Saturday	31	Passed

FIGURE 3-37 Results of Execution of Test Plan for Final Stage

CHAPTER SUMMARY

General Topics

Control Statement/Control Structure
Sequential, Selection, and Iterative Control
Relational Operators/Boolean Operators/
     Boolean Expressions
Operator Precedence and Boolean Expressions
Logically Equivalent Boolean Expressions
Short-Circuit (Lazy) Evaluation
Selection Control Statements/if Statement
Compound Statement
Multi-way Selection
While Statements

Input Error Checking
Infinite Loops
Definite vs. Indefinite Loops
Boolean Flags and Indefinite Loops
Deskchecking

Python-Specific Programming Topics

Membership Operators in, not in
if Statement in Python/else and elif headers
Indentation in Python
Multi-way Selection in Python
while Statement in Python

CHAPTER EXERCISES

Section 3.1

1. Which of the three forms of control is an implicit form of control?

2. What is meant by a "straight-line" program?

3. What is the difference between a control statement and a control structure?

Section 3.2

4. The Boolean data type contains two literal values, denoted as _____ and _____ in Python.

5. Which of the following relational expressions evaluate to `True`?
   (a) `5 < 8`   (c) `'10' < '8'`
   (b) `'5' < '8'`   (d) `'Jake' < 'Brian'`

6. Which of the following relational expressions evaluate to `False`?
   (a) `5 <= 5`   (c) `5 == 5`   (e) `5 != 10`
   (b) `5 >= 5`   (d) `5 != 5`

7. Give an appropriate expression for each of the following.
   (a) To determine if the number 24 does *not* appear in a given list of numbers assigned to variable nums.
   (b) To determine if the name `'Ellen'` appears in a list of names assigned to variable names.
   (c) To determine if a single last name stored in variable `last_name` is either `'Morris'` or `'Morrison'`.

8. Evaluate the following Python expressions.
   (a) `(12 * 2) == (3 * 8)`
   (b) `(14 * 2) != (3 * 8)`

9. What value for x makes each of the following Boolean expressions true?
   (a) `x or False`
   (b) `x and True`
   (c) `not (x or False)`
   (d) `not (x and True)`

10. Evaluate the Boolean expressions below for n = 10 and k = 20.
    (a) `(n > 10) and (k == 20)`
    (b) `(n > 10) or (k == 20)`
    (c) `not((n > 10) and (k == 20))`
    (d) `not(n > 10) and not(k == 20)`
    (e) `(n >10) or (k == 10 or k != 5)`

11. Give an appropriate Boolean expression for each of the following.
    (a) Determine if variable num is greater than or equal to 0, and less than 100.
    (b) Determine if variable num is less than 100 and greater than or equal to 0, or it is equal to 200.
    (c) Determine if either the name `'Thompson'` or `'Wu'` appears in a list of names assigned to variable `last_names`.
    (d) Determine if the name `'Thomson'` appears and the name `'Wu'` does not appear in a list of last names assigned to variable `last_names`.

12. Evaluate the following Boolean expressions for num1 = 10 and num2 = 20.
    (a) `not (num1 <1) and num2 < 10`
    (b) `not (num1 < 1) and num2 < 10 or num1 + num3 < 100`

13. Give a logically equivalent expression for each of the following.

    (a) `num != 25 or num == 0`

    (b) `1 <= num and num <= 50`

    (c) `not num > 100 and not num < 0`

    (d) `(num < 0 or num > 100)`

Section 3.3

14. Give an appropriate if statement for each of the following.

    (a) An if statement that displays `'within range'` if num is between 0 and 100, inclusive.

    (b) An if statement that displays `'within range'` if num is between 0 and 100, inclusive, and displays `'out of range'` otherwise.

15. Rewrite the following if-else statements using a single if statement and `elif` headers.

```
if temperature >= 85 and humidity > 60:
    print('muggy day today')
else:
    if temperature >= 85:
        print('warm, but not muggy today')
    else:
        if temperature >= 65:
            print('pleasant today')
        else:
            if temperature <= 45:
                print('cold today')
            else:
                print('cool today')
```

16. Regarding proper indentation,

    (a) Explain the change in indentation needed in order for the following code to be syntactically correct.

    (b) Indicate other changes in the indentation of the code that is not strictly needed, but would make the code more readable.

```
if level <= 1:
    print('Value is well within range')
    print('Recheck in one year')
elif level <= 2:
      print('Value is within range')
      print('Recheck within one month')
elif level <= 3:
      print('Value is slightly high)
        print('Recheck in one week')
elif level <= 4:
      print('Value abnormally high')
      print('Shut down system immediately')
```

Section 3.4

17. Write a program segment that uses a while loop to add up all the even numbers between 100 and 200, inclusive.

18. The following while loop is meant to multiply a series of integers input by the user, until a sentinel value of 0 is entered. Indicate any errors in the code given.

```
product = 1
num = input('Enter first number: ')
while num != 0:
        num = input('Enter first number: ')
        product = product * num
    print('product = ', product)
```

19. For each of the following, indicate which is a definite loop, and which is an indefinite loop.

    (a) `num = input('Enter a non-zero value: ')`
```
    while num == 0:
        num = input('Enter a non-zero value: ')
```
    (b) `num = 0`
```
    while n < 10:
        print 2 ** n
        n = n + 1
```

PYTHON PROGRAMMING EXERCISES

P1. Write a Python program in which the user enters either 'A', 'B', or 'C'. If 'A' is entered, the program should display the word 'Apple'; if 'B' is entered, it displays 'Banana'; and if 'C' is entered, it displays 'Coconut'. Use nested if statements for this as depicted in Figure 3-13.

P2. Repeat question P1 using an if statement with elif headers instead.

P3. Write a Python program in which a student enters the number of college credits earned. If the number of credits is greater than 90, 'Senior Status' is displayed; if greater than 60, 'Junior Status' is displayed; if greater than 30, 'Sophomore Status' is displayed; else, 'Freshman Status' is displayed.

P4. Write a program that sums a series of (positive) integers entered by the user, excluding all numbers that are greater than 100.

P5. Write a program, in which the user can enter any number of positive and negative integer values, that displays the number of positive values entered, as well as the number of negative values.

P6. Write a program containing a pair of nested while loops that displays the integer values 1–100, ten numbers per row, with the columns aligned as shown below,

```
 1  2  3  4  5  6  7  8  9 10
11 12 13 14 15 16 17 18 19 20
21 22 23 24 25 26 27 28 29 30
 .
 .
91 92 93 94 95 96 97 98 99 100
```

P7. Display the integer values 1–100 as given in question P6 using only *one* while loop.

PROGRAM MODIFICATION PROBLEMS

M1. Temperature Conversion Program: Input Error Checking

Modify the Temperature Conversion program in Figure 3-19 to perform input error checking of entered temperatures. On the Fahrenheit scale, absolute zero is -459.67. Therefore, all valid Fahrenheit temperatures start at that value (with no upper limit). On the Celsius scale, absolute zero is -273.15. The program should reprompt the user for any invalid entered temperatures.

M2. Temperature Conversion Program: Addition of Kelvin Scale

Modify the Temperature Conversion program in Figure 3-19 to add an additional option of converting to and from degrees Kelvin. The formula for conversion to Kelvin (K) from Celsius (C) is $K = C + 273.15$.

M3. Number of Days in Month Program: Input Error Checking

Modify the Number of Days in Month Program of section 3.3.4 so that the program prompts the user to re-enter any month (not in the range 1–12) or year that is an invalid value.

M4. Number of Days in Month Program: Indication of Leap Years

Modify the Number of Days in Month program of section 3.3.4 so that the program displays, in addition to the number of days in the month, that the year is a leap year or not as shown below.

```
Enter the month (1-12): 2
Please enter the year (e.g., 2010): 2000
There are 29 days in the month (a leap year)
```

M5. Oil Change Notification Program: Number of Miles before Change

Modify the Oil Change Notification program in Figure 3-21 so that the program displays the number of miles left before the next oil change, or the number of miles overdue for an oil change, as appropriate.

M6. Coin Change Exercise Program: Addition of Half-Dollar Coins

Modify the Coin Change Exercise program in section 3.4.6 to allow for the use of half-dollar coins. Make all necessary changes in the program.

M7. Coin Change Exercise Program: Raising the Challenge

Modify the Coin Change Exercise program in section 3.4.6 so that the least possible number of coins must be entered. For example, the least number of coins that total to 43 cents is 6 (one quarter, one dime, one nickel, and three pennies).

M8. Calendar Month Program: Indication of Leap Year

Modify the final version of the Calendar Month program in section 3.5 so that for leap years, the month heading is displayed as in the following,

```
June    1984 (leap year)
                            1    2
    3    4    5    6    7    8    9
   10   11   12   13   14   15   16
   17   18   19   20   21   22   23
   24   25   26   27   28   29   30
```

M9. Calendar Month Program: User Entry of Month Name

Modify the final version of the Calendar Month program to allow the user to enter a month's name (e.g., 'January') rather than a number (e.g., 1). Make all appropriate changes in the program as a result of this change.

M10. Calendar Month Program: Day of the Week Headings

Modify the final version of the Calendar Month program in section 3.5 so that there is day heading for each of the columns as shown below.

```
          January   1800

          Su  Mo  Tu  We  Th  Fr  Sa
                       1   2   3   4
           5   6   7   8   9  10  11
          12  13  14  15  16  17  18
          19  20  21  22  23  24  25
          26  27  28  29  30  31
```

M11. Sage Program Modification

Following is the output of an "all knowing" Sage program that replies with random responses to questions posed by the user. The responses generated have no meaningful connection to the questions asked.

```
What is your question?:
When will I finally finish the book?

You ask me "When will I finally finish the book?" . . .
You know the answer to that already, don't you?

Do you have another question? (y/n): y
What is your question?:
Do you really know what I am asking?

You ask me "Do you really know what I am asking?" . . .
I would focus my thoughts on something else.

Do you have another question? (y/n): y
What is your question?:
Can't you answer my questions directly?

You ask me "Can't you answer my questions directly?" . . .
The probabilities are in your favor.

Do you have another question? (y/n): y
What is your question?:
So, what's the difference between an orange?

You ask me "So, what's the difference between an orange?" . . .
It is close to certainty.

Do you have another question? (y/n): y
What is your question?:
I think you are bogus, aren't you?

You ask me "I think you are bogus, aren't you?" . . .
Someone you would not expect can be most helpful about this.

Do you have another question? (y/n): n
Goodbye ... hope I was of some help!
>>>
```

In the 1960s, a program called Eliza was developed that was able to behave as a psychotherapist. It did not really understand anything, it only looked for certain words to turn the patient's comments or questions back to the patient. For example, if a patient said, "My mom drives me crazy," it might reply with "Tell me more about your mom." Modify this program so that it appears to have understanding by similar means of word recognition as used in the Eliza program. Specifically, incorporate a set of "trigger" words that, if found, causes a specific response to be given. For example, if the word "I" appears in the question (for example, "Will I ever be rich?" or "Am I always going to be happy?"), the response may be "You are in charge of your own destiny." If the word "new" appears in the question (for example, "Will I find a new boyfriend soon?" or "Will I find a new life?," the response may be "Changes are up to you and the unpredictable events in life."

Be creative. In order to determine if a given word (or phrase) appears in a given question, make use of the `in` membership operator.

```
1  # Fortune Teller Program
2  import random
3
4  have_question = 'y'
5
6  while have_question == 'y':
7      question = input('What is your question?:\n')
8      print('\nYou ask me', '"' + question + '" . . .')
9
10     rand_num = random.randint(1,8)
11
12     if rand_num == 1:
13         print ('The probabilities are in your favor')
14     elif rand_num == 2:
15         print ("I wouldn't make any definite plans")
16     elif rand_num == 3:
17         print ('The outlook is dim')
18     elif rand_num == 4:
19         print ('I would focus my thoughts on something else')
20     elif rand_num == 5:
21         print ('You are the only one that can answer that!')
22     elif rand_num == 6:
23         print ("You know the answer to that already, don't you?")
24     elif rand_num == 7:
25         print ('Someone unexpected can be most helpful with this')
26     elif rand_num == 8:
27         print ('It is close to certainty')
28
29     have_question = input('\nDo you have another question? (y/n): ')
30
31 print('Goodbye ... hope I was of some help!')
```

PROGRAM DEVELOPMENT PROBLEMS

D1. Metric Conversion

Develop and test a Python program that converts pounds to grams, inches to centimeters, and kilometers to miles. The program should allow conversions both ways.

D2. Leap Years to Come

Develop and test a Python program that displays future leap years, starting with the first occurring leap year from the current year, until a final year entered by the user. (HINT: Module `datetime` used in the Age in Seconds Program of Chapter 2 will be needed here.)

D3. The First-Time Home Buyer Tax Credit

Develop and test a Python program that determines if an individual qualifies for a government First-Time Home Buyer Tax Credit of $8,000. The credit was only available to those that (a) bought a house that cost less than $800,000, (b) had a combined income of under $225,000 and (c) had not owned a primary residence in the last three years.

D4. Home Loan Amortization

Develop and test a Python program that calculates the monthly mortgage payments for a given loan amount, term (number of years) and range of interest rates from 3% to 18%. The fundamental formula for determining this is A/D, where A is the original loan amount, and D is the discount factor. The discount factor is calculated as,

$$D = ((1 + r)^n - 1) / r(1 + r)^n$$

where n is the number of total payments (12 times the number of years of the loan) and r is the interest rate, expressed in decimal form (e.g., .05), divided by 12. A monthly payment table should be generated as shown below,

```
        Loan Amount: $350,000  Term: 30 years
        Interest Rate              Monthly Payment
            3%                         1475.61
            4%                         1670.95
            5%                         1878.88
            6%                         2098.43
             .                            .
             .                            .
            18%                        5274.80
```

Check your results with an online mortgage calculator.

D5. Life Signs

Develop and test a program that determines how many breaths and how many heartbeats a person has had in their life. The average respiration (breath) rate of people varies with age. Use the breath rates given below for use in your program,

	Breaths per Minute
Infant	25–60
1–4 years	20–30
5–14 years	15–25
15–18 years	11–23

For heart rate, use an average of 67.5 beats per second.

## CHAPTER 4

Lists

In this chapter, we look at a means of structuring and accessing a collection of data. In particular, we look at a way of organizing data in a linear sequence, generally referred to as a list.

OBJECTIVES

After reading this chapter and completing the exercises, you will be able to:

♦ Explain what a list is in programming

♦ Describe the typical operations performed on lists

♦ Explain what is meant by list traversal

♦ Effectively create and use lists in Python

♦ Explain the difference between lists and tuples in Python

♦ Explain what a sequence is in Python

♦ Describe the sequence operations common to lists, tuples, and strings in Python

♦ Effectively use nested lists and tuples in Python

♦ Effectively iterate over lists (sequences) in Python

♦ Effectively use for statements for iterative control in Python

♦ Use the `range` function in Python

♦ Explain how list representation relates to list assignment in Python

♦ Effectively use list comprehensions in Python

♦ Write Python programs using sequences

CHAPTER CONTENTS

Motivation

Fundamental Concepts

4.1 List Structures

4.2 Lists (Sequences) in Python

MOTIVATION

The way that data is organized has a significant impact on how effectively it can be used. One of the most obvious and useful ways to organize data is as a list. We use lists in our everyday lives—we make shopping lists, to-do lists, and mental checklists. Various forms of lists are provided by programming languages, differing in the elements they can store (mixed type?), their size (variable size?), whether they can be altered (mutable?), and the operations that can be performed on them (see Figure 4-1).

Lists also occur in nature. Our DNA is essentially a long list of molecules in the form of a double helix, found in the nucleus of all human cells and all living organisms. Its purpose is also to store information—specifically, the instructions that are used to construct all other cells in the body—that we call *genes*. Given the 2.85 billion nucleotides that make up the human genome, determining their sequencing (and thus understanding our genetic makeup) is fundamentally a computational problem.

In this chapter, we look at the use of lists and other sequences in Python.

List Characteristics	Elements
Element Type	All elements of the same type
	Elements of different types
Length	Fixed length
	Varying length
Modifiability	Mutable (alterable)
	Immutable (unalterable)
Common Operations	Determine if a list is empty
	Determine the length of a list
	Access (retrieve) elements of a list
	Insert elements into a list
	Replace elements of a list
	Delete elements of a list
	Append elements to (the end of) a list

FIGURE 4-1   List Properties and Common Operations

FUNDAMENTAL CONCEPTS

4.1 List Structures

In this section we introduce the use of lists in programming. The concept of a list is similar to our everyday notion of a list. We read off (access) items on our to-do list, add items, cross off (delete) items, and so forth. We look at the use of lists next.

4.1.1 What Is a List?

A **list** is a *linear data structure*, meaning that its elements have a linear ordering. That is, there is a first element, a second element, and so on. Figure 4-2 depicts a list storing the average temperature for each day of a given week, in which each item in the list is identified by its *index value*.

The location at index 0 stores the temperature for Sunday, the location at index 1 stores the temperature for Monday, and so on. It is customary in programming languages to begin numbering sequences of items with an index value of 0 rather than 1. This is referred to as *zero-based indexing*. This is important to keep in mind to avoid any "off by one" errors in programs, as we shall see. We next look at some common operations performed on lists.

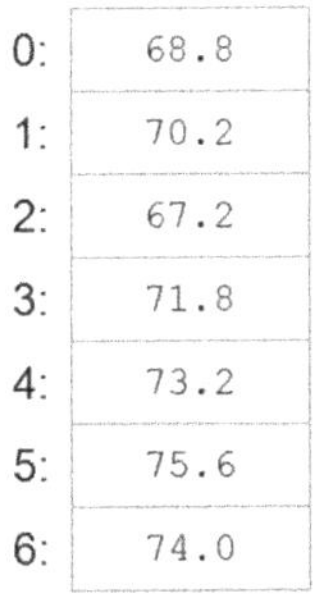

Index	Value
0:	68.8
1:	70.2
2:	67.2
3:	71.8
4:	73.2
5:	75.6
6:	74.0

FIGURE 4-2
Indexed Data
Structure `daily_temperatures`

A **list** is a linear data structure, thus its elements have a linear ordering.

4.1.2 Common List Operations

Operations commonly performed on lists include retrieve, update, insert, delete (remove) and append. Figure 4-3 depicts these operations on a list of integers.

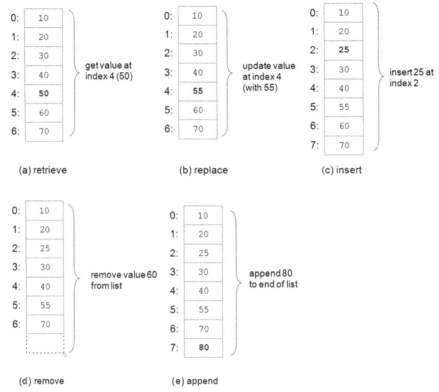

FIGURE 4-3 Common List Operations

The operation depicted in (a) retrieves elements of a list by index value. Thus, the value 50 is retrieved at index 4 (the fifth item in the list). The replace operation in (b) updates the current value at index 4, 50, with 55. The insert operation in (c) inserts the new value 25 at index 2, thus shifting down all elements below that point and lengthening the list by one. In (d), the remove operation deletes the element at index 6, thus shifting up all elements below that point and shortening the list by one. Finally, the append operation in (e) adds a new value, 80, to the end of the list. In the following sections we will see how these operations are accomplished in Python. First, we look at what is called *list traversal*, a way of accessing each of the elements of a given list.

Operations commonly performed on lists include retrieve, update, insert, remove, and append.

4.1.3 List Traversal

A **list traversal** is a means of accessing, one-by-one, the elements of a list. For example, to add up all the elements in a list of integers, each element can be accessed one-by-one, starting with the first, and ending with the last element. Similarly, the list could be traversed starting with the last element and ending with the first. To find a particular value in a list also requires traversal. We depict the tasks of summing and searching a list in Figure 4-4.

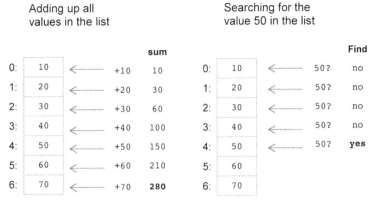

FIGURE 4-4   List Traversal

A **list traversal** is a means of accessing, one-by-one, the elements of a list.

Self-Test Questions

1. What would be the range of index values for a list of 10 elements?
    (a) 0–9   **(b)** 0–10   **(c)** 1–10

2. Which one of the following is NOT a common operation on lists?
    (a) access   **(b)** replace   **(c)** interleave   **(d)** append   **(e)** insert
    (f) delete

3. Which of the following would be the resulting list after inserting the value 50 at index 2?

    ```
    0:  35
    1:  15
    2:  45
    3:  28
    ```

    (a)
    ```
    0:  35
    1:  50
    2:  15
    3:  45
    4:  28
    ```

    (b)
    ```
    0:  35
    1:  15
    2:  50
    3:  45
    4:  28
    ```

    (c)
    ```
    0:  50
    1:  35
    2:  15
    3:  45
    4:  28
    ```

4.2 Lists (Sequences) in Python

Next, we look at lists (and other sequence types) in Python.

4.2.1 Python List Type

A **list** in Python is a mutable, linear data structure of variable length, allowing mixed-type elements. *Mutable* means that the contents of the list may be altered. Lists in Python use zero-based indexing. Thus, all lists have index values 0 . . . n-1, where n is the number of elements in the list. Lists are denoted by a comma-separated list of elements within square brackets as shown below,

```
[1, 2, 3]        ['one', 'two', 'three']     ['apples', 50, True]
```

An **empty list** is denoted by an empty pair of square brackets, []. (We shall later see the usefulness of the empty list.) Elements of a list are accessed by using an index value within square brackets,

```
lst = [1, 2, 3]      lst[0] → 1    access of first element
                     lst[1] → 2    access of second element
                     lst[2] → 3    access of third element
```

Thus, for example, the following prints the first element of list lst,

```
print(lst[0])
```

The elements in list lst can be summed as follows,

```
sum = lst[0] + lst[1] + lst[2]
```

For longer lists, we would want to have a more concise way of traversing the elements. We discuss this below. Elements of a list can be updated (replaced) or deleted (removed) as follows (for lst = [1, 2, 3]),

```
lst[2] = 4      [1, 2, 4]   replacement of 3 with 4 at index 2
del lst[2]      [1, 2]      removal of 4 at index 2
```

Methods insert and append also provide a means of altering a list,

```
lst.insert(1, 3)    [1, 3, 2]      insertion of 3 at index 1
lst.append(4)       [1, 3, 2, 4]   appending of 4 to end of list
```

In addition, methods sort and reverse reorder the elements of a given list. These list modifying operations are summarized in Figure 4-5.

Operation	fruit = ['banana', 'apple, 'cherry']	
Replace	`fruit[2] = 'coconut'`	`['banana', 'apple', 'coconut']`
Delete	`del fruit[1]`	`['banana', 'cherry']`
Insert	`fruit.insert(2, 'pear')`	`['banana', 'apple', 'pear', 'cherry']`
Append	`fruit.append('peach')`	`['banana', 'apple', 'cherry', 'peach']`
Sort	`fruit.sort()`	`['apple', 'banana', 'cherry']`
Reverse	`fruit.reverse()`	`['cherry', 'banana', 'apple']`

FIGURE 4-5   List Modification Operations in Python

Methods, and the associated *dot notation* used, are fully explained in Chapter 6 on Objects and Their Use. We only mention methods here for the sake of completeness in covering the topic of list operations.

LET'S TRY IT

From the Python Shell, enter the following and observe the results.

```
>>> lst = [10, 20, 30]          >>> del lst[2]
>>> lst                         >>> lst
???                             ???

>>> lst[0]                      >>> lst.insert(1, 15)
???                             >>> lst
                                ???

>>> lst[0] = 5                  >>> lst.append(40)
>>> lst                         >>> lst
???                             ???
```

A **list** in Python is a mutable linear data structure, denoted by a comma-separated list of elements within square brackets, allowing mixed-type elements.

4.2.2 Tuples

A **tuple** is an *immutable* linear data structure. Thus, in contrast to lists, once a tuple is defined, it cannot be altered. Otherwise, tuples and lists are essentially the same. To distinguish tuples from lists, tuples are denoted by parentheses instead of square brackets as given below,

```
nums = (10, 20, 30)
student = ('John Smith', 48, 'Computer Science', 3.42)
```

Another difference between tuples and lists is that *tuples of one element must include a comma following the element.* Otherwise, the parenthesized element will not be made into a tuple, as shown below,

CORRECT   WRONG

```
>>> (1,)          >>> (1)
(1)               1
```

An **empty tuple** is represented by a set of empty parentheses, `()`. (We shall later see the usefulness of the empty tuple.) The elements of tuples are accessed the same as lists, with square brackets,

```
>>> nums[0]       >>> student[0]
10                'John Smith'
```

Any attempt to alter a tuple is invalid. Thus, delete, update, insert, and append operations are not defined on tuples. For now, we can consider using tuples when the information to represent should not be altered. We will see additional uses of tuples in the coming chapters.

LET'S TRY IT

From the Python Shell, enter the following and observe the results.

```
>>> t = (10, 20, 30)          >>> t.insert(1, 15)
>>> t[0]                      >>> ???
???                           ???

>>> del t[2]                  >>> t.append(40)
???                           ???
```

A **tuple** in Python is an *immutable* linear data structure, denoted by a comma-separated list of elements within parentheses, allowing mixed-type elements.

4.2.3 Sequences

A **sequence** in Python is a linearly ordered set of elements accessed by an index number. Lists, tuples, and strings are all sequences. Strings, like tuples, are immutable; therefore, they cannot be altered. We give sequence operations common to strings, lists, and tuples in Figure 4-6.

For any sequence s, `len(s)` gives its length, and `s[k]` retrieves the element at index k. The slice operation, `s[index1:index2]`, returns a subsequence of a sequence, starting with the first index location up to *but not including* the second. The `s[index:]` form of the slice operation returns a string containing all the list elements starting from the given index location to the end of the sequence. The `count` method returns how many instances of a given value occur within a sequence, and the `find` method returns the index location of the *first occurrence* of a specific item, returning -1 if not found. For determining only if a given value occurs within a

Operation		String s = 'hello' w = '!'	Tuple s = (1,2,3,4) w = (5,6)	List s = [1,2,3,4] w = [5,6]
Length	`len(s)`	5	4	4
Select	`s[0]`	`'h'`	1	1
Slice	`s[1:4]` `s[1:]`	`'ell'` `'ello'`	(2, 3, 4) (2, 3, 4)	[2, 3, 4] [2, 3, 4]
Count	`s.count('e')` `s.count(4)`	1 *error*	0 1	0 1
Index	`s.index('e')` `s.index(3)`	1 --	-- 2	-- 2
Membership	`'h' in s`	True	False	False
Concatenation	`s + w`	`'hello!'`	(1, 2, 3, 4, 5, 6)	[1, 2, 3, 4, 5, 6]
Minimum Value	`min(s)`	`'e'`	1	1
Maximum Value	`max(s)`	`'o'`	4	4
Sum	`sum(s)`	*error*	10	10

FIGURE 4-6   Sequence Operations in Python

sequence, without needing to know where, the `in` operator (introduced in Chapter 3) can be used instead.

The + operator is used to denote concatenation. Since the plus sign also denotes addition, Python determines which operation to perform based on the operand types. Thus the plus sign, +, is referred to as an **overloaded operator**. If both operands are numeric types, addition is performed. If both operands are sequence types, concatenation is performed. (If a mix of numeric and sequence operands is used, an `"unsupported operand type(s) for +"` error message will occur.) Operations `min/max` return the smallest/largest value of a sequence, and `sum` returns the sum of all the elements (when of numeric type). Finally, the comparison operator, ==, returns `True` if the two sequences are the same length, and their corresponding elements are equal to each other.

LET'S TRY IT

From the Python Shell, enter the following and observe the results.

```
>>> s = 'coconut'        >>> s = (10, 30, 20, 10)    >>> s = [10, 30, 20, 10]
>>> s[4:7]               >>> s[1:3]                   >>> s[1:3]
???                      ???                          ???

>>> s.count('o')         >>> s.count(10)              >>> s.count(10)
???                      ???                          ???

>>> s.index('o')         >>> s.index(10)              >>> s.index(10)
???                      ???                          ???

>>> s + ' juice'         >>> s + (40, 50)             >>> s + (40, 50)
???                      ???                          ???
```

> In Python, a **sequence** is a linearly ordered set of elements accessed by index value. Lists, tuples, and strings are sequence types in Python.

4.2.4 Nested Lists

Lists and tuples can contain elements of any type, including other sequences. Thus, lists and tuples can be nested to create arbitrarily complex data structures. Below is a list of exam grades for each student in a given class,

```
class_grades = [ [85, 91, 89], [78, 81, 86], [62, 75, 77],...]
```

In this list, for example, `class_grades[0]` equals `[85, 91, 89]`, and `class_grades[1]` equals `[78, 81, 86]`. Thus, the following would access the first exam grade of the first student in the list,

```
student1_grades = class_grades[0]
student1_exam1 = student1_grades[0]
```

However, there is no need for intermediate variables `student1_grades` and `student1_exam1`. The exam grade can be directly accessed as follows,

```
class_grades[0][0]  →  [85, 91, 89][0]  →  85
```

To calculate the class average on the first exam, a while loop can be constructed that iterates over the first grade of each student's list of grades,

```
sum = 0
k = 0
while k < len(class_grades):
    sum = sum + class_grades[k][0]
    k = k + 1
average_exam1 = sum / float(len(class_grades))
```

If we wanted to produce a new list containing the exam average for each student in the class, we could do the following,

```
exam_avgs = []
k = 0
while k < len(class_grades):
    avg = (class_grades[k][0] + class_grades[k][1] + \
           class_grades[k][2]) / 3.0
    exam_avgs.append(avg)
    k = k + 1
```

Each time through the loop, the average of the exam grades for a student is computed and appended to list `exam_avgs`. When the loop terminates, `exam_avgs` will contain the corresponding exam average for each student in the class.

LET'S TRY IT

From the Python Shell, enter the following and observe the results.

```
>>> lst = [[1, 2 ,3], [4, 5, 6], [7, 8, 9]]      >>> lst[1]
>>> lst[0]                                       ???
???                                              >>> lst[1][1]
>>> lst[0][1]                                    ???
???
```

Lists and tuples can be nested within each other to construct arbitrarily complex data structures.

4.2.5 Let's Apply It—A Chinese Zodiac Program

The following program (Figure 4-8) determines the animal and associated characteristics from the Chinese Zodiac for a given year of birth. This program utilizes the following programming features:

➤ tuples   ➤ datetime module

Example execution of the program is given in Figure 4-7.

```
This program will display your Chinese zodiac sign and associated
personal characteristics.

Enter your year of birth (yyyy): 1984
Your Chinese zodiac sign is the Rat

Your personal characteristics ...
Forthright, industrious, sensitive, intellectual, sociable

Would you like to enter another year? (y/n): y
Enter your year of birth (yyyy): 1986
Your Chinese zodiac sign is the Tiger

Your personal characteristics ...
Unpredictable, rebellious, passionate, daring, impulsive

Would you like to enter another year? (y/n): n
>>>
```

FIGURE 4-7 Execution of the Chinese Zodiac Program

Line 3 imports the `datetime` module. It provides the current year (**line 31**), used to check for invalid years of birth (only years between 1900 and the current year are considered valid). **Lines 9–24** perform the initialization for the program. The variables on lines **9–20** are assigned the characteristics of each animal. The set of `characteristics` is represented as a tuple

```
1   # Chinese Zodiac Program
2
3   import datetime
4
5   # init
6   zodiac_animals = ('Rat', 'Ox', 'Tiger', 'Rabbit', 'Dragon', 'Snake', 'Horse',
7                     'Goat', 'Monkey', 'Rooster', 'Dog', 'Pig')
8
9   rat = 'Forthright, industrious, sensitive, intellectual, sociable'
10  ox = 'Dependable, methodical, modest, born leader, patient'
11  tiger = 'Unpredictable, rebellious, passionate, daring, impulsive'
12  rabbit = 'Good friend, kind, soft-spoken, cautious, artistic'
13  dragon = 'Strong, self-assured, proud, decisive, loyal'
14  snake = 'Deep thinker, creative, responsible, calm, purposeful'
15  horse = 'Cheerful, quick-witted, perceptive, talkative, open-minded'
16  goat = 'Sincere, sympathetic, shy, generous, mothering'
17  monkey = 'Motivator, inquisitive, flexible, innovative, problem solver'
18  rooster = 'Organized, self-assured, decisive, perfectionist, zealous'
19  dog = 'Honest, unpretentious, idealistic, moralistic, easy going'
20  pig = 'Peace-loving, hard-working, trusting, understanding, thoughtful'
21
22  characteristics = (rat, ox, tiger, rabbit, dragon, snake, horse, goat, monkey,
23                     rooster, dog, pig)
24  terminate = False
25
26  # program greeting
27  print('This program will display your Chinese zodiac sign and associated')
28  print('personal characteristics.\n')
29
30  # get current year from module datetime
31  current_yr = datetime.date.today().year
32
33  while not terminate:
34
35      # get year of birth
36      birth_year = int(input('Enter your year of birth (yyyy): '))
37
38      while birth_year < 1900 or birth_year > current_yr:
39          print('Invalid year. Please re-enter\n')
40          birth_year = int(input('Enter your year of birth (yyyy): '))
41
42      # output results
43      cycle_num = (birth_year - 1900) % 12
44
45      print('Your Chinese zodiac sign is the', zodiac_animals[cycle_num],'\n')
46      print('Your personal characteristics ...')
47      print(characteristics[cycle_num])
48
49      # continue?
50      response = input('\nWould you like to enter another year? (y/n): ')
51
52      while response != 'y' and response != 'n':
53          response = input("Please enter 'y' or 'n': ")
54
55      if response == 'n':
56          terminate = True
```

FIGURE 4-8   Chinese Zodiac Program

(**line 22**), and not a list type, since the information is not meant to be altered. It associates each set of characteristics with the corresponding year of the twelve-year cycle of the zodiac based on their position in the tuple. (We could have defined `characteristics` to contain each of the twelve string descriptions, without the use of variables `rat`, `ox`, and so on. It was written this way for the sake of readability.) Variable `terminate`, initialized to `False`, is a Boolean flag used to quit the program once set to `True` (in response to the user being asked to continue with another month or not at **line 50**). **Lines 27–28** display the program greeting.

Lines 33–56 comprise the main loop of the program. The while loop at **line 38** ensures that the entered year is valid. On **line 43**, the `cycle_num` for the individual is assigned a value between 0–11, based on their year of birth. Since the year 1900 was the year of the rat in the Chinese Zodiac, the value of `cycle_num` is `(birth_year − 1900) % 12`. **Lines 45–47** then use the `cycle_num` as an index into tuple `zodiac_animals` (to get the animal for that birth year) and tuple `characteristics` (to get the associated personal characteristics) to display the results.

Self-Test Questions

1. Which of the following sequence types is a mutable type?
   (a) strings   (b) lists   (c) tuples

2. Which of the following is true?
   (a) Lists and tuples are denoted by the use of square brackets.
   (b) Lists are denoted by use of square brackets and tuples are denoted by the use of parentheses.
   (c) Lists are denoted by use of parentheses and tuples are denoted by the use of square brackets.

3. Lists and tuples must each contain at least one element. (TRUE/FALSE)

4. For `lst = [4, 2, 9, 1]`, what is the result of the following operation, `lst.insert(2, 3)`?
   (a) `[4, 2, 3, 9, 1]`   (b) `[4, 3 ,2, 9, 1]`   (c) `[4, 2, 9, 2, 1]`

5. Which of the following is the correct way to denote a tuple of one element?
   (a) [6]   (b) (6)   (c) [6,]   (d) (6,)

6. Which of the following set of operations can be applied to any sequence?
   (a) `len(s), s[i], s + w (concatenation)`
   (b) `max(s), s[i], sum(s)`
   (c) `len(s), s[i], s.sort()`

ANSWERS: 1. (b). 2. (b). 3. False. 4. (a). 5. (d). 6. (a).

4.3   Iterating Over Lists (Sequences) in Python

Python's for statement provides a convenient means of iterating over lists (and other sequences). In this section, we look at both for loops and while loops for list iteration.

4.3.1   For Loops

A **for statement** is an iterative control statement that iterates once for each element in a specified sequence of elements. Thus, for loops are used to construct definite loops. For example, a for loop is given in Figure 4-9 that prints out the values of a specific list of integers.

for statement	Example use

`for k in `*`sequence`*`:`
`  `*`suite`*
	`nums = [10, 20, 30, 40, 50, 60]`
	
	`for k in nums:`
	`    print(k)`

FIGURE 4-9   The for Statement in Python

Variable k is referred to as a **loop variable**. Since there are six elements in the provided list, the for loop iterates exactly six times. To contrast the use of for loops and while loops for list iteration, the same iteration is provided as a while loop below,

```
k = 0
while k < len(nums):
        print(nums[k])
        k = k + 1
```

In the while loop version, loop variable k must be initialized to 0 and incremented by 1 each time through the loop. In the for loop version, loop variable k *automatically* iterates over the provided sequence of values.

The for statement can be applied to all sequence types, including strings. Thus, iteration over a string can be done as follows (which prints each letter on a separate line).

```
for ch in 'Hello':
        print(ch)
```

Next we look at the use of the built-in range function with for loops.

LET'S TRY IT

From the Python Shell, enter the following and observe the results.

```
>>> for k in [4, 2 ,3, 1]:          >>> for k in ['Apple', 'Banana', 'Pear']:
        print(k)                            print(k)
???                                 ???

>>> for k in (4, 2, 3, 1):          >>> for k in 'Apple':
        print(k)                            print(k)
???                                 ???
```

A **for statement** is an iterative control statement that iterates once for each element in a specified sequence of elements.

4.3.2 The Built-in `range` Function

Python provides a built-in **range function** that can be used for generating a sequence of integers that a for loop can iterate over, as shown below.

```
sum = 0
for k in range(1, 11):
        sum = sum + k
```

The values in the generated sequence include the starting value, up to *but not including* the ending value. For example, range (1, 11) generates the sequence [1, 2, 3, 4, 5, 6, 7, 8, 9, 10]. Thus, this for loop adds up the integer values 1–10.

The range function is convenient when long sequences of integers are needed. Actually, range does not create a sequence of integers. It creates a *generator function* able to produce each next item of the sequence when needed. This saves memory, especially for long lists. Therefore, typing range (0, 9) in the Python shell does not produce a list as expected—it simply "echoes out" the call to range.

By default, the range function generates a sequence of consecutive integers. A "step" value can be provided, however. For example, range (0, 11, 2) produces the sequence [0, 2, 4, 6, 8, 10], with a step value of 2. A sequence can also be generated "backwards" when given a negative step value. For example, range (10, 0, −1) produces the sequence [10, 9, 8, 7, 6, 5, 4, 3, 2, 1]. Note that since the generated sequence always begins with the provided starting value, "up to" but not including the final value, the final value here is 0, and not 1.

LET'S TRY IT

From the Python Shell, enter the following and observe the results.

```
>>> for k in range(0, 11):        >>> for k in range(2, 102, 2):
        print(k)                          print(k)
???                               ???

>>> for k in range[0, 11]:        >>> for k in range(10, −1, −2):
        print(k)                          print(k)
???                               ???
```

Python provides a built-in **range** function that can be used for generating a sequence of integers that a for loop can iterate over.

4.3.3 Iterating Over List Elements vs. List Index Values

When the elements of a list need to be accessed, but not altered, a loop variable that iterates over each list element is an appropriate approach. However, there are times when the loop variable must iterate over the *index values* of a list instead. A comparison of the two approaches is shown in Figure 4-10.

Loop variable iterating over the elements of a sequence	Loop variable iterating over the index values of a sequence
nums = [10, 20, 30, 40, 50, 60]	nums = [10, 20, 30, 40, 50, 60]

for k in nums:
    sum = sum + k
	for k in range(len(nums)):
	    sum = sum + nums[k]

FIGURE 4-10 Iterating Over the Elements vs. the Index Values of a Given Sequence

Suppose the average of a list of class grades named `grades` needs to be computed. In this case, a for loop can be constructed to iterate over the grades,

```
for k in grades:
    sum = sum + k

print('Class average is', sum/len(grades))
```

However, suppose that the instructor made a mistake in grading, and a point needed to be added to each student's grade? In order to accomplish this, the index value (the location) of each element must be used to update each grade value. Thus, the loop variable of the for loop must iterate over the index values of the list,

```
for k in range(len(grades)):
    grades[k] = grades[k] + 1
```

In such cases, the loop variable k is also functioning as an *index variable*. An **index variable** is a variable whose *changing value is used to access elements of an indexed data structure*. Note that the range function may be given only one argument. In that case, the starting value of the range defaults to 0. Thus, `range(len(grades))` is equivalent to `range(0,len(grades))`.

LET'S TRY IT

From the Python Shell, enter the following and observe the results.

```
>>> nums = [10, 20, 30]              >>> for k in range(len(nums)-1, -1, -1):
                                             print(nums[k])
>>> for k in range(len(nums)):       ???
    print(nums[k])
???
```

An **index variable** is a variable whose changing value is used to access elements of an indexed data structure.

4.3.4 While Loops and Lists (Sequences)

There are situations in which a sequence is to be traversed while a given condition is true. In such cases, a while loop is the appropriate control structure. (Another approach for the partial traversal of a sequence is by use of a for loop containing `break` statements. We avoid the use of `break` statements in this text, favoring the more structured while loop approach.)

Let's say that we need to determine whether the value 40 occurs in list nums (equal to [10, 20, 30]). In this case, once the value is found, the traversal of the list is terminated. An example of this is given in Figure 4-11.

Variable k is initialized to 0, and used as an index variable. Thus, the first time through the loop, k is 0, and nums[0] (with the value 10) is compared to `item_to_find`. Since they are not equal, the second clause of the if statement is executed, incrementing k to 1. The loop continues until either the item is found, or the complete list has been traversed. The final if statement determines

```
k = 0
item_to_find = 40
found_item = False

while k < len(nums) and not found_item:
    if nums[k] == item_to_find:
        found_item = True
    else:
        k = k + 1

if found_item:
    print('item found')
else:
    print('item not found')
```

FIGURE 4-11   List Search in Python

which of the two possibilities for ending the loop occurred, displaying either `'item found'` or `'item not found'`. Finally, note that the correct loop condition is `k < len(nums)`, and not `k <= len(nums)`. Otherwise, an "index out of range" error would result.

LET'S TRY IT

Enter and execute the following Python code and observe the results.

```
k = 0
sum = 0
nums = range(100)

while k < len(nums) and sum < 100:
    sum = sum + nums[k]
    k = k + 1

print('The first', k, 'integers sum to 100 or greater')
```

For situations in which a sequence is to be traversed while a given condition is true, a while loop is the appropriate control structure to use.

4.3.5   Let's Apply It—Password Encryption/Decryption Program

The following program (Figure 4-13) allows a user to encrypt and decrypt passwords containing uppercase/lowercase characters, digits, and special characters. This program utilizes the following programming features:

➤ for loop   ➤ nested sequences (tuples)

Example program execution is given in Figure 4-12.

Lines 4–9 perform the initialization needed for the program. Variable `password_out` is used to hold the encrypted or decrypted output of the program. Since the output string is created by appending to it each translated character one at a time, it is initialized to the empty string.

```
Program Execution ...

This program will encrypt and decrypt user passwords

Enter (e) to encrypt a password, and (d) to decrypt: e
Enter password: Pizza2Day!
Your encrypted password is: Njaam2Fmc!
>>>

Program Execution ...

This program will encrypt and decrypt user passwords

Enter (e) to encrypt a password, and (d) to decrypt: d
Enter password: Njaam2Fmc!
Your decrypted password is: Pizza2Day!
```

FIGURE 4-12   Execution of Password Encryption/Decryption Program

Variable `encryption_key` holds the tuple (of tuples) used to encrypt/decrypt passwords. This tuple contains as elements tuples of length two,

$$\texttt{encryption\_key = (('a', 'm'), ('b', 'h'), etc.}$$

The first tuple, `('a', 'm')`, for example, is used to encode the letter `'a'`. Thus, when encrypting a given file, each occurrence of `'a'` is replaced by the letter `'m'`. When decrypting, the reverse is done—all occurrences of letter `'m'` are replaced by the letter `'a'`.

   Line 12 contains the program greeting. **Line 15** inputs from the user whether they wish to encrypt or decrypt a password. Based on the response, variable `encrypting` is set to either `True` or `False` (**line 20**).

   The program section in **lines 26–47** performs the encryption and decryption. If variable `encrypting` is equal to `True`, then `from_index` is set to 0 and `to_index` is set to 1, causing the "direction" of the substitution of letters to go from the first in the pair to the second (`'a'` replaced by `'m'`). When encrypting is `False` (and thus decryption should be performed), the direction of the substitution is from the second of the pair to the first (`'m'` replaced by `'a'`).

   Variable `case_changer` (**line 33**) is set to the difference between the encoding of the lowercase and the uppercase letters (recall that the encoding of the lowercase letters is greater than that of the uppercase letters). The for loop at **line 38** performs the iteration over the pairs of letters in the encryption key. The first time through the loop, `t = ('a', 'm')`. Thus, `t[from_index]` and `t[to_index]` refer to each of the characters in the pair. Since all characters in the encryption key are in lowercase, when uppercase letters are found in the password, they are converted to lowercase by use of variable `case_changer` (**line 43**) before being compared to the (lowercase) letters in the encryption key. This works because the character encoding of all lowercase letters is greater than the corresponding uppercase version,

```
>>> ord('A')          >>> ord('a')          >>> ord('a') - ord('A')
65                    97                    32
```

A similar approach is used for converting from lowercase back to uppercase. Finally, on **lines 50–53**, the encrypted and decrypted versions of the password are displayed to the user.

```
 1  # Password Encryption/Decryption Program
 2
 3  # init
 4  password_out = ''
 5  case_changer = ord('a') - ord('A')
 6  encryption_key = (('a','m'), ('b','h'), ('c','t'), ('d','f'), ('e','g'),
 7     ('f','k'), ('g','b'), ('h','p'), ('i','j'), ('j','w'), ('k','e'),('l','r'),
 8     ('m','q'), ('n','s'), ('o','l'), ('p','n'), ('q','i'), ('r','u'), ('s','o'),
 9     ('t','x'), ('u','z'), ('v','y'), ('w','v'), ('x','d'), ('y','c'), ('z','a'))
10
11  # program greeting
12  print('This program will encrypt and decrypt user passwords\n')
13
14  # get selection (encrypt/decrypt)
15  which = input('Enter (e) to encrypt a password, and (d) to decrypt: ')
16
17  while which != 'e' and which != 'd':
18      which = input("\nINVALID - Enter 'e' to encrypt, 'd' to decrypt: ")
19
20  encrypting = (which == 'e')  # assigns True or False
21
22  # get password
23  password_in = input('Enter password: ')
24
25  # perform encryption / decryption
26  if encrypting:
27      from_index = 0
28      to_index = 1
29  else:
30      from_index = 1
31      to_index = 0
32
33  case_changer = ord('a') - ord('A')
34
35  for ch in password_in:
36      letter_found = False
37
38      for t in encryption_key:
39          if ('a' <= ch and ch <= 'z') and ch == t[from_index]:
40              password_out = password_out + t[to_index]
41              letter_found = True
42          elif ('A' <= ch and ch <= 'Z') and chr(ord(ch) + 32) == t[from_index]:
43              password_out = password_out + chr(ord(t[to_index]) - case_changer)
44              letter_found = True
45
46      if not letter_found:
47          password_out = password_out + ch
48
49  # output
50  if encrypting:
51      print('Your encrypted password is:', password_out)
52  else:
53      print('Your decrypted password is:', password_out)
```

FIGURE 4-13 Password Encryption/Decryption Program

The substitution occurs in the nested for loops in **lines 35–47**. The outer for loop iterates variable ch over each character in the entered password (to be encrypted or decrypted). The first step of the outer for loop is to initialize letter_found to False. This variable is used to indicate if each character is a (uppercase or lowercase) letter. If so, it is replaced by its corresponding encoding character. If not, it must be a digit or special character, and thus appended as is (**line 47**). The code on **lines 39–41** and **lines 42–46** is similar to each other. The only difference is that since the letters in the encryption key are all lowercase, any uppercase letters in the password need to be converted to lowercase before being compared to the letters in the key.

Self-Test Questions

1. For nums = [10,30,20,40], what does the following for loop output?

   ```
   for k in nums:
       print(k)
   ```

   (a) 10   **(b)** 10   **(c)** 10
        20   30   30
        30   20   20
        40   40

2. For nums = [10, 30, 20, 40], what does the following for loop output?

   ```
   for k in range(1, 4):
       print(nums[k])
   ```

   (a) 10   **(b)** 30   **(c)** 10
        30   20   30
        20   40   20
                                     40

3. For fruit = 'strawberry', what does the following for loop output?

   ```
   for k in range(0, len(fruit), 2):
       print(fruit[k], end='')
   ```

   (a) srwer   **(b)** tabry

4. For nums = [12, 4, 11, 23, 18, 41, 27], what is the value of k when the while loop terminates?

   ```
   k = 0
   while k < len(nums) and nums[k] != 18:
       k = k + 1
   ```

   (a) 3   **(b)** 4   **(c)** 5

ANSWERS: 1. (b), 2. (b), 3. (a), 4. (b)

4.4 More on Python Lists

In this section, we take a closer look at the assignment of lists. We also introduce a useful and convenient means of generating lists that the range function cannot produce, called *list comprehensions*.

4.4.1 Assigning and Copying Lists

Because of the way that lists are represented in Python, when a variable is assigned to another variable holding a list, list2 = list1, each variable ends up referring to the *same instance* of the list in memory. This is depicted in Figure 4-14.

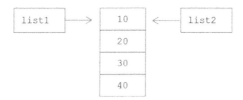

FIGURE 4-14 Assignment of Lists

This has important implications. For example, if an element of list1 is changed, then the corresponding element of list2 will change as well,

```
>>> list1 = [10, 20, 30, 40]
>>> list2 = list1
>>> list1[0] = 5
>>> list1
[5, 20, 30, 40]     change made in list1
>>> list2
[5, 20, 30, 40]     change in list1 causes a change in list2
```

Knowing that variables list1 and list2 refer to the same list explains this behavior. This issue does not apply to strings and tuples, since they are immutable and therefore cannot be modified.

When needed, a copy of a list can be made as given below,

```
list2 = list(list1)
```

In this case, we get the following results,

```
>>> list1 = [10, 20, 30, 40]
>>> list2 = list(list1)
>>> list1[0] = 5
>>> list1
[5, 20, 30, 40]     change made in list1
>>> list2
[10, 20, 30, 40]    change in list1 does NOT cause any change in list2
```

When copying lists that have sublists, another means of copying, called *deep copy*, may be needed. We will discuss this further in Chapter 6 when discussing objects in Python.

LET'S TRY IT

From the Python Shell, enter the following and observe the results.

```
>>> list1 = ['red', 'blue', 'green']        >>> list1 = ['red', 'blue', 'green']

>>> list2 = list1                           >>> list2 = list(list1)
>>> list1[2] = 'yellow'                      >>> list1[2] = 'yellow'

>>> list1                                    >>> list1
???                                          ???

>>> list2                                    >>> list2
???                                          ???
```

> When a variable is assigned to another variable holding a list, each variable ends up referring to the *same instance* of the list in memory.

4.4.2 List Comprehensions

The `range` function allows for the generation of sequences of integers in fixed increments. **List comprehensions** in Python can be used to generate more varied sequences. Example list comprehensions are given in Figure 4-15.

Example List Comprehensions	Resulting List
(a) `[x**2 for x in [1, 2, 3]]`	`[1, 4, 9]`
(b) `[x**2 for x in range(5)]`	`[0, 1, 4, 9, 16]`
(c) `nums = [-1, 1, -2, 2, -3, 3, -4, 4]` `    [x for x in nums if x >= 0]`	`[1, 2, 3, 4]`
(d) `[ord(ch) for ch in 'Hello']`	`[72, 101, 108, 108, 111]`

(e) `vowels = ('a', 'e', 'i', 'o', 'u')`
`    w = 'Hello'`
`    [ch for ch in w if ch in vowels]`
	`['e', 'o']`

FIGURE 4-15   List Comprehensions

In the figure, (a) generates a list of squares of the integers in list `[1, 2, 3]`. In (b), squares are generated for each value in `range(5)`. In (c), only positive elements of list `nums` are included in the resulting list. In (d), a list containing the character encoding values in the string `'Hello'` is created. Finally, in (e), tuple `vowels` is used for generating a list containing only the vowels in string w. List comprehensions are a very powerful feature of Python.

LET'S TRY IT

From the Python Shell, enter the following and observe the results.

```
>>> temperatures = [88, 94, 97, 89, 101, 98, 102, 95, 100]
>>> [t for t in temperatures if t >= 100]
???

>>> [(t - 32) * 5/9 for t in temperatures]
???
```

> **List comprehensions** in Python provide a concise means of generating a more varied set of sequences than those that can be generated by the `range` function.

COMPUTATIONAL PROBLEM SOLVING

4.5 Calendar Year Program

In this section, we extend the calendar month program given in the Computational Problem Solving section of Chapter 3 to display a complete calendar year.

4.5.1 The Problem

The problem is to display a calendar year for any year between 1800 and 2099, inclusive. The format of the displayed year should be as depicted in Figure 4-16.

```
2015

January                    February                   March
          1  2  3            1  2  3  4  5  6  7         1  2  3  4  5  6  7
 4  5  6  7  8  9 10         8  9 10 11 12 13 14         8  9 10 11 12 13 14
11 12 13 14 15 16 17        15 16 17 18 19 20 21        15 16 17 18 19 20 21
18 19 20 21 22 23 24        22 23 24 25 26 27 28        22 23 24 25 26 27 28
25 26 27 28 29 30 31                                    29 30 31


April                      May                        June
          1  2  3  4                     1  2          1  2  3  4  5  6
 5  6  7  8  9 10 11         3  4  5  6  7  8  9         7  8  9 10 11 12 13
12 13 14 15 16 17 18        10 11 12 13 14 15 16        14 15 16 17 18 19 20
19 20 21 22 23 24 25        17 18 19 20 21 22 23        21 22 23 24 25 26 27
26 27 28 29 30             24 25 26 27 28 29 30        28 29 30
                           31

July                       August                     September
          1  2  3  4                          1                 1  2  3  4  5
 5  6  7  8  9 10 11         2  3  4  5  6  7  8         6  7  8  9 10 11 12
12 13 14 15 16 17 18         9 10 11 12 13 14 15        13 14 15 16 17 18 19
19 20 21 22 23 24 25        16 17 18 19 20 21 22        20 21 22 23 24 25 26
26 27 28 29 30 31          23 24 25 26 27 28 29        27 28 29 30
                           30 31

October                    November                   December
          1  2  3            1  2  3  4  5  6  7                 1  2  3  4  5
 4  5  6  7  8  9 10         8  9 10 11 12 13 14         6  7  8  9 10 11 12
11 12 13 14 15 16 17        15 16 17 18 19 20 21        13 14 15 16 17 18 19
18 19 20 21 22 23 24        22 23 24 25 26 27 28        20 21 22 23 24 25 26
25 26 27 28 29 30 31       29 30                        27 28 29 30 31
```

FIGURE 4-16 Calendar Month Display

4.5.2 Problem Analysis

The computational issues for this problem are similar to the calendar month program of Chapter 3. We need an algorithm for computing the first day of a given month for years 1800–2099. However, since the complete year is being displayed, only the day of the week for January 1st of the given year needs be computed—the rest of the days follow from knowing the number of days in each month (including February for leap years). The algorithm previously developed to display a calendar month, however, is not relevant for this program. Instead, the information will first be stored in a data structure allowing for the months to be displayed three across.

4.5.3 Program Design

Meeting the Program Requirements

We will develop and implement an algorithm that displays the calendar year as shown in Figure 4-16. We shall request the user to enter the four-digit year to display, with appropriate input error checking.

Data Description

The program needs to represent the year entered, whether it is a leap year, the day of the week for January 1st of the year, and the number of days in each month (accounting for leap years). The names of each of the twelve months will also be stored for display in the calendar year. Given this information, the calendar year can be appropriately constructed and displayed.

We make use of nested lists for representing the calendar year. The data structure will start out as an empty list and will be built incrementally as each new calendar month is computed. The list structures for the calendar year and calendar month are given below,

```
calendar_year = [ [calendar_month], [calendar_month], etc.] ]

calendar_month = [ week_1, week_2, ..., week_k ]
```

Each italicized month is represented as a list of four to six strings, with each string storing a week of the month to be displayed (or a blank line for alignment purposes).

FEBRUARY 2015   MAY 2015

Sun	Mon	Tues	Wed	Thur	Fri	Sat
1	2	3	4	5	6	7
8	9	10	11	12	13	14
15	16	17	18	19	20	21
22	23	24	25	26	27	28

4 lines

Sun	Mon	Tues	Wed	Thur	Fri	Sat
					1	2
3	4	5	6	7	8	9
10	11	12	13	14	15	16
17	18	19	20	21	22	23
24	25	26	27	28	29	30
31						

6 lines

The strings are formatted to contain all the spaces needed for proper alignment when displayed. For example, since the first week of May 2015 begins on a Friday, the string value for this week would be,

'   1 2'

The complete representation for the calendar year 2015 is given below, with the details shown for the months of February and May.

```
[[ January ],
 ['  1  2  3  4  5  6  7', '  8  9 10 11 12 13 14',
   ' 15 16 17 18 19 20 21', ' 22 23 24 25 26 27 28'],
 [ March ],
 [ April ],
 ['             1  2', '  3  4  5  6  7  8  9',
   ' 10 11 12 13 14 15 16', ' 17 18 19 20 21 22 23',
   ' 24 25 26 27 28 29 30', ' 31                '],
 [ June ],
 [ July ],
 [ August ],
 [ September ],
 [ October ],
 [ November ],
 [ December ]]
```

February

May

(Typically, yearly calendars combine the one or two remaining days of the month on the sixth line of a calendar month onto the previous week. We shall not do that in this program, however.)

Algorithmic Approach

We make use of the algorithm for determining the day of the week previously used. For this program, however, the only date for which the day of the week needs to be determined is January 1 of a given year. Thus, the original day of the week algorithm can be simplified by removing variable day and replacing its occurrence on line 6 with 1, given in Figure 4-17.

To determine the day of the week for January 1 of a given **year**:

1. Let **century_digits** be equal to the first two digits of the year.
2. Let **year_digits** be equal to the last two digits of the year.
3. Let **value** be equal to **year_digits** + floor(**year_digits** / 4)
4. If **century_digits** equals 18, then add 2 to **value**, else if **century_digits** equals 20, then add 6 to **value**.
5. If **year** is not a leap year then add 1 to **value**.
6. Set **value** equal to (**value** + 1) mod 7.
7. If **value** is equal to 1 (Sunday), 2 (Monday), ... 0 (Saturday).

FIGURE 4-17 Simplified Day of the Week Algorithm

Overall Program Steps

The overall steps in this program design are given in Figure 4-18.

4.5.4 Program Implementation and Testing

Stage 1—Determining the Day of the Week (for January 1st)

We first develop and test the code for determining the day of the week for January 1st of a given year. This modified code from the calendar month program is given in Figure 4-19.

Program Initialization

Program Greeting

Get Year from User

Determine if Leap Year

Determine Day of the Week

Construct Calendar Year

Display Calendar Year

FIGURE 4-18   Overall Steps of Calendar Year Program

Line 4 initializes Boolean flag terminate to False. If the user enters −1 for the year (in **lines 10–13**), terminate is set to True and the while loop at **line 7** terminates, thus terminating the program. If a valid year is entered, **lines 19–42** are executed.

Lines 19–22 determine if the year is a leap year using the same code as in the calendar month program, assigning Boolean variable leap_year accordingly. **Lines 25–40** implement the simplified day of the week algorithm for determining the day of the week for January 1 of a given year in Figure 4.17, with the result displayed on **line 42**.

Stage 1—Testing

We show a sample test run of this stage of the program in Figure 4-20.

Figure 4-21 displays the test cases used for this program.

Since all test cases passed, we can move on to the next stage of program development.

Stage 2—Constructing the Calendar Year Data Structure

Next we develop the part of the program that constructs the data structure holding all of the calendar year information to be displayed. The data structure begins empty and is incrementally built, consisting of nested lists, as previously discussed.

```
 1  # Calendar Year Program (Stage 1)
 2
 3  # initialization
 4  terminate = False
 5
 6  # prompt for years until quit
 7  while not terminate:
 8
 9      # get year
10      year = int(input('Enter year (yyyy) (-1 to quit): '))
11
12      while (year < 1800 or year > 2099) and year != -1:
13          year = int(input('INVALID - Enter year(1800-2099): '))
14
15      if year == -1:
16          terminate = True
17      else:
18          # determine if leap year
19          if (year % 4 == 0) and (not (year % 100 == 0) or (year % 400 == 0)):
20              leap_year = True
21          else:
22              leap_year = False
23
24          # determine day of the week
25          century_digits = year // 100
26          year_digits = year % 100
27
28          value = year_digits + (year_digits // 4)
29
30          if century_digits == 18:
31              value = value + 2
32          elif century_digits == 20:
33              value = value + 6
34
35          # leap year check
36          if not leap_year:
37              value = value + 1
38
39          # determine first day of month for Jan 1
40          first_day_of_month = (value + 1) % 7
41
42          print('Day of week is:', first_day_of_month)
```

FIGURE 4-19   Stage 1 of the Calendar Year Program

```
Enter year (yyyy) (-1 to quit): 1800
Day of week is: 4
Enter year (yyyy) (-1 to quit): 1900
Day of week is: 2
Enter year (yyyy) (-1 to quit): 1984
Day of week is: 1
Enter year (yyyy) (-1 to quit): 1985
Day of week is: 3
Enter year (yyyy) (-1 to quit): 3000
INVALID - Enter year(1800-2099): 2000
Day of week is: 0
Enter year (yyyy) (-1 to quit): 2009
Day of week is: 5
Enter year (yyyy) (-1 to quit): -1
>>>
```

FIGURE 4-20   Example Output of First Stage Testing

Calendar Month	Expected Results first day of month	Actual Results first day of month	Evaluation
January 1800	4 (Wednesday)	4	Passed
January 1900	2 (Monday)	2	Passed
January 1984	1 (Sunday)	1	Passed
January 1985	3 (Tuesday)	3	Passed
January 2000	0 (Saturday)	0	Passed
January 2009	5 (Thursday)	5	Passed

FIGURE 4-21   Test Cases for Stage 1 of the Calendar Year Program

Figure 4-22 shows an implementation of this stage of the program.

Lines 4–14 perform the required initialization. Tuples `days_in_month` and `month_names` have been added to the program to store the number of days for each month (with February handled as an exception) and the month names. On **line 11**, `calendar_year` is initialized to the empty list. It will be constructed month-by-month for the twelve months of the year. There is the need for strings of blanks of various lengths in the program, initialized as `month_separator`, `blank_week`, and `blank_col` (**lines 12–14**). The `calendar_year` data structure will contain all the space characters needed for the calendar months to be properly displayed. Therefore, there will be no need to develop code that determines how each month should be displayed as in the calendar month program. The complete structure will simply be displayed row by row.

Lines 17–49 are the same as the first stage of the program for determining the day of the week of a given date. Once the day of the week for January 1st of the given year is known, the days of the week for all remaining dates simply follow. Thus, there is no need to calculate the day of the week for any other date.

Line 52 begins the for loop for constructing each of the twelve months. On **line 53**, the month name is retrieved from tuple `month_names` and assigned to `month_name`. Variable `current_day`, holding the current day of the month, is initialized to 1 for the new month (**line 56**). In **lines 57–60**, `first_day_of_current_month`, determined by the day of the week algorithm, is converted to the appropriate column number. Thus, since 0 denotes Saturday, if `first_day_of_current_month` equals 0, `starting_col` is set to 7. Otherwise, `starting_col` is set to `first_day_of_current_month` (e.g., if `first_day_of_current_month` is 1, then `starting_col` is set to 1).

In **lines 62–64**, the initialization for a new month finishes with the reassignment of `current_col`, `calendar_week`, and `calendar_month`. Each calendar week of a given month is initially assigned to the empty string, with each date appended one-by-one. Variable `current_col` is used to keep track of the current column (day) of the week, incremented from 0 to 6. Since the first day of the month can fall on any day of the week, the first week of any month may contain blank ("skipped") columns. This includes the columns from `current_col` up to but not including `starting_col`. The while loop in **lines 67–69** appends any of these skipped columns to empty string `calendar_week`.

Lines **72–75** assign `num_days_this_month` to the number of days stored in tuple `days_in_month`. The exception for February, based on whether the year is a leap year or not, is handled as a special case. The while loop at **line 77** increments variable `current_day` from 1 to the number of

```
1  # Calendar Year Program (Final Version)
2
3  # initialization
4  terminate = False
5  days_in_month = (31, 28, 31, 30, 31, 30, 31, 31, 30, 31, 30, 31)
6
7  month_names = ('January', 'February', 'March', 'April', 'May', 'June'
8                 'July', 'August', 'September', 'October', 'November',
9                 'December')
10
11 calendar_year = []
12 month_separator = format(' ', '8')
13 blank_week = format(' ', '21')
14 blank_col = format(' ', '3')
15
16 # prompt for years until quit
17 while not terminate:
18
19     # get year
20     year = int(input('Enter year (yyyy) (-1 to quit): '))
21     while (year < 1800 or year > 2099) and year != -1:
22         year = int(input('INVALID - Enter year(1800-2099): '))
23
24     if year == -1:
25         terminate = True
26     else:
27         # determine if leap year
28         if (year % 4 == 0) and (not (year % 100 == 0) or
29             (year % 400 == 0)):
30             leap_year = True
31         else:
32             leap_year = False
33
34         # determine day of the week
35         century_digits = year // 100
36         year_digits = year % 100
37         value = year_digits + (year_digits // 4)
38
39         if century_digits == 18:
40             value = value + 2
41         elif century_digits == 20:
42             value = value + 6
43
44         # leap year check
45         if not leap_year:
46             value = value + 1
47
48         # determine first day of month for Jan 1
49         first_day_of_current_month = (value + 1) % 7
50
51         # construct calendar for all 12 months
52         for month_num in range(12):
53             month_name = month_names[month_num]
54
55             # init for new month
56             current_day = 1
57             if first_day_of_current_month == 0:
58                 starting_col = 7
59             else:
60                 starting_col = first_day_of_current_month
61
62             current_col = 1
63             calendar_week = ''
64             calendar_month = []
65
```

FIGURE 4-22 Stage 2 of the Calendar Year Program (*Continued*)

```
66          # add any needed leading space for first week of month
67          while current_col < starting_col:
68              calendar_week = calendar_week + blank_col
69              current_col = current_col + 1
70
71          # store month as separate weeks
72          if (month_name == 'February') and leap_year:
73              num_days_this_month = 29
74          else:
75              num_days_this_month = days_in_month[month_num]
76
77          while current_day <= num_days_this_month:
78
79              # store day of month in field of length 3
80              calendar_week = calendar_week + \
81                  format(str(current_day),'>3')
82
83              # check if at last column of displayed week
84              if current_col == 7:
85                  calendar_month = calendar_month + [calendar_week]
86                  calendar_week = ''
87                  current_col = 1
88              else:
89                  current_col = current_col + 1
90
91              # increment current day
92              current_day = current_day + 1
93
94          # fill out final row of month with needed blanks
95          calendar_week = calendar_week + \
96           blank_week[0:(7-current_col+1) * 3]
97          calendar_month = calendar_month + [calendar_week]
98
99          # reset values for next month
100         first_day_of_current_month = current_col
101         calendar_year = calendar_year + [calendar_month]
102         calendar_month = []
103
104     print(calendar_year)
105
106     #reset for another year
107     calendar_year = []
```

FIGURE 4-22 Stage 2 of the Calendar Year Program

days in the month. In **lines 80–81** each date is appended to calendar_week right-justified as a string of length three by use of the format function. Thus, a single-digit date will be appended with two leading blanks, and a double-digit date with one leading blank so that the columns of dates align.

For each new date appended to calendar_week, a check is made on **line 84** as to whether the end of the week has been reached. If the last column of the calendar week has been reached (when column_col equals 7) then the constructed calendar_week string is appended to the calendar_month (**line 85**). In addition, calendar_week is re-initialized to the empty string, and current_col is reset to 1 (**lines 86–87**). If the last column of the calendar week has not yet been reached, then current_col is simply incremented by 1 (**line 89**). Then, on **line 92**, variable current_day is incremented by 1, whether or not a new week is started.

When the while loop (at **line 77**) eventually terminates, variable current_week holds the last week of the constructed month. Therefore, as with the first week of the month, the last week may contain empty columns. This is handled by **lines 95–97**. Before appending calendar_week to calendar_month, any remaining unfilled columns are appended to it (the reason that these final columns must be blank-filled is because months are displayed side-by-side, and therefore are needed to keep the whole calendar properly aligned),

```
calendar_week = calendar_week + blank_week[0:(7-current_col+1) * 3]
```

Thus, the substring of `blank_week` produced will end up as an empty string if the value of `current_col` is 6 (for Saturday, the last column) as it should. **Line 100** sets variable `first_day_of_current_month` to `current_col` since `current_col` holds the column value of the next column that *would have been* used for the current month, and thus is the first day of the following month. On **line 101**, the completed current month is appended to list `calendar_year`. And on **line 102**, `calendar_month` is reset to an empty list in anticipation of the next month to be constructed.

Finally, on **line 104**, the complete `calendar_year` list is displayed. Because the program prompts the user for other years to be constructed and displayed, the `calendar_year` list is reset to the empty list (**line 107**).

Stage 2—Testing

The program terminates with an error on line 53,

```
Enter year (yyyy) (-1 to quit): 2015
Traceback (most recent call last):
  File "C:\My Python Programs\CalendarYearStage2.py", line 54, in <module>
    month_name = month_names[month_num]
IndexError: tuple index out of range
```

This line is within the for loop at line 52,

```
        for month_num in range(12):
            month_name = month_names[month_num]
```

For some reason, index variable `month_num` is out of range for tuple `month_names`. We look at the final value of `month_num` by typing the variable name into the Python shell,

```
            >>> month_num
            11
```

Since `month_names` has index values 0–11 (since of length 12), an index value of 11 should not be out of range. How, then, can this index out of range error happen? Just to make sure that `month_names` has the right values, we display its length,

```
            >> len(month_names)
            11
```

This is not right! The tuple `month_names` should contain all twelve months of the year. That is the way it was initialized on line 7, and tuples, unlike lists, cannot be altered, they are immutable. This does not seem to make sense. To continue our investigation, we display the value of the tuple,

```
>> month_names
('January', 'February', 'March', 'April', 'May', 'JuneJuly', 'August',
'September', 'October', 'November', 'December')
>>>
```

Now we see something that doesn't look right. Months June and July are concatenated into one string value 'JuneJuly' making the length of the tuple 11, and not 12 (as we discovered). *That* would explain why the index out of range error occurred.

What, then, is the problem. Why were the strings 'June' and 'July' concatenated? We need to look at the line of code that creates this tuple,

```
month_names = ('January', 'February', 'March', 'April', 'May', 'June'
               'July', 'August', 'September', 'October', 'November', 'December')
```

It looks OK. Strings 'June' and 'July' were written as separate strings. We then decide to count the number of items in the tuple. Since items in tuples and lists are separated by commas, we count the number of items between the commas. We count the items up to 'May', which is five items as it should be, then 'June', which is six items . . . ah, there is no comma after the string 'June'! *That* must be why strings 'June' and 'July' were concatenated, and thus the source of the index out of range error. We try to reproduce this in the shell,

```
>>> 'June' 'July'
'JuneJuly'
```

That's it! We have found the problem and should feel good about it. After making the correction and re-executing the program, we get the following results,

```
Enter year (yyyy) (-1 to quit): 2015
[['              1  2  3', '  4  5  6  7  8  9 10', ' 11 12 13 14 15 16 17', ' 1
8 19 20,21 22 23 24', ' 25 26 27 28 29 30 31','                      '], ['  1
2  3  4  5  6  7', '  8  9 10 11 12 13 14', ' 15 16 17 18 19 20 21', ' 22 23 24
25 26 27 28', '                      '], ['  1  2  3  4  5  6  7', '  8  9 10 11
12 13 14', ' 15 16 17 18 19 20 21', ' 22 23 24 25 26 27 28', ' 29 30 31
   '], ['              1  2  3  4', '  5  6  7  8  9 10 11', ' 12 13 14 15 16 17 18
', ' 19 20 21 22 23 24 25', ' 26 27 28 29 30        '], ['                 1  2',
'  3  4  5  6  7  8  9', ' 10 11 12 13 14 15 16', ' 17 18 19 20 21 22 23', ' 24
25 26 27 28 29 30', ' 31                   '], ['        1  2  3  4  5  6', '  7  8
 9 10 11 12 13', ' 14 15 16 17 18 19 20', ' 21 22 23 24 25 26 27', ' 28 29 30
       '], ['              1  2  3  4', '  5  6  7  8  9 10 11', ' 12 13 14 15 16
17 18', ' 19 20 21 22 23 24 25', ' 26 27 28 29 30 31    '], ['
 1', '  2  3  4  5  6  7  8', '  9 10 11 12 13 14 15', ' 16 17 18 19 20 21 22',
' 23 24 25 26 27 28 29', ' 30 31                '], ['           1  2  3  4  5', '
 6  7  8  9 10 11 12', ' 13 14 15 16 17 18 19', ' 20 21 22 23 24 25 26', ' 27 28
29 30          '], ['              1  2  3', '  4  5  6  7  8  9 10', ' 11 12 13
14 15 16 17', ' 18 19 20 21 22 23 24', ' 25 26 27 28 29 30 31', '
       '], ['  1  2  3  4  5  6  7', '  8  9 10 11 12 13 14', ' 15 16 17 18 19 2
0 21', ' 22 23 24 25 26 27 28', ' 29 30                '], ['           1  2  3  4
5', '  6  7  8  9 10 11 12', ' 13 14 15 16 17 18 19', ' 20 21 22 23 24 25 26', '
27 28 29 30 31        ']]
Enter year (yyyy) (-1 to quit):
```

We can see if the output looks like the structure that we expect. The first item in the list, the structure for the month of January, is as follows,

```
[['              1  2  3', '  4  5  6  7  8  9 10', ' 11 12 13 14 15 16 17',
' 18 19 20 21 22 23 24', ' 25 26 27 28 29 30 31', '                      ']
```

In checking against available calendar month calculators, we see that the first day of the month for January 2015 is a Thursday. Thus, the first week of the month should have four skipped days, followed by 1, 2, and 3 each in a column width of 3. We find that there are fourteen blank characters in the first line. The first twelve are for the four skipped columns, and the last two are for the right-justified string '1' in the column of the first day of the month,

Since there are five weeks in the month, there should be one extra "blank week" at the end of the list to match the vertical spacing of all other months. We see, in fact, that the last (sixth) string is a string of blanks.

Since the `calendar_year` structure looks correct, we now develop the final stage of the program that displays the complete calendar year.

Stage 3—Displaying the Calendar Year Data Structure

We now give the complete calendar year program in Figure 4-23. In this final version, the only change at the start of the program is that a program greeting is added on **line 19**. The rest of the program is the same up to **line 105**, the point where the calendar year has been constructed. (The `print(calendar_year)` line and re-initialization of `calendar_year` to the empty list have been removed from the previous version, since they were only there for testing purposes.)

The new code in this version of the program is in **lines 107–141**, which displays the calendar year. The calendar year output is given in Figure 4-24.

On **line 108** the year is displayed. Because the months are displayed three across, as shown in Figure 4-16, the for loop on **line 111** iterates variable `month_num` over the values [0, 3, 6, 9]. Thus, when `month_num` is 0, months 0-2 (January–March) are displayed. When `month_num` is 3, months 3-5 (April–June) are displayed, and so forth.

The for loop at **line 114** displays the month names for each row (for example, January, February, and March). Each is displayed left-justified in a field width of 19. A leading blank character is appended to the formatting string to align with the first column of numbers displayed for each month. The `print(. . ., end=' ')` form of print is used, which prevents the cursor from moving to the next line. Thus, the months can be displayed side-by-side. Variable `month_separator` contains the appropriate number of blank spaces (initialized at the top of the program) to provide the required amount of padding between the months, as shown below,

Lines 119–120 perform the initialization needed for the following while loop (at **line 122**), which displays each week, one-by-one, of the current three months. Variable `week` is initialized to zero for each month and is used to keep count of the number of weeks displayed. Variable `lines_to_print` is initialized to `True` to start the execution of the following while loop.

At **line 125** within the while loop, `lines_to_print` is initialized to `False`. It is then set to `True` by any (or all) of the current three months being displayed only if they still have more calendar lines (weeks) to print, thus causing the while loop to continue with another

```
1  # Calendar Year Program (Final Version)
2
3  # initialization
4  terminate = False
5  days_in_month = (31, 28, 31, 30, 31, 30, 31, 31, 30, 31, 30, 31)
6
7  month_names = ('January', 'February', 'March', 'April', 'May', 'June',
8                 'July', 'August', 'September', 'October', 'November',
9                 'December')
10
11 calendar_year = []
12 month_separator = format(' ', '8')
13 blank_week = format(' ', '21')
14 blank_col = format(' ', '3')
15
16 # prompt for years until quit
17 while not terminate:
18
19     # program greeting
20     print ('This program will display a calendar year for a given year')
21
22     # get year
23     year = int(input('Enter year (yyyy) (-1 to quit): '))
24     while (year < 1800 or year > 2099) and year != -1:
25         year = int(input('INVALID - Enter year(1800-2099): '))
26
27     if year == -1:
28         terminate = True
29     else:
30         # determine if leap year
31         if (year % 4 == 0) and (not (year % 100 == 0) or
32             (year % 400 == 0)):
33             leap_year = True
34         else:
35             leap_year = False
36
37         # determine day of the week
38         century_digits = year // 100
39         year_digits = year % 100
40         value = year_digits + (year_digits // 4)
41
42         if century_digits == 18:
43             value = value + 2
44         elif century_digits == 20:
45             value = value + 6
46
47         # leap year check
48         if not leap_year:
49             value = value + 1
50
51         # determine first day of month for Jan 1
52         first_day_of_current_month = (value + 1) % 7
53
54         # construct calendar for all 12 months
55         for month_num in range(12):
56             month_name = month_names[month_num]
57
58             # init for new month
59             current_day = 1
60             if first_day_of_current_month == 0:
61                 starting_col = 7
62             else:
63                 starting_col = first_day_of_current_month
64
```

FIGURE 4-23   Final Stage of the Calendar Year Program (*continued*)

```
            current_col = 1
            calendar_week = ''
            calendar_month = []

            # add any needed leading space for first week of month
            while current_col < starting_col:
                calendar_week = calendar_week + blank_col
                current_col = current_col + 1

            # store month as separate weeks
            if (month_name == 'February') and leap_year:
                num_days_this_month = 29
            else:
                num_days_this_month = days_in_month[month_num]

            while current_day <= num_days_this_month:

                # store day of month in field of length 3
                calendar_week = calendar_week + \
                    format(str(current_day),'>3')

                # check if at last column of displayed week
                if current_col == 7:
                    calendar_month = calendar_month + [calendar_week]
                    calendar_week = ''
                    current_col = 1
                else:
                    current_col = current_col + 1

                # increment current day
                current_day = current_day + 1

            # fill out final row of month with needed blanks
            calendar_week = calendar_week + \
                        blank_week[0:(7-current_col+1) * 3]
            calendar_month = calendar_month + [calendar_week]

            # reset values for next month
            first_day_of_current_month = current_col
            calendar_year = calendar_year + [calendar_month]
            calendar_month = []

    # print calendar year
    print('\n', year,'\n')

    # each row starts with January, April, July, or October
    for month_num in [0,3,6,9]:

        # displays three months in each row
        for i in range(month_num, month_num + 3):
            print(' ' + format(month_names[i],'19'),
                    month_separator, end='')

        # display each week of months on separate lines
        week = 0
        lines_to_print = True
```

FIGURE 4-23   Final Stage of the Calendar Year Program (*continued*)

```
122        while lines_to_print:
123
124            # init
125            lines_to_print = False
126
127            # another week to display for first month in row?
128            for k in range(month_num, month_num + 3):
129                if week < len(calendar_year[k]):
130                    print(calendar_year[k][week], end='')
131                    lines_to_print = True
132                else:
133                    print(blank_week, end='')
134
135                print(month_separator, end='')
136
137            # move to next screen line
138            print()
139
140            # increment week
141            week = week + 1
```

FIGURE 4-23 Final Stage of the Calendar Year Program

iteration. This occurs within the for loop at **lines 128–135**. Since variable month_num indicates the current month being displayed, the number of weeks in the month is determined by the length of the tuple of strings for the current month k.

$$len(calendar\_year[k])$$

Note that some months may have no more weeks to display, whereas others may. This is the case for the first three months of 2015,

```
January                    February                   March

            1  2  3         1  2  3  4  5  6  7        1  2  3  4  5  6  7
 4  5  6  7  8  9 10         8  9 10 11 12 13 14        8  9 10 11 12 13 14
11 12 13 14 15 16 17        15 16 17 18 19 20 21       15 16 17 18 19 20 21
18 19 20 21 22 23 24        22 23 24 25 26 27 28       22 23 24 25 26 27 28
25 26 27 28 29 30 31                                   29 30 31
```

In this case, the while loop needs to continue to iterate in order to display the last lines of January and March even though the last line of February has been displayed. Therefore, in cases where a given month has a line to print but another month doesn't, a blank line is displayed in order to maintain the correct alignment of month weeks. After the week of dates (or blank week) is output for each of the three months, the cursor is moved to the start of the next line (on **line 138**) and variable week is incremented by one (**line 141**) before the loop begins the next iteration for displaying the next row of calendar weeks.

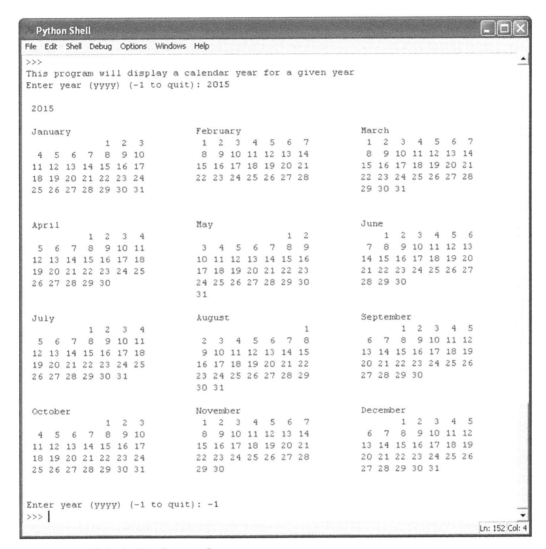

FIGURE 4-24   Calendar Year Program Output

Finally, the while loop at line 122 continues to iterate until there are no more lines to display for all of the three months currently being displayed—that is, until `lines_to_print` is `False`.

Figure 4-25 displays the results of testing this final version by using the test plan from the Calendar Month program of Chapter 3. The test plan passed for all test cases.

CHAPTER SUMMARY

General Topics

Linear Data Structures
List Operations
List Traversal

The Empty List and Its Use
Nested Lists
List Iteration
Loop Variable/Index Variable

Calendar Month	Expected Results first day	num days	Actual Results first day	num days	Evaluation
January 1800	Wednesday	31	Wednesday	31	Pass
February 1800	Saturday	28	Saturday	28	Pass
April 1860	Sunday	30	Sunday	30	Pass
July 1887	Friday	31	Friday	31	Pass
February 1904	Monday	29	Monday	29	Pass
March 1945	Thursday	31	Thursday	31	Pass
September 1960	Thursday	30	Thursday	30	Pass
October 1990	Monday	31	Monday	31	Pass
November 1992	Sunday	30	Sunday	30	Pass
February 2000	Tuesday	29	Tuesday	29	Pass
August 2006	Tuesday	31	Tuesday	31	Pass
May 2014	Thursday	31	Thursday	31	Pass
December 2019	Sunday	31	Sunday	31	Pass
June 2084	Thursday	30	Thursday	30	Pass

FIGURE 4-25 Final Calendar Year Program Testing

Python-Specific Programming Topics

Lists in Python

List Operations in Python

Empty Lists and Tuples in Python

Lists, Tuples, and Strings as Sequences in Python

Additional Sequence Operations

Nested Lists and Tuples in Python

For/While Loops and List Iteration in Python

Built-in Range Function in Python

Iterating over List (Sequence) Elements vs.
Iterating over Index Values in Python

Assigning Lists in Python

List Comprehensions in Python

CHAPTER EXERCISES

Section 4.1

1. **(a)** Give the index values of all the odd numbers in the following list representation, assuming zero-based indexing.

23
16
14
33
19
6
11

(b) How many elements would be looked at when the list is traversed (from top to bottom) until the value 19 was found?

Section 4.2

2. Which of the following lists are syntactically correct in Python?
   (a) `[1, 2, 3, 'four']`   (b) `[1, 2, [3, 4]]`   (c) `[[1, 2, 3] ['four']]`

3. For `lst = [4, 2, 9, 1]`, what is the result of each of the following list operations?
   (a) `lst[1]`   (b) `lst.insert(2, 3)`   (c) `del lst[3]`   (d) `lst.append(3)`

4. For `fruit = ['apple', 'banana', 'pear', 'cherry']`, use a list operation to change the list to `['apple', 'banana', 'cherry']`.

5. For a list of integers, `lst`, give the code to retrieve the maximum value of the second half of the list.

6. For variable `product_code` containing a string of letters and digits,
   (a) Give an if statement that outputs "Verified" if `product_code` contains both a "Z" and a "9", and outputs "Failed" otherwise.
   (b) Give a Python instruction that prints out just the last three characters in `product_code`.

7. Which of the following are valid operations on tuples (for tuples `t1` and `t2`)?
   (a) `len(t1)`   (b) `t1 + t2`   (c) `t1.append(10)`   (d) `t1.insert(0, 10)`

8. For `str1 = 'Hello World'`, answer the following,
   (a) Give an instruction that prints the fourth character of the string.
   (b) Give an instruction that finds the index location of the first occurrence of the letter `'o'` in the string.

9. For a nested list `lst` that contains sublists of integers of the form `[n1, n2, n3]`,
   (a) Give a Python instruction that determines the length of the list.
   (b) Give Python code that determines how many total integer values there are in list `lst`.
   (c) Give Python code that totals all the values in list `lst`.
   (d) Given an assignment statement that assigns the third integer of the fourth element (sublist) of `lst` to the value 12.

Section 4.3

10. For a list of integers named `nums`,
    (a) Write a while loop that adds up all the values in `nums`.
    (b) Write a for loop that adds up all the values in `nums` in which the loop variable is assigned each value in the list.
    (c) Write a for loop that adds up all the elements in `nums` in which the loop variable is assigned to the index value of each element in the list.
    (d) Write a for loop that displays the elements in `nums` backwards.
    (e) Write a for loop that displays every other element in `nums`, starting with the first element.

Section 4.4

11. For `list1 = [1, 2, 3, 4]` and `list2 = [5, 6, 7, 8]`, give the values of `list1[0]` and `list2[0]` where indicated after the following assignments.
    (a) `list1[0] = 10`
    `list2[0] = 50`   `list1[0]` _____   `list2[0]` _____
    (b) `list2 = list1`   `list1[0]` _____   `list2[0]` _____
    (c) `list2[0] = 15`   `list1[0]` _____   `list2[0]` _____
    (d) `list1[0] = 0`   `list1[0]` _____   `list2[0]` _____

12. Give an appropriate list comprehension for each of the following.

    (a) Producing a list of consonants that appear in string variable w.

    (b) Producing a list of numbers between 1 and 100 that are divisible by 3.

    (c) Producing a list of numbers, `zero_values`, from a list of floating-point values, `data_values`, that are within some distance, `epsilon`, from 0.

PYTHON PROGRAMMING EXERCISES

P1. Write a Python program that prompts the user for a list of integers, stores in another list only those values between 1–100, and displays the resulting list.

P2. Write a Python program that prompts the user for a list of integers, stores in another list only those values that are in tuple `valid_values`, and displays the resulting list.

P3. Write a Python program that prompts the user for a list of integers and stores them in a list. For all values that are greater than 100, the string `'over'` should be stored instead. The program should display the resulting list.

P4. Write a Python program that prompts the user to enter a list of first names and stores them in a list. The program should display how many times the letter `'a'` appears within the list.

P5. Write a Python program that prompts the user to enter a list of words and stores in a list only those words whose first letter occurs again within the word (for example, `'Baboon'`). The program should display the resulting list.

P6. Write a Python program that prompts the user to enter types of fruit, and how many pounds of fruit there are for each type. The program should then display the information in the form *fruit*, *weight* listed in alphabetical order, one fruit type per line as shown below,

```
Apple, 6 lbs.
Banana, 11 lbs.
etc.
```

P7. Write a Python program that prompts the user to enter integer values for each of two lists. It then should displays whether the lists are of the same length, whether the elements in each list sum to the same value, and whether there are any values that occur in both lists.

PROGRAM MODIFICATION PROBLEMS

M1. Chinese Zodiac Program: Japanese and Vietnamese Variations

Modify the Chinese Zodiac program in the chapter to allow the user to select the Chinese Zodiac, the Japanese Zodiac, or the Vietnamese Zodiac. The Japanese Zodiac is the same as the Chinese Zodiac, except that "Pig" is substituted with "Wild Boar." The Vietnamese Zodiac is also the same except that the "Ox" is substituted with "Water Buffalo" and "Rabbit" is replaced with "Cat."

M2. Chinese Zodiac Program: Improved Accuracy

The true Chinese Zodiac does not strictly follow the year that a given person was born. It also depends on the month and date as well, which vary over the years. Following are the correct range of dates for each of the Zodiac symbols for the years 1984 to 2007 (which includes two full cycles of the zodiac). Modify

鼠 Rat	Feb 02, **1984** – Feb 19, 1985
牛 Ox	Feb 20, **1985** – Feb 08, 1986
虎 Tiger	Feb 09, **1986** – Jan 28, 1987
兔 Rabbit	Jan 29, **1987** – Feb 16, 1988
龍 Dragon	Feb 17, **1988** – Feb 05, 1989
蛇 Snake	Feb 06, **1989** – Jan 26, 1990
馬 Horse	Jan 27, **1990** – Feb 14, 1991
羊 Sheep	Feb 15, **1991** – Feb 03, 1992
猴 Monkey	Feb 04, **1992** – Jan 22, 1993
鷄 Rooster	Jan 23, **1993** – Feb 09, 1994
狗 Dog	Feb 10, **1994** – Jan 30 1995
猪 Pig	Jan 31, **1995** – Feb 18, 1996

鼠 Rat	Feb 19, **1996** – Feb 06, 1997
牛 Ox	Feb 07, **1997** – Jan 27, 1998
虎 Tiger	Jan 28, **1998** – Feb 15, 1999
兔 Rabbit	Feb 16, **1999** – Feb 04, 2000
龍 Dragon	Feb 05, **2000** – Jan 23, 2001
蛇 Snake	Jan 24, **2001** – Feb 11, 2002
馬 Horse	Feb 12, **2002** – Jan 31, 2003
羊 Sheep	Feb 01, **2003** – Jan 21, 2004
猴 Monkey	Jan 22, **2004** – Feb 08, 2005
鷄 Rooster	Feb 09, **2005** – Jan 28, 2006
狗 Dog	Jan 29, **2006** – Feb 17, 2007
猪 Pig	Feb 18, **2007** – Feb 06, 2008

the Chinese Zodiac program in the chapter so that the user is prompted to enter their date of birth, including month and day, and displays the name and characteristics of the corresponding Chinese Zodiac symbol based on the more accurate zodiac provided here.

M3. Password Encryption/Decryption Program: Multiple Executions

Modify the Password Encryption/Decryption program in the chapter so that it allows the user to continue to encrypt and decrypt passwords until they quit.

M4. Password Encryption/Decryption Program: Secure Password Check

Modify the Password Encryption/Decryption program in the chapter so that the program rejects any entered password for encryption that is not considered "secure" enough. A password is considered secure if it contains at least eight characters, with at least one digit and one special character (!, #, etc).

M5. Password Encryption/Decryption Program: Random Key Generation

Modify the Encryption/Decryption program in the chapter so that a new encryption key is randomly generated each time the program is executed. (See the Python 3 Programmers' Reference for information on the Random module.)

M6. Calendar Year Program: Multilingual Version

Modify the Calendar Year program so that the user can select the language with which the calendar months are labeled. Give the user the choice of at least three different languages from which to select. Find the month names for the other languages online.

M7. Calendar Year Program: Flexible Calendar Format

The program as is always displays three months per row. Modify the Calendar Year program so that the user can select how many months are displayed per row. Allow the user to select either two, three, or four months per row.

PROGRAM DEVELOPMENT PROBLEMS

D1. Morse Code Encryption/Decryption Program

Develop and test a Python program that allows a user to type in a message and have it converted into Morse code, and also enter Morse code and have it converted back to the original message. The encoding of Morse code is given below.

A	• —	N	— •
B	— • • •	O	— — —
C	— • — •	P	• — — •
D	— • •	Q	— — • —
E	•	R	• — •
F	• • — •	S	• • •
G	— — •	T	—
H	• • • •	U	• • —
I	• •	V	• • • —
J	• — — —	W	• — —
K	— • —	X	— • • —
L	• — • •	Y	— • — —
M	— —	Z	— — • •

Format the original message (containing English words) so that there is one sentence per line. Format the Morse code file (containing dots and dashes) so that there is one letter per line, with a blank line following the last letter of each word, and two blank lines following the end of each sentence (except the last).

D2. Holidays Calendar

Develop and test a Python program that displays the day of the week that the following holidays fall on for a year entered by the user,

♦ New Year's Eve
♦ Valentine's Day
♦ St. Patrick's Day
♦ April Fool's Day
♦ Fourth of July
♦ Labor Day
♦ Halloween
♦ User's Birthday

Note that Labor Day, as opposed to the other holidays above, does not fall on the same date each year. It occurs each year on the first Monday of September.

D3. The Game of Battleship

Battleship is a game involving ships at sea for each of two players. The ships are located in a grid in which each column of the grid is identified by a letter, and each row by a number, as shown below.

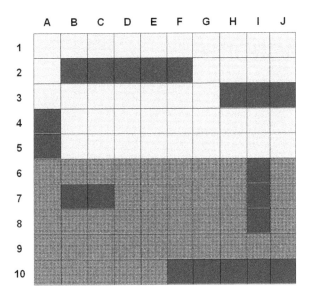

The top half of the board contains the ships of player 1, and the bottom half the ships of player 2. The darkened areas indicate the size and location of ships. Each player starts with the same number and types of ships. The location of each player's ships is determined by the player. Players take turns taking a shot at the opponent's ships by "calling out" a particular grid location. For example, if player 1 calls out "C10," no ship would be hit in this example. If, however, they were to call out "G10," then player 2's ship (on the bottom half of the board) would be hit. Each player calls out "hit" or "miss" when they are shot at by the other player. When all grid locations of a given ship have been hit, the ship is sunk, and the opponent gets the number of points based on the ship's size (given below).

The number of grid locations that a given ship takes up indicates its type and point value. A typical set of ships is given below.

Type of Ship	Size of Ships
aircraft carrier	5
battleship	4
cruiser	3
submarine	3
destroyer	2

Develop and test a Python program that can play the game of battleship. The user should be able to select the skill level. The higher the skill level, the larger the grid that is created for play. All games start with exactly one of each type of ship for each player. The locations of the computer's ships will be randomly placed. The user, however, must be able to enter the location of each of their ships. The computer's shots into the opponent's grid area should be randomly generated.

D4. Heuristic Play for the Game of Battleship

A heuristic is a general "rule of thumb" for solving a problem. Modify the Game of Battleship program from the previous problem so that the locations of the shots that the computer makes into the opponent's grid area are based on heuristics, rather than being randomly generated. Include an explanation of the heuristics developed.

## CHAPTER 5

Functions

Up until this point, we have viewed a computer program as a single series of instructions. Most programs, however, consist of distinct groups of instructions, each of which accomplishes a specific task. Such a group of instructions is referred to as a "routine." Program routines, called "functions" in Python, are fundamental building blocks in software development. We take our first look at functions in this chapter.

OBJECTIVES

After reading this chapter and completing the exercises, you will be able to:

♦ Explain the concept of a program routine

♦ Explain the concept of parameter passing

♦ Explain the concept of value-returning and non-value-returning functions

♦ Explain the notion of the side-effects of a function call

♦ Differentiate between local scope and global scope

♦ Define and use functions in Python

♦ Explain the concept of keyword and default arguments in Python

♦ Write a Python program using programmer-defined functions

♦ Effectively use trace statements for program testing

CHAPTER CONTENTS

MOTIVATION

So far, we have limited ourselves to using only the most fundamental features of Python— variables, expressions, control structures, input/print, and lists. In theory, these are the only instructions needed to write any program (that is, to perform any computation). From a *practical* point-of-view, however, these instructions alone are not enough.

The problem is one of complexity. Some smart phones, for example, contain over 10 million lines of code (see Figure 5-1). Imagine the effort needed to develop and debug software of that size. It certainly cannot be implemented by any one person, it takes a team of programmers to develop such a project.

In order to manage the complexity of a large problem, it is broken down into smaller subproblems. Then, each subproblem can be focused on and solved separately. In programming, we do the same thing. Programs are divided into manageable pieces called *program routines* (or simply *routines*). Doing so is a form of *abstraction* in which a more general, less detailed view of a system can be achieved. In addition, program routines provide the opportunity for code reuse, so that systems do not have to be created from "scratch." Routines, therefore, are a fundamental building block in software development.

In this chapter, we look at the definition and use of program routines in Python.

Term	Number of Lines of Code (LOC)	Equivalent Storage
KLOC	1,000	Application programs
MLOC	1,000,000	Operating systems / smart phones
GLOC	1,000,000,000	Number of lines of code in existence for various programming languages

FIGURE 5-1   Measures of Lines of Program Code

FUNDAMENTAL CONCEPTS

5.1   Program Routines

We first introduce the notion of a program routine. We then look in particular at program routines in Python, called *functions*. We have already been using Python's built-in functions such as len, range, and others. We now look more closely at how functions are used in Python, as well as how to define our own.

5.1.1   What Is a Function Routine?

A **routine** is a named group of instructions performing some task. A routine can be **invoked** (*called*) as many times as needed in a given program, as shown in Figure 5-2.

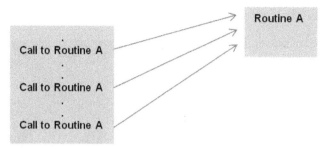

FIGURE 5-2 Program Routine

When a routine terminates, execution automatically returns to the point from which it was called. Such routines may be predefined in the programming language, or designed and implemented by the programmer.

A **function** is Python's version of a program routine. Some functions are designed to return a value, while others are designed for other purposes. We look at these two types of functions next.

A program **routine** is a named group of instructions that accomplishes some task. A routine may be **invoked** (called) as many times as needed in a given program. A **function** is Python's version of a program routine.

5.1.2 Defining Functions

In addition to the built-in functions of Python, there is the capability to define new functions. Such functions may be generally useful, or specific to a particular program. The elements of a function definition are given in Figure 5-3.

```
Function Header  ▶   def avg(n1, n2, n3):
                        ------
Function Body           ------
(suite)          ▶      ------
                        ------
```

FIGURE 5-3 Example of Python Function Definition

The first line of a function definition is the *function header*. A function header starts with the keyword `def`, followed by an identifier (`avg`), which is the function's name. The function name is followed by a comma-separated (possibly empty) list of identifiers (`n1, n2, n3`) called **formal parameters**, or simply "parameters." Following the *parameter list* is a colon (:). Following the function header is the body of the function, a suite (program block) containing the function's instructions. As with all suites, the statements must be indented at the same level, relative to the function header.

The number of items in a parameter list indicates the number of values that must be passed to the function, called **actual arguments** (or simply "arguments"), such as the variables num1, num2, and num3 below.

```
>>> num1 = 10
>>> num2 = 25
>>> num3 = 16

>>> avg(num1,num2,num3)
```

Functions are generally defined at the top of a program. However, *every function must be defined before it is called.*

We discuss more about function definition and use in the following sections.

Actual arguments, or simply "arguments," are the values passed to functions to be operated on. **Formal parameters**, or simply "parameters," are the "placeholder" names for the arguments passed.

Value-Returning Functions

A **value-returning function** is a program routine called for its return value, and is therefore similar to a mathematical function. Take the simple mathematical function $f(x) = 2x$. In this notation, "x" stands for any numeric value that function f may be applied to, for example, $f(2) = 2x = 4$. Program functions are similarly used, as illustrated in Figure 5-4.

Function avg takes three arguments (n1, n2, and n3) and returns the average of the three. The *function call* avg(10, 25, 16), therefore, is an expression that evaluates to the returned function value. This is indicated in the function's *return statement* of the form return *expr*, where *expr* may be any expression. Next, we look at a second form of program routine called for a purpose other than a returned function value.

Function Definition

Function Value

```
def avg(n1, n2, n3):
    return (n1 + n2 + n3) / 3.0
```

17.0

```
result = avg(10, 25, 16) * factor
```

Function Call

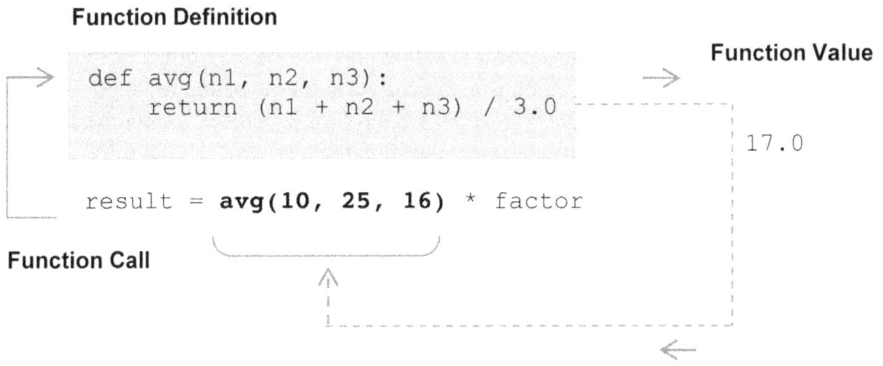

FIGURE 5-4   Call to Value-Returning Function

LET'S TRY IT

From the Python Shell, first enter the following function, making sure to indent the code as given. Hit return twice after the last line of the function is entered. Then enter the following function calls and observe the results.

```
>>> def avg(n1, n2, n3):          >>> avg(40, 10, 25)
        return (n1 + n2 + n3) / 3.0    ???

>>> avg(10, 25, 40)                >>> avg(40, 25, 10)
???                                 ???
```

A **value-returning function** in Python is a program routine called for its return value, and is therefore similar to a mathematical function.

Non-Value-Returning Functions

A **non-value-returning function** is called not for a returned value, but for its *side effects*. A **side effect** is an action other than returning a function value, such as displaying output on the screen. There is a fundamental difference in the way that value-returning and non-value-returning functions are called. A call to a value-returning function is an expression, as for the call to function avg: result = **avg(10, 25, 16)** * factor.

When non-value-returning functions are called, however, the function call is a *statement*, as shown in Figure 5-5. Since such functions do not have a return value, it is incorrect to use a call to a non-value-returning function as an expression.

Function Definition

```
def displayWelcome():
    print('This program will convert between Fahrenheit and Celsius')
    print('Enter (F) to convert Fahrenheit to Celsius')
    print('Enter (C) to convert Celsius to Fahrenheit')

# main
    .
displayWelcome()
```

FIGURE 5-5   Call to Non-Value-Returning Function

In this example, function displayWelcome is called only for the side-effect of the screen output produced. Finally, every function in Python is technically a value-returning function since *any function that does not explicitly return a function value (via a return statement) automatically returns the special value* None. We will, however, consider such functions as non-value-returning functions.

LET'S TRY IT

From the Python Shell, first enter the following function, making sure to indent the code as given. Then enter the following function calls and observe the results.

```
>>> def hello(name):              >>> name = 'John'
        print('Hello', name + '!')    >>> hello(name)
                                       ???
```

A **non-value-returning function** is a function called for its *side effects*, and not for a returned function value.

5.1.3   Let's Apply It—Temperature Conversion Program (Function Version)

The following is a program (Figure 5-7) that allows a user to convert a range of values from Fahrenheit to Celsius, or Celsius to Fahrenheit, as presented in Chapter 3. In this version, however, the program is designed with the use of functions. This program utilizes the following programming features.

➤ value-returning functions   ➤ non-value-returning functions

Example execution of the program is given in Figure 5-6.

```
This program will convert a range of temperatures
Enter (F) to convert Fahrenheit to Celsius
Enter (C) to convert Celsius to Fahrenheit

Enter selection: F
Enter starting temperature to convert: 65
Enter ending temperature to convert: 95

  Degrees  Degrees
Fahrenheit Celsius
    65.0     18.3
    66.0     18.9
    67.0     19.4
    68.0     20.0
    69.0     20.6
    70.0     21.1
    71.0     21.7
    72.0     22.2
    73.0     22.8
    74.0     23.3
    75.0     23.9
    76.0     24.4
    77.0     25.0
    78.0     25.6
    79.0     26.1
    80.0     26.7
    81.0     27.2
    82.0     27.8
    83.0     28.3
    84.0     28.9
    85.0     29.4
    86.0     30.0
    87.0     30.6
    88.0     31.1
    89.0     31.7
    90.0     32.2
    91.0     32.8
    92.0     33.3
    93.0     33.9
    94.0     34.4
    95.0     35.0
```

FIGURE 5-6   Execution of Temperature Conversion Program

```
1   # Temperature Conversion Program (Celsius-Fahrenheit / Fahrenheit-Celsius)
2
3   def displayWelcome():
4
5       print('This program will convert a range of temperatures')
6       print('Enter (F) to convert Fahrenheit to Celsius')
7       print('Enter (C) to convert Celsius to Fahrenheit\n')
8
9   def getConvertTo():
10
11      which = input('Enter selection: ')
12      while which != 'F' and which != 'C':
13          which = input('Enter selection: ')
14
15      return which
16
17  def displayFahrenToCelsius(start, end):
18
19      print('\n  Degrees', ' Degrees')
20      print('Fahrenheit', 'Celsius')
21
22      for temp in range(start, end + 1):
23          converted_temp = (temp - 32) * 5/9
24          print('  ', format(temp, '4.1f'), '    ', format(converted_temp, '4.1f'))
25
26  def displayCelsiusToFahren(start, end):
27
28      print('\n  Degrees', ' Degrees')
29      print('  Celsius', 'Fahrenheit')
30
31      for temp in range(start, end + 1):
32          converted_temp = (9/5 * temp) + 32
33          print('  ', format(temp, '4.1f'), '    ', format(converted_temp, '4.1f'))
34
35  # ---- main
36
37  # Display program welcome
38  displayWelcome()
39
40  # Get which converion from user
41  which = getConvertTo()
42
43  # Get range of temperatures to convert
44  temp_start = int(input('Enter starting temperature to convert: '))
45  temp_end = int(input('Enter ending temperature to convert: '))
46
47  # Display range of converted temperatures
48  if which == 'F':
49      displayFahrenToCelsius(temp_start, temp_end)
50  else:
51      displayCelsiusToFahren(temp_start, temp_end)
```

FIGURE 5-7   Temperature Conversion Program (Function Version)

In **lines 3–29** are defined functions displayWelcome, getConvertTo, displayFahren-ToCelsius, and displayCelsiusToFahren. The functions are directly called from the main module of the program in **lines 32–48**.

On **line 35**, the non-value-returning function displayWelcome is called. Its job is to display information about the program to the user. It does not need to be passed any arguments since it performs the same output each time it is called. Next, on **line 38**, value-returning function get-ConvertTo is called. This function also is not passed any arguments. It simply asks the user to enter either 'F' or 'C' to indicate whether they want to convert from Fahrenheit to Celsius, or Celsius to Fahrenheit. The input value entered is returned as the function value.

The instructions on **line 41–42** then prompt the user for the start and end range of temperatures to be converted. This task does not warrant the construction of a function since there are only two input instructions to accomplish this.

The final part of the program displays the converted range of temperatures. Two non-value-returning functions are defined for accomplishing this task—displayFahrenToCelsius and displayCelsiusToFahren. Each is passed two arguments, temp_start and temp_end, which indicate the range of temperature values to be converted.

What is left to look at is the implementation of each of the individual functions. The implementation of function displayWelcome (**lines 3–6**) is very straightforward. It simply contains three print instructions. Function getConvertTo (**lines 8–13**) contains a call to input followed by a while loop that performs input validation. The user is forced to enter either 'F' or 'C', and is continually prompted to re-enter as long as a value other than these two values is entered. When the loop terminates, variable which is returned by the return statement in **line 13**.

Function displayFahrenToCelsius (**lines 15–21**) and function displayCelsius-ToFahren (**lines 23–29**) are similar in design. Each contains two parameters—start and end (which are each passed actual arguments temp_start and temp_end in the main section of the program). Each first prints the appropriate column headings followed by a for statement that iterates variable temp over the requested temperature range. The conversion formula is different in each, however. Each has the same final print instruction to print out the original temperature and the converted temperature in each of the columns.

Self-Test Questions

1. The values passed in a given function call in Python are called,
   (**a**) formal parameters
   (**b**) actual arguments

2. The identifiers of a given Python function providing names for the values passed to it are called,
   (**a**) formal parameters
   (**b**) actual arguments

3. Functions can be called as many times as needed in a given program. (TRUE/FALSE)

4. When a given function is called, it is said to be,
   (**a**) subrogated   (**b**) invoked   (**c**) activated

5. Which of the following types of functions must contain a return statement,
   (**a**) value-returning functions   (**b**) non-value-returning functions

6. Value-returning function calls are,
   (**a**) expressions   (**b**) statements

7. Non-value-returning function calls are,
   (**a**) expressions   (**b**) statements

8. Which of the following types of routines is meant to produce side effects?
   (**a**) value-returning functions   (**b**) non-value-returning functions

5.2 More on Functions

In this section we further discuss issues related to function use, including more on function invocation and parameter passing.

5.2.1 Calling Value-Returning Functions

Calls to value-returning functions can be used anywhere that a function's return value is appropriate,

```
result = max(num_list) * 100
```

Here, we apply built-in function `max` to a list of integers, `num_list`. Examples of additional allowable forms of function calls are given below.

```
(a) result = max(num_list1) * max(num_list2)
(b) result = abs(max(num_list))
(c) if max(num_list) < 10:...
(d) print('Largest value in num_list is ', max(num_list))
```

The examples demonstrate that an expression may contain multiple function calls, as in (a); a function call may contain function calls as arguments, as in (b); conditional expressions may contain function calls, as in (c); and the arguments in print function calls may contain function calls, as in (d).

What if a function is to return more than one value, such as function `maxmin` to return *both* the maximum and minimum values of a list of integers? In Python, we can do this by returning the two values as a single tuple,

function definition
```
def maxmin(num_list):
        return (max(num_list), min(num_list))
```

function use
```
weekly_temps = [45, 30, 52, 58, 62, 48, 49]
```

```
(a) highlow_temps = maxmin(weekly_temps)
(b) high, low = maxmin(weekly_temps)
```

In (a) above, the returned tuple is assigned to a single variable, `highlow_temps`. Thus, `highlow_temps[0]` contains the maximum temperature, and `highlow_temps[1]` contains the minimum temperature. In (b), however, a *tuple assignment* is used. In this case, variables `high` and `low` are each assigned a value of the tuple based on the order that they appear. Thus, `high` is assigned to the tuple value at index 0, and `low` the tuple value at index 1 of the returned tuple.

Note that it does not make sense for a call to a value-returning function to be used as a statement, for example,

```
max(num_list)
```

Such a function call does not have any utility because the expression would evaluate to a value that is never used and thus is effectively "thrown away."

Finally, we can design value-returning functions that do not take any arguments, as we saw in the `getConvertTo` function of the previous temperature conversion program. Empty parentheses are used in both the function header and the function call. This is needed to distinguish the identifier as denoting a function name and not a variable.

LET'S TRY IT

Enter the definitions of functions `avg` (from section 5.1.2) and `minmax` given above. Then enter the following function calls and observe the results.

```
>>> avg(10,25,40)
???
```

```
>>> avg(10,25,40) + 10
???
```

```
>>> if avg(10,25,-40) < 0:
        print 'Invalid avg'
???
```

```
>>> avg(avg(2,4,6),8,12)
???
```

```
>>> avg(1,2,3) * avg(4,5,6)
???
```

```
>>> num_list = [10,20,30]
```

```
>>> max_min = maxmin(num_list)
>>> max_min[0]
???
```

```
>>> max_min[1]
???
```

```
>>> max, min = maxmin(num_list)
>>> max
???
```

```
>>> min
???
```

Function calls to value-returning functions can be used anywhere that a function's return value is appropriate.

5.2.2 Calling Non-Value-Returning Functions

As we have seen, non-value-returning functions are called for their side effects, and not for a returned function value. Thus, such function calls are statements, and therefore can be used anywhere that an executable statement is allowed. Consider such a function call to `display-Welcome` from Figure 5-7,

```
displayWelcome()
```

It would not make sense to treat this function call as an expression, since no meaningful value is returned (only the default return value `None`). Thus, for example, the following assignment statement would not serve any purpose,

```
welcome_displayed = displayWelcome()
```

Finally, as demonstrated by function `displayWelcome()`, functions called for their side effects can be designed to take no arguments, the same as we saw for value-returning functions. Parentheses are still included in the function call to indicate that identifier `displayWelcome` is a function name, and not a variable.

LET'S TRY IT

Enter the definition of function `hello` given below, then enter the following function calls and observe the results.

```
>>> def sayHello():                    >>> def buildHello(name):
        print('Hello!')                        return 'Hello' + name + '!'
>>> sayHello()                         >>> greeting = buildHello('Charles')
???                                    >>> print(greeting)
>>> t = sayHello()                     ???
???                                    >>> buildHello('Charles')
>>> t                                  ???
???                                    >>> buildHello()
>>> t == None                          ???
???
```

Function calls to non-value-returning functions can be used anywhere that an executable statement is allowed.

5.2.3 Parameter Passing

Now that we have discussed how functions are called, we take a closer look at the passing of arguments to functions.

Actual Arguments vs. Formal Parameters

Parameter passing is the process of passing arguments to a function. As we have seen, actual arguments are the values passed to a function's formal parameters to be operated on. This is illustrated in Figure 5-8.

```
        def ordered(n1, n2):  ◄─────────────      formal parameters
                                                   n1 and n2
            return n1 < n2


        birthYr = int(input('Year of birth? '))
        HSGradYr = int(input('Year graduated high school? '))
        colGradYr = int(input('Year graduated college? '))
        while not (ordered(birthYr, HSGradYr) and  ◄───   actual arguments
                                                          birthYr, HSGradYr
                    ordered(HSGradYr, colGradYr)):  ◄───  actual arguments
                                                          HSGradYr, colGradYr

            print('Invalid Entry - Please Reenter')
            birthYr = int(input('Year of birth? '))
            HSGradYr = int(input('Year graduated high school? '))
            colGradYr = int(input('Year graduated college? '))
```

FIGURE 5-8 Parameter Passing

Here, the values of birthYr (the user's year of birth) and HSGradYr (the user's year of high school graduation) are passed as the actual arguments to formal parameters n1 and n2. Each call is part of the same Boolean expression ordered(birthYr, HSGradYr) and ordered(HSGradYr, colGradYr). In the second function call of the expression, a *different* set of values HSGradYr and colGradYr are passed. Formal parameter names n1 and n2, however, remain the same.

Note that the correspondence of actual arguments and formal parameters is determined by the *order* of the arguments passed, and not their names. Thus, for example, it is perfectly fine to pass an actual argument named num2 to formal parameter n1, and actual argument num1 to formal parameter n2, as given in Figure 5-9.

```
def ordered(n1, n2):
    return n1 < n2


num1 = int(input('Enter your age: '))
num2 = int(input('Enter your brother's age: '))

if ordered(num1, num2):
    print('He is your older brother')
else:
    if ordered(num2, num1):
        print('He is your younger brother')
    else:
        print('Are you twins?')
```

FIGURE 5-9   Parameter Passing and Argument Names

In this example, function ordered is called once with arguments num1, num2 and a second time with arguments num2, num1. Each is a proper function call and each is what is logically needed in this instance.

LET'S TRY IT

Enter the definition of function ordered given above into the Python Shell. Then enter the following and observe the results.

```
>>> nums_1 = [5,2,9,3]          >>> ordered(max(nums_1), max(nums_2))
>>> nums_2 = [8,4,6,1]          >>> ???

                                >>> ordered(min(nums_1), max(nums_2))
                                ???
```

The correspondence of actual arguments and formal parameters is determined by the *order* of the arguments passed, and not their names.

Mutable vs. Immutable Arguments

There is an issue related to parameter passing that we have yet to address. We know that when a function is called, the current values of the arguments passed become the initial values of their corresponding formal parameters,

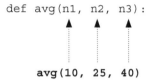

In this case, literal values are passed as the arguments to function avg. When variables are passed as actual arguments, however, as shown below,

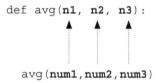

there is the question as to whether any changes to formal parameters n1, n2, and n3 in the function result in changes to the corresponding actual arguments num1, num2, and num3. In this case, function avg doesn't assign values to its formal parameters, so there is no possibility of the actual arguments being changed. Consider, however, the following function,

```
def countDown(n):
    while n >= 0:
        if (n != 0):
            print(n, '..', end='')
        else:
            print(n)
        n = n - 1
```

This function simply displays a countdown of the provided integer parameter value. For example, function call countDown(4) produces the following output,

```
4 . . 3 . . 2 . . 1 . . 0
```

What if the function call contained a variable as the argument, for example, countDown(num_tics)? Since function countDown alters the value of formal parameter n, decrementing it until it reaches the value –1, does the corresponding actual argument num_tics have value –1 as well?

```
>>> num_tics = 10
>>> countDown(num_tics)
>>> num_tics
???
```

If you try this, you will see that `num_tics` is unchanged. Now consider the following function,

```
def sumPos(nums):                >>> nums_1 = [5, -2, 9, 4, -6, 1]
    for k in range(0, len(nums)):    >>> total = sumPos(nums_1)
        if nums[k] < 0:          >>> total
            nums[k] = 0          19
                                 >>> nums_1
    return sum(nums)             [5,0,9,4,0,1]
```

Function `sumPos` returns the sum of only the positive numbers in the provided argument. It does this by first replacing all negative values in parameter `nums` with 0, then summing the list using built-in function `sum`. We see above that the corresponding actual argument `nums_1` has been altered in this case, with all of the original negative values set to 0.

The reason that there was no change in integer argument `num_tics` above but there was in list argument `nums_1` has to do with their types. Lists are mutable. Thus, arguments of type list will be altered if passed to a function that alters its value. Integers, floats, Booleans, strings, and tuples, on the other hand, are immutable. Thus, arguments of these types cannot be altered as a result of any function call.

It is generally better to design functions that do not return results through their arguments. In most cases, the result should be returned as the function's return value. What if a function needs to return more than one function value? The values can be returned in a tuple, as discussed above.

LET'S TRY IT

Enter the following and observe the results.

```
>>> num = 10          >>> nums_1 = [1,2,3]        >>> nums_2 = (1,2,3)
>>> def incr(n):      >>> def update(nums):       >>> update(nums_2)
        n = n + 1             nums[1] = nums[1] + 1  >>> ???
>>> incr(num)         >>> update(nums_1)
>>> num               >>> nums_1
???                   ???
```

Only arguments of mutable type can be altered when passed as an argument to a function. In general, function results should be through a function's return value, and not through altered parameters.

5.2.4 Keyword Arguments in Python

The functions we have looked at so far were called with a fixed number of positional arguments. A **positional argument** is an argument that is assigned to a particular parameter based on its position in the argument list, as illustrated below.

$$\text{def mortgage\_rate(amount, rate, term)}$$

$$\text{monthly\_payment} = \text{mortgage\_rate(350000, 0.06, 20)}$$

This function computes and returns the monthly mortgage payment for a given loan amount (`amount`), interest rate (`rate`), and number of years of the loan (`term`).

Python provides the option of calling any function by the use of keyword arguments. A **keyword argument** is an argument that is specified by parameter name, rather than as a positional argument as shown below (note that keyword arguments, by convention, do not have a space before or after the equal sign),

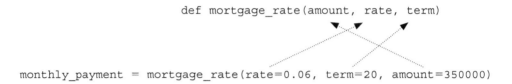

```
def mortgage_rate(amount, rate, term)
```

```
monthly_payment = mortgage_rate(rate=0.06, term=20, amount=350000)
```

This can be a useful way of calling a function if it is easier to remember the parameter names than it is to remember their order. It is possible to call a function with the use of both positional and keyword arguments. However, all positional arguments must come before all keyword arguments in the function call, as shown below.

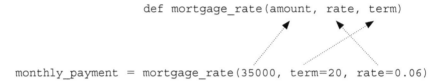

```
def mortgage_rate(amount, rate, term)
```

```
monthly_payment = mortgage_rate(35000, term=20, rate=0.06)
```

This form of function call might be useful, for example, if you remember that the first argument is the loan amount, but you are not sure of the order of the last two arguments `rate` and `term`.

LET'S TRY IT

Enter the following function definition in the Python Shell. Execute the statements below and observe the results.

```
>>> def addup(first, last):

        if first > last:
            sum = -1
        else:
            sum = 0
            for i in range(first, last+1):
                sum = sum + i
        return sum
```

```
>>> addup(1,10)
???

>>> addup(first=1, last=10)
???

>>> addup(last=10, first=1)
???
```

A **positional argument** is an argument that is assigned to a particular parameter based on its position in the argument list. A **keyword argument** is an argument that is specified by parameter name.

5.2.5   Default Arguments in Python

Python also provides the ability to assign a default value to any function parameter allowing for the use of default arguments. A **default argument** is an argument that can be optionally provided, as shown here.

```
def mortgage_rate(amount, rate, term=20)
```

```
monthly_payment = mortgage_rate(35000, 0.62)
```

In this case, the third argument in calls to function `mortgage_rate` is optional. If omitted, parameter `term` will default to the value 20 (years) as shown. If, on the other hand, a third argument is provided, the value passed replaces the default parameter value. All positional arguments must come before any default arguments in a function definition.

LET'S TRY IT

Enter the following function definition in the Python Shell. Execute the statements below and observe the results.

```
>>> def addup(first, last, incr=1):

        if first > last:
            sum = -1
        else:
            sum = 0
            for i in range(first, last+1, incr):
                sum = sum + i
        return sum
```

```
>>> addup(1,10)
???
>>> addup(1,10,2)
???
>>> addup(first=1, last=10)
???
>>> addup(incr=2, first=1,
          last=10)
???
```

A **default argument** is an argument that can be optionally provided in a given function call. When not provided, the corresponding parameter provides a default value.

5.2.6   Variable Scope

Looking back at the temperature conversion program in section 5.1.3, we see that functions `displayFahrenToCelsius` and `displayCelsiusToFahren` each contain variables named `temp` and `converted_temp`. We ask, "Do these identifiers refer to common entities, or does each function have its own distinct entities?" The answer is based on the concept of identifier *scope*, which we discuss next.

Local Scope and Local Variables

A **local variable** is a variable that is only accessible from within a given function. Such variables are said to have **local scope**. In Python, any variable assigned a value in a function becomes a local variable of the function. Consider the example in Figure 5-10.

```
def func1():
    n = 10
    print('n in func1 = ', n)

def func2():
    n = 20
    print('n in func2 before call to func1 = ', n)
    func1()
    print('n in func2 after call to func1 = ', n)
>>> func2()
n in func2 before call to func1 =  20
n in func1 =   10
n in func2 after call to func1 =  20
```

FIGURE 5-10 Defining Local Variables

Both func1 and func2 contain identifier n. Function func1 assigns n to 10, while function func2 assigns n to 20. Both functions display the value of n when called—func2 displays the value of n both *before* and *after* its call to func1. If identifier n represents the same variable, then shouldn't its value change to 10 after the call to func1? However, as shown by the output, the value of n remains 20. This is because there are *two* distinct instances of variable n, each local to the function assigned in and inaccessible from the other.

Now consider the example in Figure 5-11. In this case, the functions are the same as above except that the assignment to variable n in func1 is commented out.

```
def func1():
    # n = 10
    print('n in func1 = ', n)

def func2():
    n = 20
    print('n in func2 before call to func1 = ', n)
    func1()
    print('n in func2 after call to func1 = ', n)
>>> func2()
n in func2 before call to func1 =  20
Traceback (most recent call last):
    .
    .
    print('n in func1 = ', n)
NameError: global name 'n' is not defined
```

FIGURE 5-11 Inaccessibility of Local Variables

In this case, we get an error indicating that variable n is not defined within func1. This is because variable n defined in func2 is inaccessible from func1. (In this case, n is expected to be a *global* variable, discussed next.)

The period of time that a variable exists is called its **lifetime**. Local variables are automatically created (allocated memory) when a function is called, and destroyed (deallocated) when the function terminates. Thus, the lifetime of a local variable is equal to the duration of its function's execution. Consequently, the values of local variables are not retained from one function call to the next.

The concept of a local variable is an important one in programming. It allows variables to be defined in a function without regard to the variable names used in other functions of the program. It also allows previously written functions to be easily incorporated into a program. The use of global variables, on the other hand, brings potential havoc to programs, discussed next.

LET'S TRY IT

Enter the following function definition in the Python Shell. Execute the statements below and observe the results.

```
>>> def func1():
        some_var = 10
```

```
>>> func1()
>>> some_var
???
```

A **local variable** is a variable that is only accessible from within the function it resides. Such variables are said to have **local scope**.

Global Variables and Global Scope

A **global variable** is a variable that is defined outside of any function definition. Such variables are said to have **global scope**. This is demonstrated in Figure 5-12.

```
max = 100   # global variable

def func1(count):
    if count < max:        ◄———————  global variable max
        .                             accessed


def func2(count):
    for i in range(1, max):  ◄—————  global variable max
        .                             accessed
```

FIGURE 5-12 Access to Value of Global Variable

Variable max is defined outside func1 and func2 and therefore "global" to each. As a result, it is directly accessible by both functions. For this reason, *the use of global variables is generally considered to be bad programming style.* Although it provides a convenient way to share values among functions, *all* functions within the scope of a global variable can access and alter it. This may include functions that have no need to access the variable, but none-the-less may unintentionally alter it.

Another reason that the use of global variables is bad practice is related to code reuse. If a function is to be reused in another program, the function will not work properly if it is reliant on the existence of global variables that are nonexistent in the new program. Thus, it is good programming practice to design functions so all data needed for a function (other than its local variables) are explicitly passed as arguments, and not accessed through global variables.

> A **global variable** is a variable defined outside of any function definition. Such variables are said to have **global scope**. The use of global variables is considered bad programming practice.

5.2.7 Let's Apply It—GPA Calculation Program

The following program (Figure 5-14) computes a semester GPA and new cumulative GPA for a given student. This program utilizes the following programming features:

➤ tuple assignment

Figure 5-13 illustrates an example execution of the program.

```
This program calculates semester and cumulative GPAs

Enter total number of earned credits: 30
Enter your current cumulative GPA: 3.25

Enter grade (hit Enter if done): A
Enter number of credits: 4
Enter grade (hit Enter if done): A
Enter number of credits: 3
Enter grade (hit Enter if done): B
Enter number of credits: 3
Enter grade (hit Enter if done): B
Enter number of credits: 3
Enter grade (hit Enter if done): A
Enter number of credits: 3
Enter grade (hit Enter if done):

Your semester GPA is 3.62
Your new cumulative GPA is 3.38
>>>
```

FIGURE 5-13 Execution of GPA Calculation Program

```
1  # Semester GPA Calculation
2
3  def convertGrade(grade):
4      if grade == 'F':
5          return 0
6      else:
7          return 4 - (ord(grade) - ord('A'))
8
9  def getGrades():
10     semester_info = []
11     more_grades = True
12     empty_str = ''
13
```

FIGURE 5-14 GPA Calculation Program (*Continued*)

```
14        while more_grades:
15            course_grade = input('Enter grade (hit Enter if done): ')
16            while course_grade not in ('A','B','C','D','F',empty_str):
17                course_grade = input('Enter letter grade received: ')
18                if course_grade == empty_str:
19                more_grades = False
20            else:
21                num_credits = int(input('Enter number of credits: '))
22                semester_info.append([num_credits, course_grade])
23
24    def calculateGPA(sem_grades_info, cumm_gpa_info):
25        sem_quality_pts = 0
26        sem_credits = 0
27        current_cumm_gpa, total_credits = cumm_gpa_info
28
29        for k in range(len(sem_grades_info)):
30            num_credits, letter_grade = sem_grades_info[k]
31
32            sem_quality_pts = sem_quality_pts + \
33                            num_credits * convertGrade(letter_grade)
34
35            sem_credits = sem_credits + num_credits
36
37        sem_gpa = sem_quality_pts / sem_credits
38        new_cumm_gpa = (current_cumm_gpa * total_credits + sem_gpa * \
39                        sem_credits) /(total_credits + sem_credits)
40
41        return (sem_gpa, new_cumm_gpa)
42
43    # ---- main
44
45    # program greeting
46    print('This program calculates new semester and cummulative GPAs\n')
47
48    # get current GPA info
49    total_credits = int(input('Enter total number of earned credits: '))
50    cumm_gpa = float(input('Enter your current cummulative GPA: '))
51    cumm_gpa_info = (cumm_gpa, total_credits)
52
53    # get current semester grade info
54    print()
55    semester_grades = getGrades()
56
57    # calculate semester gpa and new cummulative gpa
58    semester_gpa, cumm_gpa = calculateGPA(semester_grades, cumm_gpa_info)
59
60    # display semester gpa and new cummulative gpa
61    print('\nYour semester GPA is', format(semester_gpa, '.2f'))
62    print('Your new cummulative GPA is', format(cumm_gpa, '.2f'))
```

FIGURE 5-14   GPA Calculation Program

The program begins with the display of the program greeting on **line 49**. **Lines 49–50** get the number of earned credits (`total_credits`) and current cumulative GPA (`cumm_gpa`) from the user. These two variables are bundled into a tuple named `cumm_gpa_info` on **line 51**. Since they are always used together, bundling these variables allows them to be passed to functions as one parameter rather than as separate parameters.

Function `getGrades` is called on **line 55**, which gets the semester grades from the user and assigns it to variable `semester_grades`. The value returned by function `getGrades` is a list of sublists, in which each sublist contains the letter grade for a given course, and the associated number of credits,

$$[['A', 3], ['B', 4], ['A', 3], ['C', 3]]$$

On **line 58**, function calculateGPA is called with arguments semester_grades and cumm_gpa_info. The function returns a tuple containing the semester GPA and new cumulative GPA of the user. A tuple assignment is used to unpack the two values into variables semester_gpa and cumm_gpa. Finally, these values are displayed on **lines 61** and **62**.

Function calculateGPA is defined in **lines 24–41** with parameters sem_grades_info and cumm_gpa_info. A GPA is calculated as the total quality points earned for a given set of courses, divided by the total number of credits the courses are worth. The number of *quality points* for a given course is defined as a course grade times the number of credits the course is worth. Thus, assuming a grade of A is worth 4 points, B worth 3 points, and grades of C, D, and F worth 2, 1 and 0 points, respectively, to calculate the semester GPA for a student receiving A's in two four-credit courses, B's in two three-credit courses, and a C in a one-credit course would be,

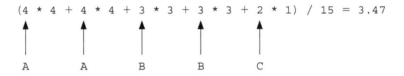

$$(4 * 4 + 4 * 4 + 3 * 3 + 3 * 3 + 2 * 1) / 15 = 3.47$$

where 15 is the total number of credits of all courses.

Similarly, in order to calculate a new cumulative GPA, the total quality points of the current cumulative GPA plus the total quality points of the new semester GPA is divided by the total number of credits the student has earned to date. Thus, to calculate a new cumulative GPA for a current cumulative GPA of 3.25 earning thirty credits, and a new semester GPA as given above (3.47 earning fifteen credits) would be,

$$(3.25 * 30 + 3.47 * 15) / 45 = 3.32$$

with 45 total earned credits. Thus, in function calculateGPA, local variables sem_quality_pts and sem_credits are initialized to zero. Their values for the courses provided in parameter sem_grades_info are computed in the for loop on **lines 29–35**. This loop also calculates the semester quality points and the number of credits of the current semester, assigned to local variables sem_quality_pts and sem_credits, respectively (at **lines 32** and **35**). Note that in the calculation of the semester quality points, function convertGrade is called to convert each letter grade to its corresponding numerical value. Finally, at the end of function calculateGPA, local variable sem_gpa is assigned to the total semester quality points divided by the total semester credits. Similarly, local variable new_cumm_gpa is assigned to the total quality points to date (current_cumm_gpa * total_credits + sem_gpa * sem_credits) divided by the total number of credits earned to date (num_credits + sem_credits). Finally, on **line 41**, a tuple is returned containing both of these computed values.

The remaining functions defined in this program are convertGrade and getGrades. Function convertGrade is passed a letter grade, and returns the corresponding numerical value. Since the ordinal value (via the ord function) of letters in Python are sequential integers, determining the difference between the ordinal value of A and the ordinal value of a given letter grade allows the numerical value of the letter grade to be determined. For example, for a letter grade of A through D, its numerical value is determined and returned as,

```
return 4 - (ord('A') - ord('A')) → return 4
return 4 - (ord('B') - ord('A')) → return 3
return 4 - (ord('C') - ord('A')) → return 2
return 4 - (ord('D') - ord('A')) → return 1
```

Since there is no letter of grade E used, a grade of F has to be handled separately.

Finally, function `getGrades` returns a list of sublists of grades and credits entered by the user, as mentioned above. Thus, local variable `semester_info` is initialized to an empty list on **line 10**. The while loop at **line 14** iterates until Boolean variable `more_grades` is `False`, initialized to `True` in **line 11**. The loop continues to iterate and append another pair of grade/credits to the list until the user hits the Enter key when prompted for a course grade (**line 15**).

Self-Test Questions

1. A function call can be made anywhere within a program in which the return type of the function is appropriate. (TRUE/FALSE)

2. An expression may contain more than one function call. (TRUE/FALSE)

3. Function calls may contain arguments that are function calls. (TRUE/FALSE)

4. All value-returning functions must contain at least one parameter. (TRUE/FALSE)

5. Every function must have at least one mutable parameter. (TRUE/FALSE)

6. A local variable in Python is a variable that is,
   (a) defined inside of every function in a given program
   (b) local to a given program
   (c) only accessible from within the function it is defined

7. A global variable is a variable that is defined outside of any function definition. (TRUE/FALSE)

8. The use of global variables is a good way to allow different functions to access and modify the same variables. (TRUE/FALSE)

ANSWERS: 1. True, 2. True, 3. True, 4. False, 5. False, 6. (c), 7. True, 8. False

COMPUTATIONAL PROBLEM SOLVING

5.3   Credit Card Calculation Program

In this section, we design, implement, and test a program that will allow us to determine the length of time needed to pay off a credit card balance, as well as the total interest paid.

5.3.1   The Problem

The problem is to generate a table showing the decreasing balance and accumulating interest paid on a credit card account for a given credit card balance, interest rate, and monthly payment, as shown in Figure 5-15.

Year	Balance	Interest Paid
1	330.18	5.17
	315.13	10.13
	299.85	14.85
	284.35	19.35
	268.62	23.62
	252.65	27.65
	236.44	31.44
	219.98	34.98
	203.28	38.28
	186.33	41.33
	169.13	44.13
2	151.66	46.66
	133.94	48.94
	115.95	50.95
	97.69	52.69
	79.15	54.15
	60.34	55.34
	41.25	56.25
	21.86	56.86
	2.19	57.19
	0.00	57.22

FIGURE 5-15 Example Execution of the Credit Card Calculation Program

5.3.2 Problem Analysis

The factors that determine how quickly a loan is paid off are the amount of the loan, the interest rate charged, and the monthly payments made. For a fixed-rate home mortgage, the monthly payments are predetermined so that the loan is paid off within a specific number of years. Therefore, the total interest that will be paid on the loan is made evident at the time the loan is signed.

For a credit card, there is only a minimum payment required each month. It is not always explicitly stated by the credit card company, however, how long it would take to pay off the card by making only the minimum payment. The minimum payment for a credit card is dependent on the particular credit card company. However, it is usually around 2–3% of the outstanding loan amount each month, and no less than twenty dollars. Thus, calculating this allows us to project the amount of time that it would take before the account balance becomes zero, as well as the total interest paid.

5.3.3 Program Design

Meeting the Program Requirements

No particular format is specified for how the output is to be displayed. All that is required is that the user be able to enter the relevant information and that the length of time to pay off the loan and the total interest paid is displayed. The user will also be given the choice of assuming the monthly payment to be the required minimum payment, or a larger specified amount.

Data Description

All that needs to be represented in this program are numerical values for the loan amount, the interest rate, and the monthly payment made. There is no need to create a data structure as the table of payments can be generated as it is displayed.

Algorithmic Approach

The only algorithm needed for this problem is the calculation of the required minimum payment. The minimum payment is usually calculated at 2% or 3% of the outstanding balance, with a lower limit of around $20. Therefore, we will assume a worst case scenario of a minimum payment calculated at 2%, with a minimum payment of $20.

Overall Program Steps

The overall steps in this program design are given in Figure 5-16.

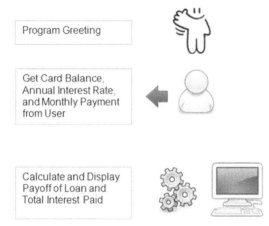

FIGURE 5-16   Overall Steps of the Credit Card
Calculation Program

5.3.4   Program Implementation and Testing

Stage 1—Developing the Overall Program Structure

We first develop and test the overall program structure given in Figure 5-17.

The program begins on **line 15** with a call to function `displayWelcome()`. Next, the current credit card balance and annual interest rate (APR) are input from the user (**lines 18–19**), each read as an integer value. Since the monthly interest rate is what will be used in the calculations, the value in `apr` is divided by 1200 (on **line 21**). This converts the value to a monthly interest rate, as well as converting it to decimal form (for example, 18% as 0.18).

The final value input from the user is the monthly payments that they wish to have the payoff calculated with. They have a choice of either going with the minimum required monthly payment, assumed to be $20 for testing purposes (**line 28**), or a specified monthly payment (**line 31**). The credit card balance, annual percentage rate, and the assumed monthly payments are passed to function `displayPayments` (on **line 34**) to calculate and display the pay down of the balance as well as the interest paid over each month of the payoff period.

```
 1  # Credit Card Calculation Program (Stage 1)
 2
 3  def displayWelcome():
 4      print('\n.... Entering function display welcome')
 5
 6  def displayPayments(balance, int_rate, monthly_payment):
 7      print('\n.... Entering function displayPayments')
 8      print('parameter balance =', balance)
 9      print('parameter int_rate =', int_rate)
10      print('parameter monthly_payment =', monthly_payment)
11
12  # ---- main
13
14  # display welcome screen
15  displayWelcome()
16
17  # get current balance and APR
18  balance = int(input('\nEnter the balance on your credit card: '))
19  apr = int(input('Enter the interest rate (APR) on the card: '))
20
21  monthly_int_rate = apr/1200
22
23  # determine monthly payment
24  response = input('Use the minimum monthly payment? (y/n): ')
25
26  if response in ('y','Y'):
27      print('Minimum payment selected')
28      monthly_payment = 20
29  else:
30      print('User-entered monthly payments selected')
31      monthly_payment = input('Enter monthly payment: ')
32
33  # display monthly payoff
34  displayPayments(balance, monthly_int_rate, monthly_payment)
```

FIGURE 5-17   Credit Card Calculation Program (Stage 1)

Functions displayWelcome (**line 3**) and displayPayments (**line 6**) consist only of **trace statements**. A trace statement prints, for testing purposes, a message indicating that a certain point in the program has been reached. Trace statements are also used to display the value of certain variables. Once this part of the program is working, we can focus on implementing the functions and further developing the main program section.

Stage 1 Testing

We show sample test runs of this version of the program in Figure 5-18.

From the test results, we see that the appropriate values are being input and passed to function displayPayments. So it looks like the overall structure of this stage of the program is working correctly.

Stage 2—Generating an Unformatted Display of Payments

We next implement function displayWelcome, and develop an initial implementation of function displayPayments, given in Figure 5-19. We remove the two print instructions that were included only for test purposes in stage 1 of the program (previously on **lines 27** and **30**).

```
.... Entering function display welcome

Enter the balance on your credit card: 1500
Enter the interest rate (APR) on the card: 18
Use the minimum monthly payment? (y/n): n
User-entered monthly payments selected
Enter monthly payment: 100

.... Entering function displayPayments
parameter balance = 1500
parameter int_rate = 0.015
parameter monthly_payment = 100
>>>
```

```
.... Entering function display welcome

Enter the balance on your credit card: 1500
Enter the interest rate (APR) on the card: 18
Use the minimum monthly payment? (y/n): y
Minimum payment selected

.... Entering function displayPayments
parameter balance = 1500
parameter int_rate = 0.015
parameter monthly_payment = 20
>>>
```

FIGURE 5-18   Output of First Stage Testing

Also, the minimum required monthly payment is computed (**lines 45–48**) rather than being set to 20.

Function `displayPayments` is where most of the work is done in the program. Therefore, we shall develop this function in stages as well. At this point, we develop the function to display, for each month during the loan payoff, the year, the current balance, and the total interest paid to date. We delay issues of screen formatting for the alignment of numbers, and only include formatting for rounding numeric values to two decimal places.

The while loop on **line 21** iterates while `balance`, passed as an argument to the function, is greater than zero. The function will keep count of the number of months (lines) displayed, as well as the total interest paid. Variables `num_months` and `total_int_paid` are used for this purpose, and are therefore initialized before the loop to 0 (**lines 11–12**). On **lines 15–18** the initial information for the calculation is displayed. Within the while loop, on **line 22**, the monthly interest paid (`monthly_int`) is computed as the current balance of that month during the payoff period (`balance`), times the monthly interest rate (`int_rate`). The total interest paid is then updated on **line 23**. On **line 24**, the new balance is computed as the current balance, plus the interest for the month, minus the monthly payment.

The next step is to display these computed values. Since time is kept track of in terms of months, the current year to be displayed is computed using integer division (**line 26**), adding one so that the first year is displayed as 1, and not 0. Then on **line 27**, the line representing the payment for the current month is displayed. Formatting is used so that all numerical values are displayed with two decimal places. Finally, variable `num_months` is incremented by one for the next iteration of the loop.

Stage 2 Testing

We test this program once for a specified monthly payment amount, and once for the option of minimum monthly payments. The results are given in Figures 5-20 and 5-21.

```
1   # Credit Card Calculation Program (Stage 2)
2
3   def displayWelcome():
4       print('This program will determine the time to pay off a credit')
5       print('card and the interest paid based on the current balance,')
6       print('the interest rate, and the monthly payments made.')
7
8   def displayPayments(balance, int_rate, monthly_payment):
9
10      # init
11      num_months = 0
12      total_int_paid = 0
13
14      # display loan info
15      print('PAYOFF SCHEDULE')
16      print('\nCredit card balance: $' + format(balance,'.2f'))
17      print('Annual interest rate:', str(1200 * int_rate)+'%')
18      print('Monthly payment: $', format(monthly_payment,'.2f'))
19
20      # display year-by-year account status
21      while balance > 0:
22          monthly_int = balance * int_rate
23          total_int_paid = total_int_paid + monthly_int
24          balance = balance + monthly_int - monthly_payment
25
26          year = (num_months // 12) + 1
27          print(year, format(balance,'.2f'), format(total_int_paid,'.2f'))
28
29          num_months = num_months + 1
30
31  # ---- main
32
33  # display welcome screen
34  displayWelcome()
35
35  # determine current balance and APR
36  balance = int(input('\nEnter the balance on your credit card: '))
37  apr = int(input('Enter the interest rate (APR) on the card: '))
38
39  monthly_int_rate = apr/1200
40
41  # determine monthly payment
42  response = input('Use the minimum monthly payment? (y/n): ')
43
44  if response in ('y','Y'):
45      if balance < 1000:
46          monthly_payment = 20
47      else:
48          monthly_payment = balance * .02
49  else:
50      monthly_payment = input('Enter monthly payment: ')
51
52  # display monthly payoff
53  displayPayments(balance, monthly_int_rate, monthly_payment)
```

FIGURE 5-19 Credit Card Calculation Program (Stage 2)

```
This program will determine the time to pay off a credit
card and the interest paid based on the current balance,
the interest rate, and the monthly payments made.

Enter the balance on your credit card: 1500
Enter the annual interest rate (APR) on the card: 18
Use the minimum monthly payment? (y/n): n
Enter monthly payment: 100
PAYOFF SCHEDULE

Credit card balance: $1500.00
Annual interest rate: 18.0%
Traceback (most recent call last):
  File "C:\My Python Programs\CreditCardCalc-Stage2 with
error.py", line 53, in <module>
    displayPayments(balance, monthly_int_rate, monthly_payment)
  File "C:\My Python Programs\CreditCardCalc-Stage2 with
error.py", line 18, in displayPayments
    print('Monthly payment: $', format(monthly_payment,'.2f'))
ValueError: Unknown format code 'f' for object of type 'str'
>>>
```

FIGURE 5-20 Output of Second Stage Testing (User-Entered Payment)

```
This program will determine the time to pay off a credit
card and the interest paid based on the current balance,
the interest rate, and the monthly payments made.

Enter the balance on your credit card: 350
Enter the annual interest rate (APR) on the card: 18
Use the minimum monthly payment? (y/n): y
PAYOFF SCHEDULE

Credit card balance: $350.00
Annual interest rate: 18.0%
Monthly payment: $ 20.00
1 335.25 5.25
1 320.28 10.28
1 305.08 15.08
1 289.66 19.66
1 274.00 24.00
1 258.11 28.11
1 241.99 31.99
1 225.62 35.62
1 209.00 39.00
1 192.13 42.13
1 175.02 45.02
1 157.64 47.64
2 140.01 50.01
2 122.11 52.11
2 103.94 53.94
2 85.50 55.50
2 66.78 56.78
2 47.78 57.78
2 28.50 58.50
2 8.93 58.93
2 -10.94 59.06
>>>
```

FIGURE 5-21 Output of Second Stage Testing (Minimum Payment)

Clearly, there is something wrong with this version of the program. The `ValueError` generated in Figure 5-20 indicates that the format specifier `.2f` is an unknown format code for a string type value, referring to **line 18**. Thus, this must be referring to variable `monthly_payment`. But that should be a numeric value, and not a string value! How could it have become a string type? Let's check if the problem also occurs when selecting the minimum payment option (Figure 5-21).

In this case the program works. Since the problem only occurred when the user entered the monthly payment (as opposed to the minimum payment option), we next try to determine what differences there are in the program related to the assignment of variable `monthly_payment`.

```
# determine monthly payment
response = input('Use the minimum monthly payment? (y/n): ')
if response in ('y', 'Y'):
    if balance < 1000:
        monthly_payment = 20
    else:
        monthly_payment = balance * .02
else:
    monthly_payment = input('Enter monthly payment: ')
```

When the user selects the minimum monthly payment option, variable `monthly_payment` is set to integer value `20` (or 2% of the current balance if balance is greater than 1000). Otherwise, its value is input from the user. This variable is not redefined anywhere else in the program. Since the variable `monthly_payment` is not a local variable, we can display its value directly from the Python shell,

```
>>> monthly_payment
'140'
```

It *is* a string value. We immediately realize that the input value for variable `monthly_payment` was not converted to an integer type, and was thus left as a string type! We fix this problem by replacing the line with the following,

```
monthly_payment = int(input('Enter monthly payment: '))
```

This explains why the problem did not appear in the testing of stage 1 of the program. In that version, variable `monthly_payment` was never formatted as a numeric value, and also never used in a numerical calculation (both of which would have generated an error).

At this point, we execute a number of test cases for various initial balances, interest rates, and monthly payments. The result is given in Figure 5-22, checked against online loan payoff calculator tools. We next move on to the final stage of program development.

Stage 3—Formatting the Displayed Output

In this final stage of the program, input error checking is added. The program is also modified to allow the user to continue to enter various monthly payments for recalculating a given balance payoff. Output formatting is added to make the displayed information more readable. Finally, we correct the display of a negative balance at the end of the payoff schedule, as appears in Figure 5-21. The final version of the program is given in Figure 5-23.

Payoff Information			Expected Results		Actual Results		
Balance	Interest Rate	Monthly Payment	Num Months	Interest Paid	Num Months	Interest Paid	Evaluation
250	18%	$20 (min)	14	28.93	14	28.93	Passed
600	14%	$20 (min)	38	142.80	38	142.80	Passed
12,000	20%	$240 (min)	109	14,016.23	109	14,016.23	Passed
250	18%	$40	7	14.54	7	14.54	Passed
600	14%	$50	14	50.15	14	50.15	Passed
12,000	20%	$400	42	4,773.98	42	4,773.98	Passed

FIGURE 5-22   Test Cases for Stage 2 of the Credit Card Calculation Program

```
1  # Credit Card Calculation Program (Final Version)
2
3  def displayWelcome():
4      print('This program will determine the time to pay off a credit')
5      print('card and the interest paid based on the current balance,')
6      print('the interest rate, and the monthly payments made.')
7
8  def displayPayments(balance, int_rate, monthly_payment):
9
10     # init
11     num_months = 0
12     total_int_paid = 0
13     payment_num = 1
14
15     empty_year_field = format(' ', '8')
16
17     # display heading
18     print('\n', format('PAYOFF SCHEDULE','>20'))
19     print(format('Year','>10') + format('Balance','>10') +
20           format('Payment Num', '>14') + format('Interest Paid','>16'))
21
22     # display year-by-year account status
23     while balance > 0:
24         monthly_int = balance * int_rate
25         total_int_paid = total_int_paid + monthly_int
26
27         balance = balance + monthly_int - monthly_payment
28
29         if balance < 0:
30             balance = 0
31
32         if num_months % 12 == 0:
33             year_field = format(num_months // 12 + 1, '>8')
34         else:
35             year_field = empty_year_field
36
37         print(year_field + format(balance, '>12,.2f') +
38               format(payment_num, '>9') +
39               format(total_int_paid, '>17,.2f'))
40
41         payment_num = payment_num + 1
42         num_months = num_months + 1
43
```

FIGURE 5-23   Final Stage of the Credit Card Calculation Program (*Continued*)

```
44  # ---- main
45
46  # display welcome screen
47  displayWelcome()
48
49  # get current balance and APR
50  balance = int(input('\nEnter the balance on your credit card: '))
51  apr = int(input('Enter the interest rate (APR) on the card: '))
52
53  monthly_int_rate = apr/1200
54
55  yes_response = ('y','Y')
56  no_response = ('n','N')
57
58  calc = True
59  while calc:
60
61      # calc minimum monthly payment
62      if balance < 1000:
63          min_monthly_payment = 20
64      else:
65          min_monthly_payment = balance * .02
66
67      # get monthly payment
68      print('\nAssuming a minimum payment of 2% of the balance ($20 min)')
69      print('Your minimum payment would be',
70              format(min_monthly_payment, '.2f'),'\n')
71
72      response = input('Use the minimum monthly payment? (y/n): ')
73      while response not in yes_response + no_response:
74          response = input('Use the minimum monthly payment? (y/n): ')
75
76      if response in yes_response:
77          monthly_payment = min_monthly_payment
78      else:
79          acceptable_payment = False
80
81          while not acceptable_payment:
82              monthly_payment = int(input('\nEnter monthly payment: '))
83
84              if monthly_payment < balance * .02:
85                  print('Minimum payment of 2% of balance required ($' +
86                          str(balance * .02) + ')')
87
88              elif monthly_payment < 20:
89                  print('Minimum payment of $20 required')
90              else:
91                  acceptable_payment = True
92
```

FIGURE 5-23   Final Stage of the Credit Card Calculation Program (*Continued*)

```
 93        # check if single payment pays off balance
 94        if monthly_payment >= balance:
 95            print('* This payment amount would pay off your balance *')
 96        else:
 97            # display month-by-month balance payoff
 98            displayPayments(balance, monthly_int_rate, monthly_payment)
 99
100            # calculate again with another monthly payment?
101            again = input('\nRecalculate with another payment? (y/n): ')
102            while again not in yes_response + no_response:
103                again = input('Recalculate with another payment? (y/n): ')
104
105            if again in yes_response:
106                calc = True   # continue program
107                print('\n\nFor your current balance of $' + str(balance))
108            else:
109                calc = False  # terminate program
```

FIGURE 5-23   Final Stage of the Credit Card Calculation Program

The first set of changes in the program provides some input error checking. (We will address means of more complete error checking in Chapter 7.) In **lines 55–56**, tuples yes_response and no_response are defined. These are used to check if input from the user is an appropriate yes/no response. For example, the while statement on **line 73** checks that the input from **line 72** is either 'y', 'Y' ,'n', or 'N',

```
while response not in yes_response + no_response:
```

by checking if response is in the concatenation of tuples yes_response and no_response. For determining the specific response, the tuples can be used individually (**line 76**),

```
if response in yes_response:
```

Similar input error checking is done on **line 101**.

The next set of changes allows a number of payoff schedules for an entered balance to be calculated. A while statement is added at **line 59**, with its condition based on the value of Boolean variable calc (initialized to True on **line 58**). To accommodate the recalculation of payoff schedules, variables num_months, total_int_paid and payment_num are each reset to 0 in function displayPayments (**lines 11–13**).

Output formatting is added in function displayPayments. On **line 18**, 'PAYOFF SCHEDULE' is displayed right-justified within a field of twenty. On **lines 19–20**, the column headings are displayed with appropriate field widths. **Lines 37–39** display the balance, payment number and interest of each month, aligned under the column headings. **Lines 32–35** ensure that each year is displayed only once. Finally, in **lines 29–30** variable balance is set to zero if it becomes negative so that negative balances are not displayed.

Stage 3 Testing

We give example output of this version of the program for both a payoff using the required minimum monthly payment, and for a user-entered monthly payment in Figures 5-24 and 5-25.

Figure 5-25 depicts a portion of the output for the sake of space. We run the same set of test cases used in the testing of the previous (stage 2) version of the program, given in Figure 5-26.

Based on these results, we can assume that the program is functioning properly.

```
This program will determine the time to pay off a credit
card and the interest paid based on the current balance,
the interest rate, and the monthly payments made.

Enter the balance on your credit card: 1500
Enter the interest rate (APR) on the card: 18

Assuming a minimum payment of 2% of the balance ($20 min)
Your minimum payment would be 30.00

Use the minimum monthly payment? (y/n): n

Enter monthly payment: 100

      PAYOFF SCHEDULE
      Year   Balance    Payment Num     Interest Paid
       1     1,422.50        1               22.50
             1,343.84        2               43.84
             1,264.00        3               64.00
             1,182.95        4               82.95
             1,100.70        5              100.70
             1,017.21        6              117.21
               932.47        7              132.47
               846.45        8              146.45
               759.15        9              159.15
               670.54       10              170.54
               580.60       11              180.60
               489.31       12              189.31
       2       396.65       13              196.65
               302.60       14              202.60
               207.13       15              207.13
               110.24       16              210.24
                11.89       17              211.89
                 0.00       18              212.07

Recalculate with another payment? (y/n): n
>>>
```

FIGURE 5-24 Output of Third Stage Testing (User-Entered Payment)

```
This program will determine the time to pay off a credit
card and the interest paid based on the current balance,
the interest rate, and the monthly payments made.

Enter the balance on your credit card: 1500
Enter the interest rate (APR) on the card: 18

Assuming a minimum payment of 2% of the balance ($20 min)
Your minimum payment would be 30.00

Use the minimum monthly payment? (y/n): y

     PAYOFF SCHEDULE
     Year   Balance    Payment Num   Interest Paid
       1    1,492.50        1             22.50
            1,484.89        2             44.89
            1,477.16        3             67.16
            1,469.32        4             89.32
                 .          .              .
                 .          .              .
                 .          .              .
       7     517.51        73          1,207.51
             495.28        74          1,215.28
             472.70        75          1,222.70
             449.79        76          1,229.79
                 .          .              .
                 .          .              .
                 .          .              .
       8     227.51        85          1,277.51
             200.92        86          1,280.92
             173.94        87          1,283.94
             146.55        88          1,286.55
             118.74        89          1,288.74
              90.53        90          1,290.53
              61.88        91          1,291.88
              32.81        92          1,292.81
               3.30        93          1,293.30
               0.00        94          1,293.35

Recalculate with another payment? (y/n): n
>>>
```

FIGURE 5-25 Output of Third Stage Testing (Minimum Payment)

Payoff Information			Expected Results		Actual Results		Evaluation
Balance	Interest Rate	Monthly Payment	Num Months	Interest Paid	Num Months	Interest Paid	
250	18%	$20 (min)	14	28.93	14	28.93	Passed
600	14%	$20 (min)	38	142.80	38	142.80	Passed
12,000	20%	$240 (min)	109	14,016.23	109	14,016.23	Passed
250	18%	$40	7	14.54	7	14.54	Passed
600	14%	$50	14	50.15	14	50.15	Passed
12,000	20%	$400	42	4,773.98	42	4,773.98	Passed

FIGURE 5-26 Test Cases for Stage 3 of the Credit Card Calculation Program

CHAPTER SUMMARY

General Topics

Program Routines
Value-Returning vs. Non-Value-Returning Functions
Side Effects (of Function Calls)
Parameter Passing: Actual Arguments vs.
    Formal Parameters
Local Scope and Local Variables
Global Scope and Global Variables
Variable Lifetime

Python-Specific Programming Topics

Defining Functions in Python
Built-in Functions of Python
Value-Returning and Non-Value-Returning
    Functions in Python
Tuple Assignment in Python
Mutable vs. Immutable Arguments in Python
Local vs. Global Variables in Python

CHAPTER EXERCISES

Section 5.1

1. Function `avg` returns the average of three values, as given in the chapter. Which of the following statements, each making calls to function `avg`, are valid? (Assume that all variables are of numeric type.)

    (a) `result = avg(n1, n2)`

    (b) `result = avg(n1, n2, avg(n3, n4, n5))`

    (c) `result = avg(n1 + n2, n3 + n4, n5 + n6)`

    (d) `print(avg(n1, n2, n3))`

    (e) `avg(n1, n2, n3)`

2. Which of the following statements, each involving calls to function `displayWelcome` displaying a welcome message on the screen as given in the chapter, are valid?

    (a) `print(displayWelcome)`

    (b) `displayWelcome`

    (c) `result = displayWelcome()`

    (d) `displayWelcome()`

Section 5.2

3. Suppose there are nine variables, each holding an integer value as shown below, for which the average of the largest value in each line of variables is to be computed.

    ```
    num1 = 10      num2 = 20      num3 = 25      |   max1 = 25
    num4 = 5       num5 = 15      num6 = 35      |   max2 = 35
    num7 = 20      num8 = 30      num9 = 25      |   max3 = 30

    average = (max1 + max2 + max3) / 3.0
            = (25 + 35 + 30) / 3.0
            = 30.0
    ```

    Using functions `avg` and `max`, give an expression that computes the average as shown above.

4. Assume that there exists a Boolean function named `isLeapYear` that determines if a given year is a leap year or not. Give an appropriate if statement that prints "Year is a Leap Year" if the year passed is a leap year, and "Year is Not a Leap Year" otherwise, for variable `year`.

5. For the following function definition and associated function calls,

```
def somefunction(n1, n2):
    .
    .
    .
# main
num1 = 10
somefunction(num1, 15)
```

(a) List all the formal parameters.
(b) List all the actual arguments.

6. For the following function, indicate whether each function call is proper or not. If improper, explain why.

```
def gcd(n1, n2):
```
function gcd calculates the greatest common divisor of n1 and n2, with the requirement that n1 be less than or equal to n2, and n1 and n2 are integer values.

(a)
```
a = 10
b = 20
result = gcd(a, b)
```
(b)
```
a = 10.0
b = 20
result = gcd(a, b)
```
(c)
```
a = 20
b = 10
result = gcd(b, a)
```
(d)
```
a = 10
b = 20
c = 30
result = gcd(gcd(a, b), c)
```
(e)
```
a = 10
b = 20
c = 30
print(gcd(a, gcd(c, b)))
```

PYTHON PROGRAMMING EXERCISES

P1. Write a Python function named `zeroCheck` that is given three integers, and returns true if any of the integers is 0, otherwise it returns false.

P2. Write a Python function named `ordered3` that is passed three integers, and returns true if the three integers are in order from smallest to largest, otherwise it returns false.

P3. Write a Python function named `modCount` that is given a positive integer, n, and a second positive integer, m <= n, and returns how many numbers between 1 and n are evenly divisible by m.

P4. Write a Python function named `helloWorld` that displays "Hello World, my name is *name*", for any given name passed to the routine.

P5. Write a Python function named `printAsterisks` that is passed a positive integer value n, and prints out a line of n asterisks. If n is greater than 75, then only 75 asterisks should be displayed.

P6. Write a Python function named `getContinue` that displays to the user "Do you want to continue (y/n): ", and continues to prompt the user until either uppercase or lowercase `'y'` or `'n'` is entered, returning (lowercase) `'y'` or `'n'` as the function value.

P7. Implement a Python function that is passed a list of numeric values and a particular threshold value, and returns the list with all values above the given threshold value set to 0. The list should be altered as a side effect to the function call, and not by function return value.

P8. Implement the Python function described in question P7 so that the altered list is returned as a function value, rather than by side effect.

PROGRAM MODIFICATION PROBLEMS

M1. Temperature Conversion Program: Adding Kelvin Scale
Modify the Temperature Conversion program in section 5.1.3 so that it allows the user to select temperature conversion to include degrees Kelvin, in addition to degrees Fahrenheit and degrees Celsius. Include input error checking for inappropriate temperature values. (NOTE: Refer to questions M1 and M2 from Chapter 3.)

M2. GPA Calculation Program: Accommodating First-Semester Students
Modify the GPA Calculation program in section 5.2.7 so that it asks the student if this is their first semester. If so, the program should only prompt for their current semester grades, and not their cumulative GPA and total earned credits, and display their semester GPA and cumulative GPA accordingly.

M3. GPA Calculation Program: Allowing for Plus/Minus Grading
Modify the GPA Calculation program in section 5.2.7 so that it is capable of calculating a GPA for plus/minus letter grades: A, A−, B+, B, B−, and so forth.

M4. Credit Card Calculation Program: Summarized Output
Modify the Credit Card Calculation program in section 5.3 so that the user is given the option of either displaying the balance and interest paid month-by-month as currently written, or to simply have the total number of months and the total interest paid without the month-by-month details.

M5. Credit Card Calculation Program: Adjustable Minimum Payment
Modify the Credit Card Calculation program in section 5.3 so that the user can enter the percentage from which the minimum monthly payment is calculated. Also modify the program so that this minimum payment percentage is displayed along with the other credit card related information.

M6. Credit Card Calculation Program: Recalculation with New Balance
Modify the Credit Card Calculation program in section 5.3 so that the program will allow the user to recalculate a new payoff schedule for a new entered balance.

PROGRAM DEVELOPMENT PROBLEMS

D1. Metric Conversion Program
Develop and test a Python program that allows the user to convert between the metric measurements of millimeter, centimeter, meter, kilometer, and inches, feet, yards, and miles. The program should be written so that any one measurement can be converted to the other.

D2. GPA Projection Program
Develop and test a Python program that lets the user enter their current cumulative GPA, their total credits earned, and the number of credits they are currently taking. The program should then request from the

user a target cumulative GPA that they wish to achieve, and display the GPA of the current semester needed to achieve it.

D3. Tic-Tac-Toe Two-Player Program

Develop and test a Python program that lets two players play tic-tac-toe. Let player 1 be X and player 2 be O. Devise a method for each player to indicate where they wish to place their symbol. The program should terminate if either there is a winner, or if the game results in a tie. The tic-tac-toe board should be displayed after every move as shown below.

```
X  ---  X
O   O   --
X   X   O
```

D4. Tic-Tac-Toe Automated Play

Develop and test a Python program that plays tic-tac-toe against the user. Develop an appropriate strategy of play and implement it in your program. The program should be designed to allow the user to continue to play new games until they decide to quit. The program should display the total number of wins by the computer versus the player at the start of each new game.

## CHAPTER 6

Objects and Their Use

In procedural programming, functions are the primary building blocks of program design. In object-oriented programming, objects are the fundamental building blocks in which functions (methods) are a component. We first look at the use of individual software objects in this chapter, and in Chapter 10 look at the use of objects in object-oriented design.

OBJECTIVES

After reading this chapter and completing the exercises, you will be able to:

♦ Explain the concept of an object

♦ Explain the difference between a reference and dereferenced value

♦ Describe the use of object references

♦ Explain the concept of memory allocation and deallocation

♦ Describe automatic garbage collection

♦ Explain the fundamental features of turtle graphics

♦ Effectively use objects in Python

♦ Develop simple turtle graphics programs in Python

CHAPTER CONTENTS

MOTIVATION

An object is one of the first concepts that a baby understands during its development. They understand an object as something that has a set of *attributes* ("big," "red" ball) and a related set of *behaviors* (it rolls, it bounces).

"Billard," No-w-ay, used under a Creative Commons Attribution 2.5 Generic license

The idea of incorporating "objects" into a programming language came out of work in computer simulation. Given the prevalence of objects in the world, it was natural to provide the corresponding notion of an object within a simulation program.

In the early 1970s, Alan Kay at Xerox PARC (Palo Alto Research Center) fully evolved the notion of object-oriented programming with the development of a programming language called Smalltalk. The language became the inspiration for the development of graphical user interfaces (GUIs)—the primary means of interacting with computers today. Before that, all interaction was through typed text. In fact, it was a visit to Xerox PARC by Steve Jobs of Apple Computers that led to the development of the first commercially successful GUI-based computer, the Apple Macintosh in 1984. Figure 6-1 lists some of the most commonly used programming languages and whether they support procedural (imperative) programming, object-oriented programming, or both. In this chapter, we look at the creation and use of objects in Python.

Programming Language	Programming Paradigm Supported	
	Procedural	Object-oriented
C (early 1970s)	X	
Smalltalk (1980)		X
C++ (mid 1980s)	X	X
Python (early 1990s)	X	X
Java (1995)		X
Ruby (mid 1990s)	X	X
C # (2000)	X	X

FIGURE 6-1   Common Programming Languages Supporting Procedural and/or Object-Oriented Programming

FUNDAMENTAL CONCEPTS

6.1   Software Objects

Objects are the fundamental component of object-oriented programming. Although we have not yet stated it, *all* values in Python are represented as objects. This includes, for example, lists, as well as numeric values. We discuss object-oriented programming in Chapter 10. In this chapter, we discuss what objects are and how they are used.

6.1.1 What Is an Object?

The notion of software objects derives from objects in the real world. All objects have certain *attributes* and *behavior*. The attributes of a car, for example, include its color, number of miles driven, current location, and so on. Its behaviors include driving the car (changing the number of miles driven attribute) and painting the car (changing its color attribute), for example.

Similarly, an **object** contains a set of attributes, stored in a set of **instance variables**, and a set of functions called **methods** that provide its behavior. For example, when sorting a list in procedural programming, there are two distinct entities—a sort function and a list to pass it, as depicted in Figure 6-2.

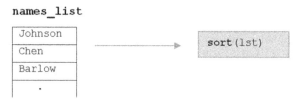

FIGURE 6-2   Procedural Programming Approach

In object-oriented programming, the sort routine would be *part of* the object containing the list, depicted in Figure 6-3.

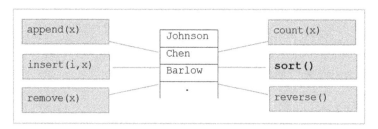

FIGURE 6-3   Object names_list

Here, names_list is an object instance of the Python built-in list type. All list objects contain the same set of methods. Thus, names_list is sorted by simply calling that object's sort method,

```
names_list.sort()
```

The period is referred to as the *dot operator*, used to select a member of a given object—in this case, the sort method. Note that no arguments are passed to sort. That is because methods operate on the data of the object that they are part of. Thus, the sort method does not need to be told which list to sort.

Suppose there were another list object called part_numbers, containing a list of automobile part numbers. Since all list objects behave the same, part_numbers would contain the identical set of methods as names_list. The data that they would operate on, however, would be different. Thus, two objects of the same type differ only in the particular set of values that each holds. This is depicted in Figure 6-4.

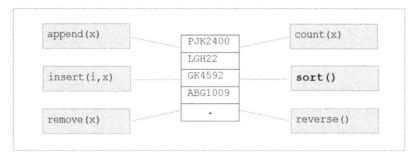

FIGURE 6-4   Object `part_numbers`

In order to sort *this* list, therefore, the `sort` method of object `part_numbers` is called,

`part_numbers.sort()`

The `sort` routine is the same as the `sort` routine of object `names_list`. In this case, however, the list of part numbers is sorted instead. Methods `append`, `insert`, `remove`, `count`, and `reverse` also provide additional functionality for lists, as was discussed in Chapter 4. We next discuss the way that objects are represented in Python.

> An **object** contains a set of attributes, stored in a set of **instance variables**, and a set of functions called **methods** that provide its behavior.

6.1.2   Object References

In this section we look at how objects are represented (which all values in Python are), and the effect it has on the operations of assignment and comparison, as well as parameter passing.

References in Python

In Python, objects are represented as a *reference* to an object in memory, as shown in Figure 6-5.

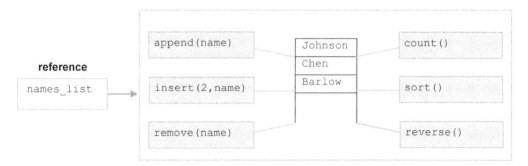

FIGURE 6-5   Object Reference

A **reference** is a value that references, or "points to," the location of another entity. Thus, when a new object in Python is created, *two* entities are stored—the object, and a variable holding a reference to the object. All access to the object is through the reference value. This is depicted in Figure 6-6.

numeric   n = 10

string   name = 'Chen'

list   nums = [10, 20, 30]

FIGURE 6-6   Object References to Python Values

The value that a reference points to is called the **dereferenced value**. This is the value that the variable represents, as shown in Figure 6-7.

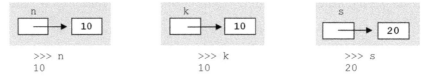

```
>>> n          >>> k          >>> s
10             10             20
```

FIGURE 6-7   Variables' Dereferenced Values

We can get the reference value of a variable (that is, the location in which the corresponding object is stored) by use of **built-in function id**.

```
>>> id(n)        >>> id(k)        >>> id(s)
505498136        505498136        505498296
```

We see that the dereferenced values of n and k, 10, is stored in the same memory location (505498136), whereas the dereferenced value of s, 20, is stored in a different location (505498296). Even though n and k are each separately assigned literal value 10, they reference the *same instance* of 10 in memory (505498136). We would expect there to be separate instances of 10 stored. Python is using a little cleverness here. Since integer values are immutable, it assigned both n and k to the same instance. This saves memory and reduces the number of reference locations that Python must maintain. From the programmer's perspective however, they can be treated as if they are separate instances.

LET'S TRY IT

From the Python Shell, first enter the following and observe the results.

```
>>> n = 10                    >>> n = 20
>>> k = 20                    >>> k = 20

>>> id(n)                     >>> id(n)
???                           ???
>>> id(k)                     >>> id(k)
???                           ???
```

A **reference** is a value that references, or "points to," the location of another entity. The value that a reference points to is called the **dereferenced value**. A variable's reference value can be determined with **built-in function** id.

The Assignment of References

With our current understanding of references, consider what happens when variable n is assigned to variable k, depicted in Figure 6-8.

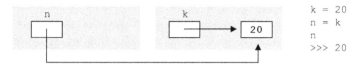

FIGURE 6-8   The Assignment of References

When variable n is assigned to k, it is the *reference value* of k that is assigned, not the dereferenced value 20, as shown in Figure 6-8. This can be determined by use of the built-in id function, as demonstrated below.

```
>>> id(k)              >>> id(k) == id(n)
505498136              True

>>> id(n)              >>> n is k
505498136              True
```

Thus, to verify that two variables refer to the same object instance, we can either compare the two id values by use of the comparison operator, or make use of the provided is operator (which performs id(k) == id(n)).

Thus, both n and k reference the same instance of literal value 20. This occurred in the above example when n and k were *separately* assigned 20 because integers are an immutable type, and Python makes attempts to save memory. In this case, however, n and k reference the same instance of 20 because assignment in Python assigns reference values. We must be aware of the fact, therefore, that when assigning variables referencing mutable values, such as lists, both variables reference the same list instance as well. We will discuss the implication of this next.

Finally, we look at what happens when the value of one of the two variables n or k is changed, as depicted in Figure 6-9.

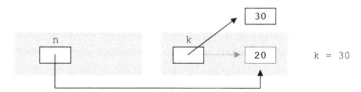

FIGURE 6-9   Reassignment of Reference Value

Here, variable k is assigned a reference value to a *new* memory location holding the value 30. The previous memory location that variable k referenced is retained since variable n is still referencing it. As a result, n and k point to different values, and therefore are no longer equal.

LET'S TRY IT

From the Python Shell, first enter the following and observe the results.

```
>>> k = 10                              >>> k = 30
>>> n = k                               >>> id(k)
>>> id(k)                               ???
???                                     >>> id(n)
>>> id(n)                               ???
???                                     >>> id(k) == id(n)
>>> id(k) == id(n)                      ???
???                                     >>> n is k
>>> n is k                              ???
???
```

When one variable is assigned to another, it is the *reference value* that is assigned, not the dereferenced value.

Memory Deallocation and Garbage Collection

Next we consider what happens when in addition to variable k being reassigned, variable n is reassigned as well. The result is depicted in Figure 6-10.

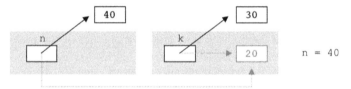

FIGURE 6-10 Inaccessible Values

After n is assigned to 40, the memory location storing integer value 20 is no longer referenced—thus, it can be *deallocated*. To **deallocate** a memory location means to change its status from "currently in use" to "available for reuse." In Python, memory deallocation is automatically performed by a process called *garbage collection*. **Garbage collection** is a method of automatically determining which locations in memory are no longer in use and deallocating them. The garbage collection process is ongoing during the execution of a Python program.

Garbage collection is a method of determining which locations in memory are no longer in use, and deallocating them.

List Assignment and Copying

Now that we understand the use of references in Python, we can revisit the discussion on copying lists from Chapter 4. We know that when a variable is assigned to another variable referencing a list, each variable ends up referring to the *same instance* of the list in memory, depicted in Figure 6-11.

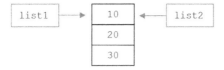

FIGURE 6-11   List Assignment

Thus, any changes to the elements of `list1` results in changes to `list2`,

```
>>> list1[0] = 5
>>> list2[0]
5
```

We also learned that a copy of a list can be made as follows,

```
>>> list2 = list(list1)
```

`list()` is referred to as a *list constructor*. The result of the copying is depicted in Figure 6-12.

FIGURE 6-12   Copying of Lists by Use of the List Constructor

A copy of the list structure has been made. Therefore, changes to the list elements of `list1` will *not* result in changes in `list2`.

```
>>> list1[0] = 5
>>> list2[0]
10
```

The situation is different if a list contains sublists, however.

```
>>> list1 = [[10, 20], [30, 40], [50, 60]]
>>> list2 = list(list1)
```

The resulting list structure after the assignment is depicted in Figure 6-13.

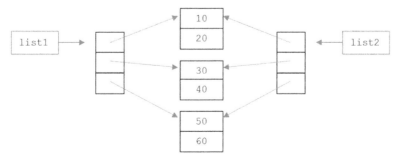

FIGURE 6-13   Shallow Copy List Structures

We see that although copies were made of the top-level list structures, the elements *within* each list were not copied. This is referred to as a **shallow copy**. Thus, if a top-level element of one list is reassigned, for example `list1[0] = [70, 80]`, the other list would remain unchanged, as shown in Figure 6-14.

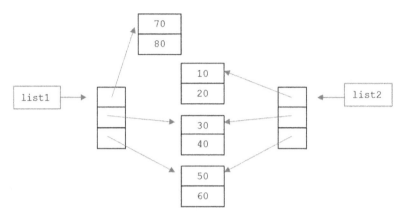

FIGURE 6-14 Top-Level Reassignment of Shallow Copies

If, however, a change to one of the sublists is made, for example, `list1[0][0] = 70`, the corresponding change would be made in the other list. That is, `list2[0][0]` would be equal to 70 also, as depicted in Figure 6-15.

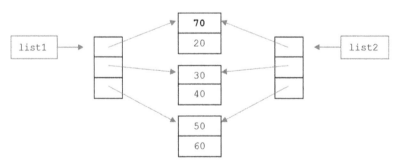

FIGURE 6-15 Sublevel Reassignment of Shallow Copies

A **deep copy** operation of a list (structure) makes a copy of the *complete* structure, including sublists. (Since immutable types cannot be altered, immutable parts of the structure may not be copied.) Such an operation can be performed with the `deepcopy` method of the `copy` module,

```
>>> import copy
>>> list2 = copy.deepcopy(list1)
```

The result of this form of copying is given in Figure 6-16.

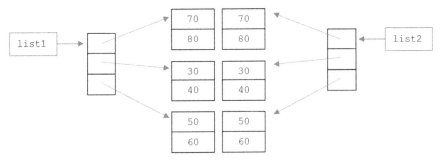

FIGURE 6-16 Deep Copy List Structures

Thus, the reassignment of any part (top level or sublist) of one list will not result in a change in the other. It is up to you as the programmer to determine which form of copy is needed for lists, and other mutable types, such as dictionaries and sets covered in Chapter 9.

LET'S TRY IT

From the Python Shell, enter the following and observe the results.

```
>>> import copy

>>> list1 = [10, 20, 30, 40]
>>> list2 = list1
>>> id(list1) == id(list2)
???
>>> list1[0] = 60
>>> list1
???
>>> list2
???

>>> list1 = [10, 20, 30, [40]]
>>> list2 = list(list1)
>>> id(list1) == id(list2)
???
>>> list1[0] = 60
>>> list1[3][0] = 90
>>> list1
???
>>> list2
???
```

```
>>> list1 = [10, 20, 30, [40]]
>>> list2 = copy.deepcopy(list1)
>>> id(list1) == id(list2)
???
>>> list1[0] = 60
>>> list1[3][0] = 90
>>> list1
???
>>> list2
???

>>> list1 = [10, 20, 30, (40)]
>>> list2 = copy.deepcopy(list1)
>>> list1[3][0] = 90
???
>>> list1[3] = (100,)
>>> list1
???
>>> list2
???
```

The list constructor `list()` makes a copy of the top level of a list, in which the sublist (lower-level) structures are shared is referred to as a **shallow copy**. A **deep copy** operation makes a complete copy of a list. A deep copy operator is provided by method `deepcopy` of the `copy` module in Python.

Self-Test Questions

1. All objects have a set of _____ and _____.

2. The _____ operator is used to select members of a given object.

3. Functions that are part of an object are called _____.

4. There are two values associated with every object in Python, the _____ value and the _____ value.

5. When memory locations are *deallocated*, it means that,
   (a) The memory locations are marked as unusable for the rest of the program execution.
   (b) The memory locations are marked as available for reuse during the remaining program execution.

6. Garbage collection is the process of automatically identifying which areas of memory can be deallocated. (TRUE/FALSE)

7. Indicate which of the following is true,
   (a) When one variable is assigned to another holding an integer value, if the second variable is assigned a new value, the value of the first variable will change as well.
   (b) When one variable is assigned to another holding a list of integer values, if the second variable assigns a new integer value to an element in the list, the list that the first variable is assigned to will be changed as well.

ANSWERS: 1. attributes/behavior, 2. dot, 3. methods, 4. reference/dereferenced, 5. (b), 6. True, 7. (b)

6.2   Turtle Graphics

Turtle graphics refers to a means of controlling a graphical entity (a "turtle") in a graphics window with x,y coordinates. A turtle can be told to draw lines as it travels, therefore having the ability to create various graphical designs. Turtle graphics was first developed for a language named Logo in the 1960s for teaching children how to program. Remnants of Logo still exist today.

Python provides the capability of turtle graphics in the `turtle` Python standard library module. There may be more than one turtle on the screen at once. Each turtle is represented by a distinct object. Thus, each can be individually controlled by the methods available for turtle objects. We introduce turtle graphics here for two reasons—first, to provide a means of better understanding objects in programming, and second, to have some fun!

Turtle graphics refers to a means of controlling a graphical entity (a "turtle") in a graphics window with x,y coordinates.

6.2.1   Creating a Turtle Graphics Window

The first step in the use of turtle graphics is the creation of a turtle graphics window (a *turtle screen*). Figure 6-17 shows how to create a turtle screen of a certain size with an appropriate title bar.

Assuming that the `import turtle` form of import is used, each of the turtle graphics methods must be called in the form `turtle.`*methodname*. The first method called, `setup`,

```
import turtle

# set window size
turtle.setup(800, 600)

# get reference to turtle window
window = turtle.Screen()

# set window title bar
window.title('My First Turtle Graphics Program')
```

FIGURE 6-17   Creating a Turtle Graphics Window

creates a graphics window of the specified size (in pixels). In this case, a window of size 800 pixels wide by 600 pixels high is created. The center point of the window is at coordinate (0,0). Thus, x-coordinate values to the right of the center point are positive values, and those to the left are negative values. Similarly, y-coordinate values above the center point are positive values, and those below are negative values. The top-left, top-right, bottom-left, and bottom-left coordinates for a window of size (800, 600) are as shown in Figure 6-18. A turtle graphics window in Python is also an object. Therefore, to set the title of this window, we need the reference to this object. This is done by call to method Screen.

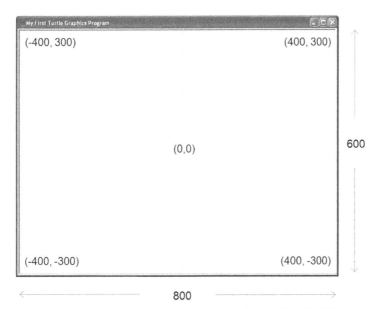

FIGURE 6-18   Python Turtle Graphics Window (of size 800 × 600)

The background color of the turtle window can be changed from the default white background color. This is done using method bgcolor,

```
window = turtle.Screen()
window.bgcolor('blue')
```

See the discussion about pen color below for details on the specification of color values.

The first step in the use of turtle graphics is to create a **turtle graphics window** of a specific size with an appropriate title.

6.2.2 The "Default" Turtle

A "turtle" is an entity in a turtle graphics window that can be controlled in various ways. Like the graphics window, turtles are objects. A "default" turtle is created when the setup method is called. The reference to this turtle object can be obtained by,

```
the_turtle = turtle.getturtle()
```

A call to getturtle returns the reference to the default turtle and causes it to appear on the screen. The initial position of all turtles is the center of the screen at coordinate (0,0), as shown in Figure 6-19.

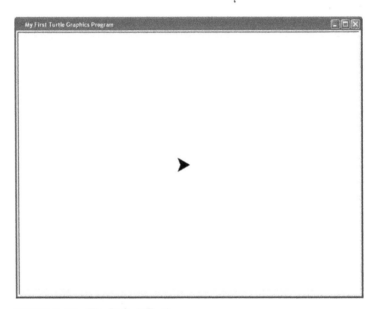

FIGURE 6-19 The Default Turtle

The default turtle shape is an arrowhead. (The size of the turtle shape was enlarged from its default size for clarity.) A turtle's shape can be set to basic geometric shapes, or even made from a provided image file (shown in section 6.2.4).

A **default turtle** is created when the setup method is called. A call to method getturtle returns the reference to the default turtle and causes it to appear on the screen.

6.2.3   Fundamental Turtle Attributes and Behavior

Recall that objects have both attributes and behavior. Turtle objects have three fundamental attributes: *position, heading* (orientation), and *pen* attributes. We discuss each of these attributes next.

Absolute Positioning

Method `position` returns a turtle's current position. For newly created turtles, this returns the tuple `(0, 0)`. A turtle's position can be changed using *absolute positioning* by moving the turtle to a specific x,y coordinate location by use of method `setposition`. An example of this is given in Figure 6-20.

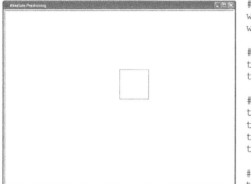

```
# set window title
window = turtle.Screen()
window.title('Absolute Positioning')

# get default turtle and hide
the_turtle = turtle.getturtle()
the_turtle.hideturtle()

# create square (absolute positioning)
the_turtle.setposition(100, 0)
the_turtle.setposition(100, 100)
the_turtle.setposition(0, 100)
the_turtle.setposition(0, 0)

# exit on close window
turtle.exitonclick()
```

FIGURE 6-20   Absolute Positioning of Turtle

The turtle is made invisible by a call to method `hideturtle`. Since newly created turtles are positioned at coordinates `(0, 0)`, the square will be displayed near the middle of the turtle window. To draw the square, the turtle is first positioned at coordinates `(100, 0)`, 100 pixels to the right of its current position. Since the turtle's pen is down, a line will be drawn from location `(0, 0)` to location `(100, 0)`. The turtle is then positioned at coordinates `(100, 100)`, which draws a line from the bottom-right corner to the top-right corner of the square. Positioning the turtle to coordinates `(0, 100)` draws a line from the top-right corner to the top-left corner. Finally, positioning the turtle back to coordinates `(0, 0)` draws the final line from the top-left corner to the bottom-left corner.

> A turtle's position can be changed using *absolute positioning* by use of method `setposition`.

Turtle Heading and Relative Positioning

A turtle's position can also be changed through *relative positioning*. In this case, the location that a turtle moves to is determined by its second fundamental attribute, its heading. A newly created turtle's heading is to the right, at 0 degrees. A turtle with heading 90 degrees moves up; with a heading 180 degrees moves left; and with a heading 270 degrees moves down. A turtle's heading can be changed by turning the turtle a given number of degrees left, `left(90)`, or right, `right(90)`. The `forward` method moves a turtle in the direction that it is currently heading. An example of relative positioning is given in Figure 6-21.

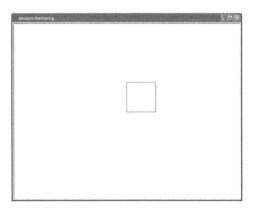

```
# set window title
window = turtle.Screen()
window.title('Relative Positioning')

# get default turtle and hide
the_turtle = turtle.getturtle()
the_turtle.hideturtle()

# create box (relative positioning)
the_turtle.forward(100)
the_turtle.left(90)
the_turtle.forward(100)
the_turtle.left(90)
the_turtle.forward(100)
the_turtle.left(90)
the_turtle.forward(100)

# exit on close window
turtle.exitonclick()
```

FIGURE 6-21   Relative Positioning of Turtle

In this example, the turtle is controlled using relative positioning, drawing the same square as in Figure 6-20 above. Since turtles are initially positioned at coordinates (0, 0) with an initial heading of 0 degrees, the first step is to move the turtle forward 100 pixels. That draws the bottom line of the square. The turtle is then turned left 90 degrees and again moved forward 100 pixels. This draws the line of the right side of the square. These steps continue until the turtle arrives back at the original coordinates (0, 0), completing the square.

Methods `left` and `right` change a turtle's heading relative to its current heading. A turtle's heading can also be set to a specific heading by use of method `setheading`: `the_turtle.set-heading(90)`. In addition, method `heading` can be used to determine a turtle's current heading.

> A turtle's position can be changed using *relative positioning* by use of methods `setheading`, `left`, `right`, and `forward`.

Pen Attributes

The pen attribute of a turtle object is related to its drawing capabilities. The most fundamental of these attributes is whether the pen is currently "up" or "down," controlled by methods `penup()` and `pendown()`. When the pen attribute value is "up," the turtle can be moved to another location without lines being drawn. This is especially needed when drawing graphical images with disconnected segments. Example use of these methods is given in Figure 6-22.

In this example, the turtle is hidden so that only the needed lines appear. Since the initial location of the turtle is at coordinate (0, 0), the pen is set to "up" so that the position of the turtle can be set to (-100, 0) without a line being drawn as it moves. This puts the turtle at the bottom of the left side of the letter. The pen is then set to "down" and the turtle is moved to coordinate (0, 250), drawing as it moves. This therefore draws a line from the bottom of the left side to the top of the "A." The turtle is then moved (with its pen still down) to the location of the bottom of the right side of the letter, coordinate (100, 0). To cross the "A," the pen is again set to "up" and the turtle is moved to the location of the left end of the crossing line, coordinate (-64, 90). The pen is then set to "down" and moved to the end of the crossing line, at coordinate (64, 90), to finish the letter.

```
turtle.setup(800, 600)
window = turtle.Screen()
window.title('Drawing an A')

the_turtle = turtle.getturtle()
the_turtle.hideturtle()
the_turtle.penup()
the_turtle.setposition(-100, 0)
the_turtle.pendown()
the_turtle.setposition(0, 250)
the_turtle.setposition(100, 0)
the_turtle.penup()
the_turtle.setposition(-64, 90)
the_turtle.pendown()
the_turtle.setposition(64, 90)

turtle.exitonclick()
```

FIGURE 6-22   Example Use of Methods penup and pendown

The pen size of a turtle determines the width of the lines drawn when the pen attribute is "down." The pensize method is used to control this: the_turtle.pensize(5). The width is given in pixels, and is limited only by the size of the turtle screen. Example pen sizes are depicted in Figure 6-23.

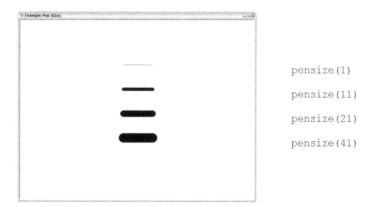

```
pensize(1)

pensize(11)

pensize(21)

pensize(41)
```

FIGURE 6-23   Example Turtle Pen Sizes

The pen color can also be selected by use of the pencolor method: the_turtle. pencolor('blue'). The name of any common color can be used, for example 'white', 'red', 'blue', 'green', 'yellow', 'gray', and 'black'. Colors can also be specified in RGB (red/green/blue) component values. These values can be specified in the range 0–255 if the color mode attribute of the turtle window is set as given below,

```
turtle.colormode(255)
the_turtle.pencolor(238, 130, 238) # violet
```

This provides a means for a full spectrum of colors to be displayed.

The pen attributes that can be controlled include whether the pen is down or up (using methods penup and pendown), the pen size (using method `pensize`), and the pen color (using method `pencolor`).

6.2.4 Additional Turtle Attributes

In addition to the fundamental turtle attributes already discussed, we provide details on other attributes of a turtle that may be controlled. This includes whether the turtle is visible or not, the size (both demonstrated above), shape, and fill color of the turtle, the turtle's speed, and the tilt of the turtle. We will discuss each of these attributes next.

Turtle Visibility

As we saw, a turtle's visibility can be controlled by use of methods `hideturtle()` and `showturtle()` (in which an invisible turtle can still draw on the screen). There are various reasons for doing this. A turtle may be made invisible while being repositioned on the screen. In gaming, a turtle might be made invisible when it meets its "demise." Or maybe a given turtle needs to blink, as we will see at the end of the chapter.

Methods `showturtle()` and `hideturtle()` control a turtle's visibility.

Turtle Size

The size of a turtle shape can be controlled with methods `resizemode` and `turtlesize` as shown in Figure 6-24.

```
# set to allow user to change turtle size
the_turtle.resizemode('user')

# set a new turtle size
the_turtle.turtlesize(3, 3)
```

FIGURE 6-24 Changing the Size of a Turtle

The first instruction sets the resize attribute of a turtle to 'user'. This allows the user (programmer) to change the size of the turtle by use of method `turtlesize`. Otherwise, calls to `turtlesize` will have no effect. The call to method `turtlesize` in the figure is passed two parameters. The first is used to change the *width* of the shape (perpendicular to its orientation), and the second changes its *length* (parallel to its orientation). Each value provides a factor by which the size is to be changed. Thus, the_turtle.turtlesize(3, 3) stretches both the width and length of the current turtle shape by a factor of 3. (A third parameter can also be added that determines the thickness of the shape's outline.)

There are two other values that method `resizemode` may be set to. An argument value of `'auto'` causes the size of the turtle to change with changes in the pen size, whereas a value of `'noresize'` causes the turtle shape to remain the same size.

> The size of a given turtle shape can be controlled with methods `resizemode` and `turtlesize`.

Turtle Shape

There are a number of ways that a turtle's shape (and fill color) may be defined to something other than the default shape (the arrowhead) and fill color (black). First, a turtle may be assigned one of the following provided shapes: `'arrow'`, `'turtle'`, `'circle'`, `'square'`, `'triangle'`, and `'classic'` (the default arrowhead shape), as shown in Figure 6-25.

FIGURE 6-25 Available Turtle Shapes

The shape and fill colors are set by use of the `shape` and `fillcolor` methods,

```
the_turtle.shape('circle')
the_turtle.fillcolor('white')
```

New shapes may be created and registered with (added to) the turtle screen's *shape dictionary*. One way of creating a new is shape by providing a set of coordinates denoting a polygon, as shown in Figure 6-26.

```
turtle.setup(800, 600)
window = turtle.Screen()
window.title('My Polygon')
the_turtle = turtle.getturtle()

turtle.register_shape('mypolygon',
((0, 0), (100, 0), (140, 40)))

the_turtle.shape('mypolygon')
the_turtle.fillcolor('white')
```

FIGURE 6-26 Creating a New Polygon Turtle Shape

In the figure, method `register_shape` is used to register the new turtle shape with the name `mypolygon`. The new shape is provided by the tuple of coordinates in the second argument. These coordinates define the polygon shown in the figure. Once the new shape is defined, a turtle can be set to that shape by calling the `shape` method with the desired shape's name. The `fillcolor` method is then called to make the fill color of the polygon white (with the edges remaining black). It is also possible to create turtle shapes composed of various individual polygons called *compound shapes*. We refer the reader to the official online Python documentation of the turtle module for details (see http://docs.python.org/py3k/library/turtle.html#module-turtle).

The creation of this polygon may not seem too exciting, but the orientation of a turtle can be changed. In addition, a turtle is able to *stamp* its shape on the screen, which remains there even after the turtle is repositioned (or relocated). That means that we can create all sorts interesting graphic patterns by appropriately repositioning the turtle, as shown in Figure 6-27.

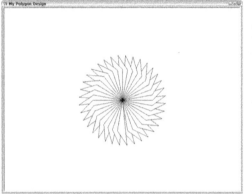

```
turtle.setup(800, 600)
window = turtle.Screen()
window.title('My Polygon Design')
the_turtle = turtle.getturtle()

turtle.register_shape('mypolygon',
((0, 0), (100, 0), (140, 40)))
the_turtle.shape('mypolygon')
the_turtle.fillcolor('white')

for angle in range(0, 360, 10):
    the_turtle.setheading(angle)
    the_turtle.stamp()
```

FIGURE 6-27 Creating a Design from a Turtle using a Polygon Shape

Only a few lines of code are needed to generate this design. The for loop in the figure iterates variable `angle` over the complete range of degrees, 0 to 360, by increments of 10 degrees. Within the loop the turtle's heading is set to the current angle, and the `stamp()` method is called to stamp the polygon shape at the turtle's current position. By varying the shape of the polygon and the angles that the turtle is set to, a wide range of such designs may be produced.

Another way that a turtle shape can be created is by use of an image. The image file used must be a "gif file" (with file extension .`gif`). The name of the file is then registered and the shape of the turtle set to the registered name,

```
register_shape('image1.gif')
the_turtle.shape('image1.gif')
```

The final program of this chapter gives an example of the use of image shapes.

A turtle's shape may be set to one of the provided shapes, a described polygon (or collection of polygons), or an image.

Turtle Speed

At times, you may want to control the speed at which a turtle moves. A turtle's speed can be set to a range of speed values from 0 to 10, with a "normal" speed being around 6. To set the speed of the turtle, the `speed` method is used, `the_turtle.speed(6)`. The following speed values can be set using a descriptive rather than a numeric value,

```
10: 'fast'    6: 'normal'    3: 'slow'    1: 'slowest'    0: 'fastest'
```

Thus, a normal speed can also be set by `the_turtle.speed('normal')`. When using the turtle for line drawing only, the turtle will move more quickly if it is made invisible (by use of the `hideturtle` method).

The speed of a turtle can be controlled by use of the `speed` method.

6.2.5 Creating Multiple Turtles

So far, we have seen examples in which there is only one turtle object, the default turtle created with a turtle window. However, it is possible to create and control any number of turtle objects. To create a new turtle, the `Turtle()` method is used,

```
turtle1 = turtle.Turtle()
turtle2 = turtle.Turtle()
etc.
```

By storing turtle objects in a list, any number of turtles may be maintained,

```
turtles = []
turtles.append(turtle.Turtle())
turtles.append(turtle.Turtle())
etc.
```

An example of using multiple turtle objects is given in the following "Let's Apply It" section.

Any number of turtle objects can be created by use of method `Turtle()`.

6.2.6 Let's Apply It—Bouncing Balls Program

Following is a program (Figure 6-29) that displays one or more bouncing balls within a turtle screen. This program utilizes the following programming features.

➤ turtle module   ➤ time module   ➤ random module

Example execution of the program is given in Figure 6-28.

Program Execution ...

```
This program simulates one or more bouncing balls on a turtle screen.
Enter number of seconds to run: 30
Enter number of balls in simulation: 5
```

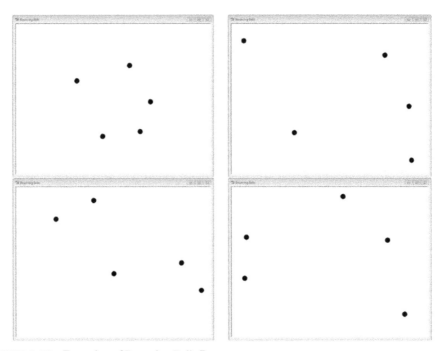

FIGURE 6-28   Execution of Bouncing Balls Program

In addition to the `turtle` graphics module, this program makes use of the `time` and `random` Python standard library modules to allow control of how long (in seconds) the simulation is executed, as indicated by the user, and to generate the random motion of the bouncing balls.

The main section of the program begins on **line 52** with the programming greeting. On **lines 58–60**, the size of the turtle screen (in pixels) is hard-coded into the program, assigned to variables `screen_width` and `screen_height`. Since all references to the screen size are through these variables, the desired window size can be altered by simply altering these variables.

```
 1  # Bouncing Balls Simulation Program
 2
 3  import turtle
 4  import random
 5  import time
 6
 7  def atLeftEdge(ball, screen_width):
 8      if ball.xcor() < -screen_width / 2:
 9          return True
10      else:
11          return False
12
13  def atRightEdge(ball, screen_width):
14      if ball.xcor() > screen_width / 2:
15          return True
16      else:
17          return False
18
19  def atTopEdge(ball, screen_height):
20      if ball.ycor() > screen_height / 2:
21          return True
22      else:
23          return False
24
25  def atBottomEdge(ball, screen_height):
26      if ball.ycor() < -screen_height / 2:
27          return True
28      else:
29          return False
30
31  def bounceBall(ball, new_direction):
32      if new_direction == 'left' or new_direction == 'right':
33          new_heading = 180 - ball.heading()
34      elif new_direction == 'down' or new_direction == 'up':
35          new_heading =  360 - ball.heading()
36
37      return new_heading
38
39  def createBalls(num_balls):
40      balls = []
41      for k in range(0, num_balls):
42          new_ball = turtle.Turtle()
43          new_ball.shape('circle')
44          new_ball.fillcolor('black')
45          new_ball.speed(0)
46          new_ball.penup()
47          new_ball.setheading(random.randint(1, 359))
48          balls.append(new_ball)
49
50      return balls
51
```

FIGURE 6-29   Bouncing Balls Program (*Continued*)

On **lines 63–64**, the turtle screen is created and its reference value assigned to variable `window`. The title of the window is assigned through a call to the `title` method. Following that, the user is prompted to enter the number of seconds for the simulation, as well as the number of simultaneously bouncing balls.

```
52  # ---- main
53  # program greeting
54  print('This program simulates bouncing balls in a turtle screen')
55  print('for a specified number of seconds')
56
57  # init screen size
58  screen_width = 800
59  screen_height = 600
60  turtle.setup(screen_width, screen_height)
61
62  # create turtle window
63  window = turtle.Screen()
64  window.title('Bouncing Balls')
65
66  # prompt user for execution time and number of balls
67  num_seconds = int(input('Enter number of seconds to run: '))
68  num_balls = int(input('Enter number of balls in simulation: '))
69
70  # create balls
71  balls = createBalls(num_balls)
72
73  # set start time
74  start_time = time.time()
75
76  # begin simulation
77  terminate = False
78
79  while not terminate:
80      for k in range(0, len(balls)):
81          balls[k].forward(15)
82
83          if atLeftEdge(balls[k], screen_width):
84              balls[k].setheading(bounceBall(balls[k], 'right'))
85          elif atRightEdge(balls[k], screen_width):
86              balls[k].setheading(bounceBall(balls[k], 'left'))
87          elif atTopEdge(balls[k], screen_height):
88              balls[k].setheading(bounceBall(balls[k], 'down'))
89          elif atBottomEdge(balls[k], screen_height):
90              balls[k].setheading(bounceBall(balls[k], 'up'))
91
92          if time.time() - start_time > num_seconds:
93              terminate = True
94
95  # exit on close window
96  turtle.exitonclick()
```

FIGURE 6-29 Bouncing Balls Program

Function createBalls is called (on **line 71**) to create and return a list of turtle objects with a ball shape. The function definition (**lines 39–50**) initializes an empty list named balls and creates the requested number of balls one-by-one, each appended to the list, by use of the for loop at **line 41**. Each ball is created with shape 'circle', fill color of 'black', speed of 0 (fastest speed), and with pen attribute 'up'. In addition, the initial heading of each turtle is set to a random angle between 1 and 359 (**line 47**).

Back in the main program section at **line 74**, the current time (in seconds) is obtained from a call to method `time` of the `time` module: `time.time()`. The current time value is stored in variable `start_time`. (The current time is the number of seconds since the "epoch," which is January 1, 1970. This will be discussed further in the Horse Racing program that follows.) The while loop beginning on **line 79** begins the simulation. The loop iterates as long as Boolean variable `terminate` is `False` (initialized to `False` on **line 77**). The for loop at **line 80** moves each of the specified number of balls a small distance until reaching one of the four edges of the window (left, right, top, or bottom edge). Boolean functions `atLeftEdge`, `atRightEdge`, `atTopEdge`, and `atBottomEdge` are used to determine when a ball is at an edge (defined in **lines 7–29**). Function `bounceBall` is called to bounce the ball in the opposite direction it is heading, and returns the new heading of the ball, passed as the argument to that ball's `setheading` method. Finally, on **line 92** a check is made to determine whether the user-requested simulation time has been exceeded. If so, Boolean variable `terminate` is set to `True`, and the program terminates. Because of the call to `exitonclick()` on **line 96**, the program will properly shut down when the close button of the turtle window is clicked.

Self-Test Questions

1. A turtle screen is an 800-pixel wide by 600-pixel high graphics window. (TRUE/FALSE).

2. The three main attributes of a turtle object are _____, _____, and _____.

3. A turtle can be moved using either _____ or _____ positioning.

4. A turtle can only draw lines when it is not hidden. (TRUE/FALSE)

5. A turtle shape is limited to an arrow, turtle, circle, square, triangle, or classic (default) shape. (TRUE/FALSE)

6. What attribute of a turtle determines the size of the lines it draw?
   (a) Pen size
   (b) Turtle size

7. A turtle can draw in one of seven colors. (TRUE/FALSE)

8. A turtle can leave an imprint of its shape on the screen by use of the _____ method.

9. In order to create a new turtle object, the _____ method is called.

ANSWERS: 1. False. 2. position, heading, pen. 3. absolute/relative 4. False. 5. False. 6. (a). 7. False. 8. stamp. 9. Turtle

COMPUTATIONAL PROBLEM SOLVING

6.3   Horse Race Simulation Program

In this section, we design, implement and test a program that simulates a horse race.

6.3.1 The Problem

The problem is to create a visualization of a horse race in which horses are moved ahead a random distance at fixed intervals until there is a winner, as shown in Figure 6-30.

FIGURE 6-30 Example Horse Race Simulation

6.3.2 Problem Analysis

The program needs a source of random numbers for advancing the horses a random distance in the race. We can use the random number generator of the Python standard library module `random` that we used in Chapter 3 in the Coin Change Exercise example. The remaining part of the problem is in the creation of appropriate graphics for producing a visualization of a horse race. We shall make use of the turtle graphics module from the Python standard library to do this.

6.3.3 Program Design

Meeting the Program Requirements

There are no specific requirements for this problem, other than to create an appropriate simulation of a horse race. Therefore, the requirement is essentially the generation of a horse race in which the graphics look sufficiently compelling, and each horse has an equal chance of winning a given race. Since a specific number of horses was not specified, we will design the program for ten horses in each race.

Data Description

The essential information for this program is the current location of each of the ten horses in a given race. Each turtle is an object, whose attributes include its shape and its coordinate position on the turtle screen. Therefore, we will maintain a list of ten turtle objects with the shape attribute of a horse image for this purpose. Thus, suitable horse images must be found or created for this purpose.

Algorithmic Approach

There is no algorithm, per se, needed in this program other than to advance each horse a random distance at fixed time intervals until one of the horses reaches a certain point on the turtle screen (the "finish line").

Overall Program Steps

The overall steps in this program design are given in Figure 6-31.

FIGURE 6-31   Overall Steps of the Horse Race Simulation Program

6.3.4 Program Implementation and Testing

Stage 1—Creating an Initial Turtle Screen Layout

We first develop and test an initial program that lays out the positions of the starting horses on the turtle graphics screen, as shown in Figure 6-32. Figure 6-33 provides this first stage of the program.

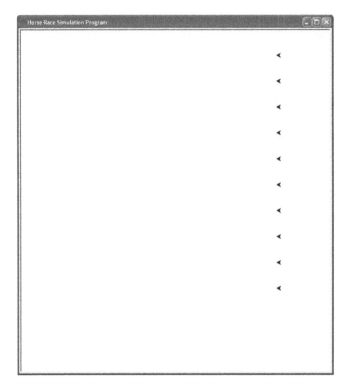

FIGURE 6-32 Output of Stage 1 of the Horse Race Simulation Program

At **line 3** the turtle module is imported. Since the `import module_name` form of import is used, each call to a method of this module must be prefixed with the module name. For example, `turtle.setup(750, 800)` on **line 31** (which sets the turtle screen size to a width of 750 and a height of 800 pixels).

The intent of this version of the program is to ensure that the turtle screen is appropriately sized and that the initial layout of horse locations is achieved. Therefore, only the default turtle shape is used at this point. In the next version we will focus on generating a set of horse images on the screen. Thus, on **line 34**, the turtle screen object is retrieved (by the call to `turtle.Sreen()`) and its reference assigned to variable `window`. The start location of the first (lowest) horse is set to an x coordinate value of 240, and a y coordinate value of −200. This puts the turtle screen object at the lower right corner of the screen. The amount of vertical separation between the horses is assigned to variable `track_separation`. These values were determined from knowledge of the screen coordinates in turtle graphics and a little trial and error.

Next, on **line 44** a call is made to function `generateHorses` (at **lines 9–15**). This function returns a list of ten new turtle objects, and assigned to variable `horses`. Function `newHorse` (**lines 5–7**) is called by function `generateHorses` to create each new horse turtle object. At this stage, function `newHorse` simply creates and returns a regular turtle object. In the next stage however, it will be responsible for returning new turtle objects with an appropriate horse shape.

The position for each of these horses is determined by function `placeHorses` on **lines 17–23**. It is passed the list of horse turtle objects, the location of the first turtle, and the amount of separation between each (established as 60 pixels on **line 41**). Function `placeHorses`, therefore,

```
 1   # Horse Racing Program (Stage 1)
 2
 3   import turtle
 4
 5   def newHorse():
 6       horse = turtle.Turtle()
 7       return horse
 8
 9   def generateHorses(num_horses):
10       horses = []
11       for k in range(0, num_horses):
12           horse = newHorse()
13           horses.append(horse)
14
15       return horses
16
17   def placeHorses(horses, loc, separation):
18       for k in range(0, len(horses)):
19           horses[k].hideturtle()
20           horses[k].penup()
21           horses[k].setposition(loc[0], loc[1] + k * separation)
22           horses[k].setheading(180)
23           horses[k].showturtle()
24
25   # ---- main
26
27   # init number of horses
28   num_horses = 10
29
30   # set window size
31   turtle.setup(750, 800)
32
33   # get turtle window
34   window = turtle.Screen()
35
36   # set window title bar
37   window.title('Horse Race Simulation Program')
38
39   # init screen layout parameters
40   start_loc = (240, -200)
41   track_separation = 60
42
43   # generate and init horses
44   horses = generateHorses(num_horses)
45
46   # place horses at starting line
47   placeHorses(horses, start_loc, track_separation)
48
49   # terminate program when close window
50   turtle.exitonclick()
```

FIGURE 6-33   Stage 1 of the Horse Race Simulation Program

contains a for loop that iterates over the list of horse objects and makes them initially hidden with their pen up (**lines 19–20**), moves each to its starting position (**line 21**), sets the heading of each to 180 degrees to move left (**line 22**), and then makes each visible (**line 23**). Finally, method exiton-click() is called so that the program will terminate when the user clicks on the program window's close box.

In the next stage, we further develop the program to include the specific shapes and images for the simulation.

Stage 2—Adding the Appropriate Shapes and Images

We next develop and test the program with additional code that adds the horse shapes (images) needed. The resulting turtle screen is shown in Figure 6-34. Figure 6-35 shows this second stage of the program.

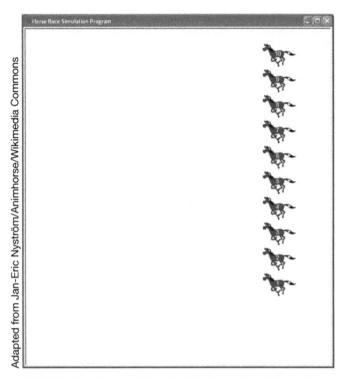

FIGURE 6-34   Output of Stage 2 of the Horse Race Simulation Program

In this stage of the program we add functions getHorseImages and registerHorseImages, called from **lines 61** and **62** of the main program section. Function getHorseImages returns a list of GIF image files. Each image contains the same horse image, each with a unique number 1 to 10. Function registerHorseImages does the required registering of images in turtle graphics by calling method turtle.register_shape on each.

Function generateHorses (**lines 26–32**) is implemented the same way as in stage 1 to return a list of horse turtle objects, except that it is altered to be passed an argument containing a list of horse images. Thus, the call to generateHorses in **line 65** is altered to pass the list of images in variable horse_images. Function newHorse (**lines 19–24**) is altered as well to be passed a particular horse image for the horse that is created, horse.shape(image_file).

Stage 3—Animating the Horses

Next we develop and test the program with additional code that animates the horses so that they are randomly advanced until a horse crosses the finish line. The resulting turtle screen is shown in Figure 6-36. Figure 6-37 provides this third stage of the program.

```
1  # Horse Racing Program (Stage 2)
2
3  import turtle
4
5  def getHorseImages(num_horses):
6      # init empty list
7      images = []
8
9      # get all horse images
10     for k in range(0, num_horses):
11         images = images + ['horse_' + str(k + 1) + '_image.gif']
12
13     return images
14
15 def registerHorseImages(images):
16     for k in range(0, len(images)):
17         turtle.register_shape(images[k])
18
19 def newHorse(image_file):
20     horse = turtle.Turtle()
21     horse.hideturtle()
22     horse.shape(image_file)
23
24     return horse
25
26 def generateHorses(images, num_horses):
27     horses = []
28     for k in range(0, num_horses):
29         horse = newHorse(images[k])
30         horses.append(horse)
31
32     return horses
33
34 def placeHorses(horses, loc, separation):
35     for k in range(0, len(horses)):
36         horses[k].hideturtle()
37         horses[k].penup()
38         horses[k].setposition(loc[0], loc[1] + k * separation)
39         horses[k].setheading(180)
40         horses[k].showturtle()
41
```

FIGURE 6-35   Stage 2 of the Horse Simulation Race Program (*Continued*)

Two new functions are added in this version of the program, startHorses and display-Winner. Function startHorses (**lines 44–58**) is passed the list of horse turtle objects, the location of the finish line (as an x coordinate value on the turtle screen) and the fundamental increment amount—each horse is advanced by one to three times this amount. The while loop for incrementally moving the horses is on **line 49**. The loop iterates until a winner is found, that is, until the variable have_winner is True. Therefore, have_winner is initialized to False in **line 46**. Variable k, initialized on **line 48**, is used to index into the list of horse turtle objects. Since each horse in turn is advanced some amount during the race, variable k is incremented by one, modulo the number of horses in variable num_horses (10) (**line 57**). When k becomes equal to num_horses −1 (9), it is reset to 0 (for horse 1).

The amount that each horse is advanced is a factor of one to three randomly determined by call to method randint(1,3) of the Python standard library module random in **line 51**. Variable forward_incr is multiplied by this factor to move the horses forward an appropriate amount.

```
42  # ---- main
43
44  # init number of horses
45  num_horses = 10
46
47  # set window size
48  turtle.setup(750, 800)
49
50  # get turtle window
51  window = turtle.Screen()
52
53  # set window title bar
54  window.title('Horse Race Simulation Program')
55
56  # init screen layout parameters
57  start_loc = (240, -200)
58  track_separation = 60
59
60  # register images
61  horse_images = getHorseImages()
62  registerHorseImages(horse_images)
63
64  # generate and init horses
65  horses = generateHorses(horse_images)
66
67  # place horses at starting line
68  placeHorses(horses, start_loc, track_separation)
69
70  # terminate program when close window
71  turtle.exitonclick()
```

FIGURE 6-35   Stage 2 of the Horse Simulation Race Program

Adapted from Jan-Eric Nyström/Animhorse/Wikimedia Commons

FIGURE 6-36   Output of Stage 3 of the Horse Race Simulation Program

```
1   # Horse Racing Program (Stage 3)
2
3   import turtle
4   import random
5
6   def getHorseImages(num_horses):
7       # init empty list
8       images = []
9
10      # get all horse images
11      for k in range(0, num_horses):
12          images = images + ['horse_' + str(k+1) + '_image.gif']
13
14      return images
15
16  def registerHorseImages(images):
17      for k in range(0, len(images)):
18          turtle.register_shape(images[k])
19
20  def newHorse(image_file):
21      horse = turtle.Turtle()
22      horse.hideturtle()
23      horse.shape(image_file)
24
25      return horse
26
27  def generateHorses(images, num_horses):
28      horses = []
29      for k in range(0, num_horses):
30          horse = newHorse(images[k])
31          horses.append(horse)
32
33      return horses
34
35  def placeHorses(horses, loc, separation):
36      for k in range(0, len(horses)):
37          horses[k].hideturtle()
38          horses[k].penup()
39          horses[k].setposition(loc[0], loc[1] + k * separation)
40          horses[k].setheading(180)
41          horses[k].showturtle()
42          horses[h].pendown()
43
44  def startHorses(horses, finish_line, forward_incr):
45      # init
46      have_winner = False
47
48      k = 0
49      while not have_winner:
50          horse = horses[k]
51          horse.forward(random.randint(1, 3) * forward_incr)
52
53          # check for horse over finish line
54          if horse.position()[0] < finish_line:
55              have_winner = True
56          else:
57              k = (k + 1) % len(horses)
58      return k
59
```

FIGURE 6-37   Stage 3 of the Horse Race Simulation Program (*Continued*)

```
60  def displayWinner(winning_horse):
61      print('Horse', winning_horse, 'the winner!')
62
63  # ---- main
64
65  # init number of horses
66  num_horses = 10
67
68  # set window size
69  turtle.setup(750, 800)
70
71  # get turtle window
72  window = turtle.Screen()
73
74  # set window title bar
75  window.title('Horse Race Simulation Program')
76
77  # init screen layout parameters
78  start_loc = (240, -200)
79  finish_line = -240
80  track_separation = 60
81  forward_incr = 6
82
83  # register images
84  horse_images = getHorseImages(num_horses)
85  registerHorseImages(horse_images)
86
87  # generate and init horses
88  horses = generateHorses(horse_images, num_horses)
89
90  # place horses at starting line
91  placeHorses(horses, start_loc, track_separation)
92
93  # start horses
94  winner = startHorses(horses, finish_line, forward_incr)
95
96  # display winning horse
97  displayWinner(winner + 1)
98
99  # terminate program when close window
100 turtle.exitonclick()
```

FIGURE 6-37   Stage 3 of the Horse Race Simulation Program

The value of forward_incr is initialized in the main program section. This value can be adjusted to speed up or slow down the overall speed of the horses.

Function displayWinner displays the winning horse number in the Python shell (**lines 60–61**). This function will be rewritten in the next stage of program development to display a "winner" banner image in the turtle screen. Thus, this implementation of the function is for testing purposes only.

The main program section (**lines 63–100**) is the same as in the previous stage of program development, except for the inclusion of the calls to functions startHorses and displayWinner in **lines 94** and **97**.

Final Stage—Adding Race Banners

Finally, we add the code for the displaying of banners at various points in the race as shown earlier in Figure 6-30. In Figure 6-38 is the final stage of the program. This final version imports one additional module, Python Standard Library module `time` (**line 5**), used to control the blink rate of the winning horse.

While the race progresses within the while loop at **line 102**, checks for the location of the lead horse are made in two places—before and after the halfway mark of the race (on **line 108**). If the

```
1   # Horse Racing Program (Final Stage)
2
3   import turtle
4   import random
5   import time
6
7   def getHorseImages(num_horses):
8       # init empty list
9       images = []
10
11      # get all horse images
12      for k in range(0, num_horses):
13          images = images + ['horse_' + str(k + 1) + '_image.gif']
14
15      return images
16
17  def getBannerImages(num_horses):
18      # init empty list
19      all_images = []
20
21      # get "They're Off" banner image
22      images = ['theyre_off_banner.gif']
23      all_images.append(images)
24
25      # get early lead banner images
26      images = []
27      for k in range(0, num_horses):
28          images = images + ['lead_at_start_' + str(k + 1) + '.gif']
29      all_images.append(images)
30
31      # get mid-way lead banner images
32      images = []
33      for k in range(0, num_horses):
34          images = images + ['looking_good_' + str(k + 1) + '.gif']
35      all_images.append(images)
36
37      # get "We Have a Winner" banner image
38      images = ['winner_banner.gif']
39      all_images.append(images)
40
41      return all_images
42
43  def registerHorseImages(images):
44      for k in range(0, len(images)):
45          turtle.register_shape(images[k])
46
```

FIGURE 6-38   Final Stage of the Horse Race Simulation Program (*Continued*)

```
47   def registerBannerImages(images):
48       for k in range(0, len(images)):
49           for j in range(0, len(images[k])):
50               turtle.register_shape(images[k][j])
51
52   def newHorse(image_file):
53       horse = turtle.Turtle()
54       horse.hideturtle()
55       horse.shape(image_file)
56
57       return horse
58
59   def generateHorses(images, num_horses):
60       horses = []
61       for k in range(0, num_horses):
62           horse = newHorse(images[k])
63           horses.append(horse)
64
65       return horses
66
67   def placeHorses(horses, loc, separation):
68       for k in range(0, len(horses)):
69           horses[k].hideturtle()
70           horses[k].penup()
71           horses[k].setposition(loc[0], loc[1] + k * separation)
72           horses[k].setheading(180)
73           horses[k].showturtle()
74           horses[k].pendown()
75
76   def findLeadHorse(horses):
77       # init
78       lead_horse = 0
79
80       for k in range(1, len(horses)):
81           if horses[k].position()[0] <  \
82               horses[lead_horse].position()[0]:
83                   lead_horse = k
84       return lead_horse
85
86   def displayBanner(banner, position):
87       the_turtle = turtle.getturtle()
88       the_turtle.setposition(position[0], position[1])
89       the_turtle.shape(banner)
90       the_turtle.stamp()
91
```

FIGURE 6-38   Final Stage of the Horse Race Simulation Program (*Continued*)

x coordinate location of the lead horse is less then 125, the "early lead banner" is displayed on **line 117** by a call to function displayBanner. Otherwise, if one second has elapsed, then the "midrace lead banner" is displayed on **line 111**.

The sleep method of the time module is used to control the blinking of the winning horse in function displayWinner. A "count-down" variable, blink_counter, is set to 5 on **line 133**. This will cause the winning horse to blink five times. The following while loop decrements

```
92   def startHorses(horses, banners, finish_line, forward_incr):
93       # init
94       have_winner = False
95       early_leading_horse_displayed = False
96       midrace_leading_horse_displayed = False
97
98       # display "They're Off" banner image
99       displayBanner(banner_images[0][0], (70, -300))
100
101      k = 0
102      while not have_winner:
103          horse = horses[k]
104          horse.forward(random.randint(1, 3) * forward_incr)
105
106          # display mid-race lead banner
107          lead_horse = findLeadHorse(horses)
108          if horses[lead_horse].position()[0] < -125 and \
109             not midrace_leading_horse_displayed:
110
111              displayBanner(banners[2][lead_horse], (40, -300))
112              midrace_leading_horse_displayed = True
113
114          # display early lead banner
115          elif horses[lead_horse].position()[0] < 125 and \
116             not early_leading_horse_displayed:
117              displayBanner(banners[1][lead_horse], (10, -300))
118              early_leading_horse_displayed = True
119
120          # check for horse over finish line
121          if horse.position()[0] < finish_line:
122              have_winner = True
123          else:
124              k = (k + 1) % len(horses)
125      return k
126
```

FIGURE 6-38   Final Stage of the Horse Race Simulation Program (*Continued*)

blink_counter and continues to iterate until blink_counter is 0. Variable show, initialized to False on **line 132**, is used to alternately show and hide the turtle based on its current (Boolean) value, which is toggled back and forth between True and False each time through the loop. The sleep method is called on **line 143** to cause the program execution to suspend for four-tenths of a second so that the switch between the visible and invisible horse appears slowly enough to cause a blinking effect. This version of displayWinner replaces the previous version that simply displayed the winning horse number in the Python shell window.

Added functions getBannerImages (**lines 17–41**), registerBannerImages (**lines 47–50**), and displayBanner (**lines 86–90**) incorporate the banner images into the program the same way that the horse images were incorporated in the previous program version. Function startHorses was modified to take another parameter, banners, containing the list of registered banners displayed during the race, passed to it from the main program section.

```
127 def displayWinner(winning_horse, winner_banner):
128     # display "We Have a Winner" banner
129     displayBanner(winner_banner, (20, -300))
130
131     # blink winning horse
132     show = False
133     blink_counter = 5
134     while blink_counter != 0:
135         if show:
136             winning_horse.showturtle()
137             show = False
138             blink_counter = blink_counter - 1
139         else:
140             winning_horse.hideturtle()
141             show = True
142
143         time.sleep(.4)
144
145 # ---- main
146
147 # init number of horses
148 num_horses = 10
149
150 # set window size
151 turtle.setup(750, 800)
152
153 # get turtle window
154 window = turtle.Screen()
155
156 # set window title
157 window.title('Horse Race Simulation Program')
158
159 # hide default turtle and keep from drawing
160 the_turtle.hideturtle()
161 the_turtle.penup()
162
163 # init screen layout parameters
164 start_loc = (240, -200)
165 finish_line = -240
166 track_separation = 60
167 forward_incr = 6
168
169 # register images
170 horse_images = getHorseImages()
171 banner_images = getBannerImages()
172 registerHorseImages(horse_images)
173 registerBannerImages(banner_images)
174
```

FIGURE 6-38   Final Stage of the Horse Race Simulation Program (*Continued*)

Finally, the default turtle (created with the turtle graphics window) is utilized in function displayBanners and in the main section. It is used to display the various banners at the bottom of the screen. To do this, the turtle's "shape" is changed to the appropriate banner images stored in list banner_images. To prevent the turtle from drawing lines when moving from the initial (0, 0) coordinate location to where banners are displayed, the default turtle is hidden and its pen attribute is set to "up" (**lines 160–161**).

```
175  # generate and init horses
176  horses = generateHorses(horse_images)
177
178  # place horses at starting line
179  placeHorses(horses, start_loc, track_separation)
180
181  # start horses
182  winner = startHorses(horses, banner_images, finish_line,
183                       forward_incr)
184
185  # light up for winning horse
186  displayWinner(horses[winner], banner_images[3][0])
187
188  # terminate program when close window
189  turtle.exitonclick()
```

FIGURE 6-38 Final Stage of the Horse Race Simulation Program

CHAPTER SUMMARY

General Topics

Software Objects/Methods
References/Reference vs. Dereferenced Values
Reference Assignment
Memory Allocation/Deallocation

Garbage Collection
Shallow vs. Deep Copy Operations

Python-Specific Programming Topics

Objects and Turtle Graphics in Python

CHAPTER EXERCISES

Section 6.1

1. Indicate exactly what the contents of lst1 and lst2 would be after each of the following set of assignments,

   (a) `lst1 = [10, 20, 30]`
     `lst2 = [10, 20, 30]`
     `lst1[2] = 50`

   (b) `lst1 = [10, 20, 30]`
     `lst2 = lst1`
     `lst1[2] = 50`

   (c) `lst1 = [10, 20, 30]`
     `lst2 = list(lst1)`
     `lst1[2] = 50`

2. Indicate which of the following set of assignments would result in automatic garbage collection in Python.

   (a) `lst1 = [1, 2, 3]`
     `lst2 = [5, 6, 7]`
     `lst1 = lst2`

   (b) `str1 = 'Hello World'`
     `str2 = 'Nice Day'`
     `str3 = str1`

   (c) `tuple1 = (1, 2, 3)`
     `tuple2 = tuple1`
     `tuple1 = (4, 5, 6)`

3. For the set of assignments in question 1, indicate how both the `id` method and `is` operator can be used to determine if lists lst1 and lst2 are each referencing the same list instance in memory.

Section 6.2

4. Give a set of instructions to create a turtle window of size 400 pixels wide and 600 pixels high, with a title of `'Turtle Graphics Window'`.

5. Give a set of instructions that gets the default turtle and sets it to an actual turtle shape.

244 CHAPTER 6 Objects and Their Use

6. For each of the following method calls on turtle `the_turtle`, indicate in what part of the screen the turtle will be placed relative to the center of the screen.
   (a) `the_turtle.setposition(0, 0)`
   (b) `the_turtle.setposition(−100, 0)`
   (c) `the_turtle.setposition(−50, 0)`
   (d) `the_turtle.setposition(0, −50)`

7. For the following method calls on turtle `the_turtle`, describe the shape that will be drawn.
```
the_turtle.penup()
the_turtle.setposition(−100, 0)
the_turtle.pendown()
the_turtle.setposition(100, 0)
the_turtle.setposition(100, 50)
the_turtle.setposition(−100, 50)
the_turtle.setposition(−100, 0)
```

8. What color line will be drawn in the following?
```
turtle.colormode(255)
the_turtle.pencolor(128, 0, 0)
the_turtle.pendown()
the_turtle.forward(100)
```

9. What will be displayed by the following turtle actions?
```
the_turtle.pendown()
the_turtle.showturtle()
the_turtle.forward(25)
the_turtle.penup()
the_turtle.hide_turtle()
the_turtle.forward(25)
the_turtle.pendown()
the_turtle.showturtle()
the_turtle.forward(25)
```

PYTHON PROGRAMMING EXERCISES

P1. Give a set of instructions for controlling the turtle to draw a line from the top-left corner of the screen to the bottom-right corner, and from the top-right corner to the bottom-left corner, thereby making a big X on the screen. There should be no other lines drawn on the screen.

P2. Using relative positioning, give a set of instructions for controlling the turtle to draw an isosceles triangle on the screen (that is, a triangle with two equal-length sides).

P3. Give a set of instructions for controlling the turtle to draw the letter W using relative positioning.

P4. Give a set of instructions for controlling the turtle to create three concentric circles, each of different color and line width.

P5. Give a set of instructions that sets the turtle to an actual turtle shape, and moves it from the bottom of the screen towards the top, getting smaller as it moves along.

P6. Give a set of instructions that moves the turtle with an actual turtle shape from the bottom of the screen toward the top, changing its fill color when it crosses the x axis of the grid coordinates.

P7. Give a set of instructions to create your own polygon shape and create an interesting design with it.

P8. Give a set of instructions so that the turtle initially moves slowly around the edge of the screen, then moves faster and faster as it goes around.

P9. Give a set of instructions to create two turtle objects each with circle shape that move to various locations of the turtle screen, each stamping their circle shape of varying sizes and colors.

PROGRAM MODIFICATION PROBLEMS

M1. Bouncing Balls with Color
Modify the bouncing balls simulation program so that exactly three balls are created, each with a different color.

M2. Bouncing Balls with Changing Color
Modify the bouncing balls simulation program so that each time a ball hits an edge of the turtle graphics screen, it changes color.

M3. Bouncing Balls with Trailing Lines
Modify the bouncing balls simulation program so that a trail is left on the screen of each ball's path.

M4. Bouncing Ball Chase
Modify the bouncing balls simulation program so that there are exactly three balls generated, with the first ball started in a random direction (heading), and the other two balls following it closely behind.

M5. Horse Racing Program: Multiple Races and Score Keeping
Modify the Horse Racing program so that the user can continue to play another race without having to rerun the program. Also, the cumulative wins of all the horses should be displayed in the shell window. This allows the user to see if some horses are a more "winning" horse than others.

M6. Horse Racing Program: Handicap Racing
Modify the Horse Racing program so that the user can assign a handicap to one or more horses on a scale of 1 to 5. (A "handicap" in racing is a means of giving advantage to less competitive horses over more competitive ones.) If a horse is assigned a handicap of 1, it should move ahead one-fifth farther than usual. A handicap of 2 would increase its move by two-fifths, and so forth. The list of handicaps should be displayed in the shell window each time before the race begins.

M7. Horse Racing Program: Pari-mutuel Betting
Modify the Horse Racing program to allow individuals to enter their name to "register themselves" to place bets. The program should be modified so that races can be consecutively run without having to re-start the program. Before each race, bets can be placed by registered players. Each bet is for which horse will win. The payout will be based on the rules of *pari-mutuel betting* described below. The amount of money gained or lost by each registered player should be constantly displayed in the shell.

Example of pari-mutuel betting
Each horse has a certain amount of money wagered on it (assuming eight horses):

1	2	3	4	5	6	7	8
$30.00	$70.00	$12.00	$55.00	$110.00	$47.00	$150.00	$40.00

Thus, the total *pool* of money on this particular wagering event is $514.00. Following the start of the event, no more wagers are accepted. The event is decided and the winning outcome is determined to be outcome 4 with $55.00 wagered. The *payout* is now calculated. First, the *commission* or *take* for the wagering company is deducted from the pool. For example, with a commission rate of 14.25% the pool is: $514 \times (1 - 0.1425) = $440.76. This remaining amount in the pool is now distributed to those who wagered on outcome 4: $440.76 / $55 ≈ $8 per $1 wagered. This payout includes the $1 wagered plus an additional $7 profit. Thus, the odds of outcome 4 are 7-to-1.

Wikipedia contributors. "Parimutuel betting." *Wikipedia, The Free Encyclopedia*. Wikipedia, The Free Encyclopedia, May 7, 2011. Web, May 11, 2011.

PROGRAM DEVELOPMENT PROBLEMS

D1. Drunkard's Walk

A *random walk* is a trajectory taken by a sequence of random steps. Random walks can be used to model the travel of molecules, the path that animals take when looking for food, and financial fluctuations, for example. A specific form of random walk is called the "Drunkard's Walk." A (drunken) man tries to find his way home. He does so by making a random choice at each street intersection of which of the four paths to take: continue in the same direction; go back from the direction he came; turn left; or turn right. Thus, the man is traveling the same distance after each choice of direction (one city block). Implement and test a Python program using turtle graphics to display random walks. Select an appropriate number of pixels as the length of a city block.

D2. Name Reversal

Implement and test a Python program using turtle graphics to allow the user to enter their first name, and have it displayed in the turtle window as a reverse mirror image.

D3. Battleship Game Visualization

Implement and test a Python program using turtle graphics to provide a visualization for the game of Battleship discussed in Program Development problem D3 in Chapter 4.

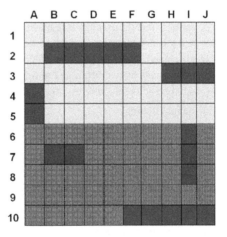

## CHAPTER 7

Modular Design

Until now, we have looked at programs comprised of a set of individual functions. In complex software systems, however, programs are organized at a higher level as a set of modules, each module containing a set of functions (or objects). Modules, like functions, are a fundamental building block in software development.

OBJECTIVES

After reading this chapter and completing the exercises, you will be able to:

♦ Explain the use of modular design in software development

♦ Explain the specification of modules

♦ Explain the process of top-down design

♦ Describe the concept of a stack

♦ Differentiate between unit testing and integration testing

♦ Become familiar with the use of docstrings in Python

♦ Explain the use of modules and namespaces in Python

♦ Describe and use the different forms of module import in Python

♦ Develop well-specified Python programs using top-down design

CHAPTER CONTENTS

Motivation

Fundamental Concepts

7.1 Modules

7.2 Top-Down Design

7.3 Python Modules

Computational Problem Solving

7.4 Calendar Year Program (function version)

MOTIVATION

Software systems are some of the most complex entities ever created. Web browsers and operating systems, for example, contain as many as 50–100 million lines of code. Developing programs of such size and complexity can easily take 10,000 person-years of effort to develop. It is natural, therefore, to find ways to divide the task of software development among various individuals (or groups of individuals).

We can make complex systems more manageable by designing them as a set of subsystems, or modules. For example, NASA's space shuttle (Figure 7-1) is one of the most complex systems ever engineered, containing more than 2.5 million parts. The major components are the orbiter vehicle, a large external liquid-fuel tank, and two solid rocket boosters. The orbiter vehicle itself is composed of several subsys-

NASA/Space Shuttle Columbia launching/ Wikimedia Commons

FIGURE 7-1   Space Shuttle

tems (e.g., the communications system), which in turn may be composed of sub-subsystems (e.g., the data network system), as shown in Figure 7-2.

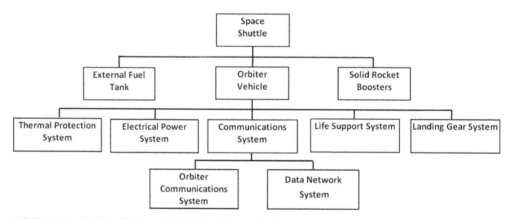

FIGURE 7-2   Modular Design of the NASA Space Shuttle

Although many of the technicians involved with the shuttle may understand its overall design, only a few select individuals need to understand or be involved with the detailed design, implementation, and testing of any specific subsystem. The same is true for the modular design of software. In this chapter, we look at the issue of modular program design.

FUNDAMENTAL CONCEPTS

7.1   Modules

7.1.1   What Is a Module?

An important aspect of well-designed software is that programs are designed as a collection of modules. The term "module," broadly speaking, refers to the design and/or implementation of specific functionality to be incorporated into a program. While an individual function may be considered a module, modules generally consists of a collection of functions (or other entities). The Python turtle module is an example of a software module. The use of modules has a number of advantages as shown in Figure 7-3.

- SOFTWARE DESIGN
  - provides a means for the development of well-designed programs

- SOFTWARE DEVELOPMENT
  - provides a natural means of dividing up programming tasks
  - provides a means for the reuse of program code

- SOFTWARE TESTING
  - provides a means of separately testing parts of a program
  - provides a means of integrating parts of a program during testing

- SOFTWARE MODIFICATION AND MAINTENANCE
  - facilitates the modification of specific program functionalities

FIGURE 7-3 Advantages of Modular Programming

Modular design allows large programs to be broken down into manageable size parts, in which each part (module) provides a clearly specified capability. It aids the software development process by providing an effective way of separating programming tasks among various individuals or teams. It allows modules to be individually developed and tested, and eventually integrated as a part of a complete system. Finally, modular design facilitates program modification since the code responsible for a given aspect of the software is contained within specific modules, and not distributed throughout the program.

The term "**module**" refers to the design and/or implementation of specific functionality to be incorporated into a program.

7.1.2 Module Specification

Every module needs to provide a *specification* of how it is to be used. This is referred to as the module's **interface**. Any program code making use of a particular module is referred to as a **client** of the module. A module's specification should be sufficiently *clear* and *complete* so that its clients can effectively utilize it. For example, numPrimes is a function that returns the number of primes in a given integer range, as shown in Figure 7-4.

```
def numPrimes(start, end):

    """ Returns the number of primes between start and end. """
```

FIGURE 7-4 docstring Specification

The function's specification is provided by the line immediately following the function header, called a *docstring* in Python. A **docstring** is a string literal denoted by triple quotes given as the first line of certain program elements. The docstring of a particular program element can be displayed by use of the __doc__ extension,

```
>>> print(numPrimes.__doc__)
Returns the number of primes between start and end.
```

This provides a convenient way for discovering how to use a particular function without having to look at the function definition itself. Some software development tools also make use of docstrings. Let's consider how complete this specification is for this function. At first look it may seem sufficient. However, it does not answer whether the number of primes returned includes the endpoints of the range or not. Also, it is not clear what will happen if the function is called with a first argument (start) greater than the second (end). Thus, a more complete specification is needed. This is given in Figure 7-5.

```
def numprimes(start, end):

    """ Returns the number of primes between start and end, inclusive.

        Returns -1 if start is greater than end.
    """
```

FIGURE 7-5 A More Complete docstring Specification

This is now a reasonable specification of the function. This docstring follows the Python convention of putting a blank line after the first line of the docstring, which should be an overall description of what the function does, followed by an arbitrary number of lines providing additional details. These additional lines must be indented at the same level, as shown in the figure. Appropriate use of this function by a client is given below.

```
.

.

first_num = int(input('Enter the start of the range: '))
second_num = int(input('Enter the end of the range: '))

result = numprimes(first_num, second_num)
    if result == -1:
        print('* Invalid range entered *')
    else:
        print('The number of primes between', first_num, 'and', second_num,
            'is', result)
```

In this example, the user inputs a start and end value for the range of integers to check. Since the user may inappropriately enter a start value greater than the value of the end value, a check is made for a returned value of −1 after the call to numprimes. If −1 is found, then an error message is output; otherwise, the result is displayed.

There are potential problems when returning both a computed result and an error result as a function's return value. First, there is no guarantee that the client will perform the necessary check for the special error value. Thus, an incorrect result may be displayed to the user,

```
The number of primes between 100 and 1 is -1
```

Second, there may not be a special value that *can* be returned for error reporting. For example, if there is a function meant to return any integer value, including negative numbers, there is no special integer value that can be returned. We will see a better means of error reporting by a function when we discuss exception handling in Chapter 8.

A module's **interface** is a specification of what it provides and how it is to be used. Any program code making use of a given module is called a **client** of the module. A **docstring** is a string literal denoted by triple quotes used in Python for providing the specification of certain program elements.

Self-Test Questions

1. Which of the following is not an advantage in the use of modules in software development?
   (a) Provides a natural means of dividing up programming tasks.
   (b) Provides a means of reducing the size of a program.
   (c) Provides a means for the reuse of program code.
   (d) Provides a means of separately testing individual parts of a program.
   (e) Provides a means of integrating parts of a program during testing.
   (f) Facilitates the modification of specific program functionalities.

2. A specification of how a particular module is used is called the module's _____.

3. Program code that makes use of a given module is called a _____ of the module.

4. Indicate which of the following are true. A docstring in Python is
   (a) A string literal denoted by triple or double quotes.
   (b) A means of providing specification for certain program elements in Python.
   (c) A string literal that may span more than one line.

ANSWERS: 1. (b), 2. interface, 3. client, 4. (b), (c)

7.2   Top-Down Design

One method of deriving a modular design is called **top-down design**. In this approach, the overall design of a system is developed first, deferring the specification of more detailed aspects of the design until later steps. We next consider a modular design using a top-down approach for the calendar year program from Chapter 4.

Top-down design is an approach for deriving a modular design in which the overall design of a system is developed first, deferring the specification of more detailed aspects of the design until later steps.

7.2.1   Developing a Modular Design of the Calendar Year Program

We will develop a modular design for the calendar year program from Chapter 4 (implemented there without the use of functions) using a top-down design approach. The three overall steps of the program are getting the requested year from the user, creating the calendar year structure, and displaying the year. This is depicted in Figure 7-6.

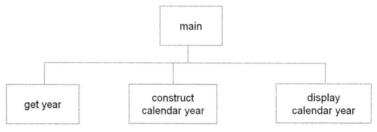

FIGURE 7-6 First Stage of a Modular Design of the Calendar Year Program

We then consider whether any of these modules needs to be further broken down. Making such a decision is more of an art than a science. The goal of modular design is that each module provides clearly defined functionality, which collectively provide all of the required functionality of the program. Modules get year and display calendar year are not complex enough to require further breakdown. Module construct calendar year, on the other hand, is where most of the work is done, and is therefore further broken down. Figure 7-7 contains the modules of this next design step.

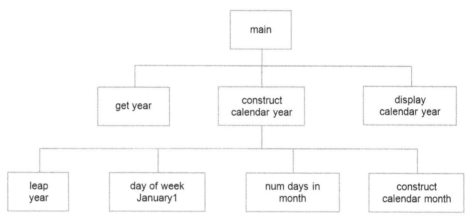

FIGURE 7-7 Second Stage of Modular Design of a Calendar Year Program

In order to construct a calendar year, it must be determined whether the year is a leap year, what day of the week January 1st of that year falls on, and how many days are in each month (accounting for leap years). Thus, modules leap year, day of week January1, and num days in month are added as *submodules* of module construct calendar year. The calendar month for each of the twelve months must then be individually constructed, handled by module construct calendar month.

> The goal of top-down design is that each module provides clearly defined functionality, which collectively provide all of the required functionality of the program.

7.2.2 Specification of the Calendar Year Program Modules

The modular design of the calendar year program provides a high-level view of the program. However, there are many issues yet to resolve in the design. Since each module is to be implemented as a function, we need to specify the details of each function. For example, for each function it needs to be decided if it is a value-returning function or a non-value-returning function; what parameters it will take; and what results it will produce. We give such a specification in Figure 7-8 using Python docstrings.

This stage of the design provides sufficient detail from which to implement the program. The main module provides the overall construction of the program. It simply displays the program

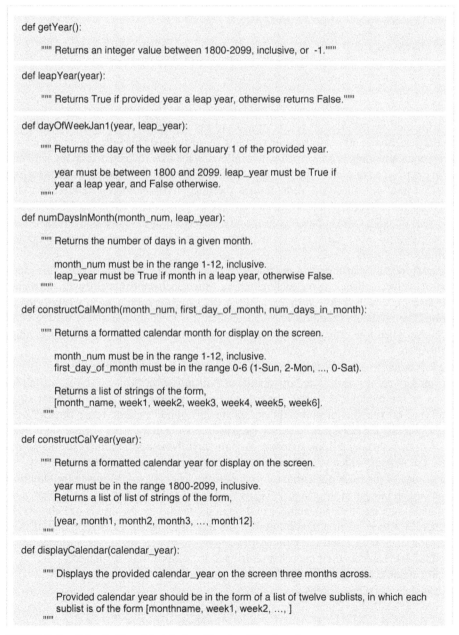

```
def getYear():

    """ Returns an integer value between 1800-2099, inclusive, or  -1."""

def leapYear(year):

    """ Returns True if provided year a leap year, otherwise returns False."""

def dayOfWeekJan1(year, leap_year):

    """ Returns the day of the week for January 1 of the provided year.

        year must be between 1800 and 2099. leap_year must be True if
        year a leap year, and False otherwise.
    """

def numDaysInMonth(month_num, leap_year):

    """ Returns the number of days in a given month.

        month_num must be in the range 1-12, inclusive.
        leap_year must be True if month in a leap year, otherwise False.
    """

def constructCalMonth(month_num, first_day_of_month, num_days_in_month):

    """ Returns a formatted calendar month for display on the screen.

        month_num must be in the range 1-12, inclusive.
        first_day_of_month must be in the range 0-6 (1-Sun, 2-Mon, ..., 0-Sat).

        Returns a list of strings of the form,
        [month_name, week1, week2, week3, week4, week5, week6].
    """

def constructCalYear(year):

    """ Returns a formatted calendar year for display on the screen.

        year must be in the range 1800-2099, inclusive.
        Returns a list of list of strings of the form,

        [year, month1, month2, month3, ..., month12].
    """

def displayCalendar(calendar_year):

    """ Displays the provided calendar_year on the screen three months across.

        Provided calendar year should be in the form of a list of twelve sublists, in which each
        sublist is of the form [monthname, week1, week2, ..., ]
    """
```

FIGURE 7-8   Calendar Year Module Specification (*Continued*)

```
# main
terminate = False

print('This program will display a calendar year for a given year')

while not terminate:
    year = getYear()

    if year == -1:
        terminate = True
    else:
        calendar_year = constructCalYear(year)
        displayCalendar(calendar_year)
```

FIGURE 7-8 Calendar Year Module Specification

greeting, calls module getYear to get the year from the user, calls module constructCalYear to construct the year, and finally calls module displayCalendar to display the calendar year. The only detail that the main module is concerned with is allowing the user to keep displaying another calendar year, or enter -1 to terminate the program. This is controlled by Boolean variable terminate.

The first module called, getYear, returns the integer value entered by the user. The module's specification indicates that it returns an integer value between 1800 and 2099, inclusive; or -1 (if the user decides to terminate the program). Therefore, it is the responsibility of the module to ensure that no other value is returned. This relieves the main module of having to check for bad input.

The next module that the main module uses is module constructCalYear. This module returns a list of twelve sublists, one for each month, in which each sublist begins with the name of the month (as a string value), followed by each of the weeks in the month, each week formatted as a single string. The module's specification indicates that it is to be passed a year between 1800 and 2099, inclusive. Therefore, any year given to it that is outside that range violates its condition for use, and therefore the results are not guaranteed.

The last module called from the main module is module displayCalendar. It is given a constructed calendar year, as constructed by module constructCalMonth.

Based on the modular design of the calendar year program, constructCalYear is the only module relying on the use of submodules, specifically modules leapYear, dayOfWeekJan1, numDaysInMonth, and constructCal. The leapYear module determines whether a given a year is a leap year or not, returning a Boolean result. Module dayOfWeekJan1 returns the day of the week for January 1st of the provided year. Boolean value leap_year must also be provided to the module, needed in the day of the week algorithm on which the module is based. Module numDaysInMonth must be passed an integer in the range 1–12, as well as a Boolean value for leap_year. This is so that the module can determine the number of days in the month for the month of February. Finally, constructCalMonth is given a month number, the day of the week of the first day of the month (1-Sun, 2-Mon, . . ., 0-Sat) and the number of days in the month. With this information, module constructCalYear can construct the calendar list and its sublists to be displayed.

Finally, module displayCalendarMonth is given a formatted calendar year. Its job is to display the calendar year three months across.

This more detailed modular design provides the details of how each module is to be incorporated into a complete program. We will discuss the implementation of this design at the end of the chapter.

Self-Test Questions

1. In top-down design (select one),
  (a) The details of a program design are addressed before the overall design.
  (b) The overall design of a program is addressed before the details.

2. All modular designs are a result of a top-down design process. (TRUE/FALSE)

3. In top-down design, every module is broken down into the same number of submodules. (TRUE/FALSE)

4. Which of the following advantages of modular design apply to the design of the calendar program.
  (a) Provides a means for the development of well-designed programs.
  (b) Provides a natural means of dividing up programming tasks.
  (c) Provides a means of separately testing individual parts of a program.

ANSWERS: 1. (b), 2. False, 3. False, 4. (a), (b), (c)

7.3   Python Modules

7.3.1   What Is a Python Module?

A Python module is a file containing Python definitions and statements. When a Python file is directly executed, it is considered the *main module* of a program. Main modules are given the special name __main__. Main modules provide the basis for a complete Python program. They may *import* (include) any number of other modules (and each of those modules import other modules, etc.). Main modules are not meant to be imported into other modules.

As with the main module, imported modules may contain a set of statements. The statements of imported modules are executed only once, the first time that the module is imported. The purpose of these statements is to perform any initialization needed for the members of the imported module. The Python Standard Library contains a set of predefined *Standard (built-in) modules*. We have in fact seen some of these modules already, such as the math and random Standard Library modules.

Python modules provide all the benefits of modular software design we have discussed. By convention, modules are named using all lower case letters and optional underscore characters. We will look more closely at Python modules in the next section.

LET'S TRY IT

Create a Python module by entering the following in a file name simple.py. Then execute the instructions in the Python shell as shown and observe the results.

```
# module simple                          >>> import simple
print('module simple loaded')           ???
                                         >>> simple.func1()
def func1():                             ???
    print('func1 called')
                                         >>> simple.func2()
def func2():                             ???
    print('func2 called')
```

A **Python module** is a file containing Python definitions and statements. The Python Standard Library contains a set of predefined **standard (built-in) modules**.

7.3.2 Modules and Namespaces

A **namespace** is a container that provides a named context for a set of identifiers. Namespaces enable programs to avoid potential *name clashes* by associating each identifier with the namespace from which it originates. In software development, a **name clash** is when two otherwise distinct entities with the same name become part of the same scope. Name clashes can occur, for example, if two or more Python modules contain identifiers with the same name and are imported into the same program, as shown in Figure 7-9.

```
# module1

def double(lst):

    """Returns a new list with each
       number doubled, for example,
       [1, 2, 3] returned as [2, 4, 6]
    """
```

```
# module2

def double(lst):

    """Returns a new list with each
       number duplicated, for example,
       [1, 2, 3] returned as
       [(1, 1), (2, 2), (3, 3)]
    """
```

```
import module1
import module2

# main
    .
    num_list = [3, 8, 14]
    result = double(num_list)   ⟵······ ambiguous reference for
    .                                    identifier double
```

FIGURE 7-9 Example Name Clash of Imported Functions

In this example, module1 and module2 are imported into the same program. Each module contains an identifier named double, which return very different results. When the function call double(num_list) is executed in main, there is a name clash. Thus, it cannot be determined which of these two functions should be called. Namespaces provide a means for resolving such problems.

In Python, each module has its own namespace. This includes the names of all items in the module, including functions and global variables—variables defined within the module and outside the scope of any of its functions. Thus, two instances of identifier double, each defined in their own module, are distinguished by being *fully qualified* with the name of the module in which each is defined: module1.double and module2.double. Figure 7-10 illustrates the use of fully qualified identifiers for calls to function double.

The use of namespaces to resolve problems associated with duplicate naming is not restricted to computer programming. In fact, it occurs in everyday situations. Imagine, for instance, that you

```
import module1
import module2


# main

    ans1 = module1.double(...)   <········      references function double from
                                                module1's namespace

    ans2 = module2.double(...)   <········      references function double from
                                                module2's namespace
```

FIGURE 7-10 Example Use of Fully Qualified Function Names

run into a friend who tells you that "Paul is getting married." In fact, you have two friends in common named Paul. Because you are not certain which Paul your friend is referring to, you may respond "Paul from back home, or Paul from the dorm?" In this case, you are asking your friend to respond with a fully qualified name to resolve the ambiguity: "home:Paul" vs. "dorm:Paul." Next, we look at different ways that Python modules can be imported.

LET'S TRY IT

Enter each of the following functions in their own modules named mod1.py and mod2.py. Enter and execute the following and observe the results.

```
# mod1                                    >>> import mod1, mod2
def average(lst):                         >>> mod1.average([10, 20, 30])
    print('average of mod1 called')       ???
                                          >>> mod2.average([10, 20, 30])
# mod2                                     ???
def average(lst):                         >>> average([10, 20, 30])
    print('average of mod2 called')       ???
```

A **namespace** provides a context for a set of identifiers. Every module in Python has its own namespace. A **name clash** is when two otherwise distinct entities with the same identifier become part of the same scope.

7.3.3 Importing Modules

In Python, the **main module** of any program is the first ("top-level") module executed. When working interactively in the Python shell, the Python interpreter functions as the main module, containing the *global namespace*. The namespace is reset every time the interpreter is started (or when selecting Shell → Restart Shell). Next we look at various means of importing modules in Python. (We note that module __builtins__ is automatically imported in Python programs, providing all the built-in constants, functions, and classes.)

In Python, the **main module** of any program is identified as the first ("top-level") module executed.

The "import *modulename*" Form of Import

When using the `import` *modulename* form of import, the namespace of the imported module becomes *available to*, but not *part of*, the importing module. Identifiers of the imported module, therefore, must be fully qualified (prefixed with the module's name) when accessed. Using this form of import prevents any possibility of a name clash. Thus, as we have seen, if two modules, `module1` and `module2`, both have the same identifier, `identifier1`, then `module1.identifier1` denotes the entity of the first module and `module2.identifier1` denotes the entity of the second module.

LET'S TRY IT

Enter the following into the Python shell and observe the results.

```
>>> factorial(5)              >>> import math
???                           >>> factorial(5)
                              ???
>>> math.factorial(5)
???                           >>> math.factorial(5)
                              ???
```

With the `import` *modulename* form of import in Python, the namespace of the imported module becomes available to, but does not become part of, the namespace of the importing module.

The "from-import" Form of Import

Python also provides an alternate import statement of the form

$$\textbf{from } modulename \textbf{ import } something$$

where *something* can be a list of identifiers, a single renamed identifier, or an asterisk, as shown below,

    (a) **from** *modulename* **import** func1, func2
    (b) **from** *modulename* **import** func1 **as** new_func1
    (c) **from** *modulename* **import** *

In example (a), only identifiers `func1` and `func2` are imported. In example (b), only identifier `func1` is imported, renamed as `new_func1` in the importing module. Finally, in example (c), *all* of the identifiers are imported, except for those that begin with two underscore characters, which are meant to be private in the module, which will be discussed later.

There is a fundamental difference between the `from` *modulename* `import` and `import` *modulename* forms of import in Python. When using `import` *modulename*, the namespace of the imported module does not become part of the namespace of the importing module, as mentioned. Therefore, identifiers of the imported module must be fully qualified (e.g., *modulename*.`func1`) in the importing module. In contrast, when using `from-import`, the imported module's namespace *becomes part of* the importing module's namespace. Thus, imported identifiers are referenced without being fully qualified (e.g., `func1`).

The `from` *modulename* `import` func1 `as` new_func1 form of import is used when identifiers in the imported module's namespace are known to be identical to identifiers of the importing module. In such cases, the renamed imported function can be used without needing to be fully qualified. Finally, using the `from modulename import *` form of import in example (c), although convenient, makes name clashes more likely. This is because the names of the imported identifiers are not explicitly listed in the import statement, creating a greater chance that the programmer will unintentionally define an identifier with the same name as in the importing module. And since the `from-import` form of import allows imported identifiers to be accessed without being fully qualified, it is unclear in the importing module where these identifiers come from. We provide an example of this in Figure 7-11.

```
# module somemodule

def func1(n):
  return n * 10

def func2(n1, n2):
  return n1 * n2
```

```
# ---- main

from somemodule import *

# NAMESPACES AND FUNCTION USE

def func2(n):
    return n * n              # definition of func2 masks imported func2

print(func1(8))              # outputs 80 (func1 of somemodule called)
print(somemodule.func1(8))   # NameError: name 'somemodule' is not defined

print(func2(5))              # outputs 25 (func2 of MAIN called)
print(func2(3, 8))           # TypeError: func2() takes exactly 1 argument

print(somemodule.func2(3, 8)) # NameError: name 'somemodule' is not
                                defined
```

FIGURE 7-11 Example Use of `from-import` Form of Import

Module `somemodule` contains functions `func1` and `func2`. Since `somemodule` is imported with `from somemodule import *`, identifiers `func1` and `func2` become part of the main module's namespace. However, since the module's namespace already contains identifier `func2` (denoting the function defined there), access to `func2` of `somemodule` is *masked*, and therefore is inaccessible. Using the fully qualified form `somemodule.func2` does not work either, since `somemodule` is not part of the imported namespace for this form of import.

Finally, it is recommended Python style that standard modules be imported before the programmer-defined ones, with each section of imports separated by a blank line as shown below.

```
import standardmodule1          # standard modules
import standardmodule2

import somemodule1              # programmer-defined modules
import somemodule2
```

LET'S TRY IT

Enter the following into the Python shell and observe the results.

```
>>> from math import factorial          >>> from math import factorial as fact
>>> factorial(5)                         >>> fact(5)
???                                      ???

>>> def factorial(n):                    >>> def factorial(n):
        print('my factorial')                    print('my factorial')

>>> factorial(5)                         >>> factorial(5)
???                                      ???

>>> math.factorial(5)                    >>> fact(5)
???                                      ???
```

With the `from-import` form of import, imported identifiers become part of the importing module's namespace. Because of the possibility of name clashes, `import modulename` is the preferred form of import in Python.

Module Private Variables

In Python, all identifiers in a module are "public"—that is, accessible by any other module that imports it. Sometimes, however, entities (variables, functions, etc.) in a module are meant to be "private"—used within the module, but not meant to be accessed from outside it.

Python does not provide any means for preventing access to variables or other entities meant to be private. Instead, there is a convention that names beginning with two underscores (_) are intended to be private. Such entities, therefore, *should not* be accessed. It does not mean that they *cannot* be accessed, however. There is one situation in which access to private variables is restricted. When the `from modulename import *` form of import is used to import *all* the identifiers of a module's namespace, names beginning with double underscores are not imported. Thus, such entities become inaccessible from within the importing module.

In Python, all the variables in a module are "public," with the convention that variables beginning with an two underscores are intended to be private.

7.3.4 Module Loading and Execution

Each imported module of a Python program needs to be located and loaded into memory. Python first searches for modules in the current directory. If the module is not found, it searches the directories specified in the PYTHONPATH environment variable. If the module is still not found (or PYTHON-PATH is not defined), a Python installation-specific path is searched (e.g., `C:\Python32\Lib`). If the program still does not find the module, an error (`ImportError` exception) is reported. For our purposes, all of the modules of a program will be kept in the same directory. However, if you wish to develop a module made available to other programs, then the module can be saved in your own Python modules directory specified in the PYTHONPATH, or stored in the particular Python installation Lib directory.

When a module is loaded, a compiled version of the module with file extension .pyc is automatically produced. Then, the next time that the module is imported, the compiled .pyc file is loaded, rather than the .py file, to save the time of recompiling. A new compiled version of a module is automatically produced whenever the compiled version is out of date with the source code version of the module when loading, based on the dates that the files were created/modified.

Built-in Function `dir()`

Built-in function `dir()` is very useful for monitoring the items in the namespace of the main module for programs executing in the Python shell. For example, the following gives the namespace of a newly started shell,

```
>>> dir()
['__builtins__', '__doc__', '__name__', '__package__']
```

The following shows the namespace after importing and defining variables,

```
>>> import random
>>> n = 10
>>> dir()
['__builtins__', '__doc__', '__name__', '__package__', 'n', 'random']
```

Selecting Shell → Restart Shell (Ctrl-F6) in the shell resets the namespace,

```
(after Restart Shell selected)
>>> dir()
['__builtins__', '__doc__', '__name__', '__package__']
```

LET'S TRY IT

Create the following Python module named `simplemodule`, import it, and call function `display-Greeting` as shown from the Python shell and observe the results.

```
# simplemodule

def displayGreeting():
    print('Hello World!')
```

```
>>> import simplemodule
>>> simplemodule.displayGreeting()
```

Modify module `simplemodule` to display 'Hey there world!', import and again execute function `displayGreeting` as shown. Observe the results.

```
>>> import simplemodule
>>> simplemodule.displayGreeting()
```

Finally, reload the module as shown and again call function `displayGreeting`.

```
>>> reload(simplemodule)
>>> simplemodule.displayGreeting()
???
```

When a module is loaded, a compiled version of the module with file extension `.pyc` is automatically produced. When using the Python shell, an updated module can be forced to be reloaded and recompiled by use of the `reload()` function.

7.3.5   Local, Global, and Built-in Namespaces in Python

During a Python program's execution, there are as many as three namespaces that are referenced ("active")—the built-in namespace, the global namespace, and the local namespace. The **built-in namespace** contains the names of all the built-in functions, constants, and so on, in Python. The **global namespace** contains the identifiers of the currently executing module. And the **local namespace** is the namespace of the currently executing function (if any).

When Python looks for an identifier, it first searches the local namespace (if defined), then the global namespace, and finally the built-in namespace. Thus, if the same identifier is defined in more than one of these namespaces, it becomes masked, as depicted in Figure 7-12.

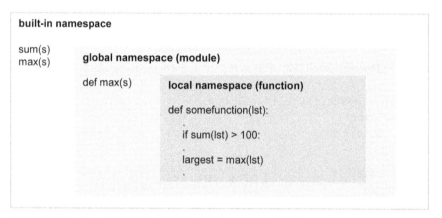

FIGURE 7-12   Local, Global, and Built-in Namespaces of Python

Functions `sum` and `max` are built-in functions in Python, and thus in the built-in namespace. Built-in function `sum` returns the sum of a sequence (list or tuple) or integers. Built-in function `max` returns the largest value of a string, list, tuple, and other types.

In the module (and thus part of the global namespace) is defined another function named `max`. This programmer-defined function returns the index of the largest value from an ordered collection of items, not the value itself as built-in function `max` is designed to do. This is demonstrated below.

```
max([4, 2, 7, 1, 9, 6])      →     9 (built-in function max)
max([4, 2, 7, 1, 9, 6])      →     4 (programmer-defined function max)
```

Which specific functions are called from within `somefunction` depends on where the functions are defined. Function `sum`, for example, is not defined within the global namespace. Therefore, built-in function `sum` of the built-in namespace is called. The call to function `max`, on the other hand, does not access the built-in function `max`; rather, it calls function `max` of the more closely defined global namespace. This demonstrates how issues of scope, if not clearly considered, can result in subtle and unexpected program errors. Consider the example program in Figure 7-13.

```
# grade_calc module

def max(grades):
    largest = 0

    for k in grades:
        if k > 100:
            largest = 100
        elif k > largest:
            largest = k

    return largest

def grades_highlow(grades):
    return (min(grades), max(grades))
```

```
# classgrades (main module)

from grade_calc import *

class_grades = [86, 72, 94, 102, 89, 76, 96]

low_grade, high_grade = grades_highlow(class_grades)
print('Highest adjusted grade on the exam was', high_grade)
print('Lowest grade on the exam was', low_grade)

print('Actual highest grade on exam was', max(class_grades))
```

FIGURE 7-13 Inadvertent Masking of Identifier in the Built-in Namespace

This program is meant to read in the exam grades of a class. (The grades are hard-coded here for the sake of an example.) The main module imports module `grade_calc` that contains function `grades_highlow`, which returns as a tuple the highest grade (with extra credit grades over 100 returned as 100) and lowest grade in a list of grades. Upon executing this program, we find the following results,

```
Highest adjusted grade on the exam was 100
Lowest grade on the exam was 72
The actual highest grade on the exam was 100
>>>
```

For the list of grades 86, 72, 94, 102, 89, 76, 96, the high and low grades of 72 and 100 is correct (counting the grade 102 as a grade of 100). Then the program is to display the actual highest grade of 102. However, a grade of 100 is displayed instead.

The problem is that the `grade_calc` module was imported using `from grade_calc import *`. Thus, all of the entities of the module were imported, including the defined `max` function. This function returns a "truncated" maximum grade of 100 from a list of grades, used as a supporting function for function `grades_highlow`. However, since it is defined in the global (module) namespace of the `classgrades` program, that definition of function `max` masks the built-in max function of the built-in namespace. Thus, when called from within the class-grades program, it also produces a truncated highest grade, thus returning the actual highest grade of 100 instead of 102.

This example shows the care that must be taken in the use and naming of global identifiers, especially with the from-import * form of import. Note that if function max were named as a private member of the module, __max, then it would not have been imported into the main module and the actual highest grade displayed would have been correct.

LET'S TRY IT

Enter the following in the Python shell:

```
>>> sum([1, 2, 3])
???

>>> def sum(n1, n2, n3):
        total = n1 + n2 + n3

        return total
>>> sum([1, 2, 3])
???

>>> sum(1, 2, 3)
???
```

Create a file with the following module:

```
# module max_test_module
def test_max():
        print 'max =', max([1, 2, 3])
```

Create and execute the following program:

```
import max_test_module

def max():
        print('max:local namespace called')

print(max_test_module.test_max())
```

At any given point in a Python program's execution, there are three possible namespaces referenced ("active")—the **built-in namespace**, the **global namespace**, and the **local namespace**.

7.3.6 A Programmer-Defined Stack Module

In order to demonstrate the development of a programmer-defined module, we present an example stack module. A **stack** is a very useful mechanism in computer science. Stacks are used to temporarily store and retrieve data. They have the property that the last item placed on the stack is the first to be retrieved. This is referred to as LIFO—"last in, first out." A stack can be viewed as a list that can be accessed only at one end, as depicted in Figure 7-14.

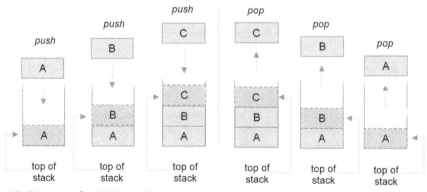

FIGURE 7-14   Stack Mechanism

In this example, three items are *pushed* on the stack, denoted by A, B, and C. First, item A is pushed, followed by item B, and then item C. After the three items have been placed on the stack, the only item that can be accessed or removed is item C, located at the *top of stack*. When C is retrieved, it is said to be *popped* from the stack, leaving item B as the top of stack. Once item B is popped, item A becomes the top of stack. Finally, when item A is popped, the stack becomes empty. It is an error to attempt to pop an empty stack.

In Figure 7-15 is a Python module containing a set of functions that implements this stack behavior. For demonstration purposes, the program displays and pushes the values 1 through 4 on the stack. It then displays the numbers popped off the stack, retrieved in the reverse order that they were pushed.

The stack module consists of five functions—getStack, isEmpty, top, push, and pop. The stack is implemented as a list. Only the last element in the list is accessed—that is where

```
 1   # stack Module
 2
 3   def getStack():
 4
 5       """Creates and returns an empty stack."""
 6
 7       return []
 8
 9   def isEmpty(s):
10
11       """Returns True if stack empty, otherwise returns False. """
12
13       if s == []:
14           return True
15       else:
16           return False
17
18   def top(s):
19
20       """Returns value of the top item of stack, if stack not empty.
21          Otherwise, returns None.
22       """
23
24       if isEmpty(s):
25           return None
26       else:
27           return s[len(s) - 1]
28
29   def push(s, item):
30
31       """Pushes item on the top of stack. """
32
33       s.append(item)
34
35   def pop(s):
36
37       """Returns top of stack if stack not empty. Otherwise, returns None."""
38
39       if isEmpty(s):
40           return None
41       else:
42           item = s[len(s) - 1]
43           del s[len(s) - 1]
44           return item
```

FIGURE 7-15   Programmer-Defined Stack Module

all items are "pushed" and "popped" from. Thus, the end of the list logically functions as the "top" of stack.

Function getStack (**lines 3–7**) creates and returns a new empty stack as an empty list. Function isEmpty (**lines 9–16**) returns whether a stack is empty or not (by checking if an empty list). Function top (**lines 18–27**) returns the top item of a stack without removing it. Functions push (**lines 29–33**) and pop (**lines 35–44**) provide the essential stack operations. The push function pushes an item on the stack by appending it to the end of the list. The pop function removes the item from the top of stack by retrieving the last element of the list, and then deleting it. If either pop or top are called on an empty stack, the special value None is returned.

```
   # main
1  import stack
2
3  mystack = stack.getStack()
4
5  for item in range(1, 5):
6      stack.push(mystack, item)
7      print('Pushing', item, 'on stack')
8
9  while not stack.isEmpty(mystack):
10     item = stack.pop(mystack)
11     print('Popping', item,'from stack')
```

FIGURE 7-16 Demonstration of the Programmer-Defined Stack Module

The small program in Figure 7-16 demonstrates the use of the stack module. First, a new stack is created by assigning variable mystack to the result of the call to function getStack (**line 3**). Even though a list is returned, it is intended to be more specifically a stack type. Therefore, only the stack-related functions should be used with this variable—the list should not be directly accessed, otherwise the stack may become corrupted. Then the values 1 through 4 are pushed on the stack, and popped in the reverse order,

```
Pushing 1 on stack
Pushing 2 on stack
Pushing 3 on stack
Pushing 4 on stack
Popping 4 from stack
Popping 3 from stack
Popping 2 from stack
Popping 1 from stack
```

Ensuring that only the provided functions can be used on the stack represents a fundamental advantage of objects. Since an object consists of data and methods (routines), only the methods of the object can be used to access and alter the data. Thus, the stack type is best implemented as an object, as all other values in Python are. We will see how do to this after the introduction of object-oriented programming in Chapter 10.

7.3.7 Let's Apply It—A Palindrome Checker Program

The program in Figure 7-18 determines if a given string is a palindrome. A palindrome is something that reads the same forwards and backwards. For example, the words "level" and "radar" are palindromes. The program imports the stack module developed in the previous section. This program utilizes the following programming feature:

➤ Programmer-defined module

Example execution of the program is given in Figure 7-17.

```
Program execution ...


This program can determine if a given string is a palindrome

(Enter return to exit)
Enter string to check: look
look is NOT a palindrome

Enter string to check: radar
radar is a palindrome

Enter string to check:
>>>
```

FIGURE 7-17   Execution of the Palindrome Checker Program

The stack module is imported on **line 3** of the program. The "import *modulename*" form of import is used. Therefore, each stack function is referenced by `stack.function_name`. **Lines 6–7** displays a simple program welcome. The following lines perform the required initialization for the program. **Line 10** sets `char_stack` to a new empty stack by call to `getStack()`. **Line 11** initializes variable `empty_string` to the empty string. This is used in the program for determining if the user has finished entering all the words to check.

The string to check is input by the user on **line 14**. If the string is of length one, then by definition the string is a palindrome. This special case is handled in **lines 17–18**. Otherwise, the complete string is checked. First, variable `palindrome` is initialized to `True`. On **line 24**, variable `compare_length` is set to half the length of the input string, using integer division to truncate the length to an equal number of characters. This represents the number of characters from the front of the string (working forward) that must match the number of characters on the rear of the string (working backwards). If there are an odd number of characters, then the middle character has no other character to match against.

On **lines 27–28** the second half of the string chars are pushed character-by-character onto the stack. Then, on lines **31–37** the characters are popped from the stack one by one, returning in the reverse order that they were pushed. Thus, the first character popped (the *last* character pushed on the stack) is compared to the *first* character of the complete string. This continues until there are no more characters to be checked. If characters are found that do not match, then `is_palindrome` is set to `False` (**lines 34–35**) and the while loop terminates. Otherwise, `is_palindrome` remains `True`. **Lines 40–43** output whether the input string is a palindrome or not, based on the final value of `is_palindrome`. **Lines 45–46** prompt the user for another string to enter, and control returns to the top of the while loop.

```
1   # Palindrome Checker Program
2
3   import stack
4
5   # welcome
6   print('This program can determine if a given string is a palindrome\n')
7   print('(Enter return to exit)')
8
9   # init
10  char_stack = stack.getStack()
11  empty_string = ''
12
13  # get string from user
14  chars = input('Enter string to check: ')
15
16  while chars != empty_string:
17      if len(chars) == 1:
18          print('A one letter word is by definition a palindrome\n')
19      else:
20          # init
21          is_palindrome = True
22
23          # to handle strings of odd length
24          compare_length = len(chars) // 2
25
26          # push second half of input string on stack
27          for k in range(compare_length, len(chars)):
28              stack.push(char_stack, chars[k])
29
30          # pop chars and compare to first half of string
31          k = 0
32          while k < compare_length and is_palindrome:
33              ch = stack.pop(char_stack)
34              if chars[k].lower() != ch.lower():
35                  is_palindrome = False
36
37              k = k + 1
38
39          # display results
40          if is_palindrome:
41              print(chars, 'is a palindrome\n')
42          else:
43              print(chars, 'is NOT a palindrome\n')
44
45      # get next string from user
46      chars = input('Enter string to check: ')
```

FIGURE 7-18   Palindrome Checker Program

It is important to mention that the problem of palindrome checking could be done more efficiently without the use of a stack. A for loop can be used that compares the characters k locations from each end of the given string. Thus, our use of a stack for this problem was for demonstration purposes only. We leave the checking of palindromes by iteration as a chapter exercise.

Self-Test Questions

1. Any initialization code in a Python module is only executed once, the first time that the module is loaded. (TRUE/FALSE)

2. With the "import *moduleName*" form of import, any utilized entities from the imported module must be prefixed with the module name. (TRUE/FALSE)

3. By convention, variables names in a module beginning with two _____ characters are meant to be treated as private variables of the module.

4. When importing modules, all Python Standard Library modules must be imported before any programmer-defined modules, otherwise a runtime error will occur. (TRUE/FALSE)

5. If a particular module is imported more than once in a Python program, the Python interpreter will ensure that the module is only loaded and executed the first time that it is imported. (TRUE/FALSE)

6. The _____ command can be used to force the reloading of a given module, useful for when working interactively in the Python shell.

7. The three active namespaces that may exist during the execution of any given Python program are the _____, _____ and _____ namespaces.

ANSWERS: 1. True. 2. True. 3. Underscore. 4. False. 5. True. 6. reload. 7. built-in, global, local

COMPUTATIONAL PROBLEM SOLVING

7.4 Calendar Year Program (function version)

In this section, we implement and test the modular design for the calendar year program in section 7.2.

7.4.1 The Problem

The problem is the same as that given in Chapter 4—to display a calendar year from 1800 to 2099, displayed as shown in Figure 7-19.

7.4.2 Problem Analysis

Since the same problem is being solved, the algorithms utilized are also the same—an algorithm for computing the day of the week (for the years 1800 to 2099), an algorithm for storing the calendar year, and a means of displaying a calendar year three months across.

7.4.3 Program Design

The program requirements, data structures, algorithms, and overall program steps are the same as specified in Chapter 4. This program will only differ in that we will utilized a modular design for the program, as introduced in section 7.2. This will result in a program that is more easily understood, more easily modified, and more amenable to program testing.

7.4.4 Program Implementation and Testing

Now that we are using modular design, we can more easily incrementally test the program. Given the specification of each module (function), we can first test each function separately to see if the implementation correctly meets the specification. The individual testing of modules is called **unit testing**. Once each module is individually tested, they can all be tested together.

```
2015

January                         February                        March
         1  2  3               1  2  3  4  5  6  7              1  2  3  4  5  6  7
 4  5  6  7  8  9 10           8  9 10 11 12 13 14              8  9 10 11 12 13 14
11 12 13 14 15 16 17          15 16 17 18 19 20 21             15 16 17 18 19 20 21
18 19 20 21 22 23 24          22 23 24 25 26 27 28             22 23 24 25 26 27 28
25 26 27 28 29 30 31                                           29 30 31


April                           May                             June
         1  2  3  4                           1  2                 1  2  3  4  5  6
 5  6  7  8  9 10 11            3  4  5  6  7  8  9              7  8  9 10 11 12 13
12 13 14 15 16 17 18          10 11 12 13 14 15 16             14 15 16 17 18 19 20
19 20 21 22 23 24 25          17 18 19 20 21 22 23             21 22 23 24 25 26 27
26 27 28 29 30                24 25 26 27 28 29 30             28 29 30
                              31


July                            August                          September
         1  2  3  4                              1                    1  2  3  4  5
 5  6  7  8  9 10 11            2  3  4  5  6  7  8              6  7  8  9 10 11 12
12 13 14 15 16 17 18           9 10 11 12 13 14 15             13 14 15 16 17 18 19
19 20 21 22 23 24 25          16 17 18 19 20 21 22             20 21 22 23 24 25 26
26 27 28 29 30 31             23 24 25 26 27 28 29             27 28 29 30
                              30 31


October                         November                        December
            1  2  3            1  2  3  4  5  6  7                    1  2  3  4  5
 4  5  6  7  8  9 10           8  9 10 11 12 13 14              6  7  8  9 10 11 12
11 12 13 14 15 16 17          15 16 17 18 19 20 21             13 14 15 16 17 18 19
18 19 20 21 22 23 24          22 23 24 25 26 27 28             20 21 22 23 24 25 26
25 26 27 28 29 30 31          29 30                            27 28 29 30 31
```

FIGURE 7-19 Calendar Year Display

This is called **integration testing**. We demonstrate unit testing and integration testing of the calendar program in this section.

Implementation of the Calendar Year Program

Figure 7-20 shows an implementation of the Calendar Year program based on the modular design developed.

The main section of the program, **lines 188–207**, follows directly from our modular design, developed in section 7.2. The first function call is to function getYear (**lines 3–12**). This function simply contains an input statement and while loop to ensure that the year returned is in the range 1800 to 2099, inclusive.

Next, function constructCalYear (**lines 121–147**) is called. As seen from the modular design, it relies on calls to functions leapYear, dayOfWeekJan1, numDaysInMonth, and constructCalMonth. This function essentially consists of a for loop that iterates once for each of the twelve months, calling constructCalMonth to construct each month and append each to the list calendar_year. The constructed year is a list of lists as given below,

```
[year, [month, week1, week2,...], [month, week1, week2,...],...]
```

```
 1  # Calendar Year Program (Function Version)
 2
 3  def getYear():
 4
 5      """Returns a year between 1800-2099, inclusive, or the value -1."""
 6
 7      year = int(input('Enter year (yyyy) (-1 to quit): '))
 8      while (year < 1800 or year > 2099) and year != -1:
 9          print('INVALID INPUT - Year must be between 1800 and 2099')
10          year = int(input('Enter year (1-12): '))
11
12      return year
13
14  def leapYear(year):
15
16      """Returns True if year a leap year, otherwise returns False."""
17
18      if (year % 4 == 0) and (not (year % 100 == 0) or
19          (year % 400 == 0)):
20          leap_year = True
21      else:
22          leap_year = False
23
24      return leap_year
25
26  def dayOfWeekJan1(year, leap_year):
27
28      """Returns the day of the week for January 1 of a given year.
29
30          year must be between 1800 and 2099. leap_year must be True if
31          year a leap year, and False otherwise.
32      """
33      century_digits = year // 100
34      year_digits = year % 100
35      value = year_digits + (year_digits // 4)
36
37      if century_digits == 18:
38          value = value + 2
39      elif century_digits == 20:
40          value = value + 6
41
42      # adjust for leap years
43      if not leap_year:
44          value = value + 1
45
46      # return first day of month for Jan 1
47      return (value + 1) % 7
48
```

FIGURE 7-20   Implementation of the Calendar Year Program (*Continued*)

Functions dayOfWeekJan1 (**lines 26–47**) and numDaysInMonth (**lines 49–63**) are straightforward, neither relying on a call to any other function.

Function constructCalMonth is the largest of all the functions. It uses the same basic approach as before to properly align the weeks for display. In this function, a list of strings is created to be output to the screen. Finally, function displayCalendar is given a particular calendar year structure and displays it in four rows of months, with three months across each row.

```
49  def numDaysInMonth(month_num, leap_year):
50  #------------------------------------------------------------------
51      """Returns the number of days in a given month.
52
53          month_num in the range 1-12, inclusive.
54          leap_year True if month in a leap year, otherwise False.
55      """
56      num_days_in_month = (31, 28, 31, 30, 31, 30, 31, 31, 30, 31, 30, 31)
57
58      # special check for February in leap year
59      if (month_num == 2) and leap_year:
60          num_days = 29
61      else:
62          num_days = num_days_in_month[month_num - 1]
63      return num_days
64
65  def constructCalMonth(month_num, first_day, num_days_in_month):
66  #------------------------------------------------------------------
67      """Returns a formatted calendar month for display on the screen.
68
69          month_num in the range 1-12, inclusive.
70          first_day in the range 0-6 (1-Sun, 2-Mon, ..., 0-Sat)
71
72          Returns a list of strings of the form,
73          [month_name, week1, week2, week3, week4, ...]
74      """
75      # init
76      empty_str = ''
77      blank_col = format(' ', '3')
78      blank_week = format(' ', '21')
79      month_names = ('January', 'February', 'March', 'April', 'May',
80                     'June', 'July', 'August', 'September', 'October',
81                     'November', 'December')
82
83      calendar_month = [' ' + format(month_names[month_num - 1], '<20')]
84      current_day = 1
85      current_col = 1
86      calendar_week = ''
87
88      # init starting column
89      if first_day == 0:
90          starting_col = 7
91      else:
92          starting_col = first_day
93
94      # add any needed leading spaces for first week of month
95      while current_col < starting_col:
96          calendar_week = calendar_week + blank_col
97          current_col = current_col + 1
98
```

FIGURE 7-20 Implementation of the Calendar Year Program (*Continued*)

```
 99        # construct month for proper number of days
100        while current_day <= num_days_in_month:
101
102            # store day of month in field of length 3
103            calendar_week = calendar_week + format(str(current_day), '>3')
104
105            # append new week to month if at end of week
106            if current_col == 7:
107                calendar_month = calendar_month + [calendar_week]
108                calendar_week = empty_str
109                current_col = 1
110            else:
111                current_col = current_col + 1
112
113            current_day = current_day + 1
114
115        # if there is a final week, append to constructed month
116        if calendar_week != empty_str:
117            calendar_month = calendar_month + [calendar_week]
118
119        return calendar_month
120
121  def constructCalYear(year):
122
123      """Returns a formatted calendar year for display on the screen.
124
125         year in the range 1800-2099, inclusive
126         Returns a list beginning with the year, followed by
127         twelve constructed months
128
129             [year, month1, month2, week3, ..., month12]
130      """
131      # init
132      leap_year = leapYear(year)
133      first_day_of_month = dayOfWeekJan1(year, leap_year)
134      calendar_year = [year]
135
136      # construct calendar from twelve constructed months
137      for month_num in range(1, 13):
138          num_days_in_month = numDaysInMonth(month_num, leap_year)
139
140          calendar_year = calendar_year + \
141                      constructCalMonth(month_num, first_day_of_month,
142                                        num_days_in_month)
143
144          first_day_of_month = (first_day_of_month + \
145                                num_days_in_month) % 7
146
147      return calendar_year
148
```

FIGURE 7-20 Implementation of the Calendar Year Program (*Continued*)

```
149  def displayCalendar(calendar_year):
150
151      """Displays a calendar_year on the screen three months across."""
152
153      # init
154      month_separator = format(' ', '8')
155      blank_week = format(' ', '21')
156
157      # display year
158      print('\n', calendar_year[0])
159
160      # display months three across
161      for month_index in [1, 4, 7, 10]:
162
163          # init
164          week = 1
165          lines_to_print = True
166
167          while lines_to_print:
168
169              # init
170              lines_to_print = False
171
172              # print weeks of months side-by-side
173              for k in range(month_index, month_index + 3):
174                  if week < len(calendar_year[k]):
175                      print(calendar_year[k][week-1], end='')
176                      lines_to_print = True
177                  else:
178                      print(blank_week, end='')
179
180                  print(month_separator, end='')
181
182              # move to next screen line
183              print()
184
185              # increment week
186              week = week + 1
187
188  # --- main
189
190  # initialization
191  terminate = False
192
193  # program greeting
194  print('This program will display a calendar year for a given year')
195
```

FIGURE 7-20   Implementation of the Calendar Year Program (*Continued*)

Development and Unit Testing of Individual Modules

To begin, we can create a program that contains each of the function headers and docstring specifications, and implement and test them one by one. This is given in Figure 7-21, with an implementation for function getYear.

Running this version of the program will not produce any output. However, it will define function getYear. Therefore, this function can be unit tested in the Python shell,

```
>>> getYear()
Enter year (yyyy) (−1 to quit): 1800
1800
```

```
196  # continue to display calendar years until -1 entered
197  while not terminate:
198      year = getYear()
199
200      if year == -1:
201          terminate = True
202      else:
203          # construct calendar
204          calendar_year = constructCalYear(year)
205
206          # display calendar
207          displayCalendar(calendar_year)
```

FIGURE 7-20 Implementation of the Calendar Year Program

```
# Calendar Year Program
# This program will display any calendar year between 1800-2099.

def getYear():

    """Returns a year between 1800-2099, inclusive, or -1 if end of
        user input
    """

    year = int(input('Enter year (yyyy) (-1 to quit): '))

    while (year < 1800 or year > 2099) and year != -1:
        print('INVALID INPUT - Year must be between 1800 and 2099')
        year = int(input('Enter year: '))

    return year


#def leapYear(year):

#    """Returns True if year a leap year, otherwise returns False. """
 .
 .
```

FIGURE 7-21 Implementation and Unit Testing of Function getyear

```
>>> getYear()
Enter year (yyyy) (-1 to quit): 2099
2099
>>> getYear()
Enter year (yyyy) (-1 to quit): 1985
1985
>>> getYear()
Enter year (yyyy) (-1 to quit): 1799
INVALID INPUT - Year must be between 1800 and 2099
Enter year: 2100
INVALID INPUT - Year must be between 1800 and 2099
Enter year: 2050
2050
>>>
```

Since the `getYear` function tested OK, we can next implement and test the `leapYear` function. This is given in Figure 7-22.

```
# Calendar Year Program
# This program will display any calendar year between 1800-2099.

##def getYear():

##      """Returns a year between 1800-2099, inclusive, or -1 if end of
##          user input.
##      """
##      year = int(input('Enter year (yyyy) (-1 to quit): '))
##
##      while (year < 1800 or year > 2099) and year != -1:
##          print('INVALID INPUT - Year must be between 1800 and 2099')
##          year = int(input('Enter year: '))
##
##      return year

def leapYear(year):

    """Returns True if year a leap year, otherwise returns False."""

    if (year % 4 == 0) and (not (year % 100 == 0) or \
        (year % 400 == 0)):
        leap_year = True
    else:
        leap_year = False

    return leap_year
 .
 .
```

FIGURE 7-22   Implementation and Unit Testing of Function `leapYear`

Running this version of the program defines function `leapYear`, which can then be unit tested.

```
>>> leapYear(1803)
False
>>> leapYear(1800)
False
>>> leapYear(1860)
True
>>> leapYear(1900)
False
>>> leapYear(1964)
True
>>> leapYear(2000)
True
>>> leapYear(2012)
True
```

Based on the test results, both `getYear` and `leapYear` are properly working. Next, we will unit test function `dayOfWeekJan1`. The implementation of this function is given in Figure 7-23.

```
 .
 .
##def leapYear(year):

##    """Returns True if year a leap year, otherwise returns False. """
##
##    if (year % 4 == 0) and (not (year % 100 == 0) or
##        (year % 400 == 0)):
##        leap_year = True
##    else:
##        leap_year = False
##
##    return leap_year

def dayOfWeekJan1(year, leap_year):

    """Returns the day of the week for January 1 of a given year.

        year must be between 1800 and 2099. leap_year must be True if
        year a leap year, and False otherwise.
    """
    century_digits = year // 100
    year_digits = year % 100
    value = year_digits + (year_digits // 4)

    if century_digits == 18:
        value = value + 2
    elif century_digits == 20:
        value = value + 6

    # adjust for leap years
    if not leap_year:
        value = value + 1

    # return first day of month for Jan 1
    return (value + 1) % 7

 .
 .
```

FIGURE 7-23   Implementation and Unit Testing of Function dayOfWeekJan1

As with previous stages of development, running this version of the program defines function leapYear, which we can then unit test.

```
>>> dayOfWeekJan1(1800, False)
4
>>> dayOfWeekJan1(1864, True)
6
>>> dayOfWeekJan1(1900, False)
2
>>> dayOfWeekJan1(2000, True)
0
>>> dayOfWeekJan1(2012, True)
1
>>> dayOfWeekJan1(2013, False)
3
```

Recalling that the values 0–6 represent the days of the week Saturday to Sunday (where Saturday is 0), checking these results with other sources, they are found to be correct. Next, we unit test function numDaysInMonth as shown in Figure 7-24.

```
.
.
##      # adjust for leap years
##      if not leap_year:
##          value = value + 1
##
##      # return first day of month for Jan 1
##      return (value + 1) % 7


def numDaysInMonth(month_num, leap_year):

    """Returns the number of days in a given month.

        month_num in the range 1-12, inclusive.
        leap_year True if month in a leap year, otherwise False.
    """
    num_days_in_month = (31, 28, 31, 30, 31, 30, 31, 31, 30, 31, 30, 31)

    # special check for February in leap year
    if (month_num == 2) and leap_year:
        num_days = 29
    else:
        num_days = num_days_in_month[month_num]

    return num_days
```

FIGURE 7-24   Implementation and Unit Testing of Function numDaysInMonth

By executing this version of the program and unit testing function numDaysInMonth, we get the following results.

```
>>> numDaysInMonth(1, False)
28
>>> numDaysInMonth(2, False)
31
>>> numDaysInMonth(2, True)
29
>>> numDaysInMonth(3, False)
30
>>> numDaysInMonth(12,False)
Traceback (most recent call last):
  File "<pyshell#5>", line 1, in <module>
    numDaysInMonth(12,False)
  File "C:\My Python Programs\CalendarYearFunc.py", line 65, in
numDaysInMonth
    num_days = num_days_in_month[month_num]
IndexError: tuple index out of range
>>>
```

Obviously, something is wrong with this function. First, we have to make sure that we called it with proper values. The function specification indicates that it should be given values in the range 1 to 12, inclusive, as the first argument, and a Boolean value (indicating whether the year is a leap year or not) for the second. Therefore, it is being called correctly.

Looking at the results produced for the consecutive months tested, it seems that the results are off by one month. That is, numDaysInMonth(1, False) is giving the result 28, which would be correct for February (of a non-leap year), and numDaysInMonth(2, False) is giving the result 31, which would be the correct results for March (of either a leap year or a non-leap year). So, if the index value used to index list num_days_in_month were one greater than it should be, this would be consistent with the test results. Furthermore, the fact that an index out of range error occurs for a month number of 12 further supports the likely "off by one" error.

However, there is one result that is inconsistent with this hypotheses. For February of a leap year, numDaysInMonth(2, True), we get the correct result of 29. This could be explained if the case of February in a leap year is handled as a special case in the function code. In fact, that is exactly the case by the if-else statement. Therefore, we make the needed correction in the function, given in Figure 7-25.

```
def numDaysInMonth(month_num, leap_year):

    """Returns the number of days in a given month.

        month_num in the range 1-12, inclusive.
        leap_year True if month in a leap year, otherwise False.
    """
    num_days_in_month = (31, 28, 31, 30, 31, 30, 31, 31, 30, 31, 30, 31)

    # special check for February in leap year
    if (month_num == 2) and leap_year:
        num_days = 29
    else:
        num_days = num_days_in_month[month_num - 1]

    return num_days
```

FIGURE 7-25   Corrected numDaysInMonth Function

We again test the function, and this time get the correct result for each test case.

```
>>> numDaysInMonth(1, False)
31
>>> numDaysInMonth(2, False)
28
>>> numDaysInMonth(2, True)
29
>>> numDaysInMonth(3, False)
31
>>> numDaysInMonth(4, False)
30
etc.
```

Since there are only 13 possible sets of input values to the function (including two sets for February), we test each one and find that the function is working for each of these cases.

Function `constructCalMonth` is tested next. It is passed a month number (1 to 12), a day of the week value (0 to 6) and the number of days in the month, and returns a constructed calendar month as given below,

```
>>> constructCalMonth(1, 0, 31)
[' January               ', '                         1', ' 2  3  4  5  6  7  8',
 ' 9 10 11 12 13 14 15', ' 16 17 18 19 20 21 22', ' 23 24 25 26 27 28 29',
 ' 30 31']
>>>
```

Additional testing of this function indicates that it is working correctly.

Integration Testing of Modules

The remaining functions to test are `constructCalYear` and `displayCalendar`. Function `constructCalYear` relies on the use of functions `leapYear`, `dayOfWeekJan1`, `numDaysInMonth`, and `constructCalMonth`. Since each of these has been tested and found correct, we can now perform integration testing of all these functions with function `constructCalYear`. We therefore execute a version of the program in which all the code developed so far, except these functions, are commented out, as depicted in Figure 7-26.

```
##
##    # if there is a final week, append to constructed month
##    if calendar_week != empty_str:
##        calendar_month = calendar_month + [calendar_week]
##
##    return calendar_month

def constructCalYear(year):

    """Returns a formatted calendar year for display on the screen.

        year in the range 1800-2099, inclusive
        Returns a list beginning with the year, followed by
        twelve constructed months

           [year, month1, month2, week3, ..., month12]
    """
    # init
    leap_year = leapYear(year)
    first_day_of_month = dayOfWeekJan1(year, leap_year)
    calendar_year = [year]

    # construct calendar from twelve constructed months
    for month_num in range(1, 13):
        num_days_in_month = numDaysInMonth(month_num, leap_year)

        calendar_year = calendar_year + \
                    constructCalMonth(month_num, first_day_of_month,
                                      num_days_in_month)

        first_day_of_month = (first_day_of_month + num_days_in_month) % 7

    return calendar_year
```

FIGURE 7-26 Integration Testing with Function `constructCalYear`

Test results from a call to ConstructCalYear are given below.

```
>>> constructCalYear(2012)
[2012, [' January              ', '  1  2  3  4  5  6  7', '  8  9 10 11 12 13 14
', ' 15 16 17 18 19 20 21', ' 22 23 24 25 26 27 28', ' 29 30 31'], [' February
        ', '              1  2  3  4', '  5  6  7  8  9 10 11', ' 12 13 14 15 16
17 18', ' 19 20 21 22 23 24 25', ' 26 27 28 29'], [' March              ', '
        1  2  3', '  4  5  6  7  8  9 10', ' 11 12 13 14 15 16 17', ' 18 19 2
0 21 22 23 24', ' 25 26 27 28 29 30 31', [' April              ', '  1  2  3
4  5  6  7', '  8  9 10 11 12 13 14', ' 15 16 17 18 19 20 21', ' 22 23 24 25 26
27 28', ' 29 30'], [' May              ', '        1  2  3  4  5', '  6  7  8
  9 10 11 12', ' 13 14 15 16 17 18 19', ' 20 21 22 23 24 25 26', ' 27 28 29 30 3
1'], [' June              ', '                 1  2', '  3  4  5  6  7  8  9',
 ' 10 11 12 13 14 15 16', ' 17 18 19 20 21 22 23', ' 24 25 26 27 28 29 30'], ['
July              ', '  1  2  3  4  5  6  7', '  8  9 10 11 12 13 14', ' 15 16
 17 18 19 20 21', ' 22 23 24 25 26 27 28', ' 29 30 31'], [' August
', '              1  2  3  4', '  5  6  7  8  9 10 11', ' 12 13 14 15 16 17 18', '
19 20 21 22 23 24 25', ' 26 27 28 29 30 31'], [' September              ', '
        1', '  2  3  4  5  6  7  8', '  9 10 11 12 13 14 15', ' 16 17 18 19
 20 21 22', ' 23 24 25 26 27 28 29', ' 30'], [' October              ', '     1
2  3  4  5  6', '  7  8  9 10 11 12 13', ' 14 15 16 17 18 19 20', ' 21 22 23 24
25 26 27', ' 28 29 30 31'], [' November              ', '           1  2  3', '
  4  5  6  7  8  9 10', ' 11 12 13 14 15 16 17', ' 18 19 20 21 22 23 24', ' 25 2
6 27 28 29 30',] [' December              ', '              1', '  2  3  4
5  6  7  8', '  9 10 11 12 13 14 15', ' 16 17 18 19 20 21 22', ' 23 24 25 26 27
28 29', ' 30 31']]
>>>
```

The constructed year looks correct, and so we include the final function to be tested, displayCalendar, in this integration testing. Test results from a call to displayCalendar are given below.

```
This program will display a calendar year for a given year
Enter year (yyyy) (−1 to quit): 2012

2012
J
a      1      8
n
u
a      2      9
r
y             1
       3      0
              1
       4      1
              1
       5      2

.
.
.
```

This output does not look even close to what it should be. The output displayed by function `displayCalendar` depends on providing it with a correctly structured calendar year. So maybe we should think through each step of function `displayCalendar` with the test output from function `constructCalYear` to see if we can gain any insight into the problem. The output from function `constructCalYear` for the year 2012 is partially reproduced below.

```
>>> constructCalYear(2012)
[2012, ' January                ', '  1  2  3  4  5  6  7', '  8  9 10 11 12 13 14
', ' 15 16 17 18 19 20 21', ' 22 23 24 25 26 27 28', ' 29 30 31'], [' February
      ', '             1  2  3  4', '  5  6  7  8  9 10 11', ' 12 13 14 15 16
17 18', ' 19 20 21 22 23 24 25', ' 26 27 28 29'], [' March               ', '
```

The body of function `constructCalYear`, for parameter `year`, is shown below.

```
 1 # init
 2 leap_year = leapYear(year)
 3 first_day_of_month = dayOfWeekJan1(year, leap_year)
 4 calendar_year = [year]
 5
 6 # construct calendar from twelve constructed months
 7 for month_num in range(1, 13):
 8     num_days_in_month = numDaysInMonth(month_num, leap_year)
 9
10     calendar_year = calendar_year + \
11                     constructCalMonth(month_num, first_day_of_month,
12                                       num_days_in_month)
13
14     first_day_of_month = (first_day_of_month + num_days_in_month) % 7
15
16 return calendar_year
```

Lines 2 and **3** make calls to functions `leapYear` and `dayOfWeekJan1`, which have both been tested, so we can assume, for now, that the results of these function calls are correct. On **line 4**, list `calendar_year` is initialized to a list of one element, the integer representing the year. The for loop at **line 7** is used to construct each of the calendar months one at a time, appending each to list `calendar_year`.

One thing to double-check is the range of the for loop, since there is always a chance that we have an "off by one" error. In this case, `range` is called with a first argument of 1, and a second argument of 13. Thus, variable `month_num` will be assigned to the values 1, 2, . . . , 12. The loop will iterate, therefore, 12 times—once for each of the 12 months. This is the correct number of iterations. Now we should check to see if they are the correct range of values.

Variable `month_num` is only used in the call to function `constructCalMonth` on **line 11**. Thus, we check the specification of the function to see if it requests month values in the range 1–12, or if it requests their index values 0–11. Looking back at the specification for this function in Figure 7-8, 1–12 is the correct range of month values to be passed to it.

Next, we consider the concatenation of `calendar_year` with a newly constructed calendar month each time through the loop. This occurs in **lines 10–12**, given below.

```
calendar_year = calendar_year + \
              constructCalMonth(month_num,first_day_of_month,
                                num_days_in_month)
```

We know that `calendar_year` is initialized to the list `[2012]`. Also, calls to `constructCalMonth` return a constructed calendar month as a list of the form,

```
[' January               ', '                        1', '  2  3  4  5  6  7  8', '  9
10 11 12 13 14 15', ' 16 17 18 19 20 21 22', ' 23 24 25 26 27 28 29', ' 30 31']
```

Thus, the above instruction would result in the following,

```
calendar_year = [2012] + [' January               ', '                        1',
'  2  3  4  5  6  7  8', '  9 10 11 12 13 14 15', ' 16 17 18 19 20 21 22', ' 23
24 25 26 27 28 29', ' 30 31']
```

Now we realize something. The structure of a calendar year is designed to be,

```
[year, [month, week1, week2,...], [month, week1, week2,...],....]
```

So we check the initial result of the structure of `calendar_year` after doing a simplified version of the above concatenation in the Python shell,

```
>>> [2012] + [' January ', ' 1']
[2012, ' January ', ' 1']
```

Here is a problem! The result of the concatenations should be a list of lists, with each sublist containing a constructed month. The result above is a *single* list of values. That would certainly be a cause for the `displayCalYear` function not working correctly. The error is that instead of concatenating the two lists, each constructed month should be *appended* to the calendar year list, as given below.

```
calendar_year.append(constructCalMonth(
                    month_num,
                    first_day_of_month,
                    num_days_in_month))
```

Testing again in the Python shell, this gives the following (correct) results.

```
>>> [2012] + [[' January ', ' 1']]
[2012, [' January ', ' 1']]
```

Therefore, we make the correction and retest function `displayCalYear`. This time we get a correctly displayed calendar year, as shown in Figure 7-27. (Note that the width of the shell window needs to be adjusted for the weeks of the calendar year to properly align.)

```
This program will display a calendar for a given year
Enter year (yyyy) (-1 to quit): 2012

2012
January                      February                     March
 1  2  3  4  5  6  7                  1  2  3  4                          1  2  3
 8  9 10 11 12 13 14           5  6  7  8  9 10 11           4  5  6  7  8  9 10
15 16 17 18 19 20 21          12 13 14 15 16 17 18          11 12 13 14 15 16 17
22 23 24 25 26 27 28          19 20 21 22 23 24 25          18 19 20 21 22 23 24

April                        May                          June
 1  2  3  4  5  6  7                  1  2  3  4  5                             1  2
 8  9 10 11 12 13 14           6  7  8  9 10 11 12           3  4  5  6  7  8  9
15 16 17 18 19 20 21          13 14 15 16 17 18 19          10 11 12 13 14 15 16
22 23 24 25 26 27 28          20 21 22 23 24 25 26          17 18 19 20 21 22 23

July                         August                       September
 1  2  3  4  5  6  7                  1  2  3  4                                   1
 8  9 10 11 12 13 14           5  6  7  8  9 10 11           2  3  4  5  6  7  8
15 16 17 18 19 20 21          12 13 14 15 16 17 18           9 10 11 12 13 14 15
22 23 24 25 26 27 28          19 20 21 22 23 24 25          16 17 18 19 20 21 22
                                                            23 24 25 26 27 28 29

October                      November                     December
    1  2  3  4  5  6                        1  2  3                                1
 7  8  9 10 11 12 13           4  5  6  7  8  9 10           2  3  4  5  6  7  8
14 15 16 17 18 19 20          11 12 13 14 15 16 17           9 10 11 12 13 14 15
21 22 23 24 25 26 27          18 19 20 21 22 23 24          16 17 18 19 20 21 22
                                                            23 24 25 26 27 28 29

Enter year (yyyy) (-1 to quit):
```

FIGURE 7-27   Calendar Year Program Output

CHAPTER SUMMARY

General Topics

Modules/Module Interface/Specification
Top-Down Design
Stacks
Namespaces and Name Clashes
Global Scope/Global Variables

Python-Specific Programming Topics

Python Docstring Specification
Built-in/Global/Local Namespaces in Python
Main Modules/Standard Modules in Python
Forms of Module Import in Python
Global vs. Private Module Variables in Python
Module Loading and Execution in Python

CHAPTER EXERCISES

Section 7.1

1. For the following function,

```
def hours_of_daylight(month, year)
```

(a) Give an appropriate docstring specification where hours_of_daylight returns the total number of hours of daylight for the month and year given (each passed an integer value) designed so that the function does not check for invalid parameter values.

(b) Give a print statement that displays the docstring for this function.

Section 7.2

2. Develop a modular design depicting the components of a typical computer, similar to that for the Space Shuttle in Figure 7-2. Assume that the major components of a computer system consist of a CPU (central processing unit), busses (connections between components), main memory (RAM), secondary memory (hard drive, USB drive, etc.), and input/output devices (mouse, keyboard, etc.). Search online for more specific subsystems and devices to complete your design.

3. For the hours_of_daylight function in exercise 1, give a code segment that prompts the user for a month and year, and appropriately calls function hours_of_daylight according to its docstring specification, displaying the result.

Section 7.3

4. For module1, module2, and the client module shown below, indicate which of the imported identifiers would result in a name clash if the imported identifiers were not fully qualified.

```
# module1

def func_1(n):
    etc.

def func_2(n):
    etc.
```

```
# module2

def func_2(n):
    etc.

def func_3(n):
    etc.
```

```
from module1 import *
from module2 import *

def func_3(n):
    etc.
```

5. Depict what is left on stack s after the following series of push and pop operations (starting with the first column of operations and continuing with the second). Assume that the stack is initially empty.

```
push(s,10)        push(s,50)
push(s,20)        push(s,60)
push(s,40)        push(s,80)
pop(s)            pop(s)
pop(s)            pop(s)
```

6. For the program in Figure 7-9 that imports modules module1 and module1, indicate how many total namespaces exist for this program.

7. For the Palindrome Checker program in section 7.3.7, describe the changes that would be needed in the program if the import statement were changed from import Stack to from Stack import *.

8. For the following program and the imported modules, describe any name clashes that would occur for both program version1 and version 2.

```
# module m1

def total(items):

def convert(items):

def show(items)
```

```
# module m2

def totalSum(items):

def convert(items):

def display(items)
```

```
from m1 import *
from m2 import *

def display()

def calc()

def getItems()

# ---- main

items = getItems()
items = convert(items)
show(items)
```

```
import m1
import m2

def display()

def calc()

def getItems()

# ---- main

items = getItems()
items = m2.convert(items)
display(items)
```

Version 1   Version 2

PYTHON PROGRAMMING EXERCISES

P1. Write a function called convertStatus that is passed status code 'f', 's', 'j', or 'r' and returns the string 'freshman', 'sophomore', 'junior', or 'senior', respectively. Design your function so that if an inappropriate letter is passed, an error value is returned. Make sure to include an appropriate docstring with your function.

P2. Write a function called palindromeChecker using iteration to return True if a provided string is a palindrome, and False otherwise. Make sure to include docstring specification for the function.

P3. Implement a set of functions called getData, extractValues, and calcRatios. Function getData should prompt the user to enter pairs of integers, two per line, with each pair read as a single string, for example,

```
Enter integer pair (hit Enter to quit):
134 289 (read as '134 289')
    etc.
```

These strings should be passed one at a time as they are being read to function extractValue, which is designed to return the string as a tuple of two integer values,

```
extractValues('134 289') returns (134, 289)
    etc.
```

Finally, each of these tuples is passed to function calcRatios one at a time to calculate and return the ratio of the two values. For example,

```
calcRatios( (134, 289) ) returns 0.46366782006920415
    etc.
```

Implement a complete program that displays a list of ratios for an entered series of integer value pairs. Make sure to include docstring specification for each of the functions.

PROGRAM MODIFICATION PROBLEMS

M1. Stack Module: Limited Stack Size

For the stack module given in Figure 7-15, suppose that the implementation is to limit stacks to no more than 100 items. Redesign and re-implement the relevant parts of the module that need to be changed. Write a small program to demonstrate this new version of the stack module.

M2. Stack Module: Ability to "Peek" in Stack

For the stack module given in Figure 7-15, redesign and re-implement the relevant parts of the module to allow the ability to "peek" into the stack to find out if a given element is on the stack or not. Write a small program to demonstrate this new version of the stack module.

M3. Stack Module: Double-Ended Stacks

A double-ended stack is essentially a pair of stacks that share a fixed amount of storage (memory). The two stacks are designed so that the top of stack of each begins at each end of a list structure. Each top of stack moves towards the other when an element is pushed, as depicted below. This stack implementation has the advantage of more effectively utilizing a fixed amount of memory than if each stack were allocated its own storage.

top
(stack 1)

top
(stack 2)

Modify and test the stack module to behave as a double-ended stack.

M4. Calendar Year Program: Optional Month/Year Display

Modify the Calendar Year Program so the user can select whether they want to display a complete calendar year, or just a specific calendar month.

M5. Calendar Year Program: Flexible Layout of Months

Modify the Calendar Year Program so the user can select whether they want the calendar displayed "row oriented" (with January, February, and March in the first row, April, May, and June in the second row, etc.) or "column oriented" (with January, February, March, and April in the first column, May, June, July, and August in the second column, etc.).

PROGRAM DEVELOPMENT PROBLEMS

D1. Parentheses Matching Program

Implement and test a Python program that determines if all parentheses in an entered line of code form matching pairs. Note: Pairs of parentheses may be nested.

D2. Determining Body Mass Index (BMI)

Following is a chart for determining one's body mass index (BMI). BMI is a general indication of the amount of body fat that a person has. The formula for computing BMI is,

$$BMI = mass / height^2$$

Implement a Python program that prompts a user for their height and weight. Height should be entered as inches and weight should be entered in pounds. Perform the calculation in units of kilograms and meters as shown in the chart. Compare the result to the information in the chart. Use functions in your program design.

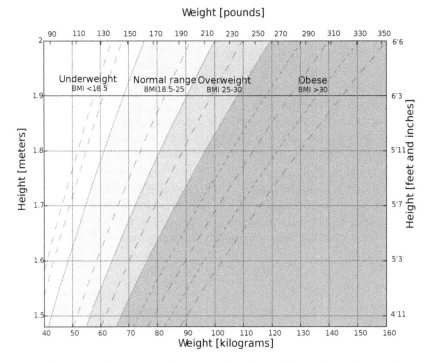

D3. Create interesting geometric animations by the use of turtle graphics and the stack module provided in the chapter. A snapshot of an example is shown below.

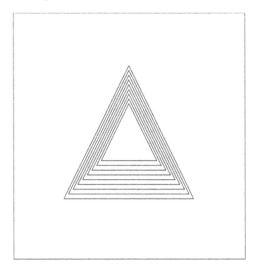

To do this, create a geometric shape in turtle graphics. Then, create multiple invisible turtle objects of this shape, each scaled down to a smaller size than the previous and pushed on a stack. Once the stack has been "loaded" with a sufficient number of such turtle objects, continually pop the stack and make each visible on the screen, pushing the popped turtle object onto a second stack. When the first stack is empty, reverse the process using the second stack (pushing the popped turtle objects from the second stack back onto the first stack), making each visible again. Use the `sleep` function of the `time` module of Python to control the speed of the animation.

## CHAPTER 8

Text Files

We have, up to now, been storing data only in the variables and data structures of programs. However, such data is not available once a program terminates. Therefore, in order for information to persist from one program execution to the next, the data must be stored in a data file. In this chapter we discuss the use of one particular type of data file, text files.

OBJECTIVES

After reading this chapter and completing the exercises, you will be able to:

♦ Explain what a text file is

♦ Differentiate between a text file and a binary file

♦ Explain the process of opening and closing a file

♦ Explain the process of reading and writing files

♦ Explain the process of exception handling

♦ Explain the process of unit testing using test drivers

♦ Effectively utilize text files in Python

♦ Effectively perform string processing in Python

♦ Catch and handle exceptions in Python

CHAPTER CONTENTS

MOTIVATION

The vast amount of information being generated today means that there must also be vast amounts of storage for all this data. Information sharing on the web through Wikipedia, social networks, and other means keeps driving this growth. *It has been estimated that 90% of all the data in the world has been generated in the last two years.*

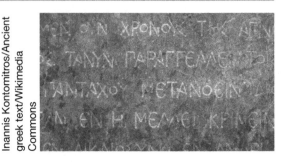

Throughout the age of computing, data has always been shared in some manner. In the early days data had to be physically carried on storage media such as reels of magnetic tapes. Later, early developments in computer networks allowed the sharing of data between a small number of large and expensive connected computers. With the advent of the Internet, computers are not directly connected, but indirectly through routers that temporarily store and forward data toward its destination. The World Wide Web has made access to information easy and intuitive by the incorporation of hypertext—text that can be clicked on to retrieve more text—effectively making text "three-dimensional."

The evolving technology of "cloud computing" is a further step in the sharing of information. Not only is data easily shared, but also the programs and other services needed to use that data. Figure 8-1 shows the various information storage devices in use today. (Note that a volatile memory device is one that loses its contents when power is lost, whereas a nonvolatile device retains its contents.)

Storage Technology	Example	Characteristics
Magnetic Storage	Hard drive	Nonvolatile
	Magnetic Tape Storage	Nonvolatile
Semiconductor Memory	Main memory	Volatile
	USB (Thumb) Drive	Nonvolatile
Optical Storage	CD, DVD	Nonvolatile

FIGURE 8-1   Types of Storage Technology

FUNDAMENTAL CONCEPTS

8.1   What Is a Text File?

A **text file** is a file containing characters, structured as individual lines of text. In addition to printable characters, text files also contain the *nonprinting* newline character, \n, to denote the end of each text line. As discussed in Chapter 2, the newline character causes the screen cursor to move to the beginning of the next screen line. Thus, text files can be directly viewed and created using a text editor.

In contrast, **binary files** can contain various types of data, such as numerical values, and are therefore not structured as lines of text. Such files can only be read and written via a computer program.

Any attempt to directly view a binary file will result in "garbled" characters on the screen. Our purpose is not to cover all of types of files in Python. Rather, we cover enough to be able to perform simple reading and writing of text files.

LET'S TRY IT

Let's view both a text file and a binary file using a simple text editor like notepad. First, create a simple file within IDLE named `hello.py` containing only two lines :

```
print 'Hello'
print 'There'
```

Execute the program. From the shell window that the program displays the results in, enter the following,

```
>>> import hello
```

This will both execute the program and compile it into a binary file named hello.pyc. Open the Python source file using notepad (or other simple text editor). The two print statements of the program should be displayed. Open the Python compiled file of this program using notepad and observe what is displayed.

A **text file** is a file containing characters, structured as lines of text. A **binary file** is a file that is formatted in a way that only a computer program can read.

8.2 Using Text Files

Fundamental operations of all types of files include *opening* a file, *reading* from a file, *writing* to a file, and *closing* a file. Next we discuss each of these operations when using text files in Python.

8.2.1 Opening Text Files

All files must first be opened before they can be read from or written to. In Python, when a file is (successfully) opened, a file object is created that provides methods for accessing the file. We look how to open files for either reading (from) or writing (to) a file in this section.

All files must first be opened before they can be used. In Python, when a file is opened, a file object is created that provides methods for accessing the file.

Opening for Reading

To open a file for reading, the built-in `open` function is used as shown,

```
input_file = open('myfile.txt','r')
```

The first argument is the file name to be opened, `'myfile.txt'`. The second argument, `'r'`, indicates that the file is to be opened for reading. (The second argument is optional when opening a file for reading.) If the file is successfully opened, a file object is created and assigned to the provided identifier, in this case identifier `input_file`.

When opening a file for reading, there are a few reasons why an *I/O error* may occur. (We look at how to include the ability of a program to catch and handle such errors in the discussion of exception handling in section 8.4.) First, if the file name does not exist, then the program will terminate with a "no such file or directory" error,

```
>>> open('testfile.txt','r')
Traceback (most recent call last):
  File "<pyshell#1>", line 1, in <module>
    open('testfile.txt','r')
IOError: [Errno 2] No such file or directory:
'testfile.txt'
```

This error can also occur if the file name is not found in the location looked for (uppercase and lowercase letters are treated the same for file names). When a file is opened, it is first searched for in the same folder/directory that the program resides in. The programs in the text are written this way. However, an alternate location can be specified in the call to `open` by providing a path to the file,

```
input_file = open('data/myfile.txt','r')
```

In this case, the file is searched for in a subdirectory called `data` of the directory in which the program is contained. Thus, its location is relative to the program location. (Although some operating systems use forward slashes, and other backward slashes in path names, directory paths in Python are always written with forward slashes and are automatically converted to backward slashes when required by the operating system executing on.) Absolute paths can also be provided giving the location of a file anywhere in the file system,

```
input_file = open('C:/mypythonfiles/data/myfile.txt','r')
```

When the program has finished reading the file, it should be closed by calling the `close` method on the file object,

```
input_file.close()
```

Once closed, the file may be reopened (with reading starting at the beginning of the file) by the same, or another program. Next, we look at how to open files for writing in Python.

LET'S TRY IT

In a new Python file window, enter the following lines,

```
Line one
Line two
Line three
```

Save the file under the name `data.txt`. (Make sure to save it with extension `'.txt'` and not `'.py'`.) Then, in the same folder (directory) as the data file, create the following Python program,

```
file_name = input('Enter file name: ')
input_file = open(file_name, 'r')
```

Run this program twice. The first time, enter the file name `garbage.txt`. The second time, enter the correct file name `data.txt` and observe the results.

To open a file for reading in Python, the built-in function open is called with (optional) argument value 'r'.

Opening for Writing

To open a file for writing, the open function is used as shown below,

```
output_file = open('mynewfile.txt','w')
```

Note that, in this case, 'w' is used to indicate that the file is to be opened for writing. If the file already exists, it will be overwritten (starting with the first line of the file). When using a second argument of 'a', the output will be appended to an existing file instead.

It is important to close a file that is written to, otherwise the tail end of the file may not be written to the file (discussed below),

```
output_file.close()
```

When opening files for writing, there is not much chance of an I/O error occurring. The provided file name does not need to exist since it is being created (or overwritten). Thus, the only error that may occur is if the file system (such as the hard disk) is full.

LET'S TRY IT

In a new Python file window, enter the following lines,

```
file_name = input('Enter file name: ')
file = open(file_name, 'w')
file.close()
```

Save the file under the name createfile.py and run it. When the program requests a file name, give it any file name you wish with the extension '.txt'. Then, look in the folder in which the program resides to see if a new file with the file name that you entered exists. (This file will be empty—we will see how to write to a file next.)

Modify the open instruction above, changing 'w' to 'r' and rerun the program. When it requests a file name, enter the name of the file you just created. Run it a second time; this time give it the wrong file name. Observe the different results in each case.

To open a file for writing in Python, the built-in function open is called with a second argument of 'w'. A second argument of 'a' will open a file for appending to instead.

8.2.2   Reading Text Files

The readline method returns as a string the next line of a text file, including the end-of-line character, \n. When the end-of-file is reached, it returns an empty string as demonstrated in the while loop of Figure 8-2.

Text File `myfile.txt`

```
input_file = \
    open('myfile.txt','r')
empty_str = ''

line = input_file.readline()

while line != empty_str:
    print(line)
    line = input_file.readline()

input_file.close()
```

Screen Output

```
Line One
Line Two
Line Three
```

Text file box:
```
Line One\n
Line Two\n
Line Three\n
```

Screen output box:
```
Line One

Line Two

Line Three
```

FIGURE 8-2   Reading from a Text File

It is also possible to read the lines of a file by use of the for statement,

```
input_file = \
    open('myfile.txt','r')
for line in input_file:
```

Using a for statement, *all* lines of the file will be read one by one. Using a while loop, however, lines can be read until a given value is found, for example.

Finally, note the blank lines in the screen output. Since `read_line` returns the newline character, and `print` adds a newline character, *two* newline characters are output for each line displayed, resulting in a skipped line after each. We will see an easy way to correct this when we discuss string methods.

LET'S TRY IT

Create a text file named `'myfile.txt'`. Enter and execute the following program and observe the results. Make sure that the program and text file reside in the same folder.

```
input_file = open('myfile.txt','r')
for line in input_file:
    print(line)
```

The `readline` method returns the next line of a text file, including the end-of-line character. If at the end of the file, an empty string is returned.

8.2.3 Writing Text Files

The `write` method is used to write strings to a file, as demonstrated in Figure 8-3.

Text File
`myfile.txt`

```
empty_str = ''
input_file = open('myfile.txt','r')
output_file = open('myfile_copy.txt','w')

line = input_file.readline()

while line != empty_str:
    output_file.write(line)
    line = input_file.readline()

output_file.close()
```

Text File
`myfile_copy.txt`

Text file box (myfile.txt):
```
Line One\n
Line Two\n
Line Three\n
```

Text file box (myfile_copy.txt):
```
line one
line two
line three
```

FIGURE 8-3   Writing to a Text File

This code copies the contents of the input file, `'myfile.txt'`, line by line to the output file, `'myfile_copy.txt'`. In contrast to `print` when writing to the screen, *the `write` method does not add a newline character to the output string*. Thus, a newline character will be output only if it is part of the string being written. In this case, each line read contains a newline character.

Finally, when writing to a file, data is first placed in an area of memory called a *buffer*. Only when the buffer becomes full is the data actually written to the file. (This makes reading and writing files more efficient.) Since the last lines written may not completely fill the buffer, the last buffer's worth of data may not be written. The `close()` method *flushes* the buffer to force the buffer to be written to the file.

LET'S TRY IT

In the Python shell, open an existing file `myfile.txt` and do the following.

```
>>> input_file = ('myfile.txt','r')
>>> output_file = ('newfile.txt','w')
>>> line = input_file.readline()
>>> output_file.write(line)
>>> output_file.close()
```

Observe that `newfile.txt` has been created, and examine its contents.

Use the `write()` method to output text to a file. To ensure that all data has been written, call the `close()` method to close the file after all information has been written.

Self-Test Questions

1. Only files that are written to need to be opened first. (TRUE/FALSE)

2. Indicate which of the following reasons an IOError (exception) may occur when opening a file.
   (a) Misspelled file name **(c)** File not found in directory searched
   (b) Unmatched uppercase and lowercase letters

3. Which one of the following is true?
   (a) When calling the built-in `open` function, a second argument of `'r'` or `'w'` must always be given
   (b) When calling the built-in `open` function, a second argument of `'r'` must always be given when opening a file for reading
   (c) When calling the built-in `open` function, a second argument of `'w'` must always be given when opening a file for writing

4. Which one of the following is true?
   (a) There is more chance of an I/O error when opening a file for reading.
   (b) There is more chance of an I/O error when opening a file for writing.

5. The `readline` method reads every character from a text file up to and including the next newline character `'\n'`. (TRUE/FALSE)

6. It is especially important to close a file that is open for writing. (TRUE/FALSE)

8.3 String Processing

The information in a text file, as with all information, is most likely going to be searched, analyzed, and/or updated. Collectively, the operations performed on strings is called *string processing*. We have already seen some operations on strings—for example, str[k], for accessing individual characters, and len(str) for getting the length of a string. In this section, we revisit sequence operations that apply to strings, and look at additional string-specific methods.

> *String processing* refers to the operations performed on strings that allow them to be accessed, analyzed, and updated.

8.3.1 String Traversal

We saw in Chapter 4 how any sequence can be traversed, including strings. This is usually done by the use of a for loop. For example, if we want to read a line of a text file and determine the number of blank characters it contains, we could do the following,

```
space = ' '
num_spaces = 0

line = input_file.readline()
    for k in range(0,len(line)):
        if line[k] == space:
            num_spaces = num_spaces + 1
```

We also saw that the last lines can be done more simply without the explicit use of an index variable,

```
for chr in line:
    if chr == space:
        num_spaces = num_spaces + 1
```

Given the ability to traverse a string, each character can be individually "looked at" for various types of string processing. We look at some string processing operations next.

> The characters in a string can be easily traversed, without the use of an explicit index variable, using the for *chr* in *string* form of the for statement.

8.3.2 String-Applicable Sequence Operations

Because strings (unlike lists) are immutable, sequence-modifying operations are not applicable to strings. For example, one cannot add, delete, or replace characters of a string. Therefore, *all string operations that "modify" a string return a new string that is a modified version of the original string*. Sequence operations relevant to string processing are given in Figure 8-4. We look at string-specific operations in the next section.

Sequences Operations Applicable to Strings			
Length	len(*str*)	Membership	'h' in s
Select	s[*index_val*]	Concatenation	s + w
Slice	s[*start*:*end*]	Minimum Value	min(s)
Count	s.count(*char*)	Maximum Value	max(s)
Index	s.index(*char*)	Comparison	s == w

FIGURE 8-4 Sequence Operations on Strings

Recall that as we saw with lists, the slice operator s[start:end] returns the substring starting with index start, *up to but not including* index end. Also, s.index(chr) returns the index of the first occurrence of chr in s. Finally, min and max as applied to strings return the smallest (largest) character based on the underlying Unicode encoding. Thus, for example, all lowercase letters are larger (have a larger Unicode value) than all uppercase letters. We give examples of each of these operations for s = 'Hello Goodbye!'.

```
>>> len(s)         s.count('o')      >>> s + '!!'
14                 3                  'Hello Goodbye!!!'

>>> s[6]           >>> s.index('b')  >>> min(s)
'G'                10                 ' '

>>> s[6:10]        >>> 'a' in s       >>> max(s)
'Good'             False              'y'
```

We next look at methods in Python that are specific to strings.

Because strings are immutable, sequence modifying operations do not modify the string applied to. Rather, they construct *new* strings that are a modified version of the original.

8.3.3 String Methods

There are a number of methods specific to strings in addition to the general sequence operations. We discuss these methods next.

Checking the Contents of a String

There are times when the individual characters in a string (or substring) needs to be checked. For example, to check whether a character is an appropriate denotation of a musical note, we could do the following,

```
if char not in ('A', 'B', 'C', 'D', 'E', 'F', 'G'):
    print('Invalid musical note found')
```

Checking the Contents of a String			
`str.isalpha()`	Returns True if *str* contains only letters.	s = 'Hello'	s.isalpha() → True
		s = 'Hello!'	s.isalpha() → False
`str.isdigit()`	Returns True if *str* contains only digits.	s = '124'	s.isdigit() → True
		s = '124A'	s.isdigit() → False
`str.islower()` `str.isupper()`	Returns True if *str* contains only lower (upper) case letters.	s = 'hello'	s.islower() → True
		s = 'Hello'	s.isupper() → False
`str.lower()` `str.upper()`	Return lower (upper) case version of *str*.	s = 'Hello!'	s.lower() → 'hello!'
		s = 'hello!'	s.upper() → 'HELLO!'
Searching the Contents of a String			
`str.find(w)`	Returns the index of the first occurrence of w in *str*. Returns -1 if not found.	s = 'Hello!'	s.find('l') → 2
		s = 'Goodbye'	s.find('l') → -1
Replacing the Contents of a String			
`str.replace(w,t)`	Returns a copy of *str* with all occurrences of w replaced with t.	s = 'Hello!'	s.replace('H', 'J') → 'Jello'
		s = 'Hello'	s.replace('ll', 'r') → 'Hero'
Removing the Contents of a String			
`str.strip(w)`	Returns a copy of *str* with all leading and trailing characters that appear in w removed.	s = ' Hello! ' s = 'Hello\n'	s.strip(' !') → 'Hello' s.strip('\n') → 'Hello'
Splitting a String			
`str.split(w)`	Returns a list containing all strings in *str* delimited by w.	s = 'Lu, Chao'	s.split(',') → ['Lu', 'Chao']

FIGURE 8-5 String Methods in Python

Since the `in` operator can also be applied to strings, we can also do the following,

```
if char not in 'ABCDEFG':
    print('Invalid musical note character found')
```

We could take a similar approach for determining if a given character is a lowercase or uppercase letter or digit character; for example,

```
char in 'ABCDEFGHIJKLMNOPQRSTUVWXYZ' or \          letter?
char in 'abcdefghijklmnopqrstuvwxyz' or \
char in '0123456789'
```

Since checking for uppercase/lowercase and digit characters is common in programming, Python provides string methods `isalpha`, `isdigit`, `isupper`, and `islower` (among others).

For example, to perform error checking on an entered credit card number could be done as follows,

```
if not credit_card.isdigit():
    print('Invalid card number')
```

The method `isdigit` returns `True` if and only if each character in string `credit_card` is a digit. If only *part* of a string is to be checked, then a method can be applied to a slice of a string. For example, if the part numbers of a given company all begin with three letters, a check for invalid part numbers could be done as follows,

```
if not part_num[0:3].isalpha():
    print('Invalid part number')
```

in which `isalpha` returns `True` if and only if the first three characters in `part_num` are letters. Additional string methods are listed in Figure 8-5. We look at the issue of string search and string modification next.

> Python provides a number of methods specific to strings, in addition to the general sequence operations.

Searching and Modifying Strings

String processing involves search. For example, to determine the user name and domain parts of an email address, the ampersand character separating the two would be searched for,

```
>>> email_addr = 'jsmith@somecollege.edu'
>>> amper_index = email_addr.find('@')
>>> username = email_addr[0:amper_index]
>>> domain = email_addr[amper_index + 1:len(email_addr)]
>>> print('Username:', username, 'Domain:', domain)
Username: jsmith Domain: somecollege.edu
```

The find method returns the index location of the *first occurrence* of a specified substring. Since in Python strings are immutable, to update the email address, a *new* string would be constructed with the desired replacement as shown,

```
>>> email_addr = username + '@' + 'newcollege.edu'
>>> email_addr
jsmith@newcollege.edu
```

The `replace` method produces a new string with *every occurrence* of a given substring within the original string replaced with another,

```
>>> word = 'common'              >>> word = 'common'
>>> word.replace('m', 't')       >>> word = word.replace('m', 't')
'cotton'                         'cotton'
>>> word                         >>> word
'common'                         'cotton'
```

Note that for all string modifications, the variable references the same string until it is reassigned.

Python also provides a `strip` method that "strips off" leading and trailing characters from a string. This is especially useful for stripping off the newline character, \n, from the end of a line in text processing if needed,

```
>>> line = 'Hello\n'
>>> print(line)
'Hello'

>>>
```

```
>>> line = 'Hello\n'
>>> print(line.strip('\n'))
'Hello'
>>>
```

The `find`, `replace`, and `strip` methods in Python can be used to search and produce modified strings.

8.3.4 Let's Apply It—Sparse Text Program

Sparse data is data that lacks "density." A diary containing entries only for holidays and special occasions would contain sparse data. Sparse data can often be compressed. Compressed data should retain all (or most) of the original information. To explore this, the program in Figure 8-7 removes all occurrences of the letter 'e' from a provided text file. How much of the compressed text can be understood indicates how much of the information is retained. This program utilizes the following programming features:

➤ text files   ➤ string methods (replace, strip)

Figure 8-6 shows the file produced by the Sparse Text Program for a passage from *Alice's Adventures in Wonderland.*

The main section of the program begins on **line 32**. The program welcome is displayed on **lines 33–34**. In **lines 37–38**, the file name entered by the user is opened for reading and assigned to file object `input_file`. In **lines 37–40**, a file is opened for writing with the same file name as the input file but with 'e_' added to the beginning and assigned to the file object `output_file`.

The creation of the modified file is handled by function `createModifiedFile` (**lines 3–28**) called on **line 44**. The function returns a tuple containing how many occurrences of letter `'e'` were removed, and the total character count of the file. The values of the tuple are therefore assigned to variables `num_total_char` and `num_removals`. (Note that Python allows such a multiple assignment on lists, tuples, and even on strings.) The input and output files are closed on **lines 47–48**. Finally, both the number of characters removed and the percentage of the file that the removed characters comprised are displayed (**lines 52–54**).

What remains is function `createModifiedFile`. On **lines 9–11**, variable `empty_str` is initialized to the empty string, and variables `num_total_chars` and `num_removals` are initialized to 0. On **line 16**, variable `orig_line_length` is set to the length of the currently read line (in variable `line`) minus one. This is so that the newline character (\n) at the end of the line is not counted.

A Mad Tea-Party (original version)

There was a table set out under a tree in front of the house, and the March Hare and the Hatter were having tea at it: a Dormouse was sitting between them, fast asleep, and the other two were using it as a cushion, resting their elbows on it, and talking over its head. 'Very uncomfortable for the Dormouse,' thought Alice; 'only, as it's asleep, I suppose it doesn't mind.' The table was a large one, but the three were all crowded together at one corner of it: 'No room! No room!' they cried out when they saw Alice coming. 'There's PLENTY of room!' said Alice indignantly, and she sat down in a large arm-chair at one end of the table.

```
Program Execution ...

This program will display the contents of a provided text file with all
occurrences of the letter 'e' removed.

Enter file name (including file extension): alice_tea_party.txt

Thr was a tabl st out undr a tr in front of th hous, and th
March Har and th Hattr wr having ta at it: a Dormous was sitting
btwn thm, fast aslp, and th othr two wr using it as a cushion,
rsting thir lbows on it, and talking ovr its had. 'Vry uncomfortabl
for th Dormous,' thought Alic; 'only, as it's aslp, I suppos it doesn't
mind.' Th tabl was a larg on, but th thr wr all crowdd togthr
at on cornr of it: 'No room! No room!' thy crid out whn thy saw Alic
coming. 'Thr's PLNTY of room!' said Alic indignantly, and sh sat down in
a larg arm-chair at on nd of th tabl

70 occurrences of the letter 'e' removed
Percentage of data lost: 11 %
Modified text in file e_alice_tea_party.txt
```

FIGURE 8-6   Execution of the Sparse Text Program

On **line 20**, variable `modified_line` is then set to the new string produced by the `replace` method applied to the current line. Each occurrence of `'e'` and `'E'` is replaced with the empty string, thus removing these occurrences from the string. Note the consecutive calls to the `replace` method,

```
modified_line = line.replace('e',empty_str).replace('E',empty_str)
```

This is possible to do when the first method call returns a value (object) for which the second method call can be applied. In this case, `line.replace('e',empty_str)` returns a string (consisting of a copy of the original string with all occurrences of the letter `'e'` removed), which is then operated on by the second instance of the method call to remove all instances of `'E'`.

On **line 21**, the number of characters removed (`num_removals`) is updated. The number removed from the current line is determined by taking the difference between the original line length (without the newline character) and the length of the new modified line minus one, so that the newline character in the modified line is not counted. Finally, the modified line of output to the screen (as well as to the output file) is displayed so the user may observe the results of the file processing as it is occurring. A tuple including the number of total characters in the file and the number of removed characters is returned as the function value.

```
1   # Sparse Text Program
2
3   def createModifiedFile(input_file, outputfile):
4
5       """For text file input_file, creates a new version in file outputfile
6          in which all instances of the letter 'e' are removed.
7       """
8
9       empty_str = ''
10      num_total_chars = 0
11      num_removals = 0
12
13      for line in input_file:
14
15          # save original line length
16          orig_line_length = len(line) - 1
17          num_total_chars = num_total_chars + orig_line_length
18
19          # remove all occurrances of letter 'e'
20          modified_line = line.replace('e',empty_str).replace('E',empty_str)
21          num_removals = num_removals + \
22                          (orig_line_length - (len(modified_line)-1))
23
24          # simulataneouly output line to screen and output file
25          print(modified_line.strip('\n'))
26          output_file.write(modified_line)
27
28      return (num_total_chars, num_removals)
29
30  # --- main
31
32  # program welcome
33  print("This program will display the contents of a provided text file")
34  print("with all occurrences of the letter 'e' removed.\n")
35
36  # open files for reading and writing
37  file_name = input('Enter file name (including file extension): ')
38  input_file = open(file_name,'r')
39  new_file_name = 'e_' + file_name
40  output_file = open(new_file_name,'w')
41
42  # create file with all letter e removed
43  print()
44  num_total_chars, num_removals = createModifiedFile(input_file, output_file)
45
46  # close current input and output files
47  input_file.close()
48  output_file.close()
49
50  # display percentage of characters removed
51  print()
52  print(num_removals, "occurrences of the letter 'e' removed")
53  print('Percentage of data lost:',
54        int((num_removals / num_total_chars) * 100), '%')
55  print('Modified text in file', new_file_name)
```

FIGURE 8-7   Sparse Text Program

Self-Test Questions

1. Some string methods alter the string they are called on, while others return a new altered version of the string. (TRUE/FALSE)

2. The find method returns the number of occurrences of a character or substring within a given string. (TRUE/FALSE)

3. Which of the results below does s[2:4] return for the string s = 'abcdef'.
   (a) 'cd'   **(b)** 'bcd'   **(c)** 'bc'   **(d)** 'cde'

4. Indicate which of the following is true.
   (a) String method isdigit returns true if the string applied to contains any digits.
   (b) String method isdigit returns true if the string applied to contains only digits.

5. Indicate which of the following s.replace('c','e') returns for s = 'abcabc'.
   (a) 'abeabc'   **(b)** 'abeabe'

6. Which of the results below does s.strip('-') return for the string s = '---ERROR---'.
   (a) '---ERROR'   **(b)** 'ERROR---'   **(c)** 'ERROR'

ANSWERS: 1. False, 2. False, 3. (a), 4. (b), 5. (b), 6. (c)

8.4   Exception Handling

Various error messages can occur when executing Python programs. Such errors are called *exceptions*. So far we have let Python handle these errors by reporting them on the screen. Exceptions can be "caught" and "handled" by a program, however, to either correct the error and continue execution, or terminate the program gracefully. We take this opportunity to discuss the fundamentals of exception handling in the use of text files.

8.4.1   What Is an Exception?

An **exception** is a value (object) that is *raised* ("thrown") signaling that an unexpected, or "exceptional," situation has occurred. Python contains a predefined set of exceptions referred to as **standard exceptions**. We list some of the standard exceptions in Figure 8-8.

ImportError	raised when an import (or from…import) statement fails
IndexError	raised when a sequence index is out of range
NameError	raised when a local or global name is not found
TypeError	raised when an operation or function is applied to an object of inappropriate type
ValueError	raised when a built-in operation or function is applied to an appropriate type, but of inappropriate value
IOError	raised when an input/output operation fails (e.g., "file not found")

FIGURE 8-8   Some Standard Exceptions in Python

The standard exceptions are defined within the `exceptions` module of the Python Standard Library, which is automatically imported into Python programs. We have seen a number of these exceptions before in our programming,

```
>>> lst = [1, 2, 3]
>>> lst[3]
Traceback (most recent call last):
    File "<pyshell#4>", line 1, in
        <module> lst[3]
IndexError: list index out of range
>>> 2 + '3'
Traceback (most recent call last):
    File "<pyshell#7>", line 1, in
        <module> 2 + '3'
TypeError: unsupported operand
type(s) for +: 'int' and 'str'
```

```
>>> lsst[0]
Traceback (most recent call last):
    File "<pyshell#5>", line 1, in
        <module> lsst[0]
NameError: name 'lsst' is not defined
>>> int('12.04')
Traceback (most recent call last):
    File ",pyshell#9.", line 1, in
        <module> int('12.04')
ValueError: invalid literal for
int() with base 10: '12.04'
```

Raising an exception is a way for a function to inform its client a problem has occurred that *the function itself cannot handle*. For example, suppose a function called `getYN` prompts a user to enter `'y'` or `'n'`. If the user enters something other than these two values, the function can simply prompt the user to re-enter. On the other hand, if a function called `isEven` is to be passed a numeric value, but is passed a string instead, it cannot correct the problem. It can only notify the client of the problem, leaving it up to the client to determine what to do. We next discuss in detail the raising and catching of exceptions.

An **exception** is a value (object) that is "raised" by a function signaling that an unexpected, or "exceptional," situation has occurred that the function itself cannot handle.

8.4.2 The Propagation of Raised Exceptions

Raised exceptions are not required to be handled in Python. When an exception is raised and not handled by the client code, it is automatically propagated back to the *client's* calling code (and *its* calling code, etc.) until handled. If an exception is thrown all the way back to the top level (main module) and not handled, then the program terminates and displays the details of the exception as depicted in Figure 8-9.

For example, a program might not be able to determine whether a password is valid at the source of the input. Rather, the password must be verified in a password file that is accessed only after a *chain* of function calls have been made. If the password is found invalid, an exception is propagated from the function identifying the error all the way back to the function responsible for user input, which can then prompt the user to re-enter their password.

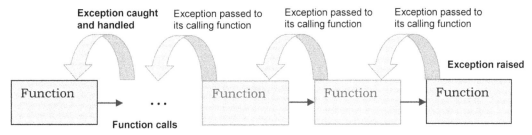

FIGURE 8-9 The Propagation of Exceptions

An exception is either handled by the client code, or automatically propagated back to the client's calling code, and so on, until handled. If an exception is thrown all the way back to the main module (and not handled), the program terminates displaying the details of the exception.

8.4.3 Catching and Handling Exceptions

Many of the functions in the Python Standard Library raise exceptions. For example, the factorial function of the Python math module raises a `ValueError` exception when a negative value is passed to it, as shown in Figure 8-10.

```
import math

num = int(input('Enter number to compute factorial of: '))
print('The factorial of', num, 'is', math.factorial(num))
```

```
Enter number to computer factorial of: -5
The factorial of -5 is
Traceback (most recent call last):
  File "C:\My Python Programs\exception_example1.py", line 4, in <module>
    print 'The factorial of', num, 'is', math.factorial(num)
ValueError: factorial() not defined for negative values
```

FIGURE 8-10 Simple Program without Exception Handling

When −5 is passed to the `factorial` function, an exception is raised, thrown back to the client code to catch and handle. Since the client code (here, the code in the main module) does not attempt to catch the exception, the exception is caught by the Python interpreter, causing the program to terminate and display an error message indicating the exception type. The last line of the message indicates that a `ValueError` exception occurred within the `factorial` function. The previous lines indicate where in the client code this function was called (line 4). In Figure 8-11 we give a version of the program that catches the raised exception.

```
import math

num = int(input('Enter number to compute factorial of: '))
try:
    print(math.factorial(num))
except ValueError:
    print('Cannot compute the factorial of negative numbers')
```

```
Enter number to compute factorial of: -5
Cannot compute the factorial of negative numbers
```

FIGURE 8-11   Simple Program with Exception Handling

The call to the factorial function is contained within a **try suite** (**try block**)—the block of code surrounded by try and except headers. The suite following the except header is referred to as an **exception handler**. This exception header "catches" exceptions of type ValueError. The exception handler in this case simply outputs an error message to the user before terminating the program. This program termination is much more user-friendly than the previous version.

Finally we show a version of the program that recovers from the exception. Rather than terminating the program, the user is prompted again for input so that the program can continue executing. This new version is given in Figure 8-12.

```
import math

num = int(input('Enter number to compute factorial of: '))
valid_input = False

while not valid_input:
    try:
,--------- result = math.factorial(num)
:            print(result)
:            valid_input = True
:    except ValueError:
'-------->   print('Cannot compute factorial of negative numbers')
            num = int(input('Please re-enter: '))
```

```
Enter number to compute factorial of: -5
Cannot compute the factorial of negative numbers
Please re-enter: 5
120
```

FIGURE 8-12   Program Recovery via Exception Handling

Note that within a try suite in Python, any statement making a call (either directly or indirectly) to a function that raises an exception causes the rest of the statements in the suite to be skipped, as depicted in the figure.

Exceptions are caught and handled in Python by use of a **try block** and **exception handler**.

8.4.4 Exception Handling and User Input

Besides exceptions raised by built-in functions, programmer-defined functions may raise exceptions as well. Suppose we prompted the user to enter the current month as a number,

```
month = input('Enter current month (1-12): ')
```

The input function will return whatever is entered as a string. We can do integer type conversion on this value to make it an integer type,

```
month = int(input('Enter current month (1-12): '))
```

If the input string contained non-digit characters (except for + and −), the int function would raise a ValueError exception. However, there also needs to be a check for values outside the range 1–12. This can be done as shown in Figure 8-13.

```
valid = False

while not valid:
    try:
        month = int(input('Enter current month (1-12): '))

        while month < 1 or month > 12:
            print('Invalid Input - Must be in the range 1-12'
            month = int(input('Enter current month (1-12): '))
        valid = True
    except ValueError:
        print('Invalid Month Value')
```

FIGURE 8-13 Input Error Checking (Version 1)

Athough this works, a better approach is to design a function called getMonth that raises a ValueError exception for either error condition—if the user enters non-digit characters, or if the user enters a numeric value outside the range 1–12. Such a function is given in Figure 8-14.

```
def getMonth():
    month = int(input('Enter current month (1-12): '))

    if month < 1 or month > 12:
        raise ValueError('Invalid Month Value')

    return month
```

FIGURE 8-14 Programmer-Defined Function with Raised Exception

In this version of `getMonth`, if non-digit characters are entered, the `ValueError` exception is automatically raised by the built-in `int` type conversion function,

```
>>> getMonth()
Enter current month (1-12): 1a
Traceback (most recent call last):
    File "<pyshell#18>", line 1, in <module>
      getMonth()
    File " C:\My Python Programs\exception /Raising Excpt Test.py",
line 2, in getMonth
      month = int(input('Enter current month (1-12): '))
ValueError: invalid literal for int() with base 10: '1a'
```

Since there is no try block around the input assignment statement, the exception is not caught and therefore is thrown back to the Python interpreter. If a valid numeric string is entered, but the value is outside the range 1–12, then a `ValueError` is raised by function `getMonth` and is thrown back to the client,

```
>>> getMonth()
Enter current month (1-12): 14
Traceback (most recent call last):
    File "<pyshell#23>", line 1, in <module>
        getMonth()
    File " C:\My Python Programs\exception /Raising Excpt Test.py",
line 5, in getMonth
        raise ValueError('Invalid Month Value')
ValueError: Invalid Month Value
```

Note that raised exceptions can optionally have a description that further describes the error, as has been done here,

```
raise ValueError('Invalid Month Value')
```

This error message is displayed when the `ValueError` generated is the one thrown by function `getMonth`. With this function, the less elegant error checking code in Figure 8-13 can now be replaced with that in Figure 8-15.

```
valid = False

while not valid:
    try:
        month = getMonth()
        valid = True
    except ValueError:
        print('Invalid Month Entry\n')
```

FIGURE 8-15   Input Error Checking (Version 2)

In this case, when an invalid input is entered, we get the following,

```
Enter current month (1-12): 1a
Invalid Month Value
Enter current month (1-12): 14
Invalid Month Value
```

This is a much cleaner error reporting for the user. The error message `Invalid Month Value`, however, doesn't indicate *why* the input was invalid (that is, either that an invalid character was found, or an integer outside the range 1–12 was entered). We could go one step further and output the error message associated with the specific `ValueError` exception thrown, as shown in Figure 8-16.

```
valid = False

while not valid:
    try:
        month = getMonth()
        valid = True
    except ValueError as err_mesg:
        print(err_mesg,'\n')
```

FIGURE 8-16 Input Error Checking (Version 3)

The line `except ValueError as err_mesg` not only catches the `ValueError` exceptions, but with as *identifier* added (here as `err_mesg`), the error message of the particular `ValueError` exception is assigned to the specified identifier name,

```
Enter current month (1-12): 1a
invalid literal for int() with base 10: '1a'
Enter current month (1-12): 14
Invalid Month Value
Enter current month (1-12): 12
>>>
```

We next look at exception handling related to file processing.

> Programmer-defined functions may raise exceptions in addition to the exceptions raised by the built-in functions of Python.

8.4.5 Exception Handling and File Processing

We saw that when opening a file for reading, an exception is raised if the file cannot be found. In this case, the standard `IOError` exception is raised and the program terminates with a `'No such file or directory'` error message. We can catch this exception and handle the error as shown in Figure 8-17.

```
file_name = input('Enter file name: ')
empty_str = ''

input_file_opened = False

while not input_file_opened:
    try:
        input_file = open(file_name, 'r')
        input_file_opened = True

        line = input_file.readline()

        while line != empty_str:
            print(line.strip('\n'))
            line = input_file.readline()
    except IOError:
        print('File Open Error\n')
        file_name = input('Enter file name: ')
```

FIGURE 8-17   Exception Handling of Open File Error

Variable file_name stores the file name entered by the user. Variable input_file_opened is initialized to False. The while loop continues to iterate as long as input_file_opened is False. Because of the try block within the loop, every time that open(file_name, 'r') raises an exception, the remaining lines in the try block are skipped, and the exception handler following the except header is executed. Only when the call to open does not throw an exception do all the instructions in the try block get executed, with the program continuing after the while loop. A similar, but much less likely exception can be raised when opening a file for writing and the file system (hard disk, for example) we want to write to is full.

Note that when reading from a text file, the readline method does not raise any exceptions. When the end of file is reached, readline returns an empty string rather than throwing an exception.

IOError exceptions raised as a result of a file open error can be caught and handled.

8.4.6   Let's Apply It—Word Frequency Count Program

The following Python program (Figure 8-19) prompts the user for the name of a text file to open and a word to search for, and displays the number of times that the word occurs within the file. This program utilizes the following Python programming features:

➤ text files/readline()
➤ string methods lower(), index()

Example execution of the program is given in Figure 8-18.

Program execution begins at **line 77**. First, the program welcome is displayed. On **line 81**, function getFile is called, which prompts the user for the file name to open for reading. It returns a tuple containing both the file name and the associated input file object, assigned to variables file_name and input_file, respectively.

```
Text File: wordtest.txt

This is a sample text file.
The word 'the' in this file is to be counted.
Must be careful not to count words like their and there.
Should only count the word "the" when it is a separate word.
This is the last line of the file.
```

```
Program Execution ...

This program will display the number of occurrences of a
specified word within a given text file

Enter input file name: word
Input file not found - please reenter

Enter input file name: wordtest.txt
Enter word to search: apple
No occurrences of word 'apple' found in file wordtest.txt
```

Program Execution ...

This program will display the number of occurrences of a
specified word within a given text file

Enter input file name: wrdtest.txt
Input file not found - please reenter

Enter input file name: wordtest.txt
Enter word to search: the
The word 'the' occurs 6 times in file wordtest.txt

FIGURE 8-18   Execution of the Word Frequency Count Program

On **line 84** the user is prompted for the word to search for, stored in variable search_word. In the following line, search_word is reassigned to all lowercase characters by use of method lower(). The file lines read in function countWords are also converted to lowercase so that the matching of words does not depend on whether letters are in uppercase or lowercase (in other words, so that it is not *case sensitive*).

The function that does most of the work, function countWords, is called on **line 88**. It is passed the file object, input_file, as well as the words to search for. The function returns, as an integer, the number of occurrences found. Finally, in **lines 91–98**, the results of the search are displayed.

The getFile function called from the main section of the program prompts the user for a file name to open (**line 12**). The file is opened for reading on **line 13**. If the file is not found, an IOException is raised and caught by the except clause on **line 15**. In this case, an error message is printed (**line 16**) and the while loop at **line 10** iterates again, prompting the user to re-enter. If an exception is not thrown, then **line 14** is executed setting input_file_opened to True, causing the loop to terminate and the function to return both the file name and input file object as a tuple.

Function countWords, the final function of the program, is on **lines 21–72**. It is passed the input_file object and the search word, and returns the number of occurrences of the search word within the file. **Lines 28–31** perform the initialization for the function. Variable space is assigned to a string containing only a single blank character (to aid in the readability of the program). Variable num_occurrences, which keeps count of the number of times the search word appears in the file, is initialized to 0. And word_delimiters is set to a tuple

```
 1  # Word Frequency Count Program
 2
 3  def getFile():
 4
 5      """Returns the file name and associated file object for reading
 6         the file as a tuple of the form (file_name, input_file).
 7      """
 8
 9      input_file_opened = False
10      while not input_file_opened:
11          try:
12              file_name = input('Enter input file name: ')
13              input_file = open(file_name, 'r')
14              input_file_opened = True
15          except IOError:
16              print('Input file not found - please reenter\n')
17
18      return (file_name, input_file)
19
20
21  def countWords(input_file, search_word):
22
23      """Returns the number of occurrences of search_word in the
24         provided input_file object.
25      """
26
27      # init
28      space = ' '
29      num_occurrences = 0
30      word_delimiters = (space, ',', ';', ':', '.','\n',
31                         "'",'"', '(', ')')
32
33      search_word_len = len(search_word)
34
35      for line in input_file:
36          end_of_line = False
37
38          # convert line read to all lower case chars
39          line = line.lower()
40
41          # scan line until end of line reached
42          while not end_of_line:
43              try:
44                  # search for word in current line
45                  index = line.index(search_word)
46
47                  # if word at start of line followed by a delimiter
48                  if index == 0 and line[search_word_len] in
49                     word_delimiters:
50                          found_search_word = True
51
```

FIGURE 8-19   Word Frequency Count Program (*Continued*)

containing all the possible word delimiters—a space character, a comma, a semicolon, a colon, a period, and a newline character.

Because the length of the search word is used multiple times, it is calculated once and stored in variable search_word_len (**line 33**). The for loop on **line 35** reads each line of the file. Each line is scanned for all occurrences of the search word. Variable end_of_line is initialized to

```
53              # if search word within line, check chars before/after
54              elif line[index - 1] in word_delimiters and \
55                  line[index + search_word_len] in word_delimiters:
56                  found_search_word = True
57
58              # if found within other letters, then not search word
59              else:
60                  found_search_word = False
61
62              # if search word found, increment count
63              if found_search_word:
64                  num_occurrences = num_occurrences + 1
65
66              # reset line to rest of line following search word
67              line = line[index + search_word_len: len(line)]
68
69          except ValueError:
70              end_of_line = True
71
72      return num_occurrences
73
74  # ---- main
75
76  # program welcome
77  print('This program will display the number of occurrences of a')
78  print('specified word within a given text file\n')
79
80  # open file to search
81  file_name, input_file = getFile()
82
83  # get search word
84  search_word = input('Enter word to search: ')
85  search_word = search_word.lower()
86
87  # count all occurrences of search word
88  num_occurrences = countWords(input_file, search_word)
89
90  # display results
91  if num_occurrences == 0:
92      print('No occurrences of word', "'" + search_word + "'",
93          'found in file', file_name)
94  else:
97      print('The word', "'" + search_word + "'", 'occurs',
98          num_occurrences, 'times in file', file_name)
```

FIGURE 8-19   Word Frequency Count Program

False (**line 36**) for the while loop below it. On **line 39**, all characters in the line are converted to lowercase to allow for the matching of words of different case (mentioned above). Then, beginning on **line 42**, a while loop is used to search for all occurrences of the search word in the current line, continuing until the end of line is found.

On **line 45** the index string method is called on the current line to search for the first occurrence of the search word. It therefore performs the same task as the find method. However, whereas find returns a −1 if the string is not found, the index method raises a ValueError exception instead. Since we have now introduced exception handling in Python, we here use the index method.

The if statement on **line 48** checks if the search string matches the beginning characters of the line (followed by a delimiter). This determines if the first word of the current line matches the search string. If so, then found_search_string is set to True (**line 50**). Otherwise, a check is made on **line 54** to see if the matched string in the current line is immediately preceded and followed by a delimiter. If found, then found_search_string is also set to True, otherwise, found_search_string is set to False. On **lines 63–64**, if found_search_word is True, num_occurences is incremented by 1.

Variable line is reassigned to the substring following the last word found (**line 67**). This is needed because the index method only finds the *first* occurrence of a given substring within a string, and not *all* occurrences. Therefore, the line is continually shortened and scanned until no further instances of the word are found within the line. Once the complete line is scanned, the while loop terminates and control is returned to the top of the for loop (on **line 35**). When there are no more lines of the file to read, execution continues at **line 72** and the value of num_occurrences is returned.

Self-Test Questions

1. An exception is,
   (**a**) an object   (**b**) a standard module   (**c**) a special function

2. Which of the following is not a standard exception in Python?
   (**a**) ValueError   (**b**) AssignmentError   (**c**) NameError   (**d**) IOError

3. The standard exceptions are automatically imported into Python programs. (TRUE/FALSE)

4. All raised standard exceptions must be handled in Python. (TRUE/FALSE)

5. Which one of the following is true?
   (**a**) When calling the built-in open function for file handling, it *must* be called from within a try block with an appropriate exception handler.
   (**b**) When calling the built-in open function for file handling, it *should* be called from within a try block with an appropriate exception handler.

6. In addition to catching standard exceptions in Python, a program may also raise standard exceptions. (TRUE/FALSE)

ANSWERS: 1. (a). 2. (b). 3. True. 4. False. 5. (b). 6. True

COMPUTATIONAL PROBLEM SOLVING

8.5   Cigarette Use/Lung Cancer Correlation Program

In this section, we design a program using data from the Centers for Disease Control and Prevention (CDC) for computing the correlation between cigarette use and incidences of lung cancer (Figure 8-20). One data set gives the percentage of the population that smoke cigarettes within the United States by state. The other gives the rate of lung cancer per 100,000 individuals by state. The computed correlation, along with other factors, can be used to determined if there is a causal relationship between the two.

8.5.1 The Problem

The problem is to calculate a correlation value for two sets of data. Correlation is measured on a scale of −1 to 1, with 1 indicating a *perfect positive correlation*, and −1 a *perfect negative correlation*. For example, there is a positive correlation between the amount of ice cream sold and the current temperature—as temperatures rise, so do the sales of ice cream. There is a negative correlation between the number of snow blowers sold and the current temperature—as temperatures rise, the number of snow blowers sold decreases.

In a perfect correlation, knowing one value allows one to determine the *exact* value of the other. In real-world situations, perfect correlations are almost never found. For example, many other factors can affect exactly how much ice cream is sold—there may be a truckers' strike reducing deliveries, there may be a recall of a certain brand of ice cream, and so forth. Therefore, most correlation values fall somewhere between −1 and 1.

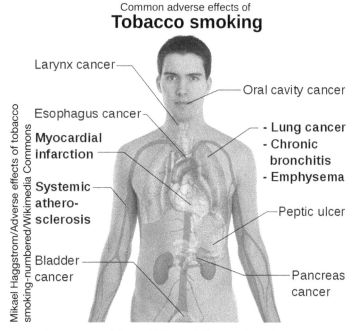

FIGURE 8-20 Adverse Effects of Cigarette Smoking

8.5.2 Problem Analysis

In the two sets of data provided in Figure 8-21, one contains the percentage of the population that smokes state-by-state in the United States, and the other the state-by-state rates of incidence of lung cancer per 100,000 individuals.

The mathematical formula for computing correlation is given below.

$$ r = \frac{N \sum xy - \sum x \sum y}{\sqrt{(N \sum x^2 - (\sum x)^2)(N \sum y^2 - (\sum y)^2)}} $$

where,

   N is equal to the number of pairs of values in the data
   x and y are a given pair of values
   $\sum xy$ is the sum of the products of paired scores
   $\sum x$ is the sum of the scores of one data set
   $\sum y$ is the sum of the scores of the other data set
   $\sum x^2$ is the sum of the squares of the scores of one data set
   $\sum y^2$ is the sum of the squares of the scores of the other data set

For our data, N is equal to 48 (all states except Arizona and Wisconsin, which were not provided in the data sets from the CDC). An example of x and y values are the two values for Alabama, $x = 23.3$ (percent of population that smokes) and $y = 75.1$ (lung cancer cases per 100,000 individuals). Note that to apply this formula, the values of x and y do not have to be in the same units.

```
State, Percent Cigarette Smokers
Alabama,23.3
Alaska,24.2
Arkansas,23.7
California,14.9
Colorado,17.9
Connecticut,17
Delaware,21.7
Florida,21
Georgia,20
Hawaii,17.5
Idaho,16.8
Illinois,20.5
Indiana,24.1
Iowa,21.5
Kansas,20
Kentucky,28.6
Louisiana,23.4
Maine,20.9
Maryland,17.8
Massachusetts,17.8
Michigan,22.4
Minnesota,18.3
Mississippi,25.1
Missouri,23.3
Montana,19
Nebraska,18.6
Nevada,22.2
New Hampshire,18.7
New Jersey,18.1
New Mexico,20.2
New York,18.3
North Carolina,22.1
North Dakota,19.6
Ohio,22.5
Oklahoma,25.1
Oregon,18.5
Pennsylvania,21.5
Rhode Island,19.3
South Carolina,22.3
South Dakota,20.4
Tennessee,22.6
Texas,18.1
Utah,9.8
Vermont,18
Virginia,19.3
Washington,17.1
West Virginia,25.7
Wyoming,21.6
```

```
Cases Lung Cancer per 100,000
Alabama,75.1
Alaska,69.8
Arkansas,77.7
California,51.6
Colorado,48.4
Connecticut,68.3
Delaware,83.5
Florida,68.7
Georgia,71
Hawaii,51.7
Idaho,54
Illinois,71.4
Indiana,77.2
Iowa,67.1
Kansas,68.4
Kentucky,97.2
Louisiana,77.5
Maine,80.1
Maryland,62.9
Massachusetts,64.5
Michigan,72
Minnesota,55.8
Mississippi,77.1
Missouri,77.9
Montana,60.8
Nebraska,61.3
Nevada,73.3
New Hampshire,66.8
New Jersey,64.5
New Mexico,43.9
New York,63
North Carolina,75.3
North Dakota,53
Ohio,72.8
Oklahoma,80.8
Oregon,64.4
Pennsylvania,70
Rhode Island,69.5
South Carolina,70.7
South Dakota,59.2
Tennessee,82.2
Texas,62
Utah,28
Vermont,79.2
Virginia,65.8
Washington,65.2
West Virginia,91
Wyoming,48.9
```

CDC Data on the Percentage of the Population that Smoke Cigarettes within the U.S. by State (2006)

CDC Data on the Rate of Lung/Bronchus Cancer per 100,000 Individuals within the U.S. by State (2006)

FIGURE 8-21 Cigarette Smoking and Incidence of Lung Cancer Data

8.5.3 Program Design

The data is provided in two comma-separated (CSV) files. Thus, we must first read the data from these file. Using this data, we must then compute the correlation of the two sets of data on a scale of -1 (a perfect negative correlation) to 1 (a perfect positive correlation).

Meeting the Program Requirements

The program must only display the correlation value between the two sets of data. Since the program requirements do not specify how the result is to be presented (for example, on a scale), the raw numerical value will simply be displayed on the screen.

Data Description

The data from the files will be stored in two lists so that the values can be easily accessed during the calculation of the correlation. Thus, the data is simply organized as two corresponding "parallel" lists of floating-point values.

Algorithmic Approach

The algorithm for this program is the means of calculating the correlation values using the mathematical formula given above.

Overall Program Steps

The overall steps in the program design are given in Figure 8-22.

FIGURE 8-22   Overall Steps of the Smoking/
Lung Cancer Correlation Program

Modular Design

The modular design for this program is given in Figure 8-23.

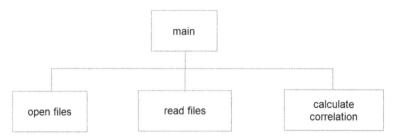

FIGURE 8-23 Modular Design of the Smoking/Lung Cancer Correlation Program

Following this modular design, there are three functions in the program: `openFiles`, `readFiles`, and `calculateCorrelation`. The main module utilizing these functions is given in Figure 8-24.

```
1  # ---- main
2
3  # program greeting
4  print('This program will determine the correlation between')
5  print('cigarette smoking and incidences of lung cancer\n')
6
7  try:
8      # open data files
9      smoking_datafile, cancer_datafile = openFiles()
10
11     # read data
12     smoking_data, cancer_data = readFiles(smoking_datafile, cancer_datafile)
13
14     # calculate correlation value
15     correlation = calculateCorrelation(smoking_data, cancer_data)
16
17     # display correlation value
18     print('r_value = ', correlation)
19 except IOError as e:
20     print(str(e))
21     print('Program terminated ...')
```

FIGURE 8-24 Main Module of the Smoking/Lung Cancer Correlation Program Design

8.5.4 Program Implementation and Testing

We develop and test the program in stages by developing and unit testing each of the three functions of the modular design. We begin with function `openFiles`.

Development and Unit Testing of Function `openFiles`

In the main module, we see that `openFiles` is designed as a value-returning function with no arguments, returning file objects for each of the opened data files. An implementation of this function is given in Figure 8-25.

```
 1  # Module module_openFiles
 2
 3  def openFiles():
 4      """
 5          Prompts the user for the file names to open, opens the files, and
 6          returns the file objects for each in a tuple of the form
 7          (smoking_datafile, cancer_datafile).
 8
 9          Raises an IOError exception if the files are not successfully
10          opened after four attempts of entering file names.
11      """
12      # init
13      smoking_datafile_opened = False
14      cancer_datafile_opened = False
15      num_attempts = 4
16
17      # prompt for file names and attempt to open files
18      while ((not smoking_datafile_opened) or (not cancer_datafile_opened)) \
19              and (num_attempts > 0):
20          try:
21              if not smoking_datafile_opened:
22                  file_name = input('Enter smoking data file name: ')
23                  smoking_datafile = open(file_name, 'r')
24                  smoking_datafile_opened = True
25
26              if not cancer_datafile_opened:
27                  file_name = input('Enter lung cancer data file name: ')
28                  cancer_datafile = open(file_name, 'r')
29                  cancer_datafile_opened = True
30          except IOError:
31              print('File not found:', file_name + '.', 'Please reenter\n')
32              num_attempts = num_attempts - 1
33
34      # if one of more file not opened, raise IOError exception
35      if not smoking_datafile_opened or not cancer_datafile_opened:
36          raise IOError
37      else:
38          return (smoking_datafile, cancer_datafile)
```

FIGURE 8-25   Implementation of Function openFiles

Function `openFiles` is initially put in its own Python file so that it can be easily imported for unit testing. The function handles the task of inputting from the user the data file names (for both the smoking-related data file and the lung cancer–related data file), opening the files for reading, and returning the two file objects created as a tuple of the form (`smoking_datafile, cancer_datafile`).

In the init section, variables `smoking_datafile_opened` and `cancer_datafile_opened` are initialized to `False` (**lines 13–14**). They are used in the control of the following while loop so that the user is continually prompted until correct file names for the data files are entered. On **line 15**, variable `num_attempts` is initialized to 4. This variable is decremented each time that an invalid file name (for either file) is entered. If the counter reaches 0, the while loop terminates and the final if statement checks if the files have been successfully opened. If not, then an `IOError` exception is raised, terminating the function.

The while loop at **line 18** continues to iterate as long as either of the two data files has not been successfully opened, and as long as the value of variable num_attempts is greater than zero. The statements in the loop are contained within a try block (**lines 21–29**), used to catch any IOError exceptions raised when attempting to open either of the two data files by call to method open,

$$smoking\_datafile = open(file\_name, 'r')$$
$$cancer\_datafile = open(file\_name, 'r')$$

Following the calls to method *open* for the smoking data file (**line 23**) and the cancer data file (**line 28**) is an assignment statement that assigns smoking_datafile_opened and cancer_datafile_opened, respectively, to True. Since these statements would not be reached if the call to the open method raised an exception, these Boolean variables provide a means of determining which, if any, of the two files has been opened successfully. If either call to method open raises an exception, it is caught by the except clause (**line 30**). As a result, on **line 31** the error message 'File not found: *filename*. Please reenter', for the *filename* in variable file_name is displayed. In addition, variable num_attempts is decremented by 1 (**line 32**), and control returns to the top of the while loop. Finally, when the loop terminates with both files successfully opened, a tuple containing each of the file objects is returned (**line 38**).

Function openFiles is not easily tested interactively in the Python shell. Therefore, we develop a *test driver* program that simply calls function openFile (imported from module_openFiles) to open the data files, and displays the first line of each file on the screen. The test driver program is given in Figure 8-26.

```
1  # TEST DRIVER for Function openFiles of Smoking/Cancer Correlation Program
2
3  from module_openFiles import *
4
5  empty_str = ''
6  print('TESTING FUNCTION openFiles')
7
8  try:
9      # open data files
10     smoking_datafile, cancer_datafile = openFiles()
11
12     # display sucessfully opened
13     print('Data files successfully opened')
14
15     # display first line of smoking data file
16     print('\nReading first line of smoking data file ...')
17     line = smoking_datafile.readline()
18     print(line.strip('\n'))
19
20     # display first line of cancer data file
21     print('\nReading first line of cancer data file ...')
22     line = cancer_datafile.readline()
23     print(line.strip('\n'))
24 except IOError:
25     print('Too many attempts of opening input files')
26     print('Program terminated ...')
```

FIGURE 8-26 Test Driver for Function openFiles

Since function `openFiles` is designed to raise an `IOError` exception if the files are not successfully opened after four attempts, we test this aspect of the program by purposely entering incorrect file names four times. The result of this testing is given in Figure 8-27.

```
TESTING FUNCTION openFiles
Enter smoking data file name: CDC_Cigarette_Smking_Data.csv
File not found: CDC_Cigarette_Smking_Data.csv. Please reenter

Enter smoking data file name: CDC_Cigarette_Smokin_Data.csv
File not found: CDC_Cigarette_Smokin_Data.csv. Please reenter

Enter smoking data file name: CDC_Cigarette_Smoking_Data.csv
Enter file name with lung cancer data: CDC_Lng_Cancer_Data.csv
File not found: CDC_Lng_Cancer_Data.csv. Please reenter

Enter lung cancer data file name: CDC_Lung_Caner_Data.csv
File not found: CDC_Lung_Caner_Data.csv. Please reenter

Too many attempts of reading input file
Program terminated ...
>>>
```

FIGURE 8-27 Invalid File Names Test Case for Function openFiles

Thus, this aspect of the function appears to be working. We next give it correct file names to see if the function successfully opens and correctly displays the first line of each file. The results are shown in Figure 8-28.

```
TESTING FUNCTION openFiles
Enter smoking data file name: CDC_Cigarette_Smoking_Data.csv
Enter lung cancer data file name: CDC_Lung_Cancer_Data.csv
Data files successfully opened

Reading first line of smoking data file ...
State, Percent Cigarette Smokers , CDC 2006 Data (except AZ, WI)

Reading first line of cancer data file ...
Cases Lung Cancer per 100000 CDC Data 2006 (except AZ,WI)
>>>
```

FIGURE 8-28 Valid File Names Test Case for Function openFiles

The output is as expected. We can assume that function `openFiles` is implemented correctly. We therefore unit test function `readFiles` next.

Development and Unit Testing of Function `readFiles`

As done for function `openFiles`, we put function `readFiles` in its own file to be imported by its test driver, named `module_readFiles.py`. An implementation of function `readFiles`, implemented as a separate module, is given in Figure 8-29.

```
1   # Module module_readFiles
2
3   def readFiles(smoking_datafile, cancer_datafile):
4
5       """Reads the data from the provided file objects smoking_datafile
6          and cancer_datafile. Returns a list of the data read from each
7          in a tuple of the form ([smoking data], [cancer data]).
8       """
9
10      # init
11      smoking_data = []
12      cancer_data = []
13      empty_str = ''
14
15      # read past file headers
16      smoking_datafile.readline()
17      cancer_datafile.readline()
18
19      # read data files
20      eof = False
21
22      while not eof:
23
24          # read line of data from each file
25          s_line = smoking_datafile.readline()
26          c_line = cancer_datafile.readline()
27
28          # check if at end-of-file of both files
29          if s_line == empty_str and c_line == empty_str:
30              eof = True
31
32          # check if end of smoking data file only
33          elif s_line == empty_str:
34              raise IOError('Unexpected end-of-file: smoking data file')
35
36          # check if at end of cancer data file only
37          elif c_line == empty_str:
38              raise IOError('Unexpected end-of-file: cancer data file')
39
40          # append line of data to each list
41          else:
42              smoking_data.append(s_line.strip().split(','))
43              cancer_data.append(c_line.strip().split(','))
44
45      # return list of data from each file
46      return (smoking_data, cancer_data)
```

FIGURE 8-29   Implementation of Function readFiles

Function `readFiles` parameters are passed the file objects of the smoking-related and cancer-related data files (**line 3**). It reads the data from each file and returns it in two lists. On **lines 11–12**, variables `smoking_data` and `cancer_data` are initialized to an empty list, and on **line 13** variable `empty_str` is assigned to an empty string. The first line is then read from each file (**line 16–17**), which contain file headers (descriptions of the file contents),

```
State, Percent Cigarette Smokers      (header of smoking-related data file)
Cases Lung Cancer per 100,000         (header of cancer-related data file)
```

On **line 20**, variable `eof` is set to `False`. The value of this variable indicates whether the end-of-file has been reached for the files. The while loop at **line 22** continues to iterate as long as `eof` is `False`. A line from each file is then read (**line 25–26**) and stored in variables `s_line` (from the smoking-related data file) and `c_line` (from the cancer-related data file). The following if state-ment (**line 29**) checks if each of these variables is equal to the empty string. If true, then the end of file of each has been reached, and thus variable `eof` is assigned to `True` (**line 30**) If not, then a check is made (on **line 33** and **line 37**) if either `s_line` or `c_line` is equal to the empty string. If so, then the end of one file has been reached before the other. In that case, an `IOError` exception is raised (on **line 34** or **38**) with one of the following error message strings,

'Unexpected end-of-file: smoking data file'

or

'Unexpected end-of-file: cancer data file'

If the strings in variables `s_line` and `c_line` are each found non-empty, then on **lines 42–43** they are appended to lists `smoking_data` and `cancer_data`, respectively. Since each line returned by `readLine` contains a final newline character, method `strip` is used to strip off the last char-acter of each line. Also, because each line of the files is of the form

state_name, data_value

the `split` string method is used to split each string into two values (`state_name` and `data_value`) using the comma as the separation character. This returns the two values in a list of the form

[*state_name, data_value*]

Finally, when all the lines of the files have been read, the data in lists `smoking_data` and `cancer_data` are returned as a tuple.

As we did for function `openFile`, we develop a simple test driver program for testing func-tion `readFiles`. The test driver (in Figure 8-30) first prompts the user for each of the file names

```
1   # TEST DRIVER for Function readFiles of Smoking/Cancer Correlation Program
2
3   from module_readFiles import *
4
5   try:
6       file_name = input('Enter file name with smoking data: ')
7       smoking_datafile = open(file_name, 'r')
8
9       file_name = input('Enter file name with lung cancer data: ')
10      cancer_datafile = open(file_name, 'r')
11
12      smoking_data, cancer_data = readFiles(smoking_datafile, cancer_datafile)
13
14      print('\nList of smoking data read')
15      print(smoking_data)
16      print('\nList of cancer data read')
17      print(cancer_data)
18  except IOError as e:
19      print(str(e))
```

FIGURE 8-30   Test Driver for Function readFiles

without doing any I/O error checking. This is because in the complete program version, function `openFile` will handle this, and therefore we can alleviate the test driver of that. Thus, the files are opened (assuming that correct file name are given) and the contents read and displayed on the screen.

Function `readFiles` raises an exception if the two data files do not have the same number of lines. Therefore, we test for that condition by purposely entering the names of two data files in which one file is shorter than the other. The results of this test case is given in Figure 8-31.

```
Enter file name with smoking data: CDC_Cigarette_Smoking_Data.csv
Enter file name with lung cancer data: CDC_Lung_Cancer_Data_Short.csv
Unexpected end-of-file: cancer data file
>>>
```

FIGURE 8-31   Unexpected End-of-File Test Case for Function readFiles

We next enter the names of equal length data files to test if the lists returned by `readFiles` contain the proper data. The results are given in Figure 8-32.

```
Enter file name with smoking data: CDC_Cigarette_Smoking_Data.csv
Enter file name with lung cancer data: CDC_Lung_Cancer_Data.csv

List of smoking data read
[['Alabama',      '23.3'],      ['Alaska',      '24.2'],      ['Arkansas',      '23.7'],
['California',      '14.9'],      ['Colorado',      '17.9'],      ['Connecticut',      '17'],
['Delaware',   '21.7'],   ['Florida',   '21'],   ['Georgia',   '20'],   ['Hawaii',
'17.5'],   ['Idaho',   '16.8'],   ['Illinois',   '20.5'],   ['Indiana',   '24.1'],
['Iowa',   '21.5'],   ['Kansas',   '20'],   ['Kentucky',   '28.6'],   ['Louisiana',
'23.4'],   ['Maine',   '20.9'],   ['Maryland',   '17.8'],   ['Massachusetts',   '17.8'],
['Michigan',      '22.4'],      ['Minnesota',      '18.3'],      ['Mississippi',      '25.1'],
['Missouri',   '23.3'],   ['Montana',   '19'],   ['Nebraska',   '18.6'],   ['Nevada',
'22.2'],   ['New Hampshire',   '18.7'],   ['New Jersey',   '18.1'],   ['New Mexico',
'20.2'],   ['New York',   '18.3'],   ['North Carolina',   '22.1'],   ['North Dakota',
'19.6'],   ['Ohio',   '22.5'],   ['Oklahoma',   '25.1'],   ['Oregon',   '18.5'],
['Pennsylvania',   '21.5'],   ['Rhode   Island',   '19.3'],   ['South   Carolina',
'22.3'],   ['South Dakota',   '20.4'],   ['Tennessee',   '22.6'],   ['Texas',   '18.1'],
['Utah',   '9.8'],   ['Vermont',   '18'],   ['Virginia',   '19.3'],   ['Washington',
'17.1'],   ['West Virginia',   '25.7'],   ['Wyoming',   '21.6']]

List of cancer data read
[['Alabama',      '75.1'],      ['Alaska',      '69.8'],      ['Arkansas',      '77.7'],
['California',      '51.6'],      ['Colorado',      '48.4'],      ['Connecticut',      '68.3'],
['Delaware',   '83.5'],   ['Florida',   '68.7'],   ['Georgia',   '71'],   ['Hawaii',
'51.7'],   ['Idaho',   '54'],   ['Illinois',   '71.4'],   ['Indiana',   '77.2'],
['Iowa',   '67.1'],   ['Kansas',   '68.4'],   ['Kentucky',   '97.2'],   ['Louisiana',
'77.5'],   ['Maine',   '80.1'],   ['Maryland',   '62.9'],   ['Massachusetts',   '64.5'],
['Michigan',      '72'],      ['Minnesota',      '55.8'],      ['Mississippi',      '77.1'],
['Missouri',   '77.9'],   ['Montana',   '60.8'],   ['Nebraska',   '61.3'],   ['Nevada',
'73.3'],   ['New Hampshire',   '66.8'],   ['New Jersey',   '64.5'],   ['New Mexico',
'43.9'],   ['New York',   '63'],   ['North Carolina',   '75.3'],   ['North Dakota',
'53'],   ['Ohio',   '72.8'],   ['Oklahoma',   '80.8'],   ['Oregon',   '64.4'],
['Pennsylvania',   '70'],   ['Rhode   Island',   '69.5'],   ['South   Carolina',
'70.7'],   ['South Dakota',   '59.2'],   ['Tennessee',   '82.2'],   ['Texas',   '62'],
['Utah',   '28'],   ['Vermont',   '79.2'],   ['Virginia',   '65.8'],   ['Washington',
'65.2'],   ['West Virginia',   '91'],   ['Wyoming',   '48.9']]
>>>
```

FIGURE 8-32   Proper Data Files Test Case for Function readFiles

Looking at the output, it appears that the data from both files has been properly read and properly constructed in each list.

Development and Unit Testing of Function `calculateCorrelation`

The final function of the program to unit test is function `calculateCorrelation`. An implementation of this function is given in Figure 8-33.

```python
1  import math
2
3  def calculateCorrelation(smoking_data, cancer_data):
4
5      """ Calculates and returns the correlation value for the data
6          provided in lists smoking_data and cancer_data
7      """
8
9      # init
10     sum_smoking_vals = sum_cancer_vals = 0
11     sum_smoking_sqrd = sum_cancer_sqrd = 0
12     sum_products = 0
13
14     # calculate intermediate correlation values
15     num_values = len(smoking_data)
16
17     for k in range(0,num_values):
18         sum_smoking_vals = sum_smoking_vals + float(smoking_data[k][1])
19         sum_cancer_vals = sum_cancer_vals + float(cancer_data[k][1])
20
21         sum_smoking_sqrd = sum_smoking_sqrd +  \
22                                 float(smoking_data[k][1]) ** 2
23         sum_cancer_sqrd = sum_cancer_sqrd +  \
24                                 float(cancer_data[k][1]) ** 2
25
26         sum_products = sum_products + float(smoking_data[k][1]) *  \
27                         float(cancer_data[k][1])
28
29     # calculate and display correlation value
30     numer = (num_values * sum_products) - \
31             (sum_smoking_vals * sum_cancer_vals)
32
33     denom = math.sqrt(abs( \
34         ((num_values * sum_smoking_sqrd) - (sum_smoking_vals ** 2)) * \
35         ((num_values * sum_cancer_sqrd) - (sum_cancer_vals ** 2)) \
36         ))
37
38     return numer / denom
```

FIGURE 8-33   Implementation of Function calculateCorrelation

The test driver for this function is given in Figure 8-34. For testing the correctness of the calculation performed by function `calculateCorrelation`, we do not use the data from the data files. Instead, we use data for which we know what the calculated correlation value is. Therefore, three sets of data are hard-coded in the test driver—values in which there is a perfect correlation, another set of values with no correlation, and a final set of values in which there is a perfect negative correlation.

```
 1  # TEST DRIVER for Function calculateCorrelation of Smoking/Cancer
 2  # Correlation Program
 3
 4  from module_calculateCorrelation import *
 5
 6  # calculate perfect positive correlation
 7  print('Calculating perfect positive correlation ...')
 8  smoking_data = [['A', 10], ['B', 20], ['C', 30], ['D', 40]]
 9  cancer_data = [['A', 100], ['B', 200], ['C', 300], ['D', 400]]
10
11  print('Correlation value:', calculateCorrelation(smoking_data, cancer_data))
12
13  # calculate zero correlation
14  print('\nCalculating zero correlation ...')
15  smoking_data = [['A', 10], ['B', 20], ['C', 30], ['D', 40]]
16  cancer_data = [['A', 100], ['B', 0], ['C', 300], ['D', 0]]
17
18  print('Correlation value:', calculateCorrelation(smoking_data,
19  cancer_data))
20
21  # calculate perfect negative correlation
22  print('\nCalculating perfect negative correlation ...')
23  smoking_data = [['A', 10], ['B', 20], ['C', 30], ['D', 40]]
24  cancer_data = [['A', 400], ['B', 300], ['C', 200], ['D', 100]]
25
26  print('Correlation value:', calculateCorrelation(smoking_data, cancer_data))
```

FIGURE 8-34   Test Driver for Function calculateCorrelation

In the first set of lists, the values in list smoking_data (**line 8**) range from 10 to 40 in increments of ten. The values in list cancer_data (**line 9**) range from 100 to 400, in increments of 100. Since the rise in value in each list in proportion to the other, there is a perfect correlation; thus there is, a correlation value of 1. (Note that we simply use the letters 'A', 'B', etc., for the names of the states since this information is irrelevant for this testing.)

In the second set of lists, half of the values in list cancer_data (**line 15**) rise as the values in list smoking_data rise (**line 16**), and the other half of values decrease as the values in smoking_data rise (each by proportional amounts). Therefore, there is no correlation between these two lists of values; thus, there is a correlation value of 0.

Finally, in the third set of lists, the values in list smoking_data (**line 23**) increase as the values in list cancer_data decrease (**line 24**), each by proportional amounts. Therefore, there is a perfect negative correlation; thus there is a correlation value of −1. The results of the execution of the test driver are given in Figure 8-35.

At this point, each of the three functions has been successfully unit tested. What follows next is to perform integrating testing by incorporating each of the functions into the main module and testing the program as a whole.

Integration Testing of the Smoking/Cancer Correlation Program

For the purposes of unit testing, we developed each function in its own module. Now that we are ready to perform integration testing, we put all function definitions into one program file with the main module. The complete program is given in Figure 8-36.

```
Calculating perfect positive correlation ...
Correlation value: 1.0

Calculating zero correlation ...
Correlation value: 0.0

Calculating perfect negative correlation ...
Correlation value: -1.0
>>>
```

FIGURE 8-35   Test Results for Function calculateCorrelation

```
1  Cigarette Use / Lung Cancer Correlation Program
2  import math
3
4  def openFiles():
5
6      """ Prompts the user for the file names to open, opens the files,
7          and returns the file objects for each in a tuple of the form
8          (smoking_datafile, cancer_datafile).
9
10         Raises an IOError exception if the files are not successfully
11         opened after four attempts.
12     """
13
14     # init
15     smoking_datafile_opened = False
16     cancer_datafile_opened = False
17     num_attempts = 4
18
19     # prompt for file names and attempt to open files
20     while ((not smoking_datafile_opened) or \
21            (not cancer_datafile_opened)) \
22           and (num_attempts > 0):
23         try:
24             if not smoking_datafile_opened:
25                 file_name = input('Enter smoking data file name: ')
26                 smoking_datafile = open(file_name, 'r')
27                 smoking_datafile_opened = True
28
29             if not cancer_datafile_opened:
30                 file_name = input('Enter lung cancer data file name: ')
31                 cancer_datafile = open(file_name, 'r')
32                 cancer_datafile_opened = True
33         except IOError:
34             print('File not found:',file_name + '.','Please reenter\n')
35             num_attempts = num_attempts - 1
36
37     # if one of more file not opened, raise IOError exception
38     if not smoking_datafile_opened or not cancer_datafile_opened:
39         raise IOError('Too many attempts of reading input files')
40
41     # return file objects if successfully opened
42     else:
43         return (smoking_datafile, cancer_datafile)
44
```

FIGURE 8-36   Cigarette Use/Lung Cancer Correlation Program (*Continued*)

```
45  def readFiles(smoking_datafile, cancer_datafile):
46
47      """ Reads the data from the provided file objects smoking_datafile
48          and cancer_datafile. Returns a list of the data read from each
49          in a tuple of the form (smoking_datafile, cancer_datafile).
50      """
51
52      # init
53      smoking_data = []
54      cancer_data = []
55      empty_str = ''
56
57      # read past file headers
58      smoking_datafile.readline()
59      cancer_datafile.readline()
60
61      # read data files
62      eof = False
63
64      while not eof:
65
66          # read line of data from each file
67          s_line = smoking_datafile.readline()
68          c_line = cancer_datafile.readline()
69
70          # check if at end-of-file of both files
71          if s_line == empty_str and c_line == empty_str:
72              eof = True
73
74          # check if end of smoking data file only
75          elif s_line == empty_str:
76              raise IOError('Unexpected end-of-file: smoking data file')
77
78          # check if at end of cancer data file only
79          elif c_line == empty_str:
80              raise IOError('Unexpected end-of-file: cancer data file')
81
82          # append line of data to each list
83          else:
84              smoking_data.append(s_line.strip().split(','))
85              cancer_data.append(c_line.strip().split(','))
86
87      # return list of data from each file
88      return (smoking_data, cancer_data)
89
90  def calculateCorrelation(smoking_data, cancer_data):
91
92      """ Calculates and returns the correlation value for the data
93          provided in lists smoking_data and cancer_data
94      """
95
96      # init
97      sum_smoking_vals = sum_cancer_vals = 0
98      sum_smoking_sqrd = sum_cancer_sqrd = 0
99      sum_products = 0
100
```

FIGURE 8-36 Cigarette Use/Lung Cancer Correlation Program (*Continued*)

```
101       # calculate intermediate correlation values
102       num_values = len(smoking_data)
103
104       for k in range(0,num_values):
105
106           sum_smoking_vals = sum_smoking_vals + float(smoking_data[k][1])
107           sum_cancer_vals = sum_cancer_vals + float(cancer_data[k][1])
108
109           sum_smoking_sqrd = sum_smoking_sqrd + \
110                              float(smoking_data[k][1]) ** 2
111           sum_cancer_sqrd = sum_cancer_sqrd + \
112                             float(cancer_data[k][1]) ** 2
113
114           sum_products = sum_products + float(smoking_data[k][1]) * \
115                          float(cancer_data[k][1])
116
117       # calculate and display correlation value
118       numer = (num_values * sum_products) - \
119              (sum_smoking_vals * sum_cancer_vals)
120
121       denom = math.sqrt(abs( \
122           ((num_values * sum_smoking_sqrd) - (sum_smoking_vals ** 2)) * \
123           ((num_values * sum_cancer_sqrd) - (sum_cancer_vals ** 2)) \
124           ))
125
126       return numer / denom
127
128 # ---- main
129
130 # program greeting
131 print('This program will determine the correlation (-1 to 1) between')
132 print('data on cigarette smoking and incidences of lung cancer\n')
133
134 try:
135     # open data files
136     smoking_datafile, cancer_datafile = openFiles()
137
138     # read data
139     smoking_data, cancer_data = readFiles(smoking_datafile, cancer_datafile)
140
141     # calculate correlation value
142     correlation = calculateCorrelation(smoking_data, cancer_data)
143
144     # display correlation value
145     print('r_value = ', correlation)
146 except IOError as e:
147     print(str(e))
148     print('Program terminated ...')
```

FIGURE 8-36 Cigarette Use/Lung Cancer Correlation Program

We test the program with the same data used for the unit testing of function `calculate-Correlation`. In this case, however, the data is contained in files to be opened and read by the program. The files and their contents are given below.

```
Smoking Test Data 1
A, 10
B, 20
C, 30
D, 40
```

```
Cancer Test Data 1
A, 100
B, 200
C, 300
D, 400
```

```
Smoking Test Data 2
A, 10
B, 20
C, 30
D, 40
```

```
Cancer Test Data 2
A, 100
B, 0
C, 300
D, 0
```

```
Smoking Test Data 3
A, 10
B, 20
C, 30
D, 40
```

```
Cancer Test Data 3
A, 400
B, 300
C, 200
D, 100
```

The three test results of the program for the data sets above is given below in Figure 8-37.

The results are as expected. We get the same results as in the unit testing of `calculateCorrelation`. Therefore, all three functions are properly integrated into the program. We next run the program on the actual data files `CDC_Cigaratte_Smoking_Data` and `CDC_Lung_Cancer_Data`.

```
This program will determine the correlation (-1 to 1) between
data on cigarette smoking and incidences of lung cancer

Enter smoking data file name: Smoking_Test_Data_1.csv
Enter lung cancer data file name: Cancer_Test_Data_1.csv
r_value =  1.0
>>> ================================ RESTART ================================
>>>
This program will determine the correlation (-1 to 1) between
data on cigarette smoking and incidences of lung cancer

Enter smoking data file name: Smoking_Test_Data_2.csv
Enter lung cancer data file name: Cancer_Test_Data_2.csv
r_value =  0.0
>>> ================================ RESTART ================================
>>>
This program will determine the correlation (-1 to 1) between
data on cigarette smoking and incidences of lung cancer

Enter smoking data file name: Smoking_Test_Data_3.csv
Enter lung cancer data file name: Cancer_Test_Data_3.csv
r_value =  -1.0
>>>
```

FIGURE 8-37   Integration Testing Results for Cigarette Use/Lung Cancer Correlation Program

8.5.5   Determining the Correlation Between Smoking and Lung Cancer

The output from the execution of this program on the actual data is given in Figure 8-38.

```
This program will calculate the correlation value (-1 to 1) between
provided data on cigarette smoking and incidences of lung cancer

Enter the names of the two data files, including file extension
(files must contain same number of lines of data)

Enter name of cigarette smoking file: CDC Cigarette Smoking Data.csv
Enter name lung cancer file: CDC_Lung_Cancer_Data.csv
r_value =  0.786159246886
```

FIGURE 8-38   Output of the Cigarette Use/Lung Cancer Correlation Program

In the output, we see a correlation value of approximately 0.79. That indicates a very strong correlation, depicted in Figure 8-39.

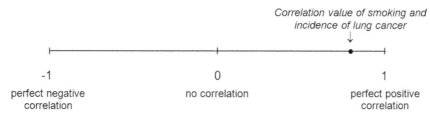

FIGURE 8-39   Depiction of Results on a Correlation Scale

So, can we conclude from this result alone that smoking *causes* lung cancer? No. Causation cannot be easily determined even with a perfect correlation. For example, there is a strong correlation between the amount of ice cream sold and the number of drownings that occur in the United States. Does that mean that eating ice cream raises the likelihood of drowning? Common sense tells us no, that the correlation results from them both being summertime activities.

To interpret our results, we have to decide that either (a) smoking causes lung cancer; (b) lung cancer causes the urge to smoke; (c) there exists a third factor simultaneously causing the desire for smoking and lung cancer; or (d) there is no causal relationship. Since a strong correlation is not enough to argue that causation exists, other evidence needs to be considered, such as the lung tissue of those who have died from lung cancer. This, in fact, is what medical research has investigated. Based on the findings, along with the demonstrated correlation, tells us that yes, smoking does cause lung cancer.

CHAPTER SUMMARY

General Topics

Text Files vs. Binary Files
Opening and Closing Files
Reading and Writing Text Files
String Processing
Exception Handling
Comma Separated Data Files

Python-Specific Programming Topics

Built-in Functions open and close in Python
File Object Methods readline and write in
    Python
String Methods in Python
Catching and Handling Exceptions in Python
Standard Exceptions in Python

CHAPTER EXERCISES

Section 8.1

1. Explain the difference in how numbers are represented in a text file versus how they are represented in a binary file containing numerical values.

2. Explain why binary files do not contain newline characters.

Section 8.2

3. Give an instruction in Python that opens a file named `'datafile.txt'` for reading and assigns identifier `input_file` to the file object created.

4. Give an instruction in Python that opens a file named `'datafile2.txt'` for writing and assigns identifier `output_file` to the file object created.

5. Assume that `input_file` is a file object for a text file open for reading, and `output_file` is a file object for a text file open for writing. Explain the contents of the output file after the following code is executed,

```
empty_str = ''
line = input_file.readline()

while line != empty_str:
    output_file.write(line + '\n')
    line = input_file.readline()
```

Section 8.3

6. Give a for loop that counts all the letter characters in string `line`.

7. For variable `month` which contains the full name of any given month, give an instruction to display just the first three letters of the month.

8. Give an instruction that displays `True` if the letter 'r' appears in a variable named `month`, otherwise displays `False`.

9. Give an instruction for determining how many times the letter 'r' appears in a variable named `month`.

10. For variables `first_name` and `last_name`, give an instruction that displays the person's name in the form *last name, first name*.

11. Give an instruction that determines if a variable named `ss_num` contains any non-digit characters, other than a dash.

12. Give an instruction that determines the index of the '@' character in an email address in variable `email_addr`.

13. For variable `date` containing a date of the form 12/14/2012, write a function that produces the same date, but with all slashes characters replaced with dashes.

14. For a variable named `err_mesg` that contains error messages in the form `** error message **`, give an instruction that produces a string containing the error message without the leading and trailing asterisks and blank characters.

Section 8.4

15. Identify the error in the following code,

```
input_file_opened = False

while not input_file_opened:
```

```
try:
    file_name = input('Enter file name: ')
    input_file = open(file_name, 'r')
except:
    print('Input file not found - please reenter')
```

PYTHON PROGRAMMING EXERCISES

P1. Write a Python function called `reduceWhitespace` that is given a line read from a text file and returns the line with all extra whitespace characters between words removed,

'This line has extra space characters' → 'This line has extra space characters'

P2. Write a Python function named `extractTemp` that is given a line read from a text file and displays the one number (integer) found in the string,

'The high today will be 75 degrees' → 75

P3. Write a Python function named `checkQuotes` that is given a line read from a text file and returns `True` if each quote characters in the line has a matching quote (of the same type), otherwise returns `False`.

'Today's high temperature will be 75 degrees' → `False`

P4. Write a Python function named `countAllLetters` that is given a line read from a text file and returns a list containing every letter in the line and the number of times that each letter appears (with upper/lower case letters counted together),

'This is a short line' → [('t', 2), ('h', 2), ('i', 3), ('s', 3), ('a', 1),
('o', 1), ('r', 1), ('l', 1), ('n', 1), ('e', 1)]

P5. Write a Python function named `interleaveChars` that is given *two* lines read from a text file, and returns a single string containing the characters of each string interleaved,

'Hello', 'Goodbye' → 'HGeololdobye'

P6. Write a program segment that opens and reads a text file and displays how many lines of text are in the file.

P7. Write a program segment that reads a text file named `original_text`, and writes every other line, starting with the first line, to a new file named `half_text`.

P8. Write a program segment that reads a text file named `original_text`, and displays how many times the letter 'e' occurs.

PROGRAM MODIFICATION PROBLEMS

M1. Sparse Text Program: User-Selected Letter Removed
Modify the Sparse Text program in section 8.3.4 so that instead of the letter 'e' being removed, the user is prompted for the letter to remove.

M2. Sparse Text Program: Random Removal of Letters
Modify the Sparse Text program in section 8.3.4 so that instead of a particular letter removed, a percentage of the letters are randomly removed based on a percentage entered by the user.

M3. Word Frequency Count Program: Display of Scanned Lines
Modify the Word Frequency Count program in section 8.4.6 so that the text lines being scanned are at the same time displayed on the screen.

M4. Word Frequency Count Program: Counting of a Set of Words
Modify the Word Frequency Count Program so that the user can enter any number of words to be counted within a given text file.

M5. Word Frequency Count Program: Counting of All Words
Modify the Word Frequency Count program so that all the words in a given text file are counted.

M6. Word Frequency Count Program: Outputting Results to a File
Modify the Word Frequency Count program so that the counts of all words in a given text file are output to a file with the same name as the file read, but with the file extension ' .wc ' (for 'word count').

M7. Lung Cancer Correlation Program: Air Pollution and Lung Cancer
Modify the cigarettes and lung cancer correlation program in the Computational Problem Solving section of the chapter to correlate lung cancer with air pollution instead. Use the data from the following ranking of states from highest to lowest amounts of air pollution given below.

Rank	State	Added cancer risk (per 1,000,000)	Rank	State	Added cancer risk (per 1,000,000)
1.	NEW YORK	1900	26.	UTAH	500
2.	NEW JERSEY	1400	27.	WASHINGTON	490
3.	DISTRICT OF COLUMBIA	1100	28.	NORTH CAROLINA	480
4.	CALIFORNIA	890	29.	NEW HAMPSHIRE	470
5.	MASSACHUSETTS	890	30.	MISSOURI	460
6.	MARYLAND	870	31.	ARIZONA	440
7.	DELAWARE	860	32.	COLORADO	440
8.	PENNSYLVANIA	860	33.	ALABAMA	400
9.	CONNECTICUT	850	34.	SOUTH CAROLINA	390
10.	ILLINOIS	800	35.	NEBRASKA	390
11.	OHIO	730	36.	KANSAS	360
12.	INDIANA	720	37.	IOWA	340
13.	RHODE ISLAND	670	38.	NEVADA	340
14.	MINNESOTA	660	39.	ARKANSAS	330
15.	GEORGIA	650	40.	OKLAHOMA	330
16.	MICHIGAN	640	41.	MISSISSIPPI	320
17.	VIRGINIA	620	42.	VERMONT	270
18.	LOUISIANA	590	43.	IDAHO	260
19.	WEST VIRGINIA	560	44.	MAINE	240
20.	TEXAS	550	45.	NEW MEXICO	230
21.	WISCONSIN	540	46.	NORTH DAKOTA	200
22.	KENTUCKY	540	47.	SOUTH DAKOTA	190
23.	TENNESSEE	520	48.	MONTANA	180
24.	OREGON	520	49.	WYOMING	140
25.	FLORIDA	510			

PROGRAM DEVELOPMENT PROBLEMS

D1. Sentence, Word, and Character Count Program
Develop and test a Python program that reads in any given text file and displays the number of lines, words, and total number of characters there are in the file, including spaces and special characters, but not the newline character, ' \n ' .

D2. Variation on a Sparsity Program
Develop and test a program that reads the text in a given file, and produces a new file in which the *first occurrence only* of the vowel in each word is removed, unless the removal would leave an empty word (for example, for the word "I"). Consider how readable the results are for various sample text.

D3. Message Encryption/Decryption Program
Develop and test a Python program that reads messages contained in a text file, and encodes the messages saved in a new file. For encoding messages, a simple substitution key should be used as shown below,

A	F
B	G
C	L
D	R
E	P
.	.
.	.

Each letter in the left column is substituted with the corresponding letter in the right column when encoding. Thus, to decode, the letters are substituted the opposite way. Unencrypted message files will be simple text files with file extension .txt. Encrypted message files will have the same file name, but with file extension .enc. For each message encoded, a new substitution key should be randomly generated and saved in a file with the extension '.key'. Your program should also be able to decrypt messages given a specific encoded message and the corresponding key.

D4. Morse Code Encryption/Decryption Program

Develop and test a Python program that allows a user to open a text file containing a simple message using only the (uppercase) letters A . . . Z, and saves a Morse code version of the message, that is, containing only the characters dash ("-"), dot ("."). In the encoded version, put the encoding of each character on its own line in the text file. Use a blank line to indicate the end of a word, and two blank lines to indicate the end of a sentence. Your program should be able to both convert an English message file into Morse code, and a Morse code file into English. The Morse code for each letter is given below.

A	· −	N	− ·
B	− · · ·	O	− − −
C	− · − ·	P	· − − ·
D	− · ·	Q	− − · −
E	·	R	· − ·
F	· · − ·	S	· · ·
G	− − ·	T	−
H	· · · ·	U	· · −
I	· ·	V	· · · −
J	· − − −	W	· − −
K	− · −	X	− · · −
L	· − · ·	Y	− · − −
M	− −	Z	− − · ·

D5. Universal Product Code Check Digit Verification Program

A *check digit* is a digit added to a string of digits that is derived from other digits in the string. Check digits provide a form of redundancy of information, used for determining if any of the digits in the string are incorrect or misread.

The Universal Product Code on almost all purchase items utilizes a bar code to allow for the scanning of items. Below the bar code is the sequence of digits that the bar code encodes, as illustrated below.

The last digit of the product code (2) is a check digit computed as follows,

1. Add up all digits in the odd numbered positions (first, third, fifth, etc., starting with the leftmost digit) excluding the last check digit, and multiply the result by 3,

$$0 + 6 + 0 + 2 + 1 + 5 = 14, \ 14 * 3 = 42$$

2. Add up all digits in the even numbered positions (second, fourth, etc.) excluding the last check digit,

$$3 + 0 + 0 + 9 + 4 = 16$$

3. Take the sum of the two previous results mod 10,

$$(42 + 16) \bmod 10 = 58 \bmod 10 = 8$$

4. Subtract the result from 10 to get the checksum digit.

$$10 - 8 = \mathbf{2}$$

Develop and test a Python program that verifies the check digit of Universal Product Codes.

Dictionaries and Sets

CHAPTER 9

Since Chapter 4, we have been using linear (sequential) data structures—lists, tuples, and strings—in which elements are accessed by their index value (that is, by location). There also exist data structures in which elements are not accessed by location, but rather by an associated key value, called dictionaries in Python. We look at both dictionaries and sets in Python in this chapter.

OBJECTIVES

After reading this chapter and completing the exercises, you will be able to:

♦ Explain the concept of an associative data structure

♦ Define and use dictionaries in Python

♦ Define and use sets in Python

♦ Write Python programs using dictionaries and sets

♦ Perform unit testing using test stubs (and test drivers)

CHAPTER CONTENTS

Motivation

Fundamental Concepts

MOTIVATION

The vast amounts of data being stored today could not be effectively utilized without being organized in some way. Databases do not simply store large amounts of data. Rather, they provide a complete database management system (DBMS) used in conjunction with stored data to allow the data to be associated and accessed in various ways.

Database management systems provide access to data without needing to know how the data is physically structured, only how it is *logically* organized. Access is provided by a *query language* that allows arbitrarily complex queries to be made of the data. For example, one can construct a query that returns the set of students who have a perfect 4.0 GPA and are graduating at the end of the current semester. Or, one could construct a more complex query that returns the set of students that have a GPA of 3.6 or above, with senior status, female, a computer science major, and has taken at least twelve credits of biology or eight credits of biology and four credits of chemistry.

Some of the concerns of database management systems include: *integrity of data*—that is, data that is accessible and properly organized; *security* in the control of who has what level of access; and management of *concurrency* issues when multiple users are accessing the same data. Data mining (Figure 9-1) is a relatively new field in which database management systems are used in conjunction with methods from statistics and artificial intelligence to extract patterns from very large amounts of data.

Areas	Data Mining Application
Business	Customer Relationship Management (e.g., to find, attract, retain customers)
Genetics	DNA Analysis (e.g., to understand individual variations in human DNA in relation to disease susceptibility)
National Security	Behavioral Patterns (e.g., to identify possible terrorist activities)
Information Retrieval	Music Information Retrieval (to discover musical patterns used in music retrieval)

FIGURE 9-1 Data Mining Applications

FUNDAMENTAL CONCEPTS

9.1 Dictionary Type in Python

In this section we introduce the notion of an *associative data structure*. Elements of indexed linear data structures, such as lists, are ordered—the first element (at index 0), second element (at index 1), and so forth. In contrast, the elements of an associative data structure are unordered, instead accessed by an associated key value. In Python, an associative data structure is provided by the *dictionary type*. We look at the use of dictionaries in Python next.

9.1.1 What Is a Dictionary?

A **dictionary** is a mutable, associative data structure of variable length. The syntax for declaring dictionaries in Python is given below.

```
daily_temps = {'sun': 68.8, 'mon': 70.2, 'tue': 67.2, 'wed': 71.8,
               'thur': 73.2, 'fri': 75.6, 'sat': 74.0}
```

Dictionary `daily_temps` stores the average temperature for each day of the week, as we did earlier in Chapter 4 using a list. However, in this case, each temperature has associated with it a unique key value (`'sun'`, `'mon'`, etc.). Strings are often used as key values. The syntax for accessing an element of a dictionary is the same as for accessing elements of sequence types, except that a key value is used within the square brackets instead of an index value: `daily_temps['sun']`. A comparison of accessing indexed data structures vs. associative data structures is given in Figure 9-2.

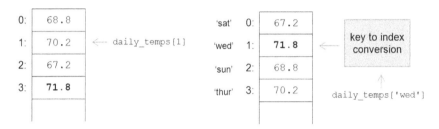

indexed data structure   associative data structure

FIGURE 9-2 Indexed vs. Associative Data Structure

On the left is an indexed data structure, and on the right an associative data structure. Although the elements of the associative data structure are physically ordered, the ordering is irrelevant to the way that the structure is utilized. *The location that an element is stored in and retrieved from within an associative data structure depends only on its key value,* thus there is no logical first element, second element, and so forth. The specific location that a value is stored is determined by a particular method of converting key values into index values called *hashing*. Example use of dictionary `daily_temps` is given below.

```
if daily_temps['sun'] > daily_temps['sat']:
    print 'Sunday was the warmer weekend day'
else
    if daily_temps['sun'] < daily_temps['sat']:
        print 'Saturday was the warmer weekend day'
    else:
        print 'Saturday and Sunday were equally warm'
```

Although strings are often used as key values, any immutable type may be used as well, such as a tuple (shown in Figure 9-3). In this case, the temperature for a specific date is retrieved by,

```
temps[('Apr', 14, 2001)]  →  74.6
```

```
temps = { ('Jan', 2,2004): 34.8,          ('Apr', 14, 2001) :    74.6
          ('Mar', 6, 2000): 68.2,
          ('Nov', 30, 2003): 61.0,         ('Dec', 21, 2002):     28.8
          ('Apr', 14, 2001): 74.6,
          ('Dec', 21, 2002): 28.8}         ('Nov', 30, 2003):     61.0

                                           ('Jan', 2, 2004):      34.8

                                           ('Mar', 6, 2000):      68.2
```

FIGURE 9-3   Associative Data Structure Using Tuple Key Values

Note that this key contains both string and integer values. To give an example of when an associative array may be of benefit over an indexed type, we give two versions of a program that displays the recorded average temperature for any day of the week—one using a list, and the other using a dictionary. We first give the list version of the program in Figure 9-4, which allows a user to enter a day of the week and have the average temperature for that day displayed.

```
# Temperature Display Program (List Version)

daily_temps = [68.8, 70.2, 67.2, 71.8, 73.2, 75.6, 74.0]

print('This program will display the average temperature for a given day')
terminate = False

while not terminate:

    day = input("Enter 'sun', 'mon', 'tue', 'wed', 'thur', 'fri', or 'sat': ")

    if day == 'sun':
        dayname = 'Sunday'
        temp = daily_temps[0]
    elif day == 'mon':
        dayname = 'Monday'
        temp = daily_temps[1]
    elif day == 'tue':
        dayname = 'Tuesday'
        temp = daily_temps[2]
    elif day == 'wed':
        dayname = 'Wednesday'
        temp = daily_temps[3]
    elif day == 'thur':
        dayname = 'Thursday'
        temp = daily_temps[4]
    elif day == 'fri':
        dayname = 'Friday'
        temp = daily_temps[5]
    elif day == 'sat':
        dayname = 'Saturday'
        temp = daily_temps[6]

    print('The average temperature for', dayname, 'was', temp, 'degrees\n')

    response = input('Continue with another day? (y/n): ')
    if response == 'n':
        terminate = True
```

FIGURE 9-4   Temperature Display Program (Indexed Array Version)

The program prompts the user for the day of the week (as `'sun'`, `'mon'`, `'tue'`, etc.) to display the average temperature for. The average temperatures are stored in list `daily_temps`. Once read, an if statement (with `elif` headers) is used to set variable `dayname` to the full name of the day entered, as well as retrieve the corresponding temperature from list `daily_temps`. The result is then displayed to the user. An example execution of this program is given below.

```
This program will display the average temperature for a given day
Enter 'sun', 'mon', 'tue', 'wed', 'thur', 'fri', or 'sat': wed
The average temperature for Wednesday was 71.8 degrees
>>>
```

The program in Figure 9-5 provides the identical functionality, but instead using an associative array instead of a list for storing the average daily temperatures.

```
# Temperature Display Program (Dictionary Version)

daily_temps = {'sun': 68.8, 'mon': 70.2, 'tue': 67.2, 'wed': 71.8,
               'thur': 73.2, 'fri': 75.6, 'sat': 74.0}

daynames = {'sun': 'Sunday', 'mon': 'Monday', 'tue': 'Tuesday',
            'wed': 'Wednesday', 'thur': 'Thursday', 'fri': 'Friday',
            'sat': 'Saturday'}

print('This program will display the average temperature for a given day')
day = input("Enter 'sun', 'mon', 'tue', 'wed', 'thur', 'fri', or 'sat': ")
print('The average temperature for', daynames[day], 'was',
      daily_temps[day], 'degrees')
```

FIGURE 9-5 Temperature Display Program (Dictionary Version)

This version of the program is much more concise and elegant than the previous one. Rather than using a series of conditions in an if-elif statement for checking the day of the week entered by the user, the entered day is directly used for retrieving the corresponding average temperature from dictionary `daily_temps`. A second associative array is also used in the program for storing the corresponding full day names, accessed by the same set of key values.

In the previous example, the values of the dictionaries are "hard-coded" into the program. Dictionaries, however, may also be created and modified dynamically (that is, during program execution). There are cases where this capability is needed. For example, if a given dictionary contains thousands of elements, too many to hard-code into a program, then the key/value pairs can be read from a file and the dictionary "built" at runtime. Or, it may be that some of the values to be stored are not yet known, and therefore, the dictionary needs to be expanded and updated at execution time (for example, when storing user-selected passwords). The operations related to the dynamic creation and updating of dictionaries are shown in Figure 9-6.

Operation	Results
dict()	Creates a new, empty dictionary
dict(s)	Creates a new dictionary with key values and their associated values from sequence s, for example, fruit_prices = dict(fruit_data) where fruit_data is (possibly read from a file): [['apples', .66],…,['bananas', .49]]
len(d)	Length (num of key/value pairs) of dictionary d.
d[key] = value	Sets the associated value for key to value, used to either add a new key/value pair, or replace the value of an existing key/value pair.
del d[key]	Remove key and associated value from dictionary d.
key in d	True if key value key exists in dictionary d, otherwise returns False.

FIGURE 9-6 Some Operations for Dynamically Manipulating Dictionaries

---

LET'S TRY IT

From the Python Shell, enter the following and observe the results.

```
>>> fruit_prices = {'apples': .66, 'pears': .25,
                    'peaches': .74, 'bananas': .49}
>>> fruit_prices['apples']
???
>>> fruit_prices[0]
???
>>> veg_data = [['corn', .25], ['tomatoes', .49], ['peas', .39]]
>>> veg_prices = dict(veg_data)
>>> veg_prices
???
>>> veg_prices['peas']
???
```

A **dictionary** in Python is a mutable, associative data structure of variable length denoted by the use of curly braces.

9.1.2 Let's Apply It—Phone Number Spelling Program

The following Python program (Figure 9-8) generates all the possible spellings of the last four digits of any given phone number. The program utilizes the following programming features:

➤ dictionaries

Example execution of the program is given in Figure 9-7.

The program begins at **line 55**. First, a program welcome is displayed on **lines 55–56**. On **line 59**, variable terminate is assigned False. This variable controls the while loop at **line 61**. It is set to True, which terminates the loop, when the user indicates that they do not wish to enter any more phone numbers (**line 69**).

Within the loop, functions getPhoneNum and displayAllSpellings are called. Function getPhoneNum (**lines 3–32**) reads a phone number from the user of the form 123-456-7890.

```
Program execution ...

This program will generate all possible spellings of the
last four digits of any phone number

Enter phone number (xxx-xxx-xxxx): 410-555-7324
410-555-pdag
410-555-pdah
410-555-pdai
410-555-pdbg
410-555-pdbh
410-555-pdbi
410-555-pdcg
410-555-pdch
410-555-pdci
410-555-peag
410-555-peah
410-555-peai
410-555-pebg
410-555-pebh
410-555-pebi
.
.
Enter another phone number? (y/n): y
Enter phone number (xxx-xxx-xxxx): 410-555-4267
410-555-gamp
410-555-gamq
410-555-gamr
410-555-gams
410-555-ganp
410-555-ganq
410-555-ganr
410-555-gans
410-555-gaop
410-555-gaoq
410-555-gaor
410-555-gaos
.
.
```

FIGURE 9-7 Execution of Phone Number Spelling Program

On **line 8**, variable `valid_ph_num` is initialized to `False`, used to control the while loop on **line 12**. Only when a valid phone number has been entered is this variable set to `True`, which terminates the loop and returns the (valid) entered phone number.

Within the while loop, the entered phone number is input as a string (**line 13**). Two checks are made for the validity of the entered string. First, a check (**line 16**) is made as to whether the string is the wrong length (should be twelve characters long) or if the fourth (index 3) or eighth (index 7) characters are not a dash. If any of these errors are found, an error message is displayed (**line 18**) and another iteration of the while loop is executed. If, however, no error is found at this point, a second check is made that the remaining characters in the string (other than the two dashes) are digit characters. In this case, the string is assumed to contain proper digit characters (that is, `valid_ph_num` is set to True on **line 22**), unless found otherwise (by use of string method `isdigit` on **line 26**). Thus, if a non-digit character is found, `valid_ph_num` is set to `False` and the inner while loop terminates, continuing with another execution of the outer while loop (at **line 12**). If, however, no non-digits are found, `valid_ph_num` remains `True`, thus terminating the outer while loop and returning the entered phone number.

```
1  # Phone Number Spelling Program
2
3  def getPhoneNum():
4
5      """Returns entered phone number in the form 123-456-7890."""
6
7      # init
8      valid_ph_num = False
9      empty_str = ''
10
11     # prompt for phone number
12     while not valid_ph_num:
13         phone_num = input('Enter phone number (xxx-xxx-xxxx): ')
14
15         # check if valid form
16         if len(phone_num) != 12 or phone_num[3] != '-' or \
17            phone_num[7] != '-':
18             print('INVALID ENTRY - Must be of the form xxx-xxx-xxxx\n')
19         else:
20             # check for non-digits
21             k = 0
22             valid_ph_num = True
23             phone_num_digits = phone_num.replace('-', empty_str)
24
25             while valid_ph_num and k < len(phone_num_digits):
26                 if not phone_num_digits[k].isdigit():
27                     print('* Non-digit:', phone_num_digits[k],'*\n')
28                     valid_ph_num = False
29                 else:
30                     k = k + 1
31
32     return phone_num
33
34  def displayAllSpellings(phone_num):
35
36      """Displays all possible phone numbers with the last four digits
37         replaced with a corresponding letter from the phone keys
38      """
39      translate =  {'0': ('0'), '1':('1'), '2': ('a','b','c'),
40                    '3': ('d','e','f'),'4': ('g','h','i'),
41                    '5': ('j','k','l'), '6': ('m','n','o'),
42                    '7': ('p','q','r','s'),'8': ('t','u','v'),
43                    '9': ('w','x','y','z')}
44
45      # display spellings
46      for let1 in translate[phone_num[8]]:
47          for let2 in translate[phone_num[9]]:
48              for let3 in translate[phone_num[10]]:
49                  for let4 in translate[phone_num[11]]:
50                      print(phone_num[0:8] + let1 + let2 + let3 + let4)
51
```

FIGURE 9-8 Phone Number Spelling Program (*Continued*)

In function `displayAllSpellings` (**lines 34–50**), we see our first example of the use of deeply nested (for) loops. Because we want to generate all combinations of each of the four possible letters of the last four digits of the entered phone number, we utilize for loops nested four deep (**line 46**). Each digit ranges over its particular set of letters that appear on phone keys. Dictionary `translate` is defined for this purpose. In the dictionary, each digit 0–9 is a key value. The value associated with each key is a tuple containing the associated keypad letters for that

```
52  #---- main
53
54  # program welcome
55  print('This program will generate all possible spellings of the')
56  print('last four digits of any phone number\n')
57
58  # get phone number and display spellings
59  terminate = False
60
61  while not terminate:
62
63      phone_num = getPhoneNum()
64      displayAllSpellings(phone_num)
65
66      # continue?
67      response = input('Enter another phone number? (y/n): ')
68      if response == 'n':
69          terminate = True
```

FIGURE 9-8 Phone Number Spelling Program

digit. (Digits `'0'` and `'1'` return a string equal to themselves, since these phone digits do not have any letters associated with them.) For example, within the first for statement, dictionary `translate` contains the list of letters associated with the digit currently in the eighth position (the digit right after the second dash) of the entered phone number. Let's say that digit is 7. Then the retrieved tuple would be `('p','q','r','s')`. Therefore, all combinations of strings starting with these letters will be generated, as shown in Figure 9-9.

```
let1 = 'p','q','r','s'
    let2 = 'd','e','f'
        let3 = 'a','b','c'
            let4 = 'g','h','i'
                410-555-pdag
                410-555-pdah
                410-555-pdai

                410-555-pdbg
                410-555-pdbh
                410-555-pdbi

                410-555-pdcg
                410-555-pdch
                410-555-pdci

                410-555-peag
                410-555-peah
                410-555-peai

            etc.
```

FIGURE 9-9 Nested for Loops in the
Generation of Phone Number Spellings

On **line 67**, the user is prompted if they want to continue with another phone number. If they respond no (`'n'`), variable `terminate` is set to `True`, which terminates the outer while loop, and thus ends the program; otherwise, the program prompts for another number.

Self-Test Questions

1. A dictionary type in Python is an associative data structure that is accessed by a
    _____ rather than an index value.

2. Associative data structures such as the dictionary type in Python are useful for,
    (a) accessing elements more intuitively than by use of an indexed data structure
    (b) maintaining elements in a particular order

3. Which of the following types can be used as a key in Python dictionaries?
    (a) strings
    (b) lists
    (c) tuples
    (d) numerical values

4. Which of the following is a syntactically correct sequence, s, for dynamically creating a
    dictionary using `dict(s)`.
    (a) `s = [[1: 'one'], [2: 'two'], [3: 'three']]`
    (b) `s = [[1, 'one'], [2, 'two'], [3, 'three']]`
    (c) `s = {1:'one', 2:'two', 3:'three'}`

5. For dictionary `d = {'apples':0.66,'pears':1.25,'bananas':0.49}`, which
    of the following correctly updates the price of bananas.
    (a) `d[2]  = 0.52`
    (b) `d[0.49]  = 0.52`
    (c) `d['bananas']  = 0.52`

ANSWERS: 1. key value. 2. (a). 3. (a), (c), (d). 4. (b). 5. (c)

9.2   Set Data Type

9.2.1   The Set Data Type in Python

A **set** is a mutable data type with nonduplicate, unordered values, providing the usual mathematical
set operations as shown in Figure 9-10.

Set operator	Set A = {1,2,3}	Set B = {3,4,5,6}	
membership	`1 in A`	True	*True if 1 is a member of set*
add	`A.add(4)`	{1,2,3,4}	*Adds new member to set*
remove	`A.remove(2)`	{1,3}	*Removes member from set*
union	`A	B`	{1,2,3,4,5,6}	*Set of elements in either set A or set B*
intersection	`A & B`	{3}	*Set of elements in both set A and set B*
difference	`A - B`	{1,2}	*Set of elements in set A, but not set B*
symmetric difference	`A ^ B`	{1,2,4,5,6}	*Set of elements in set A or set B, but not both*
size	`len(A)`	3	*Number of elements in set (general sequence operation)*

FIGURE 9-10   Set Operators

One of the most commonly used set operators is the `in` operator (which we have been already using with sequences) for determining membership,

```
>>> fruit = {'apple', 'banana', 'pear', 'peach'}
>>> fruit
{'pear', 'banana', 'peach', 'apple'}

>>> 'apple' in fruit
True
```

Note that the items in the set are not displayed in the order that they were defined. Sets, like dictionaries, do not maintain a logical ordering. The order that items are stored is determined by Python, and not by the order in which they were provided. Therefore, it is invalid and makes no sense to access an element of a set by index value.

The `add` and `remove` methods allow sets to be dynamically altered during program execution, as shown below,

```
>>> fruit.add('pineapple')
>>> fruit
{'pineapple', 'pear', 'banana', 'peach', 'apple'}
```

To define an initially empty set, or to initialize a set to the values of a particular sequence, the `set` constructor is used,

```
>>> set1 = set()     >>> vegs = ['peas', 'corn']    >>> vowels = 'aeiou'
>>> len(set1)        >>> set(vegs)                  >>> set(vowels)
0                    {'corn', 'peas'}               {'a', 'i', 'e', 'u', 'o'}
```

Note that `set()`, and not empty braces are not used to create an empty set, since that notation is used to create an empty dictionary. Because sets do not have duplicate elements, adding an already existing item to a set results in no change to the set.

Finally, there are two set types in Python—the mutable `set` type, and the immutable `frozenset` type. Methods `add` and `remove` are not allowed on sets of `frozenset` type. Thus, all its members are declared when it is defined,

```
>>> apple_colors = frozenset(['red', 'yellow', 'green'])
```

As shown, the values of a set of type `frozenset` must be provided in a single list when defined. (A frozenset type is needed when a set is used as a key value in a given dictionary.)

LET'S TRY IT

From the Python shell, enter the following and observe the results.

```
>>> s = {1,2,3}                    >>> s = set(['apple', 'banana', 'pear'])
>>> 1 in s                         >>> s
???                                ???

>>> s.add(4)                       >>> s.add('pineapple')
>>> s                              ???
???
                                   >>> s = frozenset(['apple', 'banana', 'pear'])
>>> s = set('abcde')               >>> s.add('pineapple')
>>> s                              >>> ???
???
```

A **set** is a mutable data structure with nonduplicate, unordered values, providing the usual set operations. A **frozenset** is an immutable set type.

9.2.2 Let's Apply It—Kitchen Tile Visualization Program

The following Python program (Figure 9-12) allows the user to select a particular kitchen tile size, a primary and secondary tile color, the frequency in which the secondary color is to be placed, and a grout color. It then displays the resulting tile pattern. This program utilizes the following programming features:

➤ sets

Example execution of the program is given in Figure 9-11 (shown as grey tones in this image).

Program execution begins on **line 154**. Variable `tile_area` is assigned to a dictionary that holds the width and height of the turtle window to be created. Variable `grout_color_selection` is assigned to a set containing string values `'white'`, `'gray'`, `'brown'`, and `'black'`. These strings are recognized in turtle graphics as color values. The user is prompted to enter one of these values as the grout color, which is set as the background color of the turtle screen within function `layoutTile`. Variable `scaling` is used to appropriately adjust the size of the displayed tile. Changing this value will make tiles appear larger or smaller on the screen.

Function `greeting` is called on **line 159** to display an explanation of the program to the user. On **line 162**, the `getTileSelections` function is called. This function prompts the user for the tile width and length, the primary and secondary colors of the tiles, the number of primary colors that should be displayed for each secondary tile color, and the grout color. These values are returned in a dictionary of the form,

```
{'tile_size':{'length':tile_length, 'width':tile_width},
 'primary_color':color1, 'secondary_color':color2,
 'tile_skip':skip, 'grout_color':grout}
```

```
Program Execution ...

This program will display the tile pattern for a selected
pair of tile colors, tile size, and grout color.

The repeat frequency for the secondary tile color can be selected:
if skip = 1, secondary tile color placed every other tile,
if skip = 2, secondary tile color placed every third tile, etc.

Enter tile length (1-4 inches): 4
Enter tile width (1-4 inches): 4
Enter primary tile color (6-digit RGB): 006400
Enter secondary tile color (6-digit RGB): D2B4AC
Enter frequency of secondary tile color (1-10): 2
Enter grout color (white, gray, brown or black): white
```

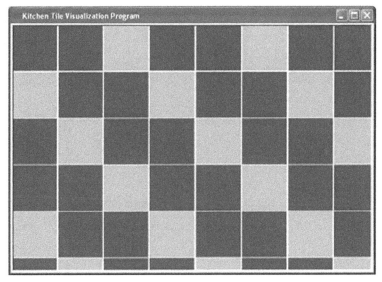

FIGURE 9-11   Execution of the Kitchen Tile Visualization Program

Thus, for example, for variable `selections` assigned to this dictionary, `selections['tile_size']` gets the selected tile length and width, and `selections['primary_color']` gets the primary tile color. Note that the value associated with key `'tile_size'` is itself a dictionary of the form,

$$\{'length':tile\_length, \ 'width':tile\_width\}$$

Thus, for variable `tile_size` assigned to this dictionary, `tile_size['length']` returns the user-selected tile length, and `tile_size['height']` returns the height.

On **line 165**, the `setup` method of turtle graphics is called to establish the turtle screen. On **line 168**, the reference to the screen created is assigned to variable `window`. For this particular program, the normal coordinate system in turtle graphics with coordinate (0,0) at the center of the screen is not the most "natural" coordinate system. Turtle graphics allows the coordinate system to be redefined by specifying the coordinates of the bottom-left corner and the top-right corner of the

```
 1   # Kitchen Tile Visualization Program
 2
 3   import turtle
 4
 5   def greeting():
 6
 7       """Displays the program greeting on the screen."""
 8
 9       print('This program will display the tile pattern for a selected')
10       print('pair of tile colors, tile size, and grout color.\n')
11       print('The repeat frequency for the secondary tile color can be selected:')
12       print('if skip = 1, secondary tile color placed every other tile,')
13       print('if skip = 2, secondary tile color placed every third tile, etc.\n')
14
15   def getTileSelections(grout_color_options):
16
17       """Returns dictionary of the form,
18
19           {'tile_size':dict, 'color1':str, 'color2':str, 'skip':int, 'grout':str}
20
21           where the value of tile_size is a dictionary of the form
22           {'tile_length': value, 'tile_width': value},
23
24           color1 and color2 are the selected primary and secondary color code
25           strings in hexadecimal format, skip is an integer indicating the
26           number of primary colors that occur for every secondary color, and
27           grout contains the selected grout color in hexadecimal format.
28       """
29
30       # init
31       empty_set = set()
32       hex_digits = {'0','1','2','3','4','5','6','7','8','9',
33                     'A','B','C','D','E','F','a','b','c','d','e','f'}
34
35       # prompt user for tile size (length and width)
36       tile_length = int(input('Enter tile length (1-4 inches): '))
37       while tile_length <1 or tile_length > 4:
38           tile_length = int(input('INVALID SIZE SELECTED - please re-enter: \n'))
39
40       tile_width = int(input('Enter tile width (1-4 inches): '))
41       while tile_width < 1 or tile_width > 4:
42           tile_width = int(input('INVALID SIZE SELECTED - please re-enter: \n'))
43
44       # prompt user for primary tile color
45       color1 = input('Enter primary tile color (6-digit RGB): ')
46       while (len(color1) != 6) or \
47             (set(color1) - hex_digits != empty_set):
48           color1 = input('INVALID RGB color, please re-enter: ')
49
50       # prompt user for secondary tile color
51       color2 = input('Enter secondary tile color (6-digit RGB): ')
52       while (len(color2) != 6) or \
53             (set(color2) - hex_digits != empty_set):
54           color2 = input('INVALID RGB color, please re-enter: ')
55
56       # prompt user for skip pattern for colors
57       skip = int(input('Enter frequency of secondary tile color (1-10): '))
58       while (skip < 1 or skip > 10):
59           skip = int(input('INVALID - Please enter 1,2,3,etc. '))
60
```

FIGURE 9-12 Kitchen Tile Visualization Program (*Continued*)

```
61         # prompt user for grout color
62         grout = input('Enter grout color (white, gray, brown or black): ')
63         while (grout not in grout_color_options):
64             grout = input('INVALID grout color selection, please re-enter: ')
65
66         # prepend hash sign to indicate RGB string
67         color1 = '#' + color1
68         color2 = '#' + color2
69
70         # create dictionary of selections
71         selections = {'tile_size':{'length':tile_length, 'width':tile_width},
72                       'primary_color':color1, 'secondary_color':color2,
73                       'tile_skip':skip, 'grout_color':grout}
74
75         return selections
76
77     def layoutTiles(window, selections, tile_area, scaling):
78
79         """Displays the tiles in the window starting with the top and working
80            towards the bottom of the window. This function requires that the
81            coordinate (0,0) be set as the top corner of the window.
82         """
83
84         # set background color (as grout color)
85         window.bgcolor(selections['grout_color'])
86
87         # get selected tile size
88         tile_size = selections['tile_size']
89
90         # get turtle
91         the_turtle = turtle.getturtle()
92
93         # scale size of tiles for display
94         scaled_length = scaling * tile_size['length']
95         scaled_width = scaling * tile_size['width']
96
97         # scale grout spacing
98         tile_spacing = 6
99
100        # create tile shape
101        turtle.register_shape('tileshape',
102                               ((0,0), (0, scaled_length),
103                                (scaled_width, scaled_length), (scaled_width, 0)))
104
105        # set turtle attributes
106        the_turtle.setheading(0)
107        the_turtle.shape('tileshape')
108        the_turtle.hideturtle()
109        the_turtle.penup()
110
111        # place first tile at upper left corner
112        loc_first_tile = (-10, tile_area['height'] + 10)
113        the_turtle.setposition(loc_first_tile)
114
115        # init first tile color and counters
116        first_tile_color = 'primary_color'
117        skip_counter = selections['tile_skip']
118        row_counter = 1
119
```

FIGURE 9-12   Kitchen Tile Visualization Program (*Continued*)

```
120        terminate_layout = False
121        while not terminate_layout:
122
123            # check if current row of tiles is before right edge of window
124            if the_turtle.xcor()< tile_area['width']:
125
126                # check if need to switch to secondary tile color
127                if skip_counter == 0:
128                    the_turtle.color(selections['secondary_color'])
129                    skip_counter = selections['tile_skip']
130                else:
131                    the_turtle.color(selections['primary_color'])
132                    skip_counter = skip_counter - 1
133
134                # place current tile color at current turtle location
135                the_turtle.stamp()
136
137                # move turtle to next tile location of current row
138                the_turtle.forward(scaled_length + tile_spacing)
139
140            # check if current row of tiles at bottom edge of window
141            elif turtle.ycor() + scaled_width > 0:
142
143                the_turtle.setposition(loc_first_tile[0],
144                                       loc_first_tile[1]- row_counter *
145                                       scaled_width - row_counter * tile_spacing)
146
147                row_counter = row_counter + 1
148            else:
149                terminate_layout = True
150
151 # ---- main
152
153 # init
154 tile_area = {'width': 660, 'height': 440}
155 grout_color_selection = {'white', 'gray', 'brown', 'black'}
156 scaling = 20
157
158 # program greeting
159 greeting()
160
161 # get tile selection and layout details
162 selections = getTileSelections(grout_color_selection)
163
164 # set window size
165 turtle.setup(tile_area['width'], tile_area['height'])
166
167 # get reference to turtle window
168 window = turtle.Screen()
169
170 # set window title
171 window.title('Kitchen Tile Visualization Program')
172
173 # set coordinate system
174 window.setworldcoordinates(0, 0, tile_area['width'], tile_area['height'])
175 window.mode('world')
176
177 # layout tiles in window
178 layoutTiles(window, selections, tile_area, scaling)
179
180 # terminate program when window closed
181 turtle.exitonclick()
```

FIGURE 9-12 Kitchen Tile Visualization Program

screen. This is done by call to method `setworldcoordinates` on **line 174**. We therefore set the bottom-left corner to be coordinate (0,0), and the top-right corner to be coordinate `(tile_area['width'], tile_area['height'])`. Thus, for the current tile width of 660 and tile height of 400, the top-right coordinate would be (660,400). This is depicted in Figure 9-13.

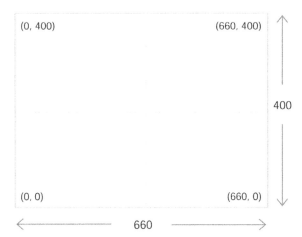

FIGURE 9-13   Screen Coordinates for the Kitchen Tile Visualization Program

In order to utilize the new coordinate system, the turtle screen mode must be set to `'world'` (on line **175**).

The final steps of the program includes a call (**line 178**) to function `layoutTiles`. It is passed variable `window`, holding a reference to the turtle screen created, variable `selections`, which holds all the user-selected options, variable `tile_area`, which holds the dimensions of the turtle screen, and variable `scaling`, which indicates how the tile dimensions in dictionary `selections` are to be scaled. In the last line of the program, **line 181**, turtle method `exitonclick()` is called so that the program terminates when the turtle window is closed.

We now look at program functions `getTileSelections` and `layoutTile`. Function `getTileSelections` (**lines 15–75**) begins by setting variable `empty_set` to an empty set, `empty_set = set()`. Recall that empty braces are used to create an empty dictionary, and therefore `set()` is used to created an empty set. Variable `empty_set` is used for input error checking as we will see. Variable `hex_digits` is assigned to a set containing each of the digits 0–9, as well as the uppercase and lowercase letters A–F. Collectively, these are the symbols used in denoting hexadecimal numbers. This set is also used for input error checking. In **lines 35–64**, the user is prompted to enter all the tile selection options. At **line 36**, the user is prompted for the tile length, limited to a size of four inches. Following, at **line 40**, the user is likewise prompted for the tile width, also limited to four inches. At **line 45**, the user is prompted for the primary tile color. This is the color that will appear most often (or just as often, if the selected pattern is one primary color followed by one secondary color, etc.). Finally, at **line 51**, the user is prompted for the secondary color.

Color values are entered as six hexadecimal digits in the range `000000` (black) to `FFFFFF` (white). Since color values may contain the letters `A-F` (`a-f`), as well as the digits `0-9`, any entered color value containing characters other than that is invalid. Example color values are given in Figure 9-14.

white	FFFFFF	DarkSalmon	E9967A	Amethyst	9966CC
ivory	FFFFF0	LightSalmon	FFA07A	DarkViolet	9400D3
Linen	FAF0E6	FireBrick	B22222	DarkOrchid	9932CC
Beige	F5F5DC	DarkRed	8B0000	DarkMagenta	8B008B
LightGray	D3D3D3	Tomato	FF6347	Indigo	4B0082
DarkGray	A9A9A9	OrangeRed	FF4500	CornSilk	FFF8DC
SlateGray	708090	DarkOrange	FF8C00	BlanchedAlmond	FFEBCD
PaleGreen	98FB98	Orange	FFA500	Bisque	FFE4C4
SeaGreen	2E8B57	Gold	FFD700	Wheat	F5DEB3
DarkSlateGray	2F4F4F	Yellow	FFFF00	BurlyWood	DEB887
DarkGreen	006400	LightYellow	FFFFE0	Tan	D2B48C
Olive	808000	LemonChiffon	FFFACD	SandyBrown	F4A460
Teal	008080	Moccasin	FFE4B5	GoldenRod	DAA520
Aquamarine	7FFFD4	PaleGoldenrod	EEE8AA	DarkGoldenrod	B8860B
CadetBlue	5F9EA0	Thistle	D8BFD8	Peru	CD853F
SkyBlue	87CEEB	Plum	DDA0DD	Chocolate	D2691E
CornFlowerBlue	6495ED	MediumPurple	9370DB	SaddleBrown	8B4513
SteelBlue	4682B4	Orchid	DA70D6	Sienna	A0522D
Navy	000080	MediumOrchid	BA55D3	Brown	A52A2A

FIGURE 9-14 Selected Hexadecimal Color Codes

The check for invalid color values occurs on **lines 46** and **52**. First, the color values must be six characters long. Then, the color value strings are converted into a set using set(color1) and set(color2). Thus, for example, for color1 equal to FF3243, set(color1) would produce the following set,

$$\{\,'3',\ '2',\ '4',\ 'F'\,\}$$

Then, the set difference operator, −, is applied to this set, and the set hexdigits defined at the start of the function,

$$\text{set(color1)} \ - \ \text{hexdigits}$$

Recall that the set difference operator, A − B, returns any items that are in set A, but not in set B. Since set A is the entered color string and set hexdigits contains all the valid characters of a hexadecimal number, if this difference is not empty (the empty set), then color1 (or color 2) must contain invalid characters.

The final items for which the user is prompted is the skip pattern of the tiles and the grout color. The value of skip indicates how many primary color tiles are placed before a secondary color tile is placed. Thus, for a skip value of 1, the primary and secondary tiles will alternate every other tile. For a skip value of 2, two primary color tiles will be placed for every secondary color tile, and so forth. The grout color entered by the user must be one of the string values in set `grout_color_options`. Thus, if the entered string is not in this set, the user is prompted to re-enter.

Finally, on lines **67** and **68**, the `'#'` symbol is prepended to each of the color strings, `color1` and `color2`. This indicates in Python that the string contains a hexadecimal value. At **line 71**, a dictionary is built containing all of the selected values to be returned as the function value (**line 75**).

Function `layoutTile`, **lines 77–153**, is passed all the information needed to lay out the tiles according to the turtle screen size, the user's selections, and the scaling factor to be used. On **line 85**, the background color of the turtle screen is set to the user-selected grout color. On **line 88**, variable `tile_size` is set to the value for key `'tile_size'` in the selections dictionary. Recall that this value is itself a dictionary. Thus, variable `tile_size` is holding a dictionary with keys `'length'` and `'width'`.

On **line 91**, the reference to the turtle is set to variable `the_turtle`. On **lines 94–95** the dimensions of each tile are scaled by the scaling factor in variable `scaling`, and assigned to variables `scaled_length` and `scaled_width`. Since the user is entering tile size in inches, a four-inch by four-inch tile would be displayed as four pixels by four pixels, which is too small for the purpose of displaying tile patterns. Thus, with a scaling factor of 20, for example, a four-by-four inch tile would be displayed as 80 pixels by 80 pixels. The spacing between tiles (in pixels) is set to 6, assigned to variable `tile_spacing` on **line 98**.

In order to create the appropriate tile shape as specified by the user, the `register_shape` method in turtle graphics is used to both describe the shape and provide a shape name. Thus, on **line 101**, `register_shape` is called with the name `'tileshape'` as the first parameter value, followed by a list of coordinate values defining the desired shape. The coordinate values are specified in terms of the values `scaled_length` and `scaled_width` to define the specific size of the tile shape to match the user's specified size.

On **lines 106–109**, the turtle attributes are set for laying out tiles. Since the tiles will be laid out from the top of the screen going left to right, the turtle heading is set to 0 (facing right) and the shape is set to `'tileshape'` (on **lines 106–107**). Since the turtle is used to stamp its image where each tile is to be placed, and not be visible or draw lines on the screen, the turtle is hidden (**line 108**) with its pen set to up (**line 109**).

In order for the tile to appear in the correct location, a ten-pixel adjustment is made. Thus, on **line 112**, variable `loc_first_tile` is set to the coordinate `(-10, tile_area['height'] + 10)`. The turtle is then positioned at this location (**line 113**) to begin the placement of tiles. Since the primary color tile is always the first tile placed, variable `first-tile-color` is set to the key value `'primary_color'` (of dictionary `selections`). Variable `skip_counter` is also set to the skip value stored in the selections dictionary with the key value `'tile_skip'`. In order to determine where to begin the placement of tiles for each new row, variable `row_counter` is initialized to 1 and incremented for each next row of tiles. Thus, knowing the number of each new row allows for the coordinate value of each new row to be calculated (since each row of tiles is the same height).

Lines 120–149 perform the placement of tiles. Variable `terminate_layout` is initialized to `False` on **line 120**, which controls the while loop on **line 121**. It is not set to `True` until the last row of tiles has been completed. The if statement at **line 124** checks whether the x-coordinate value of the turtle's current location is past the right edge of the screen. If not, then the color of the next tile to be placed is determined based on the current value of variable `skip_counter`. This variable is used as a "count-down" counter. That is, it is decremented by one each time another tile has been placed. When `skip_counter` reaches 0, the next tile is set to the secondary color, and the `skip_counter` is reset to the value in variable `tile_skip` to again count down to zero (**lines 127–132**). Once the color of the tile has been determined, the stamp method is called on the turtle to "imprint" its image on the screen (**line 135**). The turtle is then moved forward (to the right) by an amount equal to the tile length plus the amount of tile spacing (**line 138**). Thus, the turtle is positioned for the placement of the next tile, and execution returns to the top of the while loop.

If the condition of the if statement on **line 124** is false, that is, the current tile is past the right edge of the screen, then a check is made on **line 141** if the current tile position is past the bottom of the screen (that is, `the_turtle.ycor()` is less than zero). If not, then the turtle is repositioned to the beginning of the next row of tiles (**lines 143–145**) making use of variable `row_counter`, as mentioned. Because a new row of tiles is started, `row_counter` is incremented by one. Finally, if the conditions at both **line 124** and **line 141** are found false (that is, the current turtle position is at the end of the last row of tiles), then `terminate_layout` is set to `True` and thus the while loop terminates, also terminating the function.

Self-Test Questions

1. Indicate all of the following that are syntactically correct for creating a set.
   (a) `set([1, 2, 3])`
   (b) `set((1, 2, 3))`
   (c) `{1, 2, 3}`

2. For set s containing values 1, 2, 3, and set t containing 3, 4, 5, which of the following are the correct results for each given set operation?
   (a) `s | t` → `{3}`
   (b) `s & t` → `{1, 2, 3, 4, 5}`
   (c) `s - t` → `{1, 2}`
   (d) `s ^ t` → `{1, 2, 4, 5}`

3. For set s containing values 1, 2, 3 and set w of type `frozenset` containing values `'a','b','c'`, which of the following are valid set operations?
   (a) `'a' in s`
   (b) `'a' in w`
   (c) `len(s) + len(w)`
   (d) `s.add(4)`
   (e) `w.add('d')`
   (f) `s | w`
   (g) `s & w`
   (h) `s - w`

ANSWERS: 1. (a), (b), (c). 2. (c), (d). 3. (a), (b), (c), (d), (f), (g).

COMPUTATIONAL PROBLEM SOLVING

9.3 A Food Co-op's Worker Scheduling Simulation

In this section, we develop a program for simulating the number of people that show up for work at a food co-op using two different worker scheduling methods—one in which workers sign up for certain time slots, and the other in which workers show up whenever they want.

9.3.1   The Problem

A food co-op in a university town found an interesting solution to a scheduling problem. The co-op offered two prices for everything—one price for members, and a higher price for nonmembers. To qualify for the lower prices, each member had to volunteer to work at the co-op for a couple hours each week.

Jim Thompson/Albuquerque Journal/ZUMAPRESS.com/ NewsCom

The problem was that the co-op needed two people to be working at all times. Members would be asked to sign up for time slots, limited to two workers for each slot. Too often, however, members who had signed up for a given time did not show up, leaving the co-op either completely or partially uncovered.

The co-op eventually devised an effective, albeit daring solution to this problem. They decided to just let members come in to work whenever they wanted to, with no planned scheduling! This unscheduled approach ran the risk of there being times in which the co-op was left without any workers. What was interesting was that they found this approach to be a better solution than the scheduled approach. (We will look at whether this is also better for the individual members or not.)

In this section, we develop a program capable of performing a simulation of both approaches based on assumed probabilities of typical human behavior. We then compare the effectiveness of the scheduled vs. the unscheduled approach both from the co-op's and the members' point of view.

9.3.2   Problem Analysis

The computational issue for this problem is to model and simulate the behavior of individuals for assumed probabilities of certain actions. The behaviors in this case are related to fulfilling a commitment to work a given number of hours each week. In one scenario, workers sign up in advance to work certain time slots; in the other scenario, workers show up to work whenever they feel like it.

Besides assumed probabilities of workers showing up for work, there are also assumed probabilities of workers showing up late or leaving early. Since each of these actions is probabilistic, there needs to be a computational means of determining when such actions take place. We use a random number generator for this. For example, if there is an assumed 10% chance that any given person may show up late, a random number between 1 and 10 is generated. If the generated value is 1, the action is assumed to occur; otherwise, the action is assumed not to occur.

We will assume a certain schedule of hours that the co-op is open, given below.

Sunday	12:00 pm–6:00 pm
Monday–Thursday	8:00 am–6:00 pm
Friday, Saturday	8:00 am–8:00 pm

We also assume that every time slot is two hours long. Thus, for example, there would be three time slots on Sundays, 12:00–2:00 pm, 2:00–4:00 pm, and 4:00–6:00 pm. Based on this, there are 35 time slots in a week. We also assume that the co-op has 75 members.

Because of the different natures of the two scheduling approaches, we assume different probabilities for the behaviors of members. For the scheduled approach, we assume a probability of 15% that a given member *will not* show up for their time slot. For the unscheduled approach, we assume a probability that any given worker *will* decide to show up for a given time slot to be 5%. Also, we assume that the chance that a scheduled worker will show up late for the start of the time slot is greater than in the unscheduled approach, since in the unscheduled approach workers show up for the time slot that is convenient for them. On the other hand, we assume a greater chance that unscheduled workers will leave fifteen minutes earlier than scheduled workers, since they may feel less committed to working the complete time slot. We assume the probabilities for these behaviors as given in Figure 9-15.

Scheduled Approach Probabilities	Unscheduled Approach Probabilities
Chance of arriving 15 minutes late is 15%.	Chance of arriving 15 minutes late is 5%.
Chance of arriving 30 minutes late is 5%.	Chance of arriving 30 minutes late is 2%.
Chance of arriving 45 minutes late is 2%.	Chance of arriving 45 minutes late is 1%.
Chance of leaving 15 minutes early is 5%	Chance of leaving 15 minutes early is 10%
Chance of leaving 30 minutes early is 3%	Chance of leaving 30 minutes early is 3%
Chance of not showing up at all is 15%	Change of deciding to show up is 5%

FIGURE 9-15 Assumed Probabilities for the Food Co-op Simulation Program

9.3.3 Program Design

Meeting the Program Requirements

The program must simulate the number of workers that show up for each of the time slots that the co-op is open by utilizing assumed probabilities. The co-op requires two workers in the store at all times that it is open. The program must also utilize the probabilities that workers will show up 15, 30, or 45 minutes late for work, or leave 15 or 30 minutes early.

Data Description

The data that needs to be represented in this program includes the number of co-op members (stored as an integer), the two-hour time slots that a worker may work (stored as a tuple), the probabilities of each of the actions that may occur (stored as a dictionary), and the names of the days of the week (stored as a tuple) as given below:

```
num_members = 75
time_slots = ('8:00am','10:00am','12:00pm','2:00pm','4:00pm','6:00pm')
days = ('Sunday','Monday','Tuesday','Wednesday','Thursday','Friday',
        'Saturday')
sched_probabilities = {'CLate_15':15, 'CLate_30':5, 'CLate_45':2,
                       'CLEarly_15':5, 'CLEarly_30':3,'CNoshow':15}
unsched_probabilities = {'CLate_15':5, 'CLate_30':2, 'CLate_45':1,
                         'CLEarly_15':10, 'CLEarly_30':3,'CShowup':5}
```

In dictionary probabilities, CLate_15, CLate_30, and CLate_45 contain the chances that a worker will arrive 15, 30, or 45 minutes late, respectively; CLEarly_15 and CLEarly_30 contain the chances that a worker will leave 15 or 30 minutes early, respectively; CNoshow contains the chance that a scheduled worker will not show up for their time slot; and CShowup is the chance that an unscheduled worker will decide to show up to work.

Algorithmic Approach

The algorithmic approach for this problem relies on the use of randomization to run the simulation. One complete week of co-op staffing is simulated, including the number of workers showing up for each of the 35 time slots in a week, how many show up a given number of minutes late, and how many leave a given number of minutes early. For the assumed probability of each of these actions, a random number will be generated for simulating whether each event has occurred or not.

Overall Program Steps

The overall steps of the program are given in Figure 9-16.

Import random Module

Random Module

Program Initialization

Get Random Seed Value
from System Clock

Get Scheduled or
Unscheduled Scheduling
Selection from User

Start Simulation

FIGURE 9-16   Overall Steps of Food Co-op Program

Modular Design

The modular design for this program is given in Figure 9-17. Following this design, there are six functions in the program. Function `executeScheduledSimulation` determines the time slots for a given day of the week by calling function `displayScheduledWorkerHours` to probabilistically determine whether a scheduled worker shows up, and if so, if they show up a certain number of minutes late and/or leave a certain number of minutes early. The function, in turn, relies on the use of function `eventOccurred`, which is provided a probability value, and returns `True` or `False` to

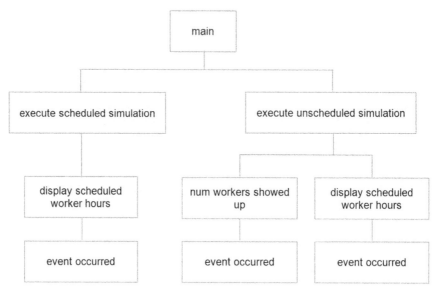

FIGURE 9-17 Modular Design of the Food Co-op Simulation Program

simulate whether the event has occurred or not. Function executeUnscheduledSimulation is designed similarly, except that it also needs to determine how many (unscheduled) workers decide to show up at their convenience. Thus, the function relies on function numWorkersShowedUp (which in turn relies on function eventOccurred). We give the specification for each of these functions in Figure 9-18. From this we can begin to implement and test the program.

9.3.4   Program Implementation and Testing

The implementation of the main module of this program is given in Figure 9-19. The main module gives the overall steps of the program. First, all values that determine the model's behaviors are initialized. Variable num_members is assigned the assumed number of co-op members for the simulation, 75 (**line 4**). Tuple time_slots is assigned the start time of all the two-hour time slots that workers may work (**line 5**), and tuple days is assigned the days of the week that the co-op is open (every day of the week) on **line 8**. The dictionary sched_probabilities contains the assumed probabilities for when scheduled workers show up late, leave early, or don't show up at all (**lines 11–12**). The dictionary unsched_probabilities contains the assumed probabilities for when unscheduled workers show up late, leave early, and decide to show up to work for a given time slot (**lines 14–15**).

On **line 18**, the seed function for the random number generator is called (the required import random statement is provided at the top of the program). When random.seed() is called without an argument, the seed value is taken from the system clock (usually from the lower order digits of the time in the milliseconds range). This ensures that each time the program is run, a different sequence of random numbers most likely will be generated.

The remainder of the program handles the task of prompting the user for the type of simulation to execute ("scheduled" or "unscheduled"). Based on the user's response, either function executeScheduledSimulation (at **line 36**) or function executeUnscheduledSimulation (at **line 40**) is called. Variable valid_input is initialized to False (at **line 23**), set to True only when a valid response of 1 or 2 is entered for the desired simulation (at **line 43**). Thus,

```
def eventOccurred(chances):

    """For given integer value chances as a percentage value (1-100), returns
       True if randomly generated number in range (1,100) is less than or equal
       to chances, otherwise returns False.
    """

def numWorkersShowedUp(indiv_chance, num_individuals):

    """For given integer values indiv_chance and num_individuals, returns how
       many times that num_individual calls to event_occurred with argument
       indiv_chance returns True.
    """

def displayScheduledWorkerHours(workernum, probabilities):

    """For workernum equal to 1 or 2, and the proability values given in dictionary
       probabilities of the form,

           {'CLate_15':<num>, 'CLate_30':<num>, 'CLate_45':<num>,
            'CLEarly_15':<num>, 'CLEarly_30':<num>,'CNoshow':<20>,
            'CShowup':<num>}

       where each <num> is a value between 1-100, displays one of

           worker <worker_num> -- no show --   or
           worker <worker_num> <mins_late> mins late  and/or
           worker <worker_num> left <mins_early> mins early

       where <mins_late> is 15, 30, or 45,   <mins_early> is 15 or 30.
    """

def displayUnscheduledWorkerHours(workernum, probabilities):

    """For workernum equal to 1 or 2, and the proabilities given in dictionary
       probabilities of the form,

           {'CLate_15':<num>, 'CLate_30':<num>, 'CLate_45':<num>,
            'CLEarly_15':<num>, 'CLEarly_30':<num>,'CNoshow':<20>,
            'CShowup':<num>}

       where each <num> is a value between 1-100, displays one of

           worker <worker_num> -- no show --   or
           worker <worker_num> <mins_late> mins late  and/or
           worker <worker_num> left <mins_early> mins early

       where <mins_late> is 15 or 30,
             <mins_early> is 15 or 30.
    """

def executeScheduledSimulation(probabilities, days, time_slots):

    """Displays a simulated week of workers in attendance for all time slots,
       based on a scheduled worker schedule.

    """

def executeUnscheduledSimulation(probabilities, days, time_slots):

    """Displays a simulated week of workers in attendance for all time slots,
       based on an unscheduled worker schedule.
    """
```

FIGURE 9-18 Function Specifications of the Food Co-op Simulation Program

```
1   # ---- main
2
3   # init
4   num_members = 75
5   time_slots = ('8:00am', '10:00am', '12:00pm', '2:00pm', '4:00pm',
6                 '6:00pm')
7
8   days = ('Sunday', 'Monday', 'Tuesday', 'Wednesday', 'Thursday',
9           'Friday', 'Saturday')
10
11  sched_probabilities = {'CLate_15':15, 'CLate_30':5, 'CLate_45':2,
12                         'CLEarly_15':5, 'CLEarly_30':3,'CNoshow':15}
13
14  unsched_probabilities = {'CLate_15':5, 'CLate_30':2, 'CLate_45':1,
15                           'CLEarly_15':10, 'CLEarly_30':3,'CShowup':5}
16
17  # seed random number generator with system clock
18  random.seed()
19
20  # get type of simulation
21  print('Welcome to the Food Co-op Schedule Simulation Program')
22
23  valid_input = False
24  while not valid_input:
25      try:
26          response = \
27              int(input('(1)scheduled, (2)unscheduled simulation? '))
28
29          while (response != 1) and (response != 2):
30              print('Invalid Selection\n')
31              response = \
32                  int(input('(1)scheduled, (2)unscheduled simulation? '))
33
34          if response == 1:
35              print('<< SCHEDULED WORKER SIMULATION >>\n')
36              executeScheduledSimulation(sched_probabilities, days,
37                                         time_slots)
38          else:
39              print('<< UNSCHEDULED WORKER SIMULATION >>\n')
40              executeUnscheduledSimulation(unsched_probabilities,
41                                           days, time_slots)
42
43          valid_input = True
44
45      except ValueError:
46          print('Please enter numerical value 1 or 2\n')
```

FIGURE 9-19   Main Module of the Food Co-op Simulation Program

the while loop continues to execute as long as an invalid response is entered. Because the input value is converted to an integer type,

```
response = int(input('(1) scheduled, (2) unscheduled simulation? '))
```

a ValueError will be raised (by function input) if the user enters a non-digit character. There-fore, this line (and the rest of the code) is placed within a try-except block (within **lines 25–45**). Thus, if a non-digit is entered, the raised exception is caught by the except ValueError clause, and the message `'Please enter numerical value 1 or 2'` is displayed (at **line 46**). Since `valid_input` is still `False` in this case, the while loop performs another iteration, again prompting the user for their selection.

Because a user may enter a numerical value other than 1 or 2, the while loop at **line 29** catches such errors and immediately re-prompts the user. Once the loop terminates, the input is known to be valid. Therefore, based on the selection, either function `executeScheduledSimulation` or function `executeUnscheduleSimulation` is called, and `valid_input` is set to `True` causing the outer while loop at **line 24** to terminate.

Test Drivers and Test Stubs

In the development of the smoking/lung cancer correlation program of Chapter 8, we utilized unit testing, testing each function separately by developing an appropriate test driver for each. This was followed by integration testing, which tested the complete program with all functions working together.

We use unit testing and integration testing for this program as well. However, in the smoking/lung cancer program, there were only three functions, each directly called by the main module as given below.

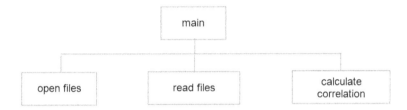

Since these functions did not call any other function of the program, they were simply individually implemented and tested. However, based on the design of the current program, there are functions that call other functions. Thus, these functions cannot be tested without having some version of the other functions to call. This is true for function `executeScheduledSimulation` for example, shown in Figure 9-20.

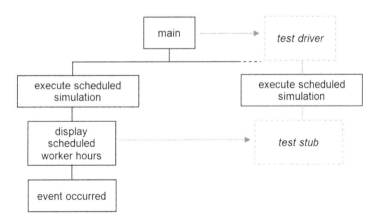

FIGURE 9-20   Unit Testing of Function executeScheduledSimulation

As shown in the figure, both a test driver and a test stub are needed for testing the function. A *test driver*, as we saw in Chapter 8, is code developed simply for calling and testing a given function.

A *test stub*, on the other hand, is a simple, incomplete implementation of a function for testing functions that call it. For example, a test stub for a function designed to calculate the GPA of a given student might be implemented to simply return an arbitrary floating-point value, *as if* it were a calculated result. Thus, test drivers and test stubs are developed for testing purposes only, and do not become part of the ultimate implementation.

Unit Testing Function `executeScheduledSimulation`

We begin with the unit testing of function executeScheduledSimulation, given in Figure 9-21.

```
1   def executeScheduledSimulation(probabilities, days, time_slots):
2
3       """Displays a simulated week of workers in attendance for all
4          time slots, based on a scheduled worker schedule.
5       """
6
7       # for each day of the week
8       for day in days:
9           print(day)
10          print('--------')
11
12          if (day == 'Sunday'):  # sunday?
13              current_timeslot = '12:00pm'
14              num_timeslots = 3
15          elif day in days[1:5]: # mon-thurs?
16              current_timeslot = '8:00am'
17              num_timeslots = 5
18          else:  # friday, saturday
19              current_timeslot = '8:00am'
20              num_timeslots = 6
21
22          # find loc of current_timeslot in tuple time_slots
23          index_val = time_slots.index(current_timeslot)
24
25          # iterate through num_timeslots starting with current time slot
26          for time_slot in time_slots[index_val:num_timeslots]:
27              print('{0:>7}'.format(time_slot), ' ', end='')
28
29              for k in range(0,2):
30                  displayScheduledWorkerHours(k+1, probabilities)
31              print()
32          print()
```

FIGURE 9-21   Implementation of Function executeScheduledSimulation

We develop a test driver that calls function executeScheduledSimulation with values for parameters probabilities, days, and time_slots defined in the main module, given in Figure 9-22.

In addition, since the function depends on the use of function displayScheduledWorker-Hours, a test stub is developed for this function for executeScheduledSimulation to call, given in Figure 9-23. All this test stub does is display the value of workernum. The time slots and day of the week are displayed by function executeScheduledSimulation. Finally, we put function

```
# TEST DRIVER for Function executeScheduledSimulation for Food Co-op Program

from executescheduledsimulation import *

# init required data
sched_probabilities = {'CLate_15':15, 'CLate_30':5, 'CLate_45':2,
                       'CLEarly_15':5, 'CLEarly_30':3,'CNoshow':15}

days = ('Sunday', 'Monday', 'Tuesday', 'Wednesday', 'Thursday',
        'Friday', 'Saturday')

time_slots = ('8:00am', '10:00am', '12:00pm', '2:00pm', '4:00pm',
              '6:00pm', '8:00pm')

# call function
executeScheduledSimulation(sched_probabilities, days, time_slots)
```

FIGURE 9-22   Test Driver for Function executeScheduledSimulation

```
# TEST STUB for Function displayScheduledWorkerHours for Food Co-op Program

def displayScheduledWorkerHours(workernum, probabilities):

    if workernum == 1:
        print('workernum = ', workernum, end=' ')
    else:
        print('workernum = ', workernum)
```

FIGURE 9-23   Test Stub for Function displayScheduledWorkerHours

executeScheduledSimulation in its own file named executescheduledsimulation.
py, as well as the test driver and test stub to be used as modules. Since module executescheduledsimulation needs to call function stub displayScheduledWorkerHours, it
contains an import statement of the form from displayscheduledworkerhours import *.
Also, since the driver makes a call to function executeScheduledSimulation, it contains an
import statement of the form from executescheduledsimulation import *. The result of
the testing is given in Figure 9-24.

The output shows the scheduled time slots for each day of the week. However, we see an
error for the time slots for Sundays. Only one time slot is displayed (for 8:00 am) but there
should be three (8:00 am, 10:00 am, and 12:00 pm). To track down this error, we do some interactive testing in the Python shell. First, we display the value of variable days to make sure it
contains each weekday,

```
>>> days
('Sunday', 'Monday', 'Tuesday', 'Wednesday', 'Thursday', 'Friday', 'Saturday')
```

This is correct. We also check the value of variable time_slots,

```
>>> time_slots
('8:00am', '10:00am', '12:00pm', '2:00pm', '4:00pm', '6:00pm')
```

```
         Sunday
         -------
         12:00pm  workernum =  1 workernum =  2

         Monday
         -------
          8:00am  workernum =  1 workernum =  2
         10:00am  workernum =  1 workernum =  2
         12:00pm  workernum =  1 workernum =  2
          2:00pm  workernum =  1 workernum =  2
          4:00pm  workernum =  1 workernum =  2

         Tuesday
         -------
          8:00am  workernum =  1 workernum =  2
         10:00am  workernum =  1 workernum =  2
         12:00pm  workernum =  1 workernum =  2
          2:00pm  workernum =  1 workernum =  2
          4:00pm  workernum =  1 workernum =  2

         Wednesday
         -------
          8:00am  workernum =  1 workernum =  2
         10:00am  workernum =  1 workernum =  2
         12:00pm  workernum =  1 workernum =  2
          2:00pm  workernum =  1 workernum =  2
          4:00pm  workernum =  1 workernum =  2

         Thursday
         -------
          8:00am  workernum =  1 workernum =  2
         10:00am  workernum =  1 workernum =  2
         12:00pm  workernum =  1 workernum =  2
          2:00pm  workernum =  1 workernum =  2
          4:00pm  workernum =  1 workernum =  2

         Friday
         -------
          8:00am  workernum =  1 workernum =  2
         10:00am  workernum =  1 workernum =  2
         12:00pm  workernum =  1 workernum =  2
          2:00pm  workernum =  1 workernum =  2
          4:00pm  workernum =  1 workernum =  2
          6:00pm  workernum =  1 workernum =  2

         Saturday
         -------
          8:00am  workernum =  1 workernum =  2
         10:00am  workernum =  1 workernum =  2
         12:00pm  workernum =  1 workernum =  2
          2:00pm  workernum =  1 workernum =  2
          4:00pm  workernum =  1 workernum =  2
          6:00pm  workernum =  1 workernum =  2
         >>>
```

FIGURE 9-24 Unit Testing Results for Function
displayScheduledWorkerHours

This is also correct. We then consider the part of function `executeScheduledSimulation` that determines the time slots for each day,

```
for day in days:
    print(day)
    print('-------')

    if (day == 'Sunday'): # sunday?
        current_timeslot = '12:00pm'
        num_timeslots = 3
    elif day in days[1:5]: # mon-thurs?
        current_timeslot = '8:00am'
        num_timeslots = 5
    else: # friday, saturday
        current_timeslot = '8:00am'
        num_timeslots = 6

    # find loc of current_timeslot in tuple time_slots
    index_val = time_slots.index(current_timeslot)

    # iterate through num_timeslots starting with current time slot
    for time_slot in time_slots[index_val:num_timeslots]:
        print('{0:>7}'.format(time_slot), ' ', end = '')
```

We see that variable `num_timeslots` is set to 3 for Sundays. Since that seems correct, we see what happens in the following code. Variable `index` is set to the index value of the first occurrence of the first time slot for the day, held by variable `current_timeslot`. Since the value of `current_timeslot` should be `'12:00pm'`, we call method `index` to be sure of the index value returned,

```
>>> index_val = time_slots.index('12:00pm')
>>> index_val
2
```

This is correct. We therefore focus on the for loop,

```
for time_slot in time_slots[index_val: num_timeslots]:
    print('{0:>7}'.format(time_slot), ' ', end = '')
```

For all other days, this loop iterates the correct number of times, once for each time slot of each day. We check to see the slice of `time_slots` that is returned specifically for `index_value` equal to 2 and `num_timeslots` equal to 3.

```
>>> time_slots[2:3]
('12:00pm',)
```

Ah, there is a problem! The result should have been (`'12:00pm'`, `'2:00pm'`, `'4:00pm'`). But why does it work correctly for all the other days of the week? We see that Sunday is the only day that the first time slot does not begin at 8:00 am. Thus, all other slices of list `time_slots` are of the form,

```
time_slots[0:k]
```

whereas for Sunday, it is of the form,

`time_slots[3:k]`

It must come down to how the index values are used in the slice notation. We checked on this and found that we had incorrectly used the slice operation. The first index value is the starting location of the slice, and the second index value is one greater than the last index of the substring. We had written the code as if the second index indicated *how many* elements to include. So the actual code should be,

```
for time_slot in time_slots[index_val: index_val + num_timeslots]:
    print('{0:>7}'.format(time_slot), ' ', end = '')
```

It worked for all the other days of the week because in those cases, `index_val` was 0, and therefore `index_val + num_timeslots` was equal to `num_timeslots`. So that explains everything! We find a similar error in function `executeUnscheduledSimulation`, so we make the correction there as well.

We should feel good about ourselves. Not only did we find the error, but we are able to fully explain why this error created the incorrect output. As we have said, making a change that fixes a problem without knowing why the change fixes it is disconcerting and risky. We therefore make this correction to `executeScheduledSimulation` and again perform unit testing, this time getting the expected output for Sunday (as well as the rest of the days).

```
Sunday
-------
12:00pm  workernum =  1 workernum =  2
 2:00pm  workernum =  1 workernum =  2
 4:00pm  workernum =  1 workernum =  2

Monday
-------
 8:00am  workernum =  1 workernum =  2
10:00am  workernum =  1 workernum =  2
12:00pm  workernum =  1 workernum =  2
 2:00pm  workernum =  1 workernum =  2
 4:00pm  workernum =  1 workernum =  2

Tuesday
-------
 8:00am  workernum =  1 workernum =  2
10:00am  workernum =  1 workernum =  2
12:00pm  workernum =  1 workernum =  2
 2:00pm  workernum =  1 workernum =  2
 4:00pm  workernum =  1 workernum =  2

Wednesday
-------
 8:00am  workernum =  1 workernum =  2
10:00am  workernum =  1 workernum =  2
12:00pm  workernum =  1 workernum =  2
 2:00pm  workernum =  1 workernum =  2
 4:00pm  workernum =  1 workernum =  2

Thursday
-------
 8:00am  workernum =  1 workernum =  2
10:00am  workernum =  1 workernum =  2
12:00pm  workernum =  1 workernum =  2
 2:00pm  workernum =  1 workernum =  2
 4:00pm  workernum =  1 workernum =  2
```

```
Friday
-------
 8:00am   workernum =  1 workernum =  2
10:00am   workernum =  1 workernum =  2
12:00pm   workernum =  1 workernum =  2
 2:00pm   workernum =  1 workernum =  2
 4:00pm   workernum =  1 workernum =  2
 6:00pm   workernum =  1 workernum =  2

Saturday
-------
 8:00am   workernum =  1 workernum =  2
10:00am   workernum =  1 workernum =  2
12:00pm   workernum =  1 workernum =  2
 2:00pm   workernum =  1 workernum =  2
 4:00pm   workernum =  1 workernum =  2
 6:00pm   workernum =  1 workernum =  2
>>>
```

We leave as an exercise the unit testing of the remaining program functions.

Integration Testing of the Food Co-op Program

Assuming each function of the program has been unit tested, we next perform integration testing. The complete program is given in Figure 9-25.

The main section of the program is in **lines 213–267**. This part of the program has already been discussed. The displayScheduledWorkerHours, displayUnscheduledWorker-Hours, executeScheduledSimulation, and executeUnscheduledSimulation functions contain the bulk of the implementation.

Function executeScheduledSimulation (**lines 135–165**) consists of three nested for loops. The outer loop (**line 142**) iterates through each of the days in the schedule, in this simulation, all seven days. The next inner for loop (**line 160**) iterates through each of the time slots for the day. **Lines 146–154** initialize the first time slot (current_timeslot) as well as the number of time slots (num_timeslots) based on the current value of day. Variable time_slots passed to the function contains all the possible time slots for all the days that the co-op is open. In order to find that first time slot for the current day within this list time_slots, the index method is used (**line 157**), as discussed in the unit testing of this function.

Finally, for each time slot, we iterate over the number of workers for the slot in the innermost for loop in **lines 162–164**. In this case, the for loop iterates exactly two times since, in the scheduled worker approach, that is the number of workers assigned to each time slot. It is within this innermost loop that function displayScheduledWorkerHours is called (**line 163**). The argument in the function call is adjusted by 1 (k+1), because function displayScheduledWorkerHours expects to be passed worker numbers starting at 1.

Function displayScheduledWorkerHours (**lines 38–90**) generates the events that may occur for a given scheduled worker; specifically, whether the worker arrives late and/or leaves early or does not show up at all. Thus, at the start of the function (in **lines 57–58**), variables mins_late and mins_left_early are initialized to zero. Following that is an if statement (**line 60**) determining if the (scheduled) worker does not show up for their assigned time slot. The probability of this occurring is contained in the dictionary probabilities. If the event is found to be true, then mins_late is set to the special value -1, to be used later on **line 80**.

```
1  # Food Co-op Simulation Program
2
3  import random
4
5  # Probabilties for Simulation (for values between 1-100)
6  #
7  # CLate_xx = chance of being late for work,
8  # CLEarly_xx = chance of leaving early from work,
9  # CNoshow = chance that a scheduled worker WILL NOT show up for work
10 # CShowup = chance that an unscheduled worker WILL show up to work
11
12
13 def eventOccurred(chances):
14
15     """For given integer value chances as a percentage value (1-100),
16         returns True if randomly generated number in range (1,100) is
17         less than or equal to chances, otherwise returns False.
18     """
19     if random.randint(1,100) <= chances:
20         return True
21     else:
22         return False
23
24 def numWorkersShowedUp(indiv_chance, num_individuals):
25
26     """For given integer values indiv_chance and num_individuals,
27         returns how many times that num_individual calls to
28         event_occurred with argument indiv_chance returns True.
29     """
30     numworkers_arriving = 0
31
32     for i in range(num_individuals):
33         if eventOccurred(indiv_chance):
34             numworkers_arriving = numworkers_arriving + 1
35
36     return numworkers arriving
37
38 def displayScheduledWorkerHours(workernum, probabilities):
39
40     """For workernum equal to 1 or 2, and the proability values
41         given in dictionary probabilities of the form,
42
43         {'CLate_15':<num>, 'CLate_30':<num>, 'CLate_45':<num>,
44          'CLEarly_15':<num>, 'CLEarly_30':<num>,'CNoshow':<num>}
45
46
47         where each <num> is a value between 1-100, displays one of
48
49         worker <worker_num> -- no show --    or
50         worker <worker_num> <mins_late> mins late  and/or
51         worker <worker_num> left <mins_early> mins early
52
53         where <mins_late> is 15, 30, or 45,  <mins_early> is 15 or 30.
54     """
55
```

FIGURE 9-25 Food Co-op Simulation Program (*Continued*)

```
56    # init
57    mins_late = 0
58    mins_left_early = 0
59
60    if eventOccurred(probabilities['CNoshow']):
61        mins_late = -1
62    else:
63        if eventOccurred(probabilities['CLate_15']):
64            mins_late = 15
65        elif eventOccurred(probabilities['CLate_30']):
66            mins_late = 30
67        elif eventOccurred(probabilities['CLate_45']):
68            mins_late = 45
69
70        if eventOccurred(probabilities['CLEarly_15']):
71            mins_left_early = 15
72        elif eventOccurred(probabilities['CLEarly_30']):
73            mins_left_early = 30
74
75    if workernum == 1:
76        print('{0:>3}'.format('worker'), str(workernum) + ': ', end='')
77    else:
78        print('{0:>15}'.format('worker'), str(workernum) + ': ', end='')
79
80    if mins_late == -1:
81        print('-- no show --', end='')
82    else:
83        if mins_late != 0:
84            print(mins_late, 'mins late  ', end='')
85
86        if mins_left_early != 0:
87            print('left', mins_left_early, 'mins early', end='')
88
89        if (mins_late == 0) and (mins_left_early == 0):
90            print('whole time', end='')
91
92    def displayUnscheduledWorkerHours(workernum, probabilities):
93
94        """For workernum equal to 1 or 2, and the proability values
95           given in dictionary probabilities of the form,
96
97           {'CLate_15':<num>, 'CLate_30':<num>, 'CLate_45':<num>,
98            'CLEarly_15':<num>, 'CLEarly_30':<num>,'CShowup':<num>}
99
100
101       where each <num> is a value between 1-100, displays one of
102
103          worker <worker_num> -- no show --   or
104          worker <worker_num> <mins_late> mins late  and/or
105          worker <worker_num> left <mins_early> mins early
106
107       where <mins_late> is 15 or 30,
108             <mins_early> is 15 or 30.
109       """
```

FIGURE 9-25   Food Co-op Simulation Program (*Continued*)

```
110        mins_late = 0    # init
111        mins_left_early = 0
112
113        if eventOccurred(probabilities['CLate_15']):
114            mins_late = 15
115        elif eventOccurred(probabilities['CLate_30']):
116            mins_late = 30
117            elif eventOccurred(probabilities['CLate_45']):
118                mins_late = 45
119
120        if eventOccurred(probabilities['CLEarly_15']):
121            mins_left_early = 15
122        elif eventOccurred(probabilities['CLEarly_30']):
123            mins_left_early = 30
124
125        print('{0:>15}'.format('worker'), str(workernum) + ': ', end='')
126        if mins_late != 0:
127            print(mins_late, 'mins late  ', end='')
128
129        if mins_left_early != 0:
130            print('left', mins_left_early, 'mins early', end='')
131
132        if (mins_late == 0) and (mins_left_early == 0):
133            print('whole time', end='')
134
135    def executeScheduledSimulation(probabilities, days, time_slots):
136
137        """Displays a simulated week of workers in attendance for all
138            time slots, based on a scheduled worker schedule.
139        """
140
141        # for each day of the week
142        for day in days:
143            print(day)
144            print('-------')
145
146            if (day == 'Sunday'):   # sunday?
147                current_timeslot = '12:00pm'
148                num_timeslots = 3
149            elif day in days[1:5]: # mon-thurs?
150                current_timeslot = '8:00am'
151                num_timeslots = 5
152            else:   # friday, saturday
153                current_timeslot = '8:00am'
154                num_timeslots = 6
155
156            # find loc of current_timeslot in tuple time_slots
157            index_val = time_slots.index(current_timeslot)
158
159            # iterate through num_timeslots starting with current time slot
160            for time_slot in time_slots[index_val:index_val + num_timeslots]:
161                print('{0:>7}'.format(time_slot), ' ', end='')
162                for k in range(0,2):
163                    displayScheduledWorkerHours(k+1, probabilities)
164                    print()
165                print()
166
```

FIGURE 9-25 Food Co-op Simulation Program (*Continued*)

If the "no show" event does not occur, the simulation checks events for when the volunteers are 15, 30, or 45 minutes late (**lines 63–68**). Because showing up late and leaving early are independent events, the program also checks for the particular worker leaving 15 or 30 minutes early (**lines 70–73**). The remaining lines of function display_scheduledworkerhours

```
167 def executeUnscheduledSimulation(probabilities, days, time_slots):
168
169     """Displays a simulated week of workers in attendance for all
170        time slots, based on an unscheduled worker schedule.
171     """
172
173     # for each day in the week
174     for day in days:
175         print(day)
176         print('-------')
177
178         if (day == 'Sunday'):   # sunday
179             current_timeslot = '12:00pm'
180             num_timeslots = 3
181         elif day in days[1:5]: # mon-thurs?
182             current_timeslot = '8:00am'
183             num_timeslots = 5
184         else:  # fri, sat
185             current_timeslot = '8:00am'
186             num_timeslots = 6
187
188         # find loc of current_timeslot in tuple time_slots
189         index_val = time_slots.index(current_timeslot)
190
191         # iterate through num_timeslots starting with current time slot
192         for time_slot in time_slots[index_val:index_val + num_timeslots]:
193             numworkers = \
194              numWorkersShowedUp(probabilities['CShowup'], num_members)
195             print('{0:>7}'.format(time_slot), ' ', end='')
196
197             if numworkers == 1:
198                 print(numworkers, 'worker came')
199                 num_stayed = 1
200             elif numworkers == 0 or numworkers == 2:
201                 print(numworkers, 'workers came')
202                 num_stayed = numworkers
203             else:
204                 print(numworkers, 'workers came (' + \
205                 str(numworkers - 2), 'went home)' )
206                 num_stayed = 2
207
208             for k in range(num_stayed): # at most 2 workers stay to work
209                 displayUnscheduledWorkerHours(k+1, probabilities)
210
211             print()
212
```

FIGURE 9-25   Food Co-op Simulation Program (*Continued*)

(**lines 75–90**) involve checking which events occurred and displaying (and properly spacing) the appropriate output.

Functions executeUnscheduledSimulation (**lines 167–211**) and its supporting function displayUnscheduledWorkerHours (**lines 92–133**) are very similar to the corresponding functions executeScheduledSimulation and displayScheduledWorkerHours. One difference is the way that the simulation handles the number of possible workers for a given time slot in function executeUnscheduledSimulation. Because in the unscheduled approach any number of workers can show up, this section indicates how many workers actually stay to work that time

```
213  # ---- main
214
215  # init
216  num_members = 75
217  time_slots = ('8:00am', '10:00am', '12:00pm', '2:00pm', '4:00pm',
218                '6:00pm')
219
220  days = ('Sunday', 'Monday', 'Tuesday', 'Wednesday', 'Thursday',
221         'Friday', 'Saturday')
222
223  sched_probabilities = {'CLate_15':15, 'CLate_30':5, 'CLate_45':2,
224                         'CLEarly_15':5, 'CLEarly_30':3,'CNoshow':15}
225
226  unsched_probabilities = {'CLate_15':5, 'CLate_30':2, 'CLate_45':1,
227                           'CLEarly_15':10, 'CLEarly_30':3,'CShowup':5}
228
229  # seed random number generator with system clock
230  random.seed()
231
232  # get type of simulation
233  print('Welcome to the Food Co-op Schedule Simulation Program')
234
235  valid_input = False
236  while not valid_input:
237      try:
238          response = int(input('(1)scheduled, (2)unscheduled simulation? '))
239
240          while (response != 1) and (response != 2):
241              print('Invalid Selection\n')
242              response = \
243                  int(input('(1)scheduled, (2)unscheduled simulation? '))
244
245          if response == 1:
246              print('<< SCHEDULED WORKER SIMULATION >>\n')
247              executeScheduledSimulation(sched_probabilities,
248                                         days, time_slots)
249          else:
250              print('<< UNSCHEDULED WORKER SIMULATION >>\n')
251              executeUnscheduledSimulation(unsched_probabilities,
252                                           days, time_slots)
253
254          valid_input = True
255
256      except ValueError:
257          print('Please enter numerical value 1 or 2\n')
```

FIGURE 9-25   Food Co-op Simulation Program

slot—no more than two—and how many go home. Another minor difference is the way that `display-UnscheduledWorkerHours` is designed. This is due to the fact that a "no show" only applies to scheduled workers, and not to unscheduled workers since unscheduled workers never sign up for a time slot to work.

Function `event_occurred` (**lines 13–22**) is a simple function that returns a Boolean (`True`/`False`) value used to simulate whether a given event has occurred or not. The function is passed an integer value between 1 and 100 representing the probability of the event (where 100 represents certainty). It then makes a call to the random number generator to randomly generate an integer in the same range of 1 to 100 (in **line 19**). If the number is less than or equal to the value passed in parameter `chance`, then the event is assumed to have occurred, and the value `True` is returned. Otherwise, the event is assumed *not* to have occurred, and thus returns `False`. This function is what drives the simulation.

Finally, function `numworkersShowedUp` (**lines 24–36**) is a supporting function, called from **line 194** of function `executeUnscheduledSimulation`. In the simulation of the unscheduled approach, any number of members may show up for work for any given time slot. To simulate this, function `numworkershowedup` is designed to be given the chances that an individual member may show up (in parameter `indiv_chance`), as well as the total number of members in the co-op (in parameter `num_individuals`).

9.3.5   Analyzing a Scheduled vs. Unscheduled Co-op Worker Approach

We now look at the simulation results for worker coverage at the food co-op, one using a scheduled approach (Figure 9-26), and the other using an unscheduled approach (Figure 9-27).

We can compare these two simulation runs. Since each run is based on assumed probabilities of events, the results are only as accurate as the probability estimates. Also, multiple simulation runs would provide a more accurate picture of likely events. Comparative results are given in Figure 9-28.

So with these caveats in mind, what can we conclude from this simulation? We first look at the reason that the food co-op chose to try an unscheduled approach—that too often, time slots were left partially or completely uncovered. From our simulation of a scheduled approach, we do see three times in which time slots are completely uncovered, and fourteen times in which there is only partial coverage (that is, only one person showing up). In the simulation of the unscheduled approach, there were no time slots left uncovered, and only three time slots in which there was partial coverage. This, therefore, coincides with the co-op's experience that there is better coverage in an unscheduled approach.

We next focus on the number of times a worker was 15 or 30 minutes late. In the scheduled approach, members were 15 minutes late six times, 30 minutes late two times, and 45 minutes late one time. For the unscheduled approach, members were 15 minutes late six times, 30 minutes late three times, and never 45 minutes late. Thus, there is no appreciable difference in the amount of time workers arrive late based on the simulation. When we look at the number of times workers left early, we see that in the scheduled approach, workers left 15 minutes early three times and 30 minutes early four times. In the unscheduled approach, workers left 15 minutes early four times, and 30 minutes early only once. Thus, there is also no appreciable difference in the amount of times workers leave early, except that scheduled workers were more likely to leave 30 minutes early than unscheduled workers (based on our assumed probabilities of human behavior).

Overall, the results indicate that an unscheduled approach does improve the problem of uncovered time slots. This, therefore, improves the functioning of the co-op. However, is there a hidden cost to this? A downside of the unscheduled approach is that there are times when more than the

```
Welcome to the Food Co-op Schedule Simulation      4:00pm  worker 1: -- no show --
Program                                                    worker 2: whole time
(1)scheduled, (2)unscheduled simulation? 1
<< SCHEDULED WORKER SIMULATION >>                  Thursday
                                                   -------
Sunday                                              8:00am  worker 1: whole time
-------                                                     worker 2: -- no show --
12:00pm  worker 1: whole time
         worker 2: whole time                      10:00am  worker 1: -- no show --
                                                            worker 2: whole time
 2:00pm  worker 1: whole time
         worker 2: -- no show --                   12:00pm  worker 1: whole time
                                                            worker 2: 15 mins late
 4:00pm  worker 1: whole time
         worker 2: -- no show --                    2:00pm  worker 1: whole time
                                                            worker 2: whole time
Monday
-------                                             4:00pm  worker 1: whole time
 8:00am  worker 1: -- no show --                            worker 2: 15 mins late
         worker 2: whole time
                                                   Friday
10:00am  worker 1: whole time                      -------
         worker 2: whole time                       8:00am  worker 1: -- no show --
                                                            worker 2: whole time
12:00pm  worker 1: -- no show --
         worker 2: -- no show --                   10:00am  worker 1: 15 mins late
                                                            worker 2: -- no show --
 2:00pm  worker 1: left 30 mins early
         worker 2: whole time                      12:00pm  worker 1: whole time
                                                            worker 2: -- no show --
 4:00pm  worker 1: whole time
         worker 2: whole time                       2:00pm  worker 1: whole time
                                                            worker 2: left 30 mins early
Tuesday
-------                                             4:00pm  worker 1: 15 mins late
 8:00am  worker 1: -- no show --                            worker 2: whole time
         worker 2: -- no show --
                                                    6:00pm  worker 1: whole time
10:00am  worker 1: whole time                               worker 2: whole time
         worker 2: whole time
                                                   Saturday
12:00pm  worker 1: whole time                      -------
         worker 2: 15 mins late                     8:00am  worker 1: whole time
                                                            worker 2: -- no show --
 2:00pm  worker 1: whole time
         worker 2: -- no show --                   10:00am  worker 1: whole time
                                                            worker 2: left 30 mins early
 4:00pm  worker 1: whole time
         worker 2: -- no show --                   12:00pm  worker 1: 15 mins late
                                                            worker 2: whole time
Wednesday
-------                                             2:00pm  worker 1: left 15 mins early
 8:00am  worker 1: whole time                               worker 2: -- no show --
         worker 2: whole time
                                                    4:00pm  worker 1: -- no show --
10:00am  worker 1: 30 mins late                             worker 2: -- no show --
         worker 2: 30 mins late   left 15 mins early
                                                    6:00pm  worker 1: whole time
12:00pm  worker 1: 45 mins late   left 30 mins early        worker 2: -- no show --
         worker 2: whole time

 2:00pm  worker 1: left 15 mins early
         worker 2: 30 mins late
```

FIGURE 9-26   Scheduled Worker Simulation

```
Welcome to the Food Co-op Schedule Simulation
Program
(1)scheduled, (2)unscheduled simulation? 2
<< UNSCHEDULED WORKER SIMULATION >>

Sunday
-------
12:00pm  7 workers came (5 went home)
         worker 1: 15 mins late
         worker 2: whole time

 2:00pm  1 worker came
         worker 1: whole time

 4:00pm  5 workers came (3 went home)
         worker 1: whole time
         worker 2: whole time

Monday
-------
 8:00am  7 workers came (5 went home)
         worker 1: whole time
         worker 2: whole time

10:00am  4 workers came (2 went home)
         worker 1: whole time
         worker 2: whole time

12:00pm  4 workers came (2 went home)
         worker 1: whole time
         worker 2: whole time

 2:00pm  4 workers came (2 went home)
         worker 1: left 15 mins early
         worker 2: left 30 mins early

 4:00pm  4 workers came (2 went home)
         worker 1: 15 mins late
         worker 2: whole time

Tuesday
-------
 8:00am  4 workers came (2 went home)
         worker 1: whole time
         worker 2: 15 mins late

10:00am  5 workers came (3 went home)
         worker 1: 15 mins late
         worker 2: whole time

12:00pm  3 workers came (1 went home)
         worker 1: whole time
         worker 2: whole time

 2:00pm  4 workers came (2 went home)
         worker 1: 15 mins late
         worker 2: whole time

 4:00pm  1 worker came
         worker 1: whole time
```

```
Wednesday
-------
 8:00am  4 workers came (2 went home)
         worker 1: left 15 mins early
         worker 2: whole time

10:00am  3 workers came (1 went home)
         worker 1: whole time
         worker 2: left 15 mins early

12:00pm  2 workers came
         worker 1: whole time
         worker 2: left 15 mins early

 2:00pm  6 workers came (4 went home)
         worker 1: whole time
         worker 2: whole time

 4:00pm  6 workers came (4 went home)
         worker 1: whole time
         worker 2: whole time

Thursday
-------
 8:00am  6 workers came (4 went home)
         worker 1: whole time
         worker 2: whole time

10:00am  3 workers came (1 went home)
         worker 1: whole time
         worker 2: whole time

12:00pm  6 workers came (4 went home)
         worker 1: whole time
         worker 2: 30 mins late

 2:00pm  6 workers came (4 went home)
         worker 1: whole time
         worker 2: whole time

 4:00pm  5 workers came (3 went home)
         worker 1: whole time
         worker 2: whole time

Friday
-------
 8:00am  4 workers came (2 went home)
         worker 1: whole time
         worker 2: whole time

10:00am  3 workers came (1 went home)
         worker 1: whole time
         worker 2: whole time

12:00pm  3 workers came (1 went home)
         worker 1: whole time
         worker 2: whole time

 2:00pm  4 workers came (2 went home)
         worker 1: whole time
         worker 2: 30 mins late
```

FIGURE 9-27   Unscheduled Worker Simulation (*Continued*)

```
4:00pm  2 workers came                    12:00pm  9 workers came (7 went home)
          worker 1: whole time                     worker 1: whole time
          worker 2: whole time                     worker 2: whole time

6:00pm  3 workers came (1 went home)       2:00pm  1 worker came
          worker 1: whole time                     worker 1: whole time
          worker 2: whole time

Saturday                                   4:00pm  2 workers came
-------                                             worker 1: whole time
8:00am  6 workers came (4 went home)                worker 2: 30 mins late
          worker 1: whole time
          worker 2: whole time             6:00pm  4 workers came (2 went home)
                                                    worker 1: whole time
10:00am 3 workers came (1 went home)                worker 2: whole time
          worker 1: 15 mins late
          worker 2: whole time
```

FIGURE 9-27 Unscheduled Worker Simulation

two workers show up. Thus, there are expected to be times when members who show up to work are not needed, and therefore need to return another time. In our simulation, this happened 77 times, which depending on other factors (for example, how long it takes to get to the co-op, how far out of the way is it from other locations that members would typically go to, etc.) is an additional burden on individual members.

Thus, it is understandable from the co-op's point of view that an unscheduled approach to worker "scheduling" is a better approach. However, *for individual members it adds an extra burden of time, and thus it may not be considered an improvement from their perspective.*

Number of Time Slots that:	Scheduled Approach	Unscheduled Approach
No One Showed Up	3	0
Only One Person Showed Up	14	3
Number of Times that Someone was 15 Minutes Late	6	6
Number of Times that Someone was 30 minutes Late	3	3
Number of Times that Someone was 45 Minutes Late	1	0
Number of Times that Someone Left 15 Minutes Early	3	4
Number of Times that Someone Left 30 Minutes Early	4	1
Number of People Turned Away Because had Enough Workers (unscheduled only)	-	77

FIGURE 9-28 Results of Simulation Runs of Scheduled vs. Unscheduled Approach

CHAPTER SUMMARY

General Topics

Associative Data Structures
Set Operations
Hexadecimal Numbers
Computer Simulation
Test Drivers/Test Stubs

Python-Specific Programming Topics

Dictionaries in Python
Set and Frozenset Types in Python

CHAPTER EXERCISES

Section 9.1

1. Indicate whether an indexed data structure, an associative data structure, or a set type would be most appropriate for each of the following.

   (a) The number of inches of rain for each day of the year in a given locality, used for computing the average yearly rainfall.

   (b) The number of inches of rain, only for the days when there was rainfall in a given locality, used to retrieve the amount of rain for any given day as quickly as possible.

   (c) Faculty members that belong to various committees, in which each faculty member on the university senate must also be a member of at least one college committee, but may not also be a member of another university-level committee.

2. Create a dictionary named `password_lookup` that contains usernames as keys (as string types), and passwords as associated string values. Make up data for five dictionary entries.

3. Give a program segment that creates an initially empty dictionary named `password_lookup`, prompting one-by-one for usernames and passwords (until a username of `'z'` is read) entering each into the dictionary.

4. Create a dictionary named `password_hint` that contains email addresses as keys, and associated values that contain both a user's "password security question," and the answer to the question. Make up data for five dictionary entries.

5. Create a dictionary named `member_table` that contains users' email addresses as keys, and their current password as the values. Write a function that generates a temporary new password for a given user and updates it in the table.

Section 9.2

6. Declare a set named `vowels` containing the strings `'a'`,`'e'`,`'i'`,`'o'`, and `'u'`. Give a program segment that prompts the user for any English word, and displays how many vowels it contains.

7. Give a program segment that prompts the user for two English words, and displays which letters the two words have in common.

8. Give a program segment that prompts the user for two English words, and displays which letters are in the first word but not in the second.

9. Give a program segment that prompts the user for two English words, and displays which letters of the alphabet are in neither of the two words.

10. Give a program segment that prompts the user for two English words, and displays which letters are in either the first word or the second word, but not in both words.

11. Give a program segment that prompts the user for two English words, entered in no particular order, and determines if all the letters of first word are contained within the second.

PYTHON PROGRAMMING EXERCISES

P1. Write a Python function called addDailyTemp that is given a (possibly empty) dictionary meant to hold the average daily temperature for each day of the week, the day, and the day's average temperature. The function should add the temperature to the dictionary only if does not already contain a temperature for that day. The function should return the resulting dictionary, whether or not it is updated.

P2. Write a Python function named moderateDays that is given a dictionary containing the average daily temperature for each day of a week, and returns a list of the days in which the average temperature was between 70 and 79 degrees.

P3. Write a Python function named getDailyTemps that prompts the user for the average temperature for each day of the week, and returns a dictionary containing the entered information.

P4. Write a Python function named getWeekendAvgTemp that is passed a dictionary of daily temperatures, and returns the average temperature over the weekend for the weekly temperatures given.

P5. Write a Python function named addVegetable that is passed a (possible empty) set of vegetable names, and raises a ValueError exception if the given vegetable is already in the set, otherwise, the new vegetable should be added and the new set returned.

P6. Write a Python function named numVowels that is passed a string containing letters, each of which may be in either uppercase or lowercase, and returns a tuple containing the number of vowels and the number of consonants the string contains.

PROGRAM MODIFICATION PROBLEMS

M1. Word Frequency Count Program: Making Use of Sets
Modify the Word Frequency Count Program in Chapter 8 making use of the set type where possible.

M2. Phone Number Spelling Program: Modifying for Australia
In Australia, phone numbers are of the form 0x-xxxx-xxxx. Modify the Phone Number Spelling program so that it prints out Australian phone numbers with spellings for the last four digits.

M3. Kitchen Tile Visualization Program: Color Name Entry
Modify the Kitchen Tile Visualization Program so that, instead of requiring the user to enter hexadecimal RGB color codes, they are given a subset of twelve color names from which to select (from the colors listed in Figure 9-11).

M4. Kitchen Tile Visualization Program: Randomly Generated Patterns
Modify the Kitchen Tile Visualization Program so that the user can enter up to three different tile colors, as well as the grout color. The program should then display a pattern of tiles that is randomly generated using the three colors specified.

M5. Kitchen Tile Visualization Program: Automatic Complementary Colors
The complementary color of a given color is the "opposite" color (directly opposite on the color wheel). Designers often use complementary colors because of their vibrant contrast. Modify the Kitchen Tile visualization program so that the user enters one tile color, with the complementary color automatically

generated as the secondary tile color. To calculate the complementary color of a color, each of the three color values is replaced by its arithmetic complement to 255,

FFFFFF (white) → 255 255 255 → 255-255 255-255 255-255 → 000000 (black)
00FF00 (green) → 0 255 0 → 255-0 255-255 255-0 → 255 0 255 → FF00FF (magenta)
87CEEB (sky blue) → 135 206 235 → 255-135 255-206 255-235 → 120 49 20 → 783114 (brownish red)

M6. Kitchen Tile Visualization Program: Muted and Tinted Colors
Sometimes two colors are too vibrant together. Colors can be muted, or made less vibrant and "toned down," by adding some of their complementary color. Modify the Kitchen Tile Visualization Program so that the user can mute either or both of the two displayed colors to varying degrees. (See problem M5 about complementary colors.)

M7. Food Co-op Worker Schedule Simulation Program: Adjusting the Model
The program developed for the food co-op simulation allows for easy adjustment of some of the parameters in the model. This includes the assumed number of co-op members, as well as the various assumed probabilities for members' behaviors. Since the number of members in the co-op only affects the unscheduled simulation results, run the unscheduled simulation for various number of co-op members and
 (a) Plot a graph using the x-axis for the number of co-op members, and the y-axis for the number of members turned away when showing up to work over the period of one week.
 (b) Determine the optimal number of co-op members so that each time slot is covered, but with the least number of members showing up to work turned away.
 (c) Adjust the probabilities for the assumed behavior of co-op members to what you consider to be a more accurate reflection of peoples' behavior and describe the results.

M8. Food Co-op Worker Schedule Simulation Program: Multiple Simulations
Modify the Food Co-op Worker Schedule Simulation program so that the user can select the number of multiple, sequential simulations. The program should output the average results over all the simulation runs as shown below:

- ◆ average number of workers that showed up to work for any given time slot
- ◆ average number of workers that worked the complete time slot
- ◆ average number of workers that were 15, 30, and 45 minutes late
- ◆ average number of workers that left 15 or 30 minutes early
- ◆ average number of workers turned away over the week because the co-op had enough workers (for unscheduled approach)

PROGRAM DEVELOPMENT PROBLEMS

D1. Reverse Phone Spelling Program
Develop and test a program that allows the user to enter a spelled phone number for the last four digits (for example, 410-555-book) and generates the phone number that produces that spelling.

D2. Color Encoding Conversion Program
Develop and test a program that allows the user to enter six-digit hexadecimal RGB color codes and converts them to base 10. (You are *not* to use the ' # ' symbol for denoting hexadecimal values in Python in this program.) In this format, the first two hexadecimal digits represents the amount of red, the second two the amount of green, and the last two the amount of blue. Following is the hexadecimal value for the color "tomato,"

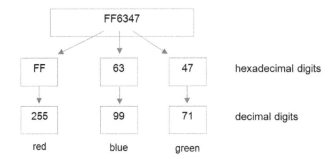

Hexadecimal numbers have place values that are powers of 16, in which the letters A–F have the values 10–15, respectively. Thus, FF in hexadecimal is equal to $15 * 16 + 15 * 1 = 240 + 15 = 255$. Likewise, 63 in hexadecimal is equal to $6 * 16 + 3 * 1 = 96 + 3 = 99$.

D3. Color Code Recording Program

Develop and test a program that allows the user to store color codes that they would like to save for future reference. The program should be designed so that they can enter a color code in either hexadecimal or decimal format (see problem D2). Whichever color code format is entered, it should be stored in both hexadecimal and decimal form. For example, if the user enters F0A514, it should be stored as both F0A514 and (240, 165, 20), and vice versa. The program should allow an annotation to be added for each color (for example, "Used this shade of green on my website"). The user should also be able to delete unwanted color entries.

Object-Oriented Programming

In Chapter 6, we learned what objects are and how they are used. We found that all values in Python are objects. Classes in object-oriented programming define objects. Thus, a class is a "cookie cutter" for creating any number of objects of that type. As with functions, there are predefined classes in Python, as well as the ability of programmers to define their own. In this chapter, we see how to define and use classes in Python.

OBJECTIVES

After reading this chapter and completing the exercises, you will be able to

♦ Explain the fundamental concepts of object-oriented programming

♦ Explain the concept of a class

♦ Define encapsulation, inheritance, and polymorphism

♦ Explain the use of subclasses as a subtype

♦ Explain the purpose of UML

♦ Explain the relationships of a UML class diagram

♦ Write simple UML class diagrams

♦ Define and use classes in Python

♦ Explain and use special methods in Python

♦ Effectively use inheritance and polymorphism in Python

CHAPTER CONTENTS

MOTIVATION

Classification can be described as the act of grouping entities into various categories that have something in common. In Biology, organisms are placed in a taxonomy based on their individual traits, for example. Libraries group books using various classification systems based on subject matter.

Most classification systems contain subcategories (and subcategories of subcategories, etc.), resulting in a hierarchy of types as shown in Figure 10.1. For example, chimpanzees are species in the Hominidae family, which is in the order Primate, which is in the mammal class, which is in the Animal Kingdom. The African elephant, on the other hand, is a species in the Elephantidae family, which is in the order Proboscidea, which is in the same class as chimpanzees, the Mammal class.

By this taxonomy, therefore, chimpanzees and African elephants have the same traits identified in the Mammal class, as well as traits of the Animal Kingdom. Their differences, on the other hand, are identified in the Primate and Proboscidea orders, as well as the traits within the Hominidae and Elephantidae families, and the chimpanzee and African elephant species. In this chapter, we see how the organization of class type and subtypes are utilized in object-oriented programming.

Nickandmel/flickr/Elephant near Ndutu/Wikimedia Commons

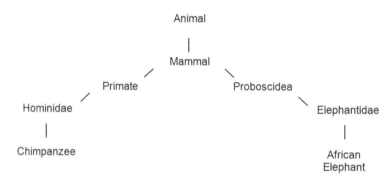

FIGURE 10-1 Taxonomy of Chimpanzees and African Elephants

FUNDAMENTAL CONCEPTS

10.1 What Is Object-Oriented Programming?

We have discussed and have been using objects in our programs. The use of objects in itself, however, does not constitute object-oriented programming. For that, we first need to introduce the concept of a class, which we discuss next.

10.1.1   What Is a Class?

A **class** specifies the set of instance variables and methods that are "bundled together" for defining a type of object. A class, therefore, is a "cookie cutter" that can be used to make as many object instances of that type object as needed. For example, strings in Python are object instances of the built-in `String` class, depicted in Figure 10-2.

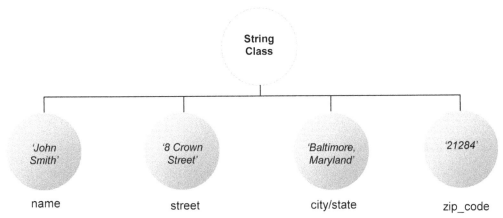

FIGURE 10-2   Object Instances of String Class

One method of the `String` class is `isdigit`. Thus, every string object has this method. The specific object whose `isdigit` method is called determines the specific string that it is applied to,

$$
\begin{array}{ll}
\texttt{name.isdigit()} \rightarrow \texttt{False} & \texttt{city\_state.isdigit()} \rightarrow \texttt{False} \\
\texttt{address.isdigit()} \rightarrow \texttt{False} & \texttt{zip\_code.isdigit()} \rightarrow \texttt{True}
\end{array}
$$

We next look at the three fundamental features of object-oriented programming.

> A **class** specifies the set of instance variables and methods that are "bundled together" for defining a type of object.

10.1.2   Three Fundamental Features of Object-Oriented Programming

Object-oriented programming languages, such as Python, provide three fundamental features that support object-oriented programming—*encapsulation*, *inheritance*, and *polymorphism*. These support a paradigm shift in software development from the focus on variables and passing of variables to functions in procedural programming, to the focus on objects and *message passing* between them.

   Message passing occurs when a method of one object calls a method of another, as depicted in Figure 10-3. For example, if Object B were a list and B1 a sorting method, then a call to B1 is a message (or request) for it to become sorted. A message to one object can result in the propagation of messages among many other objects in order to accomplish a request. In the next sections we discuss these three features of object-oriented programming, as well as introduce a means of specifying an object-oriented design using UML.

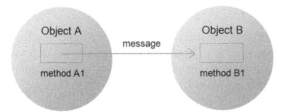

FIGURE 10-3 Message Passing in Object-Oriented Programming

Three fundamental features supporting the design of object-oriented programs are referred to as *encapsulation*, *inheritance*, and *polymorphism*.

10.2 Encapsulation

In this section we develop a Fraction class for demonstrating the notion of encapsulation. (Note that the Fraction class developed here is unrelated to the Fraction class of the Python Standard Library.)

10.2.1 What Is Encapsulation?

Encapsulation is a means of bundling together instance variables and methods to form a given type (class). Selected members of a class can be made inaccessible ("hidden") from its clients, referred to as *information hiding*. Information hiding is a form of abstraction. This is an important capability that object-oriented programming languages provide. As an example, we give a depiction of a Fraction object in Figure 10-4.

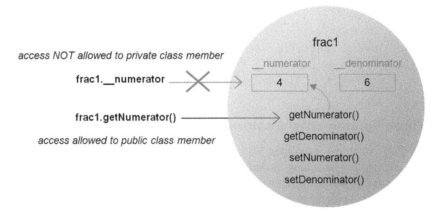

FIGURE 10-4 Fraction Object Access

The Fraction object shows private instance variables __numerator and __denominator, and four public methods. Private members of a class begin with two underscore characters, and cannot be directly accessed. For example, trying to access the instance variables of Fraction object `frac1` is invalid,

```
frac1.__numerator = 4      NOT ALLOWED
frac1.__denominator = 6    NOT ALLOWED
```

Public members of a class, on the other hand, are directly accessible. For example, the following are valid method calls,

```
frac1.getNumerator()      ALLOWED
frac1.getDenominator()    ALLOWED
frac1.setNumerator(4)     ALLOWED
frac1.setDenominator(6)   ALLOWED
```

These methods are referred to as **getters** and **setters** since their purpose is to get (return) and set (assign) private instance variables of a class. Restricting access to instance variables via getter and setter methods allows the methods to control what values are assigned (such as not allowing an assignment of 0 to the denominator), and how they are represented when retrieved. Thus, the instance variables of a class are generally made private, and the methods of the class generally made public.

> **Encapsulation** is a means of bundling together instance variables and methods to form a given type, as well as a way of restricting access to certain class members.

10.2.2   Defining Classes in Python

In this section, we develop a Python Fraction class.

Defining a Fraction Class

The first stage in the development of a Fraction class is given in Figure 10-5.

The `class` keyword is used to define classes, much as `def` is used for defining functions. All lines following the class declaration line are indented. Instance variables are initialized in the `__init__` special method. (We discuss special methods in the following.) Being private, instance variables `__numerator` and `__denominator` are not meant to be directly accessed.

```
>>> frac1.__numerator
AttributeError: 'Fraction' object has no attribute '__numerator'
```

In actuality, however, private members *are* accessible if written as follows:

```
>>> frac1._Fraction__numerator
```

```
class Fraction(object):
                                                              Special Methods

    def __init__(self, numerator, denominator):
        """Inits Fraction with values numerator and denominator."""

        self.__numerator = numerator
        self.__denominator = denominator
        self.reduce()

    def getNumerator(self):                           Getter and Setter Methods
        """Returns the numerator of a Fraction."""

        return self.__numerator

    def getDenominator(self):
        """Returns the denominator of a Fraction."""

        return self.__denominator

    def setNumerator(self, value):
        """Sets the numerator of a Fraction to the provided value."""

        self.__numerator = value

    def setDenominator(self, value):
        """Sets the denominator of a Fraction to the provided value.

        Raises a ValueError exception if a value of zero provided.
        """

        if value == 0:
            raise ValueError('Divide by Zero Error')

        self.__denominator = value
```

FIGURE 10-5 Initial Fraction Class

To understand this, all private class members are automatically renamed to begin with a single underscore character followed by the class name. Such renaming of identifiers is called *name mangling*. Unless the variable or method is accessed with its complete (mangled) name, it will not be found. Name mangling prevents unintentional access of private members of a class, while still allowing access when needed.

The methods of a class, as we have seen, are essentially functions meant to operate on the instance variables of the class. In Python, functions serving as a method must have an extra first parameter, by convention named `self`. This parameter contains a reference to the object instance to which the method belongs. When a method accesses any other member of the same class, the member name must be preceded by 'self' (self.__numerator). Getter and setter methods are also defined. Note that setDenominator raises an exception when passed a value of 0 to ensure that Fraction objects cannot be set to an invalid value. We further discuss special methods in Python next.

LET'S TRY IT

Enter and execute the following Python class. Then enter the given instructions within the Python shell and observe the results.

```
class SomeClass(object):                    >>> obj = SomeClass()
    def __init__(self):                     >>> obj.__n
        self.__n = 0                        ???
        self.n2 = 0                         >>> obj._SomeClass__n
                                            ???
                                            >>> obj.n2
                                            ???
```

The `class` keyword is used to define a class in Python. Class members beginning with two underscore characters are intended to be private members of a class. This is effectively accomplished in Python by the use of *name mangling*.

Special Methods in Python

Method names that begin and end with two underscore characters are called *special methods* in Python. Special methods are automatically called. For example, the __init__ method of the Fraction class developed is automatically called whenever a new Fraction object is created,

$$\text{frac1} = \text{Fraction}(1,2) \quad \text{– creates new fraction with value 1/2}$$
$$\text{frac2} = \text{Fraction}(6,8) \quad \text{– creates new fraction with value 6/8}$$

The values in parentheses are arguments to the __init__ method to initialize a new Fraction object to a specific value. Note that although there are three parameters defined (self, numerator, denominator), the first is always implied. Therefore, only the remaining arguments (numerator and denominator) are explicitly provided when creating a Fraction object.

Two other special methods of Python are __str__ and __repr__. These methods are used for representing the value of an object as a string. The __str__ method is called when an object is displayed using print (and when the str conversion function is used.) The __repr__ function is called when the value of an object is displayed in the Python shell (when interactively using Python). This is demonstrated below.

```
class DemoStrRepr():                >>> s = DemoStrRepr()

    def __repr__(self):             >>> print(s)
        return '__repr__ called'    __str__ called

    def __str__(self):              >>> s
        return '__str__ called'     __repr__ called
```

The difference in these special methods is that __str__ is for producing a string representation of an object's value that is most readable (for humans), and __repr__ is for producing a string representation that Python can evaluate. If special method __str__ is not implemented, then special method __repr__ is used in its place. An implementation of __repr__ for the Fraction class is given below.

```
def __repr__(self):
    return str(self.__numerator) + '/' + str(self.__denominator)
```

This, therefore, will display Fraction values as we normally write them:

```
>>> frac1 = Fraction(3,4)      >>> print('Value of frac1 is', frac1)
>>> frac1                      Value of frac1 is 3/4
3/4
```

We give special method __repr__ of the Fraction class (to also serve as the implementation of special method __str__) in Figure 10-6.

```
class Fraction(object):

                                              Additional Special Methods

    def __repr__(self):
        """Returns Fraction value as x/y."""

        return str(self.__numerator) + '/' + str(self.__denominator)
```

FIGURE 10-6   Additional Special Method repr

We will look at more Python special methods in the next section.

LET'S TRY IT

Enter and save the following class definition in a Python file and execute it. Then enter the given instructions in the Python shell and observe the results.

```
class XYcoord(object):            >>> coord = XYcoord(5, 2)
                                  >>> print(coord)
    def __init__(self, x, y):     ???
        self.__x = x
        self.__y = y              >>> str(coord)
                                  ???

    def __repr__(self):
        return '(' + str(self.__x) + ',' \      >>> coord
                   + str(self.__y) + ')'        ???
```

Special methods in Python have names that begin and end with two underscore characters, and are automatically called in Python.

Adding Arithmetic Operators to the Fraction Class

Special methods used to provide arithmetic operators for class types are shown in Figure 10-7.

Operator	Example Use	Special Method
- (negation)	-frac1	__neg__
+ (addition)	frac1 + frac2	__add__
- (subtraction)	frac1 - frac2	__sub__
* (multiplication)	frac1 * frac2	__mul__

FIGURE 10-7 Arithmetic Operator Special Methods

The expression `frac1 + frac2`, for example, evaluates to the returned value of the `__add__` method in the class, where the left operand (`frac1`) is the object on which the method call is made: `frac1.__add__(frac2)`. Arithmetic methods for the `Fraction` class are given in Figure 10-8.

```
                                        Arithmetic Operator Special Methods
def __neg__(self):
    """Returns a new Fraction equal to the negation of self."""

    return Fraction(-self.__numerator, self.__denominator)

def __add__(self, rfraction):
    """Returns a new reduced Fraction equal to self + rfraction."""

    numer = self.__numerator * rfraction.getDenominator() + \
            rfraction.getNumerator() * self.__denominator

    denom = self.__denominator * rfraction.getDenominator()

    resultFrac = Fraction(numer, denom)
    return resultFrac.reduce()

def __sub__(self, rfraction):
    """Returns a new reduced Fraction equal to self - rfraction."""

    return self + (-rfraction)

def __mul__(self, rfraction):
    """Returns a new reduced Fraction equal to self * rfraction."""

    numer = self.__numerator * rfraction.getNumerator()
    denom = self.__denominator * rfraction.getDenominator()

    resultFrac = Fraction(numer, denom)
    resultFrac.reduce()

    return resultFrac
```

FIGURE 10-8 Arithmetic Operators of the Fraction Class

Special method `__add__` is implemented to add the numerator and denominator of each fraction based on a common denominator as shown below,

```
2/4 + 1/5      →      (2 * 5)/(4 * 5) + (1 * 4)/(5 * 4)
               →      10/20 + 4/20
               →      14/20
               →      7/10     (after call to method reduce)
```

Note that a `reduce` method of the class (not given) is called on the resulting fraction to return the result in simplest form. Thus, rather than returning $14/20$, the value $7/10$ is returned.

The `__sub__` special method has a very simple and elegant implementation. It simply adds the first fraction to the negation of the second fraction, relying on the implementation of the `__add__` and `__neg__` methods. Finally, the `__mul__` special method multiplies the numerators of each of the fractions, as well as the denominators of each, building a new `Fraction` object from the results, and reducing the new fraction to simplest form by call to method `reduce`. (We omit the special method for the division operator here.)

Just as with the other arithmetic operators, a new (negated) `Fraction` object is returned by the `__neg__` method, rather than the original fraction object being altered. To negate a fraction, reassignment would be used instead,

$$frac1 = -frac1$$

LET'S TRY IT

Enter and save the following class definition in a Python file, and execute. Then enter the given instructions in the Python shell and observe the results.

```
class XYcoord(object):

    def __init__(self, x, y):
        self.__x = x
        self.__y = y

    def __repr__(self)
        return '(' + str(self.__x) + ',' \
                   + str(self.__y) + ')'

    def __add__(self, rCoord):
        new_x = self.__x + rCoord.__x
        new_y = self.__y + rCoord.__y

        return XYCoord(new_x, new_y)
```

```
>>> coord_1 = XYcoord(4,2)
>>> coord_2 = XYCoord(6,10)
>>> coord_1 + coord_2
???

>>> coord = coord_1 + coord_2
>>> print(coord)
???
```

Adding Relational Operators to the Fraction Class

We have yet to add the capability of applying relational operators to `Fraction` objects. The set of relational operator special methods that can be implemented is shown in Figure 10-9.

Operator	Example Use	Special Method
< (less than)	frac1 < frac2	__lt__
<= (less than or equal to)	frac1 <= frac2	__le__
== (equal to)	frac1 == frac2	__eq__
!= (not equal to)	frac1 != frac2	__ne__
> (greater than)	frac1 > frac2	__gt__
>= (greater than or equal to)	frac1 >= frac2	__ge__

FIGURE 10-9 Relational Operator Special Methods

The special methods for providing the relational operators of the `Fraction` class are given in Figure 10-10.

```
                                                        Relational Operators
def __eq__(self, rfraction):
    """Returns True if self arithmetically equal to rfraction.
       Otherwise, returns False.
    """

    temp_frac1 = self.copy()
    temp_frac2 = rfraction.copy()
    temp_frac1.reduce()
    temp_frac2.reduce()

    return temp_frac1.getNumerator() == temp_frac2.getNumerator() and \
        temp_frac1.getDenominator() == temp_frac2.getDenominator()

def __neq__(self, rfraction):
    """Returns True if Fraction not arithmetically equal to rfraction.
       Otherwise, returns False.
    """

    return not self.__eq__(rfraction)


def __lt__(self, rfraction):
    """Returns True if self less than rfraction."""

    if self.getDenominator() == rfraction.getDenominator():
        return self.getNumerator() < rfraction.getNumerator()
    else:
        temp_frac1 = self.copy()
        temp_frac2 = rfraction.copy()

        saved_denom = temp_frac1.getDenominator()
        temp_frac1.__adjust(temp_frac2.getDenominator())
        temp_frac2.__adjust(saved_denom)

        return temp_frac1.getNumerator() < temp_frac2.getNumerator()

def __le__(self, rfraction):
    """Returns True if self less than or equal to rfraction."""

    return not (rfraction < self)

def __gt__(self, rfraction):
    """Returns True if self greater than rfraction."""

    return not(self <= rfraction)

def __ge__(self, rfraction):
    """Returns True if self greater than or equal to rfraction."""

    return not(self < rfraction)
```

FIGURE 10-10 Relational Operators of the Fraction Class

Each of the special methods for the relational operators is implemented. For example, `frac1 < frac2` is determined by call to method `__lt__` on the first object, `frac1`, with the second object, `frac2`, passed as an argument,

$$\text{frac1.\_\_lt\_\_(frac2)}$$

In order to compare two fractions, they must have common denominators. Therefore, method `__lt__` first checks if the denominators are equal. If so, then the result of `self.__getNumerator() < rfraction.__getNumerator()` is returned. Otherwise, since we do not want the two fractions to be altered as a result of the comparison, a copy of each is made, assigned to `temp_frac1` and `temp_frac2`. In order to convert them common denominators, the numerator and denominator of each is multiplied by the denominator of the other. This is accomplished by call to private method `__adjust`. Then, the Boolean result `temp_frac1.__getNumerator() < temp_frac2.__getNumerator()` is returned.

Most other relational operators are grounded in the implementation of the less than special method, `__lt__`. The implementation of special method `__le__` (less than or equal to) is based on the fact that a $<=$ b is the same as not (b $<$ a). Special method `__neq__` (not equal to) is simply implemented as not (a = b). Finally, special method `__gt__` (greater than) is implemented as not a $<=$ b, and special method `__ge__` (greater than or equal to) is implemented as not (a $<$ b). Finally, the implementation of methods `copy`, `reduce`, and `__adjust` are left as an exercise at the end of the chapter.

The `Fraction` type developed represents the power of abstraction, as implemented through the use of encapsulation. The `Fraction` class contains two integer instance variables and an associated set of methods. That is what it "really" is. Through the use of information hiding, however, the client is provided an abstract view, which, for all intents and purposes, *is* a `Fraction` type. The `Fraction` class can be defined within its own Python file, and thus serve as a module that can be easily imported and used by any program.

> There exist special methods for the arithmetic and relational operators in Python that can be implemented to determine how these operators are evaluated for a given object type.

10.2.3 Let's Apply It—A Recipe Conversion Program

The following Python program (Figure 10-12) will convert the measured amount of ingredients of recipes, based on a provided conversion factor, to vary the number of servings. The program utilizes the following programming features:

➤ programmer-defined class

Example execution of the program is given in Figure 10-11.

The program makes use of the fraction class module developed in section 10.2.2, imported on **line 3**. Since there is only one item to be imported (the class), the choice of using `import Fraction` vs. `from Fraction import *` only affects whether Fraction objects are created as `frac1 = Fraction.Fraction(1,2)` for the first form of import, or `frac1 = Fraction(1,2)` for the second

Chocolate Chip Cookies Recipe

4 1/2 cups all-purpose flour
2 teaspoons baking soda
2 cups butter, softened
1 1/2 cups packed brown sugar
1/2 cup white sugar
2 packages instant vanilla pudding mix
4 eggs
2 teaspoons vanilla extract
4 cups semisweet chocolate chips
2 cups chopped walnuts

```
This program will convert a given recipe to a different
quantity based on a specified conversion factor. Enter a
factor of 1/2 to halve, 2 to double, 3 to triple, etc.

Enter file name: ChocChipCookiies.txt
File Open Error

Enter file name: ChocChipCookies.txt
Enter the conversion factor: 2
Converted recipe in file:  conv_ChocChipCookies.txt
```

Chocolate Chip Cookies Recipe
9 cups all-purpose flour
4 teaspoons baking soda
4 cups butter, softened
3 cups packed brown sugar
1 cup white sugar
4 packages instant vanilla pudding mix
8 eggs
4 teaspoons vanilla extract
8 cups semisweet chocolate chips
4 cups chopped walnuts

```
Enter file name: ChocChipCookies.txt
Enter the conversion factor: 1/2
Converted recipe in file:  conv_ChocChipCookies.txt
```

Chocolate Chip Cookies Recipe
9/4 cups all-purpose flour
1 teaspoons baking soda
1 cups butter, softened
3/4 cups packed brown sugar
1/4 cup white sugar
1 packages instant vanilla pudding mix
2 eggs
1 teaspoons vanilla extract
2 cups semisweet chocolate chips
1 cups chopped walnuts

FIGURE 10-11   Execution of the Recipe Conversion Program

form. We therefore choose the from-import form of import. Note that the methods of a class are called the same way regardless of the form of import used to import the class.

The main section of the program is in **lines 106–143**. The program welcome is provided on **lines 109–111**. The rest of the code is encompassed within a try block for catching any IOError exceptions. There is one instance of an IOError exception that is raised by the program (in addition to those raised by the Python standard functions) in function getFile (**lines 5–28**).

The getFile function prompts for a file name to open, returning both the file name and associated file object as a tuple. If, after three attempts the file fails to open successfully, an IOError exception is raised containing the error message 'Exceeded number of open file attempts' (**line 26**). Thus, a try block is used to catch each IOError exception raised by the open function. When such an exception is caught, variable num_attempts is incremented (**line 22**) in the corresponding exception handler (**lines 21–23**). When an input file is successfully opened, the loop terminates and file_name and input_file are returned as a tuple.

Back in the main module of the program, the user is prompted for the conversion factor (**line 119**). Since all calculations in the program are executed as Fraction types, the conversion factor is scanned (read) by call to function scanAsFraction (**lines 45–84**). If a single integer value (read as a string) is entered, for example '2', then scanAsFraction returns the Fraction value 2/1. If a single fraction value is entered, such as '2/4', then the Fraction value (in reduced form) 1/2 is returned. If an integer and fraction are entered, such as '1 1/2', then a Fraction equal to the sum of both is returned, 3/2.

Function scanAsFraction returns, as a Fraction value, the total value of the initial part of the parameter string passed.

4 1/2 cups all-purpose flour

```
1   # Recipe Conversion Program
2
3   from fraction import *
4
5   def getFile():
6
7       """Returns as a tuple the file name entered by the user and the
8          open file object. If the file exceeds three attempts of opening
9          successfully, an IOError exception is raised.
10      """
11
12      file_name = input('Enter file name: ')
13      input_file_opened = False
14      num_attempts = 1
15
16      while not input_file_opened and num_attempts < 3:
17          try:
18              input_file = open(file_name, 'r')
19              input_file_opened = True
20          except IOError:
21              print('File Open Error\n')
22              num_attempts = num_attempts + 1
23              file_name = input('Enter file name: ')
24
25      if num_attempts == 3:
26          raise IOError('Exceeded number of file open attempts')
27
28      return (file_name, input_file)
29
30  def removeMeasure(line):
31
32      """Returns provided line with any initial digits and fractions
33         (and any surrounding blanks) removed.
34      """
35
36      k = 0
37      blank_char = ' '
38
39      while k < len(line) and (line[k].isdigit() or \
40                               line[k] in ('/', blank_char)):
41          k = k + 1
42
43      return line[k:len(line)]
44
45  def scanAsFraction(line):
46
47      """Scans all digits, including fractions, and returns as a
48         Fraction object. For example, '1/2' would return as Fraction
49         value 1/2, '2' would return as Fraction 2/1, and '2 1/2' would
50         return as Fraction value 3/2.
51      """
52
```

FIGURE 10-12   Recipe Conversion Program (*Continued*)

```
53          completed_scan = False
54          value_as_frac = Fraction(0,1)
55
56          while not completed_scan:
57              k = 0
58              while k < len(line) and line[k].isdigit():
59                  k = k + 1
60
61              numerator = int(line[0:k])
62
63              if k < len(line) and line[k] == '/':
64                  k = k + 1
65                  start = k
66                  while k < len(line) and line[k].isdigit():
67                      k = k + 1
68
69                  denominator = int(line[start:k])
70              else:
71                  denominator = 1
72
73              value_as_frac = value_as_frac + Fraction(numerator,
74                                                        denominator)
75
76              if k == len(line):
77                  completed_scan = True
78              else:
79                  line = line[k:len(line)].strip()
80
81                  if not line[0].isdigit():
82                      completed_scan = True
83
84          return value_as_frac
85
86  def convertLine(line, factor):
87
88      """If line begins with a digit, returns line with the value
89         multiplied by factor. Otherwise, returns line unaltered
90         (e.g., for a factor of 2, '1/4 cup' returns as '1/2 cup'.)
91      """
92
93      if line[0].isdigit():
94          blank_char = ' '
95          frac_meas = scanAsFraction(line) * factor
96
97          if frac_meas.getDenominator() == 1:
98              frac_meas = frac_meas.getNumerator()
99
100         conv_line = str(frac_meas) + blank_char + removeMeasure(line)
101     else:
102         conv_line = line
103
104     return conv_line
105
```

FIGURE 10-12   Recipe Conversion Program (*Continued*)

```
106  # ---- main
107
108  # display welcome
109  print('This program will convert a given recipe to a different')
110  print('quantity based on a specified conversion factor. Enter a')
111  print('factor of 1/2 to halve, 2 to double, 3 to triple, etc.\n')
112
113  try:
114
115      # get file name and open file
116      file_name, input_file = getFile()
117
118      # get conversion factor
119      conv_factor = input('Enter the conversion factor: ')
120      conv_factor = scanAsFraction(conv_factor)
121
122      # open output file named 'conv_' + file_name
123      output_file_name = 'conv_' + file_name
124      output_file = open(output_file_name, 'w')
125
126      # convert recipe
127      empty_str = ''
128      recipe_line = input_file.readline()
129
130      while recipe_line != empty_str:
131          recipe_line = convertLine(recipe_line, conv_factor)
132          output_file.write(recipe_line)
133          recipe_line = input_file.readline()
134
135      # close files
136      input_file.close()
137      output_file.close()
138
139      # display completion message to user
140      print('Converted recipe in file: ', output_file_name)
141
142  except IOError as err_mesg:  # catch file open error
143      print(err_mesg)
```

FIGURE 10-12 Recipe Conversion Program

First, variable `completed_scan` is initialized to `False` (**line 53**) and set to `True` when the initial digit (and `'/'`) characters have been scanned. Then variable `value_as_frac` (**line 54**) is initialized to the `Fraction` value `0/1`, so that it can be used to accumulate values (**line 73**) when both an integer and a fractional value are found, as shown. Within the while loop, index variable k is initialized to `0` (**line 57**). Following that, k is incremented to scan past each character in `line` that is a digit character (as long as k is less than the length of the line). This places k at the index location of the first non-digit. Then, the range of characters scanned so far, `line[0:k]`, is converted to an integer type and assigned to `numerator`. The next character is then scanned for the '/' character (indicating that a fraction notation exists), as long as the end of line has not been reached (that is, k < `len(line)`). If the slash character is found, then there is a denominator to go with the numerator value just scanned. Thus, the following characters are scanned until a non-digit is found (**lines 66–67**).

The current location of k is first stored in variable `start` (**line 65**) so that the beginning of the new substring of digits can be scanned. At that point, `denominator` is set to the integer value of the digits from index `start` to `k−1` (`line[start:k]`). Then, on **line 73**, variable `value_as_frac` is set to the current value of `value_as_frac` plus the newly created `Fraction` object with the current values of `numerator` and `denominator`. If a slash character is not found, then `denominator` is set to one (**line 71**) so that the integer value scanned, for example 2, is returned as `2/1`.

On **line 76** a check is made to determine if the end of the line has been reached. (This would not normally be true of a recipe line, but would be `True` when scanning a conversion value.) If the end has been reached, then `completed_scan` is set to `True`, which terminates the main while loop, causing the final return statement to return the scanned value. If, however, the end of the line has not been reached, the next character is checked to see if it is a digit. If it is, then the while loop at **line 56** iterates again to scan the following value, which is expected to be a fractional value. If the next character is not a digit, then `completed_scan` is set to `True` (**line 82**), causing the function to return the (non-fractional) value scanned.

In **lines 123–124** of the main module, `output_file_name` is assigned to the name of the input file name and prepended with the string `'conv_'`, and file object `output_file` is created (where the converted recipe is written). Following that, the process of converting each line of the recipe file begins. First, `empty_str` is initialized and the first line of the recipe file is read as `recipe_line` (**lines 127–128**). The while loop at **line 130** then converts the current recipe line by a call to `convertLine`. Function `convertLine` (**lines 86–104**) first checks that the first character of the line is a digit. If not, then the line is assigned unaltered to `conv_line` on **line 102** (since there is no initial numerical value to convert). If a digit is found, then `blank_char` is initialized (**line 94**), and `frac_meas` is set to the `Fraction` value returned by `scanAsFunction` (for the given conversion factor). If the denominator of `frac_meas` is found to be 1 (e.g., `2/1`), then `frac_meas` is set to the value of the numerator (2), otherwise it is left as is. Variable `line` is set to the remaining part of the line by call to `removeMeasure` (**line 100**), and `conv_line` is set to the string representation of `frac_meas` concatenated with a blank and the remaining part of the original line, and returned. Finally, function `removeMeasure` (**lines 30–43**) scans past the initial digit, blank, and slash characters, returning the remaining part of the line.

Self-Test Questions

1. Encapsulation bundles together instance variables and methods of a class, and allows certain members of the class to be made inaccessible by use of keyword `private` in Python. (TRUE/FALSE)

2. Private members of a class are not meant to be directly accessed by methods of other classes. (TRUE/FALSE)

3. Methods of a class that provide access to privates members of the class are called _____ and _____.

4. Which of the following are special methods in Python?
   (**a**) Getter and setters
   (**b**) Method names that begin and end with two underscore characters
   (**c**) Methods that are part of any Python built-in type

5. Which of the following is a special method for defining an operator in a class?
   (a) `__init__`
   (b) `__add`
   (c) `__add__`

10.3 Inheritance

The true capabilities of object-oriented programming present themselves when inheritance of classes is employed. In this section, we explore the use of inheritance in Python.

10.3.1 What Is Inheritance?

Inheritance, in object-oriented programming, is the ability of a class to inherit members of another class as part of its own definition. The inheriting class is called a **subclass** (also "derived class" or "child class"), and the class inherited from is called the **superclass** (also "base class" or "parent class"). Superclasses may themselves inherit from other classes, resulting in a hierarchy of classes as shown in Figure 10-13 (inherited class members are in gray).

Class A is the superclass of all the classes in the figure. Thus, subclasses B and E each inherit variable var1 and method method1 from Class A. In addition, Class B defines variable var2 and method method2, and Class E defines method5. Since Class C is a subclass of Class B, it inherits everything in Class A and Class B, adding var3 and method3 in its own definition. And since Class D is also a subclass of Class B, it inherits everything in Class A and Class B, also defining method4.

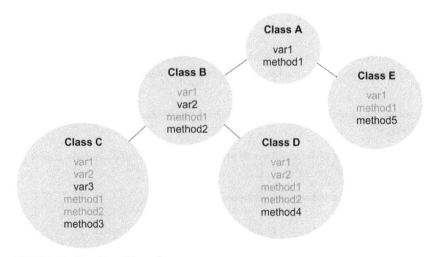

FIGURE 10-13 Class Hierarchy

Inheritance in object-oriented programming is the ability of a **subclass** (also "derived class" or "child class") to inherit members of a **superclass** (also "base class" or "parent class") as part of its own definition.

10.3.2 Subtypes

A **subtype** is something that can be substituted for and behave as its parent type (and its parent's parent type, etc.). For example, consider the characteristic features within the Animal Kingdom in Figure 10-14.

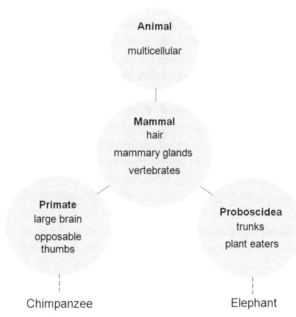

FIGURE 10-14 Hierarchy of Characteristics of Animals

Mammals are a type of animal. Therefore, they have the characteristic of being multicellular. In addition, they have the characteristics of having hair, mammary glands, and vertebrae. Primates (which include chimpanzees) are a type of mammal (and thus a type of animal). Therefore, they have the characteristics of mammals, as well as having large brains and opposable thumbs. Proboscidea (which includes elephants) are a type of mammal (and a type of animal) and thus have the characteristics of mammals, as well as having some form of trunk and being plant eaters. Thus, each classification describes a subtype of the classifications from which it derives. For example, consider the following simple story.

Andy was very interested in animals. He had many books about them, and went to see animals whenever he had the chance.

Because chimpanzees are a type of animal, an alternate version of the story can be generated by substituting "chimpanzee" for "animal,"

> *Andy was very interested in chimpanzees. He had many books about them, and went to see chimpanzees whenever he had the chance.*

Now consider the following story,

> *Andy was very interested in chimpanzees. He had many books about them, and loved to watch the chimpanzees swing from tree to tree.*

In this case, if we substitute another animal, "elephant," for "chimpanzee," we get the following story,

> *Andy was very interested in elephants. He had many books about them, and loved to watch the elephants swing from tree to tree.*

Because an elephant is not a chimpanzee, this version of the story does not make sense. Note, however, that since an elephant is a type of animal, "elephant" can be substituted in the original story just as chimpanzee was and make sense. We next look at how to create subclasses in Python.

A **subtype** is something that can be substituted for and behave as its parent type (and *its* parent type, etc.).

10.3.3   Defining Subclasses in Python

We now look at how to employ the object-oriented programming feature of inheritance in Python. We give an example of an "exploded" string class as a subclass of the built-in string class, and look at whether an exploded string can be substituted as a string type.

Class Names of the Built-In Types in Python

Recall that all values in Python are objects. Thus, there exists a class definition for each of the built-in types. To determine the type (class name) of a particular value (object) in Python, the built-in function `type` can be used.

```
>>> type(12)          >>> type(12.4)        type('')
<class 'int'>         <class 'float'>       <class 'str'>

>>> type([])          >>> type(())          type({})
<class 'list'>        <class 'tuple'>       <class 'dict'>
```

The resulting expression `<class classname>` gives the associated class name for any value. (We use some empty values here, such as the empty string, but the type of any value can be determined this way.) A detailed description of a built-in class can be displayed by use of the help function,

>>> help(int)   >>> help(str)

Partial display of the str built-in type is given in Figure 10-15.

```
>>> help(str)
Help on class str in module builtins:

class str(object)
 |  str(string[, encoding[, errors]]) -> str
 |
 |  Create a new string object from the given encoded string.
 |  encoding defaults to the current default string encoding.
 |  errors can be 'strict', 'replace' or 'ignore' and defaults to 'strict'.
 |
 |  Methods defined here:
 |
 |  __add__(...)
 |      x.__add__(y) <==> x+y
 |
 |  __contains__(...)
 |      x.__contains__(y) <==> y in x
 |
 |  __eq__(...)
 |      x.__eq__(y) <==> x==y
 |
 |      .
 |      .
 |
 |  find(...)
 |      S.find(sub[, start[, end]]) -> int
 |
 |      Return the lowest index in S where substring sub is found,
 |      such that sub is contained within S[start:end].  Optional
 |      arguments start and end are interpreted as in slice notation.
 |
 |      Return -1 on failure.
 |      .
 |      .
```

FIGURE 10-15   Description of Built-in String Class

For programmer-defined classes, such as the Fraction class developed earlier, we use the name of the class (with any required arguments) for creating objects of that type,

frac1 = Fraction(1,2)

For built-in types such as the str type, object instances are generally created using a more convenient syntax. For example, to create a new string value (object), we simply put quotes around the desired characters of the string,

name = 'John Smith'

404 CHAPTER 10 Object-Oriented Programming

For creating a new list, the list elements are surrounded by square brackets,

$$nums = [10,20,30,40]$$

We have seen a similar means of creating tuples, dictionaries, and sets. Knowing the class names of the built-in types, we can alternatively create object instances of each as follows,

```
>>> int(1)            >>> int('1')          >>> int(1.2)
1                     1                     1

>>> list([1, 2, 3])   >>> list((1,2,3))     >>> list('123')
[1, 2, 3]             [1, 2, 3]             [1, 2, 3]
```

When using the class name of a built-in type to create a new object instance, arguments of various types can be used to initialize its value. For example, an integer can be created from a provided string or float value; a list can be created from a provided tuple or string. Finally, we note that the built-in class names in Python contain only lowercase letters. Programmer-defined classes, such as Fraction however, are by convention named with a beginning uppercase letter.

LET'S TRY IT

Enter the following in the Python shell and observe the results.

```
>>> type(1)           >>> type([])          >>> help(int)
???                   ???                   ???
>>> type(1.5)         >>> type([1,2,3])     >>> help(float)
???                   ???                   ???
>>> type('')          >>> type(())          >>> help(list)
???                   ???                   ???
>>> type('Hi')        >>> type((1,2,3))     >>> help(tuple)
???                   ???
```

Built-in function type can be used to determine the type (class name) of any value in Python. Built-in function help can be used to get the class description of a built-in type.

Defining an Exploded String Type

Given the built-in string class, we can easily create a new string type that is identical to the string class, and in addition provide the option of being "exploded." By an exploded string is meant a string with spaces (blank characters) between all characters, for example, 'H e l l o'. We call this new class ExplodedStr, and give its definition in Figure 10.16.

When defining a subclass, the name of the class is followed by the name of the parent class within parentheses,

```
class ExplodedStr(str):
```

```
# Exploded String Class

class ExplodedStr(str):

    def __init__(self, value = ''):

        # call to init of str class
        str.__init__(value)


    def explode(self):

        # empty str returned unaltered
        if len(self) == 0:
            return self
        else:
            # create exploded string
            empty_str = ''
            blank_char = ' '
            temp_str = empty_str

            for k in range(0, len(self) - 1):
                temp_str = temp_str + self[k] + blank_char

            # append last char without following blank
            temp_str = temp_str + self[len(self)- 1]

            # return exploded str by joining all chars in list
            return temp_str
```

FIGURE 10-16 ExplodedStr Type as a Subclass of the Built-in str Class

Our new exploded string type can be used as shown below.

```
>>> title = ExplodedStr('My Favorite Movies')
>>> print(title.explode())
My Favorite Movies
```

Let's see how this works. The ExplodedStr class does not define any instance variables of its own. Thus, its __init__ method simply calls the __init__ method of the built-in str class to pass the value that the string is to be initialized to. If an initial value is not provided, the method has a default argument assigned to the empty string,

```
def __init__(self, value = ''):

    # call to init of str class
    str.__init__(value)
```

Here str.__init__(value) is used to call the str class's __init__ method.

Method `explode` returns the exploded version of the string. First, a check is made to see if the string is the empty string. If so, then the reference `self` is returned, thus returning its unaltered value. Otherwise, a new string is created (`temp_str`), equal to the original string referenced by `self`, with a blank appended after every character except the last. A for loop is used for this construction,

```
for k in range(0, len(self) - 1):
        temp_str = temp_str + self[k] + blank_char
```

Since the range function is called with parameters 0 and `len(self) - 1`, all except the last character of the original string is appended by this loop (since the last character should not have a blank character appended after it). Finally, the newly constructed exploded string (`temp_str`) is returned.

We can place the `ExplodedStr` class in its own module called `exploded_str` and import it when needed. Testing this new string type, we see that it behaves as desired.

```
>>> reg_str = 'Hello'            defining a regular string
>>> ex_str = ExplodedStr('Hello')   defining an exploded string
>>> reg_str                       value of regular string
'Hello'
>>> ex_str                        value of exploded string
'Hello'
>>> ex_str.explode()              call to explode method
H e l l o
>>> reg_str == ex_str             comparing the strings
True
>>>
```

LET'S TRY IT

For the following underlined string `uStr` class definition, enter and save it in a Python file, and execute. Then enter the associated instructions within the Python shell and observe the results.

```
class uStr(str):                         >>> reg_str = 'Hello'
                                         >>> u_str = uStr('Hello')
    def __init__(self, u_str):
        str.__init__(u_str)              >>> reg_str
                                         ???
    def underline(self):                 >>> u_str
                                         ???
        return str.__str__(self) + '\n' + \
            format('', '-<' + str(len(self)))   >>> u_str.underline()
                                         ???

                                         >>> reg_str == u_str
                                         ???
```

We see that exploded strings can be used as a regular string or in exploded form. Thus, it is only the added behavior of being able to be exploded that is different, not its value. As a result, the `ExplodedStr` subclass serves as a subtype of the built-in string class. We discuss the related issue of polymorphism next.

> When defining a subclass, the name of the class is followed by the name of the parent class within parentheses.

10.3.4   Let's Apply It—A Mixed Fraction Class

The following `MixedFraction` class is implemented as a subclass (subtype) of the `Fraction` class developed earlier. The program utilizes the following programming features:

➤ Inheritance of classes

The `Fraction` class that we developed only represents values as common fractions, that is, with just a numerator and denominator. Thus, the value one and a half is represented as 3/2. Mixed (compound) fractions denote values with a separate whole value and (proper) fraction—3/2 is represented as 1 1/2. In certain applications, such as in the recipe conversion program developed earlier, the latter representation is preferable. An example of this is given below for a conversion of the chocolate chip cookie recipe. Example testing of the Fraction class is shown in Figure 10-17.

```
>>> frac1 = Fraction(5,4)          >>> frac1 = MixedFraction(5,4)
>>> frac1                          >>> frac1
5/4                                1 1/4
>>> frac2 = Fraction(11,4)         >>> frac2 = MixedFraction(11,4)
>>> frac2                          >>> frac2
11/4                               2 3/4
>>> -frac1                         >>> -frac1
-5/4                               -1 1/4
>>> frac1 + frac2                  >>> frac1 + frac2
4/1                                4
>>> frac1 - frac2                  >>> frac1 - frac2
-3/2                               -1 1/2
>>> frac1 * frac2                  >>> frac1 * frac2
55/16                              3 7/16
>>>                                >>>
```

Use of **Fraction** Type   Use of **MixedFraction** Type

FIGURE 10-17   Interactive Testing of the `MixedFraction` Class

The implementation of the `MixedFraction` class is given in Figure 10-18. The `Fraction` class is imported on **line 3** using the `from-import` form of import. This class provides the (special) methods for performing arithmetic and relational operations on fractions. Therefore, the operations

```
1  # MixedFraction Class
2
3  from fraction import *
4
5  class MixedFraction(Fraction):
6
7      def __init__(self, *args):                          Special Methods
8          if len(args) == 2:
9              self.__whole_num = 0
10             Fraction.__init__(self, args[0], args[1])
11         elif len(args) == 3:
12             self.__whole_num = args[0]
13             Fraction.__init__(self, args[1], args[2])
14         else:
15             raise TypeError('MixedFraction takes 2 or 3 arguments ' + \
16                 '(' + str(len(args)) + ' given)')
17
18     def __str__(self):
19         empty_str = ''
20         blank = ' '
21
22         displayFrac = Fraction.copy(self)
23         displayFrac.reduce()
24
25         whole_num = 0
26         numer = displayFrac.getNumerator()
27         denom = displayFrac.getDenominator()
28
29         if numer == 0:
30             return '0'
31
32         if denom == 1:
33             return str(numer)
34
35         if numer < 0:
36             numer = abs(numer)
37             sign = '-'
38         else:
39             sign = empty_str
40
41         if abs(numer) > abs(denom):
42             whole_num = abs(numer) // abs(denom)
43             numer = abs(numer) % abs(denom)
44
45         if whole_num == 0:
46             return sign + str(numer) + '/' + str(denom)
47         else:
48             return sign + str(whole_num) + blank + \
49                     str(numer) + '/' + str(denom)
50
51     def __repr__(self):
52         return self.__str__()
53
```

FIGURE 10-18 MixedFraction Class (*Continued*)

of addition, subtraction, multiplication, and comparison on mixed fractions can be accomplished by the inherited methods of the Fraction class.

The difference between the Fraction class and the MixedFraction class is in how fraction values are displayed. For example, a Fraction object with the value 3/2 is displayed by the

```
54
55                                              Getter and Setter Methods
56      def getWholeNum(self):
57          return self.getNumerator() // self.getDenominator()
58
59
60      def setWholeNum(self, value):
61          self.setNumerator(self.getNumerator() + \
62                             value * self.getDenominator())
63
64      def set(self, whole_num, numer, denom):
65          Fraction.set(self, numer + whole_num * denom, denom)
66
67
68                                       Special Arithmetic Operator Methods
69      def __neg__(self):
70          return MixedFraction(-Fraction.getNumerator(self),
71                                Fraction.getDenominator(self))
72
73      def __sub__(self, rfraction):
74          tempFrac = Fraction.__sub__(self, rfraction)
75
76          return self.__createMixedFraction(tempFrac)
77
78      def __add__(self, rfraction):
79          tempFrac = Fraction.__add__(self, rfraction)
80
81          return self.__createMixedFraction(tempFrac)
82
83
84      def __mul__(self, rfraction):
85          tempFrac = Fraction.__mul__(self, rfraction)
86
87          return self.__createMixedFraction(tempFrac)
88
89      def __createMixedFraction(self, frac):
90          numer = frac.getNumerator()                Private Methods
91          denom = frac.getDenominator()
92
93          return MixedFraction(numer, denom)
94
95
```

FIGURE 10-18 MixedFraction Class

MixedFraction class as 1 1/2. For each object instance, however, the same values are stored—as an integer numerator and integer denominator value, and thus can be operated on the same way.

How fractions are displayed is determined by the implementation of the __str__ special method. In the Fraction class, the numerator and denominator values are simply concatenated with a '/' between them. In the MixedFraction class, however, the fraction value is reconstructed in three parts, a whole number part (possibly 0), and a proper fraction part in which the numerator is less than the denominator. How the fraction is displayed depends on these three values. If, for example, the whole number part is 0, then only a proper fraction is displayed,

0 + 1/2 displayed as 1/2

If the denominator is 1, then only the numerator is displayed,

4/1 displayed as 4

Otherwise, both the whole number part and the associated proper fraction part are displayed,

5/4 displayed as 1 1/4

The implementation of special method __str__ in the MixedFraction class is on **lines 18–49**. Variables empty_str and blank are initialized on **lines 19–20**. These are used in the construction of the mixed-fraction string. On **line 22** a copy is made of the object's value by use of the copy method of the Fraction class. This is so that the value of the fraction can be reduced to its simplest form, in preparation for the conversion of the fraction value to a whole number and proper fraction part. The reduction is performed by the reduce() method inherited from the Fraction class.

Once the (temporary) fraction object is reduced to simplest terms, it can be determined whether there is a whole number part to be displayed as part of the fraction value. This depends on whether the numerator is greater than the denominator. Thus, on **line 25**, variable whole_num is initialized to 0. The numerator and denominator values of the temporary displayFrac object are set to variables numer and denom, respectively (**lines 26–27**). What remains is to determine how the fraction value should be displayed based on these three values. On **line 29**, if variable numer is 0, then the fraction value is also 0; therefore '0' is returned (**line 30**). If the denominator in variable denom is 1, then the fraction value can be displayed as a single integer value (**lines 32–33**).

Next, special method __str__ handles the proper display of negative fractions. For example, $-4/3$ is stored as negative integer value 4 and positive integer value 3. When this value is displayed in mixed fraction form, the negative sign should appear as follows,

$-$ 1 1/3

Thus, on **line 35**, a check is made to determine if the numerator value in numer is negative. If so, then numer is set to its absolute value (**line 36**). This prevents a negative sign with the numerator from being displayed. Because a negative sign will need to appear with the whole number part of the displayed value, variable sign is set the dash character (**line 37**). If, on the other hand, the numerator is found to be nonnegative, then variable sign is set to the empty string (**line 39**).

In addition to checking the sign of the numerator, a check is made to see if the numerator is greater than the denominator (**line 41**). If so, then there needs to be a separate whole number value displayed along with the (proper) fraction value. Thus, if the numerator is found to be greater, then variable whole_num is set to the result of the integer division of the absolute value of the numerator by the absolute value of the denominator (**line 42**). Absolute values are used because the sign of the displayed result has already been determined (stored in variable sign). The numerator is then set to the remaining fractional part by use of the modulo operator (**line 43**). Thus, for 4/3, whole_num is set to 1 (4 // 3), and numer is set to 1 (4 % 3). Finally, if the whole number part of the value is 0, then a string containing only the proper fraction is returned (**line 46**). If not 0, then a string of the form '1 1/3' is constructed and returned (**lines 48–49**).

The remaining part of the MixedFraction class provided the needed getters and setters for mixed fractions (**lines 56–65**). It also provides a set of arithmetic operators and arithmetic methods to replace those inherited from the Fraction class (**lines 69–87**). Finally, private method __createMixedFraction is defined as a private supporting method called by the arithmetic operators in the class.

Self-Test Questions

1. A class is made a subclass of another class by the use of _____.

2. Which of the following contains terms that mean the same thing?
   (a) Parent class, derived class
   (b) Parent class, base class
   (c) Subclass, base class

3. All subclasses are a subtype in object-oriented programming. (TRUE/FALSE)

4. When defining a subclass in Python that is meant to serve as a subtype, the `subtype` Python keyword is used. (TRUE/FALSE)

5. Built-in function `type` can be used to,
   (a) Determine the type of only the built-in types in Python
   (b) Determine the type of only programmer-defined types (classes)
   (c) Determine the type of all types

ANSWERS: 1. inheritance. 2. (b). 3. False. 4. False. 5. (c)

10.4   Polymorphism

Polymorphism is a powerful feature of object-oriented programming languages. It allows for the implementation of elegant software that is well designed and easily modified. We explore the use of polymorphism in this section.

10.4.1   What Is Polymorphism?

The word *polymorphism* derives from Greek meaning "something that takes many forms." In object-oriented programming, **polymorphism** allows objects of different types, each with their own specific behaviors, to be treated as the same general type. For example, consider the Shape class and its subclasses given in Figure 10-19.

All Shape objects have an x, y coordinate (with corresponding getter and setter methods). In addition, Shape objects can also calculate their areas. How a shape's area is computed, however,

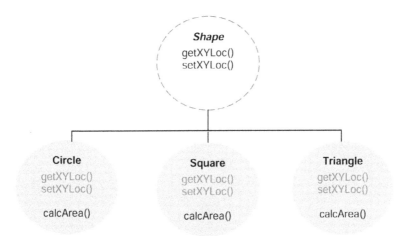

FIGURE 10-19   Polymorphic Shape Class

depends on what shape it is. Thus, it is not possible to define a `calcArea` method in the `Shape` class that serves the purposes of all types of shapes. On the other hand, we want all shape types to have a `calcArea` method. Therefore, we add an *unimplemented* version of the `calcArea` method to the `Shape` class as shown in Figure 10-20.

```
class Shape:

    def __init__(self, x, y):
        self.__x = x
        self.__y = y

    def getXYLoc(self):
        return (self.__x, self.__y)

    def setXYLoc(self, x, y):
        self.__x = x
        self.__y = y

    def calcArea(self):
        raise NotImplementedError("Method calcArea not implemented")
```

FIGURE 10-20   Abstract Shape Class

Subclasses of the `Shape` class must implement the `calcArea` method, otherwise a `NotImplementedError` exception is raised. A class in which one or more methods are unimplemented (or only implemented to raise an exception) is called an **abstract class**. Figure 10-21 gives `Circle`, `Square`, and `Triangle` subclasses of the `Shape` class.

```
class Circle(Shape):

    def __init__(self, x, y, r):
        Shape.__init__(self, x, y)
        self.__radius = r

    def calcArea(self):
        return math.pi * self.__radius ** 2

class Square(Shape):

    def __init__(self, x, y, s):
        Shape.__init__(self, x, y)
        self.__side = s

    def calcArea(self):
        return self.__side ** 2

class Triangle(Shape):

    def __init__(self, x, y, s):
        Shape.__init__(self, x, y)
        self.__side = s

    def calcArea(self):
        return (self.__side ** 2) * math.sqrt(3) / 4.0
```

FIGURE 10-21   Subclasses `Circle`, `Square`, and `Triangle`

Each of the subclasses contains an __init__ method, in which the first two arguments provide the x,y location of the shape (within a graphics window) and the third argument indicates its size. Each first calls the __init__ method of the Shape class with arguments x,y to set its location, since the x,y values are maintained by the Shape class. Note that methods getXYLoc and setXYLoc are not defined in the subclasses, as they are inherited from the Shape class.

The size of each shape is handled differently, however. In the Circle class size is stored as the radius, and in the Square and Triangle classes it is stored as the length of each side. (The Triangle class represents only equilateral triangles, those in which each side is of the same length.) Given these classes, we can now see how polymorphism works in Python.

Suppose that there was a list of Shape objects for which the total area of all shapes combined was to be calculated,

```
shapes_list = (circle1, circle2, square1, triangle1, triangle2)
```

Because each implements the methods of the Shape class, they are all of a common general type, and therefore can be treated in the same way,

```
total_area = 0

for shape in shapes_list:
    total_area = total_area + shape.calcArea()
```

LET'S TRY IT

For the following class definitions, enter and save them in a single Python file, and execute. Then enter the associated instructions within the Python shell and observe the results.

```
class Bird(object):
    def __init__(self, w):
        print('__init__ of Bird Class called')
        self.__weight = w

    def getWeight(self):
        return str(self.__weight) + 'ounces'

    def getColor(self):
        raise NotImplementedError( \
            'Method color not implemented')

class BlueJay(Bird):
    def __init__(self, w):
        Bird.__init__(self, w)

    def getColor(self):
        return 'Blue'

class Cardinal(Bird):
    def __init__(self, w):
        Bird.__init__(self, w)

    def getColor(self):
        return 'Red'

class BlackBird(Bird):
    def __init__(self, w):
        Bird.__init__(self, w)

    def getColor(self):
        return 'Black'
```

```
>>> b1 = BlueJay(1)
???

>>> b2 = Cardinal(1.4)
???

>>> b3 = BlackBird(3.5)
???

>>> b1.getWeight()
???

>>> b2.getWeight()
???

>>> b3.getWeight()
???

>>> b1.getColor()
???

>>> b2.getColor()
???

>>> b3.getColor()
???

>>> b4 = Bird(2.0)
>>> b.getColor()
```

In Python, it is not because `Circle`, `Square`, and `Triangle` are subclasses of the `Shape` class that allows them to be treated in a similar way. It is because the classes are *subtypes* of a common parent class. (Actually, in Python, any set of classes with a common set of methods, even if not subclasses of a common type, can be treated similarly. This kind of typing is called **duck typing—**that is, "if it looks like a duck and quacks like a duck, then it's a duck.")

In object-oriented programming, **polymorphism** allows objects of different types, each with their own specific behaviors, to be treated as the same general type.

10.4.2   The Use of Polymorphism

To fully appreciate the benefits of polymorphism, let's consider the development of a program for manipulating geometric shapes. We consider a graphical environment in which classes `Circle`, `Square`, and `Triangle` do not have a common set of methods, and therefore cannot be treated polymorphically.

We assume that we have a graphics program in which the user selects the geometric shape that they want (stored in variable `selected_shape`) for which the appropriate object type is created:

```
if selected_shape == 1:
    cir = Circle(0, 0, 1)
elif selected_shape == 2:
    sqr = Square(0, 0, 1)
elif selected_shape == 3:
    tri = Triangle(0, 0, 1)
```

Next, the geometric object is displayed. Since each object has its own set of methods, the appropriate method must be called. This is determined by use of another `if` statement:

```
if selected_shape == 1:
    cir.drawCircle()
elif selected_shape == 2:
    sqr.drawSquare()
elif selected_shape == 3:
    tri.drawTriangle()
```

The user may then request that the area of the graphic object be displayed. Since each of the `Circle`, `Square`, and `Triangle` classes have a different method for calculating their area, then an `if` statement must again be used:

```
if selected_shape == 1:
    area = cir.calcCircleArea()
elif selected_shape == 2:
    area = sqr.calcSquareArea()
elif selected_shape == 3:
    area = tri.calcTriangleArea()
```

And when the graphic object is repositioned, an `if` statement is again needed:

```
if selected_shape == 1:
    cir.moveCircle(x, y)
elif selected_shape == 2:
    sqr.moveSquare(x, y)
elif selected_shape == 3:
    tri.moveTriangle(x, y)
```

The design of this program becomes rather tedious and inelegant. If statements abound throughout the program. Let's now look at how the same program can be written with the use of polymorphism. First, we give a more complete `Shape` class in Figure 10-22.

```
class Shape(object):

    def __init__(self, x, y):
        self.__x = x
        self.__y = y

    def getXYLoc(self):
        return (self.__x, self.__y)

    def setXYLoc(self, x, y):
        self.__x = x
        self.__y = y

    def draw(self):
        raise NotImplementedError("Method draw not implemented")

    def calcArea(self):
        raise NotImplementedError("Method calcArea not implemented")

    def resize(self, amt):
        raise NotImplementedError("Method resize not implemented")
```

FIGURE 10-22 Methods of `Circle`, `Square`, and `Triangle` Classes Following Duck Typing

As before, the unimplemented methods of the class raise a `NotImplementedError` exception. In this case, each of the `Circle`, `Square`, and `Triangle` classes are defined as subclasses of the `Shape` class. Therefore, each is required to have methods for the unimplemented methods of the `Shape` class in order to be completely defined.

   We reconsider the implementation of a graphics program for manipulating geometric shapes. We give side-by-side listing of nonpolymorphic vs. polymorphic code in Figure 10-23.

   One benefit of polymorphism, as apparent from the example, is that the program code is much more straightforward and concise. Without polymorphism, there is constant use of if statements that clutters up the code. Another benefit is that it allows the programmer to think at a more abstract level ("this section of code needs to draw *some kind of geometric shape*") without having to keep in mind specific entities such as circles, squares, and triangles ("this section of code needs to draw *either a circle, square, or triangle*").

   The most significant benefit of polymorphism is that programs are much easier to maintain and update. Suppose, for example, that our program had to be updated to also handle rectangles.

Non-Polymorphic Code

```
# Create Appropriate Object

if selected_shape == 1:
    cir = Circle(0, 0, 1)
elif selected_shape == 2:
    sqr = Square(0, 0, 1)
elif selected_shape == 3:
    tri = Triangle(0, 0, 1)


# draw
if selected_shape == 1:
    cir.drawCircle()
elif selected_shape == 2:
    sqr.drawSquare()
elif selected_shape == 3:
    tri.drawTriangle()

# calc area
if selected_shape == 1:
    area = cir.calcCircleArea()
elif selected_shape == 2:
    area = sqr.calcSquareArea()
elif selected_shape == 3:
    area = tri.calcTriangleArea()

# resize
if selected_shape == 1:
    cir.resizeCircle(percentage)
elif selected_shape == 2:
    sqr.resizeSquare(percentage)
elif selected_shape == 3:
    tri.resizeTriangle(percentage)

# reposition
if selected_shape == 1:
    cir.setXY(x, y)
elif selected_shape == 2:
    sqr.setPosition(x, y)
elif selected_shape == 3:
    tri.moveTo(x, y)
```

Polymorphic Code

```
# Create Appropriate Object

if selected_shape == 1:
    fig = Circle(0, 0, 1)
elif selected_shape == 2:
    fig = Square(0, 0, 1)
elif selection_shape == 3:
    fig = Triangle(0, 0, 1)


# draw
fig.draw()

# calc area
area = fig.calcArea()

# resize
fig.resize(selected_percentage)

# reposition
fig.setXYLoc(x, y)
```

For the call to method draw(), the method defined in the specific subclass is the actual method called.

For the call to method calcArea(), the method defined in the specific subclass is the actual method called.

For the call to method resize(), the method defined in the specific subclass is the actual method called.

For the call to method setXYLoc(), there is no method defined in any of the subclasses. Therefore, for each particular shape, the method of the Shape class is the method called.

FIGURE 10-23   Nonpolymorphic vs. Polymorphic Code

How much of the program would need to be changed? Without polymorphism, every if statement for the selection of method calls would need to be updated. With polymorphism, however, only the first if statement that creates the appropriate type object would need to be changed to include a Rectangle type. The rest of the code would remain the same, as shown in Figure 10-24.

In the end, selection needs to occur somewhere—either within the program (in the nonpolymorphic approach), or by the programming language (with the use of polymorphism).

Polymorphism allows the programmer to think at a more abstract level during program development, and supports the development of programs that are easier to maintain and update.

```
# Create Appropriate Object

if selected_shape == 1:
    fig = Circle(0, 0, 1)
elif selected_shape == 2:
    fig = Square(0, 0, 1)
elif selected_shape == 3:
    fig = Triangle(0, 0, 1)
elif selected_shape == 4:
    fig = Rectangle(0, 0, 1)
```

FIGURE 10-24 Updated Polymorphic Code for Incorporating a New `Rectangle` Type

Self-Test Questions

1. The term *polymorphism* in object-oriented programming refers to
   (a) The ability to treat various type objects in a similar way
   (b) The ability to change an object from one type to another type
   (c) The ability to have multiple objects of the same type treated as one

2. The use of duck typing in Python results in
   (a) More restriction on the type values that can be passed to a given method
   (b) Less restriction on the type values that can be passed to a given method

3. The *biggest* reason for the use of polymorphism in a program is
   (a) There is less program code to write
   (b) The program will result in a more elegant design, and thus will be easier to maintain and update
   (c) It allows the programmer to think at a more abstract level

ANSWERS: 1. (a), 2. (b), 3. (b)

10.5 Object-Oriented Design Using UML

We have mainly focused on object-oriented *programming* (OOP). The first step in the development of any object-oriented program, however, is the development of an appropriate **object-oriented design (OOD)**. Next we discuss a specification language for denoting an object-oriented design, referred to as the *Unified Modeling Language*.

10.5.1 What Is UML?

The **Unified Modeling Language (UML)** is a standardized design specification (modeling) language for specifying an object-oriented design. The term "Unified" comes from the fact that the language is a unification of three earlier object-oriented design modeling languages.

  UML is a language-independent, *graphical* specification language. It contains numerous types of graphical diagrams for expressing various aspects of an object-oriented design. One of the most widely used graphical diagrams is called a "class diagram." A class diagram specifies the classes and their relationships of a given object-oriented design. We look at class diagrams in UML next.

> **UML** ("Unified Modeling Language") is a standardized language-independent, graphical modeling language for specifying an object-oriented design.

10.5.2 UML Class Diagrams

In UML, **class diagrams** are used to express the *static* aspects of a design, such as the instance variables and methods of individual classes, their visibility (i.e., public or private), and various relationships between classes. Other UML diagrams, called **interaction diagrams**, are used to represent the sequence of method calls between objects during program execution (the *dynamic* aspect of a design). We omit discussion of interaction diagrams and look at the UML notation for denoting the classes of an object-oriented design.

> **Class diagrams** in UML are used to express the static aspects of an object-oriented design. Other diagrams, called **interaction diagrams**, are used to represent the sequence of method calls between objects during program execution.

The Representation of Classes

A class is denoted in UML in three parts: a class name, a set of class attributes (instance variables), and a set of methods, as given below.

Class Name
instance variables
methods

We give the UML specification for the abstract Shape class and the (concrete) Circle class in Figure 10-25. The names of unimplemented (abstract) methods are denoted in italics.

Initialization methods like __init__ in Python are named create() in UML. The types of attributes (instance variables) and the return type of methods is indicated by :<type name>, for any given type (for example, :Integer). The + and − symbols are used to specify if a given member of a class has either public (+) or private (−) access.

> A class is denoted in UML in three parts: a class name, a set of class attributes (instance variables), and a set of methods.

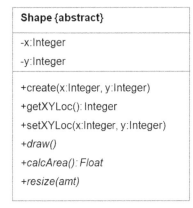

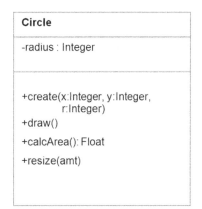

FIGURE 10-25 UML Class Diagrams for `Shape` and `Circle` Classes

Denoting Associations between Classes

Associations are the most common relationship in UML class diagrams. An **association** between two classes indicates that the methods of one class make calls to methods of the other, as shown in Figure 10-26.

FIGURE 10-26 Association in UML

In this example, it is assumed that the classes are part of a graphical design package, in which the `GraphicsWindow` class creates and can manipulate a set of `Shape` objects. (We have left out the details of the `GraphicsWindow` and `Shape` classes in this diagram.)

The numbers above the association ends are referred to as **multiplicity**. The multiplicity of `1` at the `GraphicsWindow` end of the association and `0..*` at the `Shape` end indicates that one `GraphicsWindow` object may be associated with any number of (zero or more) `Shape` objects. The `"creates"` label at the `GraphicsWindow` association end is referred to as a **role name**. Role names are used to describe an association between two classes.

Finally, the arrow denotes **navigability**. It indicates the direction of method calls made. In this example, it shows that a `GraphicsWindow` object makes method calls (sends messages) to `Shape` objects, and not the other way around.

> An **association** between two classes, denoted by a connecting solid line (and a possible arrow-head) indicates that methods of one class call methods of the other.

Denoting Subclass Relationships

Subclasses are indicated in UML by use of a solid line with a closed arrow head from a subclass to its superclass, as shown in Figure 10-27.

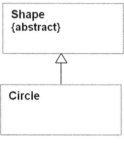

FIGURE 10-27 UML
Subclass Notation

This diagram indicates that the `Circle` class is a subclass of the abstract `Shape` class. (We again have left out the details of both the `Shape` and `Circle` classes.) Note that multiplicity is not used in subclass relationships.

> Subclass relationships in UML are indicated by use of a solid line with a closed arrow head from a subclass to a superclass.

Denoting Composition vs. Aggregation

Composition indicates a "part-of" relationship between classes (Figure 10-28). The containing object is viewed as "owning" the contained object, of which the contained object is an integral part. For example, the `Shape` class is comprised of two integers for holding the x,y location of any `Shape` type. Because these two integer values are used together, we could develop an `XYCoord` class, in which the `Shape` class contains an instance. This is an example of the use of composition.

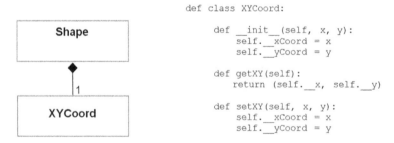

FIGURE 10-28 Composition of Classes in UML

When denoting composition, a filled diamond head is used at the end of the line connected to the containing class (the `Shape` class). With composition, it is implied that the containing class (`Shape`) makes calls to the member class (`XYCoord`), and thus composition also connotes the relationship of association.

We note that, since all values in Python are objects, *every* class with instance variables involves the use of composition, including the `Shape` class. However, the reason to indicate a non-built-in type as composition is that it provides a place to specify the details of the type.

Instance variables of a built-in type can simply be included in the class as primitive types as was done for the x and y instances variables of the Shape class above.

Aggregation, in contrast to composition, is not a part-of relationship. It is used to denote a class that groups together, or aggregates, a set of objects that exists independently of the aggregating class. An example of aggregation is given in Figure 10-29.

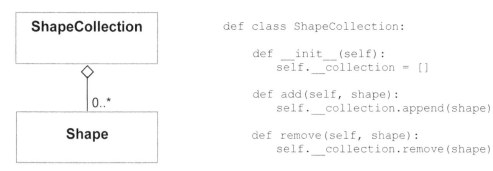

```
def class ShapeCollection:

    def __init__(self):
        self.__collection = []

    def add(self, shape):
        self.__collection.append(shape)

    def remove(self, shape):
        self.__collection.remove(shape)
```

FIGURE 10-29   Aggregation of Classes in UML

Aggregation is denoted by an unfilled diamond head. Here, the ShapeCollection class contains references to an arbitrary number of Shape objects. This might be used, for example, when a graphics window allows the user to select a group of Shape objects on the screen and change an attribute of each, such as their size, all at once.

Composition is a "part of" relationship between classes denoted by a filled diamond head in UML. **Aggregation** is a "grouping" relationship, denoted by an unfilled diamond head.

An Example Class Diagram

Although UML is a specification language for modeling object-oriented software, it can be used to specify any set of entities and their relationships. Modeling everyday concepts and entities can be instructive in understanding UML. Figure 10-30 shows a UML class diagram modeling the concept of a car.

For every car, there is one engine, an integral part of a car. Thus, a composition relationship is denoted between Car and Engine, with a multiplicity of 1 on each end. As with engines, tires are an integral part of a car, so this is also indicated by composition, with a multiplicity of four tires for each passenger car.

A car is still a car with or without a driver. Therefore, a relationship of composition is not appropriate here. There is simply an association between Car and Driver with multiplicity of 0..1 on the driver end of the association. Since a Driver is a Person, a subclass relationship is denoted between the two.

There is an association between Car and Person with a multiplicity of 0..*. Since the association denoted is not so apparent (owner? passenger?), we add the role name Passenger to the Person end of the association to be more explicit. Finally, any number of Drivers may belong to AAA (Automobile Association of America), denoted by the use of aggregation.

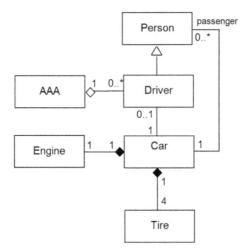

FIGURE 10-30 Passenger Car UML Class Diagram

Self-Test Questions

1. Which of the following is true of UML?
   (a) UML is a specification language for designing Python programs
   (b) UML is a specification language that can be used for designing programs in various programming languages

2. In UML, class diagrams are used to express the _____ aspects of a design, and _____ are used to denote the dynamic aspects

3. In UML, an association between two classes indicates that
   (a) The two classes have a common superclass
   (b) Objects of each of the two class types are created at the same time
   (c) Methods of one of the classes make calls to methods of the other

4. Multiplicity in UML indicates
   (a) How many objects of a given class type exist
   (b) How many objects of one given class there are in relation to another
   (c) How many subclasses of a given class there may be

5. Composition in UML indicates,
   (a) A "part of" relationship
   (b) A grouping of objects

6. Aggregation in UML indicates,
   (a) A "part of" relationship
   (b) A grouping of objects

ANSWERS: 1. (b), 2. static, interaction diagrams, 3. (c), 4. (b), 5. (a), 6. (b)

COMPUTATIONAL PROBLEM SOLVING

10.6   Vehicle Rental Agency Program

In this section, we design, implement, and test a program that will serve the needs of a vehicle rental agency.

10.6.1   The Problem

The problem is to develop an object-oriented design and implementation of a program capable of maintaining reservations for a vehicle rental agency. The agency rents out three types of vehicles—cars, vans, and moving trucks. The program should allow users to check for available vehicles, request rental charges by vehicle type, get the cost of renting a particular type vehicle for a specified period of time, and make/cancel reservations.

10.6.2   Problem Analysis

The program needs an appropriate set of objects for the vehicle rental agency domain. An obvious class to include is a Vehicle class. It can be implemented to maintain information common to all vehicle types. Subclasses of the Vehicle class can maintain information specific to each subtype.

For example, all vehicles have a miles-per-gallon rating and a vehicle identification number (VIN). Thus, this information can be maintained in the Vehicle class. However, there are different make and model cars (with either two or four doors, that hold a specific number of passengers); different make and model vans (able to hold a specific number of passengers); and moving trucks of various lengths, each providing a certain amount of cargo space. Therefore, the Vehicle class is made a superclass of classes Car, Van, and Truck, in which each subclass contains information (instance variables and/or methods) specific to that vehicle type.

For each type vehicle, there is a rental charge based on daily, weekly, and weekend rental rates. There is also a mileage charge and some number of free miles (on select vehicles), plus the cost of optional insurance. Because these costs are associated with particular types, but cost is not inherently *part* of a vehicle's attribute, we include a separate VehicleCost class.

Finally, we incorporate a Reservation class that maintains the information for each reservation made. This will include the customer name, address, credit card number, and the VIN of the vehicle rented.

10.6.3   Program Design

Meeting the Program Requirements

The general requirements for this program are for users to be able to check for the availability of vehicles of a certain type (cars, vans, or trucks); request rental charges by vehicle type; determine the rental cost for a particular vehicle and rental period; and make and cancel reservations. The specific requirements of this program are given in Figure 10-31.

The program must maintain a group of specific model vehicles for the following vehicle categories: cars, vans, and (moving) trucks with the following characteristics:

Cars: make/model, miles-per-gallon, num of passengers, num of doors, VIN
Vans: make/model, miles-per-gallon, number of passengers, VIN
Trucks: miles-per-gallon, length, number of rooms, VIN

The program must be able to display the specific vehicles available for rent by vehicle type.

The program must display the cost associated with a given type vehicle including daily, weekend and weekly rate, insurance cost, mileage charge, and number of free miles. It must also allow the user to determine the cost of a particular vehicle, for a given period of time, an estimated number of miles, and the cost of optional insurance.

The program must be able to allow a particular vehicle to be reserved and cancelled.

FIGURE 10-31   Program Requirements for the Vehicle Rental Agency Program

The specific rental costs for each vehicle type are given in Figure 10-32.

	Daily Rate	Weekly Rate	Weekend Rate	Free Miles Per Day	Per Mile Charge
Car	$24.99	$180.00	$45.00	100	0.15
Van	$35.00	$220.00	$55.00	0	0.20
Truck	$34.95	$425.00	$110.00	25	0.25

FIGURE 10-32   Rental Costs by Vehicle Type

The specific vehicles in stock at the rental agency are shown in Figure 10-33.

Data Description

All the data is stored as string types, converted to a numeric type when needed in a computation (such as the cost of daily insurance).

Algorithmic Approach

The algorithmic methods of the program will consist of simple search (for finding and retrieving the requested vehicle information by the user), updating of information (for marking vehicles as reserved or unreserved), and direct calculation (for calculating the total cost of a rental).

Make/Model	Mileage	Num Passengers	Num Doors	Vehicle #
CARS				
Chevrolet Camaro	30 mpg	4	2	WG8JM5492DY
Chevrolet Camaro	30 mpg	4	2	KH4GM4564GD
Ford Fusion	34 mpg	5	4	AB4FG5689GM
Ford Fusion Hybrid	35 mpg	5	4	GH2KL4278TK
Ford Fusion Hybrid	32 mpg	5	4	KU4EG3245RW
Chevrolet Impala	36 mpg	6	4	QD4PK7394JI
Chevrolet Impala	30 mpg	6	4	RK3BM4256YH

Make/Model	Mileage	Num Passengers	Vehicle #
Vans			
Chrysler Town&Country	25 mpg	7	DK3KG8312UE
Chrysler Town&Country	25 mpg	7	VM9RE2645TD
Chrysler Town&Country	25 mpg	7	WK8BF4287DX
Dodge Caravan	25 mpg	7	QK3FL4278ME
Dodge Caravan	25 mpg	7	KY8EW2053XT
Ford Expedition	20 mpg	8	JK2RT8364HY
Ford Expedition	20 mpg	8	KH4ME4216XW

Make/Model	Mileage	Cargo Space	Vehicle #
Trucks			
Ten-Foot	12 mpg	1 bedroom	EJ5KU2435BC
Ten-Foot	12 mpg	1 bedroom	KF8JP7293EK
Seventeen-Foot	10 mpg	2 bedrooms	KG4DM5472RK
Seventeen-Foot	10 mpg	2 bedrooms	PR8JH4893WQ
Twenty-Four-Foot	8 mpg	4 bedrooms	EP2WR3182QB
Twenty-Four-Foot	8 mpg	4 bedrooms	TY3GH4290EK
Twenty-Four-Foot	8 mpg	4 bedrooms	KU9FL4235RH

FIGURE 10-33 Specific Vehicles of the Vehicle Rental Agency

Overall Program Steps

The overall steps in this program design are given in Figure 10-34.

UML Class Diagram

We give a UML class diagram for the program in Figure 10-35. In addition to the "domain objects" that we have decided on in our analysis, we add a text-based user interface, provided by the RentalAgencyUI class.

Three classes store the information in the system—Vehicle (and its subclasses), VehicleCost, and Reservation. For each of these classes there is a corresponding aggregator class—Vehicles, VehicleCosts, and Reservations—that maintains a collection of the corresponding object type. Each aggregator class has methods for maintaining its collection of objects (for example, addVehicle in the Vehicles class and addVehicleCost in the VehicleCosts class).

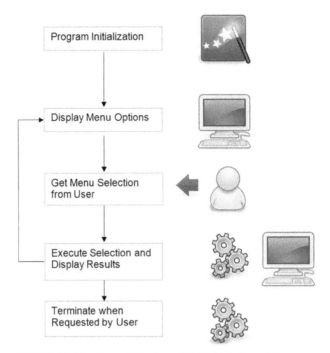

FIGURE 10-34 Overall Design of the Vehicle Rental Agency
Program

The Vehicle class has three subclasses—Car, Van, and Truck. It is responsible for maintaining a vehicle's type, its VIN, and its reservation status. Method getDescription is provided in the Vehicle class to return the information common to all vehicles: miles per gallon, and a VIN. Each subclass builds on this inherited method to include the specific information for that vehicle type. The Car class stores the maximum number of passengers and number of doors, the Van class stores the maximum number of passengers, and the Truck class stores its length and the number of rooms of storage it can hold.

The VehicleCost class does not have any subclasses. Its create (__init__) method is passed six arguments: the daily/weekly/weekend rates, the number of free miles, the per mile charge, and the daily insurance rate to initialize the object with. The getVehicleCost method of the VehicleCosts aggregating class returns the cost of a specified vehicle type as a single string for display. The Reservation and corresponding Reservations aggregator class are designed in a similar manner.

Finally, a SystemInterface class provides all the methods that any user interface would need for interacting with the system. Such a set of methods is referred to as an API—*Application Programming Interface*. Thus, the SystemInterface object is created first. It then reads all the vehicle rental agency data from text files VehiclesStock.txt and RentalCost.txt and populates the corresponding objects. Then, an instance of the RentalAgencyUI is created and initialized with a reference to the system interface. The only public method of the

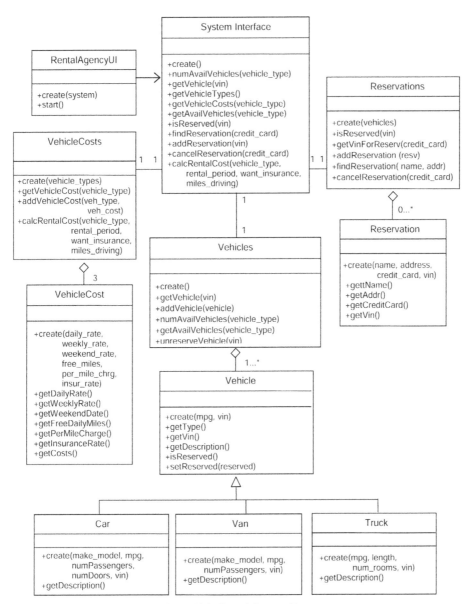

FIGURE 10-35   Class Diagram for Vehicle Rental Agency Program

RentalAgencyUI class, `start`, is called to start the console interaction. The main menu for the program is given in Figure 10-36.

Example use of the system is shown in Figure 10-37. (For the sake of space, the main menu is not repeatedly shown before each selection as in the actual program execution.)

```
<<< MAIN MENU >>>
1 - Display vehicle types
2 - Check rental costs
3 - Check available vehicles
4 - Get cost of specific rental
5 - Make a reservation
6 - Cancel a reservation
7 - Quit

Enter:
```

FIGURE 10-36 Text-Based (Console)
Interface for the Vehicle Rental Agency
Program

Display Vehicle Types

```
*****************************************************
* Welcome to the Friendly Vehicle Rental Agency *
*****************************************************

<<< MAIN MENU >>>
1 - Display vehicle types
2 - Check rental costs
3 - Check available vehicles
4 - Get cost of specific rental
5 - Make a reservation
6 - Cancel a reservation
7 - Quit

Enter: 1
--------------- Types of Vehicles Available for Rent ----------------

1 - Car
2 - Van
3 - Truck
---------------------------------------------------------------------
```

Display Rental Fees for a Given Type Vehicle

```
Enter: 2
Enter type of vehicle
1 - Car
2 - Van
3 - Truck

Enter: 1
--------------------- Rental Charges for Cars ----------------------

                        Free   Per Mile  Daily
Daily  Weekly  Weekend  Miles  Charge    Insurance
24.99  180.00  45.00    100    .15       14.99
---------------------------------------------------------------------
```

Check for Available Vehicles

```
Enter: 3
Enter type of vehicle
1 - Car
2 - Van
3 - Truck

Enter: 1
--------------------------- Available Cars --------------------------
Chevrolet Camaro       passengers: 4   doors: 2   mpg: 30   vin: WG8JM5492DY
Chevrolet Camaro       passengers: 4   doors: 2   mpg: 30   vin: KH4GM4564GD
Ford Fusion            passengers: 5   doors: 4   mpg: 34   vin: AB4FG5689GM
Ford Fusion Hybrid     passengers: 5   doors: 4   mpg: 36   vin: GH2KL4278TK
Ford Fusion Hybrid     passengers: 5   doors: 4   mpg: 36   vin: KU4EG3245RW
Chevrolet Impala       passengers: 6   doors: 4   mpg: 30   vin: QD4PK7394J1
```

Get the Cost of a Particular Rental

```
Enter: 4
Enter type of vehicle
1 - Car
```

FIGURE 10-37 Example Program Execution (*Continued*)

```
2 - Van
3 - Truck
Enter: 1
Enter the rental period:
1 - Daily   2 - Weekly  3 - Weekend

Enter: 1
How many days do you need the vehicle? 3
Would you like the insurance? (y/n): n
Number of miles expect to drive?: 240

-------------------- ESTIMATED Car RENTAL COST ----------------------
* You have opted out of the daily insurance *

Daily rental for 3 days would be $ 74.97

Your cost with an estimated mileage of 240 would be 95.97
which includes 100 free miles and a charge of 0.15 per mile
---------------------------------------------------------------------
```

Reserve a Particular Vehicle

```
Enter: 5

Enter type of vehicle
1 - Car
2 - Van
3 - Truck

Enter: 1
-------------------------- Available Cars -------------------------
1-Chevrolet Camero    passengers: 4    doors: 2    mpg: 30    vin: WG8JM5492DY
2-Chevrolet Camero    passengers: 4    doors: 2    mpg: 30    vin: KH4GM4564GD
3-Ford Fusion         passengers: 4    doors: 4    mpg: 34    vin: AB4FG5689GM
4-Ford Fusion Hybrid  passengers: 5    doors: 4    mpg: 36    vin: GH2KL4278TK
5-Ford Fusion Hybrid  passengers: 5    doors: 4    mpg: 36    vin: KU4EG3245RW
6-Chevrolet Impala    passengers: 6    doors: 4    mpg: 30    vin: QD4PK7394J1
7-Chevrolet Impala    passengers: 6    doors: 4    mpg: 30    vin: RK3BM4256YH

Enter number of vehicle to reserve: 4
Ford Fusion Hybrid   passengers: 5   doors: 4    mpg: 36   vin: GH2KL4278TK

Enter first and last name: John Smith
Enter address: 123 Main Street, Sometown 12345
Enter credit card number: 204881605
* Reservation Made *
```

Cancel a Reservation

```
Enter: 6
Please enter your credit card number: 204881605

RESERVATION INFORMATION
Name: John Smith 123 Main Street, Sometown 21252
Vehicle: Chevrolet Camaro    passengers: 4   doors: 2    mpg: 30   vin: KH4GM4564GD

Confirm Cancellation (y/n): v
* Reservation Cancelled *


Enter: 7
Thank you for using the Friendly Rental Agency
```

FIGURE 10-37   Example Program Execution

10.6.4   Program Implementation and Testing

From the UML specification, we implement and test the program. We start with the implementation of the `Vehicle` class, given in Figure 10-38. The classes will be placed in their own file, and imported into the program.

Development and Testing of the Vehicle, Car, Van, and Truck Classes

In the `Vehicle` class, the `__init__` method (**lines 10–15**) defines the attributes common to each subclass—`mpg`, `vin`, and `reserved`. There is only one setter method, `setReserved`, since the other values are defined when the object is created. Other methods include getters `getType` (**line 17**), `getVin` (**line 22**), `getDescription` (**line 27**), and Boolean `isReserved` (**line 35**).

```
1   """This module provides a Vehicle class. """
2
3   class Vehicle:
4       """The Vehicle class holds the mpg, vin and reserved flag of a vehicle.
5
6          Contains attributes common to all vehicles: mpg, vin, and reserved
7          (Boolean). Provides polymorphic behavior for method getDescription.
8       """
9
10      def __init__(self, mpg, vin):
11          """Initializes a Vehicle object with mpg and vin."""
12
13          self.__mpg = mpg
14          self.__vin = vin
15          self.__reserved = False
16
17      def getType(self):
18          """Returns the type of vehicle (car, van, truck.)"""
19
20          return type(self).__name__
21
22      def getVin(self):
23          """Returns the vin of vehicle."""
24
25          return self.__vin
26
27      def getDescription(self):
28          """Returns general description of car, not specific to type."""
29
30          descript = 'mpg:' + format(self.__mpg, '>3') + '   ' + \
31                     'vin:' + format(self.__vin, '>12')
32
33          return descript
34
35      def isReserved(self):
36          """Returns True if vehicle is reserved, otherwise returns False."""
37
38          return self.__reserved
39
40      def setReserved(self, reserved):
41          """Sets reserved flag of vehicle to provided Boolean value."""
42
43          self.__reserved = reserved
```

FIGURE 10-38 Vehicle Class

The getType methods returns the specific type of a Vehicle object (Car, Van, or Truck) by use of type(self).__name__ which returns its own type.

We can execute the file and interactively and unit test the class in the Python shell.

```
>>> v = Vehicle('32', 'ABC123')      — create instance
>>> v.getType()
'Vehicle'                            — get object type
>>> v.getVin()
'ABC123'                             — get vehicle identification number
```

We test the setReserved and isReserved methods similarily.

An implementation of the `Car` subclass is given in Figure 10-39.

```
1    """This module provides a Car class, a subtype of the Vehicle class."""
2
3    from vehicle import Vehicle
4
5    class Car(Vehicle):
6        """This class is a subtype of the Vehicle class.
7
8            Contains additional attributes of make and model, num of passengers, and
9            num of doors. Supports polymorphic behavior of method getDescription.
10       """
11
12       def __init__(self, make_model, mpg, num_passengers, num_doors, vin):
13           """Initialized with provided parameter values."""
14
15           super().__init__(mpg, vin)
16
17           self.__make_model = make_model
18           self.__num_passengers = num_passengers
19           self.__num_doors = num_doors
20
21       def getDescription(self):
22           """Returns description of car as a formatted string."""
23
24           spacing = '    '
25           descript = format(self.__make_model, '<18') + spacing + \
26                       'passengers: ' + self.__num_passengers + spacing + \
27                       'doors: ' + format(self.__num_doors, '<2') + spacing + \
28                       Vehicle.getDescription(self)
29
30           return descript
```

FIGURE 10-39   `Car` Subclass of the `Vehicle` Class

The `Car` class is defined as a subclass of the `Vehicle` class, imported on **line 3**. The methods inherited from the `Vehicle` class have already been tested. We therefore test method `getDescription` (**lines 21–30**) by executing the `Car` class file and performing the following.

```
>>> v = Car('Ford Fusion', '34', '5', '4', 'AB4FG5689GM')
>>> v.getDescription()
'Ford Fusion    passengers: 5   doors: 4   mpg: 34   vin: AB4FG5689GM'
```

These results are correct. Figure 10-40 and Figure 10-41 show similar implementations of the `Van` and `Truck` classes.

The `Van` and `Truck` classes differ from the `Car` class in the particular instance variables they contain, and the information returned by method `getDescription`. These differences support the polymorphic behavior of `Vehicle` types.

Development and Testing of the Vehicles Class

Whereas the `Vehicle` class represents the information of a single vehicle, the `Vehicles` class maintains a complete collection of `Vehicle` types. Figure 10-42 illustrates an implementation of the `Vehicles` class, maintaining the cost, availability, and reservation status of all vehicles of the rental agency.

```
1    """This module provides a Van class, a subtype of the Vehicle class."""
2
3    from vehicle import Vehicle
4
5    class Van(Vehicle):
6
7        """This class is a subtype of the Vehicle class.
8
9            Contains additional attributes of make and mode, and num of passengers.
10           Supports polymorphic behavior of method getDescription.
11       """
12       def __init__(self, make_model, mpg, num_passengers, vin):
13           """ Initializes with make-model, mpg, num_passengers, vin."""
14
15           super().__init__(mpg, vin)
16
17           self.__make_model = make_model
18           self.__num_passengers = num_passengers
19
20       def getDescription(self):
21           """Returns complete description of van"""
22
23           spacing = '  '
24           descript = format(self.__make_model, '<22') + spacing + \
25                       'passengers:' + format(self.__num_passengers, '>2') + \
26                       spacing + Vehicle.getDescription(self)
27
28           return descript
```

FIGURE 10-40 Van Subclass of the Vehicle Class

```
1    """This module provides a Truck class. a subtype of the Vehicle class."""
2
3    from vehicle import Vehicle
4
5    class Truck(Vehicle):
6
7        """This class is a subtype of the Vehicle class.
8
9            Contains additional attributes length and num of rooms storage capacity.
10           Supports polymorphic behavior of method getDescription.
11       """
12       def __init__(self, mpg, length, num_rooms, vin):
13           """ Initializes with mpg, length, num_rooms, vin."""
14
15           super().__init__(mpg, vin)
16
17           self.__length = length
18           self.__num_rooms = num_rooms
19
20       def getDescription(self):
21           """Returns complete description of truck."""
22
23           spacing = '  '
24           descript = 'length(feet):' + format(self.__length, '>3') + spacing + \
25                       'rooms:' + format(self.__num_rooms, '>2') + spacing + \
26                       Vehicle.getDescription(self)
27
28           return descript
```

FIGURE 10-41 Truck Subclass of the Vehicle Class

```
 1   """Vehicles class module. Raises InvalidFileFormatError and InvalidVinError."""
 2
 3   from vehicle import Vehicle
 4   from car import Car
 5   from van import Van
 6   from truck import Truck
 7
 8   class InvalidVinError(Exception):
 9       """Exception indicating that a provided vin was not found."""
10       pass
11
12
13   class Vehicles:
14       """This class maintains a collection of Vehicle objects."""
15
16       def __init__(self):
17           """Initializes empty list of vehicles."""
18
19           self.__vehicles = []
20
21       def getVehicle(self, vin):
22           """Returns Vehicle for provided vin. Raises InvalidVinError."""
23
24           for vehicle in self.__vehicles:
25               if vehicle.getVin() == vin:
26                   return vehicle
27
28           raise InvalidVinError
29
30       def addVehicle(self, vehicle):
31           """Adds new vehicle to list of vehicles."""
32
33           self.__vehicles.append(vehicle)
34
35       def numAvailVehicles(self, vehicle_type):
36           """Returns number of available vehicles of vehicle_type."""
37
38           return len(self.getAvailVehicles(vehicle_type))
39
40       def getAvailVehicles(self, vehicle_type):
41           """Returns a list of unreserved Vehicles objects of vehicle_type."""
42
43           return [veh for veh in self.__vehicles \
44                   if veh.getType() == vehicle_type and not veh.isReserved()]
45
46       def unreserveVehicle(self, vin):
47           """Sets reservation status of vehicle with vin to unreserved."""
48
49           k = 0
50           found = False
51
52           while not found:
53               if self.__vehicles[k].getVin() == vin:
54                   self.__vehicles[k].setReserved(False)
55                   found = True
```

FIGURE 10-42   Vehicles Class

The Vehicles class imports classes Vehicle, Car, Van, and Truck (**lines 3–6**). An In-validVinError exception class is defined (**lines 8–10**), raised when method getVehicle is called for a nonexistent VIN. Method addVehicle (**lines 30–33**) adds a new vehicle to the collection. This is called when the Vehicles object is initially populated at the start of the program (in the SystemInterface class). Method getAvailVehicles (**lines 40–44**) returns a list of vehicles that are not currently reserved.

We can easily test these classes from the Python shell as given below.

First, the needed classes are imported:

```
>>> from vehicle import Vehicle
>>> from car import Car
>>> from van import Van
>>> from truck import Truck
>>> from vehicles import Vehicles
```

Then, an instance of each type Vehicle is created:

```
>>> veh_1 = Car('Ford Fusion', '34', '5', '4', 'FG1000')
>>> veh_2 = Van('Dodge Caravan', '25', '7', 'TF1000')
>>> veh_3 = Truck('12', '10', '1', 'HG1000')
```

A Vehicles instance is created, and each Vehicle instance is added to the collection:

```
>>> v = Vehicles()
>>> v.addVehicle(veh_1)
>>> v.addVehicle(veh_2)
>>> v.addVehicle(veh_3)
```

Finally, the description of each vehicle is obtained:

```
>>> v.getAvailVehicles('Car')[0].getDescription()
'Ford Fusion          passengers: 5   doors: 4    mpg: 34  vin:    FG1000'
>>> v.getAvailVehicles('Van')[0].getDescription()
'Dodge Caravan          passengers: 7  mpg: 25   vin:      TF1000'
>>> v.getAvailVehicles('Truck')[0].getDescription()
'length(feet):   10    rooms: 1    mpg: 12    vin:      HG1000'
>>>
```

Method getAvailVehicles returns a list of available cars for the provided vehicle type. Since this returns a list of vehicles, the first vehicle in the list is selected (at index [0]), and the getDescription method is called to display the full description of the vehicle. We see that we get the correct results.

Implementation of the VehicleCost and VehicleCosts Classes

The VehicleCosts class is responsible for maintaining and providing the costs for each vehicle type. First, the VehicleCost class is given in Figure 10-43.

```
1    """This module provides a VehicleCost class."""
2
3    class VehicleCost:
4        """This class provides the methods for maintaining rental costs."""
5
6        def __init__(self, daily_rate, weekly_rate, weekend_rate,
7                     free_miles, per_mile_chrg, insur_rate):
8            """Initialzes rental rates, num free miles /mileage chrg/insur rate."""
9
10           self.__daily_rate = daily_rate
11           self.__weekly_rate = weekly_rate
12           self.__weekend_rate = weekend_rate
13           self.__free_miles = free_miles
14           self.__per_mile_chrg = per_mile_chrg
15           self.__insur_rate = insur_rate
16
17       def getDailyRate(self):
18           """Returns daily rental rate of vehicle."""
19
20           return float(self.__daily_rate)
21
22       def getWeeklyRate(self):
23           """Returns weekly rental rate of vehicle."""
24
25           return float(self.__weekly_rate)
26
27       def getWeekendRate(self):
28           """Returns weekend rental rate of vehicle."""
29
30           return float(self.__weekend_rate)
31
32       def getFreeMiles(self):
33           """Returns number of free miles for vehicle rental."""
34
35           return int(self.__free_miles)
36
37       def getPerMileCharge(self):
38           """Returns per mile charge for vehicle rental."""
39
40           return float(self.__per_mile_chrg)
41
42       def getInsuranceRate(self):
43           """Returns daily insurance rate for vehicle."""
44
45           return float(self.__insur_rate)
46
47       def getCosts(self):
48           """Returns a list containing all costs for vehicle."""
49
50           return [self.__daily_rate, self.__weekly_rate,
51                   self.__weekend_rate, self.__free_miles,
52                   self.__per_mile_chrg, self.__insur_rate]
```

FIGURE 10-43   VehicleCost Class

The VehicleCost class, like the Vehicle class, stores information accessed by the provided getter methods. The information to be stored is passed to the __init__ method (**lines 6–15**). The getCosts method (**lines 47–52**) returns all the individual cost components as a list. This method is called when the vehicle costs need to be displayed, or the cost of a particular vehicle rental needs to be determined.

We can easily test the `VehicleCost` class from the Python shell as given below.

First, the VehicleCost class is imported:

```
>>> from vehicleCost import VehicleCost
```

Then, an instance of each type VehicleCost is created:

```
>>> vc = VehicleCost('24.99', '180.00', '45.00', '100', '.15', '14.99')
```

Finally, each getter method is tested:

```
>>> vc.getDailyRate()
24.99
>>> vc.getWeeklyRate()
180.0
>>> vc.getWeekendRate()
45.0
>>> vc.getFreeMiles()
100
>>> vc.getPerMileCharge()
0.15
>>> vc.getInsuranceRate()
14.99
>>> vc.getCosts()
['24.99', '180.00', '45.00', '100', '.15', '14.99']
>>>
```

We see that we get the correct results.

In Figure 10-44, we give the `VehicleCosts` class that maintains the collection of `VehicleCost` objects.

The `vehicleCosts` class, as with the `Vehicles` class, maintains a collection of `VehicleCost` objects. The `VehicleCost` class is imported on **line 3**. On **lines 6–8** three symbolic constants are defined, `DAILY_RENTAL`, `WEEKLY_RENTAL`, and `WEEKEND_RENTAL`. The use of these constants (equal to integer values 1, 2, and 3, respectively) make the program more readable than if the corresponding integer values were used.

The `VehicleCosts` class is defined on **lines 10–89**. The vehicle costs for the three types of vehicles (cars, vans, and trucks) are stored in a dictionary using the vehicle types as key values. The `__init__` method (**lines 13–16**), therefore, initializes instance variable `vehicle_costs` to an empty dictionary. The vehicle costs are individually added to the collection of costs by method `addVehicleCost` (**lines 23–26**), called from the System-Interface class when populating the rental costs from file. Method `getVehicleCost` (**lines 18–21**) returns the costs as a list of individual costs. Finally, method `calcRentalCost` (**lines 28–89**) calculates the cost of a particular rental. We test the `VehicleCosts` class from the Python shell.

```
1    """This module provides a VehicleCosts class"""
2
3    from vehicleCost import VehicleCost
4
5    # symbol constants
6    DAILY_RENTAL = 1
7    WEEKLY_RENTAL = 2
8    WEEKEND_RENTAL = 3
9
10   class VehicleCosts:
11       """This class provides the methods for maintaining rental costs."""
12
13       def __init__(self):
14           """Initializes vehicle costs to empty."""
15
16           self.__vehicle_costs = dict()
17
18       def getVehicleCost(self, vehicle_type):
19           """Returns VehicleCost object for the specified vehicle type."""
20
21           return self.__vehicle_costs[vehicle_type]
22
23       def addVehicleCost(self, veh_type, veh_cost):
24           """Adds a vehicle cost object to dictionary with keyword veh_type."""
25
26           self.__vehicle_costs[veh_type] = veh_cost
27
28       def calcRentalCost(self, vehicle_type, rental_period,
29                          want_insurance, miles_driving):
30           """Returns estimate of rental cost for provided parameter values.
31
32              Returns dictionary with key values: {'base_charges', 'insur_rate',
33              'num_free_miles', 'per_mile_charge', 'estimated_mileage_charges'}
34           """
35
36           # get vehicle cost
37           vehicle_cost = self.getVehicleCost(vehicle_type)
38
39           # calc rental charges
40           rental_time = rental_period[1]
41
42           if rental_period[0] == DAILY_RENTAL:
43               rental_rate = vehicle_cost.getDailyRate()
44               rental_period_value = DAILY_RENTAL
45               rental_period_str = 'daily rental'
46               rental_days = rental_time
47           elif rental_period[0] == WEEKLY_RENTAL:
48               rental_rate = vehicle_cost.getWeeklyRate()
49               rental_period_value = WEEKLY_RENTAL
50               rental_period_str = 'weekly rental'
51               rental_days = rental_time * 7
52           elif rental_period[0] == WEEKEND_RENTAL:
53               rental_rate = vehicle_cost.getWeekendRate()
54               rental_period_value = WEEKEND_RENTAL
55               rental_period_str = 'weekend rental'
56               rental_days = 2
57
```

FIGURE 10-44   VehicleCosts Class (*Continued*)

```
58          elif rental_period[0] == WEEKEND_RENTAL:
59
60              rental_rate = vehicle_cost.getWeekendRate()
61              rental_period_value = WEEKEND_RENTAL
62              rental_period_str = 'weekend rental'
63              rental_days = 2
64
65          # get free miles, per mile charge and insurance rate
66          num_free_miles = vehicle_cost.getFreeMiles()
67          per_mile_charge = vehicle_cost.getPerMileCharge()
68          insurance_rate = vehicle_cost.getInsuranceRate()
69
70          # calc rental charge for selected rental period
71          if not want_insurance:
72              insurance_rate = 0
73
74          # calc base rental charges
75          base_rental_charges = rental_days * rental_rate + \
76                                rental_days * insurance_rate
77
78          miles_charged = miles_driving - num_free_miles
79
80          if miles_charged < 0:
81              miles_charged = 0
82
83          estimated_mileage_charges = miles_charged * per_mile_charge
84
85          return {'base_charges' : base_rental_charges,
86                  'insur_rate' : insurance_rate,
87                  'num_free_miles' : num_free_miles,
88                  'per_mile_charge' : per_mile_charge,
89                  'estimated_mileage_charges' : estimated_mileage_charges}
```

FIGURE 10-44 VehicleCosts Class

First, the VehicleCosts class is imported:

```
>>> from vehicleCosts import VehicleCosts
```

Then, instances of type VehicleCost are created:

```
>>> vc_1 = VehicleCost('24.99', '180.00', '45.00', '100', '.15', '14.99')
>>> vc_2 = VehicleCost('35.00', '220.00', '55.00', '0', '.20', '14.99')
>>> vc_3 = VehicleCost('55.00', '425.00', '110.00', '25', '.25', '24.99')
```

Then a VehicleCosts instance is created, and each VehicleCost instance is added to the collection:

```
>>> vc.addVehicleCost('Car', vc_1)
>>> vc.addVehicleCost('Van', vc_2)
>>> vc.addVehicleCost('Truck', vc_3)
```

Then, each getter method is tested:

```
>>> vc.getVehicleCost('Car').getCosts()
['24.99', '180.00', '45.00', '100', '.15', '14.99']
>>> vc.getVehicleCost('Van').getCosts()
['35.00', '220.00', '55.00', '0', '.20', '14.99']
>>> vc.getVehicleCost('Truck').getCosts()
['55.00', '425.00', '110.00', '25', '.25', '24.99']
```

Finally, method `calcRentalCost` is tested:

```
>>> vc.calcRentalCost('Car', (1, 3), False, 150)
{'insur_rate': 0, 'base_charges': 74.97, 'num_free_miles': 100,
'per_mile_charge': 0.15, 'estimated_mileage_charges': 7.5}
```

In the call to `calcRentalCost`, recall that the first parameter is the vehicle type, the second is the rental period (1 for DAILY_RENTAL) and the number of days (3), the third indicates if the insurance is desired, and the fourth is the expected number of miles to be driven.

We see that we get the correct results. We next give the implementation of the `Reservation` and `Reservations` classes.

Implementation of the Reservation and Reservations Classes

The remaining aggregating class in the program is the `Reservations` class. We first give the `Reservation` class in Figure 10-45.

The `Reservation` class maintains the information for a given reservation. The `__init__` method (**lines 6–14**) is provided a name, address, credit card number, and VIN when a new `Reservation` object is created, with a getter methods provided for each of these four values. We omit the testing of this class and next give the implementation of the corresponding `Reservations` class in Figure 10-46.

```
1    """This module contains a Reservation class for storing details of a rental"""
2
3    class Reservation:
4        """This class provides the methods for maintaining reservations info."""
5
6        def __init__(self, name, address, credit_card, vin):
7            """Initialzes a Reservation object with name, address, credit_card
8               and vin.
9            """
10
11           self.__name = name
12           self.__address = address
13           self.__credit_card = credit_card
14           self.__vin = vin
15
16       def getName(self):
17           """Returns first and last name for reservation."""
18
19           return self.__name
20
21       def getAddress(self):
22           """Returns address for reservation."""
23
24           return self.__address
25
26       def getCreditCard(self):
27           """Returns credit card on reservation."""
28
29           return self.__credit_card
30
31       def getVin(self):
32           """Returns vehicle identification number on reservation."""
33
34           return self.__vin
```

FIGURE 10-45 Reservation Class

```
1   """This module provides a Reservations class."""
2
3   from reservation import Reservation
4
5   class Reservations:
6       """This class provides the methods for maintaing rental reservations."""
7
8       def __init__(self):
9           """Initializes empty collection of reservations."""
10
11          self.__reservations = dict()
12
13      def isReserved(self, vin):
14          """Returns True if reservation for vin, else returns False."""
15
16          return vin in self.__reservations
17
18      def getVinForReserv(self, credit_card):
19          """Returns vin of vehicles reserved with credit_card."""
20
21          return self.__reservations[credit_card].getVin()
22
23      def addReservation(self, resv):
24          """Adds new reservation."""
25
26          self.__reservations[resv.getCreditCard()] = resv
27
28      def findReservation(self, credit_card):
29          """Returns True if reservation for credit_card, else returns False."""
30
31          return credit_card in self.__reservations
32
33      def cancelReservation(self, credit_card):
34          """Deletes reservation matching provided credit card number."""
35
36          del(self.__reservations[credit_card])
```

FIGURE 10-46   Reservations Class

The Reservation class is imported on **line 3**. The __init__ method initializes an empty dictionary for storing the reservations, with credit card numbers serving as the key values. The remaining methods of the class include method isReserved (**lines 13–16**), getVinForReserv (**lines 18–21**), addReservation (**lines 23–26**), findReservation (**lines 28–31**), and Cancel-Reservation (**lines 33–36**). We omit the testing of the Reservations class. We finally look at the implementation of the SystemInterface and RentalAgencyUI classes.

Implementation of the SystemInterface and RentalAgencyUI Classes

An implementation of the SystemInterface class is given in Figure 10-47.

The docstring for the module specifies the formatting of the files storing the vehicle and vehicle rental cost information. There is one exception raised by the module to inform the user interface when a file error has occurred. This could be due to either a file not being found, or an improperly formatted file.

The import statements on **lines 28–30** import most of the classes in the system. Symbolic constants VEHICLE_TYPES, VEHICLE_FILENAME, and VEHICLE_COSTS_FILENAME are defined (**lines 33–35**). Defining these constants makes the program more readable and modifiable.

Exception class `InvalidFileFormatError` is defined (**lines 39–49**) and used within the `SystemInterface` class. Having this exception type allows typical I/O errors (such as a file not found error) to be reported as errors specific to the file formatting requirements of the program. The exception class defines special method `__str__` to enable information to be displayed specific to the error (that is, which file header was expected and not found, in which file).

The `__init__` method (**lines 55–77**) first creates instances of the three aggregator classes of the system—`Vehicles`, `VehicleCosts`, and `Reservations`. Each is initially empty when created. The rest of the `__init__` method consists of a try block that attempts to open and read the files defined by `VEHICLES_FILENAME` and `VEHICLE_COSTS_FILENAME`. If opened successfully,

```
1   """This module provides a SystemInterface class for the Vehicle Rental Program.
2
3       Vehicles File Format
4       --------------------
5       The format for the vehicles file contains comma-separated values with the
6       indicated header lines for cars, vans, and trucks.
7
8         #CARS#
9         make-model, mpg, num-passengers, vin
10        .
11        #VANS#
12        make-model, mpg, num passengers, vin
13        .
14        #TRUCKS#
15        mpg, length, num rooms, vin
16        .
17
18
19      Vehicle Cost File Format
20      -----------------------
21      The format for the rental costs file includes a header line, followed
22      by three lines of comma-separated values for cars, vans and trucks.
23
24        daily, weekly, weekend, free miles, mileage charge, insurance
25
26      The following exceptions are raised: IOError.
27   """
28   from vehicles import Vehicles, Car, Van, Truck
29   from vehicleCosts import VehicleCost, VehicleCosts
30   from reservations import Reservations
31
32   # symbolic constants
33   VEHICLE_TYPES = ('Car', 'Van', 'Truck')
34   VEHICLES_FILENAME = 'VehiclesStock.txt'
35   VEHICLE_COSTS_FILENAME = 'RentalCost.txt'
36
37   # exception class
38
39   class InvalidFileFormatError(Exception):
40       """Exception indicating invalid file in file_name."""
41
42       def __init__(self, header, file_name):
43           self.__header = header
44           self.__file_name = file_name
45
46       def __str__(self):
47
48           return 'FILE FORMAT ERROR: File header ' + self.__header + \
49                   ' expected in file ' + self.__file_name
50
```

FIGURE 10-47 `SystemInterface` Class (*Continued*)

```
51  class SystemInterface:
52      """This class provides the system interface of the vehicle rental
53          system.
54      """
55      def __init__(self):
56          """Populates vehicles and rental costs from file. Raises IOError."""
57
58          self.__vehicles = Vehicles()
59          self.__vehicle_costs = VehicleCosts()
60          self.__reservations = Reservations()
61          self.__vehicle_info_file = None
62
63          try:
64              self.__vehicle_info_file = open(VEHICLES_FILENAME, 'r')
65              self.__rental_cost_file = open(VEHICLE_COSTS_FILENAME, 'r')
66
67              self.__populateVehicles(self.__vehicle_info_file)
68              self.__populateCosts(self.__rental_cost_file)
69          except InvalidFileFormatError as e:
70              print(e)
71              raise IOError
72          except IOError:
73              if self.__vehicle_info_file == None:
74                  print('FILE NOT FOUND:', VEHICLES_FILENAME)
75              else:
76                  print('FILE NOT FOUND:', VEHICLE_COSTS_FILENAME)
77              raise IOError
78
79      def numAvailVehicles(self, vehicle_type):
80          """Returns the number of available vehiles. Returns 0 if no
81              no vehicles available.
82          """
83
84          return self.__vehicles.numAvailVehicles(vehicle_type)
85
86      def getVehicle(self, vin):
87          """Returns Vehicle type for given vin."""
88
89          return self.__vehicles.getVehicle(vin)
90
91      def getVehicleTypes(self):
92          """Returns all vehicle types as a tuple of strings."""
93
94          return VEHICLE_TYPES
95
96      def getVehicleCosts(self, vehicle_type):
97          """Returns vehicle costs for provided vehicle type as a list.
98
99              List of form [daily rate, weekly rate, weekend rate,
100                             num free miles, per mile charge, insur rate]
101          """
102
103          return self.__vehicle_costs.getVehicleCost(vehicle_type).getCosts()
104
```

FIGURE 10-47 SystemInterface Class (*Continued*)

then each is read to populate the corresponding object. The exception handler catches two types of exceptions, InvalidFileFormatError and IOERROR, as mentioned.

A set of getter methods is provided (**lines 86–103**) for retrieving vehicle, vehicle type, and vehicle cost information. Method getAvailVehicles returns the list of vehicles that are not currently reserved. (Note that the list returned is constructed by the use of a list comprehension.) The list of unreserved vehicles is of a specified type. Four additional methods are provided (**lines 113–132**) for maintaining reservation information (isReserved, findReservation,

```
107    def getAvailVehicles(self, vehicle_type):
108        """Returns a list of descriptions of unreserved vehicles."""
109
110        avail_vehicles = self.__vehicles.getAvailVehicles(vehicle_type)
111        return [veh for veh in avail_vehicles]
112
113    def isReserved(self, vin):
114
115        return self.__reservations.isReserved(vin)
116
117    def findReservation(self, credit_card):
118
119        return self.__reservations.findReservation(credit_card)
120
121    def addReservation(self, resv):
122        """Creates reservation and marks vehicles as reserved."""
123
124        self.__reservations.addReservation(resv)
125
126    def cancelReservation(self, credit_card):
127        """Cancels reservation made with provided credit card."""
128
129        vin = self.__reservations.getVinForReserv(credit_card)
130
131        self.__vehicles.unreserveVehicle(vin)
132        self.__reservations.cancelReservation(credit_card)
133
134    def calcRentalCost(self, vehicle_type, rental_period,
135                       want_insurance, miles_driving):
136        """Returns estimate of rental cost for provided parameter values.
137
138           Returns dictionary with key values: {'base_charges', 'insur_rate',
139           'num_free_miles', 'per_mile_charge', 'estimated_mileage_charges'}
140        """
141
142        return self.__vehicle_costs.calcRentalCost(vehicle_type, rental_period,
143                                                   want_insurance, miles_driving)
144
145    # ---- Private Methods
146
147    def __populateVehicles(self, vehicle_file):
148        """Gets vehicles from vehicle_file. Raises InvalidFileFormatError."""
149
150        empty_str = ''
151
152        # init vehicle string file headers
153        vehicle_file_headers = ('#CARS#', '#VANS#', '#TRUCKS#')
154        vehicle_type_index = 0
155
156        # read first line of file (#CARS# expected)
157        vehicle_str = vehicle_file.readline()
158        vehicle_info = vehicle_str.rstrip().split(',')
159        file_header_found = vehicle_info[0]
160        expected_header = vehicle_file_headers[0]
161
```

FIGURE 10-47   SystemInterface Class (*Continued*)

addReservation, and cancelReservation). Finally, method calcRentalCost (**lines 134–143**) returns the calculated rental charges for a given vehicle type, rental period, insurance option, and expected miles driven.

The remainder of the class consists of private supporting methods. Private method populateVehicles reads the information given by VEHICLES_FILENAME and populates the Vehicles instance. Private method populateCosts reads the information given by VEHICLE_COSTS_FILENAME and populates the VehicleCosts instance.

```
164        if file_header_found != expected_header:
165            raise InvalidFileFormatError(expected_header, VEHICLES_FILENAME)
166        else:
167            # read next line of file after #CARS# header line
168            vehicle_str = vehicle_file.readline()
169
170            while vehicle_str != empty_str:
171
172                # convert comma-separated string into list of strings
173                vehicle_info = vehicle_str.rstrip().split(',')
174
175                if vehicle_info[0][0] == '#':
176                    vehicle_type_index = vehicle_type_index + 1
177                    file_header_found = vehicle_info[0]
178                    expected_header = vehicle_file_headers[vehicle_type_index]
179
180                    if file_header_found != expected_header:
181                        raise InvalidFileFormatError(expected_header,
182                                                     VEHICLES_FILENAME)
183                else:
184
185                    # create new vehicle object of the proper type
186                    if file_header_found == '#CARS#':
187                        vehicle = Car(*vehicle_info)
188                    elif file_header_found == '#VANS#':
189                        vehicle = Van(*vehicle_info)
190                    elif file_header_found == '#TRUCKS#':
191                        vehicle = Truck(*vehicle_info)
192
193                    # add new vehicle to vehicles list
194                    self.__vehicles.addVehicle(vehicle)
195
196                # read next line of vehicle information
197                vehicle_str = vehicle_file.readline()
198
199    def __populateCosts(self, cost_file):
200        """Populates RentalCost objects from provided file object."""
201
202        # skip file header / read first line of file
203        cost_file.readline()
204        cost_str = cost_file.readline()
205
206        for veh_type in VEHICLE_TYPES:
207            # strip off newline (last) character and split into list
208            cost_info = cost_str.rstrip().split(',')
209
210            for cost_item in cost_info:
211                cost_item = cost_item.strip()
212
213            # add Vehicle Type/Rental Cost key/value to dictionary
214            self.__vehicle_costs.addVehicleCost(veh_type,
215                                                VehicleCost(*cost_info))
216
217            # read next line of vehicle costs
218            cost_str = cost_file.readline()
```

FIGURE 10-47 `SystemInterface` Class

We next look at the implementation of the final class, the `RentalAgencyUI`, given in Figure 10-48.

Any user interface for the rental agency system must access it through the system interface. Thus, the `__init__` method (**lines 14–16**) of the `RentalAgencyUI` class is passed a reference to the system interface to store (in a private variable) providing it access to the system. The only

```
 1  """
 2      This module provides class RentalAgencyUI, a console user interface.
 3
 4      Method start begins execution of the interface. Raises IOError exception.
 5  """
 6  from systemInterface import VEHICLE_TYPES
 7  from vehicles import InvalidVinError
 8  from vehicleCosts import DAILY_RENTAL, WEEKLY_RENTAL, WEEKEND_RENTAL
 9  from reservations import Reservation
10
11  class RentalAgencyUI:
12      """This class provides a console interface for the rental agency system."""
13
14      def __init__(self, sys):
15          """Stores the provided reference to the vehicle rental system."""
16          self.__sys = sys
17
18      def start(self):
19          """Begins the command loop."""
20
21          self.__displayWelcomeScreen()
22          self.__displayMenu()
23
24          selection = self.__getSelection(7)
25
26          while selection != 7:
27              self.__executeCmd(selection)
28              self.__displayMenu()
29              selection = self.__getSelection(7)
30
31          print('Thank you for using the Friendly Rental Agency')
32
33
34      # Private Methods
35
36      def __displayWelcomeScreen(self):
37          """PRIVATE: Displays welcome message and general instructions."""
38
39          print('*********************************************************')
40          print('  * Welcome to the Friendly Vehicle Rental Agency *')
41          print('*********************************************************')
42
43      def __displayMenu(self):
44          """PRIVATE: Displays a list of menu options on the screen."""
45
46          print('\n<<< MAIN MENU >>>')
47          print('1 - Display vehicle types')
48          print('2 - Check rental costs')
49          print('3 - Check available vehicles')
50          print('4 - Get cost of specific rental')
51          print('5 - Make a reservation')
52          print('6 - Cancel a reservation')
53          print('7 - Quit\n')
54
```

FIGURE 10-48   RentalAgencyUI Class (*Continued*)

other public method of the class is method `start` (**lines 18–31**). This method begins the command loop when called—that is, the repeated action of displaying the main menu, getting the user's selection, and executing the selected command. The loop continues until a value of 7 (to quit the program) is entered. The rest of the methods of the class are private methods in support of the execution of commands in the `start` method.

```
55      def __getSelection(self, num_selections, prompt='Enter: '):
56          """PRIVATE: Returns user-entered value in range 1-num_selections."""
57
58          valid_input = False
59
60          selection = input(prompt)
61
62          while not valid_input:
63              try:
64                  selection = int(selection)
65
66                  if selection < 1 or selection > num_selections:
67                      print('* Invalid Entry*\n')
68                      selection = input(prompt)
69                  else:
70                      valid_input = True
71              except ValueError:
72                  selection = input(prompt)
73
74          return selection
75
76      def __displayDivLine(self, title = ''):
77          """PRIVATE: Displays line of dashes, with optional title."""
78
79          if len(title) != 0:
80              title = ' ' + title + ' '
81          print(title.center(70,'-'))
82
83      def __executeCmd(self, selection):
84          """PRIVATE: Executes command for provided menu selection."""
85
86          if selection == 1:
87              self.__CMD_DisplayVehicleTypes()
88          elif selection == 2:
89              self.__CMD_DisplayVehicleCosts()
90          elif selection == 3:
91              self.__CMD_PromptAndDisplayAvailVehicles()
92          elif selection == 4:
93              self.__CMD_DisplaySpecificRentalCost()
94          elif selection == 5:
95              self.__CMD_MakeReservation()
96          elif selection == 6:
97              self.__CMD_CancelReservation()
98
99      def __CMD_DisplayVehicleTypes(self):
100         """PRIVATE: Displays vehicle types (Cars, Vans, Trucks)."""
101
102         self.__displayDivLine('Types of Vehicles Available for Rent')
103         self.__displayVehicleTypes()
104         self.__displayDivLine()
105
```

FIGURE 10-48 RentalAgencyUI Class (*Continued*)

The methods provided by the system interface correspond to the user options given in the main menu in the user interface (as shown in Figure 10-49).

Private method displayWelcomeScreen (**lines 36–41**) provides the welcome message of the program. Private method displayMenu (**lines 43–53**) is repeatedly called to redisplay the users' options before each next command. Private method getSelection is called whenever the user is to enter a number within a provided range, such as in the main menu. Such selection occurs in other places in the program as well. Therefore, the method is designed to be passed an argument indicating the upper limit of the range of selections. (For example, for the selection of

```
106   def __CMD_DisplayVehicleCosts(self):
107       """PRIVATE: Displays rental costs for Cars, Vans, Trucks."""
108
109        empty_str = ''
110       blank_char = ' '
111
112       # get vehicle type from user
113       self.__displayVehicleTypes()
114       vehicle_type_num = self.__getSelection(len(VEHICLE_TYPES))
115       vehicle_type = VEHICLE_TYPES[vehicle_type_num - 1]
116
117       # set column headings
118       row1_colheadings = blank_char * 24 + format('Free', '7') + \
119               format('Per Mile', '10') + format('Insurance', '17')
120
121       row2_colheadings = format('Daily', '7') + format('Weekly', '8') + \
122               format('Weekend', '9') + format('Miles', '7') + \
123               format('Charge', '10') + format('(per day)', '17')
124
125       # get vehicle costs
126       costs = self.__sys.getVehicleCosts(vehicle_type)
127
128       # build costs line to display
129       costs_str = empty_str
130
131       field_widths = ('7', '8', '9', '7', '10', '17')
132       for k in range(0, len(costs)):
133           costs_str = costs_str + format(costs[k],'<' + field_widths[k])
134
135       # display headings and costs line
136       self.__displayDivLine('Rental Charges for ' + vehicle_type + 's')
137       print()
138       print(row1_colheadings + '\n' + row2_colheadings + '\n' + costs_str)
139       self.__displayDivLine()
140
141   def __CMD_DisplayAvailVehicles(self, vehicle_type, numbered=False):
142       """PRIVATE: Displays unreserved vehicles of selected type.
143          When default argument is True, lists vehicles with sequential
144          numbers at the start of the line of each vehicle description.
145       """
146
147       avail_vehicles_list = self.__sys.getAvailVehicles(vehicle_type)
148       self.__displayDivLine('Available ' + vehicle_type + 's')
149
150       if avail_vehicles_list == []:
151           print('* No Vehicles Available of this Type *')
152       elif numbered:
153           k = 1
154           for veh in avail_vehicles_list:
155               print(str(k) + '-' + veh.getDescription())
156               k = k + 1
157       else:
158           for veh in avail_vehicles_list:
159               print(veh.getDescription())
160
```

FIGURE 10-48 RentalAgencyUI Class (*Continued*)

items from the main menu, getSelection would be passed the value 7.) Two types of errors are checked by the method. One is if a value is outside of the allowable range. The other checks for invalid type of input (such as entering a letter instead of a number). The method requires that an appropriate value be entered by the user before returning.

```
161      def __CMD_PromptAndDisplayAvailVehicles(self):
162          """PRIVATE: Prompts user for vehicle type, and displays all
163              available vehicles of that type.
164          """
165
166          self.__displayVehicleTypes()
167          vehicle_type_num = self.__getSelection(len(VEHICLE_TYPES))
168          vehicle_type = VEHICLE_TYPES[vehicle_type_num - 1]
169          self.__CMD_DisplayAvailVehicles(vehicle_type)
170
171      def __CMD_DisplaySpecificRentalCost(self):
172          """PRIVATE: Prompts user for selections and displays rental cost."""
173
174          # get vehicle type and rental period from user
175          self.__displayVehicleTypes()
176          vehicle_type_num = self.__getSelection(len(VEHICLE_TYPES))
177          vehicle_type = VEHICLE_TYPES[vehicle_type_num - 1]
178
179          # assign tuple, e.g. ('DAILY_RENTAL', '4')
180          rental_period = self.__getRentalPeriod()
181
182          # prompt user for optional insurance
183          want_insurance = input('Would you like the insurance? (y/n): ')
184
185          while want_insurance not in ('y', 'Y', 'n', 'N'):
186              want_insurance = input('Would you like the insurance? (y/n): ')
187
188          # convert to Boolean value
189          want_insurance = want_insurance in ('y', 'Y')
190
191          # prompt user for num of miles expected to drive
192          print('\nNumber of miles expect to drive?')
193          num_miles = self.__getSelection(1000, prompt = 'Miles: ')
194
195          # calc base rental cost
196          rental_cost = self.__sys.calcRentalCost(vehicle_type, rental_period,
197                                              want_insurance, num_miles)
198          # display estimated rental cost
199          print()
200          self.__displayDivLine('ESTIMATED ' + vehicle_type + ' RENTAL COST')
201
202          if want_insurance:
203              print('Insurance rate of', rental_cost['insur_rate'], 'per day')
204          else:
205              print('* You have opted out of insurance coverage *')
206
207          if rental_period[0] == DAILY_RENTAL:
208              print('\nDaily rental for', rental_period[1],
209                  'days would be $', format(rental_cost['base_charges'], '.2f'))
210          elif rental_period[0] == WEEKLY_RENTAL:
211              print('\nWeekly rental for', rental_period[1],
212                  'weeks would be $', format(rental_cost['base_charges'], '.2f'))
213          elif rental_period[0] == WEEKEND_RENTAL:
214              print('\nWeekend rental is $', rental_cost['base_charges'])
215
216          est_total_cost = rental_cost['base_charges'] + \
217                          rental_cost['estimated_mileage_charges']
218
219          print('\nYour cost with an estimated mileage of',
220              num_miles, 'miles would be', format(est_total_cost, '.2f'))
221
222          print('which includes', rental_cost['num_free_miles'],
223              'free miles and a charge of',
224              format(rental_cost['per_mile_charge'], '.2f' ), 'per mile')
225
226          self.__displayDivLine()
```

FIGURE 10-48 RentalAgencyUI Class (*Continued*)

```
227    def __CMD_MakeReservation(self):
228        """PRIVATE: Prompts user for vehicle vin and reserves vehicle."""
229
230        # get vehicle type
231        self.__displayVehicleTypes()
232        vehicle_type_num = self.__getSelection(len(VEHICLE_TYPES))
233        vehicle_type = VEHICLE_TYPES[vehicle_type_num - 1]
234
235        if self.__sys.numAvailVehicles(vehicle_type) == 0:
236            print('Sorry - No available', \
237                  VEHICLE_TYPES[vehicle_type_num - 1] + 's', 'at the moment')
238        else:
239            self.__CMD_DisplayAvailVehicles(vehicle_type, numbered=True)
240            avail_vehicles = self.__sys.getAvailVehicles(vehicle_type)
241
242            valid_input = False
243
244            while not valid_input:
245                selected = input('\nEnter number of vehicle to reserve: ')
246
247                if not selected.isdigit():
248                    print('Please enter the number preceeding the vehicle')
249                elif int(selected) < 1 or \
250                     int(selected) > self.__sys.numAvailVehicles(vehicle_type):
251                    print('\nINVALID SELECTION - Please re-enter: ')
252                else:
253                    valid_input = True
254
255            vin = avail_vehicles[int(selected) - 1].getVin()
256            vehicle = self.__sys.getVehicle(vin)
257            print(vehicle.getDescription())
258
259            vehicle.setReserved(True)
260
261            name = input('\nEnter first and last name: ')
262            addr = input('Enter address: ')
263            credit_card = input('Enter credit card number: ')
264
265            reserv = Reservation(name, addr, credit_card, vin)
266            self.__sys.addReservation(reserv)
267            print('* Reservation Made *')
268
269    def __CMD_CancelReservation(self):
270        """PRIVATE: Prompts user for credit card and cancels reservation."""
271
272        credit_card = input('Please enter your credit card number: ')
273
274        if self.__sys.findReservation(credit_card):
275            print('Calling cancelReservation of sys')  # **************
276            self.__sys.cancelReservation(credit_card)
277            print('** RESERVATION CANCELLED **')
278        else:
279            print('* Reservation not Found - Invalid Credit Card Entered *')
280
```

FIGURE 10-48   RentalAgencyUI Class (*Continued*)

Method displayDivLine is called to display a row of dashes. It has a default parameter title.
Thus, the method may be called with or without a supplied argument. If an argument is not supplied,
then a complete row of dashes is displayed. If a title is displayed, it is centered within the displayed
line of dashes as given below:

```
-----------------Types of Vehicles Available for Rent-----------------
```

```
281   def __displayVehicleTypes(self):
282       """PRIVATE: Displays the numbered selection of vehicle types."""
283
284       print('\nEnter type of vehicle')
285       vehicle_types = self.__sys.getVehicleTypes()
286
287       k = 1
288
289       for veh_type in vehicle_types:
290           print(k, '-', veh_type)
291           k = k + 1
292
293       print()
```

```
295   def __getRentalPeriod(self):
296       """PRIVATE: Prompts user for desired rental period.
297
298       Returns tuple of the form (x, n), where x is one of DAILY_RENTAL,
299       WEEKLY_RENTAL or WEEKEND_RENTAL, and n is the number of those units,
300       e.g. (DAILY_RENTAL, 3) three days of a daily rental.
301       """
302       print('\nEnter the rental period:')
303       print(DAILY_RENTAL, '- Daily ', WEEKLY_RENTAL, '- Weekly ',
304           WEEKEND_RENTAL, '- Weekend\n')
305
306       valid_input = False
307
308       while not valid_input:
309           try:
310               selection = int(input('Enter: '))
311
312               while selection not in (DAILY_RENTAL, WEEKLY_RENTAL,
313                                       WEEKEND_RENTAL):
314
315                   print('* Incorrect entry. Please Re-enter *\n')
316                   selection = int(input('Enter: '))
317
318               if selection == DAILY_RENTAL:
319
320                   print('How many days do you need the vehicle?', end = '')
321                       num_days = self.__getSelection(14, prompt = ' ')
322
323                   if num_days > 6:
324                       print("Why don't you consider a weekly rental?\n")
325
326                   return (DAILY_RENTAL, num_days)
327               elif selection == WEEKLY_RENTAL:
328                   print('How many weeks do you need the vehicle? (1-3): ')
329                   num_weeks = self.__getSelection(3, prompt = 'Weeks: ')
330
331                   return (selection, num_weeks)
332
333               elif selection == WEEKEND_RENTAL:
334                   return (selection, 1)
335
336           except ValueError:
337               print('* Invalid Input - Number Expected *\n')
```

FIGURE 10-48 RentalAgencyUI Class

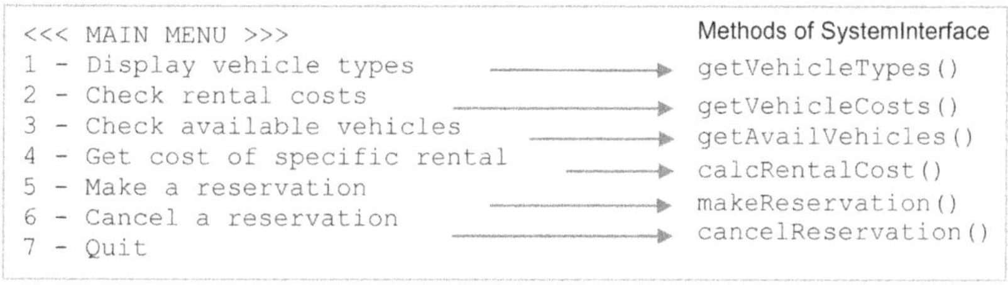

```
<<< MAIN MENU >>>                            Methods of SystemInterface
1 - Display vehicle types    ───────────▶   getVehicleTypes()
2 - Check rental costs       ───────────▶   getVehicleCosts()
3 - Check available vehicles ───────────▶   getAvailVehicles()
4 - Get cost of specific rental ─────────▶  calcRentalCost()
5 - Make a reservation       ───────────▶   makeReservation()
6 - Cancel a reservation     ───────────▶   cancelReservation()
7 - Quit
```

FIGURE 10-49   Correspondence of Menu Selections and Methods of System Interface

Method `executeCmd` (**lines 83–97**) is called to execute each command of the main menu by selection number. Rather than place the code for each command within this method, a specific command method is called for each command. Private method `CMD_DisplayVehicleTypes` (**lines 99–104**) displays the three types of vehicles (Cars, Vans, and Trucks). It in turn makes use of private method `displayVehicleTypes` (**lines 281–293**). Within this method, `getVehicleTypes` of the `systemInterface` is called to retrieve the types, since that is where they are defined.

Private method `CMD_DisplayVehicleCosts` (**lines 106–139**) displays the rental costs for a specific vehicle type:

```
Enter vehicle type: 1

------------- Following are the Rental Charges for Cars --------------

                        Free    Per Mile  Daily
Daily  Weekly  Weekend  Miles   Charge    Insurance
24.99  180.00  45.00    100     .15       14.99
----------------------------------------------------------------------
```

It displays a selection of vehicle types (**line 113**) for the user to choose from, constructs two rows of column headings (**lines 118–123**), and gets the vehicle costs for the selected vehicle type by call to method `getVehicleCosts` of the system interface (**line 126**). The rest of the method displays the information using formatted strings to align under the column headings.

Private method `CMD_DisplayAvailVehicles` displays all vehicles of a given vehicle type that are not currently reserved:

```
Enter vehicle type: 1
------------------------- Available Cars ---------------------------
Chevrolet Camaro        passengers: 4   doors: 2   mpg: 30   vin: WG8JM5492DY
Chevrolet Camaro        passengers: 4   doors: 2   mpg: 30   vin: KH4GM4564GD
Ford Fusion             passengers: 5   doors: 4   mpg: 34   vin: AB4FG5689GM
Ford Fusion Hybrid      passengers: 5   doors: 4   mpg: 36   vin: GH2KL4278TK
Ford Fusion Hybrid      passengers: 5   doors: 4   mpg: 36   vin: KU4EG3245RW
Chevrolet Impala        passengers: 6   doors: 4   mpg: 30   vin: QD4PK7394J1
Chevrolet Impala        passengers: 6   doors: 4   mpg: 30   vin: RK3BM4256YH
```

It displays a selection of vehicle types (**lines 158–159**) for the user to select from, and gets the available vehicles for the selected type from the system interface by call to method `getAvailVehicles` of the system interface (**line 147**). The rest of the method simply displays, row by row, the information for each vehicle.

Private method `CMD__PromptAndDisplayAvailVehicles` (**lines 161–169**) prompts the user for a vehicle type, and then displays the information of vehicles of that type not currently reserved. Private method `CMD_DisplaySpecificRentalCost` (**lines 171–226**) displays the costs of a particular vehicle rental based on the vehicle type, the time period rented, whether insurance is opted for, and the estimated number of miles driven:

```
-------------------- ESTIMATED Car RENTAL COST ---------------------
* You have opted out of the daily insurance *

Your cost of a daily rental would be 74.97

Your cost with an estimated mileage of 240 would be 95.97
which includes 100 free miles and a charge of 0.15 per mile
-------------------------------------------------------------------
```

First, it displays a selection of vehicle types for the user to choose from (**line 176**). It then requests the desired rental period by a call to private method `getRentalPeriod` (**line 180**). A tuple is returned containing constant value `DAILY_RENTAL`, `WEEKLY_RENTAL`, or `WEEKEND_RENTAL`, and the number of days or weeks rental period (with weekends defaulting to 1). The user is then asked if they want the optional insurance (**line 186**) and the number of miles expected to drive (**line 193**). The estimated rental cost is then calculated by a call to method `calcRentalCost` of the system interface. The rest of the method has to do with formatting and displaying the output.

Private method `makeReservation` allows the user to reserve a vehicle of a given type (**line 227**). The method first checks if there are vehicles available (**line 235**). It then calls `CMD__DisplayAvailVehicles` (**line 239**) with the default argument set to `True`. This causes the vehicle descriptions to be listed as a number list so that the desired vehicle can be selected. On **lines 242–253**, the vehicle number selected is read, checking for any invalid selections. On **line 255**, the VIN is retrieved for the selected vehicle. The VIN is needed by method `getVehicle` (of the `SystemInterface` class) to retrieve a given `Vehicle` object. Having the object, it then calls method `getDescription` (**line 257**) to display the description of the vehicle to the user. It also sets the reservation status to `True` by a call to `setReserved` (**line 259**).

The user's name, address, and credit card number are requested (**lines 261–263**) to make the reservation. It does this by creating a new `Reservation` object constructed with the provided information (**line 265**) and adds it to the collection of reservations (**line 266**). Confirmation of the reservation is displayed (**line 267**). Private method `CMD_CancelReservation` (**line 269–279**) cancels reservations by the credit card number used for making the reservation. Finally, private methods `displayVehicleTypes` and `getRentalPeriod`, supporting methods of the command methods, are given on **lines 281–337**.

Putting it All Together

Figure 10-50 shows the main module of the Vehicle Rental Agency Program that puts everything together. It first creates the vehicle rental agency system (with a system interface) and then creates a user interface containing a reference to the system, providing the user with a natural means of accessing the system.

```
 1  # Rental Agency Program
 2
 3  """ This program performs the tasks of a vehicle rental agency, including the
 4      display of vehicle information and the ability to make/cancel reservations.
 5  """
 6  from systemInterface import SystemInterface
 7  from rentalAgencyUI import RentalAgencyUI
 8
 9  try:
10      # create system with populated data from file
11      sys = SystemInterface()
12
13      # associate user interface with system
14      ui = RentalAgencyUI(sys)
15
16      # start the user interface
17      ui.start()
18
19  except IOError:
20      print('** PROGRAM TERMINATION (IO Error) **')
```

FIGURE 10-50   Rental Agency Program Main Module

The main module for the program imports the `SystemInterface` class (**line 6**) and the `RentalAgencyUI` class (**line 7**). First, an instance of the `SytemInterface` class is created (**line 11**). The `__init__` method of the class is implemented to open the vehicle information file, as well as the vehicle cost file. The information in these files is used to populate the vehicle and vehicle cost objects in the system. If any file errors occur during this process, an `IOError` exception is raised by the system interface and caught (**line 19**) to terminate the program.

Once the files are successfully opened and read, an instance of the `RentalAgencyUI` class is created (**line 14**). It is passed the needed reference to the system interface. Once the user interface is created, the `start` method of the user interface is called to begin the command loop and receive and execute commands from the user.

CHAPTER SUMMARY

General Topics

Classes
Encapsulation, Inheritance, and Polymorphism
Public vs. Private Class Members
Getters and Setters
Name Mangling
Superclass (Base Class/Parent Class)
Subclass (Derived Class/Child Class)
Subclass vs. Subtype
UML (Unified Modeling Language)
Class Diagrams in UML
Association, Multiplicity, and Role Names in UML
Composition vs. Aggregation

Python-Specific Programming Topics

Defining Classes in Python
Denoting Public and Private Class Members in
    Python
The Use of `self` in Python
Special Method `__init__` in Python
Arithmetic and Relational Special Methods in
    Python
Inheritance and Polymorphism in Python
Duck Typing in Python

CHAPTER EXERCISES

Section 10.1

1. What are the two kinds of entities "bundled" in a class?

2. What kind of entity can there be any number of instances created for a given class?

3. What are the three fundamental features that object-oriented programming languages have in support of object-oriented programming?

Section 10.2

4. What else does encapsulation provide other than the ability to bundle together instance variables and methods?

5. Describe what it means for a member of a class to be private.

6. Explain the purpose of getters and setters.

7. Explain what the special identifier `self` is used for in Python.

8. Explain the use of name mangling in Python.

9. Explain when special methods `__str__` and `__repr__` are each used in Python.

10. Give an implementation of special method `__str__` for a Range class (representing a range of integers) that contains integer instance variables, `__start` and `__end`, so that the value of Range objects are displayed as follows: `'10 . . . 16'`, when output with `print`.

11. Give an implementation of special method `__lt__` for the Range class of exercise 10 so that range1 < range2 evaluates to `True` if all the values in range1 are less than all the values in range2, and returns `False` otherwise.

Section 10.3

12. Give the one-line class definition header for a class named `MySubclass` that is a subclass of the class `MySuperclass`.

13. Explain when a subclass can serve as a subtype.

14. For an object `obj`, show how in Python the type of the object may be determined from within a program or the Python shell.

15. Show how in the Python shell information about one of the built-in types of Python can be displayed.

Section 10.4

16. Explain the concept of polymorphism in object-oriented programming.

17. Explain the advantages of using polymorphism in program design.

18. What is meant by "duck typing" in Python?

Section 10.5

19. What does the name UML stand for?

20. What are the two types of diagrams in UML mentioned in the chapter, and what aspects of a program design does each represent?

21. Give a class diagram for the `XYCoord` class in the Let's Try It box of section 10.2.2.

22. Give a class diagram that includes the partial description of the built-in `str` type in Figure 10-15, and the `ExplodedStr` subclass in Figure 10-16.

23. Give a class diagram for the `Fraction` class developed in section 10.2. Include the `MixedFraction` subclass in the diagram.

PYTHON PROGRAMMING EXERCISES

P1. Give a UML class diagram for a library. Include as entities tangible objects (such as books), persons (such as borrowers and librarians), and status (such as whether a book is checked out or not). Use multiplicity, navigation, and role names where appropriate.

P2. Design and implement a `Money` class that stores monetary values in dollars and cents. Special method `__init__` should have the following function header,

```
def __init__(self, dollars, cents)
```

Include special method `__repr__` (`__str__`) for displaying values in dollars and cents: $ 0.45, $ 1.00, $ 1.25. Also include special method `__add__`, and three getter methods that each provide the monetary value in another currency. Choose any three currencies to convert to.

P3. Implement a class named `AvgList` as a subclass of the built-in list class in Python, able to compute the average of a list of numeric values. If the list contains any nonnumeric types, a `ValueError` exception should be raised.

P4. Design and implement a `FootMeasure` class that stores a linear measurement of feet and inches. Your class should have the following function header for special method `__init__`,

```
def __init__(self, feet=0, inches=0)
```

Thus, the class should be able to create a `FootMeasure` object in various ways by use of optional keyword arguments,

```
meas = FootMeasure()
meas = FootMeasure(feet=5)
meas = FootMeasure(feet=5, inches=8)
meas = FootMeasure(inches=68)
```

Implement special method `__repr__` in the class so that measurements are displayed as follows,

```
5 ft.            NOT    5 ft. 0 in.
5 ft. 8 in.      NOT    68 in.
```

When the measurement is 0, it should be displayed as, 0 ft. 0. ins. Include special method add() for adding `FootMeasure` values. Also include all the special methods for implementing the relational operators.

P5. Develop an abstract class named `Temperature` that stores a single temperature. The class should have the following function header for special method `__init__`,

```
def __init__(self, temperature)
```

The abstract class should contain the following methods:

`__str__` — should return a string of the form "75 degrees Fahrenheit"

`aboveFreezing()` — returns `True` if temperature above the freezing point

`convertToFahren` — returns a new `Temperature` object converted to degrees Fahrenheit

`convertToCelsius` — returns a new `Temperature` object converted to degrees Celsius

`convertToKelvin` — returns a new `Temperature` object converted to degrees Kelvin

Develop the subclasses `Fahrenheit`, `Celsius` and `Kelvin` to appropriately implement each of the methods in the abstract `Temperature` class. (Note that when a meaningless conversion method is applied, for example, `temp1.convertToFahrenheit()` where `temp1` is an object of type `Fahrenheit`, then a copy of the `Temperature` object should be returned.)

Demonstrate the correctness of your classes by doing the following:

♦ Create a list of `Temperature` objects of a mix of `Temperature` types
♦ Print out the value of each temperature in the list, and add "above freezing" if the temperature is above freezing (for the specific temperature scale).
♦ Create a new list of temperatures containing each temperature of the original list converted to a common temperature scale (Fahrenheit, Celsius, or Kelvin).
♦ For each temperature object in the new list, print out its temperature value, and if it is above the freezing point.

PROGRAM MODIFICATION PROBLEMS

M1. Fraction Class—Adding a Supporting Reduce Method
Complete the `Fraction` class in section 10.2.2 by implementing the missing methods using the specifications below,

```
def copy(self):
    """Creates a copy of a given Fraction."""

def reduce(self):
    """Reduces self to simplest terms. Also removes the signs
    if both numerator and denominator are negative."""

def __adjust(self, factor):
    """Multiplies numerator and denominator by factor."""
```

M2. Vehicle Rental Agency Program—View Reservations
Modify the Vehicle Rental Agency program in section 10.6 to add the capability of viewing all current reservations.

M3. Division Operator for Fraction Class
Modify the `Fraction` class developed in section 10.2.2 to include a division operator by implementing special method `__truediv__`.

M4. Screen Display in Recipe Conversion Program
Modify the Recipe Conversion Program in section 10.2.3 so that the original recipe ingredient measurements and the converted measurements are both displayed on the screen (in addition to having the converted recipe written to a file).

M5. Adjusted Measurements in the Recipe Conversion Program
Modify the Recipe Conversion Program in section 10.2.3 so that the units of measure for teaspoons and tablespoons in a converted recipe are displayed more appropriately. For example, if a recipe that calls for 2 teaspoons of baking soda is tripled, 6 teaspoons of baking soda are currently displayed in the converted recipe. Since there are 3 teaspoons to a tablespoon, the converted measurement would be more appropriately displayed as 2 tablespoons. Similarly, since there are 16 tablespoons in a cup,

any number of tablespoons over 16 would be more appropriately displayed as one cup, plus some number of tablespoons.

M6. Revised Estimated Rental Cost in Vehicle Rental Agency Program

The rental cost for a particular type vehicle computed in the Vehicle Rental Agency Program is based on the number of days (or weeks) rented, the cost of optional insurance, and the estimated number of miles that the vehicle is expected to be driven. However, the estimate does not include the cost of gas that the customer must also pay. Since the miles per gallon (mpg) is available for all vehicles, modify the program so that this additional expense is added to the calculation of the estimated cost. The cost that is displayed should identify this additional expense. Use an instance variable in the `VehicleCosts` class to store the current price of gas per gallon.

M7. Additional Vehicle Type in Vehicle Rental Agency Program

Modify the Vehicle Rental Agency Program to include a fourth SUV vehicle type, in addition to cars, vans, and trucks. The attributes stored for an SUV object should include make and model, miles per gallon (mpg), number of passengers, whether or not it has automatic sliding doors, and the vehicle identification number (VIN). Make *all* changes in the program to incorporate this new vehicle type.

M8. Polymorphic Behavior of Vehicle Cost in Vehicle Rental Agency Program

Modify the Vehicle Rental Agency Program to include three subclasses of the `VehicleCost` class, `CarCost`, `VanCost`, and `TruckCost` so that `VehicleCost` can behave polymorphically. Make all changes to the program to incorporate these new vehicle cost types.

PROGRAM DEVELOPMENT PROBLEMS

D1. RGB/Hexadecimal Color Code Manipulation Program

Design an abstract class named `ColorCode`, and two subclass named `RGBColorCode` and `HexColorCode`. RGB color codes (as discussed in Chapter 9) are of the form (125, 80, 210), indicating the amount of red, green, and blue, respectively, for a given color. Each color value is on a scale of 0–255. Hexadecimal color codes are of the form F4F060, in which the first two hexadecimal digits indicate the amount of red, the middle two digits the amount of green, and the last two digits the amount of blue. Each pair of hexadecimal digits represent values in the range 0–255. Thus, these color encodings are just different representations of the same range of colors. Include in abstract class `ColorCode` methods for displaying a color code, for adding and reducing the amount of red, green, or blue by a given percentage, and for producing the complement of a given color. The complement is determined by subtracting each color value from 255. Develop a program in which the user can enter a series of colors in both RGB and hexadecimal form, and have them altered in the ways given above.

D2. Morse Code Translation Program

Implement a Morse code translator program from the UML design given below for translating English message files into Morse code, and Morse code files into English. The requirements for this program are as follows:

♦ English message files will be stored as text files, one sentence per line.
♦ Morse code message files will be stored as text files, one encoded character per line, where end of words are indicated by a blank line, and end of sentences by two blank lines.
♦ English message files will contain file extension `.eng`, and Morse code files file extension `.mor`.

The assumptions for this program are as follows:

♦ Messages will only contain lowercase letters, the digits 0–9, periods, commas, and question marks.

Following is the UML diagram for the program.

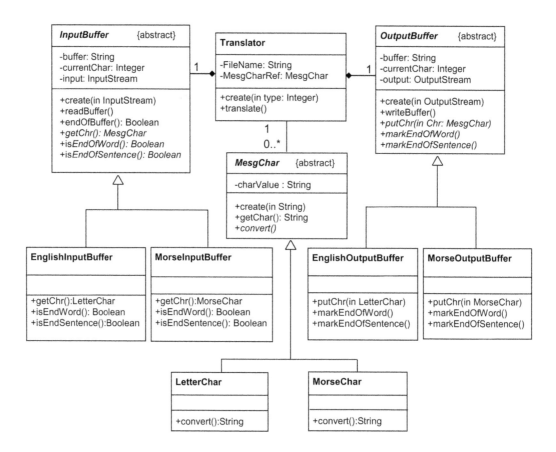

The `Translator` class coordinates the translation of messages (English to Morse code, and Morse code to English). It contains two class members through composition: `InputBuffer` and `Output-Buffer`. Thus the `Translator` class is responsible for their construction.

The `InputBuffer` contains the current message line read from the file. If the file contains an English message, then an `EnglishInputBuffer` is used; if the files contains a Morse-coded message, then a `MorseInputBuffer` is used. As the `Translator` reads the current `MesgChar` from the `InputBuffer`, it requests the `MesgChar` to translate itself, sending it to the `OutputBuffer`. When `isEndOfWord` or `isEndOfSentence` is found true, it calls the corresponding `MarkEnd-OfWord` or `MarkEndOfSentence` method of the `OuputBuffer`. If the output is in English, a space character for each end of word and a period for each end of sentence is added to the buffer; if the output is in Morse code, then a blank line for each end of word, and two blank lines for each end of sentence is added to the buffer. This is repeated until the end of file has been reached.

Note that what a given `MesgChar` is depends on the type of message file reading. If the message being read is an English message, then a `MesgChar` is a single character (letter, digit, etc.). If, however, the message being read is a Morse-code message, then a `MesgChar` is a `MorseChar` (i.e., a string containing up to six dot and dash characters). Thus, when getting and putting `MesgChars` of a given `InputBuffer` and `OutputBuffer`, the number of characters actually retrieved or placed in the buffer depends on what type of buffer is involved. The Morse Code table for this assignment is given below.

Morse Code Table

A	.-	N	-.	1	.----	.	.-.-.-
B	-...	O	---	2	..---	,	--..--
C	-.-.	P	.--.	3	...--	?	..--..
D	-..	Q	--.-	4	....-	(	-.--.
E	.	R	.-.	5	.....	)	-.--.-
F	..-.	S	...	6	-....	-	-....-
G	--.	T	-	7	--...	"	.-..-.
H	....	U	..-	8	---..	_	..--.-
I	..	V	...-	9	----.	'	.----.
J	.---	W	.--	0	-----		
K	-.-	X	-..-				
L	.-..	Y	-.--				
M	--	Z	--..				

CHAPTER 11

Recursion

In Chapter 3, we covered the fundamental types of control—sequential, selection, and iterative—used to affect the control flow of programs. There is one final form of control that we have yet to cover, referred to as recursion. We look at the use of recursion and recursive problem solving in this chapter.

OBJECTIVES

After reading this chapter and completing the exercises, you will be able to:

♦ Describe the design of recursive functions

♦ Define infinite recursion

♦ Apply recursive program solving

♦ Explain the appropriate use of iteration vs. recursion

♦ Develop recursive functions in Python

CHAPTER CONTENTS

Motivation

Fundamental Concepts

11.1 Recursive Functions

11.2 Recursive Problem Solving

11.3 Iteration vs. Recursion

Computational Problem Solving

11.4 Towers of Hanoi

MOTIVATION

Almost all computation involves the repetition of steps. Iterative control statements, such as the for and while statements, provide one means of controlling the repeated execution of instructions. Another way is by the use of *recursion*.

In *recursive problem solving*, a problem is repeatedly broken down into similar subproblems, until the subproblems can be directly solved without further breakdown. For example, consider the method of searching for a name in a sorted list of names below.

1. If the list contains only one name, then if the name found is the name you are looking for, then terminate with "name found," otherwise terminate with "name not found."

2. Otherwise, look at the middle item in the list. If that is the name you are looking for, then terminate with "name found."

3. Otherwise, continue by searching in a similar manner either the top half of the list, if the name you are looking for is alphabetically before the middle name of the list, or the bottom half of list, if the name you are looking for is alphabetically after.

The first two steps of this method are straightforward. The detail comes when the list needs to be continually broken down into sublists, and the appropriate sublists are searched. The beauty of recursive problem solving, however, is that the details of how to solve (smaller) subproblems do not need to be specified—the same steps that were used on the original list still apply. Although it is natural to try to think through all the resulting steps that are taken to recursively solve a problem, the power of "recursive thinking" is to understand that doing so is unnecessary. In this chapter, we demonstrate the power of recursive problem solving by looking at some classic examples that highlight its effectiveness.

FUNDAMENTAL CONCEPTS

11.1   Recursive Functions

Computational problem solving via the use of *recursion* is a powerful problem-solving approach. The development and use of recursive functions, however, requires a different perspective on computation than we have had so far. We discuss the design and use of recursive functions in this section.

11.1.1   What Is a Recursive Function?

A **recursive function** is often defined as "a function that calls itself." While this is an accepted definition, it is not necessarily the most appropriate explanation, for it plants in one's mind the image given in Figure 11-1.

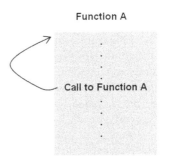

FIGURE 11-1 Recursive Function Definition

The illustration in the figure depicts a function, A, that is defined at some point to call function A (itself). The notion of a self-referential function is inherently confusing. There are two types of entities related to any function however—the *function definition*, and any current *execution instances*.

What is meant by the phrase "a function that calls itself" is a function *execution instance* that calls another *execution instance* of the same function. A function definition is a "cookie cutter" from which any number of execution instances can be created. Every time a call to a function is made, another execution instance of the function is created. Thus, while there is only one definition for any function, there can be any number of execution instances. In order to fully understand the mechanism of recursive function calls, we first consider the general mechanism of non-recursive function calls as depicted in Figure 11-2.

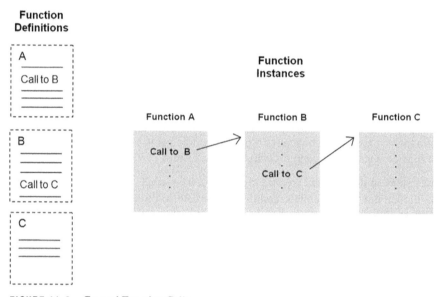

FIGURE 11-2 General Function Calls

In the function calls in the figure, there is no trouble visualizing the sequence of events that occur. First, an execution instance from the definition of function A is created and begins executing. When the call to function B is reached, the execution instance of function A is suspended while an execution instance of function B is created and begins executing. In turn, when the function call to function C is reached, function B suspends execution while an execution instance of function C is created and begins executing.

This calling and suspending of executing function instances could (theoretically) continue indefinitely. However, in this case, function C does not make a call to any other function. Thus, it simply executes until termination, returning control to the function that called it, function B. Function B then continues its execution until terminating, returning control to the function that called it, function A. Finally, function A completes and terminates, returning control to wherever it was called from.

Now, let's consider the situation when the original function, function A, is a recursive function—that is, its definition includes a call to function A (itself). As depicted in Figure 11-3, each current execution instance of function A will spawn a *new* execution instance of function A.

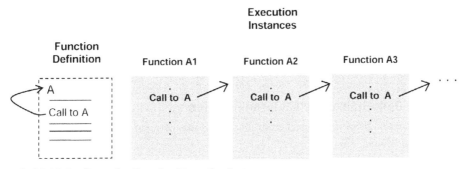

FIGURE 11-3 Recursive Function Execution Instances

Note that the execution of a series of recursive function instances is similar to the execution of a series of non-recursive instances, except that the execution instances are "clones" of each other (that is, of the same function definition). Thus, since all instances are identical, the function calls occur in exactly the same place in each.

Clearly, if the definition of a recursive function were written so that the function calls itself unconditionally, then *every* execution instance would unconditionally call another execution instance, ad infinitum. Such a nonterminating sequence of calls is referred to as **infinite recursion**, similar to the notion of an infinite loop. Therefore, *properly designed recursive functions always conditionally call another execution instance* so that eventually the chain of function calls terminates.

Now that we have better understanding of recursive functions, we can use the description of a recursive function as "a function that calls itself," understanding that this means that the function *definition* is self-referential, while the function execution instances are not. Next we will look at a classic example of a recursive function, computing the factorial of a given number.

LET'S TRY IT

From the Python Shell, enter the following and observe the results.

```
>>> def rfunc(n):
        print(n)
        if n > 0:
            rfunc(n - 1)
```

```
>>> def rfunc(n):
        if n == 1:
            return 1
        else:
            return n + rfunc(n - 1)
```

```
>>> rfunc(4)
???
```

```
>>> rfunc(1)
???
```

```
>>> rfunc(0)
???
```

```
>>> rfunc(3)
???
```

```
>>> rfunc(100)
???
```

```
>>> rfunc(100)
???
```

A **recursive function** is a function (definition) that conditionally calls itself.

11.1.2 The Factorial Function

We now look at a particular mathematical function, factorial, which is often defined by a recursive definition. We then look at how such a recursive definition can be written as a recursively defined program function.

The Recursive Definition of the Factorial Function

The factorial function is an often-used example of the use of recursion. The computation of the factorial of 4 is given as,

$$\text{factorial}(4) = 4 \cdot 3 \cdot 2 \cdot 1 = 24$$

In general, the computation of the factorial of any (positive, nonzero) integer n is,

$$\text{factorial}(n) = n \cdot (n - 1) \cdot (n - 2) \cdot \cdots 1$$

The one exception is the factorial of 0, defined to be 1. Note that if we apply this definition to the factorial of n − 1, we get factorial(n − 1) = (n − 1)(n − 2) . . . 1. Therefore, the factorial of n can be defined as n times the factorial of n − 1,

$$\text{factorial}(n) = n \cdot \underbrace{(n - 1) \cdot (n - 2) \cdot \cdots 1}_{\text{factorial}(n - 1)}$$

Thus, the complete definition of the factorial function is,

$$\begin{aligned} \text{factorial}(n) &= 1, && \text{if } n = 0 \\ &= n \cdot \text{factorial}(n - 1), && \text{otherwise} \end{aligned}$$

This definition of the factorial function is clearly defined in terms of itself, referred to as a **recursive definition**. The part of the definition "factorial(n) = 1, if n = 0" is referred to as the **base case**. The base case of a recursive definition is what terminates the repeated application of the definition (and thus the repeated function calls when executed).

Consider what would happen if the base case for the factorial function were not part of the definition,

$$\text{factorial}(n) = n \cdot \text{factorial}(n - 1), \quad \text{for all } n$$

Applying this definition, the computation of the factorial of 4 would be,

$$\text{factorial}(4) = 4 \cdot 3 \cdot 2 \cdot 1 \cdot 0 \cdot -1 \cdot -2 \cdot -3 \cdot -4 \cdot \cdots$$

The factorial of any (positive) number would be 0, since 0 would always be part of the product of values. Thus, not only is this an incorrect definition of the factorial function, if we implemented this definition as a recursive function, it would never terminate (and thus never produce a result).

Suppose, on the other hand, the base case for the definition of the factorial function is given, but that n * factorial(n − 1) were given as n * factorial(n + 1) instead,

$$\begin{aligned} \text{factorial}(n) &= 1, && \text{if } n = 0 \\ &= n \cdot \text{factorial}(n + 1), && \text{otherwise} \end{aligned}$$

Applying this definition, the computation of the factorial of 4 would be,

$$\text{factorial}(4) = 4 \cdot 5 \cdot 6 \cdot 7 \cdot 8 \cdot 9 \cdot 10 \cdot 11 \cdot 12 \cdots$$

If we implemented this (incorrect) version of factorial as a recursive function, the function would also never terminate. The problem, however, it is not because a base case is not included. It is because *the problem is not being broken down into subproblems in which the base case can be applied.*

    This highlights three important characteristics of any recursive function, given in Figure 11-4.

> 1.   There must be at least one base case (a problem instance whose solution is known without further recursive breakdown).
>
> 2.   Problems that are not a base case are broken down into subproblems that are a similar kind of problem as the original problem and work towards a base case.
>
> 3.   There is a way to derive the solution of the original problem from the solutions of the recursively solved subproblems.

FIGURE 11-4   Requirements of a Properly Designed Recursive Function

Going back to the original (correct) definition of the factorial function therefore,

$$\text{factorial}(n) = \begin{cases} 1, & \text{if } n = 0 \\ n \cdot \text{factorial}(n-1), & \text{otherwise} \end{cases}$$

we see that the first condition holds since the base case, $\text{factorial}(0) = 1$, can be applied without any future recursive breakdown of the problem. It follows the second condition since the problem is broken down into a subproblem that is a smaller instance of the original. Finally, it meets that third condition since the results of the original problem can be determined by multiplying the solution of each subproblem. Thus, this is a properly defined recursive function. We next look at an actual implementation of a recursive factorial function.

> Every properly defined recursive function must have at least one base case, and must redefine the problem into subproblems that work towards a base case such that the solution of the original problem can be derived from the solutions of the recursively solved subproblems.

A Recursive Factorial Function Implementation

Given a recursive definition of the factorial function, we can simply write it as Python program code. This is given in Figure 11-5.

```
def factorial(n):
    if n == 0:
        return 1
    else:
        return n * factorial(n-1)
```

FIGURE 11-5   Recursive Factorial Function
Implementation

Examination of this function reveals that the recursive function call is conditionally made. That is, only if n is not equal to zero is another execution instance created, otherwise the current execution instance terminates and returns a value of 1. Termination is guaranteed since the initial value of parameter n is required to be greater than or equal to 0, and each next function call operates on smaller values (i.e., n − 1). Finally, the solutions of all of the subproblems provide a solution to the original one. The sequence of function execution instances generated for the factorial of 4 is given in Figure 11-6.

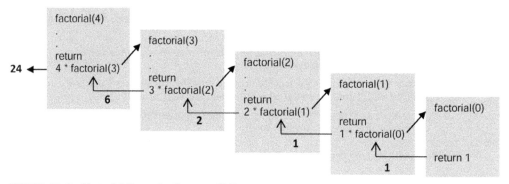

FIGURE 11-6 Factorial Recursive Instance Calls

Each execution instance of function factorial is suspended while the evaluation of expression n * factorial(n − 1) is completed. When factorial is finally called with the value 0, five execution instances of the function exist, the first four suspended until instance factorial(0) completes. When factorial(0) returns the value 1, the evaluation of expression 1 * factorial(0) can be completed, returning 1 as the value of factorial(1), and so on, until 4 * factorial(3) is evaluated and 24 is returned as the value of the original function call.

Finally, we point out that although the factorial function serves as a good example, in practice, recursion is an inappropriate choice for implementing this function. This is because an iterative version can be easily implemented, providing a much more efficient computation. (We discuss the appropriate use of recursion in section 11.3.)

LET'S TRY IT

From the Python Shell, enter the following and observe the results.

```
>>> def factorial(n):
        if n == 0:
            return 1
        return n * factorial(n - 1)


>>> factorial(4)
???
>>> factorial(0)
???
>>> factorial(100)
???
>>> factorial(10000)
???
```

```
>>> def ifactorial(n):
        result = 1
        if n == 0:
            return result
        for k in range(n, 0, -1):
            result = result * k
        return result
>>> ifactorial(0)
???
>>> ifactorial(100)
???
>>> ifactorial(10000)
???
```

Although the factorial function is an often-used example of a recursive function, the function can be executed more efficiently when implemented to use iteration.

11.1.3 Let's Apply It—Fractals (Sierpinski Triangle)

Figure 11-7 illustrates a well-known recursive set of images called the Sierpinski triangle. The Sierpinski triangle is an example of a *fractal*. A fractal is a shape that contains parts that are similar to the whole shape, thus having the property of self-similarity (Figure 11-8). The turtle graphics program in Figure 11-9 generates Sierpinski triangles at various levels of repetition. This program utilizes the following programming features:

➤ recursive functions

FIGURE 11-7 Sierpinski Triangle (Fractal Image)

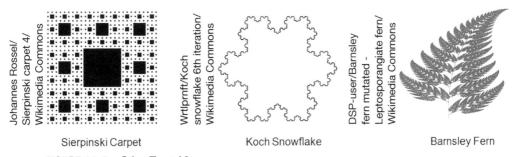

Sierpinski Carpet   Koch Snowflake   Barnsley Fern

FIGURE 11-8 Other Fractal Images

In addition to the `turtle` module, the program also imports the `math` module, needed for the square root function in the calculation of the height of a triangle (in function `triangle-Height` on **lines 21–25**). In the Sierpinski triangle, each next level in the pattern replaces each triangle with three smaller triangles. In order for the position of each next triangle to be determined (by functions `getLeftTrianglePosition`, `getRightTrianglePosition`, and `getTopTrianglePosition` at **lines 27**, **38**, and **49**, respectively) both the length of the sides of the triangle, as well as its height are needed. This is depicted in Figure 11-10.

The position of turtle shapes in turtle graphics is relative to the center of the shape. Each triangle is positioned relative to its center point (shown by the dot in the figure). Thus, method `getLeftTrianglePosition` calculates the location of the bottom left triangle as,

```
[position [0] — side / 4, position [1] — triangleHeight(side) / 4]
```

```
1   # Sierpinski Triangle Program
2
3   import turtle
4   import math
5
6   def createTriangleShape(coords):
7
8       """Creates turtle shape from coords. Registers as 'my_triangle'. """
9
10      turtle.penup()
11      turtle.begin_poly()
12      turtle.setposition(coords[0])
13      turtle.setposition(coords[1])
14      turtle.setposition(coords[2])
15      turtle.setposition(coords[0])
16      turtle.end_poly()
17
18      tri_shape = turtle.get_poly()
19      turtle.register_shape('my_triangle', tri_shape)
20
21  def triangleHeight(side):
22
23      """Returns height of equilateral triangle with length side."""
24
25      return math.sqrt(3) / 2 * side
26
27  def getLeftTrianglePosition(position, side):
28
29      """Returns position of bottom left triangle in larger triangle.
30
31         Returns (x,y) position for provided position and side length of
32         larger triangle to be placed within.
33      """
34
35      return (position[0] - side / 4,
36              position[1] - triangleHeight(side) / 4)
37
38  def getRightTrianglePosition(position, side):
39
40      """Returns position of bottom right triangle in larger triangle.
41
42         Returns (x,y) position for provided position and side length of
43         larger triangle to be placed within.
44      """
45
46      return (position[0] + side / 4,  \
47              position[1] - triangleHeight(side) / 4)
48
```

FIGURE 11-9 Sierpinski Triangle Program (*Continued*)

As a result, the x (horizontal) position of the lower left triangle is one quarter of the length of the side less than the larger triangle, therefore positioned to the left of the larger triangle's location. The y (vertical) position of the smaller triangle is one quarter of the height of the triangle less than the larger triangle, thus placed below the position of the original triangle. Positioning of the lower right triangle (by method getRightTrianglePosition) is similarly determined (positioned to the right of and below the location of the original triangle). Finally, method getTopTriangle-Position determines the position of the smaller top triangle to be at the same x location as the original triangle, and one quarter of the height of the triangle higher.

```
49  def getTopTrianglePosition(position, side):
50
51      """Returns x,y position of top triangle within larger one.
52
53         For triangle at position, with length side.
54      """
55
56      return (position[0], position[1] + triangleHeight(side) / 4)
57
58  def drawSierpinskiTriangle(t, len_side, levels):
59
60      """Recursive function that draws a Sierpinski triangle.
61
62         Draws the number of levels of triangle given in levels.
63      """
64
65      if levels == 0:
66          t.color('black')   # display triangle
67          t.showturtle()
68          t.stamp()
69
70          return
71
72      # resize triangle to half its size
73      stretch_width, stretch_length, outline = t.turtlesize()
74      t.turtlesize(0.5 * stretch_width, 0.5 * stretch_length, outline)
75
76      # determine positions for each of the three embedded triangles
77      left_triangle_position = getLeftTrianglePosition(t.position(),
78                                                       len_side)
79      right_triangle_position = getRightTrianglePosition(t.position(),
80                                                         len_side)
81      top_triangle_position = getTopTrianglePosition(t.position(),
82                                                     len_side)
83
84      # recursively display left triangle
85      t.setposition(left_triangle_position)
86      drawSierpinskiTriangle(t, len_side / 2, levels - 1)
87      t.turtlesize(0.5 * stretch_width, 0.5 * stretch_length, outline)
88
89      # recursively display right triangle
90      t.setposition(right_triangle_position)
91      drawSierpinskiTriangle(t, len_side / 2, levels - 1)
92      t.turtlesize(0.5 * stretch_width, 0.5 * stretch_length, outline)
93
94      # recursively display top triangle
95      t.setposition(top_triangle_position)
96      drawSierpinskiTriangle(t, len_side / 2, levels - 1)
97      t.turtlesize(0.5 * stretch_width, 0.5 * stretch_length, outline)
98
```

FIGURE 11-9   Sierpinski Triangle Program (*Continued*)

Once the proper positioning of the smaller triangles is determined, the rest of the program is based on the use of recursion to repeatedly apply this division of triangles until a given number of levels have been drawn. Function createTriangleShape (**lines 6–19**) creates an equilateral triangle by positioning the turtle to each of the screen locations provided in parameter coords. Because this movement occurs within the begin_poly and end_poly instructions, the polynomial

```
 99 # ---- main
100
101 # set window size
102 turtle.setup(800, 600)
103
104 # get turtle
105 the_turtle = turtle.getturtle()
106
107 # init turtle
108 the_turtle.penup()
109 the_turtle.hideturtle()
110
111 # set the number of levels
112 num_levels = 3
113
114 # create triangle shape
115 coords = ((-240, -150), (240, -150), (0, 266))
116 createTriangleShape(coords)
117 len_side = 480
118
119 # create first triangle
120 the_turtle.shape('my_triangle')
121 the_turtle.setposition(0, -50)
122 the_turtle.setheading(90)
123
124 # call recursive function
125 drawSierpinskiTriangle(the_turtle, len_side, num_levels)
126 the_turtle.hideturtle()
127
128 # terminate program when close window
129 turtle.exitonclick()
```

FIGURE 11-9 Sierpinski Triangle Program

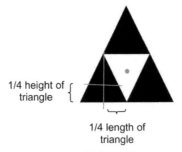

1/4 height of triangle

1/4 length of triangle

FIGURE 11-10 Relative Placement of Inner Triangles

drawn can be retrieved (**line 18**) and registered as a new turtle shape that can be used within the program (**line 19**).

The main section of the program (**lines 101–129**) does the needed preparation before drawing can begin. On **line 102** the size of the turtle window is set. On **line 105** the (default) turtle is retrieved and named the_turtle. The turtle is then initialized so that the drawing capability is off (penup) and it is hidden. This is done since the only graphics to be produced by the turtle is when its (triangle) shape is stamped. Thus, the turtle is moved and resized to create all the stamped triangle images needed for creating a given Sierpinski triangle. On **line 112** the number of levels of the triangle is set. Thus, by changing this value, a Sierpinski triangle of various levels can be created.

On **line 115** a tuple of coordinates is defined that creates an equilateral triangle. (The absolute positions of these coordinates are not relevant, only their relative positions are used for defining the shape.) The length of the triangle is specified on **line 117**, matching the length of the triangle given by the specified coordinates. The turtle specified by the_turtle is set to shape 'my_triangle'. It is then positioned at location (0, −50) of the screen (a little below the center) and the heading is set to 90 degrees (to ensure that the triangle is pointing up).

Recursive function drawSierpinskiTriangle (**lines 58–97**) is passed three arguments: the turtle (in parameter t), the length of the sides of the overall triangle, and the number of levels of the Sierpinski triangle pattern to draw (**line 125**). As a recursive function, there must be a base case in which the function no longer calls itself. Since the number of levels starts at some nonzero value, the base case is reached when the value of parameter levels is 0 (**line 65**). At that point, the turtle size and location is specified for the smallest of the embedded triangles. Therefore, since no further breakdown of the triangles is needed, these lowest-level triangles are simply displayed.

When function drawSierpinskiTriangle is called with levels not equal to zero, the size of the current triangle shape of the turtle is cut in half (**lines 73–74**). The positions of each of the three smaller triangle to fit in the area of the current turtle shape are determined, and three recursive calls are made—one for each of the smaller triangles (**lines 85–97**). For each recursive call, the turtles are first positioned (**lines 85, 90, and 95**), and the recursive function calls made (**lines 86, 91 and 95**). Because each recursive call resizes the turtle shape, on **lines 87, 92, and 97** the turtle shape is reset to what it was before each such call.

Self-Test Questions

1. A recursive function is best thought of as
   (a) A function that calls itself
   (b) A function execution instance that calls another execution instance of the same function

2. A recursive function call that never terminates is called _____.

3. What does the following recursive function return as a value, for any given positive integer argument n?

```
def rfunc(n):
    if n == 0:
        return 0
    else:
        return rfunc(n - 1) + 2
```

4. How many times does the factorial function in the chapter get called when computing the factorial of 4?

5. Iteration and recursion are two means of repeating a set of instructions. (TRUE/FALSE)

11.2   Recursive Problem Solving

11.2.1   Thinking Recursively

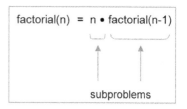

We commonly solve problems by breaking a problem into subproblems, and separately solving each subproblem. Recursive problem solving is the same, except that a problem is broken down into subproblems that are another instance of the original type problem. This was true of the factorial function in section 11.1. The problem of solving the factorial of n was bro-

FIGURE 11-11   Subproblems of Factorial Function

ken down into two subproblems—the multiplication by n as one subproblem, and the determination of the factorial of n − 1 as the other, as shown in Figure 11-11.

The factorial function is an "easy" example of recursion, because the function itself is defined recursively. Thus, the recursive function developed is just an implementation of the mathematical definition. The use of recursion is most interesting when applied to problems that are not recursively defined. To do this, we need to meet the three requirements of recursive functions given earlier in Figure 11-4.

The power of recursion is that it provides a conceptually elegant means of problem solving. The "elegance" derives from the fact that there is no need to specify or even think through all the steps that are taken to solve the problem. Since the recursive subproblems are the same kind of problem as the original, specifying the solution of the overall problem provides sufficient detail for solving each of the similar subproblems. To illustrate this, we look at some of the most well-known problems submitting to a recursive solution. We begin with an efficient means of sorting called MergeSort.

The **power of recursion** is that it provides a conceptually elegant means of problem solving.

11.2.2   MergeSort Recursive Algorithm

In this section we look at how we can apply recursive problem solving to the problem of sorting lists. In order to solve this problem recursively, we have to imagine how the problem of sorting can be broken into subproblems, so that one or more of the subproblems is also the problem of sorting a (smaller) list.

When breaking a problem down, it is often most effective to break the problem into equal size subproblems. We consider, therefore, breaking down the problem of sorting n elements, into two subproblems of sorting lists of size n/2, as depicted in Figure 11-12.

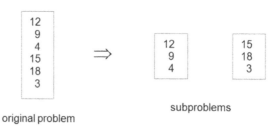

original problem

subproblems

FIGURE 11-12   Breakdown of the Problem of Sorting a List

At this point, the power of recursive thinking comes into play. Since we are developing a method for sorting lists of size n, *we can assume that any list of size less than n can be sorted, without needing to determine in detail how that is done*. (This is closely related to proof by induction in mathematics.) Thus, we can continue to develop our method for sorting lists of size n based on that fact.

The next step is to identify a base case that does not need to be broken down any further in order to be solved. The obvious base case is lists of size 1, since by definition they are sorted. Since we are dividing each list into two sublists at each step of the recursion, eventually each sublist will be of size 1. Thus, the breakdown into subproblems lead towards the base case, as required.

The last step is to determine how two (recursively solved) sorted sublists can be combined into one complete sorted list as depicted in Figure 11-13.

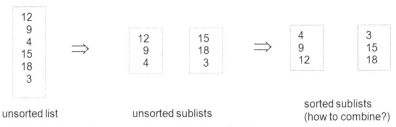

unsorted list   unsorted sublists   sorted sublists (how to combine?)

FIGURE 11-13   After Sorting Each of the Two Sublists

We cannot simply concatenate one sublist with the other. We need to somehow *merge* the values into one properly sorted list. This can be done as follows. Compare the smallest (top) item in each of the two lists. Whichever is the smaller value, move that as the first item of a new list. Cross off the item moved. Continue in the same manner until all the elements have been moved to the new list. The first steps of this process are shown in Figure 11-14.

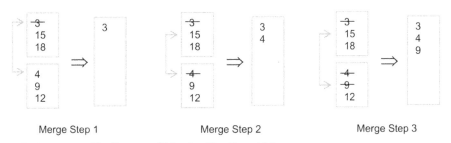

Merge Step 1   Merge Step 2   Merge Step 3

FIGURE 11-14   The Process of Merging Two Sorted Lists

Now that we have determined how to break down the problem into (smaller) subproblems, and how to combine the solutions of the subproblem into a solution of the larger problem, we can specify the complete steps of this "merge sort" algorithm.

1. Split the list into two sublists.

2. Sort each sublist.

3. Merge the sorted sublists into one sorted list.

Figure 11-15 shows how this recursive method works on a particular list.

Splitting into sublists   Merging of sublists

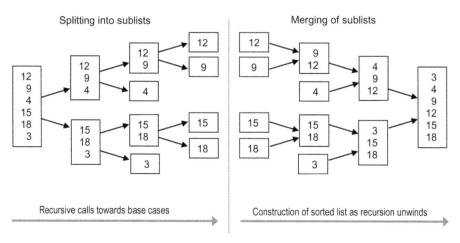

Recursive calls towards base cases   Construction of sorted list as recursion unwinds

FIGURE 11-15   Recursive Problem-Solving Example (MergeSort)

The initial problem is to sort the list 12, 9, 4, 15, 18, 3. This is broken down into the problem of sorting the sublists 12, 9, 4 and 15, 18, 3. Since each sublist will be sorted in a similar manner, let's follow how the sublist 12, 9, 4 is sorted. It is broken down into the two sublists 12, 9 and 4. Since the sublist containing only the value 4 is by definition sorted (as a base case) that subproblem does not need to be broken down any more—it is solved. So the sublist 12, 9 is broken down into the list containing 12 and another containing 9. These are now also solved since they are each a base case. The diagram indicates how the original sublist 15, 18, 3 is similarly broken down.

Now that since all base cases have been reached, the process of merging sublists begins as shown on the right side of the figure. Thus, to produce the sorted list 9, 12 the two base cases 9 and 12 are merged. We have shown how this merging can be systematically done. To produce the sublist 4, 9, 12, the *sorted* sublist 9, 12 is merged with the *sorted* sublist 4. The sorted sublist 3, 15, 18 is similarly produced. Thus, the final step is to merge the sorted versions of the original two subproblems, 4, 9, 12 and 3, 15, 18. We next give a Python implementation of this algorithm.

11.2.3   Let's Apply It—MergeSort Implementation

An implementation of the MergeSort algorithm is given in Figure 11-16. This program utilizes the following programming features.

➤ recursive functions

Function `mergesort` implements the recursive algorithm given above. When `mergesort` receives a list of length 1 (the base case), it simply returns the list (**lines 3–4**). Otherwise, the list is broken into two sublists, `sublist1` and `sublist2` (**lines 6–7**). Note that integer division is used, `len(lst)//2`, so that we don't compute non-integer lengths. Thus, when `lst` contains an uneven number of elements, for example 5, `sublist1` and `sublist2` will be of lengths 2 and 3, respectively, which makes no difference in the algorithm.

Once the list is divided into sublists, each of the sublists is sorted by a recursive call to `mergesort` (**lines 9–10**). Utilizing the power of recursive thinking, *we can assume that these recursive calls work without having to think through all the recursive steps*. Attempting to think

```
1  def mergesort(lst):
2
3      if len(lst) == 1:
4          return lst
5
6      sublist1 = lst[0:len(lst) // 2]
7      sublist2 = lst[len(lst) // 2:len(lst)]
8
9      sorted_sublist1 = mergesort(sublist1)
10     sorted_sublist2 = mergesort(sublist2)
11
12     return merge(sorted_sublist1, sorted_sublist2)
13
14
15  def merge(lst1, lst2):
16
17      merged_list = []
18
19      i = 0
20      k = 0
21
22      while i != len(lst1) and k != len(lst2):
23          if lst1[i] < lst2[k]:
24              merged_list.append(lst1[i])
25              i = i + 1
26          else:
27              merged_list.append(lst2[k])
28              k = k + 1
29
30      if i < len(lst1):
31          for loc in range(i, len(lst1)):
32              merged_list.append(lst1[loc])
33      elif k < len(lst2):
34          for loc in range(k, len(lst2)):
35              merged_list.append(lst2[loc])
36
37      return merged_list
```

FIGURE 11-16 Recursive Function `mergesort`

through the steps at each recursive level is tedious, confusing and unnecessary. Finally, the two sorted sublists are merged and returned as the final sorted list (**line 12**).

Note that supporting function `merge` is longer and more detailed than function `mergesort`. This should not be surprising, since the real work lies in the merging of sublists. In the function, the new merged list to be returned is constructed in variable `merged_list`. Thus, `merged_list` is initialized as an empty list (**line 17**). Variables `i` and `k` are used to keep track of the position of the current elements being compared in each of `sublist1` and `sublist2`; thus, each is initialized to 0 (**lines 19–20**).

The while loop in **lines 22–28** merges one more element into `merged_list` for each iteration of the loop. If the current item in `lst1` (determined by the current value of `i`) is less than the current item in `lst2` (determined by the current value of `k`), then the current item of `lst1`, `lst1[i]`, is appended to `merged_list`. Otherwise, the current item of `lst2`, `lst2[k]`, is appended. Once the while loop terminates, all of the elements of `lst1` and/or `lst2` have been merged. What is left to do is append any remaining items of either sublist whose elements have not yet been merged (when the two sublists are not of equal length). This is taken care of in **lines 30–35**. Finally, on **line 37**, the newly created merged list is returned.

We note that the MergeSort function makes two recursive calls. Such recursive functions are called *doubly recursive*. Double recursion makes the conversion of a recursive solution to an iterative one more difficult than a "singly recursive" algorithm. We shall see another example of a doubly recursive function in the Computational Problem Solving section of the chapter.

Self-Test Questions

1. Only problems that are recursively defined can be solved using recursion. (TRUE/FALSE)

2. The power of recursion is the execution speed over iteration. (TRUE/FALSE)

3. The base case in the MergeSort algorithm is,
   (**a**) an empty list   (**b**) a list of length one   (**c**) a list of length two

4. The MergeSort algorithm only works on lists of length two or more. (TRUE/FALSE)

5. The MergeSort algorithm divides a list into equal, or nearly equal, sublists in each recursive level (except for the base case). (TRUE/FALSE)

ANSWERS: 1. False, 2. False, 3. (b), 4. False, 5. True

11.3   Iteration vs. Recursion

Recursion is fundamentally a means of repeatedly executing a set of instructions. The set of instructions are those of a function, and the repetition comes from the fact that the function is repeatedly executed, once for each recursive function call. Thus, recursion and iteration are two means of accomplishing the same result. Whatever can be computed using recursion can also be computed using iteration, and vice versa.

Since iteration and recursion are equivalent in terms of what can be computed, a natural question is "When should I use recursion, and when should I use iteration?" There is no clear-cut answer to this question, but there are some guidelines. Generally, a recursive function generally takes more time to execute than an equivalent iterative approach. This is because the multiple function calls are relatively time-consuming. In contrast, while and for loops execute very efficiently. Thus, *when a problem can be solved both recursively and iteratively with similar programming effort, it is generally best to use an iterative approach*. Recall that the Factorial function was an example of such a situation. The iterative version of computing factorial is simple to implement, and executes much more efficiently.

On the other hand, some problems are very difficult to solve iteratively, and almost trivial to solve recursively. This is when recursion is most effectively used. A classic example of such a problem is the Towers of Hanoi, discussed next.

Whatever can be computed using recursion can also be computed using iteration, and vice versa.

COMPUTATIONAL PROBLEM SOLVING

11.4 Towers of Hanoi

In this section we look at a classic example of recursive problem solving in computer science, the Towers of Hanoi.

11.4.1 The Problem

The Towers of Hanoi problem (Figure 11-17) is based on a legend of unknown origin. According to the legend, there is a Vietnamese temple with a large room containing three pegs and 64 golden disks. Each disk has a hole in it so that it can be slipped onto any of the pegs. In addition, each disk is of different size. The 64 disks are moved by priests from one peg to another, with the following conditions,

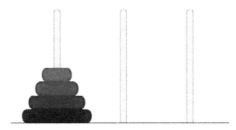

FIGURE 11-17 Towers of Hanoi

♦ Only one disk can be moved at a time.

♦ At no time can a larger disk be placed on top of a smaller one.

When the complete pile of 64 disks have been moved, the world is to end. There is not much need for concern, however—assuming that the priests moved one disk per second, it would take roughly 585 billion years to finish!

11.4.2 Problem Analysis

We will first attempt to solve this problem for three disks to gain some insight into the problem, and then develop a general solution for any number of disks. Thus, we will solve the simple problem of moving three disks from peg A to peg C as shown in Figure 11-18.

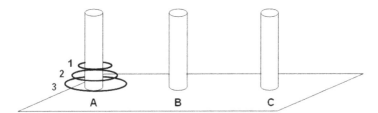

FIGURE 11-18 Towers of Hanoi Problem for Three Disks

First, let's solve this the hard way, by considering every step that must be taken. The obvious first move is to remove the smallest disk, and place it on either peg B or peg C. If we place the smallest disk on peg C, then we must place the next smallest disk on peg B, resulting in the configuration in Figure 11-19.

We then consider our third move. We can place the disk currently on peg B back on peg A, but that will be undoing what we just did in the last step. So in order to make progress, we move the smallest disk on peg C somewhere. We can move it on either peg A or peg B, since in each case it would be placed on a larger disk (thus not violating the problem's conditions). Let's assume that we

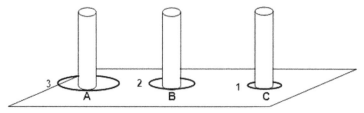

FIGURE 11-19 Towers of Hanoi after Two Moves

move the smallest disk currently on peg C on top of the second smallest disk on peg B. This move results in the configuration shown in Figure 11-20.

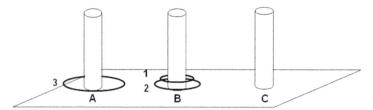

FIGURE 11-20 Towers of Hanoi after Three Moves

Now, we can move the largest disk currently on peg A to peg C (since peg C is currently empty). Then we can move the smallest disk from peg B to peg A, then move the second smallest disk from peg B to peg C, and finally move the smallest disk from peg A to peg C, thereby solving the problem as shown in Figure 11-21.

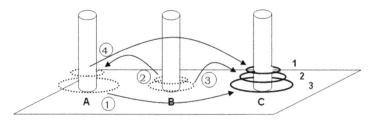

FIGURE 11-21 Towers of Hanoi Final Moves

The question is, what have we learned by thinking through the solution of this problem for three disks? What insight have we gained into the problem involving four disks? Five disks? Attempting to think through the individual steps for a larger and larger number of disks quickly becomes overwhelming.

As you should expect, there is a much more elegant solution for this problem involving recursion. The fundamental steps of a recursive solution for the Towers of Hanoi problem is given below:

Step 1: View the stack as two stacks, one on top of the other. Call the top stack Stack1, and the bottom stack Stack2.

Step 2: Recursively move Stack1 from peg A to peg B.

Step 3: Recursively move (the exposed) Stack2 from peg A to peg C.

Step 4: Recursively move Stack1 from peg B to peg C.

As we have said, in recursive problem solving, we do not need to specify the detailed steps solving any subproblem that is a smaller, similar problem to the original problem. Here, steps 2, 3, and 4 have to do with solving subproblems that are the same type of problem as the original—moving a stack of disks from one peg to another. It does not matter that the stacks being moved are different, or are being moved between different pegs. Each of the subproblems can be recursively solved in a similar way, and thus we can assume that they can be solved without explicitly specifying how. Therefore, in order to effectively solve the general problem, we only need to decide and specify the details of step 1, how to break down a stack of disks into two separate (sub)stacks. Let's consider different ways of breaking down this problem.

Suppose we start with the obvious breakdown, that is, dividing the stack of disks (six in this example) into two equal (or close to equal) size stacks. If we choose that approach, then after (recursively) moving the top half of the original stack to peg B and (recursively) moving the bottom half of the stack to peg C, we have the configuration given in Figure 11-22.

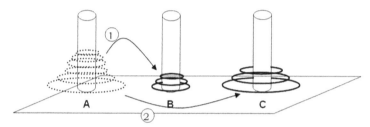

FIGURE 11-22   One Possible Breakdown of the Towers of Hanoi

Here is where we can benefit from recursive thinking. From this configuration, we need to (recursively) move the stack of disks on peg B to peg C to complete the problem solution. However, we are not allowed to move the whole stack at once, but instead must move each disk one at a time. This is accomplished by solving this problem in an identical way to the solution of the larger problem involving all disks. Without thinking through all of the details of each step, we know that the top disk on peg B must be moved at this point (since only top disks can be moved, and we do not want to move the disks on peg C, since they are currently in the correct position). So we can move the top disk from peg B to either currently empty peg A, or on top of the disks on peg C.

Note that this is the smallest disk of all disks. *Therefore, once we place this smallest disk on either peg, that peg cannot be used to place any other disks on top of it.* But the one insight we should have gained by working through the detailed solution of three disks is that there is always the need for a spare peg when moving a stack of disks from one peg to another. Thus, once the smallest disk is placed on a peg, that peg becomes unusable for placing any other disks on it (and thus unusable as a spare peg), as shown in Figure 11-23 for peg A.

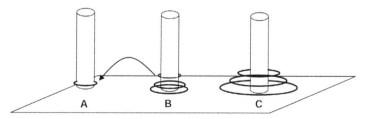

FIGURE 11-23   Inappropriate Breakdown of the Towers of Hanoi

Since we have determined that dividing the stack of disks into two (essentially) equal-size stacks will not work, we need to consider alternate methods of dividing the stack of disks. Suppose we take the opposite approach, and divide the stack into very *unequal*-sized stacks? That is, let's consider dividing the stack so that the top stack consists of the top (smallest) disk only, and the bottom stack consists of the rest of the disks. Let's see how this plays out.

Moving the top stack from peg A to peg B means moving the one smallest disk to peg B, as shown in Figure 11-24.

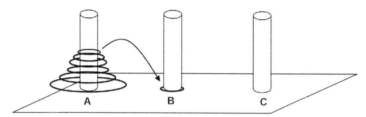

FIGURE 11-24   Another Possible Breakdown of the Towers of Hanoi

That is easy, since it is a stack of only one! Now, we must (recursively) move the bottom stack (with all the remaining disks) from peg A to peg C. We know that this cannot be done in one step, and must be done by moving one disk at a time. We also know that in order to move such a stack of disks from any peg to any other peg, we must have a spare peg. However, since the smallest disk has been placed on peg B (our spare peg), that is unavailable for use! Again, then, this approach will not work!

Finally, we consider the correct approach. We again break down the stack of disks into very unequal-sized stacks. However, this time, we break it down so that the top stack consists of *all disks except the bottom (largest) disk*. Therefore, the correct approach would be to recursively move the top stack (of n − 1 disks) from peg A to peg B. Then, simply move the largest (remaining) disk from peg A to peg C. Then recursively move the stack of disks from peg B to peg C (on top of the largest disk), as shown in Figure 11-25.

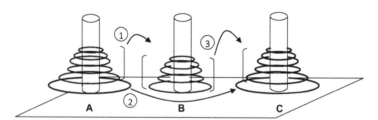

FIGURE 11-25   Correct Breakdown of the Towers of Hanoi

Note that in this case, when moving the stack of disks from peg B to peg C, we have the needed spare peg, since peg A is currently empty, and peg C has on it the largest disk, making it possible to use either as a spare peg. Thus, our recursive solution is:

Step 1:   Recursively move the top n − 1 disks from peg A to peg B.
Step 2:   Move the one (remaining) largest disk from peg A to peg C.
Step 3:   Recursively move the n − 1 disks from peg B to peg C.

As with MergeSort, this is a doubly recursive algorithm. This is a well-designed recursive solution because:

♦ *There is a base case.* When the stack of disks consists of only one disk, such a "stack" can be moved without further breakdown.

♦ *The recursive steps work towards the base case.* The subproblem involves the solution of smaller and smaller sized stacks of disks.

♦ *The solutions of the subproblems provide a solution for the original problem.* Solutions of sub-problems eventually result in all the disks being on the destination peg in the required order.

11.4.3 Program Design and Implementation

Now that we have defined a recursive solution to this problem, implementation of a program that solves it is surprisingly simple, given in Figure 11-26.

```
def towers(start_peg, dest_peg, spare_peg, num_disks):

    if num_disks == 1:
        print 'move disk from peg', start_peg, 'to peg', dest_peg
    else:
        towers(start_peg, spare_peg, dest_peg, num_disks - 1)
        print 'move disk from peg', start_peg, 'to', dest_peg
        towers(spare_peg, dest_peg, start_peg, num_disks - 1)
```

FIGURE 11-26 Recursive Function Implementation of the Towers of Hanoi

Hopefully you have gained an appreciation for the power and elegance of recursion through the examples given, and that you will be able to begin to apply "recursive thinking" in your own problem solving. We give a program utilizing turtle graphics that produces an animation of the solution of the Towers of Hanoi for a given number of disks in Figure 11-27.

In addition to the `turtle` module, the program also imports the `time` module (**lines 3 and 4**). The `time` module contains a `sleep` function used to control the speed at which the animation proceeds (**line 217**), pausing 0.5 seconds between the movement of disks.

The main module is in **lines 229–277**. On **line 230** a welcome message is displayed indicating what the program does. The call to `setup` on **line 233** establishes the turtle screen size (in pixels). The three pegs are positioned at the bottom center of the turtle screen (**line 236**) and the vertical separation of the disks on each peg is set to 24 pixels (**line 237**). (The separation between disks on a peg will be proportionally reduced in function `calcDiskLocations` so that smaller disks at the top of a stack of disks are closer together than larger disks.)

Variables `peg_A`, `peg_B`, and `peg_C` are initialized to integer values 0, 1, and 2, respectively. Thus, these values can serve as index values for lists holding both the disk objects on each peg, and a list storing all disk locations. The number of disks to solve the problem for is retrieved from the user by a call to `getNumDisks` and assigned to variable `num_disks` (**line 245**). Function `displayPegs` is then called to display the three pegs (**line 249**) for the locations in variable `peg_locations`. In **lines 252–253** the image file names the required number of disks (specified in `num_disks`) are assigned to variable `disk_images` by a call to function `getDiskImages`. The image file names are then passed to function `registerDiskImages` to be registered in turtle graphics as shapes to which turtle objects can be assigned.

The locations on each peg for where all the disks are to be placed is calculated by function `calcDiskLocations` (**lines 98–126**), called on **line 256**. The required number of disks

```
1  # Towers of Hanoi Program
2
3  from turtle import *
4  import time
5
6  def getNumDisks():
7
8      """Returns number of disks requested by user."""
9      num_disks = int(input('Enter the number of disks(2-8): '))
10
11     while num_disks < 2 or num_disks > 8:
12         print('Must select between 2 and 8 disks')
13         num_disks = int(input('Enter the number of disks (2-8): '))
14
15     return num_disks
16
17 def displayPegs(peg_locs):
18
19     """Displays peg images at peg_locs."""
20     # retrieve and register peg image
21     peg_image = 'Peg.gif'
22     register_shape(peg_image)
23
24     # set vertical offset
25     offset = 65
26
27     # create temp peg-shaped turtle
28     temp = Turtle()
29     temp.penup()
30     temp.shape(peg_image)
31
32     # stamp three images of peg-shaped turtle
33     for loc in peg_locs:
34         temp.setposition(loc[0], loc[1] + offset)
35         temp.stamp()
36
37 def getDiskImages(num):
38
39     """Returns a list of disk image file names for num requested.
40
41         Disk images in order from largest to smallest image.
42     """
43     # init empty images list
44     images = []
45
46     # init first image file name
47     disk_image = 'Disk-1.gif'
48
49     # create all disk images
50     for k in range(0,num):
51         images = ['Disk-' + str(k+1) + '.gif'] + images
52
53     return images
54
```

FIGURE 11-27 Towers of Hanoi Program (*Continued*)

(turtle objects) are created by function createDisks (**lines 80–96**) called on **line 261**. All disks are initially placed on the start peg (peg A) by function placeDisksOnStartPeg (**lines 128–132**), called on **line 264**. After being properly placed, the disks are made visible by function makeDisksVisible (**lines 134–138**) called on **line 267**. Once the disks are placed, there is a

```
55   def registerDiskImages(images):
56
57        """Registers disk image file names provided in images."""
58        for image in images:
59            register_shape(image)
60
61   def newPeg(image_file):
62
63        """Returns a new turtle with peg shape in image_file."""
64        peg = Turtle()
65        peg.hideturtle()
66        peg.shape(image_file)
67
68        return peg
69
70   def newDisk(image_file):
71
72        """Returns a new turtle with disk shape in image_file."""
73        disk = Turtle()
74        disk.penup()
75        disk.hideturtle()
76        disk.shape(image_file)
77
78        return disk
79
80   def createDisks(images):
81
82        """Returns a list of disk shape turtles for each image in images.
83
84           Disks ordered by image size from largest to smallest.
85        """
86        # init empty list of disks for all three pegs
87        disks = [[], [], []]
88
89        # create disks with all disks on first peg
90        for k in range(0, len(images)):
91
92            disks[0].append(newDisk(images[k]))
93            disks[1].append(None)
94            disks[2].append(None)
95
96        return disks
97
98   def calcDiskLocations(num_disks, peg_locs, separation):
99
100       """Returns the calculated locations of all disks for all three pegs.
101
102          Locations in order from largest (bottom) disk to smallest, with
103          decreasing separation for smaller disks.
104       """
```

FIGURE 11-27   Towers of Hanoi Program (*Continued*)

two-second delay by a call to the sleep function of the time module (**line 270**), followed by a call to the recursive function `towers` to begin the problem-solving process (**line 273**).

Function `towers` (**lines 211–225**) implements the recursive algorithm for solving the problem. When called, it is passed the peg to be treated as the start peg (from which disks are to be moved), a destination peg (where the disks are to be moved), and a spare peg (used as temporary storage while moving disks), and the number of disks to move. The base case is when there is only

```
105        # init
106        saved_separation = separation
107        all_disk_locations = []
108
109        # caculate locations of disks for all three pegs
111        for peg in range(0, 3):
112
113            disk_locs = []
114
115            for k in range(0, num_disks):
116
117                xloc = peg_locs[peg][0]
118                yloc = int(peg_locs[peg][1] + k * separation)
119
120                disk_locs.append((xloc, yloc))
121                separation = separation * 0.95
122
123            all_disk_locations.append(disk_locs)
124            separation = saved_separation
125
126        return all_disk_locations
127
128    def placeDisksOnStartPeg(start_peg, disks, locations):
129
130        """Places and displays disks on start peg in turtle graphics."""
131        for k in (range(0, len(disks[start_peg]))):
132            disks[start_peg][k].setposition(locations[start_peg][k])
133
134    def makeDisksVisible(start_peg, disks):
135
136        """Makes visible all disk-shaped turtles on start_peg."""
137        for k in range(0,len(disks[start_peg])):
138            disks[start_peg][k].showturtle()
139
140    def removeTopDisk(peg, disks):
141
142        """Returns the top disk of disks currently on peg."""
143        # init k to top-most position of disks on peg
144        k = len(disks[peg]) - 1
145        found = False
146
147        # find top-most position with disk in place
148        while k >= 0 and not found:
149
150            if disks[peg][k] != None:
151                disk = disks[peg][k]
152                disks[peg][k] = None
153                found = True
154            else:
155                k = k - 1
156
157        return disk
158
```

FIGURE 11-27   Towers of Hanoi Program (*Continued*)

one disk to move (checked for on **line 215**). In this case, the disk is simply moved from the start peg to the destination peg by call to moveDisk. Otherwise, the top num_disks − 1 are (recursively) moved from the start peg to the spare peg, the single remaining (bottom) disk is then moved from the start peg to the destination peg, and the num_disks − 1 disks on the spare peg are (recursively) moved to the destination peg.

```
159   def placeTopDisk(disk, peg, disks, disk_locations):
160
161       """Places disk on top of disks currently on peg."""
162       # init k to bottom-most position of disks on peg
163       k = 0
164       found = False
165
166       # assign disk to bottom-most position of peg with no disk
167       while k < len(disk_locations[peg]) and not found:
168
169           if disks[peg][k] == None:
170
171               disks[peg][k] = disk
172               found = True
173           else:
174               k = k + 1
175
176       return disk
177
178   def getNextAvailDiskLoc(peg, disks, disk_locations):
179
180       """Returns location for next disk on peg."""
181       # init k to bottom-most position of disks on peg
182       k = 0
183       found = False
184
185       # get bottom-most location of peg with no disk
186       while k < len(disks[peg]) and not found:
187
188           if disks[peg][k] == None:
189               loc = disk_locations[peg][k]
190               found = True
191           else:
192               k = k + 1
193
194       return loc
195
196   def moveDisk(from_peg, to_peg, disks, disk_locations):
197
198       """Moves disk on top of from_peg to top of to_peg."""
199       # get disk on top of from_peg
200       disk = removeTopDisk(from_peg, disks)
201
202       # get available loc for new disk on to_peg
202       new_loc = getNextAvailDiskLoc(to_peg, disks, disk_locations)
204
205       # move disk image
206       disk.goto(new_loc)
207
208       # add disk to to_peg list of disks
209       placeTopDisk(disk, to_peg, disks, disk_locations)
210
```

FIGURE 11-27   Towers of Hanoi Program (*Continued*)

```
211  def towers(start_peg, dest_peg, spare_peg, num_disks, disks,
212          disk_locations):
213
214      """Begins the problem solving process."""
215      if num_disks == 1:
216          moveDisk(start_peg, dest_peg, disks, disk_locations)
217          time.sleep(.5)
218
219      else:
220          towers(start_peg, spare_peg, dest_peg, num_disks - 1,
221              disks, disk_locations)
222
223          moveDisk(start_peg, dest_peg, disks, disk_locations)
224          towers(spare_peg, dest_peg, start_peg, num_disks - 1,
225              disks, disk_locations)
226
227  # ---- main
228
229  # program welcome
230  print('This program solves the Towers of Hanoi for up to eight disks')
231
232  # init turtle screen
233  setup(width=800, height=600)
234
235  # init display parameters
236  peg_locations = ((-150, -50), (0,-50), (150,-50))
237  disk_separation = 24
238
239  # initpeg numbers
240  peg_A = 0
241  peg_B = 1
242  peg_C = 2
243
244  # get number of disks
245  num_disks = getNumDisks()
246  print()
247
248  # display pegs
249  displayPegs(peg_locations)
250
251  # create and register disk images
252  disk_images = getDiskImages(num_disks)
253  registerDiskImages(disk_images)
254
255  # calc locations for all disks
256  disk_locs = calcDiskLocations(num_disks, peg_locations,
257  disk_separation)
258
259
```

FIGURE 11-27 Towers of Hanoi Program (*Continued*)

```
260   # create and position number of disks requested
261   disks = createDisks(disk_images)
262
263   # place all disks on start peg
264   placeDisksOnStartPeg(peg_A, disks, disk_locs)
265
266   # make all disks visible
267   makeDisksVisible(peg_A, disks)
268
269   # delay
270   time.sleep(2)
271
272   # start movement of disks
273   towers(peg_A, peg_C, peg_B, num_disks, disks, disk_locs)
274
275   # exit turtle screen
276   print('\nDone - Click screen to quit')
277   exitonclick()
```

FIGURE 11-27   Towers of Hanoi Program

CHAPTER SUMMARY

General Topics

Recursive Functions
Infinite Recursion
Factorial Function
Recursive Problem Solving
MergeSort
Iteration vs. Recursion
Fractals
Towers of Hanoi

Python-Specific Programming Topics

Recursive Functions in Python

CHAPTER EXERCISES

Section 11.1

1. For the following recursive functions, indicate which of the requirements of a properly designed recursive function each violates.

   (a) `def rfunc1(n):`
   `    return n + rfunc(n − 1)`

   (b) `def rfunc2(n):`
   `    if n == 0:`
   `        return 1`
   `    return n + rfunc2(n + 1)`

2. For the following Sierpinski triangle, indicate how many times function `drawSierpinskiTriangle` is called in the Sierpinski triangle program of Figure 11-9.

Sierpinski triangle evolution/
Wikimedia Commons

Section 11.2

3. Give all the steps for MergeSort in sorting the following list.

11   4   16   9   5   12   2   14

4. Indicate the results produced by the recursive function MergeSort in Figure 11-16 if line 3 was replaced with,

```
if len(lst) == 0:
```

PYTHON PROGRAMMING EXERCISES

P1. Write both a nonrecursive and recursive function that determines if a given number is even or not.

P2. Write both a nonrecursive and recursive function that determines how many times a given letter occurs in a provided string.

P3. Write both a nonrecursive and recursive function that displays a provided string backwards.

P4. Write both a nonrecursive and recursive function that converts numbers to base 2.

P5. Write both a nonrecursive and recursive function that calculates the Fibonacci number for any positive integer, defined as follows,

$$fib(0) = 0,$$
$$fib(1) = 1,$$
$$fib(n) = fib(n-1) + fib(n-2)$$

P6. Write both a nonrecursive and recursive function that displays the rows of asterisks given below,

P7. Write both a nonrecursive and recursive function that displays the rows of asterisks given below,

PROGRAM MODIFICATION PROBLEMS

M1. Towers of Hanoi: Reversal of Pegs

Modify the Towers of Hanoi program in section 11.4.3 so that the initial stack of disks is placed on peg C (as the start peg), and the final stack of disks is placed on peg A (the destination peg).

M2. Towers of Hanoi: Displayed List of Moves

Modify the Towers of Hanoi program in section 11.4.3 so that in addition to the movement of disks on the screen, the list of moves is displayed in the Python shell as given below,

```
Move disk from peg A to peg C
Move disk from peg A to peg B
Move disk from Peg C to peg A
etc.
```

M3. Sierpinski Triangle Program: Multiple Levels of Fractal Displayed

Modify the Sierpinski Triangle Program in section 11.1.3 so that it displays fours levels of the fractal as given below on the screen at once.

Sierpinski triangle evolution/ Wikimedia Commons

M4. Sierpinski Triangle Program: Modified for Creating Sierpinki Carpet

Modify the Sierpinski Triangle Program in section 11.1.3 so that it instead displays a Sierpinski carpet as the repeated pattern of a solid square surrounded by eight smaller squares as depicted below.

Johannes Rossel/ Sierpinski carpet 1, carpet 2, carpet 3, carpet 4/Wikimedia Commons

M5. Sierpinski Triangle Program: Modified for a Koch Snowflake

Modify the Sierpinski Triangle Program in section 11.1.3 so that a Koch snowflake fractal is generated instead. The progressive levels of a Koch snowflake fractal, like the Sierpinski triangle, are based on the repeated use of an equilateral triangle as given below,

1. Divide each side of the equilateral triangle into three segments.

2. Draw an equilateral triangle (of smaller size) with sides the length of the line segments above, with the base placed at the middle line segment, pointing outwards.

3. Remove the line segment forming the base of the newly placed triangle.

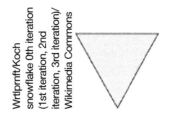

Wrtlprnft/Koch snowflake 0th iteration (1st iteration, 2nd iteration, 3rd iteration)/ Wikimedia Commons

PROGRAM DEVELOPMENT PROBLEMS

D1. Coin Change Program (Revisited)

Consider the Coin Change program in section 3.4.6 (for children learning to count change) in which the user had to enter a combination of coins that added up to a specified amount between 1 and 99 cents. Develop and test a program based on the use of recursion that "turns the tables" in which the user enters an amount between 1 and 99 cents, and the program must determine a set of coins that adds up to that amount using the least number of coins.

D2. Palindrome Checker (Revisited)

In Chapter 7 (section 7.3.7) a Palindrome Checker program was given based on the use of a stack that was also developed. Develop and test a Palindrome Checker program based on the use of recursion, instead of a stack.

D3. Phone Number Spelling Program (Revisited)

In Chapter 9 (section 9.1.2) a Phone Number Spelling program was given based on the use of deeply nested for loops. Develop and test a Phone Number Spelling program based on the use of recursion instead.

D4. Creative Designs

Using your imagination, develop and test a program using recursion that generates a fractal of your own design. As with the example fractals in the chapter, start with a basic geometric shape, and define the next level of the fractal pattern containing two or more smaller versions of the original-size shape.

D5. Develop a program that uses recursion to solve the Man, Cabbage, Goat, Wolf problem from Chapter 1.

## CHAPTER 12

Computing and Its Developments

In this final chapter, we look at the many developments and innovations that have led to present-day computing. This includes advancements in computer hardware, computer software, and computer networks, as well as theoretical developments that underlie our understanding and effective utilization of computing.

OBJECTIVES

After reading this chapter you will:

♦ Be knowledgeable about many of the developments in computing

♦ Become familiar with some of the most notable individuals in the field

♦ Be able to describe the four generations of computer technology

CHAPTER CONTENTS

Fourth-Generation Computers (early 1970s to the Present)

12.9 The Rise of the Microprocessor

12.10 The Dawn of Personal Computing

The Development of Computer Networks

12.11 The Development of Wide Area Networks

12.12 The Development of Local Area Networks (LANs)

12.13 The Development of the Internet and World Wide Web

CONTRIBUTIONS TO THE MODERN COMPUTER

12.1   The Concept of a Programmable Computer

12.1.1   "Father of the Modern Computer"—Charles Babbage (1800s)

FIGURE 12-1   Charles Babbage

In London, England, during the 1800s, **Charles Babbage** (Figure 12-1) worked on a couple of different designs for a calculating machine. The first, called the "Difference Engine," was designed to perform only certain calculations. It was to be powered by steam with a built-in "printer" that would punch out calculation tables on metal plates, important for British navigation. A partial prototype was finished in 1822. Because of technical, financial, and other problems however, his continued attempts over the next nearly twenty years to finish its construction ended in failure. If completed, it would have measured ten-feet by ten-feet by five-feet, and would have weighted two tons.

Another machine that Babbage envisioned, however, would lead to his historical imminence—the **Analytical Engine** (Figure 12-2). He completed the first workable prototype in 1837, working on its completion until his death in 1871. A major conceptual breakthrough of the Analytical Engine was that the calculations it performed were based on a set of instructions fed to it. Therefore, it could be "programmed" to solve *any* mathematical problem, not just certain problems as with the

Difference Engine. As designed, it would have been fifteen feet tall and twenty-five feet long; about the size of a small locomotive train.

The Analytical Engine was never completed due to the limited technology of the time. Its design, however, is considered one of the greatest intellectual achievements of the nineteenth century. It contained the two fundamental components of current-day computers: a *mill* (a kind of central processing unit for executing instructions, fed as punched cards), and a *store* (a kind of memory or storage area). Because of Babbage's foresight, he has been given the deserved name "Father of the Modern Computer."

FIGURE 12-2   The Analytical Engine

Charles Babbage is considered the "Father of the Modern Computer" for his work on the Analytical Engine in the 1800s.

12.1.2 "The First Computer Programmer"—Ada Lovelace (1800s)

Augusta Ada Byron (Figure 12-3), Countess of Lovelace ("**Ada Lovelace**") and daughter of the poet Lord Byron, was a talented mathematician, who first met Charles Babbage in 1833. She was intrigued with his work, and inspired Babbage to continue with his Analytical Engine. She helped write widely published scientific articles on the machine and Babbage's ideas. She showed her insightfulness by predicting that such machines were capable of processing not only numbers, but any encoded information. For example, she gave predictions that someday these machines would be able to produce graphics, compose music, and have scientific use (beyond mere scientific calculation). Because of her foresight, she is credited with being the "First Computer Programmer." The **Ada programming language** is named in her honor.

FIGURE 12-3   Ada Lovelace

Ada Lovelace is considered the "First Computer Programmer" for her work, insight and writings on the Analytical Engine.

12.2 Developments Leading to Electronic Computing

12.2.1 The Development of Boolean Algebra (mid-1800s)

We have already mentioned George Boole (Figure 12-4) in Chapter 3 in our discussions of Boolean algebra. His development of what we now call Boolean algebra, and the corresponding Boolean operators AND, OR, and NOT was conceived as a means of mathematically proving the answers to any true/false question. Later work showed that there are always some questions that cannot be answered mathematically. However, Boolean algebra became greatly applicable one hundred years later. It provides the logical foundation for the design of digital logic circuits of modern electronic computers.

FIGURE 12-4   George Boole

The development by **George Boole**, of what is now called Boolean algebra, provided the logical foundation for the development of digital circuits.

12.2.2 The Development of the Vacuum Tube (1883)

In 1883, **Thomas Edison** (Figure 12-5) invented the **vacuum tube** (Figure 12-6), an electronic device containing electrodes that electrons can travel between. The vacuum tube became the building block for the entire electronics industry at the time. A version of the device can be used as an electronic switch, which became a critical component in the development of the first modern electronic computers.

FIGURE 12-5
Thomas Edison

FIGURE 12-6   Vacuum Tubes

Thomas Edison invented the vacuum tube, which became the first form of electronic switch in electronic computers.

12.2.3 The Development of Digital Electronic Logic Gates (1903)

Serbian-born **Nikola Tesla** (Figure 12-7), who once worked for Thomas Edison, patented in 1903 the **electronic logic gate**. Such gates, composed of a small number of vacuum tubes as electronic switches, could electronically execute the logical operators of Boolean algebra—AND, OR, and NOT. Two different electrical signals representing either true or false were input to the gate, with an output electrical signal representing the true/false result, as shown in Figure 12-8. Logic gates would become fundamental to all electronic digital computers to come, the idea to be rediscovered decades later.

FIGURE 12-7   Nikola Tesla

5 volts (true) ⟩ 5 volts (true)
5 volts (true)

5 volts (true) ⟩ 0 volts (false)
0 volts (false)

FIGURE 12-8   AND Logic Gate

Nikola Tesla patented the electronic logic gate, which would become a fundamental component of all electronic computers.

12.2.4   The Development of Memory Electronic Circuits (1919)

American physicists **W. H. Eccles** (Figure 12-9) and **R. W. Jordan** in 1919 invented the **flip-flop** electronic switching circuit. These devices, based on use of vacuum tubes, were able to "flip and flop" from one stable state to another. Such a device is always in one of two states, thus provides a form of electronic storage, or "memory." Flip-flop electronic components, like Tesla's electronic logic gates, would become key components in the development of future digital electronic computers.

WilliamHenryEccles/
Wikimedia Commons

FIGURE 12-9
W. H. Eccles

W. H. Eccles and **R. W. Jordan** invented the flip-flop electronic switching circuit to become a fundamental component of all electronic computers.

12.2.5   The Development of Electronic Digital Logic Circuits (1937)

In 1937, **George Stibitz** (Figure 12-10) of Bell Laboratories, working on his kitchen table one night created the first digital electronic logic circuit. A digital electronic circuit is a circuit built out of electronic logic gates that can execute arithmetic or logical operations. Because such circuits are built out of combinations of logic gates, they are referred to as **combinatorial circuits**. Boolean algebra provides a mathematical basis for denoting, analyzing, and understanding such circuits.

The digital logic circuit that Stibitz built was for adding two binary digits, called a (full) **binary adder**. Such an adder is a fundamental component of all modern computers. Stibitz's work demonstrated the feasibility of building electronic logical and arithmetic circuits from the basic building blocks of electronic logic gates that Tesla earlier developed. This development, along with the flip-flop electronic circuit of Eccles and Jordan for the electronic storage of information, completed the technology needed for the design and construction of a fully electronic computer.

Courtesy of the Department of Mathematics and
Computer Science, Denison University

FIGURE 12-10   George Stibitz

George Stibitz created the first digital electronic logic circuit, constructed out of a combination of electronic logic gates.

12.2.6 "The Father of Information Theory"—Claude Shannon (1948)

FIGURE 12-11 Claude Shannon

While many of his colleagues were working on the hardware design of modern computers, **Claude Shannon** (Figure 12-11) at Bell Laboratories, worked on a theory of information to be processed by such machines. In 1937, at the age of 21, Shannon wrote a master's thesis that showed how Boolean algebra can be simulated electronically by simple electronic switches to perform both logical and numerical calculations—the fundamental concept of digital computing today. Some considered Shannon's result possibly the most important master's thesis of the twentieth century.

Later, in 1948, Shannon published a paper that laid the foundation for what would become the field of information theory. Shannon's *Fundamental Theorem of Information Science* states that *all* information can be represented by use of only two symbols, "0" and "1," which he called **bits** (<u>bi</u>nary di<u>gits</u>). It has been said that the digital revolution began with Shannon's work.

It was therefore clear that electronic switches could both be used for the design of digital logic circuits (e.g., a circuit for adding two numbers), and for the storage of information of any kind, not only numerical values (as Ada Lovelace foresaw). Given Shannon's demonstration of the sufficiency of binary encoding for encoding all information, the stage was set for the development of electronic binary digital computing as we know it today. For his work, Shannon is known as the "Father of Information Theory."

Such binary coding of information was already in practical use for the transmittance of messages as audible electronic signals over wire. Earlier, in 1837, **Samuel Morse** (Figure 12-12) patented his design of a telegraph, which could electronically send messages (text) in the form of two signals, dots (e.g. short beep) and dashes (long beep), called **Morse Code**. Since only two signals were used, this represented a form of binary encoding.

FIGURE 12-12 Samuel Morse

Claude Shannon developed the *Fundamental Theorem of Information Science*, stating that *all* information can be represented by only two symbols, "0" and "1," which he called bits (<u>bi</u>nary di<u>gits</u>).

FIRST-GENERATION COMPUTERS (1940s–mid-1950s)

12.3 The Early Groundbreakers

12.3.1 The Z3—The First Programmable Computer (1941)

Konrad Zuse (Figure 12-13) built a number of binary computing devices starting in 1935, at a time when other computers were being built based on the decimal system. His initial machines were the **Z1**, the first mechanical binary digital computing device, and the **Z2**, the first fully functioning electromechanical computing device, completed in 1939 as World War II was approaching. Each of these devices had limited programmability, however.

While his design of binary computers with the Z1 and Z2 was significant, his most notable accomplishment was the development of the **Z3**, the first working electromechanical *programmable* computer, completed in 1941. The Z3, like the Z2, was an electromechanical device. After serving in the German army, he realized the computing potential of a fully electronic version of his computing devices. He submitted a proposal to the German army for funding for his next generation of machine, a fully electronic calculator, the **Z4**.

FIGURE 12-13   Konrad Zuse

A fully electronic machine would have been thousands of times faster than his electromechanical versions. It would therefore have significant military use, such as for aircraft design and breaking coded messages. (We shall see that the Allies had crucial success here.) He estimated the project would take two years. His proposal was flatly turned down by the German Army Command since it was believed that Germany would soon win the war (which, of course, they lost a few years later in 1945). He went on to build the Z4 after the war, completing an electromechanical version in 1949 to become the world's first commercially available digital computer. He even wrote his own programming language for the Z4, called *Plankalkul,* with features of modern-day languages that was definitely ahead of its time.

Konrad Zuse developed the first working programmable computing device, the **Z3**, an electromechanical binary digital computer, as well as the first commercially available electronic computer, the **Z4**.

12.3.2   The Mark I—First Computer Project in the United States (1937–1943)

Howard Aiken (Figure 12-14), a mathematics instructor at Harvard University, began a project in 1937 to build a general-purpose (i.e., programmable) electromechanical calculating machine. It was the first project for the development of a modern computer in the United States (developed without knowledge of the work of Konrad Zuse). Aiken, as opposed to most others in the early computing field, knew of Babbage's work, and therefore saw himself as following through with Babbage's unfulfilled dream. Now, however, Aiken had available current-day technology that Babbage did not.

The technology available at the time was electromechanical, making use of relay switches that mechanically switched on and off by control of electrical signals. The machine, therefore, was not a fully electronic computer, and thus limited in speed by the speed of the mechanical switching of the relay switches. IBM agreed to fund the project and supplied an engineering team to build the machine following Aiken's design. When the machine was finally finished in 1943, it was eight feet tall, fifty-one feet long, two feet thick, and weighed

FIGURE 12-14   Howard Aiken

five tons (Figure 12-15). It read instructions from (punched) paper tape, and data from punched cards.

Ironically, true to technological developments of today, the Mark I was obsolete the moment it was completed, since fully electronic computers were just on the horizon. It was, however, very newsworthy at the time, and a big press release was given to announce its completion. The Mark I turned out to be very reliable compared to other electronic computers. It was able to run 24 hours a day, seven days a week, and therefore was very productive. It was used over a period of 16 years. Its development has been called the "real dawn of the computer age" (in the United States).

FIGURE 12-15 Harvard Mark I Electromechanical Computer

The **Mark I** computer, designed by **Howard Aiken** at Harvard, was the first project for the development of a modern computer in the United States. Other, more advanced computers, however, were built before the completion of the Mark I.

12.3.3 The ABC—The First Fully Electronic Computing Device (1942)

FIGURE 12-16 John Atanasoff

John V. Atanasoff (Figure 12-16), a physicist at Iowa State University, completed a design of a calculating device between 1939 and 1942 with graduate student **Clifford Berry**, called the **ABC** (Atanasoff-Berry Computer). It was the first to use vacuum tubes both for calculations (for the logic circuits) and for memory storage. Therefore, it was the first fully electronic computing device. However, since it was designed to solve only particular types of mathematical problems and could not be programmed, it was not a general-purpose computer.

The ABC was a binary computer, designed to store numerical values in base 2 (i.e., binary notation), and not base 10 as had all other machines previously built, with the exception of the computing devices developed by Konrad Zuse in Germany. Because of the war, neither Atanasoff nor Zuse knew of the others' work. Therefore each independently hit upon the novel idea of a binary computer at essentially the same time.

A functioning prototype was finished in October 1939 that could do simple addition and subtraction in binary of eight digit decimal values. In 1942, the final version was completed and tested (Figure 12-17). It was the size of a desk, weighed 700 pounds, had over 300 vacuum tubes, and contained a mile of wire.

FIGURE 12-17 The ABC Was the First Fully Electronic Computing Device

After testing of the machine was completed, Atanasoff worked on assignments for the war effort, and no further development or use of the machine followed. Given that the ABC was not a programmable device, it lacked a key feature of other machines at the time, but is credited as the first fully electronic (binary) computing device.

> **John V. Atanasoff** and **Clifford Berry** developed the **ABC** (Atanasoff-Berry Computer), a fully electronic binary computer. It was not, however, a programmable device.

12.3.4 Colossus—A Special-Purpose Electronic Computer (1943)

Karsten Sperling/EnigmaMachineLabeled/Wikimedia Commons

FIGURE 12-18 The Enigma (During World War II)

At the start of World War II, in 1939, Great Britain had decided that it would call upon the greatest mathematical and scientific minds available to break the ciphers that Germany was using for top-secret communications. The Enigma (Figure 12-18), developed at the end of World War I, generated complex coding of messages based on constantly changing alphabetic substitutions. It was believe by the Germans to be an unbreakable code.

A secret project was begun in Great Britain to build a machine capable of breaking the Enigma code. The electromechanical machine was called **Bombe** (Figure 12-19).

NSA/Bombe/Wikimedia Commons

FIGURE 12-19 Bombe

This allowed, in particular, the breaking of German naval codes, and resulted in the significant reduction of shipping losses across the Atlantic to the United States, essential for the allied support. Later, however, a second generation of encryption was developed by the Germans that was significantly more complex, using a new encryption called Lorenz code. A second new, fully electronic machine was designed and built for breaking this new code.

The machine was called the **Colossus**, a fully electronic binary machine, completed at the end of 1943. A number of machines of this design were built and used (Figure 12-20). A second version, the Colossus II, was finished on June 1, 1944. A few days after its completion, the Allies were able to intercept and decode a message from the German High Command. The message indicated that the Germans had fallen for misinformation put out by the Allies that their landing point was an area called Calais, while in fact, their planned landing location was the beaches of Normandy. As a result, commander Dwight D. Eisenhower decided to go ahead with the Normandy invasion—the infamous D-Day—on June 6, 1944 (less than a week after the Colossus II was finished). It is believed by many that the ability to break German codes brought the turning point of the war in the Allies favor.

UK/Colossus/Wikimedia Commons

FIGURE 12-20 The Colossus

The **Colossus**, built in Britain to break German codes during World War II, is believed by many to have turned the war in the Allies, favor.

12.3.5   ENIAC—The First Fully Electronic Programmable Computer

The U.S. Army's Need for a Fully Electronic Computer (1943)

When the United States entered World War II in 1941, there was a sudden increased need of people who calculated ballistic firing tables, so-called "human computers" (Figure 12-21). In order to hit their target, gunners needed to aim their weapon at the proper angle and direction based on a number of factors including the distance of the target, the wind speed, wind direction, and air temperature. Gunners depended on such firing tables to find the correct angle of fire for all the current conditions for all the different ballistic missiles.

NASA/Early NACA human computers at work/dfrc.nasa.gov

FIGURE 12-21   "Computers" During World War II

At the U.S. Army's Ballistic Research Laboratory at Aberdeen Proving Ground in Maryland, hundreds of human computers (mostly female mathematicians) were employed to calculate such tables. Two to four thousand possible trajectories had to be calculated for each pair of projectile and gun. Each human computer, using an electromechanical desk calculator, took almost three days to compute a single trajectory! By 1943, the Army was not able to keep up with the calculation of all the firing tables needed, and was desperately in need of a solution. Thus, the Army was willing to fund the construction of a fully electronic computer capable of solving this problem.

In 1943, the U.S. army was in desperate need of a means of computing the large number of firing tables needed for various ballistic missiles.

The Development of the ENIAC at the University of Pennsylvania (1945)

In August 1942, an assistant professor at The Moore School of Electrical Engineering at the University of Pennsylvania, **John W. Mauchly** (Figure 12-22) had written a paper on "The Use of High Speed Vacuum Tube Devices for Calculating." While his idea was realized by others, he understood the kinds of computing speeds that such an electronic switching device could produce over electromechanical machines—tens of thousands of operations per second. He, along with a young electronics engineer named **Presper Eckert**, was awarded a contract by the U.S. Army in June 1943 to build their electronic calculating machine, with an agreement to build a duplicate of the machine at Aberdeen Proving Grounds. (The size of computers then did not allow them to be moved around—they were permanently located!)

Courtesy of the Trustees of the University of Pennsylvania

FIGURE 12-22   John Mauchly and Presper Eckert

The **ENIAC** (for "Electronic Numerical Integrator and Computer"), shown in Figure 12-23, was finished in November 1945 (too late for its originally intended purpose) about three months after the end of the war.

It was eight feet high, eighty feet long, and weighed 30 tons. It used decimal notation, and thus was not a binary computer. When finished, however, it was roughly a thousand times faster than any other computer at the time. Whereas existing specialized calculators took fifteen to thirty minutes to compute the trajectory of a ballistic missile, the ENIAC took only twenty seconds, capable of 5,000 ten-digit additions per second.

As a demonstration of ENIAC's general-purpose functionality, the ENIAC was reprogrammed to do crucial calculations on the development of the first hydrogen bomb (an advanced weapon of the atomic bomb was used in World War II). Programming on the ENIAC, however, did not mean sitting down and typing lines at a keyboard as is done today. It had to be physically reprogrammed by changing switches and reconnecting a patchwork of wires.

FIGURE 12-23 The ENIAC Computer

The data for the currently configured program was submitted on punch cards. Its biggest problem was the unreliability of the almost 18,000 vacuum tubes it contained. In fact, the reason that base ten representation was chosen over binary was that the binary approach would have taken many more such vacuum tubes. Although ENIAC proved itself to be extremely fast at the time, the unreliability of the vacuum tube was to remain one of its shortcomings.

Because of intellectual property rights disputes in 1946 with the University of Pennsylvania, John Mauchly and Presper Eckert decided to leave the university to form the Eckert-Mauchly Computer Corporation. They believed in the potential of commercial computers, whereas others did not see the need for more than one or two computers in the whole country. They went on to design and build one the first commercial computer in the United States, the UNIVAC I (shown in Figure 12-22).

John Mauchly and **Presper Eckert** developed the ENIAC, the first fully-electronic programmable computer in the U.S.

12.3.6 EDVAC/ACE—The First Stored Program Computers (1950)

Even before Eckert and Mauchly had completed the design of the ENIAC, they conceived of the idea of a stored-program computer. In the ENIAC, only the data was stored in memory (via punched cards). To execute diffferent programs, the ENIAC had to be rewired, and later was reprogrammed through a series of switches. In a stored-program computer, the program need only be entered once and stored in memory. This concept was an important next step since high-speed computers like the ENIAC were slowed by the need to be reprogrammed this way.

In 1944, Eckert and Mauchly received another contract from the army's Ballistic Research Laboratory, this time for the development of a stored-program computer to be called EDVAC. A distinguished mathematician from Princeton named **John von Neumann** (Figure 12-24) joined the project. Even though Eckert and Mauchly

FIGURE 12-24 John von Neumann

had earlier conceived of the idea of a stored-program computer, von Neumann developed a method of how it could work, and thus is generally cited as the originator of the idea. The *von Neumann machine* remains the predominant means of stored program execution today.

> **John von Neumann** is credited with the concept of a stored-program computer. The first such computer built was called **EDVAC**. Its method of executing stored programs is utilized in essentially all computers today, called a **von Neumann machine**.

The British Stored-Program Computer—ACE (1950)

British scientists visited the Moore School of Electrical Engineering at the University of Pennsylvania soon after the end of World War II. On return to Britain, they worked on their own stored program computer named **ACE** (for "Automatic Computing Engine"). The lead designer of the project was one of the most influential and significant individuals in the history of computing, **Alan Turing**, who also played a key role in breaking German codes of World War II (Figure 12-25). A scaled-down version of the stored-program machine was completed in 1950 (before the completion of the EDVAC).

FIGURE 12-25   Alan Turing

> After the development of the EDVAC computer, Great Britain began worked on their own stored-program computer named **ACE** (for "Automatic Computing Engine"). The lead designer of the project was one of the most influential and significant individuals in the history of computing, **Alan Turing**.

12.3.7   Whirlwind—The First Real-Time Computer (1951)

In December 1944, the U.S. Navy asked MIT to do a feasibility study of the development of a special-purpose flight trainer to train pilots. This required the machine to be capable of real-time processing—that is, to compute fast enough to instantaneously respond to the actions of training pilots. A young gifted engineering graduate student, **Jay W. Forrester**, was offered the project. He changed the goal of the project from the development of a special-purpose device, to the design and development of a general electronic digital stored-program computer that could operate in real time.

The computer that Forrester developed was called **Whirlwind** (Figure 12-26). Although it operated in real time, it had one serious problem. The method of memory storage, consisting of thirty-two cathode ray tubes that rarely lasted more than a month, was unreliable, often putting the machine out of service.

FIGURE 12-26   The Whirlwind Computer

Forrester revolutionized the technology of memory storage by using magnetically charged, doughnut-shaped ceramic ferrite "cores" that could be electronically magnetized in a clockwise or counterclockwise direction (to represent "1" and "0"), shown in Figure 12-27. The cores were configured in a grid form, threaded with cross sections of wires so that any given core could be read or written by selection of the proper "vertical and horizontal" wires. The memory board in the figure is 6.5 inches square, and contained a storage capacity of 1024 bits. The term *core* is still used today—mainly in the term *core dump* referring to the raw display, or "dump" of the contents of main memory—even though computers no longer use magnetic core memory.

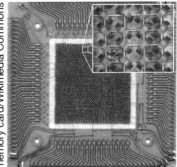

Orion 8/Ferrite core memory; Thierry46/Magnetic core; H.J. Sommer III, Professor of Mechanical Engineering, Penn State University/Magnetic core memory card/Wikimedia Commons

FIGURE 12-27 One Plane of Magnetic Core Memory

Besides the speed of this form of memory, another important feature was that each bit (or core) of memory could be read and written in the same amount of time. This was called *random access memory* (RAM), an essential characteristic of computer memory today. Core memory technology remained the main memory technology for almost thirty years.

The Whirlwind, developed by **Jay W. Forrester**, was the first real-time computer, also introducing the use of core (random access) memory.

12.4 The First Commercially Available Computers

A new stage of computer history began when companies started manufacturing commercial computers. This was the first time that computers were not thought of as unique, one-of-a-kind machines, but as particular *model* computers. A new industry was beginning that many people did not see coming. This is reflected in a quote by Thomas Watson, president of IBM in 1943: "I think there is a market for maybe five computers in the world." Two of the more notable commercially available computers first appeared at essentially the same time—the UNIVAC (mentioned earlier) in the United States, and the LEO, in Great Britain (discussed in the following).

12.4.1 The Struggles of the Eckert-Mauchly Computer Corporation (1950)

Eckert and Mauchly needed financial backing to produce their computer, the **UNIVAC I**. The Census Bureau was very interested in the development of this machine, and in 1946 gave the company their first contract to build a UNIVAC. However, the amount agreed on was not enough to cover all the development cost. By 1948, Eckert and Mauchly had five UNIVAC contracts but no completed machine, selling out to the Remington Rand Corporation in early 1950. Finally, in March 1951, the first UNIVAC (Figure 12-28) was built and delivered to the U.S. Census Bureau. Eventually, forty-six UNIVAC I computers were built and sold. The UNIVAC became very publicly known, appearing in cartoons and movies of the time. One notable event was when it was used on live TV to predict the U.S. presidential election

Matthias.Kirschner/UNIVAC I Factronic/Wikimedia Commons

FIGURE 12-28 The UNIVAC I

between Dwight D. Eisenhower and Adlai Stevenson in the 1952 election (Figure 12-29).

Most pollsters had predicted a close election race. However, UNIVAC, using data from past elections, predicted a landslide win for Eisenhower. Given the unbelievability of the results, they did not announce this prediction to the TV viewers. As it turned out, Eisenhower won by one of the biggest landslides in history. Afterwards, later that evening, news commentator Walter Cronkite had to admit that UNIVAC had earlier made the right predication—"UNIVAC was right, we were wrong!"

U.S. Census Bureau/UNIVAC 1 demo/Wikimedia Commons

FIGURE 12-29   UNIVAC Predicting the 1952 Presidential Election

The UNIVAC I was the first commercially available computer in the U.S.

12.4.2   The LEO Computer of the J. Lyons and Company (1951)

Photo by Sasha/Hulton Archive/Getty Images, Inc.

FIGURE 12-30   The J. Lyons and Company

The J. Lyons and Company of London, England, was one of the largest catering and food manufacturing companies in the world (Figure 12-30). After a trip to the United States in 1947 by two managers of the company, they realized that electronic computers would hold the key to improved efficiency of clerical procedures. Given that there was an ongoing computer project at Cambridge University, they offered some funding to the university for the project in return for advice on how to build their own computer. A recent Ph.D. graduate of Cambridge who had worked on the computer project there joined the Lyons company, and a team of technical employees was hired.

Work started on the construction of the computer, named **LEO** (for "Lyons Electronic Office"), started in January 1949 (Figure 12-31). The computer became operational in September 1951, just six months after the construction of the first UNIVAC computer in the United States. However, it took a couple more years before the machine was reliable enough to market. It became, however, the "world's first business computer."

Soon, many companies heard of the machine, and it became a big success. At first, Lyons began "renting out" time on their machine. Eventually, Lyons started building machines for sale to others, and thus became, in addition to a food service company, a computer manufacturer. Various models of the LEO computer sold moderately well until the 1960s, when American-built computers began dominating the UK computer market. Great Britain was soon after that out of the computer manufacturing business.

Courtesy of the LEO Computers Society

FIGURE 12-31   The LEO ("Lyons Electronic Office") I Computer

The **LEO** ("Lyons Electronic Office") was the first commercially available computer in the United Kingdom, with its production beginning in 1951.

SECOND-GENERATION COMPUTERS (mid-1950s to mid-1960s)

12.5   Transistorized Computers

12.5.1   The Development of the Transistor (1947)

The **transistor**, developed by **William B. Shockley**, **John Bardeen**, and **Walter H. Brattain** at Bell Telephone Laboratories in December 1947, is a solid-state, semiconductor device that enables the switching of electrical circuits "on" (e.g., "1") and "off ("0"). Thus in combination, transistors can be used to create logic circuits (such as the addition of two numbers). A transistor is referred to as a **solid-state device** because it is composed of solid material, in contrast to the previous switching technology of the vacuum tube. Vacuum tubes are similar to light bulbs in size, generate significant heat, and eventually "burn out," needing replacement. Solid-state devices do not burn out, do not generate significant heat, can be made arbitrarily small, and do not draw much power. A comparison of these two devices is shown in Figure 12-32.

FIGURE 12-32   The Vacuum Tube vs. the Transistor

www.nobelprize.org. Used by permission.

Transistors are referred to as **semiconductors** because their electrical conductivity lies between that of insulators (like rubber) and conductors (like copper). The degree of conductivity can be ectronically altered, which is what makes them a suitable electronic switching device, as shown in Figure 12-33.

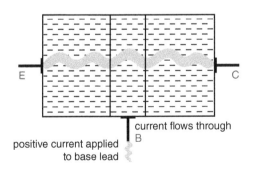

current flows through B

positive current applied to base lead

Transistor Switched On
(E – emitter   C – collector   B – base lead)

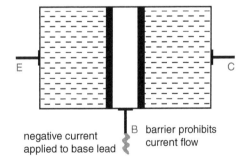

B   barrier prohibits current flow

negative current applied to base lead

Transistor Switched Off
(E – emitter   C – collector   B – base lead)

FIGURE 12-33   Transistor Switching Devices

Transistors operate through three connections, referred to as the *emitter*, the *collector*, and the *base lead*. The flow of current from emitter to collector is strictly determined by whether there is currently a positive voltage or negative voltage applied to the base lead. When a positive voltage is applied to the base lead, the material between the emitter and the collector becomes conductive, and electrons are free to flow, thus turning the connection "on." Alternatively, when a negative voltage is applied to the base lead, material between the emitter and collector becomes nonconductive, preventing electrons from freely flowing, thus turning the connection "off." These simple switching devices can be used in arbitrary combinations in order to produce any given digital logic combinatorial circuit desired. William B. Shockley, John Bardeen, and Walter H. Brattain (Figure 12-34) received the Nobel Prize in Physics in 1956 for their discovery of the transistor effect.

FIGURE 12-34 Bardeen, Brattain, and Shockley (Nobel Prize in Physics 1956)

The transistor is a solid state electronic switching device developed by **William B. Shockley**, **John Bardeen**, and **Walter H. Brattain**.

12.5.2 The First Transistor Computer (1953)

The world's first transistorized computer was completed in 1953 at the University of Manchester in the United Kingdom (Figure 12-35). A computer using all transistors as electronic switching devices rather than the vacuum tube standard at the time had a number of advantages, as mentioned above transistors do not burn out like they took much less space, and did not generated significant heat as compared to vacuum tube technology. In 1962, a transistorized computer that was developed by this research group was the fastest in the world.

FIGURE 12-35 The First Transistorized Computer

The first fully-transistorized computer was completed at the University of Manchester in 1953.

12.6 The Development of High-Level Programming Languages

12.6.1 The Development of Assembly Language (early 1950s)

In the mid-1950s, all of the computers at the time were extremely tedious to program. They needed to be programmed in either *machine code* or *assembly language*. **Machine code** (or **machine language**) is a numerical code and is the "native" language of the machine. For example, the numerical code "1001" might represent an add operation. **Assembly language** is a symbolic notation using what are called *mnemonics* in place of the numerical codes of machine language—"add" might be used in place of "1001".

Although assembly language is somewhat better than machine code, it is still a low-level language. *Low level* means that each instruction performs a very simple task. For example, to accomplish the assignment A = B + C takes a number of assembly language instructions to accomplish. Assembly language represents some improvement over numerical machine code notation. However, programming in assembly language is still very tedious. Thus, *high-level* programming languages were developed, discussed next.

> **Assembly language** is a symbolic notation using what are called *mnemonics* in place of the numerical codes of machine language.

12.6.2   The First High-Level Programming Languages (mid-1950s)

The use of assembly language, although an improvement over machine code, was only of minor help. Therefore, better programming languages needed to be designed. One of the most influential individuals in the history of computer science was **Grace Murray Hopper** (Figure 12-36). In 1951, working at Remington Rand (maker of the UNIVAC computer), she conceived a new type of programming language that could help "automate" the task of programming. The language was called a **high-level language** since the programmer could write instructions in a more natural form. For example, a programmer could write a single instruction such as A = B + C, without needing to break it down into the more primitive set of machine/assembly language instructions.

FIGURE 12-36   Navy Admiral Grace Murray Hopper

Since computers are designed to execute only machine code, in order to execute programs written in a high-level programming language, they need to first be translated into machine code. Such a translator is called a **compiler**. Whereas each line of an assembly language program is translated to one line of machine code, and thus a "one-to-one" translation, a compiler is capable of a "one-to-many" translation. Thus, one line of a program written in a high-level language is translated into many machine code instructions that accomplish it. The idea of a compiler that Grace Murray Hopper put forth was one of the most important in the development of modern computers.

IBM came out with the first programming language for commercially available computers in 1957 called **FORTRAN** ("FORmula TRANslation"). FORTRAN was a language suited for scientific programming. Other languages of note that were developed around the same time were **COBOL** ("Common Business Oriented Language") based largely on the work that Hopper did at Remington Rand, meant for business processing needs; **ALGOL** ("ALGOrithmic Language"), for general computing; **LISP** ("List Processing Language"), well suited for developing artificial intelligence programs; and **BASIC** ("Beginners All-Purpose Symbolic Instruction Code"), meant as an easy-to-learn language to make computer programming accessible to all college students, developed by **John Kemeny** at Dartmouth College in 1963. BASIC became the first programming language available on the earliest personal computers, and by the end of the 1980s, millions of school children had learned to use it.

Grace Murray Hopper, in 1951, conceived of a new type of programming language that could help "automate" the task of programming, referred to as *high-level languages*.

12.6.3 The First "Program Bug" (1947)

American engineers have been calling small flaws in machines *bugs* for over a century. Thomas Edison talked about bugs in electrical circuits in the 1870s. When the first computers were built during the early 1940s, people working on them similarly referred to "bugs" in both the hardware of the machines and in the programs that ran them.

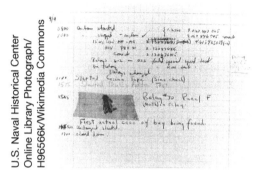

U.S. Naval Historical Center Online Library Photograph/ H96566k/Wikimedia Commons

FIGURE 12-37 The First "Computer Bug"

In 1947, engineers working on the Mark II computer at Harvard University found a moth stuck in one of the components, causing the machine to malfunction. They taped the insect in their logbook and labeled it "first actual case of bug being found (Figure 12-37)." It has become a standard part of the language of computer programmers. The log book, complete with the attached bug, is on display at the Smithsonian Institution in Washington, D.C.

In 1947, engineers working on the Mark II computer at Harvard University found a moth stuck in one of the components, causing the machine to malfunction. They taped the insect in their logbook and labeled it "first actual case of bug being found."

THIRD-GENERATION COMPUTERS (mid-1960s to early 1970s)

12.7 The Development of the Integrated Circuit (1958)

While transistors had the aforementioned advantages over vacuum tube technology, there remained the problem of how to wire together the increasing number of transistors needed for the increasingly powerful computers being designed, known as the "tyranny of numbers." This was evident with the transistorized computers. The solution to this problem was the development of the integrated circuit (or semiconductor chip), in which such wiring of components became unnecessary.

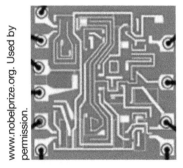

www.nobelprize.org. Used by permission.

FIGURE 12-38 Integrated (Printed) Circuit

Two different individuals, **Jack Kilby** at Texas Instruments and **Robert Noyce** at Fairchild Semiconductor, were both working hard on a solution to the problem. The elegant, practical solution that they eventually found was to replace the method of *wiring* together components on digital circuit boards with a method of *printing* the "wiring" onto a thin wafer of semiconductor material (as shown in Figure 12-38). Thus, transistors and circuits were "integrated" together in the manufacturing. This device, therefore, was called an **integrated circuit (IC)** (or semiconductor chip). This not only

made circuits smaller, but much cheaper to mass-produce. By 1961, both companies were producing commercially available integrated circuits.

It is generally agreed that Jack Kilby was first to conceive of and develop the integrated circuit in 1958, and Robert Noyce is credited with developing practical manufacturing principles that allowed for its commercialization. Jack Kilby went on to invent the portable calculator in 1967. Robert Noyce (with Gordon E. Moore, who was a cofounder of Fairchild) started in 1968 a new company named Intel (for "Integrated Electronics").

In the year 2000, Jack Kilby (Figure 12-39) was awarded the Nobel Prize in Physics for the invention of the integrated circuit. The importance of the development of the integrated circuit cannot be overstated. It forms the basis of all modern computing today, and is said to have caused a "second industrial revolution." It stands historically as one of the most important inventions of mankind.

FIGURE 12-39 Jack Kilby—Inventor of the Integrated Circuit

> *"What we didn't realize then was that the integrated circuit would reduce the cost of electronic functions by a factor of a million to one, nothing had ever done that for anything before."*—Jack Kilby

An example packaged integrated circuit ("chip") is shown in Figure 12-40.

HenkeB/Z84C0010FEC LQFP/Wikimedia Commons

FIGURE 12-40 A Modern Integrated Circuit

The integrated circuit, invented and developed by **Jack Kilby** and **Robert Noyce**, stands as one of the most important inventions of mankind.

12.7.1 The Catalyst for Integrated Circuit Advancements (1960s)

While integrated circuits had been commercially available since 1961, computer manufacturers did not jump on the new technology because it meant completely redesigning their current transistor-based machines. However, there was a politically motivated, impossible-seeming challenge that would be put forth to Americans that would speed up the development of this technology. America and the Soviet Union were about to enter a "space race."

The Beginning of the Space Race

On October 4, 1957, the Soviet Union (now Russia) launched the first artificial satellite, named "Sputnik" (Figure 12-41), sending shock waves throughout the United States. In April 1961, the Soviets had their first successful manned flight, by Cosmonaut Yuri Gagarin, with many successful manned flights following. The United States had no space program.

In response, in October 1958, **NASA** (National Aeronautics and Space Administration) was created, exactly one year after Sputnik was launched. The first U.S. manned space flight occurred on May 5, 1961. Alan B. Shepard Jr. took a 15-minute suborbital

NSSDC, NASA/Sputnik asm/ Wikimedia Commons

FIGURE 12-41 Sputnik Satellite

spaceflight that made him the first American in space. Less than a year later, on February 20, 1962, John H. Glenn Jr. became the first American to orbit the Earth. These were the first steps on a race to the moon.

On October 4, 1957, the Soviet Union (now Russia) launched the first artificial satellite, named "Sputnik" sending shock waves through the United States.

President Kennedy's Challenge of Going to the Moon (1961)

In 1961, **John F. Kennedy** was inaugurated as president. It was the height of the cold war with the Soviet Union. Although Allies in World War II, the United States and Soviet Union came out of the war distrustful of each other. The biggest arms race in history had begun.

NASA/Kennedy Giving Historic Speech to Congress-GPN-2000-001658/Wikimedia Commons

FIGURE 12-42 President Kennedy's challenge to go to the Moon

President Kennedy, concerned about the lead that the Soviets had in space, decided to raise the goal. In a speech to a special joint session of congress on May 25, 1961 (Figure 12-42), 20 days after Alan Shepard's flight, Kennedy proposed:

> *"I believe that this nation should commit itself to achieving the goal, before this decade is out, of landing a man on the moon and returning him safely to the earth. No single space project in this period will be more impressive to mankind, or more important for the long-range exploration of space; and none will be so difficult or expensive to accomplish. . . . in a very real sense, it will not be one man going to the moon . . . it will be an entire nation. For all of us must work to put him there."*—President John F. Kennedy

Thus, President Kennedy had in clear terms put out a challenge to the Soviets, a "space race," to see who could reach the moon first. It was on July 22, 1969, that Neil Armstrong, Michael Collins, and Edwin Aldren safely reached and returned from the moon (Figure 12-43)—just over five months from the end of the decade, within the timeframe that President Kennedy had proposed. What technological developments had to be made to make this happen in a little over eight years time? Because of the limited space and constrained environment of space flight, the integrated circuit was the technology needed.

NASA/The Apollo 11 Prime Crew-GPN-2000-001164/Wikimedia Commons

FIGURE 12-43 The Apollo 11 Astronauts—Armstrong, Collins, and Aldren

President Kennedy had in clear terms put out a challenge to the Soviets, a "space race," to see who could reach the moon first. Because of the limited space and constrained environment of space flight, the integrated circuit was the technology needed.

The Crucially Needed Advancements in Integrated Circuits (early 1960s)

NASA/AGC user interface/Wikimedia Commons

FIGURE 12-44   The Apollo Guidance Computer (AGC)

Integrated circuits were obviously the way to go to achieve Kennedy's goal, given their reliability and reduced weight and size over current technology. The problem was that, in 1961, integrated circuits were in their primitive stages of development, and extremely costly, at about $1,000 per chip.

The project for the development of what became called the **Apollo Guidance Computer** (AGC) (Figure 12-44) was given to MIT. The integrated circuits that were needed pushed electrical engineers to work on the development of better and more cheaply produced chips. By 1964, the cost of each chip had dropped to $25. When it was finished for the first Apollo missions using the Saturn V rocket (Figure 12-45) the AGC weight only 70 pounds, contained 4,000 integrated circuits, measuring only two feet by one foot by six inches! It was the only computer in existence completely designed using integrated circuits. The requirements of the AGC drove technological developments in the design and production of integrated circuits. By 1973, computers built completely out of integrated circuits were commonplace. By the end of the decade, integrated circuits were developed containing tens of thousands of transistors on a chip.

NASA/Ksc-69pc-442/Wikimedia Commons

FIGURE 12-45   The Saturn V Rocket

The challenge by **President John F. Kennedy** of putting a man on the moon was a catalyst for the advancements made in integrated circuits technology.

12.7.2   The Development of the Microprocessor (1971)

While integrated circuits were in use in computer systems, each chip was a special-purpose component used together in "chip sets." A different set of chip sets was needed for each particular computing device, and the cost of designing chips was expensive.

By 1969, integrated circuits were becoming more and more advanced in capability. An engineer working at Intel, named **Marcian E. ("Ted") Hoff**, hit upon a brilliant idea. Instead of Intel manufacturing numerous *special-purpose* chips for specific devices (such as handheld calculators or digital alarm clocks), why not build a *general-purpose* logic chip that could be programmed to perform any logical task. In this way, a single chip can satisfy the needs of any device. This was an advantageous approach for Intel, since they could strictly focus on the production of such general logic chips. Those incorporating them into their products would be responsible for writing the programs.

This general logic chip was equivalent to the central processing unit (CPU) in mainframe computers. In mainframes computers, however, the CPU was

Paul Sakuma/©AP/Wide World Photos

FIGURE 12-46   Marcian "Ted" Hoff (center), Inventor of the Microprocessor with co-developers Federico Faggin and Stanley Mazor

composed of a number of different circuit boards. A general logic chip compressed all those circuits onto one integrated circuit. Since this logic chip contained all the functionality of a central processing unit (the "heart" of any computer system), it became known as a **microprocessor**.

The first microprocessor was produced and made available on the open market in November 1971. It was developed with co-developers Federico Faggin and Stanley Mazor (Figure 12-46), as well as Masatoshi Shima (not shown). It was a four-bit processor called the 4004, and the first commercially available integrated circuit that could be programmed for different tasks. It contained all the necessary components of a central processing unit squeezed onto a chip one-sixth of an inch long and one-eighth of an inch wide, containing 2,250 transistors. (The term "microprocessor" was used to emphasize a complete CPU on a chip. While most CPUs are microprocessors, they are now simply referred to as a "processor.") The 4004 was used in the first scientific handheld calculators produced by Hewlett-Packard in 1972.

Marcian E. ("Ted") Hoff invented the microprocessor—a complete central processing unit on a chip.

12.8 Mainframes, Minicomputers, and Supercomputers

As computing became more and more of a commercial item, and used by various types of companies and organizations, the computing needs likewise became varied. Some required and could afford large computer systems, while others needed something less. We will see next how this diversity of needs was satisfied though the development of a more diverse set of commercial computer systems.

12.8.1 The Establishment of the Mainframe Computer (1962)

NASA/NASAComputer-Room7090.NARA/Wikimedia Commons

FIGURE 12-47 IBM 7090 Mainframe at NASA

As commercial computing developed, large computers became known as **mainframe computers** (or simply **mainframes**). Such system could consist of multiple cabinets, storing the central processing unit (before the development of the microprocessor), memory, tape drives for storage, and so forth, taking up a whole room. An example of an early mainframe was the IBM 7090, shown at NASA in 1962 in Figure 12-47.

In 1964, IBM came out with a system called the IBM 360 (Figure 12-48). It is considered by some to be one of the most successful computers in history. Various models of the 360 were developed until 1978. Its design influenced many other computer systems that followed.

The IBM 360 was actually a series of models that were compatible enough so that companies could "trade up" for a larger system without the need for significant reprogramming. It was the first series of computers offering a large range of computing needs. Customers had

Mary Evans Picture Library/Alamy Limited

FIGURE 12-48 IBM 360

the option of purchasing systems with various processor speeds and a range of main memory size, among other options.

12.8.2 The Development of the Minicomputer (1963)

Photo courtesy Queensland University of Technology, from http://commons.wikimedia.org/wiki/File:Gordon_Bell.jpg

FIGURE 12-49 Gordon Bell—"Father of the Minicomputer"

Until the early 1960s, all computers were large and expensive mainframes, costing millions of dollars, only affordable by universities and large companies. An MIT graduate, named **Kenneth Olsen**, who had worked in the research labs there, came to a realization that smaller, less expensive computers had a place in the world, so-called **minicomputers**. He formed his own company in the early 1960s, called Digital Equipment Corporation (DEC). Chief Engineer **Gordon Bell** (Figure 12-49) at DEC designed a series of computers that were small and inexpensive, transistor-based single-user systems—the PDP series.

In, 1965, DEC produced a model called the PDP-8 (Figure 12-50). This was the first widely successful minicomputer, and is considered as ushering in the minicomputer age (and eventually, personal computers). The PDP-8 was an 11-bit computer. Following the PDP-8 was the 16-bit PDP-11, and the 32-bit Vax-11. This series of computers proved to be very successful and long-lasting. The last VAX system was manufactured in 2005.

A new dimension was added to the classification of systems—by size and cost. Prior to their development, companies and other organizations that were not able to afford their own computer had to purchase time-sharing from an available mainframe over very slow phone line connections. Now a new alternative was available.

In 2010, Bell received an honorary Doctor of Science and Technology degree from Carnegie Mellon University. The university referred to him as the "Father of the Minicomputer."

Stahlkocher/DEC PDP 8e/ Wikimedia Commons

FIGURE 12-50 PDP-8 Minicomputer

Gordon Bell, in the early 1960s, designed the first minicomputers, and thus is called the "**Father of the Minicomputer**."

12.8.3 The Development of the UNIX Operating System (1969)

In the early 1960s a joint project was formed between General Electric, MIT, and Bell Labs to develop a time-shared computer called MULTICS. The project, however, ended without being as successful as hoped.

Work on the MULTICS project, however, motivated those involved from Bell Labs to continue towards the goal of interactive computing. Thus, they began work on their own time-sharing operating

FIGURE 12-51 Kenneth Thompson and Dennis Ritchie

system in 1969, to be known as **UNIX** (see www.bell-labs. com/history/unix/). The two individuals that developed UNIX were **Kenneth Thompson** and **Dennis Ritchie** (Figure 12-51).

During the development of UNIX, a new programming language named "C" was developed by Dennis Ritchie, evolved from an earlier language named "B" that Ken Thompson had developed. Eventually, the UNIX operating system was rewritten in the C language, which along with UNIX, became widely used.

The developments of UNIX and C, and their adoption by industry and academia, is one of the biggest success stories in computer science. Thompson and Ritchie received numerous prestigious awards, including the A.M. Turing Award from the Association for Computing Machinery (ACM) in 1983, the U.S. National Medal of Technology from President Bill Clinton (Figure 12-52) in 1999, and the Japan Prize for Information and Technology (2011).

UNIX and C (and its object-oriented successor **C++**) are in much use today, including a personal computer version of UNIX called **Linux**.

FIGURE 12-52 Thompson and Ritchie Receiving the National Medal of Technology

Kenneth Thompson and **Dennis Ritchie** developed the high successfully **UNIX** operating system. In addition, Dennis Ritchie developed the **C** programming language evolved from the B programming language developed by Thompson.

12.8.4 The Development of Graphical User Interfaces (early 1960s)

Another major advance in operating systems design was the move from **text-based user interfaces** (in which all commands were typed) to **graphical user interfaces** (GUIs). A GUI interface provides the familiar computer user interaction by use of a mouse. It might surprise you that the **computer mouse** was invented and first demonstrated back in the early 1960s, by a professor at Stanford University named **Doug Engelbart** (Figure 12-53). He is shown here holding a prototype of the mouse, constructed out of a wood shell and two metal wheels. Soon afterward he demonstrated the first word processor and the first hypertext, the kind of links that now exist in web pages. He has received numerous awards, including the Lemelson-MIT prize—the world's largest single prize for innovation—and the National Medal of Technology, the nation's highest technology award.

FIGURE 12-53 Doug Engelbart—Inventor of the Computer Mouse

Doug Engelbart invented the computer mouse in the early 1960s.

12.8.5 The Development of the Supercomputer (1972)

Seymour Cray-crop/Wikimedia Commons

FIGURE 12-54 Seymour Cray—
"The Father of the Supercomputer"

A supercomputer, as the name implies, is a computer system designed for maximum computational power. Whereas mainframe computers generally timeshare computations over a number of users, supercomputers focus their power on executing a few programs as quickly as possible. They are used in solving problems that require massive numbers of mathematical calculations, such as for weather forecasting.

In 1972, Seymour Cray (Figure 12-54), the "Father of Supercomputing," started a company called Cray Research. The CRAY-1, released in 1976, became one of the most successful supercomputers in history, setting a new standard for high-speed computing (Figure 12-55).

What is classified as a supercomputer is relative to current technological capabilities. A typical personal computer today would have been considered a "supercomputer" in the not so distant past. There is a website that each year lists the top 500 supercomputers worldwide (see www.top500.org). These supercomputers have demonstrated computational speeds measured in "teraflops," i.e., trillions of floating-point operations per second. The fastest supercomputer as of this writing is the Cray-XT5 HE, dubbed the "jaguar," with a speed of 1.75 petaflops (almost 2 quadrillion floating-point operations per second), with 224,000 individual processors. It is installed at the National Center for Computational Sciences at Oak Ridge National Laboratories in Tennessee.

Everett Collection, Inc./Alamy Limited

FIGURE 12-55 The CRAY-1

Seymour Cray is called the "**Father of the Supercomputer**."

FOURTH-GENERATION COMPUTERS
(early 1970s to the Present)

12.9 The Rise of the Microprocessor

12.9.1 The First Commercially Available Microprocessor (1971)

The development of the personal computer (originally "microcomputer") has been one of the biggest technical revolutions in history. It didn't emerge from the research labs of major companies and universities, but rather from a group of hobbyists interested in building and owning their own computers.

Before the development of the microprocessor in the early 1970s, it was not possible for individuals to build their own computer system. A central processing unit (CPU) was too technically sophisticated for hobbyists to build. The first microprocessor, the 4-bit 4004 released by Intel in 1971, was only powerful enough for handheld calculators. But in 1974, Intel came out with the 8080 processor (Figure 12-56). The 8080 was an 8-bit processor with a clock speed of 2 MHz (thousands of times slower than a typical CPU in personal computers today) and contained about 6,000 transistors (compared to billions of transistors today). It was powerful enough, however, to build a computer system around. Thus, the age of the personal computer was about to begin. We look at the development of the personal computer next.

Konstantin Lanzet/KL Intel D8080/ Wikimedia Commons

FIGURE 12-56 The Intel 8080 Microprocessor

The **first commercially available microprocessor** was the **Intel 4004**, a four-bit processor released in 1971.

12.9.2 The First Commercially Available Microcomputer Kit (1975)

The first commercially available microcomputer was a kit (also offered fully assembled) called the **Altair 8800** (Figure 12-57), first advertised in January 1975 on the cover of *Popular Electronics* magazine. It consisted of a box with levers and lights, used to input and display information in binary notation (i.e., light on for "1," light off for "0"). This was, especially by today's standards, a very crude and simple computer. However, given that no one until then could say that they had their own "personal computer," it was a thrill for many hobbyists.

Michael Holley/Altair 8800 Computer/Wikimedia Commons

FIGURE 12-57 The Altair 8800—The First Microcomputer Kit

The **Altair** was the **first available microcomputer** (personal computer), appearing in 1975.

12.10 The Dawn of Personal Computing

12.10.1 The Beginnings of Microsoft (1975)

In 1975, the Homebrew Computer Club began in the San Francisco area. Among the soon to be infamous members were **Paul Allen** and **Bill Gates** (Figure 12-58), who created a version of the BASIC programming language for the new Altair system, and comprised the beginnings of Microsoft. Also present at the club was **Gary Kildall**, who wrote the first programming language and disk operating system for microcomputers, among many other contributions.

In the mid-1980s, Microsoft produced the MS-DOS operating system for personal computers, which dominated the market. MS-DOS was a text-based operating system.

Ann E. Yow-Dyson/ Getty Images, Inc.

FIGURE 12-58 Bill Gates and Paul Allen

In the 1990s, Microsoft came out with the GUI-based Windows operating system, which remains the most widely used operating system today.

In 1975, **Bill Gates** and **Paul Allen** started the Microsoft Corporation. **Gary Kildall** wrote the first programming language and disk operating system specifically for microcomputers.

12.10.2 The Apple II (1977)

Two other members of the Homebrew Computer Club were **Steve Jobs** and **Steve Wozniak** (Figure 12-59). In 1977 they went on to create the most successful personal computer at the time, the **Apple II** (Figure 12-60) and form the Apple Computer company. One of the Apple II's main features was the ability to display color graphics, displaying output on a standard television monitor. Various models of the Apple II were produced until 1993.

DB Apple/picture-alliance/dpa/ NewsCom

FIGURE 12-59 Steve Jobs and Steve Wozniak

Eric Risberg/©AP/Wide World Photos

FIGURE 12-60 The Apple II

In 1977, **Steve Jobs** and **Steve Wozniak** created the most successful personal computer at the time, the **Apple II**.

12.10.3 IBM's Entry into the Microcomputer Market (1981)

IBM, which first had doubts about the future of microcomputers, saw the success of the Apple II computer and decided to develop their own microcomputer. In 1981, they came out with the **IBM-PC** (for "Personal Computer"), and before long, had sold 1 million machines (Figure 12-61). By the end of the 1980s, 65 million PCs were being used in offices, homes, and schools. Because of their size, reputation, and sales force, IBM dominated the personal computer market. Eventually, the generic name for microcomputers became "personal computer."

Ruben de Rijcke/IBM-PC 5150/ Wikimedia Commons

FIGURE 12-61 IBM-PC in 1981

In 1981, IBM came out with the IBM-PC ("personal computer"). By the end of the 1980s, 65 million PCs were in use.

12.10.4 Society Embraces the Personal Computer (1983)

In a very unconventional selection, *Time Magazine* selected the personal computer for its January 3, 1983 "Man (Machine) of the Year" cover article. In the article, it said that by the millions, computers were finding their way into offices, schools, and homes. In addition, it discussed a survey showing that the average American believed that "in the near future," computers would be as commonplace as TVs and refrigerators. The public image of what computers were had made a big change. The article stated (even in 1983) that the 30-ton ENIAC computer "could now fit on a chip the size of a pea." (In fact, as part of the fiftieth anniversary of the ENIAC at the place of its birth, the University of Pennsylvania, a group of students did just that. They made an exact logical replication of the original ENIAC on a chip about 1/3" by 1/5" in size.)

In 1983, given the widespread use and impact of the personal computer, Time Magazine selects the **personal computer as the "Man" of the Year**.

12.10.5 The Development of Graphical User Interfaces (GUIs)

An Early Machine Using a Mouse Driven Graphical User Interface (1975)

Because computers at the time were not powerful enough to support the computationally intensive graphical interactive method of computing (as demonstrated by Doug Engelbart), the idea did not initially catch on. However, in 1975, a computer was developed at Xerox Palo Alto Research Center (Xerox-PARC) that incorporated the use of a mouse device into a rather novel computer called the **Alto**. Its screen was the dimension of a normal sheet of paper, and had a graphical user interface. Although this was a notable advancement by those working at Xerox research center, it was never marketed by Xerox, leaving many of the developers feeling frustrated. Some years later, however, in 1979, Steve Jobs visited Xerox-PARC, and after seeing the Alto and its interactive mouse, immediately knew that the future of computing was about to change.

In 1975, a computer was developed at Xerox Palo Alto Research Center (Xerox-PARC) that incorporated the use of a mouse device into a rather novel computer called the **Alto**.

The First Commercially Successful Computer with GUI/Mouse (1984)

In January 1984, Apple came out with the first commercially successful computer with a graphical user interface, the **Macintosh** (Figure 12-62). In 1983, Apple had come out with another mouse/GUI system named Lisa aimed at the business market, its high selling price kept it from being commercially successful. The Macintosh, on the other hand, was priced for individuals, and highly marketed. In one of the most famous commercials in the history of television during the 1984 Super Bowl game, Apple created an image of a new wave of computing, awaking large groups of robotlike, hypnotized individuals, meant to represent the awakening of the "blind" followers of IBM (which had not yet come out with a GUI-based machine).

FIGURE 12-62   Apple Macintosh in 1984

In January 1984, Apple came out with the first commercially successful computer with a graphical user interface, the **Macintosh**.

Mouse-Driven GUI Operating Systems Predominate (1995)

Microsoft began releasing its GUI interface operating systems, Windows, in 1985 with the release of Windows 1.0. However, its Windows operating system for the IBM-PC (and clones) did not begin to catch on until the release of Windows 3.0 in 1990, some waiting until the release of Window 3.1 in 1993. However, when the much promoted and completely redesigned Windows 95 was released in August 1995, within six weeks 7 million copies had been sold. The GUI-based computing paradigm of computing had become mainstream.

With the release of the **Microsoft Windows** operating system the GUI-based computing paradigm of computing had become mainstream.

12.10.6   The Development of the C++ Programming Language

We take the opportunity here to mention one of the most widely used programming languages today, C++ (pronounced "cee plus plus"). The other widely used programming language is Java (discussed in section 12.13.4).

    C++ was developed by Bjarne Stroustrup in the early 1980s at Bell Labs (Figure 12-63). It was designed essentially as an extension of the C programming language, also developed at Bell Labs over a decade earlier. The most significant feature added to C++ is the ability to use classes, therefore facilitating object-oriented programming. However, as opposed to most object-oriented programming languages, such as Java, the use of classes is not required. Therefore, C++ program can be written strictly in the procedural style. In this way C++ is a hybrid language. There is some playfulness in the name of the language. The operator symbol "++" that exists in C (and C++)

FIGURE 12-63   Bjarne Stroustrup—Inventor of the C++ Programming Language

increments a value by 1. Since Stroustrup's new language was "an increment" of C, the name C++ was chosen.

> **Bjarne Stroustrup** invented C++ at Bell Labs in the early 1980s as an extension of the C programming language. C++ has become one of the most widely used programming languages today.

THE DEVELOPMENT OF COMPUTER NETWORKS

12.11   The Development of Wide Area Networks

12.11.1   The Idea of Packet-Switched Networks (early 1960s)

During the early 1960s, **Leonard Kleinrock** (Figure 12-64) at MIT published work on the notion of a **packet-switched network**, in which communications to be sent on a network are divided into equal-sized packets and transmitted individually. When all packets are received at the destination, they are then reassembled into the original complete communication. This is how all communication on the Internet is done. (The first experiment of having two computers—one in Massachusetts, the other in California—communicate over standard (non-packet-switched) telephone lines failed, proving Kleinrock's claim of the need for a packet-switched approach correct.) Because of the distance covered by these networks, they became known as **wide-area networks** (**WANs**).

FIGURE 12-64   Leonard Kleinrock—Inventor of Internet Technology

> **Leonard Kleinrock** invented the notion of a packet-switched network, which is how all communication on the Internet is performed.

12.11.2   The First Packet-Switched Network: ARPANET (1969)

What was needed next for wide-area computer networks was a standard "language" or communications protocol that all computers on a network could understand. By the end of 1968, a number of individuals working on packet-switched communications received funding from a military defense department, resulting in a network called **ARPANET**, becoming the first packet-switched network.

In September 1969, the first Arpanet node was installed at the University of California at Los Angeles (UCLA). Another node was installed at Stanford, and in October 1969, the first "host to host" message was sent directly from one computer to another—the beginnings of what we now know as the Internet. Over the years, more universities and companies were added to the network. In October 1972, the first public demonstration of **email** communication occurred. For the next ten years, email became the most used aspect of the new ARPANET.

> **ARPANET** was the first packet-switched network, becoming operational in 1969. The first public demonstration of **email** was in 1972.

12.12   The Development of Local Area Networks (LANs)

12.12.1   The Need for Local Area Networks

The term "wide-area network" is meant to convey communicating computers over a wide area (e.g., globally). This concept first emerged during the era of mainframe computers (in the 1960s). However, computer networking had new emerging needs with the rise in the use of minicomputers during the 1970s, and personal computers during the 1980s.

Before the use of personal computers, for example, employees in a company could communicate and share files through remote terminal screens to the company's mainframe computer. However, during the 1980s, when the personal computer began appearing on everyone's desk, something was lost. Now each employee had all the computing power that they needed right at hand, but their machine was isolated from all others in the company, each in their own "computing island."

> Computer networking had new emerging needs with the rise in the use of minicomputers during the 1970s, and personal computers during the 1980s.

12.12.2   The Development of Ethernet (1980)

Robert Metcalf (Figure 12-65) was working as a researcher for the Xerox Corporation in the early 1970s when he was asked to work on a particular problem. Xerox was in the process of developing the world's first laser printer, and wanted all the computers (hundreds of them) at the Xerox-PARC research facility where he worked to be connected to it. This problem called for a means of communication that was *fast* and allowed *many communications at once* from the hundreds of computers in the building.

His solution was the development of **local area networks (LANS)**. Local area networks are defined as a network of computers and computing devices (such as printers) within about a one-mile radius. As opposed to wide-area networks, in which the topology (i.e., the connections between computers) allows messages to be routed many different ways, Metcalf developed a network based on a simple topology. His topology consisted of a single, high-speed connection that all computing devices could share, called **Ethernet**.

FIGURE 12-65   Robert Metcalf—Inventor of Local Area Networks

Ethernet was made commercially available in 1980, and is now the most widely used local area network standard. Robert Metcalfe was awarded the National Medal of Technology from President George W. Bush for his work in 2003.

> **Robert Metcalfe** invented the concept of a local area network, which led to the development of Ethernet, the most widely used local networking standard today.

12.13 The Development of the Internet and World Wide Web

12.13.1 The Realization of the Need for "Internetworking"

The development of ARPANET proved the viability of packet-switched computer networking. However, it had its own specific protocol (i.e., specific means of communication between computers). The future was viewed, however, as developing into a number of different kinds of packet-switched networks, each with their own unique protocols. The idea of "internetworking" was the ability of individual networks, normally unable to communicate with each other, to be able to communicate using an "internetworking protocol" (IP), resulting in one big computer network.

> **Internetworking** is the ability of individual networks, normally unable to communicate, to communicate using an "internetworking protocol" (IP).

12.13.2 The Development of the TCP/IP Internetworking Protocol (1973)

A research program was initiated in 1973 to investigate ways of internetworking different packet-switched networks. The standard internetworking protocol that evolved was called TCP/IP. Since packets of a given communication travel independently in a packet-switched network, TCP/IP had the responsibility of ensuring that each packet arrived at its destination intact and reassembled into the complete original communication. The development of the TCP/IP protocol was developed by **Vinton G. Cerf** and **Robert E. Kahn** (Figure 12-66) referred to as the "Fathers of the Internet." In 2005 they each received the Medal of Freedom from President George W. Bush for their work.

Paul Morse/CerfKahn-Medal of Freedom/Wikimedia Commons

FIGURE 12-66 Vinton G. Cerf and Robert E. Kahn—"The Fathers of the Internet"

On January 1 1983, TCP/IP became the standard protocol for the internetworking of networks. On that date, all computers currently connected to the Internet (using older protocols), smoothly switched to the new protocol simultaneously, and thus was the birth of *the* **Internet** as we know it today. The Internet is now comprised of a collection of over 50,000 independent networks, on all seven continents, and even planned for use in outer space.

> **Vinton G. Cerf** and **Robert E. Kahn** developed a common network protocol called **TCP/IP** that allowed for the internetworking of computer networks. Thus, they are referred to as the "Fathers of the Internet."

12.13.3 The Development of the World Wide Web (1990)

The idea of having text that can be clicked on to lead one to more text has goes all the way back to a system developed in 1945, providing links between documents on microfiche. Doug Engelbart in the early 1960s demonstrated the notion of "mouse-clickable" text. Later, the term "hypertext" was coined. **Hypertext** documents are essentially "three-dimensional text," in that there are words "behind" other words when clicked on.

Andreas Rentz/Getty Images, Inc.

FIGURE 12-67 Tim Berners-Lee—"Father of the World Wide Web"

Tim Berners-Lee (Figure 12-67), while working at CERN in 1980 (a European center for nuclear research outside of Geneva, Switzerland), developed a simple program with hypertext properties. He later revived his idea and in 1990 developed a program he named "WorldWideWeb," the first web browser and hypertext editor. He is thus known as the "Father of the World Wide Web."

A **web browser** is an application program to properly display hypertext (web) pages, performing the necessary actions of mouse events (e.g., mouse click on a link). In May 1991, the WideWorldWeb program was released for use at CERN for the creation, searching, and cross-referencing of research papers in theoretical physics.

In 1993, a web browser was developed at the National Center for Supercomputing Applications (NCSA) at the University of Illinois named **Mosaic**, developed by **Marc Andreessen** (Figure 12-68). This was the first browser readily available to the general public, credited with popularizing the World Wide Web. Andreessen later went on to form Netscape Corporation, developing the Netscape family of browsers.

Richard Drew/©AP/Wide World Photos

FIGURE 12-68 Marc Andreessen—Developed the First Readily Available Web Browser

Tim Berners-Lee was the inventor of the World Wide Web. **Marc Andreessen** developed Mosaic, the first web browser readily available to the general public. He went on to form Netscape Corporation.

12.13.4 The Development of the Java Programming Language (1995)

The development of the World Wide Web (and Internet browsers such as Netscape) was a very significant advance for the sharing of information. However, the information was static. One could interact with the browser by clicking on a link of one page of (static) information to retrieve another page. However, the web pages themselves did not have much capability of interacting with the user. For example, a web page offering a mortgage calculation would get the input from the user, then send it back to the server for calculations to occur there, with the results downloaded in another static page. Thus, there was not a way to download within a web page programs capability of performing significant computation on the user's computer (the "client").

Peter Campbell/James Gosling 2008/Wikimedia Commons

FIGURE 12-69 James Gosling—Inventor of the Java Programming Language

As a matter of coincidence, a language perfectly suited for embedding programs in web pages emerged at the same time as the web. This was the **Java programming language**, was developed by James Gosling (Figure 12-69) at Sun Microsystems during the early 1990s.

A critical feature needed for the development of dynamic web pages was that the language used had to be executable ("understood") by all the different kinds of computers on the Internet if the capability were to be available to all. The historical coincidence that occurred was that in 1990, Sun Microsystems began work on a new programming language written with the same capability of being able to be "complied once, run anywhere." The need was related to software development for embedded systems, that is, systems containing an embedded processor, such as microwave ovens. With the new World Wide Web, it was realized the features of Java, developed for another purpose, were fundamentally suited for dynamic web pages. Java was expanded to include features especially suited for network applications, and was first released to the public in 1995, just a couple of years after the "web" became publically and freely available.

James Gosling invented the Java programming language at Sun Microsystems in the early 1990s. It has become one of the most widely used programming languages today.

Python 3 Programmers Reference

The author gratefully acknowledges the contributions of Leela Sedaghat to the style and content of this reference.

This reference provides the features of Python 3 that are most relevant for the text. Therefore, it is not intended to be an exhaustive resource. For complete coverage of the Python programming language, Standard Library and other Python-related information, we refer readers to the official web site: http://www.python.org

A. GETTING STARTED WITH PYTHON

A1. About Python

The Python programming language was created by Guido van Rossum (www.python.org/~guido) at the Centrum Wiskunde & Informatica (National Research Institute for Mathematics and Computer Science) in the Netherlands in the late 1980s. It is designed for *code readability*. It therefore has a clear and simple syntax. At the same time, Python also has a powerful set of programming features.

Python is free, open source software (http://www.python.org). The reference (standard) implementation of the Python programming language (called CPython) is managed by the non-profit Python Software Foundation. The language is bundled with a Python development environment called IDLE. The bundle is available for download at the official Python web site (see below). There are two, incompatible versions of Python currently supported: Python 2 (2.7.3) and Python 3 (3.2.3 at the time of this writing). Python 2.7.3 will be the last release version of Python 2. This text uses Python 3.

Python is growing in popularity. Many companies and organizations use Python including Google, Yahoo and YouTube. Python is also widely used in the scientific community, including the National Weather Service, Los Alamos National Laboratory, and NASA. Python also continues to gain popularity for use in introductory computer science courses.

A2. Downloading and Installing Python

To download and install the Python interpreter (and bundled IDLE program) go to http://www.python.org/download/ which displays the page shown in Figure A-1.

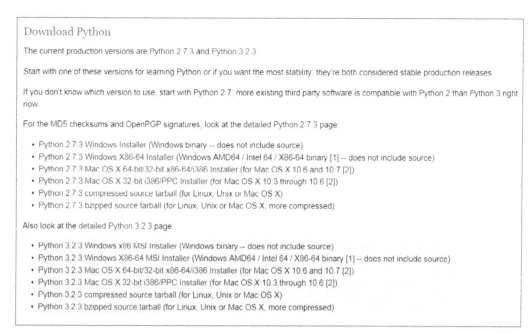

Download Python

The current production versions are Python 2.7.3 and Python 3.2.3.

Start with one of these versions for learning Python or if you want the most stability; they're both considered stable production releases.

If you don't know which version to use, start with Python 2.7; more existing third party software is compatible with Python 2 than Python 3 right now.

For the MD5 checksums and OpenPGP signatures, look at the detailed Python 2.7.3 page:

- Python 2.7.3 Windows Installer (Windows binary -- does not include source)
- Python 2.7.3 Windows X86-64 Installer (Windows AMD64 / Intel 64 / X86-64 binary [1] -- does not include source)
- Python 2.7.3 Mac OS X 64-bit/32-bit x86-64/i386 Installer (for Mac OS X 10.6 and 10.7 [2])
- Python 2.7.3 Mac OS X 32-bit i386/PPC Installer (for Mac OS X 10.3 through 10.6 [2])
- Python 2.7.3 compressed source tarball (for Linux, Unix or Mac OS X)
- Python 2.7.3 bzipped source tarball (for Linux, Unix or Mac OS X, more compressed)

Also look at the detailed Python 3.2.3 page:

- Python 3.2.3 Windows x86 MSI Installer (Windows binary -- does not include source)
- Python 3.2.3 Windows X86-64 MSI Installer (Windows AMD64 / Intel 64 / X86-64 binary [1] -- does not include source)
- Python 3.2.3 Mac OS X 64-bit/32-bit x86-64/i386 Installer (for Mac OS X 10.6 and 10.7 [2])
- Python 3.2.3 Mac OS X 32-bit i386/PPC Installer (for Mac OS X 10.3 through 10.6 [2])
- Python 3.2.3 compressed source tarball (for Linux, Unix or Mac OS X)
- Python 3.2.3 bzipped source tarball (for Linux, Unix or Mac OS X, more compressed)

FIGURE A-1   Official Download Site of Python

Select the appropriate Python 3 download for your system: Windows x86 MSI installer (for typical Windows machines), Windows x86-64 (for 64-bit Windows machines, not typical), Mac OS X 64-bit/32-bit x86-64/i386 (for newer Macs) and Mac OS X 32-bit i386/PPC (for older Macs). There are also versions for Linux and Unix, as shown. Follow the installation directions.

A3. Program Development Using IDLE

What is IDLE?   IDLE is an *integrated development environment* (IDE) for developing Python programs. An IDE consists of three major components: an **editor** for creating and modifying programs, an **interpreter** or **compiler** for executing programs, and a **debugger** for "debugging" (fixing errors in) a program.

When you execute IDLE on your system, a window such as shown in Figure A-2 will be displayed.

```
74 Python Shell
File  Edit  Shell  Debug  Options  Windows  Help
Python 3.2.2 (default, Sep  4 2011, 09:51:08) [MSC v.1500 32 bit (Intel)] on win32
Type "copyright", "credits" or "license()" for more information.
>>>
```

FIGURE A-2   The Python Shell

Note that the version of Python is displayed on the lines right before the prompt (>>>).

Interacting with the Python Shell   The Python Shell provides a means of directly interacting with the Python interpreter.

Thus, whatever Python code that is typed in will be immediately executed, as shown in Figure A-3.

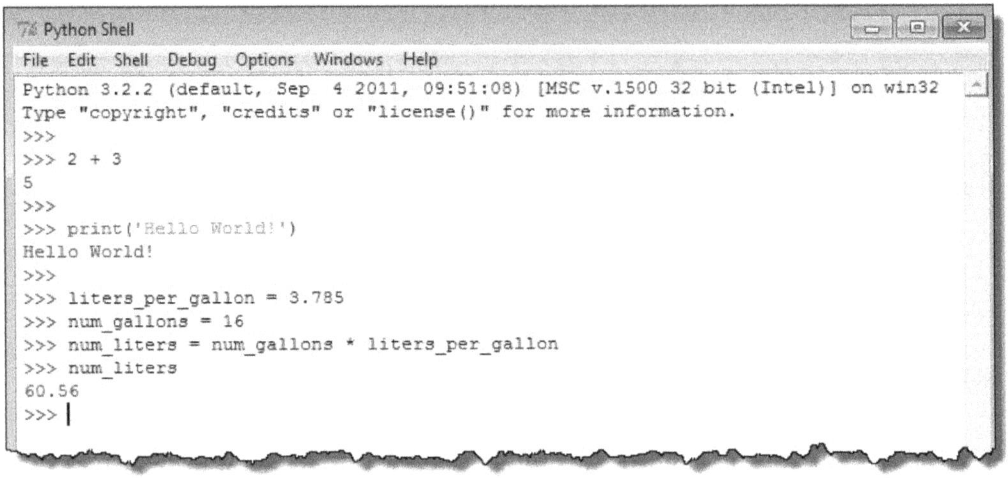

FIGURE A-3   Interacting with the Python Shell

This is referred to in programming as *interactive mode*. All variables will remain defined until the shell is either closed or restarted. To restart the shell, select **Restart Shell** from the **Shell** dropdown list, as shown in Figure A-4.

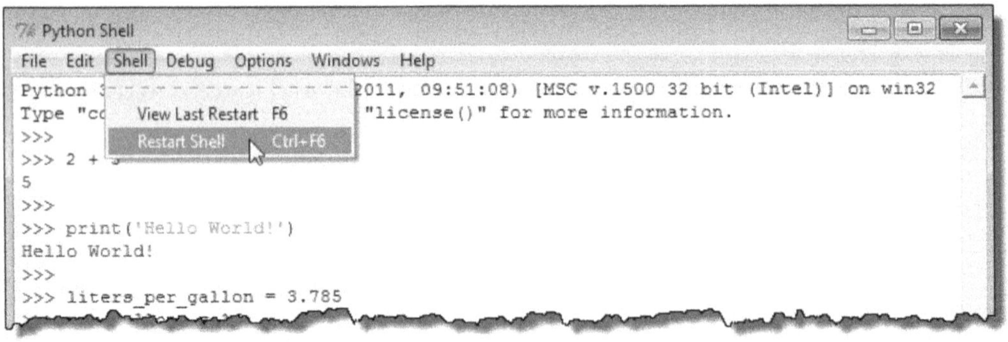

FIGURE A-4   Restarting the Python Shell

After the shell is restarted, all previously-defined variables become undefined and a "fresh" instance of the shell is executed, as shown in Figure A-5.

```
7% Python Shell                                              □  ▣  ⊠
File  Edit  Shell  Debug  Options  Windows  Help
Python 3.2.2 (default, Sep  4 2011, 09:51:08) [MSC v.1500 32 bit (Intel)] on win32  ▲
Type "copyright", "credits" or "license()" for more information.
>>>
>>> 2 + 3
5
>>>
>>> print('Hello World!')
Hello World!
>>>
>>> liters_per_gallon = 3.785
>>> num_gallons = 16
>>> num_liters = num_gallons * liters_per_gallon
>>> num_liters
60.56
>>> =============================== RESTART ================================
>>> num_liters
Traceback (most recent call last):
  File "<pyshell#9>", line 1, in <module>
    num_liters
NameError: name 'num_liters' is not defined
>>>
```

FIGURE A-5   A New Instance of the Python Shell

Being able to immediately execute instructions in the Python Shell provides a simple means of verifying the behavior of instructions in Python. For example, if one forgot the specific range of numbers that built-in function range(start, end) produces for a given start and end value, the single for statement in Figure A-6 can be easily executed to determine that.

```
7% Python Shell                                              □  ▣  ⊠
File  Edit  Shell  Debug  Options  Windows  Help
Python 3.2.2 (default, Sep  4 2011, 09:51:08) [MSC v.1500 32 bit (Intel)] on win32  ▲
Type "copyright", "credits" or "license()" for more information.
>>>
>>> for k in range(0, 10):
        print(k)


0
1
2
3
4
5
6
7
8
9
>>> |
```

FIGURE A-6   Testing Small Program Segments in the Python Shell

We can also execute Python code in the shell that requires the use of modules. To utilize a particular module in the shell, the appropriate `import` statement is first entered.

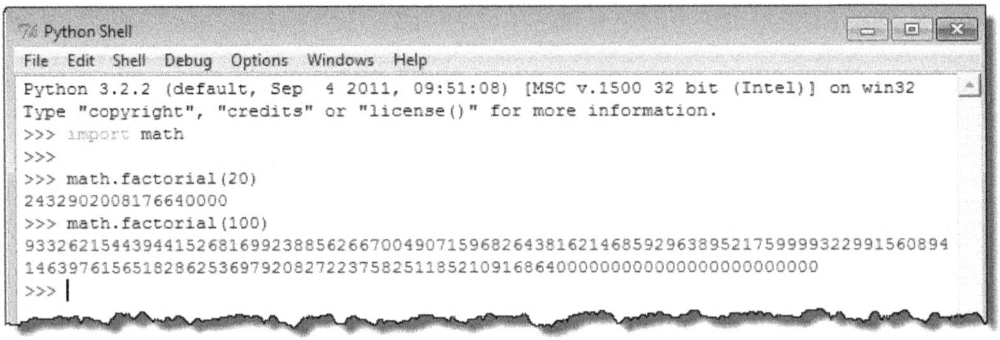

FIGURE A-7 Importing a Module into the Python Shell

Finally, when working in the interactive Python Shell, there are helpful keyboard shortcuts that the user may need to use. Some of the most commonly used commands are listed in Figure A-8.

Windows Shortcut	Mac Shortcut	Action Performed
Ctrl+C	Ctrl+C	Terminates executing program
Alt+P	Ctrl+P	Retrieves previous command(s)
Alt+N	Ctrl+N	Retrieves next command(s)

FIGURE A-8 Python Shell Shortcuts

Creating and Editing Programs in IDLE
Instructions typed into the shell are executed and then "discarded." For program development, however, we need to save instructions into a file. This is referred to as a **script** in Python. A program in Python is a script. To begin creating a script in IDLE, select New Window from the File dropdown menu, as shown in Figure A-9.

A Python program (or other text files) can be typed in this window. This program is saved by going to the File menu option and selecting Save (or by using shortcut key Ctrl+S), depicted in Figure A-10.

When selecting the Save option on a currently unnamed file, a file window appears allowing a name to be entered for the new program (Figure A-11). If the program was already named, choosing Save would save the file under the current name, overwriting the currently saved file. Using Save As allows a file to be named under a different name, such as for creating a backup file.

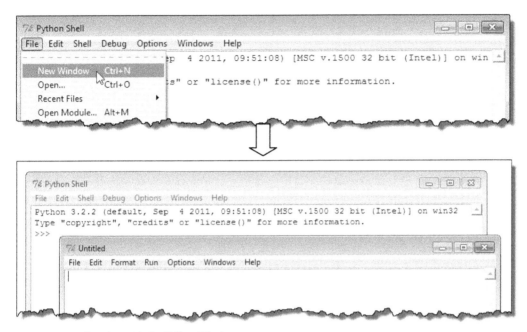

FIGURE A-9   Opening a Script Editor Window

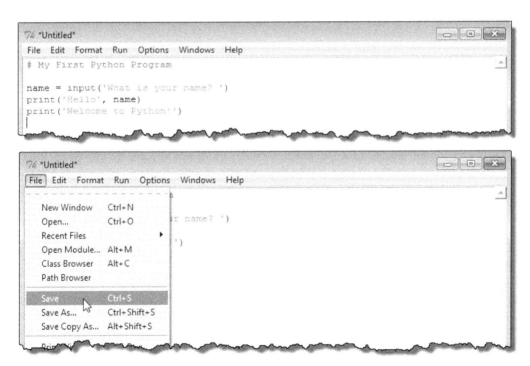

FIGURE A-10   Entering and Saving a Python Program File

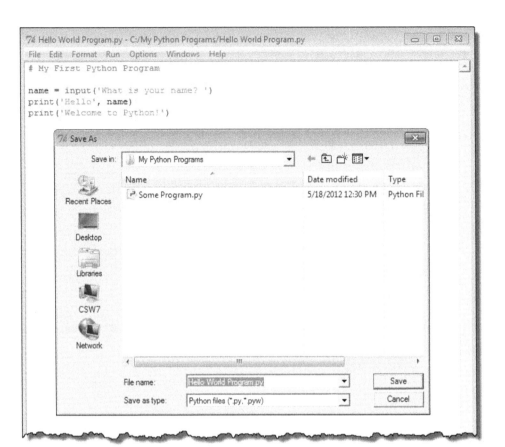

FIGURE A-11   The File Window and Naming and Saving a File

When saving a Python program, *remember to add the file extension .py to the filename*. Otherwise, the saved file will not appear in the file window when working with Python programs in IDLE. It also will not be considered a Python file by the operating system. In this case, `Hello World Program.py` will become a new file in the `My Python Programs` folder in addition to the existing file `Some Program.py`.

When creating and modifying programs, there are a number of editing features that IDLE provides. Many of these commands will likely be familiar to you. However, in addition to the familiar commands (such as "cut" and "paste") there are editing features in IDLE that are specific to Python. These commands are listed in Figure A-12.

The backspace is for deleting characters *before* the cursor, and delete deletes characters *after*. Lines may be deleted, copied and pasted within a program. For navigating a program file, there is the ability to go to a specific line number, or search for lines containing a specific search string. Once a search has begun, the shortcut Ctrl+G provides a convenient way to continue the search to each next line found.

Windows Shortcut	Mac Shortcut	Action Performed
Backspace Key	Delete	Erases character before cursor
Delete Key	-	Erases character after cursor
Ctrl+C	⌘+C	Copies highlighted set of lines to be pasted
Ctrl+X	⌘+X	Cuts highlighted set of lines to be pasted
Ctrl+V	⌘+V	Pastes most recently copied or cut highlighted lines
Alt+G	⌘+J	Prompts for line number to place cursor
Ctrl+F	⌘+F	Prompts for characters to search for
Ctrl+G	⌘+G	Continues current search
Ctrl+0	Ctrl+0	Shows the innermost matching parentheses
Ctrl+Z	⌘+Z	Undo all previous editing actions one-by-one
Ctrl+]	⌘+]	Indents selected lines
Ctrl+[	⌘+[	Unindents selected lines back to the left
Alt+3	Ctrl+3	Comments out selected lines
Alt+4	Ctrl+4	Removes ## notations from start of selected lines
Ctrl+S	⌘+S	Saves program as current file name

FIGURE A-12   Editing Commands in IDLE

The Show Matching command (Ctrl+0) identifies certain matching delimiters. The innermost set of matching parentheses, square brackets or curly braces are highlighted from the current position of the cursor. This is useful for identifying mismatched parentheses in expressions, as well as mismatched delimiters in data structures containing parentheses, square brackets and/or curly braces. The Undo command (Ctrl+Z) will undo the most recent edit change in a file. This can be used to undo all the edit changes, even before the last time the file was saved, way back to the state of the file when it was first opened (or back to an empty file if being created).

One particularly useful pair of commands are the Indent / Dedent commands. These indent and "un-indent" a selected (highlighted) set of program lines. The number of spaces of indentation by default is four, which follows the Python convention for style. Therefore, it is recommended that you do not change this value. (It can be set under the Options / Configure IDLE menu selection.) Another useful set of commands is Comment Out and Uncomment. These commands add (and remove) a "double comment" symbol, ##, on a selected set of lines. This is useful for disabling certain portions of a program during program development and testing. A summary of some of the editing commands in IDLE is given in Figure A-12. The *shortcut keys given here are worth learning so that you can be more efficient in your programming*. Each command has a corresponding menu option.

We show all the menu options in the editor window of IDLE below. The **File menu** provides the ability to open, save and print files, shown in Figure A-13.

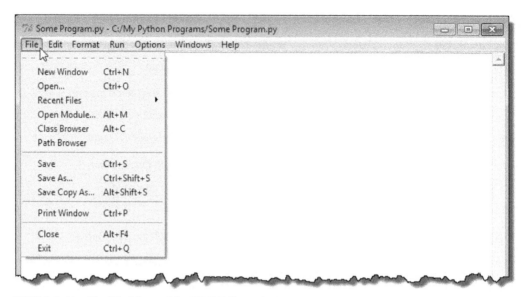

FIGURE A-13 The File Menu of the IDLE Editor Window

The **Edit menu** provides options for the usual editing commands such as Undo/Do, Copy/Cut/ Paste, Find/Replace, shown in Figure A-14.

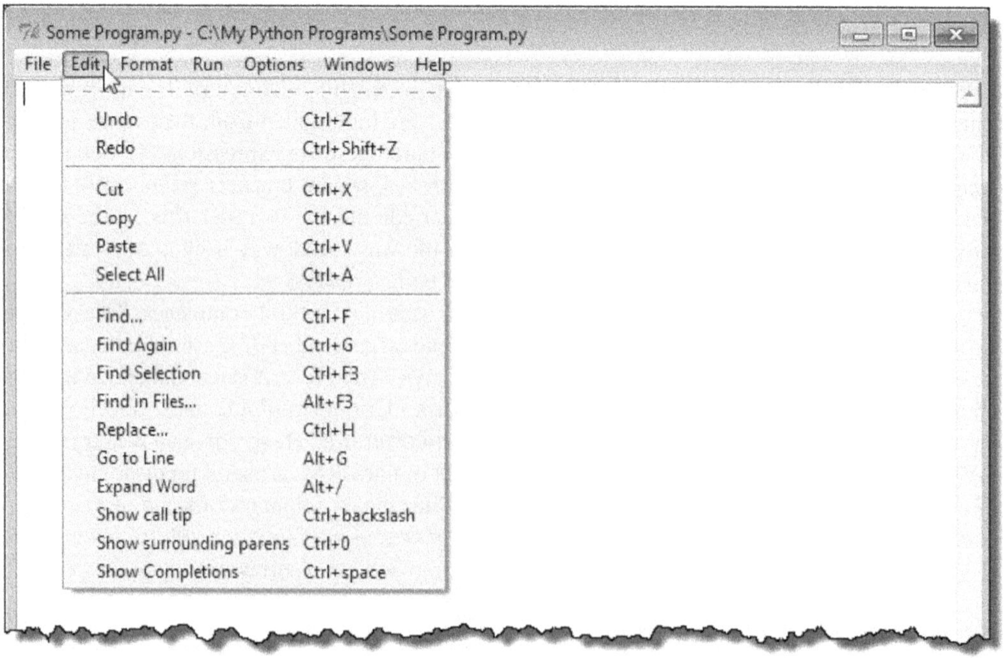

FIGURE A-14 The Edit Menu of the IDLE Editor Window

The **Format menu** provides options for Indenting / Dedenting, and Commenting Out / Uncommenting a section of code, shown in Figure A-15.

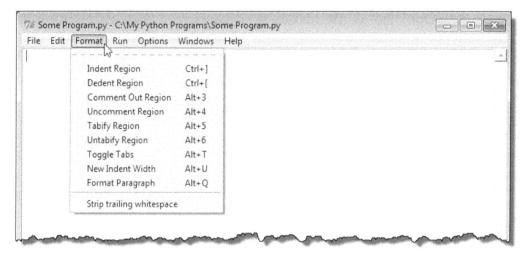

FIGURE A-15   The Format Menu of the IDLE Editor Window

The **Run menu** provides the Run Module, which executes the Python code currently in the editor window, shown in Figure A-16. *The F5 shortcut key is a convenient way to execute a program.*

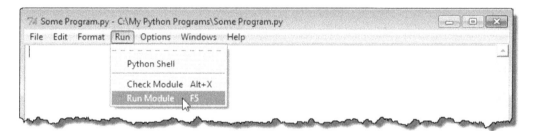

FIGURE A-16   The Run Menu of the IDLE Editor Window

The **Options menu** provides the option Configure IDLE for configuring various aspects of IDLE, including the fonts used, the color of keywords, the color of comment lines, etc., and the number of spaces used for each tab character (for indentation of program lines). Although there is a lot of control provided for the "look and feel" of IDLE, it is recommended to stick with the standard

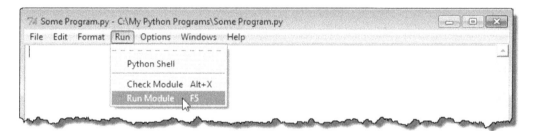

FIGURE A-17   The Options Menu of the IDLE Editor Window

configuration options. (Code Content is a feature intended to help aid in keeping track of the lines in the same program block while scrolling through a file. We do not see the benefits of this option for our purposes.)

The **Windows menu** provides options for controlling the height of the window. It also provides a list of all currently open Python windows (by file name), including the Python Shell. This provides an easy way to switch from one window to another. The menu options are shown in Figure A-18.

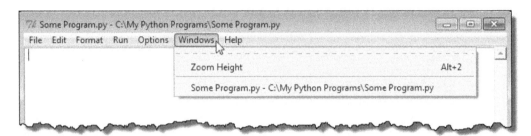

FIGURE A-18   The Windows Menu Options of the IDLE Editor Window

Finally, the **Help menu** includes About IDLE, which includes the version number of IDLE installed; and IDLE Help, which gives a brief summary of the commands of the menu bar.

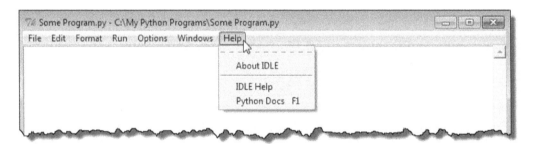

FIGURE A-19   The Help Menu Options of the IDLE Editor Window

Using Python Docs from within IDLE   A very useful feature of IDLE is the **Python Docs** option under the Help menu. This option links to the official documentation for the version of Python installed, shown in Figure A-20. The most relevant parts of the documentation for this text are marked with a (dark) checkmark. The Tutorial starts with an introduction to Python, and goes through all the features of the language, thus covering material beyond the scope of this text. It is a good starting point, however, for obtaining more information on a particular language feature. The Library Reference lists all the built-in functions, constants and types. In addition, it contains a categorized list of the Standard Library modules in Python. Finally, the Python Language Reference contains all information about the "core" of the language. This includes documentation on general syntax, expressions, statements, and compound statements (such as if and while statements). The Global Module Index, General Index and Python FAQs, indicated by lighter check marks, may also be of some help to the reader.

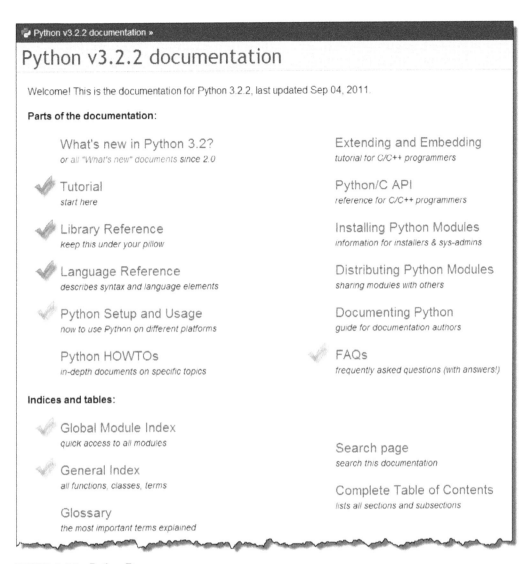

Python v3.2.2 documentation »

Python v3.2.2 documentation

Welcome! This is the documentation for Python 3.2.2, last updated Sep 04, 2011.

Parts of the documentation:

What's new in Python 3.2?
or all "What's new" documents since 2.0

Tutorial
start here

Library Reference
keep this under your pillow

Language Reference
describes syntax and language elements

Python Setup and Usage
how to use Python on different platforms

Python HOWTOs
in-depth documents on specific topics

Extending and Embedding
tutorial for C/C++ programmers

Python/C API
reference for C/C++ programmers

Installing Python Modules
information for installers & sys-admins

Distributing Python Modules
sharing modules with others

Documenting Python
guide for documentation authors

FAQs
frequently asked questions (with answers!)

Indices and tables:

Global Module Index
quick access to all modules

General Index
all functions, classes, terms

Glossary
the most important terms explained

Search page
search this documentation

Complete Table of Contents
lists all sections and subsections

FIGURE A-20   Python Docs

A4. Common Python Programming Errors

We list the typical errors for novice programmers using Python. It would be wise to use the following as a checklist when developing and debugging your Python programs.

♦ Improper Indentation

All instructions in the same suite (block) must be indented the same amount. Each tab press will move the cursor the number of character spaces that is set under Options/Configure IDLE (four spaces by default, recommended).

♦ Forgetting About Truncated (Integer) vs. Real Division

Keep in mind the difference between the / operator (5/4 → 1.25) and the // operator (5/4 → 1). This is very easy to forget when using arithmetic expressions.

♦ Confusing the Assignment Operator (=) with the Comparison Operator (==)

This is a very common error for new programmers, but one that you should learn to avoid as early as possible.

♦ Forgetting to Convert String Values when Inputting Data

Remember that the `input` function always returns a string type. It is easy to forget when reading in numeric values to convert them to integer or float before using arithmetically.

♦ Forgetting to Use Colons Everywhere Needed

Don't forget to put colons where needed. Rather than trying to memorize where they are required, a simple rule can be followed. A colon is required after any keyword (such as `if` or `while`) in which the subsequent statements are indented.

♦ Forgetting about Zero-Based Indexing

Zero-based indexing, in which the first index value of an indexed entity starts at 0, can lead to "off-by-one" errors if the programmer is not careful.

♦ Confusing Mutable and Immutable Types

Remember that the value of a mutable type can be changed without the need for reassignment, for example, `list1.append(40)`. Since tuples and strings are immutable types and thus their values cannot be changed, reassignment of the variable is needed in order to "change" it. Thus, the statement `str1 + 'There!'` does not change the value of `str1`. To change its value, it must be reassigned, `str1 = str1 +' There!'`

♦ Forgetting the Syntax for Tuples of One Element

Tuples are the only sequence type that requires a comma with tuples of only element, (1,) → (1). If the comma is left out, then the expression evaluates to that element, (1) → 1.

♦ Improperly Ended Program Lines

Forgetting to use the backslash (\) when continuing a program line to the next line.

B. PYTHON QUICK REFERENCE

The references pages contained here summarize aspects of the Python programming language most relevant to the textbook. Therefore, the functions/operators listed, and the available optional arguments for each is not meant to be comprehensive. For complete coverage, see The Python Language Reference of the official Python site at http://docs.python.org/reference/index.html.

B1. Python Coding Style

Indentation

Use four spaces for each indentation level.

Blank Lines

Use blank lines, sparingly, to separate logical sections of code.
Separate function definitions with two blank lines. (Same for class definitions)

Line Length

Limit length of lines to 79 characters (i.e., do not wrap lines around screen).

Line Continuation

Statements containing open parentheses, square brackets or curly braces can be continued on the next line (except when containing open single or open double quotes):

```
result = (num1 + num2 + num3 + num4 + num5 +
          num6 + num7 + num8 + num9 + num10)
```

Statements without such delimiters can be continued by use of the line continuation character (\):

```
response = \
    int(input('(1)continue processing, (2)quit program '))
```

Use of Whitespace in Expressions and Statements

Assignment Statements...	`This: i = i + 1` `Not This: i=i+1`
Expressions...	`This: c = (a + b) * (a - b)` `Not This: c = (a+b) * (a-b)`
Comma-Separated Items...	`This: (a, b, c, d)` `Not This: (a,b,c,d)`

Keyword Arguments...	`This:`
	`def func1(real, imag=0.0):`
	`Not This:`
	`def func1(real, imag = 0):`

Function Calls...	`This:`
	`def func1(real, imag=0.0):`
	`Not This:`
	`def func1(real, imag = 0):`

B2. Python Naming Conventions

Symbolic Constants

All uppercase, underscores used when aids readability:

```
RATIO, ANNUAL_RATE
```

Variables

All lowercase, underscores used when aids readability:

```
n, line_count
```

Functions/Methods

All lowercase using underscores when needed, or mixed case ("camel case"), in which first character is lowercase, and first letter of all other words is uppercase:

```
calcAverage, calc_average
```

Classes

Mixed case, with first character a capital letter:

```
VehicleClass
```

Modules

Short name, all lowercase, underscores used when aids readability:

```
math, conv_functions
```

Keywords in Python

```
and          del          from         None         True
as           elif         global       nonlocal     try
assert       else         if           not          while
break        except       import       or           with
class        False        in           pass         yield
continue     finally      is           raise
def          for          lambda       return
```

B3. Comment Statements in Python

Syntax

```
# Comment line
```

Description

The hash sign (#) is used to make single line comments (when at the start of a line), or an in-line comment (when within a line). All characters following the hash sign until the end of line are treated as a comment.

Examples

(1) In-line comment, e.g.,

```
state_tax_rate = 0.08  # 2008 tax rate
```

(2) Single line comment serving as program section heading, e.g.,

```
# sum all values greater than 0
for i in range(0, len(values)):
    if values[i] > 0:
        sum = sum + values[i]
```

(3) As an alternative to use of a triple-quoted docstring, e.g.,

```
def function1(n):
#-----------------------------------------------
# This function returns the largest integer
# less than or equal to n.
#-----------------------------------------------
```

Never include an in-line comment that states what is obvious from the program line, e.g.,

```
n = n + 1   # increment n
```

But this is ok,

```
n = n + 1   # adjust n to avoid off-by-one error
```

Pragmatics

- If a # appears in a line with a prior #, then the second # is taken as part of the comment.
- There is no provision for block comments in Python (i.e., commenting out a sequence of lines with one set of comment delimiters).

B4. Literal Values in Python

Special Literal Value None

None is a special "place marker" in Python that can be used when there is no available value.

Numeric Literal Values

Numeric literals never contain commas...

Yes: 1200   204231
No: 1,200   204,231

Integer literals never contain a decimal point...

Yes: 1200
No: 1200.   1200.0

Range

- There is no limit for the size of an integer
- Floats are limited to 10^{-308} to 10^{308} with 16 to 17 digits of precision

Floating-point literals must contain a decimal point...

Yes: 1200.0   1200.
No: 1200

String Literal Values

Strings are delimited ("surrounded") by single or double quotes:

Examples: 'Hello World!'   "Hello World!"

Strings must be delimited by the same type of quote characters:

Yes: 'Hello World!'
No: 'Hello World!"

Strings Containing Quote Characters
Strings containing quotes must be delimited with the other quote type:

Yes: "This is John's car"   'We all yelled "Hey John!"'
No: 'This is John's car'   "We all yelled "Hey John!""

Triple-Quoted Strings
Single and double-quoted strings must be contained on one line. Triple-quoted strings, however, can span more than one line. Triple-quoted strings may be denoted with three single quotes, or three double quote characters. These strings are mainly used as docstrings for program documentation.

Boolean Literal Values

There are only two literal values for the Boolean type:

Yes: True   False
No: true   false   TRUE   FALSE   'True'   'False'

B5. Arithmetic, Relational, and Boolean Operators in Python

Arithmetic Operators

Operator	Meaning
+	Addition
-	Subtraction
*	Multiplication
**	Exponentiation
/	Float division
//	Truncated division
%	Modulus

Relational Operators

Operator	Meaning
<	Less than
>	Greater than
<=	Less than or equal to
>=	Greater than or equal to
==	Equal
!=	Not equal

Boolean Operators

Operator	Meaning
and	logical AND
or	logical OR
not	logical NOT

Usage

Given: cond1 = True, cond2 = False

```
2 + 3 - 1 → 4          2 < 3 → True          cond1 and cond2 → False
2 * 6 → 12             3 <= 2 → False        cond1 and not cond2 → True
2 ** 6 → 64            3 == 2 → False        cond1 or cond2 → True
3 / 2 → 1.5            3 != 2 → True         not cond1 or cond2 → False
3 // 2 → 1             'A' < 'B' → True      not(cond1 and cond2) → True
3.0 // 2 → 1.0         'a' < 'B' → False     (2 < 3) and cond1 → True
2025 // 100 → 20       'Hill' < 'Wu' → True  2025 % 100 → 25
```

Operator Precedence

highest

**	exponentiation
*, /, //, %	multiplication, division, modulus (remainder)
+, -	addition, subtraction
<, <=, ... in, not in	relational, membership, and identity operators
not	Boolean not operator
and	Boolean and operator
or	Boolean or operator

lowest

NOTE: All listed operators associate left-to-right, except ** (which associates right-to-left).

B6.   Built-in Types and Functions in Python

Built-in Types

Numeric Types

`int`	Integers
`float`	Floating point numbers
`complex`	Complex numbers
`bool`	Boolean values

Mapping Types

`dict`	Dictionary

Sequence Types

`str`	Strings
`list`	Lists
`tuple`	Tuples

Set Types

`set`	Sets
`frozenset`	Immutable sets

Built-in Functions

`abs(x)`
Returns the absolute value of a number (for arguments of type int, long, and float).

`chr(i)`
Returns a string of one character whose ASCII code is the integer i. The argument must be in the range [0...255] inclusive, otherwise a `ValueError` will be raised.

`cmp(x, y)`
Compare the two objects x and y and returns a negative value if x<y, zero if x==y, and a positive value if x>y.

`dict(arg)`
Creates a new dictionary where arg is a list of the form [(attr1, value1), (attr2, value2), ...].

`float(arg)`
Returns the absolute value of a number (for arguments of type int, long, and float).

`format(value, format_spec)`
Creates a formatted string from a provided sequence of format specifiers. (See details in Section B10)

`frozenset(arg)`
Creates a frozen (immutable) set where arg is a sequence (or other iterable type).

(continued ...)

Built-in Functions   (...continued)

help(arg)
Used in interactive mode in the Python Shell. Displays a help page related to the string provided in `arg`. When an argument not provided, starts the built-in help system.

id(object)
Returns the "identity" of an `object`, which is an integer unique to all other objects, and remains the same during an object's lifetime.

input(prompt)
Prompts user with provided `prompt` argument to enter input, and returns the typed input as a string with the newline (\n) character removed. (See details in section B7)

int(arg)
Returns integer value of provided argument. Argument may be a string or an integer (in which case, the same integer value is returned).

len(arg)
Returns the length of `arg`, where `arg` may be a string, tuple, list, or dictionary.

list(arg)
Returns a list with items contained in `arg`, where `arg` may be a sequence (or other iterable type). If no argument given, returns an empty list.

max(arg)
Returns the largest value in a provided string, list or tuple.

min(arg)
Returns the smallest value in a provided string, list or tuple.

open(filename, opt_mode)
Opens and creates a file object for `filename`. Optional argument `opt_mode` either `'r'` (reading), `'w'` (writing), or `'a'` (appending). If omitted, file opened for reading.

ord(str)
Given a character (string of length one), returns the Unicode code point (character encoding value) for the character, e.g. `ord('a')` = 97.

(continued ...)

Built-in Functions

`pow(x, y)`
Returns x to the power y. Equivalent to x**y.

`print(arg1, arg2, ...)`
Prints arguments arg1, arg2, ... on the screen. (See details in section B7)

`range(opt_start, stop, opt_step)`
Creates a list of integer values of a given progression. If opt_start not provided, then sequence begins at 0. If opt_step not provided, then increments by 1.

`repr(arg)`
Returns a string which is a printable representation of arg.

`reload(module)`
Reloads a given module that has already been loaded (imported). Useful for when making changes to modules when in interactive mode.

`round(x, opt_n)`
Returns the floating point value x rounded to n decimal places. If n is omitted, decimal place returned as 0.

`set(arg)`
Returns a new set with values in arg, where arg is a sequence (or other iterable type).

`sorted(arg)`
Returns a new sorted list with values in arg, where arg is a sequence (or other iterable type).

`str(arg)`
Returns a string version of arg. If arg is omitted, returns the empty string.

`tuple(arg)`
Returns a tuple whose items are the same as in arg, where arg may be a sequence (or other iterable type). If no argument is given, returns a new empty tuple.

`type(arg)`
Returns the type of a value (object) provided in arg.

B7. Standard Input and Output in Python

Standard Input

Standard input (`sys.stdin`) is a data stream used by a program to read data. By default, standard input is from the keyboard.

Standard Output

Standard output (`sys.stdout`) is a data stream used by a program to write data. By default, standard output goes to the screen.

Built-in Functions

`input(prompt)`

The `input` function sends (optional) string parameter, `prompt`, to the standard output (the screen) to prompt the user for input. It then returns the line read from the standard input (the keyboard) as a string, with the trailing newline character removed.

`print(value, ..., sep=' ', end='\n', file=sys.stdout)`

The `print` function sends values to the standard output (the screen). Multiple values may be given, each separated by commas. The displayed values are separated by a blank character and ended with a newline character. Each of the default parameter values, `sep`, `end` and `file`, may be changed as keyword arguments.

Examples

```
(1) >>> name = input('Enter name: ')
    Enter name: Audrey Smith
    >>> name
    'Audrey Smith'

(2) >>> n = int(input('Enter age: '))
    Enter age: 28
    >>> n
    28
```

```
(3) >>> age = 38
    >>> print('His age is', age))
    His age is 38

(4) >>> print(1, 2, 3, sep='*')
    1*2*3

(5) >>> print(1, 2, 3, end='...')
    1 2 3...
```

Pragmatics

- The prompt string provided for the function `input` often is ended with a blank character to provide space between the end of the prompt and the typed user input.

- To keep the cursor on the same line when calling `print`, set default parameter end to the empty string as a keyword argument.

- The `input` function reads and returns any input by the user without generating an error. When the input is converted to another type, such as an integer in (2) above, the type conversion function used may raise an exception. Thus, exception handling is needed to check for invalid input.

B8. General Sequence Operations in Python

General Sequence Operations

`len(s)`
Returns the length of sequence s.

`s[i]` (*selection*)
Returns the item at index i in sequence s.

`s[i:j]` (*slice*)
Returns subsequence ("slice") of elements in s from index i to index j - 1.

`s[i:j:k]` (*slice with step*)
Returns subsequence ("slice") of every kth item in `s[i:j]`.

`s.count(x)`
Returns the number of occurrences of x in sequence s.

`s.index(x)`
Returns the first occurrence of x in sequence s.

`x in s` (*membership*)
Returns `True` if x is equal to one of the items in sequence s, otherwise returns `False`.

`x not in s` (*membership*)
Returns `True` if x is not equal to any of the items in sequence s, otherwise returns `False`.

`s1 + s2` (*concatenation*)
Returns the concatenation of sequence s2 to sequence s1 (of the same type).

`n * s` (or `s * n`)
Returns n (shallow) copies of sequence s concatenated.

`min(s)`
Returns the smallest item in sequence s.

`max(s)`
Returns the largest item in sequence s.

B9. String Operations in Python

String Operations

`str.find(arg) / str.index(arg)`
Both `find` and `index` return the lowest index matching substring provided. Method `find` returns `-1` if substring not found, method `index` returns `ValueError`.

`str.isalpha(arg) / str.isdigit(arg)`
Returns `True` if `str` non-empty and all characters in `str` are all letters (`isalpha`), or all digits (`isdigit`), otherwise returns `False`.

`str.isidentifier()`
Returns `True` is `str` is an identifier in Python, otherwise returns `False`.

`str.islower() / str.isupper() / str.lower() / str.upper()`
Methods `islower` / `isupper` return `True` if all letters in `str` are lower (upper) case, and there is at least one letter in `str`. Methods `lower` / `upper` return a copy of `str` with all letters in lower (upper) case.

`str.join(arg)`
Returns a string which is the concatenation of all strings in `arg`, where `arg` is a sequence (or some other iterable) type. If `arg` does not contain any strings, a `TypeError` is raised.

`str.partition(arg)`
For string separator in `arg`, returns a 3-tuple containing the substring before the separator in `str`, the separator itself, and the substring following the separator. If separator not found, returns a 3-tuple containing `str`, and two empty strings.

`str.replace(arg1, arg2)`
Returns a copy of `str` with all occurrences of `arg1` replaced by `arg2`.

`str.split(arg)`
Returns a list of words in `str` using `arg` as the delimiter string. If `arg` not provided, then whitespace (a blank space) is used as the delimiter.

`str.strip(arg)`
Returns a copy of `str` with leading and trailing chars contained in string `arg` removed. If `arg` not provided, then removes whitespace.

B10. String Formatting in Python

Syntax

`format(value, format specifier)`

Description

Built-in function `format` creates a formatted string from a provided sequence of format specifiers.

Format Strings

A format string may contain the following format specifiers in the order shown:
`fill_chr, align, width, precision, type`

Format Specifiers	Possible Values
`fill_chr`	Any character except `'{'` (requires a provided align specifier)
`align`	`'<'` (left-justified), `'>'` (right-justified), `'^'` (centered)
`width`	An integer (total field width)
`precision`	An integer (number of decimal places to display, rounded)
`type`	`'d'` (base 10), `'f'` (fixed point), `'e'` (exponential notation)

Examples

Given: `avg = 1.1275, sales = 143235 factor = 134.10456`

(1) `>>> print('Average rainfall in April:', format(avg,'.2f'), 'inches')`
`Average rainfall for April: 1.13 inches`

(2) `>>> print('Yearly Sales $', format(sales, ','))`
`Yearly Sales $ 143,235`

(3) `>>> print('Conversion factor:', format(factor, '.2e'))`
`Conversion factor: 1.34e+02`

(4) `>>> print(format('Date', '^8'), format('Num Sold', '^12'))`
`Date      Num Sold`

(5) `>>> print('\n' + format('Date', '<8') + format('Num Sold', '^12') +`
`           '\n' + format('----', '<8') + format('--------', '^12'))`

`Date      Num Sold`
`----      --------`

B11. Lists in Python

List Operations

`lst[i] = x`
Element i of lst replaced with x (for any object x).

`lst[i:j] = t`
Slice of lst from i to j-1 replaced with sequence (or other iterable type) t.

`del lst[i:j]`
Removes slice lst[i:j] from lst.

`lst[i:j:k] = t`
Replaces items lst[i:j:k] in lst with t.

`del lst[i:j:k]`
Removes slice lst[i:j:k] from lst.

`s.append(x)`
Adds x to the end of sequence s.

`s.extend(x)`
Adds the *contents* of sequence x to the end of sequence s.

`s.insert(i, x))`
Inserts x at index i in sequence s.

`s.pop(i)`
Removes and returns s[i]. When argument i not provided, removes last item in s.

`s.remove(x)`
Removes and returns the *first* item in sequence s that equals x.

`s.reverse()`
Reverses the items in sequence s.

`s.sort()`
Sorts sequence s from smallest to largest.

B12. Dictionaries in Python

Dictionary Operations

`dict(arg)`

Returns a new dictionary initialized with items in `arg`, where `arg` may be a list, tuple or string (or other iterable type). If no argument provided, returns an empty dictionary.

`len(d)`

Returns the number of items in dictionary d.

`d[key]`

Returns item of dictionary d with key `key`.

`d[key] = value`

Sets `d[key]` to value.

`del d[key]`

Removes `d[key]` from dictionary d.

`key in d`

Returns `True` if d has key `key`, otherwise returns `False`.

`key not in d`

Returns `False` if d has key `key`, otherwise returns `True`.

`d.clear()`

Removes all items from dictionary.

`d.get(key)`

Returns the value for `key` in dictionary d.

`d.pop(key)`

Removes key/value pair in d for `key` and returns the associated value.

`d.popitem()`

Removes and returns an arbitrary key/value pair from dictionary `d`.

B13. Sets in Python

Set/Frozenset Operations

set(arg) / frozenset(arg)
Returns a new set or frozenset with items provided in arg, where arg is a sequence (or other iterable type).

len(s)
Returns the number of items in set s.

x in s   (x not in s)
Returns True (False) if s has item equal to x, otherwise returns False (True).

s.add(x) / s.remove(x), s.pop(), s.clear()   *(Set type only)*
Adds / removes x, Removes-returns arbitrary item from s, Removes all items from s.

s.isdisjoint(other)
Returns True if set s had no items in common with the set provided by argument other, otherwise returns False.

s.issubset(other)   (also **set <= other**)
Returns True if every item in s is also in set other, otherwise returns False.

s.issuperset(other)   (also **set >= other**)
Returns True if every item in other is also in set s, otherwise returns False.

set < other   (set > other)
Returns True if s is a proper subset (superset) of set other

s.union(other, ...)
Returns a new set containing all items in set s and all other provided sets.

s.intersection(other, ...)
Returns a new set containing all items common to set s and all other provided sets.

s.difference(other, ...)
Returns a new set containing all items in set s that are not also in other provided sets.

s.symmetric_difference(other)
Returns a new set containing items that are in set s or set other, but not both.

B14. if Statements in Python

Syntax

```
if condition:
    statements
elif condition:
    statements
else:
    statements
```

Description

An if statement may have zero or more elif clauses, optionally followed by an else clause. As soon as the condition of a given clause is found true, that clause's statements are executed, and the rest of the clauses are skipped. If none of the clauses are found true, then the statements of the else clause are executed (if present). As with all data structures, if statements may be nested.

Examples

```
(1)  if n == 0:
         print('n is zero')

(2)  if n == 0:
         print('n is zero')
     else:
         print('n is non-zero')

(3)  if n < 0:
         print('n is less than 0')
     elif n == 0:
         print('n is zero')
     else:
         print('n is greater than zero')
```

```
(4)  if n1 == 0:
         print('n1 is zero')
     if n2 == 0:
         print('n2 is zero')

(5)  if n1 == 0:
         print('n1 is zero')
         if n2 == 0:
             print('n2 is zero')
         else:
             print 'n2 is not zero'
     else:
         print 'n1 is not zero'
```

Pragmatics

- It is not required to include elif or else clauses in if statements.

- When selecting among a set mutually exclusive conditional expressions, the if/elif (with optional else) form of if statement should be used.

Typical Errors

1. Forgetting to add a semicolon (:) after each conditional expression, and after keyword else.
2. Improper operator use when checking for equality (e.g., "==", not "=").
3. Improper Boolean expression evaluation resulting from unconsidered operator precedence.
4. Improper indentation of nested if/elif/else clause(s) resulting in faulty logic.

B15. **for Statements in Python**

Syntax

```
for k in sequence:
    statements
```

Description

The `for` statement is used to control a loop that iterates once for each element in a specified sequence of elements such as a list, string or other iterable type.

Examples

Given: `empty_str = '',  space = ' '`

(1)
```
for num in [2, 4, 6, 8]:
    print(num, end=space)
```
Output: `2 4 6 8`

(2)
```
for num in range(2, 10, 2):
    print(num, end=space)
```
Output: `2 4 6 8`

(3)
```
for num in range(10, 2, -2):
    print(num, end=space)
```
Output: `10 8 6 4`

(4)
```
for char in 'Hello':
    print(char, end=empty_str)
```
Output: `Hello`

(5)
```
lst = [2, 4, 6, 8]
for k in range(len(lst)):
    lst[k] = lst[k] + 1
print(lst)
```
Output: `3 5 7 9`

(6)
```
t = [[1, 2, 3],[4, 5, 6]]
for i in range(len(t)):
    for j in range(len(t[i])):
        print(t[i][j], end=space)
    print()
```
Output: `1 2 3`

Pragmatics

- When the elements of a sequence need to be accessed but not altered, a `for` loop that iterates over the values in the sequence is the appropriate approach (1-4).
- When the elements of a sequence need to be both accessed and updated, a `for` loop that iterates over the index values in the sequence is the appropriate approach (5,6).
- Nested `for` loops can be used to iterate through a list of sequence types (6).

Typical Errors

1. Forgetting to add a semicolon (`:`) after the loop header.
2. Improper indentation of statements contained in the body of the `for` loop.
3. Forgetting that `range(i,j)` (and `range(j)`) generates values up to, but not including j.

B16. while Statements in Python

Syntax

```
while condition:
    statements
```

Description

The `statements` contained in a while loop body continue to execute until the `condition` evaluates to `False`.

Examples

Given: `empty_str = ''`, `space = ' '`

(1)
```
i = 1
while i < 10:
    print(i, end=space)
    i = i + 1
```
Output: `1 2 3 4 5 6 7 8 9 10`

(2)
```
i = 10
while i != 0:
    print(i, end=space)
    i = i - 1
```
Output: `10 9 8 7 6 5 4 3 2 1`

(3)
```
while True:
    print('This loop keeps running!')
```
Output: `This loop keeps running!`
`This loop keeps running!`
etc.

(4)
```
file = open('filename.txt', 'r')
line = file.readline()
while line != empty_str:
    line = file.readline()
```

(5)
```
num = int(input('Enter a positive number: '))
while num < 0:
    print('Your input was invalid.')
    num = int(input('Enter a positive number: '))
```

Pragmatics

- A `while` loop can be used to implement any kind of loop, although some `while` loops are more conveniently implemented as a `for` loop (1,2).
- An *infinite loop* is caused by a condition that always evaluates to `True` (3).
- A loop to execute an indefinite number of times, such as when reading from a file, must be implemented as a `while` loop (4,5).
- A `while` loop is used when accepting and validating user input (5)

Typical Errors

1. Forgetting to add a semicolon (`:`) after the conditional expression.
2. Not making progress in the body, thereby creating a loop that never ends (i.e. an infinite loop).
3. Improper indentation of statements contained in the body of the `while` loop.

B17. Functions in Python

Description

A function is a named group of instructions accomplishing some task. A function is *invoked* (called) by providing its name, followed by a (possibly empty) list of arguments in parentheses. Calls to value-returning functions are expressions that evaluate to the returned function value. Calls to non-value returning functions are effectively statements called for their side effects. (Strictly speaking, they are value-returning functions since they return special value None).

Syntax

Value returning functions

```
def name(parameters):
    statements
    return expression
```

Non-value returning functions

```
def name(parameters):
    statements
```

Examples

Given: `num1 = 10, num2 = 25, num3 = 35, list1 = [1, 0, 3, 8, 0]`

(1)
```
def avg3(n1, n2, n3):
    '''Returns rounded avg.'''

    return round((n1 + n2 + n3) / 3)

>>> avg3(num1, num2, num3)
23
```

(2)
```
def dashLine(len, head=''):
    empty_str = ''
    space = ' '

    if head != empty_str:
        head = space + title
              + space
    print(head.center(len,'-'))

>>> dashLine(16)
----------------
>>> dashLine(16, head='price')
---- price -----
```

(3)
```
def countdown(from, to):
    for i in range(from, to-1, -1):
        print(i, end='...')

>>> countdown(from=5, to=1)
5...4...3...2...1...
```

(4)
```
def hello():
    print('Hello World!')

>>> hello()
Hello World!
```

(5)
```
def removeZeros(lst):
    for k in range(len(lst)-1, -1, -1):
        if lst[k] == 0:
            del lst[k]

>>> list1
[1, 0, 3, 8, 0]
>>> removeZeros(list1)
[1, 3, 8]
```

Pragmatics

- A triple-quoted string as the first line of a function serves as its docstring (1).
- Functions may define default arguments (2), and be called with keyword arguments (3).
- A function may be defined having no parameters (4).
- Mutable arguments passed to a function can become altered (5).

B18. Classes in Python

Syntax

```
class classname(parentclass):

    def __init__(self, args):
        '''docstring'''
        .
        .
        .
    def methodname(args):
        '''docstring'''
        .
        .
        .
    def methodname(args):
        '''docstring'''
```

Description

A class consists of a set of methods and instance variables. The instances variables are created in special method init. The init method must have an extra first parameter, by convention named self, that is not passed any arguments when the method is called.

A *docstring* is a single or multi-line string using triple quotes that provides documentation for methods, classes and modules in Python.

Example

```
class XYCoord(object):

    def __init__(self, x, y):
        self.__x = x
        self.__y = y

    def getX(self):
        return self.__x

    def setX(self, x):
        self.__x = x
        .
        .
        .
    def __repr__(self):
        return '(' + str(self.__x) + ',' + \
                     str(self.__y) + ')'

    def __eq__(self, xycoord):
        return self.__x == xycoord.getX() and \
               self.__y == xycoord.getY()
```

Special Methods

```
__init__
__repr__
__str__
__neg__
__add__
__sub__
__mul__
__truediv__
__floordiv__
__mod__
__pow__
__lt__
__le__
__eq__
__ne__
__gt__
__ge__
```

Private Members ("name mangling")

Instance variables beginning with two underscores are treated as private. They are accessible only if the mangled form of the name is used: with a single underscore followed by the class name added to the front. For example, private instance variable __x in class XYCoord becomes _XYCoord__x.

B19. Objects in Python

Syntax

identifier = classname(args)

Description

An object is an instance of a class. All values in Python are objects.

Examples

(1)	loc1 = XYCoord(5,10)	Creates a new XYCoord object, its reference assigned to loc1
(2)	loc2 = XYCoord(5,10)	Creates a new XYCoord object, its reference assigned to loc2
(3)	loc1	(5,10), dereferenced value of identifier loc1
(4)	loc2	(5,10), dereferenced value of identifier loc2
(5)	id(loc1)	37349072, reference value of identifier loc1
(6)	id(loc2)	37419120, reference value of identifier loc2
(7)	loc1 == loc2	True, comparison of their dereferenced values
(8)	loc1 is loc2	False, comparison their reference values
(9)	loc3 = loc1	Assigns reference value of loc1 to loc3
(10)	loc3 == loc1	True
(11)	loc3 is loc1	True
(12)	loc3.setX(10,10)	Changes value of loc3 to (10,10)
(13)	loc3 == loc1	False

Pragmatics

- When assigning an object to an identifier, the reference to the object is assigned, not the object itself. Thus, more than one identifier may reference the same object.

- Each newly-created object has a unique id. For variables var1 and var2, if id(var1) equals id(var2) (or var1 is var2 is True) they are referencing the same object.

- Mutable objects (e.g., lists) can be altered without reassignment:

```
>>> lst = [1, 2, 3]
>>> lst.append(4)
>>> lst
[1, 2, 3, 4]
```

- Immutable objects (e.g., strings) cannot be altered without reassignment:

```
>>> str1 = 'Hello'
>>> str1.replace('H', 'J')
>>> str1
'Hello'
>>> str1 = str1.replace('H', 'J')
>>> str1
'Jello'
```

B20. Exception Handling in Python

Syntax

```
try:
    statements
except ExceptionType:
    statements
except ExceptionType:
    statements
etc.
```

Description

Exception handling provides a means for functions and methods to report errors that cannot be corrected locally. In such cases, an *exception* (object) is *raised* that can be *caught* by its *client code* (the code that called it), or the client's client code, etc., until *handled* (i.e. the exception is caught and the error appropriately dealt with). If an exception is thrown back to the top-level code and never caught, then the program terminates displaying the exception type that occurred.

Example

```
def genAsterisks(x):
    """x an integer in range 1-79."""

    if x < 1 or x > 79:
        raise ValueError('Must enter 1-79')

    return x * '*'

#---- main
valid_input = False

while not valid_input:
    try:
        num = int(input("How Many '*'s?: "))
        print(genAsterisks(num))
        valid_input = True

    except ValueError as errorMesg:

        print(errorMesg)
```

Standard Exceptions

```
EOFError
FloatingPointError
ImportError
IOError
IndentationError
IndexError
KeyError
NameError
OverflowError
RuntimeError
SyntaxError
TypeError
ValueError
ZeroDivisionError
```

Pragmatics

- The exceptions built-in module is automatically imported in Python.
- Built-in exceptions, raised by the built-in functions/methods, may also be raised by user code.
- New exceptions may be defined as a subclass of the built-in Exception class.
- There may be any number of except clauses for a given try block.
- In addition to the except clauses, an else clause may optionally follow, only executed if the try block does not raise any exceptions. Following that, an optional finally clause, if present, is always executed, regardless of whether an exception had been raised or not. The else and finally clauses are often used for resource allocation, such as closing an open file.

B21. Text Files in Python

Description

A *text file* is a file containing characters, structured as lines of text. Text files can be directly created and viewed using a text editor. In addition to printable characters, text files also contain *non-printing* newline characters, \n, to denote the end of each line of text.

Using Input Files

A file that is open for input can be read from, but not written to.

File Operations	Action
fileref = open(filename, 'r')	Opens and creates a file object for reading filename. Raises an IOError exception if file not found.
fileref.readline()	Reads next line of file. Returns empty string if at end of file. Includes newline character ('\n') in line read.
fileref.close()	Closes file. File can be reopened to read from first line.

Example Program

```
filename = input('Enter filename: ')
inFile = open(filename, 'r')

line = inFile.readline()
while line != '':
    print(line, end='')
    line = inFile.readline()
```

Program Execution

```
Enter filename: testfile.txt
Hi,

This is a test file.
Containing five lines.
Including one blank line.
>>>
```

Using Output Files

A file that is open for output can be written to, but not read from.

File Operations	Action
fileref = open(filename, 'w')	Opens and creates a file object for writing to filename.
fileref.write(s)	Writes string s to file. Does *not* include output of '\n'.
fileref.close()	Closes file. If not closed, last part of output may be lost.

Example Program

```
filename = input('Enter filename: ')
outFile = open(filename, 'w')

line = input('Enter line of text:')
while line != '':
    outFile.write(line + '\n')
    line = input('Enter line:')

outFile.close()
```

Program Execution

```
Enter filename: newfile.txt
This is the first entered line.
This is the second entered line.
This is the last entered line.
```

Contents of file newfile.txt
```
This is the first entered line.
This is the second entered line.
This is the last entered line.
```

B22. Modules in Python

Description

A Python module is a file containing Python definitions and statements. The module that is directly executed to start a Python program is called the *main module*. Python provides standard (built-in) modules in the Python Standard Library.

Module Namespaces

Each module in Python has its own *namespace*: a named context for its set of identifiers. The *fully qualified* name of each identifier in a module is of the form `modulename.identifier`.

Forms of Import

(1) `import modulename`

Makes the namespace of `modulename` available, but not part of, the importing module. All imported identifiers used in the importing module must be fully qualified:

```
import math
print('factorial of 16 = ', math.factorial(16))
```

(2) `from modulename import identifier_1, identifier_2, ...`

`identifier_1`, `identifier_2`, etc. become part of the importing module's namespace:

```
from math import factorial
print('factorial of 16 = ', factorial(16))
```

(3) `from modulename import identifier_1 as identifier_2`

`identifier_1` becomes part of the importing module's namespace as `identifier_2`

```
from math import factorial as fact
print('factorial of 16 = ', fact(16))
```

(4) `from modulename import *`

All identifiers of `modulename` become part of the importing module's namespace (except those beginning with an underscore, which are treated as private).

```
from math import *
print('factorial of 16 = ', fact(16))
print('area of circle = ', pi*(radius**2))
```

Pragmatics

Although the `import *` form of `import` is convenient in that the imported identifiers do not have to be fully qualified in the importing module, there is the risk of a name clash. In addition, it is not apparent which identifiers are imported, or which module they are imported from.

C. PYTHON STANDARD LIBRARY MODULES

These pages contain selected modules of the Python Standard Library. For a complete listing, see the official standard library at http://docs.python.org/reference/index.html.

The Module Search Path   Python modules may be stored in various locations on a particular system. For this reason, when a module is imported, it must be searched for. The interpreter first searches for a built-in (standard) module with that name. If not found, it then searches for the module in the same directory as the executed program. If still not found, the interpreter searches in a list of directories contained in the variable `sys.path`, a variable of the built-in module `sys`. The `sys` module must be imported to access this variable:

```
>>> import sys
>>> sys.path
['C:\\Python32\\Lib\\idlelib','C:\\Windows\\system32\\python32.zip',
'C:\\Python32\\DLLs','C:\\Python32\\lib','C:\\Python32',
'C:\\Python32\\lib\\site-packages']
```

The particular value for `sys.path` depends on your particular Python installation.

The dir Built-In Function   Built-in function `dir` can be used to find out the names that a particular module defines. This may be used on any module:

```
>>> import math
>>> dir(math)
['__doc__', '__name__', '__package__', 'acos', 'acosh', 'asin',
'asinh', 'atan', 'atan2', 'atanh', 'ceil', 'copysign', 'cos', 'cosh',
'degrees', 'e', 'erf', 'erfc', 'exp', 'expm1', 'fabs', 'factorial',
'floor', 'fmod', 'frexp', 'fsum', 'gamma', 'hypot', 'isfinite', 'isinf',
'isnan', 'ldexp', 'lgamma', 'log', 'log10', 'log1p', 'modf', 'pi',
'pow', 'radians', 'sin', 'sinh', 'sqrt', 'tan', 'tanh', 'trunc']
```

Note that in addition to the available mathematical methods, there are three special identifers `__doc__`, `__name__` and `__package__` listed. The first two provide the docstring (providing brief documentation of the module's contents) and the module name, respectively:

```
>>> print(math.__doc__)
This module is always available. It provides access to the
mathematical functions defined by the C standard.
>>> print(math.__name__)
math
```

The `__package__` special identifier is used for modules that contain submodules, called packages.

C1. The math Module

Description

This module contains a set of commonly-used mathematical functions, including number-theoretic functions (such as factorial); logarithmic and power functions; trigonometric (and hyperbolic) functions; angular conversion functions (degree/radians); and some special functions and constants (including pi and e). A selected set of function from the math module are presented here.

Number-Theoretic Functions

math.ceil	returns the ceiling of x (smallest integer greater than or equal to x).
math.fabs(x)	returns the absolute value of x.
math.factorial(x)	returns the factorial of x.
math.floor()	returns the floor of x (largest integer less than x).
math.fsum(s)	returns an accurate floating-point sum of values in s (or other iterable).
math.modf()	returns the fractional and integer parts of x.
math.trunc(X)	returns the truncated value of s.

Power and Logarithmic Functions

math.exp(x)	returns e**x, for natural log base e.
math.log(x,base)	returns log x for base. If base omitted, returns log x base e.
math.sqrt(x)	returns the square root of x.

Trigonomeric Functions

math.cos(x)	returns cosine of x radians.
math.sin(x)	returns sine of x radians.
math.tan(x)	returns tangent of x radians.
math.acos(x)	returns arc cosine of x radians.
math.asin(x)	returns arc sine of x radians.
math.atan(x)	returns arc cosine of x radians.

Angular Conversion Functions

math.degrees(x)	returns x radians to degrees.
math.radians(x)	returns x degrees to radians.

Mathematical Constants

math.pi	mathematical constant pi = 3.141592 ...
math.e	mathematical constant e = 2.718281 ...

C2. The random Module

Description
This module provides a pseudorandom number generator using the Mersenne Twister algorithm, allowing users to generate random numbers with near uniform distribution over a long period.

Key Functions

```
random.random()
```
returns random float value x, where 0 <= x < 1.
```
random.uniform(a, b)
```
returns random float value x, where a <= x <= b.
```
random.randint(a, b)
```
returns random integer value x, where a <= x <= b.
```
random.randrange(start, stop, step)
```
returns random integer value x, where `start <= x < stop` and `x = start + n * step`, where n is an integer greater than or equal to zero
```
random.choice(seq)
```
returns random element from sequence seq (must be non-empty).
```
random.shuffle(seq)
```
randomly reorders sequence seq in place.
```
random.sample(seq, k)
```
returns list (length k) of unique items randomly chosen from seq.

Examples
Given: `list = ['a', 'b', 'c', 'd', 'e']`

(1) Generate random float
```
>>> random.random()
0.8568285775611655
```

(2) Generate random float in range
```
>>> random.uniform(1, 10)
9.71538746497116
```

(3) Generate random integer in range
```
>>> random.randint(1, 10)
6
```

(4) Select random item from a list
```
>>> random.choice(list)
'e'
```

(5) Generate random integer in range with step
```
>>> random.randrange(0, 10, 2)
6
>>> random.randrange(0, 10, 2)
8
>>> random.randrange(0, 10, 2)
2
```

(6) Randomly select subset from a list
```
>>> random.sample(list, 3)
['d', 'c', 'e']
```

(7) Randomly reorder a list
```
>>> random.shuffle(list)
>>> print(list)
['c', 'b', 'e', 'a', 'd']
```

Pragmatics
- The `random` module must be imported before it can be used.
- The current system time is used to initialize the random number generator. If comparability and reproducibility are important, supply a seed value x by invoking `random.seed(x)` before generating any random numbers.
- To generate only even numbers, use the `randrange` function with `start` of 0, step of 2.

C3. The turtle Module

Description

This module provides both procedure-oriented and object-oriented ways of controlling *turtle graphics*. A turtle is a graphical entity in an x/y coordinate plane (Turtle screen) that can be controlled in various ways including: its shape, size, color, position, movement (relative and absolute), speed, visibility (show/hide), and drawing status (pen up/pen down).

Creating a Turtle Graphics Window

```
# set screen size
turtle.setup(800, 600)

# get reference to turtle screen
screen = turtle.Screen()

# set window title bar
screen.title('My Turtles')
```

Creating a Turtle

```
# getting the default turtle
t = turtle.getturtle()

# creating a new turtle
t = turtle.Turtle()
```

Setting Screen Attributes

```
screen.bgcolor(args)
```  ........... background color, specified by name, (RGB) or hex
```
screen.bgpic(filename)
```  ......... sets GIF file as screen background
```
screen,clear()
```  ................. clears the screen
```
screen.reset()
```  ................. resets all turtles to their initial state
```
screen.bye()
```  ................... closes turtle screen window
```
screen.exitonclick()
```  ............ closes turtle screen window on mouse click

Setting Turtle Appearance

```
showturtle() / hideturtle()
```  ...... makes turtle visible / invisible
```
turtle.register_shape(filename)
```  .. GIF file name, registers image for use as turtle shape
```
shape(arg)
```  ...................... sets turtle to regular or registered shape

Getting Turtle's State

```
turtle.isvisible()
```  .......... returns True if turtle currently visible
```
turtle.position()
```  ........... returns current position of turtle as x, y coordinate
```
turtle.towards(x,y)
```  ......... returns angle between turtle and coordinate x, y
```
turtle.xcor()
```  .............. returns turtle's current x coordinate
```
turtle.ycor()
```  .............. returns turtle's current y coordinate
```
turtle.heading()
```  ............ returns turtle's current heading
```
turtle.distance(arg)
```  ........ returns distance to (x, y) or to another turtle

Pen Control

```
turtle.pendown()  . . . . . . . . . . . .   puts turtle's pen down so draws when it moves
turtle.penup()  . . . . . . . . . . . . . .   lift's turtle's pen so doesn't draw
turtle.isdown()  . . . . . . . . . . . . .   returns True if pen currently down
turtle.pencolor(color)  . . . . . . .   sets pen's color by color name or (RGB)
turtle.pensize(size)  . . . . . . . .   sets pen's line thickness, size a positive number
turtle.fillcolor(color)  . . . . . .   sets pen's fill color by color name or (RGB)
turtle.clear()  . . . . . . . . . . . . . .   deletes turtle's drawing from screen
turtle.write(arg)  . . . . . . . . . . .   writes text representation of arg at turtle's location
```

Controlling Turtle

```
turtle.forward(x)/backward(x) . . .   moves turtle forward/backward x pixels
turtle/right(angle)/left(x) . . . . .   moves turtle left/right by angle
turtle.goto(x,y) . . . . . . . . . . . . . .   moves turtle to coordinate (x, y)
turtle.setx(x)/sety(y)  . . . . . .   moves turtle to x/y locations
turtle.setheading(angle)  . . . .   sets heading of turtle by angle
turtle.undo()  . . . . . . . . . . . . . .   undoes last turtle action
tilt(angle) . . . . . . . . . . . . . . . . . .   rotates turtle relative to its current tile-angle
settiltangle(angle)  . . . . . . . .   sets turtle to angle
tileangle()  . . . . . . . . . . . . . . . .   returns the turtle's current tilt angle
turtle.speed(speed)  . . . . . . . .   1-slowest, 2-faster, ... 10-fast, 0-fastest
turtle.home()  . . . . . . . . . . . . . .   moves turtle to original position
turtle.circle(radius)  . . . . . . .   draws a circle if size radius
turtle.dot(size, color)  . . . . .   draws a dot with given size and color
turtle.stamp()  . . . . . . . . . . . . .   stamps turtle shape screen, return unique stamp id
turtle.clearstamp(id)  . . . . . . .   clears turtle stamp with provided id
turtle.clearstamps(n)  . . . . . . .   clears last n stamps, if argument omitted, clears all
```

Event Handling

```
turtle.onclick(func)  . . . . . . . .   func a function of two arguments called with the
                                        x,y coordinates of the location of mouse click
turtle.onrelease(func)  . . . . . . .   func a function of two arguments called with the
                                        x,y coordinates of the location of mouse release
turtle.ondrag(func)  . . . . . . . . .   func a function of two arguments called with the
                                        x,y coordinates of the location of mouse click when
                                        mouse dragged
turtle.mainloop()  . . . . . . . . . . .   starts event loop. Must be last statement in a turtle
                                        graphics program
```

C4. The webbrowser Module

Description

This module provides functionality to open Web-based documents in a browser from within a Python program. The module launches the system's default browser to open the target URL, unless a different (supported) browser is specified.

Key Functions

webbrowser.open(`url, new=0, autoraise=True`)
Opens the page at the specified `url` in a browser window. If possible, a value of 0 for `new` opens the page in an existing browser window, 1 in a new browser window, and 2 in a new browser "tab." When `autoraise` is passed as True, the browser window is raised to the top of the stack (this may happen on some systems regardless of `autoraise` value).

webbrowser.open_new(`url`) / webbrowser.open_new_tab(`url`)
Always opens the specified `url` in a new browser window or tab, respectively.

webbrowser.get(`name`)
Returns a controller object for the specified browser type `name`, allowing the user to use any browser that is registered with or predefined in the module.

Examples

(1) Open a page in the browser
```
import webbrowser
webbrowser.open('http://docs.python.org/, 0, True')
```

(2) Open a page in the browser
```
import webbrowser
webbrowser.open_new('http://docs.python.org/')
```

(3) Specify browser to open page
```
import webbrowser
browser = webbrowser.get('firefox')
browser.open('http://docs.python.org/')
```

Pragmatics

- Python scripts can be written to generate HTML code, which can then be opened in a browser as part of the program using this module.
- This module is not limited to opening Web pages. On some platforms, it can also be used to open documents and media files. Instead of passing an http URL to `open`, pass the address of the target file (e.g. `file://host/path` or, on local machine, `file:///path`).
- The functionalities of this module are also available through the command line.

Index

Q

U